EVANS'
AMERICAN BIBLIOGRAPHY

1639 - - 1820 A. D.

AMERICAN BIBLIOGRAPHY

BY

CHARLES EVANS

———

A CHRONOLOGICAL DICTIONARY

OF ALL

BOOKS PAMPHLETS AND PERIODICAL PUBLICATIONS

PRINTED IN THE

UNITED STATES OF AMERICA

FROM THE GENESIS OF PRINTING IN 1639
DOWN TO AND INCLUDING THE YEAR 1820

WITH BIBLIOGRAPHICAL AND BIOGRAPHICAL NOTES

VOLUME 12
1798-1799

O Happiness! our being's end and aim;
Good, pleasure, ease, content! whate'er thy name:
That something still, which prompts th' eternal sigh,
For which we bear to live, or dare to die.
— *Alexander Pope.*

NEW YORK
PETER SMITH
1942

FIRST PUBLISHED 1934
REPRINTED 1942

PRINTED IN THE UNITED STATES OF AMERICA

TO

CALVIN COOLIDGE OF VERMONT

4 JULY, 1872 — 5 JANUARY, 1933

FORTY-EIGHTH GOVERNOR OF THE

COMMONWEALTH OF MASSACHUSETTS

AND THIRTIETH PRESIDENT OF THE

UNITED STATES OF AMERICA

WHOSE LIFE WAS AN INSPIRATION TO THE STATE, AND TO THE NATION, FOR A RETURN TO THE UNASSUMING, FAITHFUL, CONSIDERATE, STERLING CHARACTERISTICS, WHICH DISTINGUISHED OUR PURITAN ANCESTORS, WHOSE TEACHINGS FORM THE ENDURING BASIS OF OUR GOVERNMENT; AND, OF WHOM IT MAY BE WRITTEN, AND SHOULD BE RECORDED, THAT, UNDER HIS WISE DIRECTION OF PUBLIC AFFAIRS, HE GAVE TO OUR PEOPLES — SEVEN YEARS OF THE GREATEST PEACE; THE GREATEST PROSPERITY; THE GREATEST ADVANCEMENT IN THE ARTS AND SCIENCES; OUR NATIONAL LIFE HAS EVER KNOWN; — AND, NEITHER ELATED BY SUCCESS, NOR DEPRESSED BY FAILURE, LIKE CINCINNATUS, VOLUNTARILY LEFT THE HIGH OFFICE FOR WHICH HE HAD BEEN CHOSEN, AND RETURNED TO HIS PEOPLE, AND BECAME AGAIN AS ONE OF THEM, ASSOCIATING HIMSELF, AS PRESIDENT, WITH THAT LITTLE BAND OF PATRIOT SCHOLARS WHO, FOR OVER AN HUNDRED YEARS, UNDER THE NAME OF AMERICAN ANTIQUARIAN SOCIETY, OF WORCESTER, MASSACHUSETTS, HAVE DEVOTED THEMSELVES, WITHOUT GOVERNMENT ASSISTANCE, TO THE COLLECTION AND PRESERVATION OF THE MONUMENTS OF AMERICAN LITERATURE — THE SOURCES OF OUR NATIONAL LIFE — OF WHOSE UNSELFISH LABORS THE VOLUMES OF THIS AMERICAN BIBLIOGRAPHY ARE, LARGELY, THE IMPERISHABLE RECORD, UNTIL HE RESTED AMONG THE EVER GREEN HILLS OF HIS NATIVE STATE.

This Volume is Dedicated

BY THE AUTHOR

AMERICAN BIBLIOGRAPHY

1639 - - 1820 A. D.

1798

33262   ABBOT, ABIEL   1770–1828
A MEMORIAL OF DIVINE BENEFITS. IN A SERMON, DELIVERED AT EXETER, ON THE 15TH, AND AT HAVERHILL, ON THE 29TH OF NOVEMBER, 1798, DAYS OF PUBLIC THANKSGIVING, IN NEW-HAMPSHIRE AND [MASSACHUSETTS. BY ABIEL ABBOT, PASTOR OF THE FIRST CHURCH IN HAVERHILL. [One line from] PSALM CXXXIX. 18.

Printed at Haverhill, Massachusetts; by Moore & Stebbins. Sold by them at their Printing-Office in Haverhill, and by H. Ranlet, in Exeter.—Dec. 1798. pp. [26.] 8vo.   BA. BM. CLA. JCB. LOC. UTS.

33263   ABERCROMBIE, JAMES   1758–1841
A SERMON, PREACHED IN CHRIST CHURCH AND ST. PETER'S, PHILADELPHIA: ON WEDNESDAY, MAY 9, 1798. BEING THE DAY APPOINTED BY THE PRESIDENT, AS A DAY OF FASTING, HUMILIATION, AND PRAYER THROUGHOUT THE UNITED STATES OF NORTH AMERICA. BY JAMES ABERCROMBIE, A. M. ONE OF THE ASSISTANT MINISTERS OF CHRIST CHURCH AND ST. PETER'S. PUBLISHED BY REQUEST.

Philadelphia: Printed by John Ormrod, No. 41, Chesnut-Street. [1798.] pp. (38). 8vo.   AAS. BA. HC. HSP. JCB. LOC. MHS. NYHS. NYPL.

33264   ABOLITION SOCIETIES IN THE UNITED STATES.
MINUTES OF THE PROCEEDINGS OF DELEGATES FROM THE ABOLITION SOCIETIES ESTABLISHED IN DIFFERENT PARTS OF THE UNITED STATES, ASSEMBLED AT PHILADELPHIA, ON THE FIRST DAY OF JUNE, ONE THOUSAND SEVEN HUNDRED AND NINETY-EIGHT, AND CONTINUED BY ADJOURNMENT, UNTIL THE SIXTH DAY OF THE SAME MONTH, INCLUSIVE.

Philadelphia: Printed by Zachariah Poulson, junior, No. 106, Chesnut-street, nearly opposite to the Bank of North America. 1798. pp. (20). 8vo.

                                        AAS. BU. JCB. LOC. NYHS. NYPL.

33265   ADAMS, MOSES   –1819
A SERMON, DELIVERED AT THE ORDINATION OF THE REV. LUTHER WRIGHT, TO THE PASTORAL CARE OF THE FIRST CHURCH AND CHRISTIAN SOCIETY IN MEDWAY, JUNE 13, 1798. BY MOSES ADAMS, A. M. PASTOR OF THE CHURCH IN ACTON. TO WHICH ARE ADDED THE CHARGE, BY THE REV. MR. BRIDGE, OF EAST-SUDBURY, AND THE RIGHT HAND OF FELLOWSHIP, BY THE REV. MR. PRENTISS, OF MEDFIELD.

Dedham: Printed by Mann and Adams. 1798. pp. [28.] 8vo.

                                           AAS. BA. BM. JCB. LOC.

33266   ADDISON, ALEXANDER   1759–1807
       LIBERTY OF SPEECH AND OF THE PRESS. A CHARGE TO THE GRAND JURIES OF THE
       COUNTY COURTS OF THE FIFTH CIRCUIT OF THE STATE OF PENNSYLVANIA; BY
       ALEXANDER ADDISON, PRESIDENT OF THOSE COURTS.
         Albany: Printed by L. Andrews. [1798.] pp. 16. 8vo,   LOC.

33267   —— — LIBERTY OF SPEECH, AND OF THE PRESS. A CHARGE TO THE GRAND JURIES
       OF THE COUNTY COURTS OF THE FIFTH CIRCUIT OF THE STATE OF PENNSYLVANIA.
         Washington [Pennsylvania]: Printed by John Colerick, for the Author.
       1798. pp. (24). 12mo.   AAS. BA. CLS. JCB. LOC.

33268   —— OBSERVATIONS ON THE SPEECH OF ALBERT GALLATIN, IN THE HOUSE OF REP-
       RESENTATIVES OF THE UNITED STATES, ON THE FOREIGN INTERCOURSE BILL.
       BY ALEXANDER ADDISON.
         Washington [Pennsylvania]: Printed by John Colerick. 1798. pp. (2), (2),
       52. 8vo.   AAS. BA. JCB. LCP. LOC. NYPL.

33269   —— AN ORATION ON THE RISE AND PROGRESS OF THE UNITED STATES OF AMERICA,
       TO THE PRESENT CRISIS; AND ON THE DUTIES OF THE CITIZENS. BY ALEXANDER
       ADDISON, ESQ.
         Philadelphia: Printed by John Ormrod, No. 41, Chesnut-Street. 1798. pp.
       (2), (41). 8vo.   AAS. CLS. LCP. LOC.
       Delivered at Washington, Pennsylvania, 15 May, 1798.

33270   —— — AN INFALLIBLE CURE. FOR POLITICAL BLINDNESS, IF ADMINISTERED TO
       PATIENTS POSSESSING SOUND MINDS, HONEST HEARTS, AND INDEPENDENT CIRCUM-
       STANCES. [Address to the citizens of Virginia. Signed, An old American soldier,
       June 17th, 1798.]
         [*Richmond: Printed by Thomas Nicolson, July,* 1798.] pp. (38). 16mo.
                                                      BA. LOC.

33271   —— — — AN INFALLIBLE CURE FOR POLITICAL BLINDNESS, IF ADMININSTERED
       [*sic*] TO PATIENTS POSSESSING SOUND MINDS, HONEST HEARTS, AND INDEPENDENT
       CIRCUMSTANCES.
         [*Richmond: Re-printed by Thomas Nicolson, October,* 1798.] pp. 24. 12mo.
       Consists of An Oration on the progress of the United States to the   LOC.
       present crisis, and duties in it. By Alexander Addison. With Title, and
       comments, by William Heth.

33272   AN ADDRESS TO THE VOTERS OF ANNE-ARUNDEL AND PRINCE-GEORGE'S COUN-
       TIES AND CITY OF ANNAPOLIS. [Signed, a Voter.]
         Annapolis: Printed by Frederick Green. MDCCXCVIII. pp. 16. 8vo.   BA.

33273   ÆSOPUS   619–564 B. C.
       A HISTORY OF THE LIFE OF ÆSOP, ACCORDING TO SIR ROGER L'ESTRANGE. TO
       WHICH IS ADDED, A CHOICE COLLECTION OF FABLES, WITH INSTRUCTIVE MORALS.
       FOR THE BENEFIT OF YOUTH. TAKEN FROM THE MOST EMINENT MYTHOLOGISTS.
         Philadelphia: Printed at the Southwark Office, No. 280, South Front-Street.
       1798. pp. 136, 1, 14 cuts in text. 18mo.   AAS. NYPL.

33274   —— — SELECT FABLES OF ESOP AND OTHER FABULISTS. IN THREE BOOKS. CON-
       TAINING, I. FABLES FROM THE ANCIENTS. II. FABLES FROM THE MODERNS. III.
       ORIGINAL FABLES NEWLY INVENTED. BY ROBERT DODSLEY. [Seven lines from]
       PARADISE LOST, B. 8. L. 370. A NEW EDITION.
         Philadelphia. Printed for, and sold by, Joseph and James Crukshank, No.
       87, High-Street. 1798. pp. 208, (20). 12mo.   AAS. NYPL.
       Includes, a new Life of Esop; and An essay on Fable.

33275 ALBANY. NEW YORK.
AT A . . . MEETING . . . IN THE CITY OF ALBANY, ON TUESDAY EVENING, THE 6TH INSTANT, FOR THE PURPOSE OF NOMINATING PROPER PERSONS TO FILL THE OFFICE OF GOVERNOR AND LIEUTENANT-GOVERNOR OF THIS STATE, WHICH ARE ABOUT TO BECOME VACANT . . . TO THE ELECTORS OF THE STATE OF NEW-YORK . . . [urging their support for John Jay, and Stephen Van Rensselaer. Signed, Abm. Van Vechten, and others. March 9, 1798.]
[Albany: 1798.] Broadside. NYPL.

33276 —— AT A MEETING OF A NUMBER OF MEMBERS OF BOTH HOUSES OF THE LEGISLATURE, AND CITIZENS OF THE CITY AND COUNTY OF ALBANY . . . [Announcement of the nomination of Robert R. Livingston for Governor, and Stephen Van Rensselaer, for Lieutenant-Governor, of New York. Followed by] TO THE INDEPENDENT ELECTORS . . . [urging their support. Signed, Abraham Schenck, and others.]
[Albany: 1798.] Broadside. fol. NYPL.

33277 —— CRISIS. TO THE PEOPLE OF THE STATE OF NEW-YORK. WAR! WAR! WAR! [Regarding the candidacies of Robert R. Livingston, and John Jay, for Governor.] TO THE ELECTORS OF THE STATE OF NEW-YORK . . . [defending Governor John Jay, and signed by Peter Gansevoort, jun., and others. Albany, April 16, 1798.]
[Albany: Printed by C. R. & G. Webster. 1798.] pp. (2), fol. NYPL.

33278 —— TO THE ELECTORS OF THE EASTERN DISTRICT. FELLOW CITIZENS! THE DAY APPROACHES WHEN YOU ARE TO DECIDE BY YOUR SUFFRAGES . . . [urging the re-election of Governor John Jay of New York. Signed, by Peter Gansevoort, jun., and others. Albany. April 23, 1798.]
[Albany: Printed by C. R. & G. Webster. 1798.] Broadside. fol. NYPL.

33279 THE ALBANY CENTINEL. NO. 53 OF VOL. I. TUESDAY, JANUARY 2, [– NO. 52, OF VOL. II. FRIDAY, DECEMBER 28, 1798.]
Published every Tuesday and Friday, by Loring Andrews & Co. Printers to the State, at the Printing-Office in Maiden-Lane; . . . 1798. fol. AAS.

In June, the Printing-Office was removed to Court-Street, a few rods south of the City Hall. On October 2d, the co-partnership of Thomas, Andrews and Penniman was dissolved by mutual consent: Loring Andrews continuing the Centinel, as sole proprietor.

33280 ALBANY CHRONICLE: OR, JOURNAL OF THE TIMES. EDITED BY JOHN M'DONALD. VOL. II. NO. 61. MONDAY, JANUARY 1, [– NO. 75, MONDAY, APRIL 9, 1798.]
[Albany:] Printed on Mondays by J. Fry and H. C. Southwick, corner of Dock Street and Mark Lane. 1798. fol.

With the motto: To preserve Liberty, stimulate industry and meliorate the morals of an enlightened and free people. In February ? Joseph Fry became sole Proprietor and Publisher until publication finally ceased, probably in April.

33281 THE ALBANY GAZETTE. VOL. XIV. NUMB. 1159. MONDAY, JANUARY 1, [— VOL. XV. NUMB. 1263. MONDAY, DECEMBER 31, 1798.]
Printed every Monday and Friday, by Charles R. and George Webster, in the White House, corner of State and Pearl Streets, opposite the City-Tavern. 1798. fol.

33282 THE ALBANY [N. Y. arms] REGISTER. VOL. X. NUMBER 625. MONDAY, JANUARY 1, [— VOL. XI. NUMBER 729. MONDAY, DECEMBER 31, 1798.]
Published every Monday and Friday by Barber & Southwick.—Subscriptions, advertisements, &c. for the Register, will be received at their Printing-Office, Sign of Faust's Statue, State-Street, or at their Book-Store, two doors north of the City-Hall, in Court-Street. 1798. fol. NYPL.

33283   ALLEN, JOHN   1763–1812
SPEECH OF THE HON. JOHN ALLEN, (ONE OF THE REPRESENTATIVES FROM THE STATE
OF CONNECTICUT) IN THE HOUSE OF REPRESENTATIVES OF THE UNITED STATES;
IN COMMITTEE OF THE WHOLE ON THE STATE OF THE UNION. APRIL 20, 1798.
*Albany: Printed by Charles R. & George Webster, at their Bookstore, in the
White House, corner of State and Pearl-Streets.* [1798.] pp. 13. 8vo.   LOC.

33284   —— — SPEECH OF JOHN ALLEN, ESQ., IN THE HOUSE OF REPRESENTATIVES,
FRIDAY, THE 20TH DAY OF APRIL, 1798. RELATIVE TO EMPLOYING THE ARMED
VESSELS AS CONVOYS.
Philadelphia: Published by William Cobbett, May 3, 1798. pp. 32. 8vo.
AAS. BA. BM. LOC. NYHS. Pr.PL.

33285   ALLEN, PAUL, JUNIOR   1775–1826
AN ORATION, DELIVERED AT THE BENEVOLENT CONGREGATIONAL MEETING-HOUSE
IN PROVIDENCE, BEFORE THE CORPORATION FEDERAL ADELPHI, AT THEIR ANNI-
VERSARY MEETING, ON THE 4TH DAY OF SEPTEMBER, A. D. 1798. BY PAUL ALLEN,
JUN. A. M.
Providence: Printed by Bennett Wheeler. 1798. pp. 19. 8vo.
AAS. BA. JCB. LOC. RIHS.

33286   ALLEN, THOMAS   1743–1810
BENEFITS OF AFFLICTION. A FUNERAL SERMON: OCCASIONED BY THE DEATH OF
MRS. ELIZABETH WHITE, CONSORT OF MR. WILLIAM P. WHITE; WHO DEPARTED
THIS LIFE IN LONDON, ON FRIDAY THE 2D DAY OF FEB. 1798, AND DELIVERED AT
PITTSFIELD, THE PLACE OF HER NATIVITY APRIL 22D, IN COMMEMORATION OF
THAT EVENT THE NEXT LORDS DAY AFTER THE RECEIPT OF THE MELANCHOLY
TIDINGS. BY THOMAS ALLEN, A. M. PASTOR OF THE CHURCH IN PITTSFIELD.
TO WHICH ARE ADDED TWO LETTERS FROM A RESPECTABLE GENTLEMAN, IN
LONDON, RELATING TO HER SICKNESS AND DEATH. IN THE DAY OF ADVERSITY
CONSIDER. ECCL. VII. 14.
Pittsfield: Printed by Chester Smith & Co. MDCCXCVIII. pp. [27], por-
trait. 8vo.   AAS. BA. BM. HC. NYPL.

33287   ALLEY, SARAH
AN ACCOUNT OF A TRANCE OR VISION OF SARAH ALLEY, OF BEEKMAN TOWN, DUT-
CHESS COUNTY, STATE OF NEW YORK, WHICH HAPPENED ON FIRST-DAY EVENING,
THE TWENTY-FIFTH OF SECOND MONTH, 1798. TAKEN FROM HER OWN MOUTH THE
TWENTY-SEVENTH OF THE SAME MONTH IN THE HEARING OF DIVERS PERSONS.
[Poughkeepsie: Printed by Nicholas Power.] 1798. *Price six-pence.* 12mo.
LOC.

33288   AN ALMANACK, FOR THE YEAR OF OUR LORD 1799.
Washington (Pennsylvania): Printed by John Colerick. [1798.]

33289   ALPHABETICAL LIST OF ALL THE TOWNS IN THE STATE OF NEW-YORK, AND THE
COUNTIES IN WHICH THEY ARE SITUATED.
Albany: Printed by Charles R. and George Webster. 1798. pp. 12. 24mo.

33290   AMELIA; OR, THE FAITHLESS BRITON. AN ORIGINAL AMERICAN NOVEL, FOUNDED
UPON RECENT FACTS. TO WHICH IS ADDED, AMELIA, OR MALEVOLENCE DEFEATED
[by a Lady of Massachusetts]; AND, MISS SEWARD'S MONODY ON MAJOR ANDRE.
Boston: Printed for and sold by W. Spotswood, and C. P. Wayne 1798. pp.
(2), 61, frontispiece; 22. 8vo.   AAS. LOC. NYPL.

Second title: MONODY ON MAJOR ANDRE. BY MISS SEWARD. FOURTH AMERICAN
EDITION.
Boston: Printed for and sold by W. Spotswood, and C. P. Wayne. 1798. pp. 22.
152d Massachusetts District Copyright, issued to William Spotswood,
and Caleb P. Wayne, as Proprietors, 4 October 1798.

33291   AMERICAN [cut] FARMER, AND DUTCHESS COUNTY ADVERTISER. VOL. I. No. 1 FRIDAY, JUNE 8, [— No. 30. THURSDAY, DECEMBER 27, 1798.]

Poughkeepsie, (State of New York): Printed by John Woods, by whom printing in all its branches, is executed on moderate terms. 1798. fol.   NJHS.

Established, as a weekly, by John Woods, and continued by him to the issue for July 22, 1800, when it was discontinued.

33292   AMERICAN [U. S. arms] MERCURY. VOL. XIV. No. 704. MONDAY, JANUARY 1, [— VOL. XV. No. 756. THURSDAY, DECEMBER 27, 1798.]

Published by Elisha Babcock—Hartford. 1798. fol.   AAS. CHS. YC.

33293   THE AMERICAN MORAL & SENTIMENTAL MAGAZINE, CONSISTING OF A COLLECTION OF SELECT PIECES, IN PROSE AND VERSE, FROM THE BEST AUTHORS, ON RELIGIOUS, MORAL, AND SENTIMENTAL SUBJECTS, CALCULATED TO FORM THE UNDERSTANDING, AND IMPROVE THE HEART. [Seven lines from] THOMSON. VOL. II. [MONDAY, DECEMBER 18, 1797 – MONDAY, MAY 21, 1798.]

New-York: Printed by the Editor [Thomas Kirk], 112 Chatham-Street, next door to the tea-water pump. 1798. pp. 371–766, iv, (2). 8vo.

BA. HSP. LOC. NYHS. NYPL. NYSL. WHS. YC.

Title, and imprint from the first volume. The paging is continuous, only the signatures dividing the two volumes. Discontinued at the above date.

33294   THE AMERICAN MUSICAL MISCELLANY: A COLLECTION OF THE NEWEST AND MOST APPOVED [sic] SONGS, SET TO MUSIC. [Eight lines of verse.]

Printed at Northampton, Massachusetts, by Andrew Wright, for Daniel Wright and Company. Sold by them and by S. Butler, in Northampton; by I. Thomas, jun. in Worcester; by F. Barker, in Greenfield; and by the principal Booksellers in Boston.—1798. pp. 300. 12mo.   AAS. BA. BU. JCB. LOC. MHS. NYPL. UTS.

33295   THE AMERICAN PRIMER. IMPROVED. OR, AN EASY AND PLEASANT GUIDE TO THE ART OF READING. ADORNED WITH CUTS. TO WHICH IS ADDED, THE ASSEMBLY OF DIVINES' CATECHISM.

Medford: Printed and sold by Nathaniel Coverly [junior.] (Price six pence). 1798. pp. (64). 32mo.   AAS. LOC.

33296   AMERICAN SPY. VOL. VII. NUMBER 343. TUESDAY, JANUARY 2, [—VOL. VIII. NUMBER 377. TUESDAY, AUGUST 28, 1798.]

Lansingburgh: Printed by Charles R. Webster. 1798. fol.

Discontinued at the above date. And succeeded, in September, by the Lansingburgh Gazette.

33297   AMERICAN TELEGRAPHE. BY LAZARUS BEACH, NEWFIELD, CONNECTICUT. [Motto.] VOL. III. No. 39. WHOLE No. 143. WEDNESDAY, JANUARY 3, [—VOL. IV. No. 39, WHOLE No. 195. WEDNESDAY, DECEMBER 26, 1798.]

Newfield, near Fairfield: Printed and published by Lazarus Beach, Printer, Bookseller and Stationer, opposite mr. Hinman's Inn. 1798. fol.

Before May, the motto was changed to: Use not to make any manner of lie; for the custom thereof is not good.

33298   THE AMERICAN UNIVERSAL MAGAZINE. VOL. IV. [DECEMBER 5, 1797 – MARCH 7, 1798.] [Cut.]

Philadelphia: Printed by Saml. H. Smith and Thos. Smith. [1798.] pp. (2), 430, (4), 6 plates. 8vo.   AAS. BM. BU. HSP. LCP. LOC. NYHS. NYPL. RIHS. WHS. YC.

Discontinued publication in March, as above.

33299 AMERICANISCHER Calender Aufs Jahr Christi 1799. Welches ein gemein Jahr von 365 Tagen est. [Cut of Eagle.]

Ephrata: Gedruckt bey Benjamin Mayer. [1798.] pp. (40). 4to.   AAS.

33300 AMERICANISCHER Stadt und Land Kalender Auf das 1799 ste Jahr Christi, welches ein Gemeines Jahr ist von 365 Tagen.

Philadelphia: Gedruckt und zu haben bey Carl Cist, in der Zweyten-Strasse, No. 104, nahe am Eck der Rehs-Strasse. [1798.] pp. (48). 4to.   AAS. LOC.

33301 AMUSEMENT Hall, or an easy introduction to the attainment of useful knowledge. By a Lady,

Hartford: Sold by John Babcock. January 18, 1798.

33302 ANCOURT, l'abbé d'
The Lady's preceptor, or, a letter to a young lady of distinction, upon politeness. Taken from the French of the abbe d'Ancourt, and adapted to the religion, customs, and manners of the United States.

Sag-Harbor: Printed by David Frothingham. 1798.

33303 ANDERSON, James   1680–1739
Constitutions of the ancient and honorable fraternity of Free and Accepted Masons; collected and digested from the old records, faithful traditions and lodge books for the use of lodges. Together with the history and general regulations of the Grand Lodge of Massachusetts. Compiled by the reverend Thaddeus Mason Harris, a.m. member of the Massachusetts Historical Society, and chaplain to the Grand Lodge of Massachusetts. . . . Second edition, revised and corrected; with large additions. Published under the direction of the Grand Lodge.

Printed at Worcester, Massachusetts, by brother Isaiah Thomas, in the christian era MDCCXCVIII; in the year of light IƆƆDCCXCVIII. pp. (2), (2), (2), (2), 288, frontispiece. 4to.   AAS. LOC. NYPL.

151st Massachusetts District Copyright, issued to Isaiah Thomas, as Proprietor, 21 September, 1798.

33304 ANDREWS, Samuel   1737–1818
The True means to avert national judgments. A sermon upon the solemn fast ordered through the States of America, May 9th, 1798. Delivered at the house of John Brewer, esq., in Robins-Town. upon the river Schodick, at his, and the desire of others of its inhabitants, citizens of the United States; and published at their request. By Samuel Andrews, a.m. rector of the Saint Andrew's Church, in the parish of Saint Andrews, and Province of New Brunswick; and missionary from the Society, &c.

Printed at Boston: 1798. pp. 22. 8vo.   AAS. CHS. JCB. LOC.

33305 ANDROS, Thomas   1759–1845
A Reference, not only of good but of the evil that befalls us in life, to the hand of God, an essential principle of piety: a sermon, preached to the Congregational Society in Berkley, Sept. 30, 1798, by Thomas Andros. Occasioned by the death of his wife. [Two lines from] St. Paul.

Providence: Printed by Bennett Wheeler. M,DCC,XCVIII. pp. (26). 8vo.
AAS. JCB. RIHS.

33306   THE ANNUAL VISITOR; OR ALMANAC; FOR THE YEAR OF OUR LORD, —1799,—
BEING THE THIRD AFTER LEAP-YEAR. CALCULATED FOR THE MERIDIAN OF BALTI-
MORE, BUT WITHOUT ANY CONSIDERABLE VARIATION, WILL SUIT THE STATES OF
MARYLAND, PENNSYLVANIA, VIRGINIA, KENTUCKY, OR TENNESSEE. CONTAINING,
BESIDES EVERYTHING NECESSARY IN AN ALMANAC, A VARIETY OF PIECES IN PROSE
& VERSE.—USEFUL & ENTERTAINING.

     *Baltimore: Printed by W. Pechin, No. 15, for John Hagerty, No. 104, and
Thomas, Andrews & Butler, No. 184, Market-street.* [1798.] pp. (36). 12mo. AAS.

     Contains, Directions for the management of horses when travelling.
List of post towns; and cross posts. Table of interest at 6 per cent.
Courts of law. Stamp Act. Rival candidates for the favour of Amer-
ica. Hail Columbia, etc.

33307   ARCHER, JOHN, JUNIOR   1777–1830
AN INAUGURAL DISSERTATION ON CYNANCHE TRACHEALIS, COMMONLY CALLED CROUP
OR HIVES. BY JOHN ARCHER, JUNR. HONORARY MEMBER OF THE PHILADELPHIA
MEDICAL SOCIETY, AND CITIZEN OF THE STATE OF MARYLAND. VENI, VIDI, VICI.

     Philadelphia: Printed by Way & Groff, No. 27, Arch-Street. 1798. pp. (46).
8vo.   AAS. JCB. LCP. LOC. SGO.

33308   ARCHIBALD, ROBERT
THE UNIVERSAL PREACHER; BEING AN ENQUIRY INTO THE STATE OF THE MORAL
WORLD. No. 1. BY ROBERT ARCHIBALD, V. D. M. & A. M.

     Halifax: Printed by Abraham Hodge. 1798.

33309   THE ARGUS. [Motto.] VOL. I. No. 51. MONDAY, JANUARY 1, [— No. 41 OF VOL. II.
WHOLE No. 93. SATURDAY, OCTOBER 27, 1798.]

     *Printed and published by Cornelius Sturtevant jun. & Co. at Putney, Ver-
mont.* 1798. fol.   AAS.

     On June 4, the partnership of Cornelius Sturtevant, jun. Abijah Wilder,
and Elias Sturtevant was dissolved. Cornelius Sturtevant alone continuing publication. And beginning with the issue for November 3d, the
title was changed to *Putney Argus.*

33310   ARGUS. GREENLEAF'S NEW [cut] DAILY ADVERTISER. [Motto.] NUMBER 826. MON-
DAY, JANUARY 1, [— No. 1090, MONDAY, DECEMBER 31, 1798.]

     ☞ *New-York—Edited, printed and published (every morning) by Thomas
Greenleaf, No. 54, Wall-Street—six doors from the Tontine Coffee-House.* 1798.
fol.   LOC. NYHS.

     Greenleaf died of yellow fever, September 14th, and publication was
suspended from September 16th, to November 5th, on which date it was
resumed by his widow, Ann Greenleaf.

33311   ARISTOTLE, pseudonym
KURZGEFASTES WEIBER-BUCHLEIN. ENTHALT ARISTOTELS UND ALBERTI MAGNI
HEBAMMEN-KUNST, MIT DEN DARZU GEHORIGEN RECEPTEN. [Ornaments.]

     Gedruckt im Jahr. 1798.

33312   ARISTOTLE, pseudonym, continued.
—— THE WORKS OF ARISTOTLE, THE FAMOUS PHILOSOPHER. IN FOUR PARTS. CON-
TAINING I. HIS COMPLETE MASTER-PIECE; DISPLAYING THE SECRETS OF NATURE IN
THE GENERATION OF MAN. TO WHICH IS ADDED, THE FAMILY PHYSICIAN: BEING
APPROVED REMEDIES FOR THE SEVERAL DISTEMPERS INCIDENT TO THE HUMAN
BODY. II. HIS EXPERIENCED MIDWIFE; ABSOLUTELY NECESSARY FOR SURGEONS,
MIDWIVES, NURSES, AND CHILD-BEARING WOMEN. III. HIS BOOK OF PROBLEMS,
CONTAINING VARIOUS QUESTIONS AND ANSWERS, RELATIVE TO THE STATE OF MAN'S
BODY. IV. HIS LAST LEGACY; UNFOLDING THE SECRETS OF NATURE RESPECTING
THE GENERATION OF MAN. A NEW EDITION.

Philadelphia: Printed for the Booksellers. MDCCXCVIII. pp. 72; 100; 68;
39 [*sic* 34.] 12mo.   AAS. BML.

Second title: THE EXPERIENCED MIDWIFE: ABSOLUTELY NECESSARY FOR SURGEONS,
MIDWIVES, NURSES AND CHILD-BEARING WOMEN. A NEW EDITION.

Philadelphia: Printed for the Booksellers. 1799. pp. 100.

Third title: ARISTOTLE'S BOOK OF PROBLEMS, WITH OTHER ASTRONOMERS, ASTROL-
OGERS, PHILOSOPHERS, PHYSICIANS, &C. WHEREIN ARE CONTAINED DIVERS QUES-
TIONS AND ANSWERS TOUCHING THE STATE OF MAN'S BODY. TOGETHER WITH THE
REASONS OF DIVERS WONDERS IN THE CREATION; THE GENERATION OF BIRDS,
BEASTS, FISHES, AND INSECTS; AND MANY OTHER PROBLEMS ON THE MOST WEIGHTY
MATTERS, BY WAY OF QUESTION AND ANSWER. A NEW EDITION.

Philadelphia: Printed for the Booksellers. MDCCXCII. pp. 68.

Fourth title: ARISTOTLE'S LAST LEGACY, UNFOLDING THE MYSTERIES OF NATURE
IN THE [*sic*] GENERATION OF MAN. TREATING, I. OF VIRGINITY, ITS SIGNS AND
TOKENS, AND HOW A MAN MAY KNOW WHETHER HE HATH MARRIED A VIRGIN OR
NOT. II. OF THE ORGAN OF GENERATION IN WOMEN, WITH A DESCRIPTION OF THE
WOMB. III. OF THE USE AND ACTION OF THE GENITALS IN THE WORK OF GENERA-
TION. IV. OF CONCEPTION; AND HOW TO KNOW WHETHER A WOMAN HAS CON-
CEIVED, AND WHETHER OF A MALE OR FEMALE. V. OF THE PLEASURE AND AD-
VANTAGE OF MARRIAGE; WITH THE UNHAPPY CONSEQUENCES OF UNEQUAL MATCHES,
AND MISERIES OF UNLAWFUL LOVE. VI. OF BARRENNESS, WITH REMEDIES AGAINST
IT; AND THE SIGNS OF INSUFFICIENCY BOTH IN MEN AND WOMEN. VII. DIRECTIONS
TO BOTH SEXES HOW TO MANAGE THEMSELVES IN THE ACT OF COITION, OR THEIR
VENEREAL EMBRACES. VIII. A VADE-MECUM FOR MIDWIVES AND NURSES; CON-
TAINING PARTICULAR DIRECTIONS FOR THE FAITHFUL DISCHARGE OF THEIR SEVERAL
EMPLOYMENTS. IX. EXCELLENT REMEDIES AGAINST ALL DISEASES INCIDENT TO
VIRGINS AND CHILD-BEARING WOMEN; FITTED FOR THE USE OF MIDWIVES, &C. A
NEW EDITION.

Philadelphia: Printed for the Booksellers. MDCCXCII. pp. 39 [*sic* 34.]

33313   ARMSTRONG, JOHN   1758–1843
TO THE SENATE AND REPRESENTATIVES OF THE UNITED STATES, IN CONGRESS
ASSEMBLED. [Urging repeal of the alien and sedition laws.]

[*Poughkeepsie: Printed by Nicholas Power.* 1798.] pp. (2). fol.   NYPL.

33314   ARNOLD, SAMUEL JAMES   1774–1852
AND HEAR HER SIGH ADIEU! A FAVORITE SONG SUNG IN THE OPERA OF THE SHIP-
WRECK. COMPOSED [*sic*] BY DR. ARNOLD.

New York. Printed & sold by J. Hewitt at his Musical Repository No. 131
William Street. Sold also by B. Carr Philadelphia & J. Carr Baltimore. 1798.
pp. (2). 4to.   LOC.

33315   THE ART OF CHEESE-MAKING, TAUGHT FROM ACTUAL EXPERIMENTS; BY WHICH MORE
BUTTER AND CHEESE MAY BE MADE FROM THE SAME QUANTITY OF MILK.

[*Litchfield: Printed and sold by Thomas Collier.* 1798.] pp. 16. 16mo.

33316 THE ART OF CHEESE-MAKING, continued.
—— THE ART OF CHEESE-MAKING, TAUGHT FROM ACTUAL EXPERIMENTS, BY WHICH
MORE AND BETTER CHEESE MAY BE MADE FROM THE SAME QUANTITY OF MILK.
    Windham: Printed and sold by John Byrne. 1798. pp. 8+. 16mo.   AAS.

33317 ASH, JOHN   1724-1779
GRAMMATICAL INSTITUTES, OR AN EASY INTRODUCTION TO DR. LOWTH'S ENGLISH
GRAMMAR: DESIGNED FOR THE USE OF SCHOOLS, AND TO LEAD YOUNG GENTLEMEN
AND LADIES INTO THE KNOWLEDGE OF THE FIRST PRINCIPLES OF THE ENGLISH
LANGUAGE. BY JOHN ASH, LL. D. WITH AN APPENDIX, CONTAINING, I. THE DE-
CLENSION OF IRREGULAR AND DEFECTIVE VERBS. II. THE APPLICATION OF THE
GRAMMATICAL INSTITUTES. III. SOME USEFUL OBSERVATIONS ON THE ELLIPSIS,
IV. EXERCISES OF BAD ENGLISH. V. LESSONS ON THE ENGLISH LANGUAGE. TO
WHICH ARE ADDED, SELECT LESSONS, TO INSTIL JUST SENTIMENTS OF VIRTUE INTO
YOUTH, AND A COLLECTION OF BOOKS, PROPER FOR YOUNG GENTLEMEN AND LADIES,
TO SHORTEN THE PATH TO KNOWLEDGE. A NEW EDITION, REVISED AND CORRECTED.
    *New-York: Printed by J. Buel for E. Duyckinck & Co. Robert Magill & Peter
A. Messer.* 1798. pp. 144. 24mo.   AAS. NYPL.

33318 ASPINWALL, GEORGE   1774-1804
A DISSERTATION ON THE CYNANCHE MALIGNA. BY GEORGE ASPINWALL. [Cut of eagle.]
    Dedham: Printed by Mann and Adams. 1798. pp. [20.] 8vo.
    AAS. JCB. LOC. NYPL.

33319 ASSOCIATE REFORMED CHURCH IN NORTH AMERICA.
EXTRACTS FROM THE MINUTES OF THE ACTS AND PROCEEDINGS OF THE ASSOCIATE RE-
FORMED SYNOD MET AT PHILADELPHIA, MAY 30, 1798; AND CONTINUED BY ADJOURN-
MENTS. PUBLISHED BY ORDER OF SYNOD.
    New-York: Printed by T. & J. Swords. 1798. pp. 32. 8vo.   NYPL.

33320 ATHERTON, CHARLES HUMPHREY   1773-1853
AN ORATION, PRONOUNCED IN THE FIRST PARISH AT AMHERST, N. H. ON THE ANNI-
VERSARY OF AMERICAN INDEPENDENCE, JULY 4, 1798. BY CHARLES H. ATHERTON.
[Eight lines of quotations.]
    Printed at Amherst, by Samuel Preston, July, 1798. pp. 24. 8vo.
    AAS. BM. HC. LOC.

33321 ATWOOD, JOSHUA, and JOHN
IMAGINATION IN SEARCH AFTER HAPPINESS, A POEM IN TWO CANTOS. BY JOSHUA &
JOHN ATWOOD. [Printer's mark.]
    [Boston:] Printed by Thomas Fleet, for the Author. MDCCXCVIII. pp.
(19). 12mo.   AAS.

33322 AUBORN, A. D'
THE FRENCH CONVERT: BEING A TRUE RELATION OF THE HAPPY CONVERSION OF A
NOBLE FRENCH LADY FROM THE ERRORS AND SUPERSTITIONS OF POPERY TO THE
REFORMED RELIGION, BY MEANS OF A PROTESTANT GARDENER, HER SERVANT.
WHEREIN IS SHEWN, HER GREAT AND UNPARALLELED SUFFERINGS, ON THE ACCOUNT
OF HER SAID CONVERSION; AS ALSO HER WONDERFUL DELIVERANCE FROM TWO
ASSASSINS, HIRED BY A POPISH PRIEST TO MURDER HER: AND OTHER MIRACULOUS
PRESERVATIONS IN A WOOD FOR TWO YEARS; AND HOW SHE WAS AT LAST PROVI-
DENTIALLY FOUND BY HER HUSBAND; WHO, TOGETHER WITH HER PARENTS, WERE
BROUGHT OVER TO THE EMBRACING OF THE TRUE RELIGION, AS WERE DIVERS OTH-
ERS ALSO. TO WHICH IS ADDED, A BRIEF ACCOUNT OF THE PRESENT SEVERE PER-
SECUTIONS OF THE FRENCH PROTESTANTS.
    *Brookfield (Massachusetts,) Printed by E. Merriam & Co. for G. Merriam,
Worcester, and for the Booksellers in Boston.* [1798.] pp. 112. 12mo.   LOC.

33323 AUBORN, A. D', continued.
—— — THE FRENCH CONVERT; BEING A TRUE RELATION OF THE HAPPY CONVER-
SION OF A NOBLE FRENCH LADY, FROM THE ERRORS AND SUPERSTITIONS OF POPERY,
TO THE REFORMED RELIGION, BY MEANS OF A PROTESTANT GARDENER, HER SERV-
ANT, WHEREIN IS SHEWN, HER GREAT AND UNPARALLELED SUFFERINGS, ON THE AC-
COUNT OF HER SAID CONVERSION: AS ALSO HER WONDERFUL DELIVERANCE FROM
TWO ASSASSINS, HIRED BY A POPISH PRIEST TO MURDER HER: AND OF HER MIRAC-
ULOUS PRESERVATION IN A WOOD FOR TWO YEARS; AND HOW SHE WAS AT LAST
PROVIDENTIALLY FOUND BY HER HUSBAND; WHO, TOGETHER WITH HER PARENTS
WERE BRO'T OVER TO THE EMBRACING OF THE TRUE RELIGION, AS WERE DIVERS
OTHERS ALSO.
Hartford: Printed by John Babcock, 1798. pp. 107. 12mo.   AAS. JCB. LOC.
Origen's Lamentation. pp. 99-107.

33324 —— — THE FRENCH CONVERT. BEING A TRUE RELATION OF THE HAPPY CONVER-
SION OF A NOBLE FRENCH LADY FROM THE ERRORS AND SUPERSTITIONS OF POPERY
TO THE REFORMED RELIGION, BY MEANS OF A PROTESTANT GARDENER, HER SERV-
ANT, WHEREIN IS SHEWN, HER GREAT AND UNPARALLELED SUFFERINGS, ON THE AC-
COUNT OF HER SAID CONVERSION: AS ALSO HER WONDERFUL DELIVERANCE FROM
TWO ASSASSINS, HIRED BY A POPISH PRIEST TO MURDER HER: AND OF HER MIRAC-
ULOUS PRESERVATION IN A WOOD FOR TWO YEARS: AND HOW SHE WAS AT LAST
PROVIDENTIALLY FOUND BY HER HUSBAND; WHO, TOGETHER WITH HER PARENTS
WERE BROUGHT OVER TO THE EMBRACING OF THE TRUE RELIGION, AS WERE DIVERS
OTHERS ALSO.
New-Haven, Printed by Geo. Bunce. 1798. pp. 108. 12mo.   JCB. LOC.
A Brief account of the persecutions of the French protestants. pp.
106-108.

33325 AUFRÈRE, ANTHONY   1756–1833
THE CANNIBAL'S PROGRESS, OR, THE DREADFUL HORRORS OF FRENCH INVASION! AS
DISPLAYED BY THE REPUBLICAN OFFICERS AND SOLDIERS, IN THE PERFIDY, RAPAC-
ITY, FEROCIOUSNESS, AND BRUTALITY, EXERCISED TOWARDS THE INNOCENT INHAB-
ITANTS OF GERMANY. TRANSLATED FROM THE GERMAN, BY ANTHONY AUFRER,
ESQ. [Three lines of quotations.]
Albany: Printed by Charles R. & G. Webster. [1798.]

33326 —— — THE CANNIBAL'S PROGRESS; OR THE DREADFUL HORRORS OF FRENCH
INVASION, AS DISPLAYED BY THE REPUBLICAN OFFICERS AND SOLDIERS, IN THEIR
PERFIDY, RAPACITY, FEROCIOUSNESS AND BRUTALITY, EXERCISED TOWARDS THE
INNOCENT INHABITANTS OF GERMANY. TRANSLATED FROM THE GERMAN, BY
ANTHONY AUFRER, ESQ. [Five lines of Scripture texts.]
Amherst, Newhampshire. Printed by Samuel Preston. 1798.

33327 —— — THE CANIBALS [sic] PROGRESS; OR, THE DREADFUL HORRORS OF FRENCH
INVASION, AS DISPLAYED BY THE REPUBLICAN OFFICERS AND SOLDIERS, IN THE
PERFIDY, RAPACITY, FEROCIOUSNESS, AND BRUTALITY, EXERCISED TOWARDS THE
INNOCENT INHABITANTS OF GERMANY. TRANSLATED FROM THE GERMAN, BY
ANTHONY AUFRER, ESQ.
Boston: Sold by W. P. and L. Blake. 1798. *(Price only six cents).*

33328 —— — THE CANNIBAL'S PROGRESS; OR THE DREADFUL HORRORS OF FRENCH
INVASION! AS DISPLAYED BY THE REPUBLICAN OFFICERS AND SOLDIERS, IN THEIR
PERFIDY, RAPACITY, FEROCIOUSNESS, AND BRUTALITY, EXERCISED TOWARDS THE
INNOCENT INHABITANTS OF GERMANY. TRANSLATED FROM THE GERMAN, BY
ANTHONY AUFRER, ESQ. [Three lines of quotations.]
*London: Published by Wright, Cadell, and others. And republished, at
Charleston, by Benjamin Franklin Timothy.* MDCCXCVIII. pp. 43. 8vo. SCHS.

AUFRÈRE, ANTHONY, continued.

33329 —— — THE CANNIBALS' PROGRESS; OR THE DREADFUL HORRORS OF FRENCH INVASION, AS DISPLAYED BY THE REPUBLICAN OFFICERS AND SOLDIERS, IN THEIR PERFIDY, RAPACITY, FEROCIOUSNESS, AND BRUTALITY, EXERCISED TOWARDS THE INNOCENT INHABITANTS OF GERMANY. TRANSLATED FROM THE GERMAN, BY ANTHONY AUFRER, ESQ. [Cut by Wm. Wadsworth.] [Three lines of Scripture texts.]
    London: Published by Wright, Cadel and others; and republished at Hartford, by Hudson & Goodwin. 1798. pp. 32. 8vo.   AAS. LOC. NL. UTS.

33330 —— — THE CANNIBAL'S PROGRESS, OR THE DREADFUL HORRORS OF FRENCH INVASION, CONTAINING AUTHENTIC ACCOUNTS OF THE CRUELTIES OF THE FRENCH OFFICERS AND SOLDIERS TOWARDS THE INNOCENT INHABITANTS OF GERMANY. TRANSLATED FROM THE GERMAN, BY ANTHONY AUFRERE, ESQ. . . . .
    New-Haven: Sold by Isaac Beers. 1798.

33331 —— — THE CANNIBALS' PROGRESS; OR THE DREADFUL HORRORS OF FRENCH INVASION, AS DISPLAYED BY THE REPUBLICAN OFFICERS AND SOLDIERS, IN THEIR PERFIDY, RAPACITY, FEROCIOUSNESS AND BRUTALITY, EXERCISED TOWARDS THE INNOCENT INHABITANTS OF GERMANY. TRANSLATED FROM THE GERMAN, BY ANTHONY AUFRER, ESQ. [Wood cut. Four lines of Scripture texts.]
    London: Published by Wright, Cadel and others; and republished at New-London by James Springer. [1798]. pp. 50. 12mo.   AAS.

33332 —— — THE CANNIBALS' PROGRESS; OR THE DREADFUL HORRORS OF FRENCH INVASION, AS DISPLAYED BY THE REPUBLICAN OFFICERS AND SOLDIERS, IN THEIR PERFIDY, RAPACITY, FEROCIOUSNESS AND BRUTALITY, EXERCISED TOWARDS THE INNOCENT INHABITANTS OF GERMANY. TRANSLATED FROM THE GERMAN, BY ANTHONY AUFRER, ESQ. [Three lines of Scripture texts.]
    Newburyport: Printed by Edmund M. Blunt,—State-Street. [1798.] pp. [35], (1). 8vo.   AAS. JCB.

33333 —— — THE CANNIBALS' PROGRESS; OR THE DREADFUL HORRORS OF FRENCH INVASION, AS DISPLAYED BY THE REPUBLICAN OFFICERS AND SOLDIERS, IN THEIR PERFIDY, RAPACITY, FEROCIOUSNESS AND BRUTALITY, EXERCISED TOWARDS THE INNOCENT INHABITANTS OF GERMANY. TRANSLATED FROM THE GERMAN. BY ANTHONY AUFRER, ESQ. [Wood cut. Five lines of Scripture texts.]
    London: Published by Wright, Cadel and others; and republished at Northampton, by William Butler. 1798. pp. (32). 8vo.   AAS.

33334 —— — THE CANNIBAL'S PROGRESS; OR THE DREADFUL HORRORS OF FRENCH INVASION, DISPLAYED BY THE REPUBLICAN OFFICERS AND SOLDIERS, IN THEIR PERFIDY, RAPACITY, FEROCIOUSNESS AND BRUTALITY, EXERCISED TOWARDS THE INNOCENT INHABITANTS OF GERMANY. TRANSLATED FROM THE GERMAN, BY ANTHONY AUFRER, ESQ. [Cut. Three lines of quotations.]
    London: Published by Wright, Cadel and others; and republished at Philadelphia by William Cobbett. Price only 6 cents, 11 for half a dollar, 25 for a dollar, 56 for 2 dollars, three dollars and a half per hundred. [1798.] pp. (47). 12mo.   BA. CLS. HSP. LOC.

33335 —— — THE CANNIBAL'S PROGRESS; OR THE DREADFUL HORRORS OF FRENCH INVASION, AS DISPLAYED BY THE REPUBLICAN OFFICERS AND SOLDIERS, IN THEIR PERFIDY, RAPACITY, FEROCIOUSNESS & BRUTALITY, EXERCISED TOWARDS THE INNOCENT INHABITANTS OF GERMANY. TRANSLATED FROM THE GERMAN, BY ANTHONY AUFRER, ESQ. [Three lines of quotations. Vignette.]
    Portsmouth: New-Hampshire, Printed (from the Philadelphia edition) by J. Melcher, 1798, and now selling at his Office, price only 10 cents single—7 for half a dollar & 5 dollars pr. hundred. pp. (35). 8vo.   JCB. LOC.

AUFRÈRE, ANTHONY, continued.

33336 —— — THE CANNIBAL'S PROGRESS, OR, THE DREADFUL HORRORS OF FRENCH INVASION! AS DISPLAYED BY THE REPUBLICAN OFFICERS AND SOLDIERS, IN THEIR PERFIDY, RAPACITY, FEROCIOUSNESS, AND BRUTALITY, EXERCISED TOWARDS THE INNOCENT INHABITANTS OF GERMANY. TRANSLATED FROM THE GERMAN BY ANTHONY AUFRER, ESQ. [Three lines of quotations.]
Savannah: Printed by N. Johnston and Co. 1798.

33337 —— — THE CANNIBAL'S PROGRESS; OR, THE DREADFUL HORRORS OF FRENCH INVASION DISPLAYED BY THE REPUBLICAN OFFICERS AND SOLDIERS IN THEIR PERFIDY, RAPACITY, FEROCIOUSNESS AND BRUTALITY, EXERCISED TOWARDS THE INNOCENT INHABITANTS OF GERMANY. TRANSLATED FROM THE GERMAN BY ANTHONY AUFRER. . . .
Vergennes: Printed by G. and R. Waite. 1798. pp. 47. 12mo.

33338 —— — THE CANNIBAL'S PROGRESS, OR THE DREADFUL HORRORS OF FRENCH INVASION, AS DISPLAYED BY THE REPUBLICAN OFFICERS AND SOLDIERS IN THEIR PERFIDY, RAPACITY, FEROCIOUSNESS AND BRUTALITY EXERCISED TOWARDS THE INNOCENT INHABITANTS OF GERMANY. [Six lines of verse.]
Walpole: Printed by David Carlisle, for Thomas & Thomas. 1798. pp. 47. 8vo.   AAS. MHS.

"Five thousand copies sold in Philadelphia in a few days — another edition of ten thousand copies is now in the press in that city. One large edition at Hartford, and another at Newburyport have been printed and sold very rapidly."— *New-Hampshire Gazette.* July 31, 1798.

33339 AURORA [cut] GENERAL ADVERTISER. SURGO UT PROSIM. NUM. 2174. MONDAY, JANUARY 1, [— NUM. 2441. MONDAY, DECEMBER 31, 1798.]
Published (daily) by Benj. Franklin Bache, No. 112 Market Street, between Third and Fourth Streets, Philadelphia. 1798. fol.   AAS. BM. HSP. LCP. MdHS. PSL.

Benjamin Franklin Bache died of yellow fever, September 10th, and publication was suspended to November 1st, when his widow Margaret Markoe Bache, resumed publication, with William Duane as editor, after November 14th, the imprint reading: "Published (daily) for the heirs of Benj. Franklin Bache."

33340 AUSTIN, DAVID   1759–1831
THE DOWNFALL OF MYSTICAL BABYLON; OR, A KEY TO THE PROVIDENCE OF GOD, IN THE POLITICAL OPERATIONS OF '93-4: BEING THE SUBSTANCE OF A DISCOURSE PREACHED FIRST, AT ELIZABETHTOWN, AND AFTERWARDS AT NEW-YORK, ON THE EVENING OF THE LORD'S DAY, APRIL 7, 1793, AND NOW OFFERED WITH NOTES AND ILLUSTRATIONS, IN EVIDENCE OF THE SENTIMENTS THEN DELIVERED. BY DAVID AUSTIN, A. M. MINISTER OF THE FIRST PRESBYTERIAN CHURCH AT ELIZABETHTOWN.
"Lately published and for sale by James H. Stewart, Lexington. October 2, 1798."

33341 —— A PROPHETIC LEAF. CONTAINING AN ILLUSTRATION OF THE SIGNS OF THE TIMES, AS NOW DISPLAYING THEMSELVES TO THE EYE OF A SPIRITUAL OBSERVER, IN THE NATURAL, IN THE MORAL, AND IN THE INVISIBLE HEAVENS: COLLECTED FROM THE FOUNTAIN OF TRUTH FROM THE EVENTS OF PROVIDENCE, AND FROM THE INDITINGS OF THE SPIRIT OF GRACE: DESIGNED TO UNFOLD TO AN ASTONISHED WORLD, THE PURPOSE OF GOD IN THE CONVULSIONS WHICH NOW SHAKE THE THRONES OF THE EARTH, AND THREATEN THE DEMOLITION OF THE PROPHETIC HEAVENS: PREPARATORY TO THE INTRODUCTION, IRRESISTABLE PROGRESS, AND FINAL CONSUMMATION OF THE GLORY OF THE LATTER DAY, ABSORBED IN THE PRINCELY REIGN OF THE MIGHTY REDEEMER. BY A FRIEND TO THE TRUTH. [Five lines of Scripture texts.] No. 1. SEPTEMBER, 1798. [— No. 23. OCTOBER, 1798.]
New-Haven: Printed for the Author. 1798. pp. 64. 8vo.   CHS. NYPL. YC.

Addressed to the newspapers under the title: "The Stone against the Image." "This paper will be published once every two weeks, containing one full sheet of letter press . . . and so paged and folded as to make a volume when the work is complete."

AUCTION
VALUES

33342   AUSTIN, SAMUEL   1760–1830

THE NATURE, EXTENT, AND IMPORTANCE OF THE DUTY, BINDING ON THE CHRISTIAN MINISTER, DIVINELY COMMISSIONED TO BEAR THE WARNINGS OF GOD TO MEN: ILLUSTRATED IN A SERMON, PREACHED IN FITCHBURGH, MASSACHUSETTS, ON THE 27TH DAY OF SEPTEMBER, 1797, AT THE ORDINATION OF THE REV. SAMUEL WORCESTER; AND AGAIN, BY PARTICULAR REQUEST, IN GRANVILLE, IN THE STATE OF NEW-YORK, ON THE 4TH DAY OF THE FOLLOWING OCTOBER, AT THE ORDINATION OF THE REV. NATHANIEL HALL. BY SAMUEL AUSTIN, A. M. . . .

Printed at Worcester, by Leonard Worcester. 1798. pp. 32. 8vo.

AAS. BA. HC. JCB. NYPL. YC.

33343   —— AN ORATION, PRONOUNCED AT WORCESTER, ON THE FOURTH OF JULY, 1798; THE ANNIVERSARY OF THE INDEPENDENCE OF THE UNITED STATES OF AMERICA. BY SAMUEL AUSTIN, A. M.

Printed at Worcester, by Leonard Worcester. 1798. pp. 38. 8vo.

AAS. BA. BM. HC. JCB. LOC. MHS. NYPL. YC.

33344   AUSTIN, WILLIAM   1778–1841

STRICTURES ON HARVARD UNIVERSITY.—PERSONAL SATIRE IS WORTHY OF LITTLE NOTICE—IT IS SELDOM JUST. BY A SENIOR.

Boston: Printed and sold by John W. Folsom, at his Book-Store and Printing-Office, No. 30, Union-Street. M,DCCXCVIII. pp. (35). 12mo. AAS. BA. LOC. MHS.

33345   AUSTIN, WILLIAM, editor

A SELECTION OF THE PATRIOTIC ADDRESSES, TO THE PRESIDENT OF THE UNITED STATES. TOGETHER WITH THE PRESIDENT'S ANSWERS. PRESENTED IN THE YEAR ONE THOUSAND SEVEN HUNDRED AND NINETY-EIGHT, AND THE TWENTY-SECOND OF THE INDEPENDENCE OF AMERICA.

Boston: Printed by John W. Folsom, No. 30, Union-Street. 1798. pp. 360. 12mo. AAS. BA. HC. JCB. LOC. MHS. NL. NYPL.

Dedication. To the French Directory. By the Editor. Contains a list of Subscriber's names.

33346   BABCOCK, ELISHA

THE CHILD'S SPELLING BOOK: CALCULATED TO RENDER READING COMPLETELY EASY TO LITTLE CHILDREN; TO IMPRESS UPON THEIR MINDS THE IMPORTANCE OF RELIGION, AND THE ADVANTAGES OF GOOD MANNERS. COMPILED BY A PRINTER.

Hartford [in vignette]: *Printed by John Babcock. 1798. pp. 112, frontis-piece, and cuts in text. sq. 24mo.* AAS.

Connecticut District Copyright, issued to John Babcock, as Proprietor, 2 January, 1799.

33347   BACHE'S PHILADELPHIA AURORA. No. 118. MONDAY, JANUARY 1, AND TUESDAY, JANUARY 2, [— No. ——. FRIDAY, DECEMBER 28, AND SATURDAY, DECEMBER 29, 1798.]

Published (tri-weekly) by Benj. Franklin Bache, No. 112, Market Street. 1798. fol.

Owing to the death of Bache, from yellow fever, publication was suspended from September 11th to November 2nd, when publication was resumed by William Duane "for the heirs of Benj. Franklin Bache.

33348   BACKUS, AZEL   1765–1817
ABSALOM'S CONSPIRACY: A SERMON, PREACHED AT THE GENERAL ELECTION, AT HART-
FORD IN THE STATE OF CONNECTICUT, MAY 10TH, 1798. BY AZEL BACKUS, A. M.
PASTOR OF A CHURCH IN BETHLEM. [Printers mark.]

Hartford: Printed by Hudson and Goodwin. 1798. pp. 54. 8vo.
AAS. BA. BM. JCB. LOC. MHS. NYHS. NYPL. RIHS. YC.

33349   —— — ABSALOM'S CONSPIRACY: A SERMON, PREACHED AT THE GENERAL ELECTION,
AT HARTFORD IN THE STATE OF CONNECTICUT, MAY 10TH, 1798. BY AZEL BACKUS,
A. M. PASTOR OF A CHURCH IN BETHLEM.

Hartford—printed: New-York Re-printed by John Tiebout, No. 358, *Pearl-
Street.* 1798. pp. 32. 8vo.   AAS. LOC. NYHS. NYPL. RIHS.

33350   —— — ABSALOM'S CONSPIRACY. A SERMON PREACHED AT THE GENERAL ELECTION,
AT HARTFORD, IN THE STATE OF CONNECTICUT. MAY 10TH, 1798. BY AZEL BACKUS.
A. M. PASTOR OF A CHURCH IN BETHLEM.

Hartford: Printed. Stockbridge: Re-printed by Rosseter & Willard, June,
1798. pp. 35. 8vo.   NYPL.

33351   —— — ABSALOM'S CONSPIRACY: A SERMON, PREACHED AT THE GENERAL ELECTION,
AT HARTFORD, IN THE STATE OF CONNECTICUT, MAY 10TH, 1798. BY AZEL BACKUS,
A. M. PASTOR OF A CHURCH IN BETHLEM.

Suffield: Printed by H. & O. Farnsworth. 1798. pp. 47. 8vo.   AAS. LOC.

33352   BACKUS, CHARLES   1749–1803
THE BENEVOLENT SPIRIT OF CHRISTIANITY ILLUSTRATED; IN A SERMON, DELIVERED
AT THE ORDINATION OF THE REV. THOMAS SNELL, TO THE PASTORAL CARE OF THE
SECOND CHURCH IN BROOKFIELD, MASSACHUSETTS, JUNE 27TH, 1798. BY CHARLES
BACKUS, A. M. PASTOR OF A CHURCH IN SOMERS, CONNECTICUT.

Printed at Worcester, by Leonard Worcester. 1798. pp. 39. 8vo.
AAS. BM. BU. CHS. HC. JCB. YC.

33353   —— THE PRINCIPAL CAUSES OF THE OPPOSITION TO CHRISTIANITY CONSIDERED; IN A
SERMON, DELIVERED AT THE ORDINATION OF THE REV. ZEPHANIAH SWIFT MOORE,
TO THE PASTORAL CARE OF THE CONGREGATIONAL CHURCH IN LEICESTER, MASSA-
CHUSETTS, JANUARY 10, 1798. BY CHARLES BACKUS, A. M. PASTOR OF A CHURCH
IN SOMERS, CONNECTICUT.

Printed at Worcester, by Leonard Worcester. 1798. pp. 35. 8vo.
AAS. BU. CHS. CLA. JCB. LOC. NYPL. UTS.

The Charge, by the Rev. Dr. Fiske, of Brookfield. The Right hand of
fellowship, by the Rev. Samuel Austin, of Worcester.

33354   —— THE TRUE CHRISTIAN LIVING AND DYING UNTO THE LORD. A SERMON, DELIV-
ERED AT LONG-MEADOW, MASSACHUSETTS, JANUARY 31, 1798, AT THE FUNERAL OF
MRS. SARAH STORRS, CONSORT OF THE REVEREND RICHARD SALTER STORRS, BY
CHARLES BACKUS, A. M. PASTOR OF A CHURCH IN SOMERS.

Springfield: Printed by Francis Stebbins. M,DCC,CXVIII. [1798.] pp.
[18.] 8vo.   AAS. BM. CHS. NYPL. UTS. YC.

33355   BACON, JAMES
A FUNERAL SERMON, ON THE DEATH OF NATHANIEL WATTLES, ESQ. FRANKLIN,
DELAWARE COUNTY. BY ELDER JAMES BACON.

Cooperstown: Printed by Elihu Phinney. 1798. 8vo.

AUCTION
VALUES

33356   BACON, NATHANIEL   1593–1660
A RELATION OF THE FEARFUL ESTATE OF FRANCIS SPIRA, AFTER HE TURNED APOS-
TATE FROM THE PROTESTANT CHURCH TO POPERY.
     Hartford: Printed by John Babcock. 1798. pp. 47. 8vo.   LOC.

33357   —— — A RELATION OF THE FEARFUL STATE OF FRANCIS SPIRA, AFTER HE TURNED
APOSTATE FROM THE PROTESTANT CHURCH TO POPERY. TO WHICH IS ADDED, AN
ACCOUNT OF THE MISERABLE LIVES AND WOFUL DEATHS OF MR. JOHN CHILD, WHO
HUNG HIMSELF IN BRICK LANE, SPITTLE-FIELDS, LONDON, 1684; AND MR. GEORGE
EDWARDS, WHO SHOT HIMSELF, JANUARY 4, 1704.
     Philadelphia: Printed for David Hogan.—1798. pp. 107, (1). 24mo.
                                         AAS. NYPL.

     Contains, The Remarkable history of John Diazius and his barbarous
brother. Julian the apostate. Origen.

33358   BAILEY, FRANCIS   1735–1815
BAILEY'S POCKET ALMANAC, FOR THE YEAR OF OUR LORD, MDCCXCIX; AND OF THE
INDEPENDENCE OF THE UNITED STATES, THE TWENTY-THIRD.
     *Philadelphia: Printed by Francis & Robert Bailey, at Yorick's Head, No.
116, High-Street.* [1798.] 32mo.

33359   BAILEY, KIAH
THE SUBSTANCE OF A DISCOURSE, PREACHED AT ASHBY, OCTOBER 30TH, 1796. BY
KIAH BAILEY, A. B. CANDIDATE FOR THE GOSPEL MINISTRY.
     Printed at Worcester, by Leonard Worcester. 1798. pp. 34. 8vo.   AAS. JCB.

33360   BAKER, JOHN
THE HYPOCRITE UNMASK'D. TRIAL AND CONVICTION OF JOHN BAKER, A METHODIST
TEACHER, OF THIS CITY, FOR SEDUCING MISS ANN BURNS, UNDER A PROMISE OF
MARRIAGE. HELD BEFORE THE HON. JUDGE KENT, AT THE CITY-HALL, ON FRIDAY,
AUG. 18, 1798. WITH THE PLEADINGS OF THE COUNSEL ON BOTH SIDES. IN WHICH
IS INTRODUCED A SPECIMEN OF METHODISTICAL ORTHOGRAPHY. TO WHICH IS
ADDED JUDGE KENT'S EXCELLENT CHARGE TO THE JURY.
     [New-York: 1798.] pp. 8. 8vo.   JCB.

33361   BALDWIN, ASHBEL   1757–1846
A DISCOURSE, DELIVERED ON THE 18TH OF OCTOBER IN THE BRICK MEETING-
HOUSE, NEW-HAVEN, BEFORE THE GRAND LODGE OF THE ANCIENT AND HONOR-
ABLE SOCIETY OF FREE AND ACCEPTED MASONS IN CONNECTICUT. BEING THEIR
SEMIANNUAL COMMUNICATION. BY THE REV. ASHBEL BALDWIN.
     From the Press of brother Lazarus Beach, Newfield, Connecticut. 1798. pp.
21. 8vo.   LOC.

33362   BALTIMORE. MARYLAND.
ORDINANCES OF THE CORPORATION OF THE CITY OF BALTIMORE PASSED AT THEIR
FIRST AND SECOND SESSIONS, HELD FEBRUARY 1797, AND FEBRUARY [TO MAY] 1798.
WITH THE ACT OF INCORPORATION PREFIXED; [MAKING A COMPLETE BOOK OF
THE CITY OF BALTIMORE,]
     Baltimore: Printed by T. Dobbin for Andrew Hanna. 1798. pp. 236. 8vo.
                                           LCP. LOC.

33363   BALTIMORE. MARYLAND. EGLISE DE SAINT-PATRICE.
CANTIQUES FRANCAISES À L'USAGE DU CATÉCHISME DE L' EGLISE DE SAINT-PATRICE
DE BALTIMORE.
     *A Baltimore: De l' Imprimerie de Jean Hayes, pour le compte de Jacques Rice
et Comp.* M,DCC,XCVIII. pp. 108. 12mo.   LOC.

33364   BALTIMORE.   MARYLAND.   THEATRE.
    THEATRE.   ON WEDNESDAY, SEPTEMBER 12, 1798, WILL BE PRESENTED, A TRAGEDY,
    CALLED, THE FAIR PENITENT. [Cast.] TO WHICH WILL BE ADDED A COMEDY,
    NEVER PERFORMED HERE (IN THREE ACTS) CALLED THE MIDNIGHT HOUR. [Cast.]
        [Baltimore: 1798.] Broadside. fol.   MDHS.

33365   THE BALTIMORE INTELLIGENCER. VOL. I. NO. 1. WEDNESDAY, MARCH 7, [—VOL. III.
    NO. 129. MONDAY, DECEMBER 31, 1798.]
        Baltimore: Published by William Pechin. 1798. 4to. ⁿ

    Established, as a tri-weekly, by William Pechin. The numbering runs
    irregularly, and with the issue for October 31, 1798, which is numbered
    Vol. 3, No. 103, Pechin evidently intended an extension of the number-
    ing of "The Eagle of Freedom" he established in 1796. Publication
    was continued into May, 1799, when it was absorbed into the *American
    and daily advertiser,* which continued its subscription list.

33366   THE BALTIMORE PRIMMER, OR A COMPLETE FIRST BOOK INSTRUCTION FOR YOUNG
    CHILDREN.
        Carlisle: Printed by Steel and M'Clean, for A. Loudon. [March 22, 1796.]

33367   THE BALTIMORE SONGSTER; OR FESTIVE COMPANION. A CHOICE AND APPROVED
    COLLECTION OF SONGS, INTERSPERSED WITH MANY ORIGINALS, AND THE PATRIOTIC
    SONG OF HAIL COLUMBIA! SECOND EDITION.
        Baltimore: Printed for Henry S. Keatinge. 1798.

33368   BANCROFT, AARON   1755–1839
    A SERMON, DELIVERED AT BRIMFIELD, ON THE 20TH OF JUNE, 1798, AT THE INSTAL-
    LATION OF THE REV. CLARK BROWN, TO THE PASTORAL CARE OF THE CHURCH AND
    SOCIETY IN THAT PLACE. BY AARON BANCROFT, A. M. PASTOR OF THE SECOND
    CHURCH IN WORCESTER.
        *Worcester, Massachusetts: Printed by Isaiah Thomas, jun. August—*1798.
    pp. 23. 8vo.   AAS. BA. JCB. MHS. NYPL.
        The Charge: by the Rev. Judah Nash, of Montague. Right hand of
    fellowship: by the Rev. Nathaniel Thayer, of Lancaster.

33369   BAPTISTS.
    THE BAPTIST CATECHISM.
        *"Just received and for sale at Amherst, New Hampshire, by Samuel Preston.
    April 21, 1798."*

33370   —— A CONFESSION OF FAITH, PUT FORTH BY THE ELDERS AND BRETHREN OF MANY
    CONGREGATIONS OF CHRISTIANS (BAPTIZED UPON PROFESSION OF THEIR FAITH) IN
    LONDON AND THE COUNTRY. ADOPTED BY THE BAPTIST ASSOCIATION MET AT
    PHILADELPHIA, SEPTEMBER 25, 1742. WITH TWO ADDITIONAL ARTICLES, VIZ: OF
    IMPOSITION OF HANDS, AND SINGING OF PSALMS IN PUBLIC WORSHIP. THE NINTH
    EDITION. [Three lines of Scripture texts.]
        *Philadelphia: Printed by Stephen C. Ustick, Sold at No. 79, North Third
    St. and by the Baptist ministers in the United States.* 1798. pp. vii, [52], (2);
    28. 12mo.   AAS. CTS. JCB. LOC.
        Contains, A Short treatise of church discipline. Concerning a true and
    orderly Gospel church. By Benjamin Griffith. pp. 28.

33371   —— A SUMMARY DECLARATION OF THE FAITH AND PRACTICE OF THE BAPTIST CHURCH
    OF CHRIST.
        Frankfort: Printed by Hunter and Beaumont. 1798. fol.
    "Printed on the broad side of a large sheet of paper for the purpose of
    hanging up in houses."

33372　BARBAULD, Anna Lætitia Aikin　　　　　　　　　　　1743–1825
HYMNS IN PROSE FOR CHILDREN. BY MRS. BARBAULD, AUTHOR OF LESSONS FOR
CHILDREN. THE FIFTH AMERICAN EDITION.

　*Worcester: Printed by Isaiah Thomas, jun. Sold wholesale and retail at his
Bookstore. June*—1798. pp. [46], (2), frontispiece. 24mo.　　AAS. NYPL.

33373　BARLOW, Joel　　　　　　　　　　　　　　　　　　1754–1812
THE HASTY PUDDING: A POEM IN THREE CANTOS. WRITTEN AT CHAMBERY, IN SAVOY,
JAN. 1793. BY JOEL BARLOW. OMNE TULIT PUNCTUM QUI MISCUIT UTILE DULCI.
HE MAKES A GOOD BREAKFAST WHO MIXES PUDDING WITH MOLASSES.

　Printed in Catskill, by T. & M. Croswell. [1796.] pp. 12. 12mo.　　AAS.

33374　——— — [Ornament.] THE HASTY PUDDING: A POEM, IN THREE CANTOS. WRITTEN
IN CHAMBERRY [*sic*] IN SAVOY, JAN. 1793. [Ornament.]

　Re-printed by N. Power, at Poughkeepsie, [Ornament.] [1798.] pp. 12.
12mo.　　NYHS.

33375　BARNARD, Sir John　　　　　　　　　　　　　　　1685–1764
A PRESENT FOR AN APPRENTICE: OR, A SURE GUIDE TO GAIN BOTH ESTEEM AND
ESTATE: WITH RULES FOR HIS CONDUCT TO THE MASTER, AND IN THE WORLD. BY
A LATE LORD MAYOR OF LONDON.

　Albany: Printed and sold by J. Fry, lower end of State-Street. 1798. pp.
(8), 13–160. 24mo.　　AAS.

33376　BARTGIS'S FEDERAL [U. S. arms] GAZETTE, OR THE FREDERICK COUNTY WEEKLY
ADVERTISER. VOL. V. NO. 295. WEDNESDAY, JANUARY 3, [— VOL. VI. NO. 346.
WEDNESDAY, DECEMBER 26, 1798.]

　*Printed every Wednesday, by Matthias Bartgis, at his English & German
Printing-Office, the upper end of Market-Street, Frederick-Town;* . . . 1798. fol.
　　MDHS.

33377　BARTON, Benjamin Smith　　　　　　　　　　　　　1766–1815
COLLECTIONS FOR AN ESSAY TOWARDS A MATERIA MEDICA OF THE UNITED-STATES.
READ BEFORE THE PHILADELPHIA MEDICAL SOCIETY, ON THE TWENTY-FIRST OF
FEBRUARY, 1798. BY BENJAMIN SMITH BARTON, M. D. ONE OF THE HONORARY
MEMBERS OF THE SOCIETY, AND PROFESSOR OF MATERIA MEDICA, NATURAL HIS-
TORY, AND BOTANY, IN THE UNIVERSITY OF PENNSYLVANIA. [Three lines from]
LINNÆUS. FIDEM NON ABSTULIT ERROR. [Part I.]

　Philadelphia: Printed for the Author, by Way & Groff, No. 27, Arch-Street.
1798. pp. (vii), (49). 8vo.　　AAS. BM. HC. JCB. LOC. MHS. SGO.

　204th Pennsylvania District Copyright, issued to Benjamin Smith Barton, as Author, 12 March, 1798. A Second part was published in 1804.

33378　——— NEW VIEWS OF THE ORIGIN OF THE TRIBES AND NATIONS OF AMERICA. BY BEN-
JAMIN SMITH BARTON, M. D. CORRESPONDENT MEMBER OF THE AMERICAN PHILOS-
OPHICAL SOCIETY. FELLOW OF THE AMERICAN ACADEMY OF ARTS AND SCIENCES
OF BOSTON, CORRESPONDING MEMBER OF THE MASSACHUSETTS HISTORICAL SOCIETY
AND PROFESSOR OF MATERIA MEDICA, NATURAL HISTORY AND BOTANY IN THE
UNIVERSITY OF PENNSYLVANIA. [THE SECOND EDITION, CORRECTED AND GREATLY
ENLARGED.]

　Philadelphia: Printed for the Author, by John Bioren. 1798. pp. xxviii,
cix, 133, (1), 32. 8vo.　　AAS. BA. BM. LOC. NYPL.

　216th Pennsylvania District Copyright, issued to Benjamin Smith Barton, as Author, 12 August, 1798.

33379 THE BATH GAZETTE, AND GENERAL ADVERTISER. VOL. II. No. 3. THURSDAY, JANU-
ARY 4, [— No. 52. THURSDAY, DECEMBER 13, 1798.]
Bath, County of Steuben, State of New-York: Published weekly by William
Kersey & James Edie, . . . 1798. fol.
It is presumed that publication was discontinued, probably at the end
of the second volume, this year, as above.

33380 THE BATTLE OF THE WOODEN SWORD OR THE MODERN PUGILISTS. A NEW SONG.
COPIED FROM THE PHILADELPHIA EDITION, AND PUBLISHED "ACCORDING TO ACT OF
C——SS.
Printed at Rutland, Vermont, by Josiah Fay. 1798.

33381 THE BATTLE OF TRENTON, A SONATA FOR THE PIANO-FORTE. [Portrait.] DEDICATED
TO GEN'L WASHINGTON.
New-York: Printed for James Hewitt, 131 Williams Street. [1798.]

33382 BAY, ELIHU HALL
REPORTS OF CASES, ARGUED AND DETERMINED IN THE SUPERIOR COURTS OF LAW, IN
THE STATE OF SOUTH CAROLINA, SINCE THE REVOLUTION. BY ELIHU HALL BAY,
ONE OF THE ASSOCIATE JUDGES OF THE SAID STATE. VOL. I.
Charleston, South-Carolina: Printed by Elliott & Burd, No. 47, Bay. MDCC-
XCVIII. pp. x, 500, 18, errata, (1). 8vo. MHS. NYPL.
A Second edition, in two volumes, was published in New York in 1809-
1811.

33383 BAYARD, JAMES ASHTON 1767–1815
THE SPEECH OF MR. BAYARD ON THE FOREIGN INTERCOURSE BILL. DELIVERED IN
THE HOUSE OF REPRESENTATIVES OF THE UNITED STATES, ON THE THIRD DAY OF
MARCH, 1798.
[Philadelphia: Printed by Richard Folwell. 1798.] pp. (16). 8vo.
AAS. HC. LOC. NYHS.

33384 —— — THE SPEECH OF MR. BAYARD ON THE FOREIGN INTERCOURE BILL. DELIV-
ERED IN THE HOUSE OF REPRESENTATIVES OF THE UNITED STATES, ON THE THIRD
DAY OF MARCH, 1798.
[Philadelphia: 1798.] pp. 24. 8vo. HSP. JCB.

33385 BEACH, JESSE
AN ORATION, DELIVERED AT MASON'S HALL, IN DERBY, AUG. 29, 1797. AT THE RE-
QUEST OF SOLOMON'S CHAPTER OF ROYAL ARCH MASONS. IN COMMEMORATION OF
THE DEATH OF A BROTHER, THE REV. EDWARD BLAKESLEE. BY JESSE BEACH.
Printed at Litchfield, by T. Collier. [1797.] pp. 16. 8vo. CHS.

33386 BEDELL, GREGORY
THE CLOSET COMPANION: OR, AN HELP TO SERIOUS PERSONS IN THE IMPORTANT DUTY
OF SELF-EXAMINATION. INTENDED TO BE FIXED UP IN THE CHRISTIAN'S USUAL PLACE
OF RETIREMENT, IN ORDER TO REMIND HIM OF, AS WELL AS TO ASSIST HIM IN, THE
WORK. [Three lines of Scripture texts.] [Three columns.] [Colophon:]
Boston—Printed and sold by Manning & Loring, No. 2, Cornhill. [1798.]
Broadside. fol. LOC. MHS.

33387 THE [cut] BEE. VOLUME I. NUMBER 30. WEDNESDAY, JANUARY 3, [— VOLUME II.
NUMBER 72. WEDNESDAY, DECEMBER 26, 1798.]
New-London: Printed and published by Charles Holt. 1798. fol.
AAS. LOC. NYHS. YC.
From September 5th, to November 14th, publication was suspended on
account of a "malignant disorder" in the city; and, on the latter date,
the Printing Office was removed "to the house occupied by Mr. John
Throop, innholder, a few doors below the old stand, and directly oppo-
site Mr. James Tilley's.

33388   BEERS, ANDREW   1749–1824
     BEERS'S ALMANAC FOR THE YEAR OF OUR LORD, 1799: BEING THE THIRD AFTER BIS-
SEXTILE, OR LEAP-YEAR, AND TWENTY-THIRD YEAR OF AMERICAN INDEPENDENCE,
'TILL 4TH OF JULY. CALCULATED FOR THE MERIDIAN OF HARTFORD, LATITUDE 41
DEGREES, 56 MIN. NORTH—LONGITUDE 72 DEGREES 50 MIN. WEST, AND WILL SERVE
FOR ANY OF THE ADJACENT STATES, WITHOUT ANY ESSENTIAL DIFFERENCE. CON-
TAINING ALSO, THE LUNATIONS, CONJUNCTIONS, ECLIPSES, JUDGMENT OF WEATHER,
RISING AND SETTING OF THE PLANETS, LENGTH OF DAYS AND NIGHTS, COURTS, &C.—
TOGETHER WITH USEFUL TABLES, PIECES OF INSTRUCTION AND ENTERTAINMENT,
&C. &C. BY ANDREW BEERS, PHILOM.

       Hartford: Printed by Hudson & Goodwin. [1798.] pp. [36.] 12mo.

                                      AAS. CHS. LOC. NYPL.

33389   —— THE FARMER'S AMERICAN ALMANAC, FOR THE YEAR OF OUR LORD CHRIST—
1799—AND FROM CREATION, 5748, BEING THE THIRD AFTER BISSEXTILE, OR LEAP
YEAR, AND 23D OF AMERICAN INDEPENDENCE, TILL THE 4TH OF JULY. CALCULATED
FOR THE MERIDIAN OF DANBURY, IN THE STATE OF CONNECTICUT, LATITUDE 41°
50" N. LONG. 73° 37" W. BUT MAY SERVE FOR THE ADJACENT STATES. CONTAIN-
ING, A VERY GREAT VARIETY OF USEFUL AND ENTERTAINING MATTER. BY ANDREW
BEERS, PHILOM.

       Danbury: Printed and sold by the gross, dozen or single, by Douglas & Nichols.
[1798.] 12mo.   CHS. HSP. LOC. YC.

33390   —— GLORIA THE NEW-YORK CONNECTICUT, & NEW JERSEY ALMANACK, OR DIAKY,
FOR THE YEAR OF OUR LORD, 1799: BEING THE THIRD AFTER BISSEXTILE, OR LEAP-
YEAR, THE TWENTY-THIRD OF THE INDEPENDENCE OF THE U. STATES OF AMERICA,
AND FROM CREATION (PER BIBLE) 5803. FITTED FOR THE MERIDIAN AND HORIZON
OF NEW-YORK, BUT WILL SERVE WITHOUT ESSENTIAL VARIATION, FOR CONNECTI-
CUT AND NEW JERSEY. CONTAINING USUAL ASTRONOMICAL CALCULATIONS, AND A
GREATER VARIETY OF OTHER MATTER THAN IS COMMON IN AN ALMANACK—ALL OF
WHICH IS USEFUL—CURIOUS—AND ENTERTAINING. TO WHICH IS ADDED, WITH DI-
RECTIONS. THE NEW FRENCH CALENDAR. [Cut. Six lines of verse from] MILTON.

       Printed at New-York—for John Reid. Mundi. [1798.] pp. (36). 12mo.

     Contains, The Stamp Act.   AAS. DHS. LOC. NYHS. NYPL.

33391   —— STODDARD'S DIARY: OR, THE COLUMBIA ALMANACK, FOR THE YEAR OF OUR LORD
1799: BEING THE THIRD AFTER BISSEXTILE OR LEAP YEAR, AND OF AMERICAN IN-
DEPENDENCE (WHICH WAS DECLARED THE 4TH OF JULY, 1776) PART OF THE 23D
AND 24TH YEARS: CALCULATED FOR LATITUDE 42 DEGREES NORTH, AND FOR A ME-
RIDIAN 3 DEGREES EAST OF GEORGETOWN, THE INTENDED PERMANENT RESIDENCE
OF CONGRESS. CONTAINING, BESIDES WHAT IS USEFUL AND NECESSARY IN COMPO-
SITIONS OF THIS NATURE, MANY THINGS, NEW, USEFUL AND ENTERTAINING. BY AN-
DREW BEERS, PHILOM.

       Hudson: Printed and sold by Ashbel Stoddard. ☞*Great allowance to those
who purchase quantities.* [1798.] pp. (36). 12mo.   AAS. NYPL.

33392   —— WEBSTER'S CALENDAR: OR, THE ALBANY ALMANACK, FOR THE YEAR OF OUR
LORD, 1799: BEING THE 3D AFTER BISSEXTILE OR LEAP YEAR; OF AMERICAN IN-
DEPENDENCE (WHICH WAS DECLARED THE 4TH OF JULY, 1776) PART OF THE 23D
AND 24TH YEARS: FROM THE CREATION OF THE WORLD 5748. CALCULATED FOR THE
MERIDIAN OF ALBANY; NORTH LATITUDE 42 DEGREES 45 MINUTES; FROM THE
ENGLISH OBSERVATORY, 73 DEGREES ANE 8 MINUTES WEST. BY ANDREW BEERS,
PHILOM. CONTAINING, AS USUAL, A GREAT VARIETY OF NEW, USEFUL AND ENTER-
TAINING PIECES.

       *Albany: Printed by Charles R. and George Webster, in the White-House, cor-
ner of State and Pearl Streets: Sold at their Bookstore, Albany, and by all the Post
Riders from their office. Also by G. Tracy, at his Printing-Office, Lansingburgh.*
☞*Great allowance to those who buy by wholesale.* [1798.] pp. (36). 12mo.

                                    AAS. BPL. NYHS. NYPL.

33393   BELKNAP, JEREMY   1744–1798
AMERICAN BIOGRAPHY: OR, AN HISTORICAL ACCOUNT OF THOSE PERSONS WHO HAVE
BEEN DISTINGUISHED IN AMERICA, AS ADVENTURERS, STATESMEN. PHILOSOPHERS,
DIVINES, WARRIORS, AUTHORS, AND OTHER REMARKABLE CHARACTERS. COMPRE-
HENDING A RECITAL OF THE EVENTS CONNECTED WITH THEIR LIVES AND ACTIONS.
BY JEREMY BELKNAP, D.D. VOL. II. NIL MAGNUM SINE LABORE. PUBLISHED AC-
CORDING TO ACT OF CONGRESS.

     *Printed at Boston, by Isaiah Thomas and E. T. Andrews. Sold by them, and
the other Booksellers in Boston; by I. Thomas, Worcester; by Thomas, Andrews &
Penniman, Albany; and by Thomas, Andrews & Butler, Baltimore. July*, 1798.
pp. (2), 476. 8vo.   AAS. BA. BM. BU. HC. JCB. LOC. MHS. NL. NYHS. NYPL.

     147th Massachusetts District Copyright, issued to Jeremy Belknap, as
author, 9 June, 1798. In two states: printed on thick, and on thin
paper. Owing to the death of the Author in June, the Index is by another hand. The first volume was published in Boston, in 1794. An
intended third volume was never published. Reprinted in New York, in
three volumes, 1844-1846.

33394   —— A SERMON, DELIVERED ON THE 9TH OF MAY, 1798, THE DAY OF THE NATIONAL
FAST, RECOMMENDED BY THE PRESIDENT OF THE UNITED STATES. BY JEREMY
BELKNAP, D.D. MINISTER OF THE CHURCH IN FEDERAL-STREET, BOSTON. [Orna-
ment.]

     Printed by Samuel Hall, No. 53, *Cornhill, Boston.* 1798. pp. [29]. 8vo.
         AAS. BA. BM. CHS. CLA. HC. HSP. JCB. LOC. MHS. NYPL. UTS. YC.

33395   —— — A SERMON, DELIVERED ON THE 9TH OF MAY, 1798, THE DAY OF THE
NATIONAL FAST, RECOMMENDED BY THE PRESIDENT OF THE UNITED STATES. BY
JEREMY BELKNAY, D.D. MINISTER OF THE CHURCH IN FEDERAL-STREET, BOSTON.
SECOND EDITION.

     Printed by Samuel Hall, No. 53, *Cornhill, Boston.* 1798. pp. 29. 8vo.

33396   BELLAMY, JOSEPH   1719–1790
THERON, PAULINUS, AND ASPASIO. OR, LETTERS & DIALOGUES UPON THE NATURE OF
LOVE TO GOD, FAITH IN CHRIST, ASSURANCE OF A TITLE TO ETERNAL LIFE, CON-
TAIN. SOME REMARKS ON THE SENTIMENTS OF THE REVEREND MESSIEURS HERVEY
AND MARSHAL, ON THESE SUBJECTS. PUBLISHED AT THE REQUEST OF MANY. BY
JOSEPH BELLAMY, A.M. MINISTER OF THE GOSPEL AT BETHLEM, IN NEW-ENGLAND.
[Nine lines from] HERVEY.

     *Washington [Pennsylvania]: Printed by John Colerick, and may be had of
all the Store-keepers.* 1798. pp. lx, 133. 12mo.   AAS. JCB. LOC. NYPL.

     First printed in Boston, in 1759. And reprinted in London, in 1761.

33397   —— AN ESSAY ON THE NATURE AND GLORY OF THE GOSPEL OF JESUS CHRIST: AS
ALSO ON THE NATURE AND CONSEQUENCES OF SPIRITUAL BLINDNESS, AND THE NAT-
URE AND EFFECTS OF DIVINE ILLUMINATION. DESIGNED AS A SUPPLEMENT TO THE
AUTHOR'S LETTERS AND DIALOGUES, ON THE NATURE OF LOVE TO GOD, FAITH IN
JESUS CHRIST, AND ASSURANCE OF A TITLE TO ETERNAL LIFE. BY JOSEPH BELL-
AMY, A.M. MINISTER OF THE GOSPEL IN BETHLEM, IN NEW-ENGLAND. [Three lines
from] SAINT PAUL.

     *Washington [Pennsylvania]: Printed and sold by John Colerick, at Office of
the Telegraphe.* 1798. pp. xii, 203. 12mo.   AAS. JCB. LOC. NYPL.

33398   BENHAM, ASAHEL

SOCIAL HARMONY: CONTAINING FIRST, THE RUDIMENTS OF PSALMODY MADE EASY. SECOND, A COLLECTION OF MODERN MUSIC, CALCULATED FOR THE USE OF SINGING SCHOOLS AND WORSHIPPING ASSEMBLIES. BY ASAHEL BENHAM, AUTHOR OF FEDERAL HARMONY. PUBLISHED ACCORDING TO ACT OF CONGRESS.

New-Haven: Printed by Thomas and Samuel Green. 1798. pp. 60, 32. obl. 8vo.   AAS. MHS. NYPL.

Preface dated, Wallingford, Sept. 6, 1798. Music engraved by C. Beecher.

33399   BENJAMIN, ASHER   1773–1845

THE COUNTRY BUILDER'S ASSISTANT, FULLY EXPLAINING, THE BEST METHODS FOR STRIKING REGULAR AND QUICKED MOULDINGS: FOR DRAWING AND WORKING THE TUSCAN, DORIC, IONIC AND CORINTHIAN ORDERS WITH THEIR PEDESTALS, BASES, CAPITALS AND ENTABLATURES. ARCHITRAVES FOR DOORS, WINDOWS AND CHIMNIES. CORNICES, BASES & SURBASE MOULDINGS FOR ROOMS, CHIMNEY-PIECES, DOORS AND SASHES, WITH THEIR MOULDINGS. THE CONSTRUCTION OF STAIRS WITH THEIR RAMP AND TWIST RAILS. PLAN, ELEVATION AND SECTION OF A MEETING-HOUSE, WITH A PULPIT AT LARGE. PLANS AND ELEVATIONS OF HOUSES, FENCE-POSTS AND RAILINGS. THE BEST METHOD OF FINDING THE LENGTH AND BACKING OF HIP RAFTERS. ALSO, THE TRACING OF GROINS, ANGLE BRACKETS, CIRCULAR SOFFITS IN CIRCULAR WALLS &C. CORRECTLY ENGRAVED ON THIRTY-SEVEN COPPERPLATES WITH A PRINTED EXPLANATION TO EACH. BY ASHER BENJAMIN. PUBLISHED ACCORDING TO ACT OF CONGRESS.

Boston: Printed by Spotswood and Etheridge, for the Author. Sold by him, and by Alexander Thomas, Worcester,—1798. pp. (2), 34, 37 plates. 4to.   AAS. LOC.

139th Massachusetts District Copyright, issued to Asher Benjamin, as Author, 8 February, 1798.

33400   —— PROSPECTUS OF THE COUNTRY BUILDER'S ASSISTANT.

[Boston: Printed by Spotswood and Etheridge. 1798.] Broadside.   AAS.

33401   BENNETT, AGNES MARIA   –1808

THE BEGGAR GIRL AND HER BENEFACTORS. IN THREE VOLUMES. BY MRS. BENNET, AUTHOR OF WELCH HEIRESS, JUVENILE INDISCRETIONS, AGNES DE COURCI, ELLEN COUNTESS OF CASTLE HOWEL, AND DEVALCOURT.

Philadelphia: 1798. 3 vols.

33402   BENNETT, JOHN

LETTERS TO A YOUNG LADY, ON A VARIETY OF USEFUL AND INTERESTING SUBJECTS: CALCULATED TO IMPROVE THE HEART, TO FORM THE MANNERS, AND ENLIGHTEN THE UNDERSTANDING. "THAT OUR DAUGHTERS MAY BE AS POLISHED CORNERS OF THE TEMPLE." BY THE REV. JOHN BENNETT, AUTHOR OF STRICTURES ON FEMALE EDUCATION. IN TWO VOLUMES. VOL. I. [— II.]

Hartford: Printed by Hudson & Goodwin. 1798. 2 vols. in one. pp. 129; 134. 12mo.   AAS.

33403   —— — LETTERS TO A YOUNG LADY. ON A VARIETY OF USEFUL AND INTERESTING SUBJECTS. CALCULATED TO IMPROVE THE HEART, TO FORM THE MANNERS AND ENLIGHTEN THE UNDERSTANDING. "THAT OUR DAUGHTERS MAY BE AS POLISHED CORNERS OF THE TEMPLE." BY THE REV. JOHN BENNETT. FOURTH AMERICAN EDITION. TWO VOLUMES COMPLETE IN ONE.

Printed by Isaiah Thomas, jun. Worcester, for Thomas & Andrews; sold at their Book-Store, No. 45, Newburystreet, Boston, by Thomas, Andrews & Penniman, Albany, and by Thomas, Andrews & Butler, Baltimore.—May—1798.—pp. 300. 12mo.   AAS. NYPL.

Contains a Minister's advice to a young lady. In verse. pp. 297–300.

33404　BENNEVILLE, George de　　　　　　　　　　　　1703–1793
Der merkwürdige Lebenslauf, die Sonderbare Bekehrung und Entzückungen
des ohnlängst bey Germantown in Pennsylvanien wohnenden und un-
längst verstorbenenen Dr. Benneville.

Baltimore: Gedruckt bey Samuel Saur. 1798.

Translated from the French ms. of George de Benneville, by Rev. El-
hanan Winchester.

33405　BENTLEY, William　　　　　　　　　　　　1759–1819
A Charge delivered before the Morning Star Lodge, in Worcester, Mas-
sachusetts, upon the festival of Saint John the baptist. June 25, a. l. 5798.
By the rev. brother William Bentley, of Salem, Massachusetts.

Worcester: From the Press of brother Isaiah Thomas, jun. June A.L. 5798
[1798.] pp. 36. 12mo.　　　　　　　　　AAS. BA. HC.. JCB. MHS. NYHS.

33406　BERKSHIRE Gazette. Man is man, and who is more?" Vol. i. No. 1. Wednesday, January 17, [— No. 50. Wednesday, December 26, 1798.]

Published by Merrill and Smith, Pittsfield, Massachusetts. 1798. fol.

Established, as a weekly, by Orsamus C. Merrill and Chester Smith.
In June, 1798, Merrill disposed of his interests to Nathaniel Holly
and the firm name became Holly & Smith. With the issue for March 6,
1799, Holly withdrew, and the Gazette was published by Chester Smith
to the end of the second volume in February, 1800, when it was discontinued.

33407　BERN or BERNE. Switzerland. Œconomical Society.
Essays on the spirit of legislation, in the encouragement of agriculture,
population, manufactures, and commerce.—Containing—observations on
the political systems at present pursued in various countries of Europe,
for the advancement of those essential interests. Interspersed with various remarks in the practice of agriculture. Societies of agriculture.
Rewards. Bounties. The police. Luxury. Industry. Machines. Exportation. Taxes. Inoculation. Marriage. Naturalization, &c. Translated
from the original French, which gained the premiums offered by the
Œconomical Society of Berne, in Switzerland, for the best compositions
on this subject.

*Newark: Printed by Pennington & Dodge, for William Reid, No. 442, Pearl-
Street, New-York. M,DCC,XCVIII. pp. (2),[7]-vii, 479, (4). 8vo.* AAS. IOC. NYPL.

Originally published in the Memoirs of the Berne Œconomical Society.
Republished from the London edition of 1772. Preface dated, New-
York, November 26, 1798. Contains a four-page list of Subscribers'
names.

33408　BIBLIA.
The Holy Bible, containing the Old and New Testaments: together with
the Apocrypha; translated out of the original tongues: and with the
former translations, diligently compared and revised. [Vignette of an
open "Holy Bible" throwing out rays of light, encircled by fifteen stars, and
resting upon an American Eagle.]

*Philadelphia: Printed for John Thompson & Abraham Small, [from the hot-
press of John Thompson.] M.DCC.XCVIII. Unpaged, plate. 2 vols. fol.*

BM. IOC. NYPL.

BIBLIA, continued.

Second title: THE NEW TESTAMENT OF OUR LORD AND SAVIOUR JESUS CHRIST, TRANSLATED OUT OF THE ORIGINAL GREEK: AND WITH THE FORMER TRANSLATIONS, DILIGENTLY COMPARED AND REVISED. [Vignette as above.]

Philadelphia: Printed for John Thompson and Abraham Small. M.DCC.-XCVIII. Unpaged.

The first hot-pressed edition of the Bible printed in America. Originally issued in forty numbers, at a half dollar a number, and the division into volumes arbitrary. Printing, begun in June 1796, was not completed until October, 1799. The Apocrypha is entirely in italics. There are two pages of Subscribers' names at the end.

33409 —— THE HOLY BIBLE, CONTAINING THE OLD AND NEW TESTAMENTS: TRANSLATED OUT OF THE ORIGINAL TONGUES, AND WITH THE FORMER TRANSLATIONS DILIGENTLY COMPARED AND REVISED, BY THE SPECIAL COMMAND OF KING JAMES I OF ENGLAND. [One line of Hebrew text, from Genesis II. 17, enclosed in ornamental border.]

United States of Columbia. Printed at Worcester, Massachusetts. By Isaiah Thomas. Sold by him in Worcester, by wholesale, bound or in sheets. Sold also by said Thomas and Andrews, in Boston, and by the Booksellers in the United States of Columbia. 1798. *pp.* (2), 674; (2), (288). [unpaged.] 12mo. **AAS. NYPL.**

Second title: THE NEW TESTAMENT OF OUR LORD AND SAVIOUR JESUS CHRIST. TRANSLATED OUT OF THE ORIGINAL GREEK, AND WITH THE FORMER TRANSLATIONS, DILIGENTLY COMPARED AND REVISED, BY THE SPECIAL COMMAND OF HIS MAJESTY KING JAMES I. OF ENGLAND. [Two lines of Greek text in an ornamental border.]

United States of Columbia. Printed at Worcester, Massachusetts, by Isaiah Thomas. Sold by him in worcester, by wholesale, bound or in sheets. Sold also by said Thomas and Andrews, in Boston, and by the Booksellers in the United States of Columbia. 1798. *pp.* (2), (288.) [unpaged.]

33410 —— THE BIBLE. THE NINTH EDITION.

Philadelphia: Printed for W. Jones, No. 30, N. Fourth St. 1798. 64mo.

Second title: THE HISTORY OF THE NEW TESTAMENT.

33411 —— THE HISTORY OF THE HOLY BIBLE. ILLUSTRATED WITH NOTES, AND ADORNED WITH CUTS. FOR THE USE OF CHILDREN.

Hartford: Printed by John Babcock ? 1798. 18mo.

33412 BIBLIA. OLD TESTAMENT. PSALMS.

THE PSALMS OF DAVID, WITH HYMNS AND SPIRITUAL SONGS. ALSO, THE CATECHISM, CONFESSION OF FAITH, AND LITURGY OF THE REFORMED CHURCH IN THE NETHERLANDS. FOR THE USE OF THE REFORMED DUTCH CHURCH IN NORTH AMERICA. WITH AN APPENDIX, CONTAINING, ARTICLES EXPLANATORY OF THE GOVERNMENT AND DISCIPLINE OF THE REFORMED DUTCH CHURCH IN THE UNITED STATES OF AMERICA.

New-Brunswick: Printed and sold, wholesale and retail, by Abraham Blauvelt. —1798. *pp.* xii, 348; 102; 27. 12mo. **AAS. LOC.**

Second title: THE HEIDELBERGH CATECHISM, OR, METHOD OF INSTRUCTION IN THE CHRISTIAN RELIGION: AS THE SAME IS TAUGHT IN THE REFORMED CHURCHES AND SCHOOLS OF HOLLAND. TOGETHER WITH THE ARTICLES OF FAITH, AND LITURGY OF SAID CHURCH. TRANSLATED FOR THE USE OF THE REFORMED PROTESTANT DUTCH CHURCH IN NEW YORK, TOGETHER WITH AN APPENDIX.

New-Brunswick: Printed by A. Blauvelt. 1797. *pp.* 102; 27.

33413   BIBLIA, continued.
—— THE PSALMS OF DAVID, IMITATED IN THE LANGUAGE OF THE NEW TESTAMENT,
AND APPLIED TO THE CHRISTIAN STATE AND WORSHIP. BY ISAAC WATTS, D. D. [Six
lines of Scripture texts.]

> *Boston: Printed by Joseph Bumstead   Sold by him at No. 20, Union-Street,
> and by the principal Booksellers in Boston. 1798.* pp. 595. 12mo.   AAS. NYPL.

Second title: HYMNS AND SPIRITUAL SONGS. IN THREE BOOKS. I. COLLECTED FROM
THE SCRIPTURES. II. COMPOSED ON DIVINE SUBJECTS. III. PREPARED FOR THE
LORD'S SUPPER. BY ISAAC WATTS, D. D. [Six lines of quotations.]

> *Boston: Printed by Joseph Bumstead, sold by him at No. 20, Union-Street, and
> by the principal Booksellers in Boston. 1798.* pp. (2), 319-595.

33414   —— THE PSALMS OF DAVID IN METRE: TRANSLATED AND DILIGENTLY COMPARED WITH
THE ORIGINAL TEXT AND FORMER TRANSLATIONS: MORE PLAIN, SMOOTH, AND AGREE-
ABLE TO THE TEXT, THAN ANY HERETOFORE: ALLOWED BY THE AUTHORITY OF THE
GENERAL ASSEMBLY OF THE KIRK OF SCOTLAND, AND APPOINTED TO BE SUNG IN
CONGREGATIONS AND FAMILIES. WITH NOTES, EXHIBITING THE CONNEXION, EX-
PLAINING THE SENSE; AND FOR DIRECTING AND ANIMATING THE DEVOTION. BY JOHN
BROWN, MINISTER OF THE GOSPEL IN HADDINGTON.

> *Philadelphia:* 1798. 16mo.

33415   BIBLIA. NEW TESTAMENT.
THE NEW TESTAMENT OF OUR LORD AND SAVIOUR JESUS CHRIST, NEWLY TRANS-
LATED OUT OF THE ORIGINAL GREEK: AND WITH THE FORMER TRANSLATIONS
DILIGENTLY COMPARED AND REVISED. APPOINTED TO BE READ IN CHURCHES.
[Printer's mark.]

> *New-Haven: Printed and sold by Edward O'Brien, also, sold wholesale and re-
> tail by Daniel Dunham, New-York.* M.DCC.XCVIII. unpaged. 12mo.   AAS.

33416   —— — THE NEW TESTAMENT OF OUR LORD AND SAVIOUR JESUS CHRIST, TRANS-
LATED OUT OF THE ORIGINAL GREEK; AND WITH THE FORMER TRANSLATIONS DILI-
GENTLY COMPARED AND REVISED. APPOINTED TO BE READ IN CHURCHES.

> *Wilmington: Printed and sold by Peter Brynberg.* M.DCC.XCVIII. pp. 291,
> (1). 12mo.   NYPL.

33417   —— — NEW TESTAMENT OF OUR LORD AND SAVIOUR, JESUS CHRIST: TRANSLATED
FROM THE GREEK. APPOINTED TO BE READ BY CHILDREN.

> *Hartford: Printed by John Babcock.* 1798. pp. 69,(1), wood cut. 24mo.   CHS.

Contains, a selection of "Divine Hymns." pp. 60-69.

33418   BICKERSTAFF, ISAAC   1735-1787
LIFE AND ADVENTURES OF AMBROSE GWINETT, WHO FOR A MURDER WHICH HE
NEVER COMMITTED, WAS TRIED, CONDEMNED, EXECUTED, AND HUNG IN CHAINS,
YET LIVED MANY YEARS AFTERWARD AND IN HIS TRAVELS FOUND THE MAN IN THE
WEST INDIES, ACTUALLY ALIVE, FOR THE SUPPOSED MURDER OF WHOM HE HAD
BEEN REALLY EXECUTED.

> *[Without Place:] Printed for the traveling book-sellers.* 1798. pp. 23. 12mo.

33419   BIGELOW, TIMOTHY   1767-1821
AN ORATION, DELIVERED AT AMHERST, APRIL 4, 1798, AT THE INTERMENT OF THE
HON. SAMUEL DANA, ESQ. MASTER OF THE BENEVOLENT LODGE OF FREE AND AC-
CEPTED MASONS. BY TIMOTHY BIGELOW.

> *Printed at Amherst, by Samuel Preston.* 1798. pp. 12. 8vo.   AAS. BA. LOC.

33420   BINGHAM, Caleb   1757–1817
THE AMERICAN PRECEPTOR; BEING A NEW SELECTION OF LESSONS FOR READING AND
SPEAKING. DESIGNED FOR THE USE OF SCHOOLS. BY CALEB BINGHAM, A.M. AUTHOR
OF THE COLUMBIAN ORATOR, CHILD'S COMPANION, &C. "TRAIN UP A CHILD IN THE
WAY HE SHOULD GO." THE FIFTH EDITION. PUBLISHED ACCORDING TO ACT OF
CONGRESS.
> *Boston: Printed by Manning and Loring, for the Author; and sold at his Book-*
> *Store, No. 44 Cornhill; sold also by Thomas & Andrews, D. West, J. West, J. White,*
> *E. Larkin, S. Hall, W. P. & L. Blake, &c. &c.* 1798. pp. 228. 12mo.   AAS.

33421   —— AN ASTRONOMICAL AND GEOGRAPHICAL CATECHISM. FOR THE USE OF CHILDREN.
BY CALEB BINGHAM, A.M. THE FOURTH EDITION. PUBLISHED ACCORDING TO ACT
OF CONGRESS. "THE EARTH, THE HEAVENS—ARE FRAUGHT WITH INSTRUCTION."
> *Boston: Printed and sold by S. Hall, No. 53 Cornhill. Sold also by the*
> *Author, No. 44, Cornhill.* 1798. pp. 35. 24mo.   AAS.

33422   BIRCH, Samuel   1757–1841
THE ADOPTED CHILD. A MUSICAL DRAMA, IN TWO ACTS. AS PERFORMED AT THE
HAY-MARKET THEATRE. BOSTON.
> *Boston: Printed by Benjamin Edes, Kilby-Street.* 1798.

33423   —— — SONGS IN THE MUSICAL DRAMA OF THE ADOPTED CHILD.
> *Boston: Printed by Benjamin Edes, Kilby-Street.* 1798.

33424   BIRCH, Thomas Ledlie   –1808
Caption title: [Double line.] LETTER FROM AN IRISH EMIGRANT, TO HIS FRIEND IN
THE UNITED STATES. [Double line.]
> *[New-York, September, 1798.]* pp. 56. 8vo.   AAS. NYHS.

"We sailed from Belfast, on board the Harmony of New Bedford, Captain
Asa Swift, and landed to the amount of sixty-five in number in this
City a few days ago. Some of the passengers have come hither on
mercantile affairs, but much the greater number of us have been literally
transported from his Britannic Majesty's Dominions under the sentence
of a Court Martial, or obliged to fly to avoid instant death by military
execution, which is now carrying on in all parts of that long unfortunate Island, in order to check that revolution which British tyrany
has produced and long insulted humanity has loudly called for. Many
hundreds of persons of rank and property are in a similar situation,
and all bent on coming to this Continent, forming the most respectable
emigration which has taken place to your United States since the settlement of the New-England Colonies, during the persecutions of
Queen Mary and Kings Charles I. and II. of England."

The copy in the American Antiquarian Society is interlined, and liber-
ally annotated throughout with notes exceeding even the author's own
statements.

33425   BISHOP, Abraham   1763–1844.
GEORGIA SPECULATION UNVEILED, SECOND PART. CONTAINING THE THIRD AND FOURTH
NUMBERS; WITH A CONCLUSION, ADDRESSED TO THE NORTHERN PURCHASERS.
> *Hartford: Printed by Hudson & Goodwin.* M.DCC.XCVIII. pp. (3), 44–144.
> 8vo.   AAS. BA. BM. CHS. DeRGL. LOC. MHS. NYHS. YC.

33426   BLAIR, Hugh   1798–1800
ESSAYS ON RHETORICK: ABRIDGED CHIEFLY FROM DR. BLAIR'S LECTURES ON THAT
SCIENCE. A NEW EDITION WITH ADDITIONS AND IMPROVEMENTS.
> *Albany: Printed by Barber & Southwick, and sold at their Book-Store, two*
> *doors north of the City-Hall, Court-Street, and at Faust's Statue, State-Street.*
> M,DCC,XCVIII. pp. 307, (1). 12mo.   AAS. LOC.

33427 BLAIR, SAMUEL   1741–1818
A DISCOURSE DELIVERED IN THE FIRST PRESBYTERIAN CHURCH OF PHILADELPHIA, ON WEDNESDAY, MAY 9TH, 1798, RECOMMENDED BY THE PRESIDENT OF THE UNITED STATES TO BE OBSERVED AS A DAY OF FASTING, HUMILIATION AND PRAYER, THROUGHOUT THE UNITED STATES OF NORTH AMERICA. BY SAMUEL BLAIR, D. D. PUBLISHED BY DESIRE.
Philadelphia: Published by James Watters & Co. To be had also of the principal Booksellers. 1798. pp. (2), 31. 8vo.   AAS. HSP. JCB. LOC. NYPL.

33428 BLAKE, WILLIAM P.
CATALOGUE OF BOOKS FOR SALE OR CIRCULATION BY W. P. & L. BLAKE.
Boston: Printed for W. P. and L. Blake. 1798. 12mo.   HC.

33429 BLATCHFORD, SAMUEL   1767–1828
AN ADDRESS DELIVERED AT NEWFIELD, JULY 4, 1798.
[Newfield:] Printed by Lazarus Beach. 1798. pp. 15. 8vo.

33430 —— THE VALIDITY OF PRESBYTERIAN ORDINATION MAINTAINED, IN A LETTER TO THE REV. WILLIAM SMITH, D. D., OCCASIONED BY THE PUBLICATION OF HIS SERMON, PREACHED AT THE CONSECRATION OF BISHOP JARVIS, AT NEW-HAVEN, ON THE 18TH OCTOBER, 1797. TOGETHER WITH STRICTURES ON SAID SERMON. BY SAMUEL BLATCHFORD, A. M. PASTOR OF A CHURCH AT STRATFIELD, CONNECTICUT. [Two lines of Latin quotation.]
New-Haven: Printed by George Bunce. M.DCC.XCVIII. pp. 32. 8vo.
                 AAS. BM. JCB. NYPL. UTS.

33431 BLAUVELT, ABRAHAM
BLAUVELT'S AMERICAN ALMANAC, FOR THE YEAR OF OUR LORD, 1799; BEING THE THIRD AFTER BISSEXTILE OR LEAP-YEAR AND THE TWENTY-THIRD YEAR OF AMERICAN INDEPENDENCE TILL THE FOURTH OF JULY. — CONTAINING — THE RISING AND SETTING OF THE SUN AND MOON—THE LUNATION—CONJUNCTIONS—ECLIPSES—JUDGMENTS OF THE WEATHER — RISING AND SETTING OF THE PLANETS — COURTS IN NEW-JERSEY, NEW-YORK AND PENNSYLVANIA — DISTANCES OF THE PRINCIPAL ROADS OF THE UNITED STATES. TOGETHER WITH USEFUL TABLE — ENTERTAINING MATTER BOTH IN PROSE AND VERSE — ANECDOTES, &C. CALCULATED TO SERVE EITHER OF THE MIDDLE STATES WITHOUT ANY SENSIBLE VARIATION. [Double line.]
New-Brunswick: Printed and sold by Abraham Blauvelt. [1798.] pp. (36). 12mo.   AAS.

33432 BLOODY INDIAN BATTLE, FOUGHT AT THE MIAMI VILLAGE, NOVEMBER 4, 1791. A MOURNFUL ELEGY ON THE OCCASION. AND JEMMY AND NANCY: A TRAGICAL GARLAND. [Ornament.]
New-Haven: Printed by Moses H. Woodward. [1798.] pp. 12. 12mo.

33433 BLUNT, EDMUND MARCH
THE NEW THEORETIC AND PRACTICAL NAVIGATOR, CONTAINING LATER IMPROVEMENTS PARTICULARLY IN WORKING LUNAR OBSERVATIONS, CORRECTING THE WATCH, &C. THAN ANY BOOK YET EXTANT. WHEREIN ARE SEVERAL TABLES AND MANY OTHER IMPORTANT ADDITIONS NEVER BEFORE PUBLISHED. THE TABLES OF THE SUN'S DECLINATION ARE CORRECTED AND ADAPTED TO THE ALTERATION OF STILE WHICH TAKES PLACE IN THE YEAR 1800 AND THE LOGARITHIMIC TABLES OF SINES &C. HAVE THE CORRESPONDING TIMES PREFIXED TO THE SEVERAL DEGREES AND MINUTES OF THE SUN'S ALTITUDE WITH THE REQUISITE TABLES USED WITH THE NAUTICAL ALMANAC IN DETERMINING THE LATITUDE AND LONGITUDE. REVISED AND CORRECTED BY NICHOLAS PIKE, ESQ. MEMBER OF THE AMERICAN ACADEMY OF ARTS AND SCIENCES, AND AUTHOR OF THE NEW AND COMPLETE SYSTEM OF ARITHMETIC.
Newburyport: Printed by Edmund March Blunt. 1798.

146th Massachusetts District Copyright, issued to Edmund March Blunt, as Proprietor, 22 May, 1798.

AUCTION VALUES

33434   BOOTH, ABRAHAM   1734–1806
        THE REIGN OF GRACE, FROM ITS RISE TO ITS CONSUMMATION. BY REV. ABRAHAM
        BOOTH. [Four lines of quotations.] THE THIRD AMERICAN, FROM THE FOURTH
        LONDON EDITION.
            Philadelphia: Printed by Stephen C. Ustick. Sold at No. 79, North Third
            Street. 1798. pp. 275, (7), (4). 12mo.   AAS. JCB.
            Contains, a seven-page list of Subscribers' names; and, four-page list of
            books for sale.

33435   BORDLEY, JOHN BEALE   1727–1804
        Caption title: COUNTRY HABITATIONS.
            [*Philadelphia: Printed by Charles Cist, July,*1798.] pp.(13), plate. 8vo. LOC.

33436   BOSTON. MASSACHUSETTS.
        TO JOHN ADAMS, PRESIDENT, AND TO THE CONGRESS OF THE UNITED STATES. THE
        SUBSCRIBERS, INHABITANTS, AND CITIZENS OF BOSTON, IN THE STATE OF MASSA-
        CHUSETTS . . .
            [*Boston: April 21, 1798.*] Broadside.

33437   BOSTON. MASSACHUSETTS. CHARITABLE FIRE SOCIETY.
        ARRANGEMENT OF THE PERFORMANCES FOR THE AFTERNOON . . . [Gives in full
        the Anniversary Ode, and Adams and Liberty; the Boston patriotic song, written
        for the anniversary. By Thomas Paine.]
            [*Boston: 1798.*] Broadside.   HC.

33438   BOSTON. MASSACHUSETTS. MUTUAL FIRE INSURANCE COMPANY.
        RULES AND ARTICLES OF THE MASSACHUSETTS MUTUAL FIRE INSURANCE COMPANY.
        INCORPORATED,—MARCH 1, 1798. [Two columns. And Proposal Blank. Signed,]
        CALEB BINGHAM, SEC'RY PRO TEM. BOSTON, JUNE 12, 1798.
            [*Boston: 1798.*] pp. (4). fol.   AAS.

33439   BOSTON. MASSACHUSETTS. THEATRE.
        NEVER PERFORMED IN BOSTON. ON WEDNESDAY EVENING, NOV. 28, WILL BE PRE-
        SENTED A DRAMA IN 5 ACTS, CALLED, THE CASTLE SPECTRE. WRITTEN BY THE
        AUTHOR OF THE CELEBRATED NOVEL, THE MONK. [Thirty-three lines.] TO WHICH
        WILL BE ADDED, THE MUSICAL ENTERTAINMENT OF THE DOUBLE DISGUISE. [Five
        lines.]
            [*Boston: 1798.*] Broadside. fol.   JCB. LOC. MHS.

33440   THE BOSTON [cut] GAZETTE, AND REPUBLICAN JOURNAL. [Motto.] No. 2255. MON-
        DAY, JANUARY 1, [— No. 2293. MONDAY, SEPTEMBER 17, 1798.]
            Printed by Benjamin Edes, in Kilby-Street, Boston. 1798. fol.   LOC.
            Discontinued in September, "In the forty-fourth year of the independ-
            ence of the Boston Gazette," as he expressed it, and oppressed with its
            cares, the veteran editor, and father of a family of printers and journal-
            ists, closed his honorable career, in a ringing editorial, of one of the
            best edited newspapers of the Colonial and Revolutionary periods of
            American history. The Editor's Farewell. Recites the infirmities of the
            declining period of his life—his domestic embarrassments—old age; and
            infirmity which he patiently suffers until he shall arrive at that above
            where the weary are at rest. Upwards of forty-three years hard labor
            in the "art which supports all arts" he has stood for the rights of his
            country, and during its afflicting crisis the BOSTON GAZETTE was the
            chosen herald to spread the alarm. His office was the meeting place of
            its leaders, and Adams, Hancock, Warren, with their train of co-patriots,
            were his chosen intimates. It was not the path to preferment or pecuni-
            ary reward; but as a patriot he does not mourn his own misfortunes.
            And now my fellow-citizens, I bid you farewell—maintain your virtue
            —and may the Almighty protect and defend you. B. Edes."

33441 THE BOSTON PRICE-CURRENT [cut] AND MARINE INTELLIGENCER. VOL. III. No. 34 MONDAY, JANUARY 1, [— VOL. IV. No. 26. MONDAY, JUNE 4, 1798.]

Published on Mondays and Thursdays, by John Russell, at his Office, in Quaker-Lane, Boston, 1798. fol. AAS.

The words "Russell's Commercial Gazette," in the heading, were not intended to be a part of the title. With the issue for June 11th, the title was changed to *Russell's Gazette. Commercial and political.*

33442 BOWDOINHAM. MAINE. BAPTIST ASSOCIATION.
MINUTES OF THE BOWDOINHAM ASSOCIATION, HELD AT THE BAPTIST MEETING-HOUSE IN BRUNSWICK, AUGUST 22 AND 23, 1798. [Ornament.]

Augusta (Kennebeck): Printed by Peter Edes. 1798. pp. [12.] 8vo. AAS.

33443 BOWEN, DANIEL
BOWEN'S COLUMBIAN MUSEUM AT THE HEAD OF THE MALL, BOSTON, IS OPENED EVERY DAY: AND ELEGANTLY ILLUMINATED EVERY TUESDAY, THURSDAY, & FRIDAY EVENING. . . . [one hundred and ten paintings.]

Boston: Printed by D. Bowen, at his Museum Office; where all kinds of bills, tickets, &c. are elegantly printed, on reasonable terms. [1798.] Broadside. 4to. BPL.

33444 —— BOWEN'S COLUMBIAN MUSEUM, AT THE HEAD OF THE MALL, BOSTON, IS OPEN FOR THE ENTERTAINMENT OF THE PUBLIC, EVERY DAY (EXCEPT SUNDAYS) AND ELEGANTLY ILLUMINATED EVERY TUESDAY & THURSDAY EVENING. . . . [one hundred and twelve paintings.]

[Boston: Printed by D. Bowen, at his Museum Office. 1798.] Broadside. 4to. JCB.

33445 BOWEN'S VIRGINIA GAZETTE: AND THE WINCHESTER CENTINEL. VOL. X. No. 509. FRIDAY, JANUARY 5, [— No. 520. FRIDAY, MARCH 23? 1798.]

Winchester: Printed by R. Bowen. 1798. fol.

Beginning probably in April, Bowen changed the title to: *Winchester Gazette*, with a scroll centered with the words "The Centinel" upon it.

33446 BOWERS, JAMES   –1834
A MASONIC ORATION, DELIVERED BEFORE THE WORSHIPFUL MASTER, OFFICERS AND BRETHREN, OF THE KENNEBECK LODGE, AT HALLOWELL, JUNE 27TH, 1798 — A. L. 5798; BY THE REV. BROTHER JAMES BOWERS.

Hallowell: Printed by brother Howard S. Robinson. 1798. pp. 12. 8vo. NYPL.

33447 BOWMAN, JOHN
Caption title: A NARRATIVE, &C. THE FOLLOWING LATE TRANSACTIONS, WITH SOME REMARKS UPON THEM, ARE SUBMITTED TO THE CONSIDERATION OF THE CITIZENS OF THIS STATE BY A FELLOW-CITIZEN. [Colophon:]

[Charleston, South Carolina:] Printed by W. P. Young. [27th March, 1798.] pp. 16. 8vo. NYPL

An account of the proceedings against John Bowman for contempt of the Court of Equity.

33448   BRAAM HOUCKGEEST, Andréas Everard Van   1739–1796
Voyage de l'ambassade de la Compagnie des Indes Orientales Hollandaises,
vers l'Empereur de la Chine, dans les années 1794 & 1795: où se trouve
la description de plusieurs parties de la Chine inconnues aux Européens,
& que cette ambassade à donné l'occasion de traverser: le tout tiré du
Journal d'André Everard Van Braam Houckgeest, chef de la direction
de la Compagnie des Indes Orientales Hollandaises à la Chine, & second
dans cette ambassade; ancien directeur de la Société des Sciences & Arts
de Harlem en Hollande; de la Société Philosophique de Philadelphie,
&c. &c. Et orné de cartes & de gravures. Publié en Français par m. L.
E. Moreau de Saint-Méry. Tome second.

*A Philadelphie: Et se trouve chez L'Editeur, Imprimeur-Libraire au coin de
la premiere rue Nord & de Callow-Hill. Les principaux Libraires des Etats-
Unis d'Amerique. Les Libraires des principales Villes d'Europe.* 1798. pp. xii,
520, plate, map. 4to.   BM. LOC. NYPL.

The first volume was printed in 1797. Also issued with Paris, and
London imprints.

33449   BRACKEN, Henry   1697–1764
Second American edition. Farriery improved; or, a complete treatise on
the art of farriery. Wherein are fully explained, the nature and
structure of that useful creature, a horse; with the diseases and ac-
cidents he is liable to; and the methods of cure. Exemplified by ten
elegant cuts, each the full figure of a horse, describing all the various
parts of that noble animal. Likewise, rules for breeding and training
of colts; practical receipts for the cure of common distempers incident
to oxen, cows, calves sheep, lambs, hogs, &c. To which is prefixed, ten
minutes' advice to the purchasers of horses. By Henry Bracken, m.d.

Philadelphia: Printed for Mathew Carey, by Stephen C. Ustick. Jan. 11,
1798. pp. 144, 10 plates. 18mo.   NYPL.

33450   BRADFORD, Alden   1765–1843
Two sermons, delivered in Wiscasset (Pownalborough), on the 9th of May,
1798, which the president of the United States, had previously appointed
to be religiously observed as a day of humiliation and prayer throughout
the Union. By Alden Bradford, a. m., minister of the Christian Congregational society in that place.

Wiscasset: Printed by Henry Hoskins & John W. Scott. 1798. pp. 17. (1).
8vo.   AAS. BA. CHS. JCB. LOC. MHS.

33451   BRADMAN, Arthur
Pandomicus: the grammar school-master's soliloqui [sic.] To which are
added, Poems, on various occasions. By Arthur Bradman, esq. [Ornament.]

Portland: Printed at the Office of Baker & George. 1798. pp. 16. nar. 8vo.
                                                    HC.

33452   BRIDGHAM, Samuel Willard   1774–1840
An Oration, delivered in the Benevolent Congregational meeting-house
in Providence, on the fourth of July, A. D. 1798, in commemoration of
American independence. By Samuel W. Bridgham, a. m. [Two lines of Latin
from] Horace. Published by request.

Providence: Printed by Carter and Wilkinson, and sold at their Book-Store.
1798. pp. (12). 8vo.   AAS. JCB. LOC. RIHS.

33453   BRIGGS, Isaac

AN ALMANAC; FOR THE YEAR OF OUR LORD,—1799;—BEING THE THIRD AFTER LEAP-YEAR. CONTAINING A VARIETY OF USEFUL AND ENTERTAINING PIECES. THE ASTRONOMICAL PARTS ONLY, BY ISAAC BRIGGS.

Baltimore: Printed by W. Pechin, No. 15, for John Hagerty, No. 104, and Thomas, Andrews & Butler, No.184, Market-street. [1798.] pp.(36). 12mo. LOC.

33454   —— ISAAC BRIGGS'S ALMANAC; FOR THE YEAR OF OUR LORD,—1799;—BEING THE THIRD AFTER LEAP-YEAR. THE ASTRONOMICAL PART (WHICH IS MUCH MORE COPIOUS THAN USUAL) IS ADOPTED [*sic*] TO THE LATITUDE AND MERIDIAN OF PHILADELPHIA; BUT MAY, WITHOUT MATERIAL ERROR, BE USED IN PENNSYLVANIA, NEW-JERSEY AND DELAWARE. THE SELECTED PIECES (OF WHICH THERE IS A CONSIDERABLE VARIETY IN PROSE AND VERSE) HAVE BEEN CHOSEN WITH CARE; AND NOTHING INCONSISTENT WITH THE TENENTS OF FRIENDS, IS ADMITTED INTO ANY PART OF THIS WORK.

Baltimore: Printed by W. Pechin, No. 15, Baltimore-street, for the Author. [1798.] pp. [72.] 12mo.   AAS. HSP. LOC. MHS. NYHS. NYPL.

Dated, Sharon, 10th of the 9th month, 1798.

33455   —— THE VIRGINIA ALMANACK, OR EPHEMERIS: FOR THE YEAR OF OUR LORD,—1799;—BEING THE THIRD AFTER LEAP-YEAR. THE ASTRONOMICAL PART BY ISAAC BRIGGS. [Ornament.]

Richmond, Virginia:—Printed and sold, wholesale and retail, by Samuel Pleasants, junior, third door below the Vendue-Office of M. Vandewall. [1788.] pp. (40). 12mo.   LOC. VSL.

33456   —— THE VIRGINIA ALMANAC, FOR THE YEAR OF OUR LORD, 1799; BY ISAAC BRIGGS, PHILO.

Lynchburg: Printed by John Carter & Co. [1798.]

33457   —— THE VIRGINIA & N. CAROLINA ALMANACK, FOR THE YEAR OF OUR LORD, 1799.

Norfolk: Printed and sold by Willett & O'Connor. [1798.]

33458   BRIGGS, Richard

THE NEW ART OF COOKERY; ACCORDING TO THE PRESENT PRACTICE; BEING A COMPLETE GUIDE TO ALL HOUSEKEEPERS, ON A PLAN ENTIRELY NEW; CONSISTING OF THIRTY EIGHT CHAPTERS. CONTAINING, PROPER DIRECTIONS FOR MARKETING, AND TRUSSING OF POULTRY. THE MAKING OF SOUPS AND BROTHS. DRESSING ALL SORTS OF FISH. SAUCES FOR EVERY OCCASION. BOILING AND ROASTING. BAKING, BROILING, AND FRYING. STEWS AND HASHES. MADE DISHES OF EVERY SORT. RAGOUS AND FRICASEES. DIRECTIONS FOR DRESSING ALL SORTS OF ROOTS AND VEGETABLES. ALL SORTS OF AUMLETS AND EGGS. PUDDINGS, PIES, TARTS, &C. PANCAKES AND FRITTERS. CHEESE-CAKES AND CUSTARDS. BLANCMANGE, JELLIES AND SYLLABUBS. DIRECTIONS FOR SEAFARING MEN. DIRECTIONS FOR THE SICK. PRESERVING, SYRUPS, AND CONSERVES. DRYING AND CANDYING. ALL SORTS OF CAKES. HOGS PUDDINGS, SAUSAGES, &C. POTTING AND LITTLE COLD DISHES. THE ART OF CARVING. COLLARING, SALTING, AND SOUSING. PICKLING. TO KEEP GARDEN VEGETABLES, &C. MADE WINES. CORDIAL WATERS. BREWING. ENGLISH AND FRENCH BREAD, &C. WITH BILLS OF FARE FOR EVERY MONTH IN THE YEAR. NEATLY AND CORRECTLY PRINTED. SECOND AMERICAN EDITION, IMPROVED. BY RICHARD BRIGGS, MANY YEARS COOK AT THE GLOBE TAVERN, FLEET-STREET, THE WHITE HART TAVERN, HOLBORN, AND NOW PRINCIPAL OF THE TEMPLE COFFEE-HOUSE, LONDON.

Boston: Printed [by Samuel Etheridge ?] for W. Spotswood. 1798. pp. xxiii. (25), 444. 12mo.   AAS.

BRIGGS, RICHARD, continued.

33459 —— — THE NEW ART OF COOKERY; ACCORDING TO THE PRESENT PRACTICE; BEING A COMPLETE GUIDE TO ALL HOUSEKEEPERS, ON A PLAN ENTIRELY NEW; CONSISTING OF THIRTY EIGHT CHAPTERS. CONTAINING, PROPER DIRECTIONS FOR MARKETING, AND TRUSSING OF POULTRY. THE MAKING OF SOUPS AND BROTHS. DRESSING ALL SORTS OF FISH. SAUCES FOR EVERY OCCASION. BOILING AND ROASTING. BAKING, BROILING, AND FRYING. STEWS AND HASHES. MADE DISHES OF EVERY SORT. RAGOUS AND FRICASEES. DIRECTIONS FOR DRESSING ALL SORTS OF ROOTS AND VEGETABLES. ALL SORTS OF AUMLETS AND EGGS. PUDDINGS, PIES, TARTS, &C. PANCAKES AND FRITTERS. CHEESECAKES AND CUSTARDS. BLANCMANGE, JELLIES AND SYLLABUBS. DIRECTIONS FOR SEAFARING MEN. DIRECTIONS FOR THE SICK. PRESERVING, SYRUPS, AND CONSERVES. DRYING AND CANDYING. ALL SORTS OF CAKES. HOGS PUDDINGS, SAUSAGES, &C. POTTING AND LITTLE COLD DISHES. THE ART OF CARVING. COLLARING, SALTING, AND SOUSING. PICKLING. TO KEEP GARDEN VEGETABLES, &C. MADE WINES. CORDIAL WATERS. BREWING. ENGLISH AND FRENCH BREAD, &C. WITH BILLS OF FARE FOR EVERY MONTH IN THE YEAR. NEATLY AND CORRECTLY PRINTED. SECOND AMERICAN EDITION, IMPROVED. BY RICHARD BRIGGS, MANY YEARS COOK AT THE GLOBE TAVERN, FLEET-STREET, THE WHITE HART TAVERN, HOLBORN, AND NOW PRINCIPAL OF THE TEMPLE COFFEE-HOUSE, LONDON.

Philadelphia: Printed for H. & P. Rice, and sold by J. Rice and Co. Baltimore. 1798. pp. xxiii, (25), 444. 12mo.   AAS.

33460 BROADDUS, ANDREW   1770–1848
A SELECTION OF HYMNS AND SPIRITUAL SONGS FROM THE BEST AUTHORS. BY ANDREW BROADDUS, V. D. M.
Richmond: Printed and sold by Samuel Pleasants, jun. 1798.

33461 BROWN, CHARLES BROCKDEN   1771–1810
WIELAND; OR THE TRANSFORMATION. AN AMERICAN TALE. [Four lines of verse.] COPY-RIGHT SECURED. [Ornament.]
New-York: Printed by T. & J. Swords, for H. Caritat.—1798.—pp. (2), (2), 298. 12mo.   AAS. BM. HC. JCB. LOC. NYPL.

Advertisement signed, C. B. B. September 3, 1798. 67th New York District Copyright, issued to Hocquet Caritat, as Proprietor, 5 September, 1798.

33462 BROWN, CLARK   1772–1817
Half-title: THE EMIGRATION OF POPERY.
Title: POPISH HIERARCHY SUPPRESSED BY BUONAPARTE IN ITALY; AND HIS HOLINESS EXERTING HIS INFLUENCE, IN A LATE ECCLESIASTICAL COUNCIL, HOLDEN AT BRIMFIELD, MASSACHUSETTS; CALLED, BY LETTERS MISSIVE, TO INSTAL THE REV. CLARK BROWN. BY AGATHOCLES. [Nine lines of quotations.]
Springfield: Printed by Francis Stebbins. 1798. pp. [55.] 8vo.
                                                AAS. BA. LOC. MHS.

33463 BROWN, JOHN   1722–1787
A DICTIONARY OF THE HOLY BIBLE: CONTAINING, AN HISTORICAL ACCOUNT OF THE PERSONS: A GEOGRAPHICAL AND HISTORICAL ACCOUNT OF THE PLACES: A LITERAL, CRITICAL, AND SYSTEMATICAL DESCRIPTION OF OTHER OBJECTS, WHETHER NATURAL, ARTIFICIAL, CIVIL, RELIGIOUS OR MILITARY: AND, THE EXPLICATION OF THE APPELLATIVE TERMS MENTIONED IN THE WRITINGS OF THE OLD AND NEW TESTAMENT. THE WHOLE COMPRISING WHATEVER IMPORTANT IS KNOWN CONCERNING THE ANTIQUITIES OF THE HEBREW NATION AND CHURCH OF GOD; FORMING A SACRED COMMENTARY; A BODY OF SCRIPTURE HISTORY, CHRONOLOGY, AND DIVINITY; AND SERVING IN A GREAT MEASURE AS A CONCORDANCE TO THE BIBLE. BY JOHN BROWN, MINISTER OF THE GOSPEL AT HADDINGTON. IN TWO VOLUMES. VOL. I. [— II.]
Philadelphia: Printed by and for William W. Woodward, No. 17, Chesnut Street. 1798. 2 vols. pp. (2), (2), 626, plate; (2), 653, [39], (1), plate. 8vo.   AAS. LOC.

Contains, five pages of Subscribers' names.

33464 BROWN, Thaddeus   –1803
Half-title: PHILADELPHIA REFORMED OR ELSE DESTROYED.

Title: AN ADDRESS IN CHRISTIAN LOVE TO THE INHABITANTS OF PHILADELPHIA;
ON THE AWFUL DISPENSATION OF THE YELLOW FEVER, IN 1798. BY THADDEUS
BROWN. [Three lines of Scripture texts.]

Philadelphia: Printed for the Author, by R. Aitken, No. 22, Market-Street.
1798. pp. 71. 12mo.   AAS. BM. LOC. SGO.

33465 BROWNE, Joseph
A TREATISE ON THE YELLOW FEVER; SHEWING ITS ORIGIN, CURE AND PREVENTION.
BY JOSEPH BROWNE.

New-York: Printed at the Argus Office. [1798.] pp. 31, errata. 8vo. AAS. LOC.

33466 BRUCE, James   1730–1794
AN INTERESTING NARRATIVE OF THE TRAVELS OF JAMES BRUCE, ESQ. INTO ABYSSINIA,
TO DISCOVER THE SOURCE OF THE NILE: ABRIDGED FROM THE ORIGINAL WORK.
TO WHICH ARE ADDED, NOTES AND EXTRACTS, FROM THE TRAVELS OF DR. SHAW,
M. SAVARY, AND THE MEMOIRS OF BARON DE TOTT. SECOND AMERICAN EDITION:
BEING A LITERAL COPY OF THE ENGLISH. [Printer's mark.]

Boston: Printed by Samuel Etheridge, for Alexander Thomas and George
Merriam; Sold by A. Thomas in Walpole, by G. Merriam in Worcester, and by S.
Etheridge in Boston.—1798.—pp. vii, 388. 12mo.

AAS. BM. HC. JCB. LOC. NYHS. NYPL.

33467 BRYDONE, Patrick   1743–1818
A TOUR THROUGH SICILY AND MALTA. IN A SERIES OF LETTERS TO WILLIAM BECK-
FORD, ESQ. OF SOMERLY IN SUFFOLK; FROM P. BRYDONE, F. R. S. IN TWO VOLUMES.
[Printer's mark. Vignette.]

Printed at Greenfield, Massachusetts, by Thomas Dickman, and sold at his
Bookstore in Greenfield. M,DCC,XCVIII. 2 vols. in one. pp. (2), (2), viii, 339.
12mo.   AAS. NYPL.

33468 —— — A TOUR THROUGH SICILY AND MALTA. IN A SERIES OF LETTERS TO WILLIAM
BECKFORD, ESQ. OF SOMERLY IN SUFFOLK: FROM P. BRYDONE, F. R. S. IN TWO
VOLUMES. [Printer's mark. Vignette.]

Printed at Greenfield, Massachusetts, by Thomas Dickman, for Thomas & Andrews; Sold at their Bookstore, No. 45, Newbury-Street, Boston, and by the Printer
in Greenfield. M,DCC,XCVIII. pp. (2), (2), viii, 339. 12mo.   JCB.

33469 BUCHAN, William   1729–1805
DOMESTIC MEDICINE. A TREATISE ON THE PREVENTION AND CURE OF DISEASES BY
REGIMEN AND SIMPLE MEDICINE. WITH AN APPENDIX CONTAINING A DISPENSATORY
FOR THE USE OF PRIVATE PRACTITIONERS. THE FIRST VERMONT EDITION CONTAIN-
ING ALL THE IMPROVEMENTS.

Fairhaven: Printed by and for James Lyon, at Voltaires Head. 1798. pp.
xxiv, 476, 10, (1). 8vo.   AAS. LOC. NYPL.

33470 BUCKMINSTER, Joseph   1751–1812
A DISCOURSE DELIVERED IN THE FIRST PARISH IN PORTSMOUTH, NOVEMBER 15, 1798,
A DAY OBSERVED AS AN ANNIVERSARY THANKSGIVING. BY JOSEPH BUCKMINSTER,
A. M. BY REQUEST. [Three lines of quotations.]

Portsmouth,—New-Hampshire: Printed by John Melcher. 1798. pp. (21).
8vo.   AAS. CHS. CLA. HC. JCB. LOC. MHS. NYHS. NYPL.

33471 —— A SERMON DELIVERED AT EXETER, OCTOBER 15TH, 1798, AT THE INTERMENT
OF MRS. SARAH ROWLAND, CONSORT OF THE REV. WILLIAM F. ROWLAND, AND
ELDEST DAUGHTER OF COL. ELIPHALET LADD. BY JOSEPH BUCKMINSTER, A. M.
[Three lines of Scripture texts.]

Portsmouth,—New-Hampshire: Printed by John Melcher. 1798. pp. (16).
8vo.   AAS. LOC. NYHS. YC.

33472   BUEL, Ebenezer   1713–1801
Index to the Holy Bible; which the Scriptures may be found with much greater facility, and by means of which (its curious and excellent contents coming more immediately under the eye) we shall be excited to examine the sacred volume with more pleasure and avidity, not only as christians, but as admirers of simplicity and fine writing. Printed at the desire and expence of Mr. Ebenezer Buel, aged 86, for the benefit of his posterity, and the general good.

     Printed at Litchfield, by T. Collier. [1798.] pp. 28. 8vo.   LHS.

33473   BUNYAN, John   1628–1688
The Christian pilgrim: containing an account of the wonderful adventures and miraculous escape of a christian, in his travels from the land of destruction to the New Jerusalem. First American edition.

     Worcester: Printed by Isaiah Thomas, jun. Sold, wholesale and retail at his Book-Store—October, 1798. 2 vols. pp. (2), (2), (2), (2), 7–112, frontispiece; (2), (2), (113)–219, (3). 32mo.   AAS. LOC.

     The second volume has Vol. II. on the title page, and is erroneously dated 1789.

33474   ——   The Jerusalem sinner saved; or, good news for the vilest of men. Being an help for despairing souls: shewing that Jesus Christ would have mercy in the first place offered to the biggest sinners. To which is added, an answer to those grand objections that lie in the way of them that would believe: for the comfort of those that fear they have sinned against the Holy Ghost. By John Bunyan.

     Amherst, Newhampshire: Printed by Samuel Preston. 1798. pp. 176. 16mo.
     AAS. LOC. NYPL.

33475   BURK, John Daly   1775–1808
Female patriotism or the death of Joan d'Arc: an historical play in v acts, by John Burk—author of Bunker Hill—Prince of Susa, and other dramatic pieces.

     New-York: Printed by Robert M. Hurtin, at the Literary Printing-Office, No. 29, Gold-Street. 1798. pp. 40. 12mo.   AAS. JCB. LOC. NYPL.

33476   BURNHAM, John   1780–1826
An Oration delivered on the 4th July, 1798, at Fryeburg. By John Burnham.
     Fryeburg, District of Maine. Printed by Elijah Russel. 1798.

33477   BURNS, Robert   1759–1796
Poems, chiefly in the Scottish dialect. By Robert Burns. [Third American] (From the latest European edition.) Two volumes in one.

     Philadelphia: Printed by Patterson & Cochran, No. 148, South Fourth-Street. 1798. 2 vols. in one. pp. viii, 302. 12mo.   AAS.

33478   BURROUGHS, Stephen   1765–1840
Memoirs of Stephen Burroughs. When such sad scenes the bosom pain, what eye from weeping can refrain. Copy right secured. [Ornament.]
     Printed at Hanover, Newhampshire, by Benjamin True. MDCCXCVIII. pp. (2), (2), [8]–296. 8vo.   AAS. BA. BM. HC. JCB. LOC. NYHS. NYPL. PrA.

     A second volume was printed in Boston in 1804. Reprinted in Boston circa 1840, and in New-York in 1924. Lazarus Beach issued proposals for printing this in Newfield, Connecticut, September 26, 1797.

33479   BURROUGHS, STEPHEN, continued.
—— STEPHEN BURROUGHS'S SERMON, DELIVERED IN RUTLAND, ON A HAY MOW, TO
HIS AUDITORY THE PELHAMITES, AT THE TIME WHEN A MOB OF THEM, AFTER HAVING
PURSUED HIM TO RUTLAND, IN ORDER TO APPREHEND HIM BECAUSE HE HAD
ABRUPTLY DEPARTED AND ABSCONDED FROM PELHAM, WHERE HE HAD BEEN
PREACHING THE GOSPEL; SHUT HIM INTO A BARN, INTO WHICH HE RAN FOR ASYLUM,
WHEN HE ASCENDED A HAY-MOW, WHICH WAS INACCESSIBLE, EXCEPT IN ONE PLACE,
WITH A WEAPON OF DEFENCE IN HIS HAND, WITH WHICH HE KEPT OFF HIS PURSUERS
AT PLEASURE, AS MENTIONED IN THE AUTHOR'S MEMOIRS, P. 90, 91, AND DELIVERED
TO THEM THE FOLLOWING SERMON, ON THE OCCASION.
    [Printed at Hanover, N. H. by Benjamin True. 1798.] pp. (11). 12mo.
                                                      AAS. JCB. LOC.

33480   BURTON, JOHN   1746–1806
LECTURES ON FEMALE EDUCATION AND MANNERS. BY J. BURTON. THE FOURTH
AMERICAN EDITION.
    [New-York: 1798?]

33481   BUTLER, JAMES   1755–1842
FORTUNE'S FOOT-BALL: OR, THE ADVENTURES OF MERCUTIO. FOUNDED ON MATTERS
OF FACT. A NOVEL IN TWO VOLUMES. BY JAMES BUTLER. VOL. II.
    *Harrisburgh, Pennsylvania: Printed by John Wyeth. 1798. [Entered ac-
cording to law.]* pp. 191. 12mo.   AAS. BM. JCB. LOC. NYPL.
    The first volume was printed in 1797.

33482   BUXTON, CHARLES
AN ORATION, DELIVERED BEFORE THE SOCIETY OF BLACK FRIARS, IN THE CITY OF
NEW-YORK, AT THEIR ANNIVERSARY FESTIVAL, ON TUESDAY THE 7TH OF NOV.
1797. BY CHARLES BUXTON, M. D. PUBLISHED BY ORDER OF THE SOCIETY.
    New-York: Printed by Friar M'Lean. 1798. pp. 22, (1). 8vo.   BA. LOC.

33483   CALLCOTT, JOHN WALL
WERTER TO CHARLOTTE, A FAVORITE BALLAD. COMPOSED BY JOHN WALL CALLCOTT.
    Philadelphia: Published at Carr's Musical Repository. 1798.

33484   CALLENDER, JAMES THOMSON   1758–1803
SEDGWICK & CO.; OR, A KEY TO THE SIX PER CENT. CABINET. [By James Thomson
Callender, now citizen of the United States, and one of the seven persons whom
the four Alien Bills now depending before Congress were designed to ruin.
Tartæne animus six per centibus iræ.]
    ·Philadelphia: Printed for the Author [at the Office of the Aurora.] 1798.
pp. (88). 8vo.   AAS. BA. HC. JCB. LOC. NYPL. VSL.

    "Completely developing the intrigues of Sedgwick, Smith, and others
    of that party, for the purpose of depriving the discharged Revolutionary
    soldiers, of their well-earned certificates; with other interesting remarks
    on the progress of speculation, and aristocracy in the United States of
    America; worthy of the attention of every citizen of this country."
    The bracketed part of the title page is as advertised.

33485   —— SKETCHES OF THE HISTORY OF AMERICA. BY JAMES THOMSON CALLENDER.
[ENTERED ACCORDING TO LAW.]
    *Philadelphia: From the Press of Snowden & M'Corkle, No. 47, North Fourth-
Street. 1798. [Price one dollar.]* pp. 263, (1). 8vo.
                              AAS. BA. BM. HC. JCB. LOC, NYHS. NYPL.

    202d Pennsylvania District copyright, issued to James Thomson Cal-
    lender, as Author, 8 February, 1798.

33486   CALVIN, JUNIUS, pseudonym.
THE TRIBULATIONS OF JUNIUS CALVIN, IN A SERIES OF LETTERS TO A PILGRIM.
[Four lines of verse.]
Philadelphia: Printed by Stephen C. Ustick. 1798. pp. 27. 12mo.   AAS.

33487   CAMPBELL, DONALD   1751–1804
A NARRATIVE OF THE EXTRAORDINARY ADVENTURES, AND SUFFERINGS BY SHIPWRECK
& IMPRISONMENT, OF DONALD CAMPBELL, ESQ. OF BARBRECK: WITH THE SINGULAR
HUMOURS OF HIS TARTAR GUIDE, HASSAM ARTAZ; COMPRISING THE OCCURRENCES
OF FOUR YEARS AND FIVE DAYS, IN AN OVERLAND JOURNEY TO INDIA. IN A SERIES
OF LETTERS TO HIS SON. [Three lines from] YOUNG. SECOND AMERICAN EDITION.
New-York: Printed [by John Tiebout] for Evert Duyckinck & Co. No. 110,
Pearl-Street. 1798. pp. 417, frontispiece. 12mo.   AAS. JCB. LOC. NYPL.

33488   —— PROPOSALS, FOR PUBLISHING BY SUBSCRIPTION. A NARRATIVE OF THE EXTRA-
ORDINARY ADVENTURES OF DONALD CAMPBELL, ESQ. FIRST NEW-YORK EDITION.
New-York: Printed by John Tiebout. 1799. pp. 12. 12mo.

Covering, probably, Napoleon Buonaparte's intended route to India.

33489   CAMPBELL, JOHN
THE COMPLETE SOLDIER'S POCKET COMPANION; OR, A PLAIN AND EASY METHOD OF
MILITARY DISCIPLINE. CONTAINING: THE NEW SYSTEM OF MANUAL AND PLATOON
EXERCISE, NOW PRACTISED IN THE ARMY OF GREAT-BRITAIN; TOGETHER WITH
FILING, GROUNDING, ADVANCING, HANDLING, EASING AND REVERSING OF ARMS,
WITH FIELD MANŒUVRES, CAMP AND GARRISON DUTY. TO WHICH ARE ADDED,
FORMS OF MORNING REPORTS, MONTHLY RETURNS, MUSTER ROLLS, RETURNS OF
ARMS, ACCOUTREMENTS, CLOATHING, &C. WITH A ROLL OF COUNTRY, AGE, SIZE AND
SERVITUDE. ALSO, THE FIELD PIECE AND GREAT GUN EXERCISE, WITH SOME EX-
TRACTS AND OBSERVATIONS FROM BARON STEUBEN'S PUBLICATION. BY JOHN
CAMPBELL, LATE ADJUTANT IN THE BRITISH 73D REGIMENT OF FOOT.
Philadelphia: Printed by Thomas Dobson, at the Stone-House, No. 41, *South
Second-Street.* M,DCC,XCVIII. pp. 52, 9 folded tables. 8vo.   AAS. LCP.

212th Pennsylvania District Copyright, issued to Thomas Dobson, as
Proprietor, 16 June, 1798.

33490   CAREY, JAMES
THE HOUSE OF WISDOM IN A BUSTLE; A POEM, DESCRIPTIVE OF THE NOTED BATTLE,
lately fought in C—ng—ss. BY GEOFFREY TOUCHSTONE.
Philadelphia: Printed for the Author. 1798. [*Price* 25 *cents.*] pp. 27. 8vo.
AAS. BU. REH. JCB. NYHS.

33491   —— — THE HOUSE OF WISDOM IN A BUSTLE; A POEM, DESCRIPTIVE OF THE NOTED
BATTLE LATELY FOUGHT IN C—NG—SS. BY GEOFFREY TOUCHSTONE.
Philadelphia: Printed for the Author. 1798. pp. 27, plate. 8vo.   AAS.

Reprinted in New York in 1924.

Title of folded plate: CONGRESSIONAL PUGILISTS, CONGRESS HALL IN PHIL'A FEB.
15, 1798. "He in a trice struck Lyon thrice Upon his head, enrag'd sir, Who
seiz'd the tongs to ease his wrongs, And Griswold thus engag'd sir."
[*Philadelphia:* 1798.] Broadside.

33492   —— — THE HOUSE OF WISDOM IN A BUSTLE. A POEM, DESCRIPTIVE OF THE NOTED
BATTLE LATELY FOUGHT IN C—NG—SS. BY GEOFFREY TOUCHSTONE.
New-York: Printed for the purchasers. 1798. [*Price* 25 *cents.*] pp. (24).
8vo.   AAS. BU. HSP. JCB. MHS. NYPL.

33493 CAREY, James, continued.
—— The Life of skunk Peter Porcupine and his two uncles the cobbler
and salm-singer. By Thomas Griendlief.

*[New-York:] Printed at Constantinople. At the Sign of the Heads of Tray-
tors Arnorld, Gobbet, and Blount and next door to the Knights of "the Last Ditch."*
[1798.] pp. 12. 8vo.

As advertised in New York.

33494 —— A Nosegay, for the young men from 16 to 24 years of age. A true picture of the King of England. Dedicated to his hireling skunk Porcupine.
With his petition to the Corporation, of the city of Philadelphia, &c.
&c. &c. [Seven lines of verse.] The substance of mr. Ames's speech on the
B. Treaty.

*Printed at Philadelphia [by James Carey], next door to Porcupine's Coat of
Arms, a Bull's Eye, a Baboon's Head, and a Lion's tail. Sold at the Book-
Stores,—Price one shilling.* [1798.] pp. (16). 8vo. LOC.

33495 —— —— A Nosegay, for the young men from 16 to 24 years of age. A true
picture of the King of England. Dedicated to his hireling skunk Porcupine, with his petition to the Corporation, of the city of Philadelphia,
&c. &c. &c. . . . By Thomas Griendlief.

*[New-York:] Printed at Philadelphia, next door to Porcupine's Coat of Arms,
a Bull's Eye, a Baboon's Head, and a Lion's tail. Sold at the Book-Stores,—Price
one shilling.* [1798.] pp. (16). 8vo.

As advertised in New York.

33496 CAREY'S United States' Recorder. Vol. i. No. 1. Tuesday, January 23, [—
No. 94. Thursday, August 30, 1798.]

*Philadelphia: Printed by James Carey, No. 19, Carter's-Alley; on Tuesd ays,
Thursdays, and Saturdays, at five dollars per annum.* 1798. fol. LCP.

Established, as a tri-weekly, by James Carey, in continuation of *Carey's
Daily Advertiser*, and continued by him to August 30, 1798, when it
was discontinued, owing to the yellow fever. August 2d, the Printing-
Office was removed to No. 16 Chesnut-Street; and the following motto
added to the heading: "Do thou, great Liberty, inspire our souls, and
make our lives in thy possession happy, or our deaths glorious in thy
just defence." Addison.

33497 CAREY, Mathew   1760–1839
Mathew Carey's Exchange Catalogue, [of books, Two columns.]

[Philadelphia: Printed for Mathew Carey. June 23, 1798.] Broadside.
4to. AAS.

33498 THE CAROLINA Gazette. Vol. i. No. 1. Thursday, January 4, [— No. 52.
Thursday, December 27, 1798.]

Charleston: Published by Freneau and Paine. 1798. fol. WHS.

Established, as a weekly, by Peter Freneau, and Seth Paine, in connection with their daily "City Gazette", and continued by them, and
by their successors, with the same changes in publishers as that paper,
beyond the period of this work.

33499   CARTWRIGHT, CHARLOTTE
THE LADY'S BEST COMPANION; OR, A COMPLETE TREASURY FOR THE FAIR SEX. CON-
TAINING THE WHOLE ARTS OF COOKERY — PASTRY — CONFECTIONARY — POTTING —
PICKLING — PRESERVING — CANDYING — COLLARING — BREWING, &C. WITH PLAIN
INSTRUCTIONS FOR MAKING ENGLISH WINES, FROM FRUITS, FLOWERS, &C. TO WHICH
IS ADDED, THE APPROVED FAMILY PHYSICIAN; CONSISTING OF PHYSICAL RECEIPTS,
FOR MOST DISORDERS THAT GROWN PEOPLE, AND YOUNG CHILDREN ARE SUBJECT
TO. BY MRS. CHARLOTTE CARTWRIGHT,
> *Elizabeth (Hager's) Town: Printed by Thomas Grieves, near the Court-House.*
> 1798.

33500   THE CASE OF THE COUNTY OF ORANGE, WITH OBSERVATIONS, TO SHOW THE INJUSTICE
OF THE DIVISION OF THAT COUNTY INTO TWO; AND THE PERILOUS CONSEQUENCES
OF SPLITTING THE COLONY INTO SUCH LITTLE DEPENDENT DISTRICTS, AS WILL
RENDER THEM THE PREY OF AMBITION, AND THE INSTRUMENTS OF CORRUPTION.
> *[Goshen: Printed by John G. Hurtin. 1798.]* pp. 22. 8vo.   NYPL.

33501   CATE, JAMES
REMARKS ON THE DEATH OF MR. GEORGE HANCOCK, JUN. BY JAMES CATE. [Six
lines. Cut. Fifty-one four-line verses.] FROM YOUR AFFECTIONATE FRIEND JAMES
CATE. MR. GEORGE HANCOCK, NORTHFIELD, JULY 31, 1798. [Colophon:]
> *[Exeter:] Printed by J[ohn] L[amson] for the Author.* [1798.] Broad-
> side. fol.   YC.

> Reprinted in New Haven, in an edition of two hundred and ten copies,
> in 1909.

33502   THE CATSKILL PACKET. VOL. VI. NUMBER 1. SATURDAY, JANUARY 6, [— DE-
CEMBER, 1798.]
> *Catskill, (State of New-York): Printed by Mackay Croswell.* 1798. fol.

> No numbers for this volume are known, and publication was probably
> irregular as the next volume began in March, 1799, as *The Packet.*

33503   THE CENTINEL, & COUNTRY GAZETTE. VOL. II. NO. 85. FRIDAY, JANUARY 5,
[—VOL. II. NO. 93. FRIDAY, MARCH 2, 1798.]
> *George-Town (On the Potomak). From the Press of Green, English & Co.*
> 1798. fol.
> The above is the last number located.

33504   THE CENTINEL OF FREEDOM. VOL. II. NO. 14. TOTAL NUMB. 66. WEDNESDAY,
JANUARY 2, [—VOL. III. NO. 13. TOTAL NUMB. 117. TUESDAY, DECEMBER 25,
1798.]
> *Newark, [New-Jersey]: Aaron Pennington & Daniel Dodge, Publishers.*
> 1798. fol.

33505   ——— ADDRESS PRESENTED BY THE CARRIERS TO THE PATRONS OF THE CENTINEL OF
FREEDOM, WITH THE COMPLIMENTS OF THE SEASON. JANUARY 1, 1798.
> *[Newark: Printed by Pennington and Dodge, 1798.]* Broadside. 8vo. NJHS.

33506   THE CENTINEL OF LIBERTY, AND GEORGE-TOWN ADVERTISER. [Motto.] NO. 63.
VOL. II. TUESDAY, JANUARY 2, [— NO. 62. VOL. III. FRIDAY, DECEMBER 28,
1798.]
> *From the Press of Green, English & Co. George-Town (Potomak) every Tues-*
> *day and Friday, at four dollars per annum.* 1798. fol.
> The issue for January 5th has the title: *The Centinel, & Country Gazette.*
> On January 16th, the motto was changed to: Every portion of our
> country finds the most commanding motives for carefully guarding and
> preserving the UNION of the whole. — Washington.

33507 CHARACTERISTICS IN THE PROPHECIES APPLICABLE TO, AND DESCRIPTIVE OF, THE POWER AND DURATION OF THE FRENCH REPUBLIC. ALSO A FEW OBSERVATIONS ILLUSTRATIVE OF THE PROBABLE RESULT OF THE PRESENT DISORDERED STATE OF THE CIVIL AND POLITICAL WORLD.
New-York: Printed by John Tiebout, No. 358, Pearl-Street. 1798. pp. (27). 8vo. AAS. NYPL.

33508 CHARLESTON. SOUTH CAROLINA. BAPTIST ASSOCIATION.
MINUTES OF THE CHARLESTON BAPTIST ASSOCIATION.
Charleston: 1798.

33509 CHARLESTOWN. VIRGINIA. ACADEMY.
BYE LAWS, FOR THE ORGANIZATION AND GOVERNMENT OF CHARLESTOWN ACADEMY, IN BERKELEY COUNTY, VIRGINIA; ADOPTED BY THE BOARD OF TRUSTEES, 3D FEBRUARY, 1798, AFTER MATURE DELIBERATION AT SEVERAL MEETINGS HELD PRIOR TO THAT DAY . . .
Alexandria: Printed by Henry Gird, jun. 1798. pp. 20. 12mo. NYPL.

33510 CHAUVET, DAVID
THE CONDUCT OF THE GOVERNMENT OF FRANCE TOWARDS THE REPUBLIC OF GENEVA. TRANSLATED FROM THE FRENCH. BY A CITIZEN OF TRENTON. [Between double lines.]
Trenton: Printed by G. Craft. October, 1798. pp. 16. 8vo. AAS. BA. JCB. NYHS.

33511 —— LETTER OF A GENEVAN, RESIDING AT LONDON, TO ONE OF HIS FRIENDS, AN INHABITANT OF THE PAYS DE VAUD, IN SWITZERLAND. ADD POWER TO PASSION, AND THERE IS NO WILD BEAST SO SAVAGE AS MAN. PLUT. IN VITA. CICERONIS. [Between double lines.]
Philadelphia: Published by Francis C. King, No. 42, Market-Street. 1798. Price 12½ cents. pp. 15. 8vo. NYHS.

33512 THE CHELSEA COURIER. VOL. II. NUMBER 6. WEDNESDAY, JANUARY 3, [— NUM-BER 26. WEDNESDAY, MAY 23, 1798.]
Norwich: (Chelsea Society). Printed by Thomas Hubbard. 1798. fol. CHS. HC.
Beginning with the issue for May 31st, the name was changed to The Courier.

33513 CHETWOOD, WILLIAM RUFUS   –1766
THE REMARKABLE HISTORY OF MISS VILLARS. EXTRACTED FROM THE ADVENTURES OF CAPT. ROBERT BOYLE,
Amherst, Newhampshire: From the Press of Samuel Preston. 1798.

33514 THE CHRISTIAN'S MONITOR; OR, THEOLOGICAL MAGAZINE. "TO MAKE THE SOUL BY GENTLE ADMONITION." NO. 1.— SATURDAY, DECEMBER 8, [—NO. 2.—SATUR-DAY, DECEMBER 22, 1798.]
By Rand & Burdick, Portland, Maine. [1798.] pp. (16). 8vo.
Established, as a fortnightly publication, and edited by the publishers, John Rand, and William Burdick. The last number located is No. 14. Saturday, June 8, 1799.

33515 CHRISTIANÆ MILITIÆ VIATICUM: OR, A BRIEF DIRECTORY FOR EVANGELICAL MIN-ISTERS.
Philadelphia: Printed by S. C. Ustick, No. 79, North Third St. 1798. pp. 96. 48mo. AAS.
Contains, Extracts from Cotton Mather's Manuductio ad ministerium: David Brainerd's Diary; John Rogers's Sixty memorials for a Godly life; Jonathan Edwards's Seventy Resolutions; and Dr. Owen on Spirit-ual mindedness.

33516   CISH, JANE

THE VISION AND WONDERFUL EXPERIENCE OF JANE CISH, SHEWING HOW SHE WAS CONVERTED, AND HOW SHE FELL INTO A TRANCE ON THE THIRD OF MAY, 1780, AND SAW HEAVEN AND HELL, WITH MANY OTHER STRANGE THINGS: BEING A COPY FROM HER OWN MOUTH, AND PUBLISHED AT THE REQUEST OF SEVERAL OF HER FRIENDS. COME HITHER ALL YE THAT LOVE THE LORD, AND I WILL TELL YE WHAT HE HATH DONE FOR MY SOUL.

Philadelphia: Printed in the year 1798. pp. 15. 8vo.   AAS.

33517   CITY GAZETTE AND [seal] DAILY ADVERTISER. [Motto.] VOL. XVI. No. 3249. MONDAY, JANUARY 1, [— No. 3556. MONDAY, DECEMBER 31, 1798.]

Charleston: Published by Freneau & Paine, Printers to the City, No. 47, Bay, at seven dollars per annum, payable half yearly. 1798. fol.   CLS. LOC.

33518   CLAIBORNE, JOHN

AN INAUGURAL ESSAY ON SCURVY. SUBMITTED TO THE EXAMINATION OF THE REV JOHN EWING, S. T. P. PROVOST, THE TRUSTEES, AND MEDICAL FACULTY OF THE UNIVERSITY OF PENNSYLVANIA, ON THE 22D DAY OF MAY, 1798, FOR THE DEGREE OF DOCTOR OF MEDICINE. BY JOHN CLAIBORNE, OF VIRGINIA, MEMBER OF THE PHILADELPHIA MEDICAL AND CHEMICAL SOCIETIES.

Philadelphia: Printed by Stephen C. Ustick. 1798. pp. 43. 8vo.
    AAS. JCB. LCP. LOC. SGO.

33519   CLARKE, ABRAHAM LYNSON   1768–1810

THE CATECHISM OF THE PROTESTANT EPISCOPAL CHURCH IN THE UNITED STATES OF AMERICA. WITH SELECTED QUESTIONS AND ANSWERS ON IMPORTANT SUBJECTS. BY ABRAHAM L. CLARKE, A. M. RECTOR OF ST. JOHN'S CHURCH. . . .

Providence: [Printed] By Carter & Wilkinson, opposite the Market. 1798. pp. 31. 16mo.   RIHS.

33520   CLARKE, JOHN   1755–1798

AN ANSWER TO THE QUESTION, "WHY ARE YOU A CHRISTIAN?" BY JOHN CLARKE, MINISTER OF A CHURCH IN BOSTON. [From] THE THIRD EDITION.

New-Windsor: Printed by Jacob Schultz & Abraham Lott. 1798. 12mo.   BM.

33521   CLAYPOOLE'S AMERICAN DAILY ADVERTISER. NUMBER 5846. MONDAY, JANUARY 1, [— . . . DECEMBER 31, 1798.]

Philadelphia: Printed by David C. and Septimus Claypoole, No. 48, Market-Street. 1798. fol.   AAS. BM. HSP. LCP. LOC.

Owing to yellow fever in Philadelphia, in September the publication office was removed to Germantown.

33522   CLINTON, GEORGE, JUNIOR

AN ORATION, DELIVERED ON THE FOURTH OF JULY, 1798, BEFORE THE GENERAL SOCIETY OF MECHANICS AND TRADESMEN, THE DEMOCRATIC SOCIETY, THE TAMMANY SOCIETY OR COLUMBIAN ORDER, THE NEW YORK COOPER'S SOCIETY, AND A NUMEROUS CONCOURSE OF OTHER CITIZENS. BY GEO. CLINTON, JUN., CITIZEN OF THE STATE OF NEW YORK. PUBLISHED BY ORDER OF THE SOCIETIES.

New-York: Printed by M. L. & W. A. Davis. 1798. pp. 14, (1). 8vo.
    NYHS. NYPL.

With an "Ode composed for the occasion by Margaretta V. Faugeres. The music performed by the Uranian Musical Society."

33523   COBBETT, WILLIAM   1762–1835
THE DEMOCRATIC JUDGE: OR THE EQUAL LIBERTY OF THE PRESS, AS EXHIBITED, EXPLAINED, AND EXPOSED. IN THE PROSECUTION OF WILLIAM COBBETT, FOR A PRETENDED LIBEL AGAINST THE KING OF SPAIN AND HIS EMBASSADOR, BEFORE THOMAS M'KEAN, CHIEF JUSTICE OF THE STATE OF PENNSYLVANIA. BY PETER PORCUPINE.
> *Philadelphia: Published by William Cobbett, opposite Christ-Church. March,* 1798. pp. 102. 8vo.   AAS. BA. HC. HSP. JCB. LOC. NYPL. UTS.

Reprinted in London this year, under the title of "The Republican Judge. . . . With an address to the people of England."

33524   —— THE DETECTION OF BACHE; OR FRENCH DIPLOMATIC SKILL DEVELOPED. VERY NECESSARY TO BE KEPT IN ALL FAMILIES IN TOWN AND COUNTRY. [Two columns.] PRICE ONE CENT.
> [*Philadelphia: Printed by William Cobbett, June* 18, 1798.] Broadside. fol.   HSP.

33525   —— DER FORTGANG DER MENSCHENFRESSER ODER DIE GREUEL FRANZÖSISCHEN EINFALLS. VON PETER PORCUPINE.
> *Philadelphia: Gedruckt bey H. Schweitzer.* 1798. pp. 44. 8vo.

33526   —— FRENCH ARROGANCE; OR, "THE CAT LET OUT OF THE BAG." A POETICAL DIALOGUE BETWEEN THE ENVOYS OF AMERICA, AND X.Y.Z. AND THE LADY.
> *Philadelphia: Published by Peter Porcupine, opposite Christ-Church, and sold by the principal Booksellers.* 1798. [*Price 25 cents.*] [Copy-right secured according to law.] pp. (31). 8vo.   LOC. NYHS. NYPL.

33527   —— A NEW YEAR'S GIFT TO THE DEMOCRATS; OR, OBSERVATIONS ON A PAMPHLET ENTITLED "A VINDICATION OF MR. RANDOLPH'S RESIGNATION." BY PETER POR-CUPINE. [Six lines of verse from] SWIFT. THE THIRD EDITION.
> *Philadelphia: Published by William Cobbett, opposite Christ-Church.* 1798. pp. (71). 8vo.   AAS. NL.

Preface dated, 1st January, 1796.

33528   —— BRADFORD'S FOURTH EDITION. OBSERVATIONS ON THE EMIGRATION OF DR. JO-SEPH PRIESTLEY, AND ON THE SEVERAL ADDRESSES DELIVERED TO HIM, ON HIS ARRIVAL AT NEW-YORK, WITH ADDITIONS; CONTAINING MANY CURIOUS AND INTER-ESTING FACTS ON THE SUBJECT NOT KNOWN HERE, WHEN THE FIRST EDITION WAS PUBLISHED: TOGETHER WITH A COMPREHENSIVE STORY, OF A FARMER'S BULL. BY PETER PORCUPINE. [Four lines of French from] BOILEAU.
> *Philadelphia: Published by William Cobbett, opposite Christ's Church.* 1798. pp. 88. 8vo.   BA.

33529   —— REMARKS ON THE INSIDIOUS LETTER OF THE GALLIC DESPOTS. BY PETER POR-CUPINE. THE HIRELING BACHE HAS PUBLISHED A LETTER FROM THE FRENCH MINISTER OF FOREIGN AFFAIRS TO OUR ENVOYS AT PARIS, DATED THE 18TH OF MARCH LAST. . . . I THINK IT MY DUTY TO SEND FORTH THE ANTIDOTE AFTER IT. [Four columns.]
> [*Philadelphia: Printed by William Cobbett, July*, 1798.] Price, one cent. Broadside. fol.   AAS.

33530   COCKE, WILLIAM
AN INAUGURAL DISSERTATION ON TETANUS, BY WILLIAM COCKE. OF GEORGIA.
> *Philadelphia: Printed by R. Aitkin, No. 22, Market-Street.* 1798. pp. (2), (2), (iv), [29.] 8vo.   LCP. LOC. SGO.

33531   COKE, THOMAS   1747–1814
      FOUR DISCOURSES ON THE DUTIES OF THE GOSPEL MINISTRY.

        Philadelphia: 1798. 12mo.

33532   COLES, ELISHA   1608–1688
      A PRACTICAL DISCOURSE OF GOD'S SOVEREIGNTY. WITH OTHER MATERIAL POINTS
      DERIVED THENCE. VIZ. OF THE RIGHTEOUSNESS OF GOD. OF ELECTION. OF RE-
      DEMPTION. OF EFFECTUAL CALLING. OF PERSEVERANCE. BY ELISHA COLES. WITH
      A RECOMMENDATORY PREFACE, BY THE REV. W. ROMAINE, A. M. RECTOR OF ST.
      ANDREW BY THE WARDROBE, AND ST. ANN, BLACKFRIARS; AND LECTURER OF ST.
      DUNSTAN IN THE WEST, LONDON. ALSO BY DR. OWEN, AND T. GOODWIN. [Three
      lines of Scripture texts.]

        Printed at Newburyport, by Edmund M. Blunt. MDCCXCVIII. pp. 372.
      8vo.   AAS. JCB. LOC.

33533   A COLLECTION OF MORAL AND ENTERTAINING STORIES, CALCULATED FOR THE IN-
      STRUCTION AND ENTERTAINMENT OF YOUTH. CONTAINING, I. STORY OF FRANK
      LUSON. II. FLORIO.—AN AFFECTING STORY. III. STORY OF EDWARD AND MARIA.
      IV. THE GENEROSITY OF AN INJURED DAUGHTER. V. FRATERNAL AFFECTION. VI.
      THE REMARKABLE DUEL.

        Printed at Northampton, [by Andrew Wright.] MDCCXCVIII. pp. 80+.
      16mo.   AAS.

        Second title: THE NEW PYGMALION. A NOVEL. TO WHICH IS ADDED, AMELIA: OR,
      THE FAITHLESS BRITON. AN AMERICAN TALE.

        Northampton: Printed by Andrew Wright. 1798. pp. (2), [37–80+.]

33534   COLLIN, NICHOLAS
      PHILOLOGICAL VIEW OF SOME VERY ANCIENT WORDS IN SEVERAL LANGUAGES.

        [Philadelphia: Printed by Thomas Dobson. 1798.] 4to.   BM.

      Reprinted from the fourth volume of the Transactions of the American
      Philosophical Society.

33535   COLLINS, WILLIAM   1720–1756
      THE DESPONDING NEGRO.

        Philadelphia: Printed and sold at Carr & Co's Musical Repository No. 136
      High Street. 1798.

33536   COLMAN, GEORGE, JUNIOR   1762–1836
      PAUVRE MADELON. A FAVORITE DIALOGUE & DUETT IN THE SURRENDER OF CALAIS.
      [With music.]

        New-York   Printed & sold by G. Gilfert & Co. No. 177 *Broadway.* [1798.]
      pp. (2). fol.   JCB.

33537   —— WHEN PENSIVE I THOUGHT ON MY LOVE. A FAVORITE NEW SONG. SUNG IN THE
      GRAND DRAMATIC ROMANCE OF BLUE BEARD OR FEMALE CURIOSITY. [With music.]

        New-York: Printed & sold by G. Gilfert, No. 177 *Broadway.* [1798.] pp.
      (4). fol.   JCB.

33538   COLQUHOUN, PATRICK   1745–1820
A TREATISE ON THE POLICE OF LONDON; CONTAINING A DETAIL OF THE VARIOUS
CRIMES AND MISDEMEANORS BY WHICH PUBLIC AND PRIVATE PROPERTY AND SECU-
RITY ARE, AT PRESENT, INJURED AND ENDANGERED: AND SUGGESTING REMEDIES
FOR THEIR PREVENTION. THE FIRST AMERICAN EDITION. BY A MAGISTRATE
ACTING FOR THE COUNTIES OF MIDDLESEX, SURRY, KENT, AND ESSEX.— FOR THE
CITY AND LIBERTY OF WESTMINSTER — AND FOR THE LIBERTY OF THE TOWER
OF LONDON. [Five lines of Latin.]

> *Philadelphia: Printed for Benjamin Davies, No. 68, High-Street, by Henry*
> *Sweitzer, No. 85, Race-Street.* MDCCXCVIII. pp. xii, (2), (5), 342, xxiv, table.
> 8vo.   AAS. LOC. NYPL.

33539   THE COLUMBIAN ALMANAC: OR, THE NORTH-AMERICAN CALENDAR FOR THE YEAR
OF OUR LORD 1799; BEING THE THIRD AFTER LEAP-YEAR. [Cut of] ARMS OF THE
UNITED STATES.

> *Wilmington: Printed and sold by Peter Brynberg, in Market-Street.* [1798.]
> pp. (48). 12mo.   AAS. HSP. LOC. WIPL.

33540   COLUMBIAN [U.S.A. in star] CENTINEL. VOL. XXVIII. No. 35. WEDNESDAY, JANU-
ARY 3, [— VOL. XXX. No. 34. SATURDAY, DECEMBER 29, 1798.]

> *Printed and published on Wednesdays and Saturdays, by Benjamin Russell,*
> *Printer of the Laws of the Union for the northern States—south side State Street,*
> *next to the Coffee-House, Boston, (Massachusetts).* 1798. fol.
>   AAS. BA. BM. EI. HC. LOC. MHS. NYHS. VSL.

> October 1st, Warned by the retirement of Benjamin Edes, after forty
> years service as Editor and Publisher of the Boston Gazette, in embar-
> rassed financial circumstances, the Publishers of the Centinel (published
> at an expense of 120 dollars weekly); the Mercury (published at an
> expense of 80 dollars weekly); and the Commercial Gazette (published
> at an expense of 50 dollars weekly), joined in an Address to the public,
> on their own affairs, in which the public were notified of the only terms
> upon which their respective papers, and advertisements therein could
> be had in the future. Benjamin Russell. Young & Minns, John Russell.

33541   —— THE CARRIER OF THE COLUMBIAN CENTINEL, ON THE EXIT OF 1797, AND THE
ENTRANCE OF ONE THOUSAND SEVEN HUNDRED AND NINETY-EIGHT MOST RESPECT-
FULLY TENDERS TO ALL ITS PATRONS THE CONGRATULATIONS OF THE SEASON. . . .

> [*Boston: Printed by Benjamin Russell, January* 1, 1798.] Broadside.   HSP.

33542   COLUMBIAN COURIER. VOL. I. No. 1. SATURDAY, DECEMBER 8. [— No. 4. SATUR-
DAY, DECEMBER 29, 1798.]

> *New-Bedford, Massachusetts: Printed and published by Abraham Shearman,*
> *jun.* 1798. fol.

> Established, as a weekly, by Abraham Shearman, junior, and continued
> by him to March, 1805, when it was discontinued. With the issue for
> December 3, 1802, the title was changed to *Columbian Courier, and*
> *weekly miscellany,* and this was slightly altered by substituting "or" for
> "and" in the title, with the issue for December 2, 1803.

33543   THE COLUMBIAN MIRROR AND ALEXANDRIA GAZETTE. VOL. VI. No. 738. TUES-
DAY, JANUARY 2, [— VOL. VII. No. 892. SATURDAY, DECEMBER 29, 1798.]

> *Alexandria: Printed every Tuesday, Thursday and Saturday, by Ellis Price.*
> 1798. fol.   AAS.

> With the issue for February 27th, Ellis Price withdrew, and publication
> was continued by Henry Gird junior.

AUCTION
VALUES

33544   COLUMBIAN MUSEUM & SAVANNAH ADVERTISER. [Motto.] VOL. II. No. 88. TUES-
DAY, JANUARY 2, [—VOL. III. No. 87, WHOLE NUMBER, 295. FRIDAY, DECEMBER
28, 1798.]
         Savannah—Published on Tuesday and Friday, by Gurdon I. Seymour and
Philip D. Woolhopter, on the Bay. 1798. fol.   AAS. GHS.
      With the issue for March 9th. the paper was enlarged to five columns.

33545   THE COLUMBIAN SPELLING AND READING BOOK, OR AN EASY AND ALLURING GUIDE
TO SPELLING AND READING. CONTAINING I. LESSONS IN SPELLING FROM ONE SYL-
LABLE TO SEVEN. II. A LARGE COLLECTION OF PROVERBS AND MAXIMS OF ONE AND
TWO SYLLABLES. III. EIGHTY-ONE OF DODSLEY'S FABLES, BEING MORE THAN HALF
OF THE NUMBER IN THAT ENTERTAINING BOOK, EACH ORNAMENTED WITH A HAND-
SOME METAL CUT. IV. A COLLECTION OF WORDS NEARLY ALIKE IN SOUND BUT
DIFFERENT IN SENSE. V. A TABLE OF CONTRACTIONS. VI. AN EXPLANATION OF
THE USE OF POINTS, STOPS AND CERTAIN MARKS USED IN WRITING AND PRINTING.
VII. ESSAY ON THE SOUNDS OF THE LETTERS IN THE ENGLISH LANGUAGE.
         Philadelphia: Printed for Mathew Carey. 1798.
      207th Pennsylvania District Copyright, issued to Mathew Carey, as
Proprietor, 29 May, 1798.

33546   THE COLUMBIAN WAR; OR BATTLES FOR AMERICAN INDEPENDENCE. NUMBER 1.
         New-London: Published by Charles Holt. 1798.
      The Battles delineated by E. Tisdale, junior, a citizen of Connecticut,
with vignette title page, and two other engravings, 14x19. Engraved
by C. Tiebout. To be completed in six numbers. at three dollars each.

33547   COMMERCIAL [cut of ship] ADVERTISER. VOL. I. NUMBER 79. MONDAY EVENING,
JANUARY 1, [—VOL. II. NUMBER 390. MONDAY EVENING, DECEMBER 31, 1798.]
         [New-York:] Published (daily) at No. 40, Pine-Street by Geo. F. Hopkins,
Printer of the Laws of the United States for the district of New-York. 1798. fol.
     BA. LCP. LOC. NYHS.

33548   THE COMPANION; AND COMMERCIAL CENTINEL. VOL. I. No. 1. WEDNESDAY,
MAY 2, [—No. 19. SATURDAY, SEPTEMBER 8, 1798.]
         Newport, Rhode-Island: Printed by H. & O. Farnsworth. 1798. fol.   AAS.
      Established, as a weekly, by Havila and Oliver Farnsworth, under the
above title up to the issue for September 15, 1798, when the title was
changed to *Weekly Companion; and the Commercial Centinel.* With the
issue for April 6, 1799, the partnership was dissolved, and Oliver
Farnsworth continued publication alone to the issue for June 15, 1799
— the last number located.

33549   A COMPENDIOUS VIEW AND BRIEF DEFENCE OF THE PECULIAR AND LEADING DOC-
TRINES OF THE NEW JERUSALEM CHURCH.
         Baltimore: Printed by Samuel Sower, in Fayette Street. M,DCC,XCVIII.
pp. [xxxvi], [iii]–v. 8vo.   AAS.

33550   A CONCISE SYSTEM OF FARRIERY. [Ornament.]
         Newbern: J. C. Osborn & Co. 1798. pp. (2), (2), 186. 12mo.   AAS.

33551   CONEWAGO CANAL COMPANY.
      ACCOUNT OF THE CONEWAGO-CANAL, ON THE RIVER SUSQUEHANNA. TO WHICH IS
PREFIXED, THE ACT FOR INCORPORATING THE COMPANY. [Signed, William Smith,
Henry Miller.]
         Philadelphia: Printed by William Young, Whitehall Press. 1798. pp. (6),
18. 4to.   LOC.
      Includes a Report, by John Hall.

33552   CONGREGATIONAL CHURCH IN CONNECTICUT.
ADDRESS OF THE GENERAL ASSOCIATION TO THE GOOD PEOPLE OF CONNECTICUT. [Asking for contributions towards diffusing christianity among "the inhabitants of the newly settled frontiers of our country and the heathen tribes." By Benjamin Trumbull. Dated, Hebron, June 21, 1798.]

[Without place or Printer. 1798.] Broadside. fol.

33553   CONGREGATIONAL MISSIONARY SOCIETY.
THE CONSTITUTION AND ADDRESS OF THE CONGREGATIONAL MISSIONARY SOCIETY. [Double lines.]

Stockbridge: Printed by Rosseter & Willard. 1798.] pp. 33. 12mo. NYHS.

33554   CONNECTICUT. STATE.
[Seal.] ACTS AND LAWS, MADE AND PASSED IN AND BY THE GENERAL COURT OR ASSEMBLY OF THE STATE OF CONNECTICUT, IN AMERICA, HOLDEN AT HARTFORD, (IN SAID STATE) ON THE SECOND THURSDAY OF MAY, ANNO DOMINI 1798. [Colophon:]

Hartford—Printed by Hudson & Goodwin. [1798.] pp. 481–491. 8vo.

            CHS. CSL. YC.

33555   —— — AT A GENERAL ASSEMBLY OF THE STATE OF CONNECTICUT, HOLDEN AT HARTFORD, ON THE SECOND THURSDAY OF MAY, A.D. 1798. [Resolve incorporating "The Trustees of the grammar school in the town of Hartford."]

[Hartford: Printed by Elisha Babcock. 1798.] Broadside. fol.   CHS.

33556   —— [Seal.] ACTS AND LAWS, MADE AND PASSED IN AND BY THE GENERAL COURT OR ASSEMBLY OF THE STATE OF CONNECTICUT, IN AMERICA, HOLDEN AT NEW-HAVEN (IN SAID STATE) ON THE SECOND THURSDAY OF OCTOBER, ANNO DOMINI 1798. [Colophon:]

Hartford: Printed by Hudson and Goodwin. [1798.] pp. 493–498. 8vo. PLA.

33557   —— — AT A GENERAL ASSEMBLY OF THE STATE OF CONNECTICUT HOLDEN AT NEW-HAVEN, ON THE SECOND THURSDAY OF OCTOBER, A.D. 1798. [Resolve favoring an amendment to the Constitution of the United States.]

[Hartford: Printed by Elisha Babcock. 1798.] Broadside, fol.   CHS.

33558   —— — AT A GENERAL ASSEMBLY OF THE STATE OF CONNECTICUT, HOLDEN AT NEW-HAVEN, ON THE SECOND THURSDAY OF OCTOBER, A.D. 1798. [Resolve regarding laws against Sabbath-breaking.]

[Hartford: Printed by Hudson and Goodwin. 1798.] Broadside.

33559   —— BY HIS EXCELLENCY JONATHAN TRUMBULL, ESQ. GOVERNOR AND COMMANDER IN CHIEF OF THE STATE OF CONNECTICUT, A PROCLAMATION . . . APPOINT THURSDAY, THE TWENTY-NINTH DAY OF NOVEMBER NEXT, TO BE SET APART AND RELIGIOUSLY OBSERVED AS A DAY OF PUBLIC THANKSGIVING, PRAYER AND PRAISE TO ALMIGHTY GOD, . . . ALL SERVILE LABOR ON SAID DAY IS FORBIDDEN. GIVEN UNDER MY HAND AT NEW-HAVEN, THIS TWENTY-SECOND DAY OF OCTOBER, IN THE YEAR OF OUR LORD ONE THOUSAND SEVEN HUNDRED AND NINETY-EIGHT, AND OF THE INDEPENDENCE OF THE UNITED STATES THE TWENTY-THIRD. J. TRUMBULL. BY HIS EXCELLENCY'S COMMAND, SAMUEL WYLLYS, SECRETARY.

[Hartford: Printed by Hudson and Goodwin. 1798.] Broadside. fol.

33560   —— PROCEEDINGS OF THE GENERAL ASSEMBLY, RELATIVE TO THE HARTFORD AND NEW HAVEN TURNPIKE ROAD.

[Hartford: Printed by Hudson and Goodwin. 1798.] pp. 12.

AUCTION
VALUES

33561   THE CONNECTICUT COURANT. VOL. XXXIII. NUMBER 1719. MONDAY, JANUARY 1, [— NUMBER 1771. MONDAY, DECEMBER 31, 1798.]
       Hartford: Printed by Hudson & Goodwin. 1798. fol.   AAS. CHS. YC.

33562   —— GUILLOTINA, FOR THE YEAR 1798. ADDRESSED TO THE READERS OF THE CONNECTICUT COURANT. . . . [By Lemuel Hopkins.] HARTFORD, JANUARY 1, 1798.
       Hartford: Printed by Hudson and Goodwin. 1798. pp. (2). fol.

33563   CONNECTICUT [arms] GAZETTE. QUI TRANSTULIT SUSTINET. VOL. XXXV. No. 1782. WEDNESDAY, JANUARY 3, [— VOL. XXXV. No. 1833. WEDNESDAY, DECEMBER 26. 1798.]
       New-London: Printed and published by Samuel Green, at his Office adjoining the Bank. 1798. fol.   CHS. NYHS.

33564   CONNECTICUT JOURNAL. VOL. XXXI. No. 1575. THURSDAY, JANUARY 4, [— No. 1626. THURSDAY, DECEMBER 27, 1798.]
       New-Haven: Printed by Thomas and Samuel Green, opposite the Post-Office. 1798. fol.   AAS. LOC. YC.
       The partnership of Thomas and Samuel Green, which had been continuous from 1767, was dissolved, by mutual consent, December 31, 1798, Samuel Green, died of consumption, February 13, 1799, aged 55 years. The Journal was continued by Thomas Green, and his son, Thomas Green, junior, under the firm name of Thomas Green & Son. With the issue for January 10, 1799, the title was changed to, *Connecticut Journal & Weekly Advertiser.*

33565   CONNECTICUT LAND COMPANY.
       LANDS IN NEW-CONNECTICUT, THAT PART OF THE CONNECTICUT RESERVE, OR NEW-CONNECTICUT, TO WHICH THE INDIAN TITLE HAS BEEN EXTINGUISHED, LYING WEST OF PENNSYLVANIA, AND SOUTH OF LAKE ERIE, HAVING BEEN SURVEYED AND DIVIDED. [Twenty-six lines of description.] SIMON PERKINS. AGENT OF THE ERIE COMPANY. [Colophon:]
       Printed at J. Trumbull's Press, Norwich. [1798.] Broadside. fol.   AAS.

33566   THE CONNECTICUT MAGAZINE.
       Proposals for printing the above, as a monthly publication, were made by Charles Holt, New-London, November, 1798.

33567   COOK, DAVID
       THE AMERICAN READY RECKONER, OR TRADERS ASSISTANT: SHEWING AT ONE VIEW, THE AMOUNT, OR VALUE OF ANY NUMBER OR QUANTITY OF ARTICLES FROM ONE MILL TO FOUR DOLLARS. TO WHICH IS ADDED, I. A TABLE OF SIMPLE INTEREST, AT 6 PER CENT. PER ANN. FROM HALF A DOLLAR TO 15,000 DOLLARS. II. A TABLE OF COMPOUND INTEREST, AT SIX PER CENT. PER ANN. FROM HALF A DOLLAR TO 15,000 DOLLARS. III. A TABLE OF COMMISSIONS FROM 1 TO 5 PER CENT. IV. A TABLE OF ENGLISH GOLD, REDUCED TO DOLLARS, DIMES, CENTS, AND MILLS. V. A TABLE FOR RECEIVING AND PAYING ALL KINDS OF GOLD COINS. BY DAVID COOK.
       [Printed by Thomas Green and Son, New-Haven ? 1798.]
       Connecticut District Copyright, issued to David Cook, as Author, 24 December, 1798.

33568   COOPER, SAMUEL
       THE BLOSSOMS OF MORALITY; INTENDED FOR THE AMUSEMENT AND INSTRUCTION OF YOUNG LADIES AND GENTLEMEN. BY THE EDITOR OF THE LOOKING-GLASS FOR THE MIND. WOODWARD'S SECOND EDITION.
       Philadelphia: Printed for William W. Woodward, No. 17, Chesnut Street. 1798. pp. 240. 12mo.   AAS. JCB.
       Contains a four-page list of Subcriber's names.

33569   COOPER, THOMAS   1759–1839
POLITICAL ARITHMETIC, BY THOMAS COOPER, ESQ. OF NORTHUMBERLAND. [And,
PROPOSITIONS RESPECTING THE FOUNDATION OF CIVIL GOVERNMENT; BY THOMAS
COOPER, ESQ. READ AT THE LITERARY AND PHILOSOPHICAL SOCIETY OF MAN-
CHESTER, ON MARCH 7TH, 1787, AND FIRST PUBLISHED IN THE TRANSACTIONS OF
THAT SOCIETY. VOL. 3. P. 481. ANNO 1790.]

[Philadelphia ? 1798.] pp. 40. 8vo.   AAS. LOC.

33570   COOPER, WILLIAM   1776–
THE PROMISED SEED. A SERMON PREACHED TO GOD'S ANCIENT ISRAEL THE JEWS,
AT SION CHAPEL, WHITECHAPEL, ON SUNDAY AFTERNOON, AUGUST 26, 1796. BY
WILLIAM COOPER. TO WHICH ARE ADDED, THE HYMNS THAT WERE SUNG, AND THE
PRAYERS THAT WERE OFFERED UP, BEFORE AND AFTER THE SERMON. [Ornament.]

Danbury: Re-printed by Douglas & Nichols. 1798. pp. [36.] 8vo.   AAS·

33571   ——— — THE PROMISED SEED. A SERMON PREACHED TO GOD'S ANCIENT ISRAEL
THE JEWS, AT SION-CHAPEL, WHITE CHAPLE. ON SUNDAY AFTERNOON, AUGUST
28, 1796. BY WILLIAM COOPER. TO WHICH ARE ADDED. THE HYMNS THAT WERE
SUNG, AND THE PRAYERS THAT WERE OFFERED UP, BEFORE AND AFTER THE SERMON.

*Printed by Cornelius Sturtevant, jun. & Co. at Putney, Vermont. 1798. pp.
32. 8vo.*

33572   CORNYN, DOMINICK
A POETICAL DISCRIPTION [sic] OF THE PRESENT OPPRESSIONS OF IRELAND. BY D. C.
TO WHICH IS ANNEXED, THE ANGEL OF INTELLIGENCE: AN EASTERN TALE, IN
VERSE; WITH THE EMIGRANT, AN ODE, BY THE SAME.

*Reading: Printed by J. Schneider & Comp. M,DCC,XCVIII. pp. (2), (33),
(1). 8vo.*   LOC.

33573   A CORRECT TABLE, SHEWING THE NET AMOUNT OF FUNDED 6 PER CENT. STOCK OF
THE UNITED STATES, AFTER PAYMENTS ARE MADE FOR EACH QUARTERLY DIVIDEND,
FROM THE 1ST OF JANUARY, 1796, TO THE 1ST OF JANUARY, 1819, WHEN THAT
DEBT WILL BE EXTINGUISHED ACCORDING TO LAW. COPY-RIGHT SECURED ACCORDING
TO LAW.

*Boston: Printed and sold by David West, No. 56, Cornhill. 1798. pp. [11],
folded table. 12mo.*   AAS. JCB.

33574   ——— A TABLE, SHEWING THE VALUE OF 100 DOLLARS DEFERRED STOCK, FROM 1ST
OF JANUARY, 1798, TO 1ST OF JANUARY, 1801, WHEN SAID STOCK WILL BE UPON
INTEREST AT SIX PER CENT. PER ANN. ALLOWING QUARTERLY PAYMENTS, AND COM-
POUND INTEREST ON THE SAME. N. B. THE DEFERRED STOCK WILL BEGIN TO
OPERATE IN LIKE MANNER, OF THE PRESENT SIX PER CENT. STOCKS, ON THE FIRST
OF JANUARY, 1802, AND WILL BE EXTINGUISHED ON THE 1ST OF JANUARY, 1825,
FOR WHICH THE ABOVE MENTIONED TABLE IS LIKEWISE CALCULATED.

*Boston: Printed for and sold by David West, (the Proprietor of the Copy
rights) at his Store, No. 56, Cornhill. 1798.*   AAS.

33575   ——— AN ACCURATE TABLE, SHEWING THE NET AMOUNT OF FUNDED 6 PER CENT STOCK
BEARING A PRESENT INTEREST, AFTER PAYMENTS BEING MADE FOR EACH QUARTERLY
DIVIDEND—FROM THE FIRST REIMBURSEMENT OF JANUARY 1796, UNTIL THE DEBT
SHALL HAVE BEEN EXTINGUISHED.

Portsmouth, New-Hampshire, Printed ? by Charles Peirce. March 10, 1798.

33576   THE COUNTRY PORCUPINE. VOL. I. No. 1. MONDAY, MARCH 5, [—VOL. II. No. 29. SATURDAY AND MONDAY, DECEMBER 29 AND 31, 1798.]

> *Philadelphia: Published by William Cobbett, opposite Christ Church.* 1798. fol.   AAS. LOC.

> Established, as a tri-weekly edition of his Porcupine's Gazette, by William Cobbett and discontinued with the issue for April 28, 1799. "The" in the title was dropped after 30 April, 1798.

33577   THE COURIER. VOL. II. NUMBER 27. THURSDAY, MAY 31, [VOL. III. NUMBER 5. THURSDAY, DECEMBER 27, 1798.]

> *Norwich (Chelsea Society): Printed by Thomas Hubbard.* 1798. fol.   HC.

> In continuation of *The Chelsea Courier.*

33578   COURIER OF NEW HAMPSHIRE. No. 48. VOL. VIII. WHOLE NO. 412. TUESDAY, JANUARY 2, [— No. 48. VOL. IX. WHOLE NO. 464. SATURDAY, DECEMBER 29, 1798.]

> *Devoted to news and national politicks: Published by George Hough, at Concord.* 1798. fol.

> Editorially, George Hough states in the issue for January 30th, that with that number the Courier completed its eighth year.

33579   COURRIER FRANÇAIS. (NUMÉRO 219) ANNÉE IVME PHILADELPHIE, 12 NIVÔSE (LUNDI 1ER JANVIER 1798, VIEUX STYLE) L'AN SIXIÉME DE LA RÉPUBLIQUE FRANÇAISE, UNE ET INDIVISIBLE. [—(NUMÈRO 60) ANNÉE VIME PHILADELPHIE, 15 MESSIDOR (MARDI 3 JUILLET, 1798, VIEUX STYLE) L'AN SIXIÉME DE LA RÉPUBLIQUE FRANÇAISE, UNE ET INDIVISIBLE.

> *[A Philadelphie.] Publié et Imprimé par Parent; Cinquieme Rue Sud, No. 32.* [1798.] pp. (877)–(1174 *sic* 1206); (1)–(241). fol.   NYPL.

> Beginning with Volume VI, in April, the imprint reads: Publié et Imprimé par Allain, Blocquerst et Wilson, Seconde Rue Nord, No. 147. Wilson withdrew in June, the imprint reading from 7 Juin: Allain et Blocquerst, only, until publication was discontinued as above.

33580   COUSTOS, JEAN

     AN ACCOUNT OF THE UNPARALLELED SUFFERINGS OF JOHN COUSTOS, WHO NINE TIMES UNDERWENT THE MOST CRUEL TORTURES INVENTED BY MAN, AND WAS SENTENCED TO THE GALLEY FOUR YEARS, BY COMMAND OF THE INQUISITORS AT LISBON, IN ORDER TO EXTORT FROM HIM THE SECRETS OF FREE MASONRY; FROM WHENCE HE WAS RELEASED BY THE INTERPOSITION OF THE KING OF GREAT BRITAIN: TO WHICH IS ADDED, A SELECTION OF MASONIC SONGS.

> *Norwich: Printed by John Trumbull.* 1798. pp. 40. 8vo.

33581   —— — HORRID TORTURES, OR THE UNPARALLELED SUFFERINGS OF JOHN COUSTOS. WHO NINE TIMES UNDERWENT MOST CRUEL TORTURES IN ORDER TO EXTORT FROM HIM THE SECRETS OF FREE MASONRY. TO WHICH IS ADDED A SELECTION OF MASONIC SONGS.

> *Putney: Printed by C. Sturtevant, for Justin Hinds.* MDCCXCVIII. pp. 76. 24mo.   AAS. JCB.

33582   CRÈVECŒUR, MICHEL GUILLAUME JEAN DE, called SAINT JOHN DE CREVECOUR

     LETTERS FROM AN AMERICAN FARMER; DESCRIBING CERTAIN PROVINCIAL SITUATIONS, MANNERS, AND CUSTOMS, NOT GENERALLY KNOWN; AND CONVEYING SOME IDEA OF THE LATE AND PRESENT INTERIOR CIRCUMSTANCES OF THE BRITISH COLONIES IN NORTH AMERICA. WRITTEN FOR THE INFORMATION OF A FRIEND IN ENGLAND, BY J. HECTOR ST. JOHN. A FARMER IN PENNSYLVANIA.

> *Philadelphia:* MDCCXCVIII. pp. 260. 12mo.

33583 CROSS, JOHN C.
THE WAY TO GET MARRIED. THE FAVORITE SONG. SUNG BY MRS. DAVIS AT THE ROYAL CIRCUS. THE WORDS BY MR. CROSS.
New-York: Published by G. Gilfert at his Musical Magazine, No. 177 Broadway. 1798.

33584 CUCKOLD'S CHRONICLE. NO. I. [— II.] THE CUCKOLD'S CHRONICLE. BEING SELECT TRIALS FOR ADULTERY, INCEST, IMBECILITY, RAVISHMENT, &C. &C. VOL. I.
Baltimore: 1798. 8vo.

33585 —— CUCKOLD'S CHRONICLE. VOL. I. NO. I – II.
Boston: [Printed] for those who wish to purchase. At No. 17 Kilby-Street (Edes Printing-Office.) 1798. pp. 193, (3), illustrations. 8vo.   BPL.

33586 CUDGELING AS BY LATE ACT OF CONGRESS, U. S. A. OR [Caricature of the Lyon-Griswold fracas.]
[Without place or Printer. 1798.] Broadside. obl. fol.

33587 CUMINGS, HENRY   1737–1823
A SERMON PREACHED AT BILLERICA, NOVEMBER 29, 1798, BEING THE DAY OF THE ANNIVERSARY THANKSGIVING THROUGHOUT THE COMMONWEALTH OF MASSACHUSETTS. BY HENRY CUMINGS, A. M. PASTOR OF THE CHURCH IN SAID TOWN. [Publishers mark.]
Printed by John & Thomas Fleet, Cornhill, Boston. MDCCXCVIII. pp. (31). 8vo.   AAS. BA. BM. CLA. HC. JCB. LOC. MHS. NYHS. NYPL. YC.

33588 CUMMINGS, ABRAHAM   1755–1827
BELIEVERS PROVED TO BE THE ONLY PROPER SUBJECT OF BAPTISM. IN REPLY TO A PUBLICATION, ENTITLED, "SPRINKLING THE PROPER MODE AND INFANTS THE PROPER SUBJECTS OF BAPTISM. BY NATHANIEL EMMONS, A. M." BY ABRAHAM CUMMINGS, A. M. [One line from] SOLOMON.
Boston: Printed by Manning and Loring, in Spring-Lane. 1798. pp. 64. 8vo.   AAS. LOC.

33589 CURRIE, WILLIAM   1754–1828
MEMOIRS OF THE YELLOW FEVER, WHICH PREVAILED IN PHILADELPHIA, AND OTHER PARTS OF THE UNITED STATES OF AMERICA, IN THE SUMMER AND AUTUMN OF THE PRESENT YEAR, 1798. INCLUDING, TABLES OF THE WEATHER, AND THE DAILY RETURNS OF THE SICK AND DEAD; . . . TO WHICH IS ADDED, A COLLECTION OF FACTS RESPECTING THE ORIGIN OF THE FEVER. BY WILLIAM CURRIE, S. C. M. P. . . .
Philadelphia: Printed by John Bioren, for Thomas Dobson, at the Stone-House, No. 41, South Second-Street. 1798. pp. (2), 145. 8vo.
BM. JCB. LOC. NYPL. SGO.

33590 —— OBSERVATIONS ON THE CAUSES AND CURE OF REMITTING OR BILIOUS FEVERS. TO WHICH IS ANNEXED, AN ABSTRACT OF THE OPINIONS AND PRACTICE OF DIFFERENT AUTHORS; AND AN APPENDIX, EXHIBITING FACTS AND REFLECTIONS RELATIVE TO THE SYNOCHUS ICTEROIDES, OR YELLOW FEVER, BY WILLIAM CURRIE, FELLOW OF THE COLLEGE OF PHYSICIANS OF PHILADELPHIA, &C. [Two-line quotation.]
Philadelphia: Printed for the Author, by William T. Palmer. No. 18, North Third-Street. 1798. pp. (iv), 227, (1). 8vo.   AAS. NYPL. SGO.

199th Pennsylvania District Copyright, issued to William Currie, as Author, 16 January, 1798.

33591 —— OF THE CHOLERA.
Philadelphia: Printed by William T. Palmer. 1798. pp. 14. 8vo.   SGO.

33592   CYNTHIA: WITH THE TRAGICAL ACCOUNT OF THE UNFORTUNATE LOVES OF ALMERIN AND DESDEMONA. A NOVEL. ILLUSTRATED WITH A VARIETY OF THE CHANCES OF FORTUNE; MORALIZED WITH MANY USEFUL OBSERVATIONS, WHEREBY THE READER MAY REAP BOTH PLEASURE AND PROFIT.

> *New-Haven: Printed by G. Bunce.*—1798—pp. (2), (9)-144. 24mo.   AAS. LOC.

33593   —— CYNTHIA, WITH THE TRAGICAL ACCOUNT OF THE UNFORTUNATE LOVES OF ALMERIN AND DESDEMONA: BEING A NOVEL. ILLUSTRATED WITH A VARIETY OF CHANCES OF FORTUNE; MORALIZED WITH MANY USEFUL OBSERVATIONS, WHEREBY THE READER MAY REAP BOTH PLEASURE AND PROFIT.

> *Printed at Northampton, Massachusetts, by William Butler;* M.DCC.XCVIII. pp. 108. 12mo.   AAS.

33594   D., W.
     AN ELEGANT COLLECTION OF NEW FIGURES. COMPOSED FOR THE USE OF DANCING SCHOOLS. BY W. D.

> *Amherst, Newhampshire: Printed by Samuel Preston.* 1798.

33595   DABOLL, NATHAN   1750-1818
     THE NEW-ENGLAND ALMANAC, AND GENTLEMEN AND LADIES' DIARY, ENLARGED, FOR THE YEAR OF OUR LORD CHRIST, 1799: BEING THE THIRD AFTER BISSEXTILE OR LEAP-YEAR, AND THE 23D OF AMERICAN INDEPENDENCE. [Six lines.] BY NATHAN DABOLL. [Ten lines of verse.]

> *New-London: Printed and sold by Samuel Green.* [1798.] pp. (36). 12mo.   AAS. NYPL. WL.

33596   —— SHEET ALMANAC FOR THE YEAR 1799.

> *New-London: Printed by Samuel Green.* 1798. Broadside.

33597   THE DAILY [cut of Eagle] ADVERTISER. VOL. XIV. No. 4025. MONDAY, JANUARY 1, [— No. 4336. MONDAY, DECEMBER 31, 1798.]

> *New-York: Printed by William Robins, for the Proprietor, Printer to the State, No. 71, Pine-Street.* 1798. fol.   NYHS.

     On the scroll in the Eagle's beak, is the motto, Excelsior. Printer to to the State, was dropped from the imprint before June. On July 10th, without editorial notice of the change, the name of Charles Snowden was substituted for William Robins, in the imprint.

33598   DALLAS, ALEXANDER JAMES   1759-1817
     REPORTS OF CASES RULED AND ADJUDGED IN THE SEVERAL COURTS OF THE UNITED STATES, AND OF PENNSYLVANIA, HELD AT THE SEAT OF THE FEDERAL GOVERNMENT. BY A. J. DALLAS. VOL. II. [Four lines of Latin from] GROTIUS.

> *Philadelphia: Printed for the Reporter at the Aurora Office.* M,DCC,XCVIII. pp. (2), iv, 480, xix. 8vo.   AAS. BM. DeRGL.

     218th Pennsylvania District Copyright, issued to Alexander James Dallas, as Author, 12 January, 1799.

33599   DARTMOUTH UNIVERSITY.
     CATALOGUS EORUM QUI IN UNIVERSITATE DARTMUTHENSI, A REVERENDO ELEAZARO WHEELOCK, S. T. D. INSTITUTA, IN REPUBLICA NEO HANTONIÆ, AB ANNO MDCCLXXI AD ANNUM MDCCXCVIII ALICUJUS GRADUS LAUREA DONATI SUNT. [Ornament.] QUI ALIBI INSTITUTI, VEL APUD NOS GRADU HONORARIO DONATI FUERUNT, ii LINEA SEPARATI, CLASSIUM ALUMNORUM IMO SUNT ADJECTI. [Heavy line.]

> *Leuphanæ, Typis Benjamin True. Anno Dom.* MDCCXCVIII, *et rer. pub. fœd. Amer. indep.* XXIII. pp. [15.] 8vo.   AAS. DC. BM.

33600 DARWIN, ERASMUS   1731–1802
THE BOTANIC GARDEN. A POEM IN TWO PARTS. PART I. CONTAINING THE ECONOMY
OF VEGETATION. PART II. THE LOVES OF THE PLANTS. WITH PHILOSOPHICAL
NOTES. THE FIRST AMERICAN EDITION. [Edited for republication, with a poetic
"Epistle to the Author of the Botanic garden." By Elihu Hubbard Smith.]
*New-York: Printed by T. & J. Swords, Printers to the Faculty of Physic of
Columbia College, No. 99 Pearl-street.* 1798. 2 vols. in one. pp. (2), (2), (2),
(6), (2), (6), (2), (2), 256, 8 plates; 146, (2), 9 plates. 8vo.
                                         AAS. JCB. LOC. MHS. NYHS. NYPL.

Second title: THE BOTANIC GARDEN. PART I. CONTAINING THE ECONOMY OF
VEGETATION. A POEM. WITH PHILOSOPHICAL NOTES. [Four lines of Latin from]
LUCRET. THE FIRST AMERICAN, FROM THE THIRD LONDON EDITION.
*New-York: Printed by T. & J. Swords, Printers to the Faculty of Physic of
Columbia College, No. 99 Pearl-street.* 1798. pp. (2). (2), 256, 8 plates.

Third title: THE BOTANIC GARDEN. PART II. CONTAINING THE LOVES OF THE
PLANTS. A POEM. WITH PHILOSOPHICAL NOTES. [Four lines of Latin from]
CLAUD. EPITS. THE FIRST AMERICAN, FROM THE FOURTH LONDON EDITION.
*New-York: Printed by T. & J. Swords, Printers to the Faculty of Physic of
Columbia College, No. 99 Pearl-street.* 1798. pp. 146, (2), 9 plates.

33601 —— A PLAN FOR THE CONDUCT OF FEMALE EDUCATION, IN BOARDING SCHOOLS, PRI-
VATE FAMILIES, AND PUBLIC SEMINARIES. BY ERASMUS DARWIN, M. D. F. R. S.
AUTHOR OF ZOONOMIA, AND OF THE BOTANIC GARDEN. TO WHICH ARE ADDED,
RUDIMENTS OF TASTE, IN A SERIES OF LETTERS FROM A MOTHER TO HER DAUGHTERS.
[By Mrs. Peddle.] EMBELLISHED WITH AN ELEGANT FRONTISPIECE.
Philadelphia: Printed by John Ormrod, No. 41, Chesnut-Street. 1798. pp.
(2), (2), (4), (4), [9]–188; (2), [199]–308, (4), frontispiece. 12mo. AAS. JCB. LOC.

33602 DAVENPORT, JAMES
COLUMBIA AND LIBERTY. A NEW PATRIOTIC SONG. WRITTEN BY MR. DAVENPORT.
THE MUSIC COMPOSED BY DOCTOR ARNE.
Boston: Printed & sold by Lindley and Moore, No. 19, Marlborough-Street.
1798.

154th Massachusetts District Copyright, issued to James Davenport,
Francis Linley, and John Moore, as Proprietors, 27 October, 1798.

33603 DAVIDGE, JOHN BEALE   1768–1829
A TREATISE ON THE AUTUMNAL ENDEMIAL EPIDEMICK OF TROPICAL CLIMATES, VUL-
GARLY CALLED THE YELLOW FEVER. CONTAINING ITS ORIGIN, HISTORY, NATURE
AND CURE; TOGETHER WITH A FEW REFLECTIONS ON THE PROXIMATE CAUSE OF
DISEASES. BY JOHN B. DAVIDGE, A. M. M. D.
Baltimore: Printed by W. Pechin, No. 15, Baltimore-Street. 1798. pp. 65,
(1). 8vo.   JCB. LOC. SGO.

33604 DAVIDSON, JAMES   1732–1809
AN EASY AND PRACTICAL INTRODUCTION TO THE KNOWLEDGE OF THE LATIN TONGUE:
OR AN EXEMPLIFICATION OF THE RULES OF CONSTRUCTION, CORRESPONDING TO
THOSE OF THE PHILADELPHIA GRAMMAR; WITH TWO INDEXES AND A FEW NECES-
SARY CAUTIONS, TO ASSIST YOUTH IN TRANSLATING WITH MORE ACCURACY. TO
THESE THERE IS ADDED AN EPITOME OF GENERAL HISTORY, AND SOME ACCOUNT OF
THE AFFAIRS OF GREECE, FROM THE DAYS OF EPAMINONDAS, UNTIL THEY COINCIDE
WITH THE HISTORY OF ROME. SOME EXAMPLES OF THEMES ARE ANNEXED, WITH
A FEW SELECT DISCOURSES ON VARIOUS SUBJECTS. [One line of Latin.] BY JAMES
DAVIDSON, PROFESSOR OF HUMANITY IN THE UNIVERSITY OF PENNSYLVANIA.
Philadelphia: Printed by Charles Cist, in Second-Street, near Race-Street.
M,DCC,XCVIII. pp. vi, 23. 12mo.   AAS. JCB. NYPL.

209th Pennsylvania District Copyright, issued to James Davidson, as
Author, 1 June, 1798.

33605   DAVIES, BENJAMIN
THE AMERICAN REPOSITORY, AND ANNUAL REGISTER OF THE UNITED STATES, FOR
THE YEAR 1798: CONTAINING COMPLETE AND CORRECT LISTS OF THE EXECUTIVE,
LEGISLATIVE, & JUDICIARY DEPARTMENTS OF GOVERNMENTS, AND A GREAT VARIETY
OF USEFUL TABLES, NECESSARY TO BE KNOWN IN EVERY STATE OF THE UNION.
EMBELLISHED WITH TWO HANDSOME ENGRAVINGS.

     Philadelphia: Printed for B. Davies, No. 68, High-Street, by H. Sweitzer,
1798. pp. [108], (2), 2 plates. 24mo.   HSP. LOC.

33606   DAVIES, SAMUEL   1723–1761
LITTLE CHILDREN INVITED TO JESUS CHRIST. A SERMON PREACHED IN HANOVER-
COUNTY, (VIRGINIA) MAY 8, 1758. WITH AN ACCOUNT OF THE LATE REMARKABLE
RELIGIOUS IMPRESSIONS AMONG THE STUDENTS IN THE COLLEGE OF NEW-JERSEY.
BY SAMUEL DAVIES, A. M. THE SIXTH EDITION.

     Boston: Printed by T. & J. Fleet. Re-printed at Northampton, (Massachu-
setts) By William Butler.—1798. pp. ii, 16. 8vo.   JCB. PU.

33607   DAVIS, JOHN   1776–
THE ORIGINAL LETTERS OF FERDINAND AND ELISABETH. "COME TO ME THIS NIGHT!
BRING WITH THEE POISON, BRING WITH THEE PISTOLS, AND WHEN THE CLOCK
STRIKES TWELVE WE'LL BOTH BECOME IMMORTAL!" ELISABETH TO FERDINAND.
[Between double lines.]

     New-York: Printed and sold [By H. Caritat, Bookseller, 153 Broadway.]
July, 1798. pp. 144. 12mo.   JCB. NYPL.

     With an "Elegy to the memory of the unfortunate lovers, Ferdinand
and Elisabeth." By John Davis. pp. 142-144. Nearly forty pages
(53-85) are devoted to a description of the Author's journey on foot
from New York to Philadelphia. 64th New York District Copyright,
issued to Richard Walker, as Proprietor, 17 July, 1798.

     A sordid, biological romance with the usual tragic ending. A tale, when
told by woman, still brings the sympathetic tear over a tomb in Trinity's church yard; but when told by man, with a theatrical flare, brings
only forgetfulness and obscurity, in the Bowery.

33608   —— LETTRES ORIGINALES DE DEUX AMANS HABITANS DE NEW-YORK, QUI SE SONT
TUÉS DERNIEREMENT EN CETTE VILLE. PAR UN ANGLAIS.

     New-York: Imprimés pour le compte de H. Caritat, libraire, dans Broad-
Way, No. 153. 1798. 12mo. 6 chelins.

     The French version is, probably, also the work of John Davis, who
boasted an equal facility in adapting both languages to each other.

33609   —— A TRIBUTE TO THE UNITED STATES. A POEM. BY JOHN DAVIS. [One line of
Latin from] MART.

     New-York: Printed by Robert M. Hurtin, at the Literary Printing-Office,
No. 29, *Gold-Sreet* [sic.] 1798. pp. 8. 16mo.   JCB. NYHS. NYPL.

33610   DAWSON, JOHN   1762–1814
PHILADELPHIA, JULY 19, 1798. DEAR SIR: AFTER A SESSION OF SOMEWHAT MORE
THAT EIGHT MONTHS, CONGRESS ADJOURNED ON MONDAY LAST, TO MEET ON THE
FIRST MONDAY IN DECEMBER. [Regarding laws passed at the session; and a
list of military officers appointed. Signed] J. DAWSON.

     [*Philadelphia:* 1798.] Broadside. 4to.   LOC.

33611 DAY, THOMAS 1748–1789
THE CHILDREN'S MISCELLANY; IN WHICH IS INCLUDED THE HISTORY OF LITTLE JACK.
EMBELLISHED WITH THIRTY-FIVE CUTS AND FRONTISPIECE. BY THOMAS DAY, ESQ.
AUTHOR OF THE HISTORY OF SANFORD AND MERTON.
Boston: Sold by W. Spotswood, No. 22, Marlborough-Street. 1798.

33612 DAY, THOMAS 1777–1855
AN ORATION, ON PARTY SPIRIT, PRONOUNCED BEFORE THE CONNECTICUT SOCIETY OF
CINCINNATI, CONVENED AT HARTFORD, FOR THE CELEBRATION OF AMERICAN IN-
DEPENDENCE, ON THE 4TH OF JULY, 1798. BY THOMAS DAY.
Printed at Litchfield, by T. Collier. [1798.] pp. 28. 8vo. CHS. HC. NYPL. YC.

33613 DEAR MARY, OR ADIEU TO OLD ENGLAND. PRICE 25 CENTS.
*New-York: Printed & sold at J. Hewitt's Musical Repository No. 131 Wil-
liam Street. Sold also by B. Carr Philadelphia & J. Carr Baltimore.* [1798.]
pp. (2). 4to. LOC.

33614 THE DEATH AND BURIAL OF COCK ROBIN; WITH THE TRAGICAL DEATH OF A. APPLE-
PIE: THE WHOLE TAKEN FROM THE ORIGINAL MANUSCRIPT, IN THE POSSESSION OF
MASTER MEANWELL.
Boston: Printed and sold by S. Hall, No. 53, Cornhill, 1798. pp. 32, cuts.
32mo. LOC.

33615 DECALVES, ALONSO, pseudonym.
NEW TRAVELS TO THE WESTWARD, OR UNKNOWN PARTS OF AMERICA: BEING A TOUR OF
ALMOST FOURTEEN MONTHS. CONTAINING AN ACCOUNT OF THE COUNTRY, UPWARDS
OF TWO THOUSAND MILES WEST OF THE CHRISTIAN PARTS OF NORTH AMERICA; WITH
AN ACCOUNT OF WHITE INDIANS, THEIR MANNERS, HABITS, AND MANY OTHER PAR-
TICULARS. BY DON ALONSO DECALVES. CONFIRMED BY THREE OTHER PERSONS.
TO WHICH IS ADDED, THE INTERESTING HISTORY OF CHARLES MORTIMER. AN
AMERICAN TALE.
[Without place or Printer.] Printed in the year 1797. pp. 81. 12mo.

Second title: THE INTERESTING HISTORY OF CHARLES MORTIMER. AN AMERICAN
TALE. pp. 51-81.

33616 —— — TRAVELS TO THE WESTWARD; OR UNKNOWN PARTS OF AMERICA. BEING A
TOUR OF ALMOST FOURTEEN MONTHS. CONTAINING AN ACCOUNT OF THE COUNTRY,
UPWARDS OF TWO THOUSAND MILES WEST OF THE CHRISTIAN PARTS OF NORTH AMER-
ICA; WITH AN ACCOUNT OF WHITE INDIANS, THEIR MANNERS, HABITS, AND OTHER
PARTICULARS. BY DON ALONSO DECALVES. CONFIRMED BY THREE PERSONS. THE
THIRD DOVER EDITION.
[Dover, New-Hampshire:] Printed at the Sun-Office for J. Asplund. [1798.]
pp. 41. 12mo. LOC.

33617 DE FOE, DANIEL 1661–1731
TRAVELS OF ROBINSON CRUSOE. WRITTEN BY HIMSELF.
Boston: Printed and sold by Samuel Hall. 1798. woodcuts. 48mo,

33618 DELANOE, S.
MISCELLANEOUS THOUGHTS ON THE DOCTRINE OF LIMITED ELECTION AND REPROBA-
TION, AS IT STANDS CONTRASTED WITH SCRIPTURE AND REASON. BY CANDOR.
Windsor: Printed by Alden Spooner. 1798.

Replied to this year by Ariel Kendrick. A second part was printed in
1799.

33619　　**DELAWARE. STATE.**
JOURNAL OF THE HOUSE OF REPRESENTATIVES OF THE STATE OF DELAWARE, AT A
SESSION OF THE GENERAL ASSEMBLY, WHICH WAS BEGUN AND HELD AT DOVER, ON
TUESDAY, THE SECOND DAY OF JANUARY, AND ENDED ON SATURDAY, THE TWENTY-
SEVENTH OF THE SAME MONTH, IN THE YEAR OF OUR LORD ONE THOUSAND SEVEN
HUNDRED AND NINETY-EIGHT, AND OF THE INDEPENDENCE OF THE UNITED STATES
OF AMERICA THE TWENTY-SECOND. [— 27 January, 1798.]
New-Castle: Printed by Samuel and John Adams. 1798. fol.　　　LOC.

33620　　——　JOURNAL OF THE SENATE OF THE STATE OF DELAWARE, AT A SESSION OF THE
GENERAL ASSEMBLY, COMMENCED AND HOLDEN AT DOVER, ON TUESDAY, THE SECOND
DAY OF JANUARY, IN THE YEAR OF OUR LORD ONE THOUSAND SEVEN HUNDRED AND
NINETY-EIGHT, [—27 January, 1798] PURSUANT TO THE DIRECTION OF THE FOURTH
SECTION OF THE SECOND ARTICLE OF THE CONSTITUTION OF THE SAID STATE, AND
IN THE TWENTY-SECOND YEAR OF THE INDEPENDENCE OF THE UNITED STATES.
[Arms.]
New-Castle: Printed by Samuel and John Adams. 1798. pp. 49. fol.　AAS. LOC.

33621　　——　LAWS OF THE STATE OF DELAWARE, PASSED AT A SESSION OF THE GENERAL AS-
SEMBLY, WHICH WAS BEGUN AND HELD AT DOVER, ON TUESDAY THE SECOND DAY OF
JANUARY, AND ENDED ON SATURDAY THE TWENTY-SEVENTH DAY OF THE SAME
MONTH, IN THE YEAR OF OUR LORD ONE THOUSAND SEVEN HUNDRED AND NINETY-
EIGHT, AND OF THE INDEPENDENCE OF THE UNITED STATES OF AMERICA, THE
TWENTY-SECOND. PUBLISHED BY AUTHORITY. [Double line.]
New-Castle: Printed by Samuel and John Adams. 1798. pp. 43. 4to.　NYHS.

33622　　——　THE MILITIA LAW.
New-Castle: Printed by Samuel and John Adams. 1798.

33623　　**THE DELAWARE** AND EASTERN-SHORE ADVERTISER. No. 380. MONDAY, JANUARY
1, [— No. 484, MONDAY, DECEMBER 31, 1798.]
*Wilmington: Printed on Mondays and Thursdays, by Samuel & John Adams,
corner of King and High-Streets,* . . . 1798. fol.

33624　　**THE DELAWARE** GAZETTE. No. 793. WEDNESDAY, JANUARY 3, [— No. 894. SAT-
URDAY DECEMBER 29, 1798.]
*Printed (Wednesdays & Saturdays) by W. C. Smyth, two doors below Mr.
Brinton's Tavern, High-Street, Wilmington.* 1798. fol.

William C. Smyth apparently suspended publication with the issue for
December 29th, and early in the following year he disposed of his interests to John Vaughan and Daniel Coleman, who continued publication
of the Gazette from March 14, 1799, with the same serial numbering.

33625　　**DELL, CONRAD**
SAMMLUNG GEISTLICHER LEIDER NEBST MELODIEN VON VERSCHIDENEN DICHTERN
UND COMPONISTEN HERAUSGEGEBEN UND GEDRUCKT VON CONRAD DELL.
Lancaster: Gedruckt bey Johann Albrecht und Comp. 1798. obl. 8vo.

33626　　**DENNIS, JOHN**　　　　　　　　　　　　　　1771–1807
AN ADDRESS TO THE PEOPLE OF MARYLAND, ON THE ORIGIN, PROGRESS AND PRESENT
STATE OF FRENCH AGGRESSION, WITH A SKETCH OF THE INFAMOUS ATTEMPTS TO
DEGRADE THE GOVERNMENT OF THE UNITED STATES, AND SOME REFLECTIONS ON
THE LATE PROCEEDINGS IN CONGRESS; BY A MEMBER OF THE HOUSE OF REPRE-
SENTATIVES.
Philadelphia: Printed by John Fenno. 1798. pp. (76), (1), (iv). 8vo.
BA. BM. CLS. HSP. LOC. NYPL.

33627   DERRICK. ———
THESPIAN CHAPLE. INSCRIBED TO THE MEMORY OF MR. JOHN P. MORTON, LATE OF
THE NEW THEATRE, PHILADELPHIA. THE WORDS BY MR. DERRICK.

[Philadelphia:] Published by G. Willig No. 185 Market Street. [1798.]
Broadside. 4to.   LOC.

33628   DE SAUSSURE, HENRY WILLIAM   1763–1839
AN ORATION, PREPARED, TO BE DELIVERED IN ST. PHILLIP'S CHURCH, BEFORE THE
INHABITANTS OF CHARLESTON, SOUTH-CAROLINA, ON THE FOURTH OF JULY, 1798.
IN COMMEMORATION OF AMERICAN INDEPENDENCE. BY APPOINTMENT OF THE
AMERICAN REVOLUTION SOCIETY. PUBLISHED AT THE REQUEST OF THAT SOCIETY,
AND ALSO OF THE SOUTH CAROLINA STATE SOCIETY OF CINCINNATI. BY HENRY
WILLIAM DESAUSSURE, A MEMBER OF THE REVOLUTION SOCIETY, AND INTENDANT
OF THE CITY OF CHARLESTON.

Charleston: Printed by W. P. Young, No. 43, Broad-Street. 1798. pp. (2),
iv, 45. 8vo.   AAS. BA. CLS. LOC. MHS. NYPL.

33629   A DESCRIPTION OF THE MOST REMARKABLE BIRDS. FOR THE ENTERTAINMENT OF
CHILDREN.

Hartford: Printed by John Babcock. 1798. pp. 31, 28 cuts. 32mo.   AAS.

33630   THE DESSERT TO THE TRUE AMERICAN. VOL. I. NO. 1. SATURDAY, JULY 14, [—
NO. 25, SATURDAY, DECEMBER 29, 1798.]

[Philadelphia: Published by] Samuel F. Bradford, Editor & Proprietor.
1798. 4to.   AAS. HSP. LCP. WHS. YC.

Established, as a weekly literary supplement to "The True American,"
gratis to its subscribers, and two dollars per annum to others, by Samuel F. Bradford, continuing "The Philadelphia Minerva," which he had
purchased, and continued by him to the issue for August 19, 1799—
the last number located.

33631   DER DEUTSCHE PORCUPEIN UND LANCÄSTER ANZEIGS-NACHRICHTEN. NUM. 1.
MITTWOCH, JANUAR 1, [— NUM. 52. MITTWOCH, DEZEMBER 26, 1798.]

Lancaster: Gedruckt bey Johann Albrecht und Comp. 1798. fol.   LOC.

Established, as a weekly, in continuation of *Neue Unpartheyische Lancäster Zeitung*, by Johann Albrecht and Company, and continued by them
to December 25, 1799, when, without change of numbering, the title
was changed to *Der Americanische Staatsbothe, und Lancaster Anzeigs-
Nachrichten*. Its esteemed contemporaries of the Republican (Democratic) party usually referred to it as the "Deutsche Stachelschwein."

33632   DE WITT, BENJAMIN   1774–1819
A MEMOIR ON THE ONONDAGA SALT SPRINGS AND SALT MANUFACTORIES IN THE WESTERN
PART OF THE STATE OF NEW-YORK: DESCRIBING THE SITUATION AND APPEARANCE
OF THE SPRINGS, THE NATURE AND CONTENTS OF THE WATERS, AND THE PROCESS
BY WHICH THE SALT IS PROCURED, &C. BY BENJAMIN DE WITT, M. D. CORRESPOND-
ING AND HONORARY MEMBER OF SEVERAL LEARNED MEDICAL, CHYMICAL AND
PHILOSOPHICAL SOCIETIES. READ BEFORE THE SOCIETY FOR THE PROMOTION OF
AGRICULTURE, ARTS AND MANUFACTURES OF THE STATE OF NEW-YORK, HELD AT
THE CITY OF ALBANY, FEBRUARY 28, 1798. [Double line.]

Albany: Printed by Loring Andrews. 1798. pp. 28. 4to.   HC. NYPL.

33633   DEXTER, Andrew, junior   –1816
AN ORATION, ON THE IMPORTANCE OF SCIENCE AND RELIGION, PARTICULARLY TO
AMERICAN YOUTH. PRONOUNCED IN THE BAPTIST MEETING-HOUSE IN PROVIDENCE,
AT THE COMMENCEMENT OF RHODE-ISLAND COLLEGE, SEPTEMBER 5, A. D. 1798.
BY ANDREW DEXTER, JUN. PUBLISHED AT THE REQUEST OF THE STUDENTS.

> *Providence: Printed by Carter and Wilkinson.* 1798. pp. (8). 8vo. AAS. RIHS.

33634   DIARY AND MERCANTILE ADVERTISER. No. 1837. MONDAY MORNING, JANUARY 1,
[— No. 1969 ? MONDAY, NOVEMBER 12 ? 1798.]

> *Printed and published by John Crookes, for the Proprietor, No. 68 Pine-
> Street, New-York.* 1798. fol.

With the issue for February 21st, the imprint reads "Proprietors," and
about this date James Chevalier was added to its direction. In September it again became "Proprietor" as above. The numbering would seem
to indicate suspension of publication sometime during the year. With
the issue for November 13th the title was changed to *Mercantile Advertiser*.

33635   DICK, ELISHA CULLEN   1762–1825
DOCTOR DICK'S INSTRUCTIONS FOR THE NURSING AND MANAGEMENT OF LYING-IN-
WOMEN: WITH SOME REMARKS CONCERNING THE TREATMENT OF NEW-BORN IN-
FANTS.

> *Alexandria: Printed by Thomas and Westcott, in Royal-Street, between the
> Post-Office and the Coffee-House.* M,DCC,XCVIII. pp. (16). 8vo.   AAS.

33636   DICKSON, WILLIAM, and ROBERT
DICKSON'S BALLOON ALMANAC, FOR THE YEAR OF OUR LORD 1799. THE THIRD AFTER
LEAPYEAR. ADAPTED TO PENNSYLVANIA AND THE NEIGHBOURING STATES. [Cut of
balloon ascension.]

> *Lancaster: Printed and sold by W. & R. Dickson, in Queen-Street, north of
> the court house.* [1798.] pp. (38). 12mo.   HSP.

33637   A DICTIONARY OF LOVE; WHEREIN IS A DESCRIPTION OF A PERFECT BEAUTY; THE
PICTURE OF A FOP OR MACARONI; AND A KEY TO ALL THE ARCH PHRASES, DIFFICULT
TERMS, AND PECULIAR IDIOMS, USED IN THAT UNIVERSAL LANGUAGE. WITH NOTES.

> *Philadelphia: Printed by James Carey, No. 1, South Second-Street.* [1798.]
> pp. 119. 24mo.   AAS.

33638   A DICTIONARY OF THE BIBLE: OR, AN EXPLANATION OF THE PROPER NAMES & DIFFI-
CULT WORDS IN THE OLD AND NEW TESTAMENT, ACCENTED AS THEY OUGHT TO BE
PRONOUNCED. WITH OTHER USEFUL PARTICULARS FOR THOSE WHO WOULD UNDER-
STAND THE SACRED SCRIPTURES, AND READ THEM WITH PROPRIETY. FIRST AMERI-
CAN EDITION, FROM THE SECOND LONDON EDITION, ENLARGED.

> *Printed at the Press of and for Isaiah Thomas, jun. Sold by him at his Book-
> store, also by Isaiah Thomas at the Worcester Bookstore, and by Thomas & Andrews,
> No. 45, Newbury-Street, Boston. Worcester—January—*1798. pp. iv, (229), (5).
> 12mo.   AAS. BM. JCB. NL. NYPL.

Copies of this are sometimes found bound with Thomas's Standard duodecimo edition of the Bible, printed this year.

33639   DILWORTH, THOMAS   -1780

DILWORTH'S ASSISTANT: ADAPTED TO THE COMMERCE OF THE CITIZENS OF THE UNITED STATES. BEING A COMPENDIUM OF ARITHMETIC BOTH PRACTICAL AND THEORETICAL. IN FIVE PARTS. CONTAINING I. ARITHMETIC IN WHOLE NUMBERS WHEREIN ALL THE COMMON RULES HAVING EACH OF THEM A SUFFICIENT NUMBER OF QUESTIONS WITH THEIR ANSWERS, ARE METHODICALLY AND BRIEFLY HANDLED. II. VULGAR FRACTIONS, WHEREIN SEVERAL THINGS, NOT COMMONLY MET WITH ARE DISTINCTLY TREATED OF, AND LAID DOWN IN THE MOST PLAIN AND EASY MANNER. III. DECIMALS, IN WHICH AMONG OTHER THINGS ARE CONSIDERED THE EXTRACTION OF ROOTS; INTEREST, BOTH SIMPLE AND COMPOUND; ANNUITIES REBATE AND EQUATION OF PAYMENTS. IV. A LARGE COLLECTION OF QUESTIONS WITH THEIR ANSWERS, SERVING TO EXERCISE THE FOREGOING RULES, TOGETHER WITH A FEW OTHERS BOTH PLEASANT AND DIVERTING. V. DUODECIMALS, COMMONLY CALLED CROSS MULTIPLICATION, WHEREIN THAT SORT OF ARITHMETIC IS THOROUGHLY CONSIDERED AND RENDERED VERY PLAIN AND EASY; TOGETHER WITH THE METHOD OF PROVING ALL THE FOREGOING OPERATIONS AT ONCE BY DIVISION OF SEVERAL DENOMINATIONS WITHOUT REDUCING THEM INTO THE LOWEST TERMS MENTIONED. THE WHOLE BEING DELIVERED IN THE MOST FAMILIAR WAY OF QUESTION AND ANSWER, IS RECOMMENDED BY SEVERAL EMINENT MATHEMATICIANS, ACCOMPTANTS AND SCHOOLMASTERS, AS NECESSARY TO BE USED IN SCHOOLS BY ALL TEACHERS WHO WOULD HAVE THEIR SCHOLLARS [*sic*] THOROUGHLY UNDERSTAND AND MAKE A QUICK PROGRESS IN ARITHMETIC. CAREFULLY REVISED, AND ADAPTED TO THE COMMERCE OF THE CITIZENS OF THE UNITED STATES, WITH MANY ADDITIONS IN THE VARIOUS RULES, BY JAMES GIBBONS, TEACHER OF ARITHMETIC &C, IN NEW-YORK.

       New-York: 1798.

     66th New York District Copyright, issued to James Gibbons, as Proprietor, 11 August, 1798.

33640   —— THE YOUNG BOOK-KEEPER'S ASSISTANT: SHEWING HIM IN THE MOST PLAIN AND EASY MANNER, THE ITALIAN WAY OF STATING DEBTOR AND CREDITOR; WITH PROPER AND INSTRUCTIVE NOTES UNDER EVERY ENTRY IN THE WASTE-BOOK, WHERE NECESSARY, BY WHICH THE METHOD OF JOURNALIZING IS RENDERED MORE EASY AND INTELLIGIBLE; AND ALSO THE LIKE NOTES IN THE JOURNAL AND LEDGER, INSERTED BY WAY OF INFORMATION, HOW TO POST THE JOURNAL, AND CORRECT ERRORS IN THE LEDGER: WHEREIN THERE IS A GREAT VARIETY OF EXAMPLES, NOT ONLY IN THE COMMON AND ORDINARY WAY OF BUYING AND SELLING, BUT IN THAT OF TRADING BEYOND THE SEAS, BOTH FOR A MERCHANT'S SELF AND IN COMPANY, ALL WHICH IS CONTAINED IN TWO SETTS OF BOOKS, DIRECTING THE LEARNER, NOT BY PRECEPT ONLY, BUT BY EXAMPLE, HOW TO DRAW OUT A NEW INVENTORY FROM THE OLD BOOKS, AND INSERT IT IN THE NEW ONES; AND THE TRADE CONTINUED AS IF IT WERE IN THE REAL SHOP OR COMPTING HOUSE. TO WHICH IS ANNEXED A SYNOPSIS OR COMPENDIUM OF THE WHOLE ART OF STATING DEBTOR AND CREDITOR. IN ALL THE CIRCUMSTANCES OF BOOK-KEEPING, BOTH IN PROPER FACTORAGE AND COMPANY ACCOMPTS DOMESTIC AND FOREIGN. THE THIRTEENTH EDITION. BY THOMAS DILWORTH, AUTHOR OF THE NEW GUIDE TO THE ENGLISH TONGUE, SCHOOLMASTERS ASSISTANT, &C. &C.

      Wilmington: Printed by Peter Brynberg. M,DCC,XCVIII. pp. (2), (6), (15), (8), (2), (21), (1), (52), (38), (2), (34), (4), (6). (1), (12) + 8vo.   AAS. DHS. JCB.

33641   DISBOROUGH, HENRY

AN INAUGURAL DISSERTATION ON CHOLERA INFANTUM. SUBMITTED TO THE EXAMINATION OF THE REV. JOHN EWING, S.T.P. PROVOST, THE TRUSTEES AND MEDICAL FACULTY OF THE UNIVERSITY OF PENNSYLVANIA, ON THE TWENTY-SECOND DAY OF MAY, 1798, FOR THE DEGREE OF DOCTOR OF MEDICINE. BY HENRY DISBOROUGH, OF NEW JERSEY, HONORARY MEMBER OF THE PHILADELPHIA CHEMICAL SOCIETY. [Four lines from] POPE.

      Philadelphia: Printed by Budd and Bartram, No. 58, North Second Street. May, 1798. pp. (32). 8vo.   JCB. LOC. LCP. NYPL. 8GO.

33642   A DISCOURSE ON THE PRESENT STATE OF AFFAIRS.
              Augusta: Printed by Alexander M'Millan, 1798.

33643   DIXON'S OBSERVATORY. VOL. II. NO. 126. THURSDAY, SEPTEMBER 13, [—NO. 147.
         MONDAY, NOVEMBER 26, 1798.]
              Richmond: Printed Mondays and Thursdays by John Dixon. 1798. fol.

         On December 3d, Dixon joined with Meriwether Jones in establishing
         The Examiner.

33644   DODDRIDGE, PHILIP   1702–1751
         A PLAIN AND SERIOUS ADDRESS TO THE MASTER OF A FAMILY, ON THE IMPORTANT
         SUBJECT OF FAMILY RELIGION. BY P. DODDRIDGE, D.D.
              Litchfield: Printed by Thomas Collier. 1798.

33645   ——— THE PRINCIPLES OF THE CHRISTIAN RELIGION, DIVIDED INTO LESSONS, FOR
         CHILDREN. ABRIDGED FROM THE REV. P. DODDRIDGE, D.D. ORNAMENTED WITH
         [32] CUTS DESCRIPTIVE OF THE MOST REMARKABLE PASSAGES IN SCRIPTURE.
              Hartford: Printed by John Babcock. 1798. pp. [31.] *32mo.*   AAS.

33646   DODSLEY, ROBERT   1703–1764
         THE ECONOMY OF HUMAN LIFE. IN TWO PARTS. TRANSLATED FROM AN INDIAN MANU-
         SCRIPT, WRITTEN BY A BRAMIN.
              Reprinted at Litchfield: by T. Collier. [1798.] *pp. 185. 24mo.*   LHS.

33647   DUANE, WILLIAM   1760–1835
         A CAUTION; OR, REFLECTIONS ON THE PRESENT CONTEST BETWEEN FRANCE AND
         GREAT-BRITAIN.
              [Philadelphia:] Printed by Benj. Franklin Bache, No. 112, Market-street.
         M,DCC,XCVIII. *pp.* [14.] *8vo.*   AAS. JCB. LOC. MHS. RIHS.
         Contains, An Ode on the French Revolution. Dated, January 25, 1798.

33648   ——— TRUTH WILL OUT! THE FOUL CHARGES OF THE TORIES AGAINST THE EDITOR OF
         THE AURORA REPELLED BY POSITIVE PROOF AND PLAIN TRUTH AND HIS BASE CA-
         LUMNIATORS PUT TO SHAME. [Price—two cents.]
              [Philadelphia: Printed at the Aurora Office, 1798.] pp. (2), (2), [12.] *8vo.*
                                                         AAS. HC. HSP. JCB. LOC. NYPL.

         There is a second impression with a type ornament at the foot of page 12.

33649   DUBOIS, W.
         FREE MASONS MARCH. COMPOSED BY MR. DUBOIS, ARRANGED FOR THE PIANOFORTE,
         BY MR. GENIN [sic Guenin.]
              [Philadelphia:] Published by G. Willig. Market Street, No. 185. 4to. LCP.

33650   DUNHAM, JOSIAH   1769–1844
         AN ORATION, FOR THE FOURTH OF JULY, 1798; DELIVERED IN THE MEETING-HOUSE,
         IN THE VICINITY OF DARTMOUTH-COLLEGE, AT HANOVER, IN NEWHAMPSHIRE, AT
         THE REQUEST OF THE INHABITANTS OF SAID HANOVER, AND THE ADJACENT TOWNS,
         WHO ASSEMBLED THERE FOR THE CELEBRATION OF THE 22D ANNIVERSARY OF
         AMERICAN INDEPENDENCE, AND PUBLISHED BY THEIR DESIRE. BY JOSIAH DUN-
         HAM, A.M.
              Printed at Hanover, Newhampshire, by Benjamin True. [1798.] *pp. 15. 8vo.*
                                                         AAS. BA. BM. HC. JCB. NYPL.

33651   DUNHAM, Josiah, continued.
—— Fugitive and miscellaneous poetry: consisting, principally, of early compositions, or literary amusements; among which will be found a version of the Eclogues of Virgil, with Odes in the manner of Horace, and many original scraps; interspersed with some original pieces from Parnassian friends and correspondents. [Six lines from] Burns.
     Hanover: Printed ? by Benjamin True. 1798. pp. 300.
     Proposals were issued May 7, 1798, for printing the above.

33652   DUNLAP, William   1766–1839
Andre; a tragedy, in five acts: as performed by the Old American Company, New-York, March 30, 1798. To which are added authentic documents respecting Major Andre; consisting of Letters to miss Seward, the Cow chase, Proceedings of the court martial, &c. Copyright secured.
     New-York: Printed by T. & J. Swords, No. 99 Pearl-street,—1798.—pp. 109, (1), (2). 8vo.
                   BA. BU. JCB. LCP. LOC. NYHS. NYPL.
     60th New York District Copyright, issued to William Dunlap, as Author, 6 April, 1798. Reprinted in London in 1799; and, by the Dunlap Society, in New York, in 1887.

33653   DWIGHT, Nathaniel   1770–1831
A Short but comprehensive system of the geography of the world: by way of question and answer. Principally designed for children, and common schools. By Nathaniel Dwight. The first Albany edition. From the second Hartford edition, enlarged and improved. [Four lines of quotations.]
     Albany: Printed by Charles R. & George Webster. [With privilege of Copyright.] Sold at their Bookstore, in the White-House, corner of State and Pearl Streets—MDCCXCVIII. pp. 187, (4). 12mo.   LOC.

33654   —— — A Short but comprehensive system of the geography of the world: by way of question and answer. Principally designed for children and common schools. By Nathaniel Dwight. The third Connecticut edition. [Six line quotation.] Published according to Act of Congress.
     Hartford: Printed by Hudson and Goodwin. [1798.] pp. 214. 12mo. AAS.

33655   DWIGHT, Theodore   1764–1846
An Oration, spoken at Hartford, in the State of Connecticut, on the anniversary of American independence, July 4th, 1798. By Theodore Dwight.
     Hartford: Printed by Hudson and Goodwin. 1798. pp. 31. 8vo.
                 AAS. BM. CHS. JCB. LOC. NYPL. UTS.

33656   DWIGHT, Timothy   1752–1817
The Duty of Americans, at the present crisis, illustrated in a discourse, preached on the fourth of July, 1798; by the Rev. Timothy Dwight, d.d. president of Yale-College; at the request of the citizens of New-Haven.
     New-Haven; Printed by Thomas and Samuel Green. 1798. pp. 32. 8vo.
            AAS. BA. BM. CHS. HC. JCB. LOC. MHS. NYPL. UTS. YC.
     [Copy right secured.] Connecticut District Copyright, issued to Timothy Dwight, as Author, 16 August, 1798.

33657   —— The Nature, and danger, of infidel philosophy, exhibited in two discourses, addressed to the candidates for the baccalaureate in Yale College. By the Rev. Timothy Dwight, d. d. president of Yale-College; September 9th, 1797.
     New-Haven: Printed by George Bunce. M.DCC.XCVIII. pp. 95. 8vo.
           AAS. BA. BM. CHS. HC. JCB. LOC. MHS. NYHS. NYPL. UTS. YC.
     Copy right secured. Reprinted in Bristol, England, in 1799; and in Cambridge, England, in 1804.

33658   EACKER, GEORGE I.
OBSERVATIONS ON THE NATIONAL CHARACTER OF THE AMERICANS: AN ORATION, DE-
LIVERED BEFORE THE TAMMANY SOCIETY, ON THE 12TH OF MAY, 1798. BY GEORGE
I. EACKER.
New York: Printed by William A. Davis & Co. 26, Moore Street.—1798.—
pp. 20. 8vo.   NYHS.

33659   [Cut.] THE EAGLE: OR, DARTMOUTH CENTINEL.—DEDICATED TO POLITICS AND THE
BELLES-LETTRES.—[Motto.] VOLUME V. NUMBER XXIV. MONDAY, JANUARY 1,
[— VOLUME VI. NUMBER 23. TUESDAY, DECEMBER 25, 1798.]
*Hanover, (Newhampshire) Printed and published at the Academy, by Benjamin
True: . . . 1798. fol.*   AAS.

Before August, the title was shortened to *The Eagle* only. Printed at
the northwest corner of College Square, in the Academy, by Benjamin
True.

33660   THE EASTERN COURIER; AND LINCOLN ADVERTISER.

Jan. 1, 1798, Henry Hoskins and John W. Scott, issued proposals for
printing the above, as a weekly newspaper, at Hallowell, Maine.

33661   EASTERN HERALD [cut] AND GAZETTE OF MAINE. MONDAY, JANUARY 1, [—VOL,
XIV. MONDAY, DECEMBER 31, 1798.]
*Published by John Kelse Baker, Fish-Street, Portland. [District of Maine.]
[Massachusetts.] 1798. fol.*   AAS.

With the issue for March 5th, Daniel George was admitted to partnership, as Baker & George, and this issue, for the first time, was given a
volume number, XIV.

33662   EATON, WILLIAM   1764–1811
AN ADDRESS TO MY INFLUENTIAL NEIGHBOURS, SELECTMEN AND COMMITTEES OF
BRIMFIELD.
*[Worcester:] Printed [by Leonard Worcester] at the Spy Printing-Office,
September — '98.* pp. [15.], (1). 8vo.   AAS. BA.

33663   THE ECHO: OR, FEDERAL SONGSTER. BEING A LARGE COLLECTION OF THE MOST
CELEBRATED, MODERN POETICAL WRITINGS, OF DIFFERENT AUTHORS. FIRST EDI-
TION. [Double line.]
*Brookfield: (Massachusetts,) From the Press of E. Merriam & Co. Sold by
them in Brookfield, and by G. Merriam in Worcester. [November 13, 1789.]* pp. 248.
24mo.   AAS.

With an Appendix: of Masonic Songs. A collection of the most celebrated cotillions and country dances. Toasts and sentiments.

33664   ECKLEY, JOSEPH   1756–1811
A DISCOURSE, DELIVERED ON THE PUBLIC THANKSGIVING DAY, NOVEMBER 29, 1798.
BY JOSEPH ECKLEY, D. D. MINISTER OF THE OLD SOUTH CHURCH, BOSTON. [Orna-
ment.]
Boston: Printed and sold by Manning & Loring. 1798. pp. [23.] 8vo.
AAS. BA. CHS. CLA. HC. JCB. LOC. MHS. NYHS. PU. UTS. YC.

33665   —— — A DISCOURSE, DELIVERED ON THE PUBLIC THANKSGIVING DAY, NOVEMBER
29, 1798. BY JOSEPH ECKLEY, D.D. MINISTER OF THE OLD SOUTH CHURCH, BOSTON.
SECOND EDITION. [Ornament.]
Boston: Printed and sold by Manning & Loring. 1798. pp. [23.] 8vo.
AAS. HC. LOC. NYPL. YC.

33666   EDWARD AND EMILY. A TALE [in verse.]
West-Springfield: Printed by Richard Davison. 1796. pp. 16. 16mo.   AAS.

33667 ELEGANT EXTRACTS; A COLLECTION OF THE FAVORITE MODERN SONGS FOR THE
FLUTE. BOOK III.
*Printed by J. Carr, Music Store, No. 6 Gay Street, Baltimore, and B. Carr's Mu-
sical Repositories, Market Street, Philadelphia, and William Street, New York. 1798.*

33668 ELLEN'S FATE DESERVES A TEAR. SONG.
*New-York: Published by G. Gilfert at his Musical Magazine, No. 177 Broad-
way. 1798.*

33669 ELLIOT, JAMES   1775–1839
THE POETICAL AND MISCELLANEOUS WORKS OF JAMES ELLIOT, CITIZEN OF GUILFORD,
VERMONT, AND LATE A NONCOMMISIONED OFFICER IN THE LEGION OF THE UNITED
STATES. IN FOUR BOOKS. [Thirteen lines from] POPE.
Greenfield, Massachusetts: Printed by Thomas Dickman for the Author. M,-
DCC,XCVIII. pp. 271, (4), (1). 12mo.   AAS. BA. BM. JCB. LOC.
Contains: I. Poems, which have heretofore appeared in various period-
ical publications. II. Original poems. III. Sketches, political, geo-
graphical, &c. IV. A disquisition on military establishments. Fugitive
pieces. Appendix. List of Subscribers. Errata. Three hundred copies
printed.

33670 ELLIS, ASA, JUNIOR
THE COUNTRY DYER'S ASSISTANT. BY ASA ELLIS, JUN.
Brookfield, (Massachusetts:) Printed by E. Merriam & Co. for the Author.
[1798.] pp. 139, (3), errata. 12mo.   AAS. HC. JCB. LOC.
156th Massachusetts District Copyright, issued to Asa Ellis, jun., as
Author, 13 November, 1798.

33671 EMERSON, EZEKIEL   1736–1815
A SERMON DELIVERED AT NEWCASTLE, OCTOBER 4TH, 1797, AT THE ORDINATION OF
THE REV. KIAH BAYLEY. BY EZEKIEL EMERSON, V. D. M.
Pownalborough: Printed by Laughton & Rhodes. 1798. pp. 24. 12mo.
AAS. JCB.

33672 EMERSON, SAMUEL   1765–1851
AN ORATION, PRONOUNCED AT KENNEBUNK, ON THE FOURTH OF JULY, 1798; THE
ANNIVERSARY OF AMERICAN INDEPENDENCE. BY DR. SAMUEL EMERSON.
Printed by E. A. Jenks, Portland. 1798. pp. 23. 8vo.   AAS. HC. JCB. NYHS.

33673 EMMONS, NATHANAEL   1745–1840
THE DIGNITY OF MAN. A DISCOURSE ADDRESSED TO THE CONGREGATION IN FRANK-
LIN, UPON THE OCCASION OF THEIR RECEIVING FROM DR. FRANKLIN, THE MARK OF
HIS RESPECT IN A RICH DONATION OF BOOKS APPROPRIATED TO THE USE OF A PARISH-
LIBRARY. BY NATHANAEL EMMONS, PASTOR OF THE CHURCH IN FRANKLIN.
New-York: Printed by J. Buel, for Cornelius Davis. No. 94, Water-Street.
1798. pp. 106. 18mo.   AAS. HC. JCB. NYPL.
Second title: A DISCOURSE, DELIVERED NOVEMBER 3, 1790. AT THE PARTICULAR
REQUEST OF A NUMBER OF RESPECTABLE MEN IN FRANKLIN, WHO WERE FORMING
A SOCIETY, FOR THE REFORMATION OF MORALS. AND NOW PUBLISHED AT THE DE-
SIRE OF THE HEARERS. SECOND EDITION. BY NATHANAEL EMMONS, A. M. PASTOR
OF THE CHURCH IN FRANKLIN.
New-York: Printed by J. Buel for Cornelius Davis, No. 94 Water-Street. 1798.
pp. (2), 47-80.
Third title: NATIONAL PEACE, THE SOURCE OF NATIONAL PROSPERITY. A SERMON,
DELIVERED AT FRANKLIN, ON THE DAY OF ANNUAL THANKSGIVING, DECEMBER 15,
1796. BY NATHANAEL EMMONS, PASTOR OF THE CHURCH IN FRANKLIN.
New-York: Printed by J. Buel for Cornelius Davis, No. 94 Water-Street. 1798.
pp. (2), 83-106.

33674   EMMONS, NATHANAEL, continued.
—— A DISCOURSE, DELIVERED MAY 9, 1798. BEING THE DAY OF FASTING AND PRAYER THROUGHOUT THE UNITED STATES. BY NATHANAEL EMMONS, A. M. PASTOR OF THE CHURCH IN FRANKLIN.

Printed at Wrentham, Massachusetts, by Nathaniel and Benjamin Heaton. M,DCC,XCVIII. pp. 28. 8vo.   AAS. BA. JCB. LOC. UTS. YC.

33675   —— A SERMON, PREACHED BEFORE HIS EXCELLENCY INCREASE SUMNER, ESQ. GOVERNOR; HIS HONOR MOSES GILL, ESQ. LIEUTENANT-GOVERNOR; THE HONORABLE THE COUNCIL, SENATE, AND HOUSE OF REPRESENTATIVES, OF THE COMMONWEALTH OF MASSACHUSETTS, MAY 30, 1798. BEING THE DAY OF GENERAL ELECTION.. BY NATHANAEL EMMONS, A. M. PASTOR OF THE CHURCH IN FRANKLIN.

Boston: Printed for the State. 1798. pp. [31.] 8vo.
       AAS. BA. BM. CHS. HC. JCB. LOC. MHS. NYHS. NYPL. UTS. YC.

33676   ENCYCLOPÆDIA; OR, A DICTIONARY OF ARTS, SCIENCES, AND MISCELLANEOUS LITERATURE; CONSTRUCTED ON A PLAN, BY WHICH THE DIFFERENT SCIENCES AND ARTS ARE DIGESTED INTO THE FORM OF DISTINCT TREATISES OR SYSTEMS, COMPREHENDING THE HISTORY, THEORY AND PRACTICE, OF EACH, ACCORDING TO THE LATEST DISCOVERIES AND IMPROVEMENTS; AND FULL EXPLANATIONS GIVEN OF THE VARIOUS DETACHED PARTS OF KNOWLEDGE, WHETHER RELATING TO NATURAL AND ARTIFICIAL OBJECTS, OR TO MATTERS ECCLESIASTICAL, CIVIL, MILITARY, COMMERCIAL, &C. INCLUDING ELUCIDATIONS OF THE MOST IMPORTANT TOPICS RELATIVE TO RELIGION, MORALS, MANNERS, AND THE OECONOMY OF LIFE: TOGETHER WITH A DESCRIPTION OF ALL THE COUNTRIES, CITIES, PRINCIPAL MOUNTAINS SEAS, RIVERS, &C. THROUGHOUT THE WORLD; A GENERAL HISTORY, ANCIENT AND MODERN, OF THE DIFFERENT EMPIRES, KINGDOMS AND STATES; AND AN ACCOUNT OF THE LIVES OF THE MOST EMINENT PERSONS IN EVERY NATION, FROM THE EARLIEST AGES DOWN TO THE PRESENT TIMES. COMPILED FROM THE WRITINGS OF THE BEST AUTHORS, IN SEVERAL LANGUAGES; THE MOST APPROVED DICTIONARIES, AS WELL OF GENERAL SCIENCE AS OF ITS PARTICULAR BRANCHES; THE TRANSACTIONS, JOURNALS, AND MEMOIRS, OF VARIOUS LEARNED SOCIETIES, THE MS. LECTURES OF EMINENT PROFESSORS ON DIFFERENT SCIENCES; AND A VARIETY OF ORIGINAL MATERIALS, FURNISHED BY AN EXTENSIVE CORRESPONDENCE. THE FIRST AMERICAN EDITION, IN EIGHTEEN VOLUMES GREATLY IMPROVED. ILLUSTRATED WITH FIVE HUNDRED AND FORTY-TWO COPPER PLATES. VOL. I. A–ANG. INDOCTI DISCANT, ET AMENT MEMINISSE PERITI.

Philadelphia: Printed by Thomas Dobson, at the Stone House, No. 41, South Second Street. M.DCC.XCVIII. [1790.] [Copy-right secured according to law.] pp. (2), xiv, 799, 31 plates, frontispiece. 4to.
       AAS. APS. HC. JCB. LCP. LOC. MHS. NYHS. NYPL. WC.

196th Pennsylvania District Copyright, issued to Thomas Dobson, as Proprietor, 4 January, 1798.

33677   —— ENCYCLOPÆDIA; OR, A DICTIONARY OF ARTS, SCIENCES, AND MISCELLANEOUS LITERATURE; . . . VOL. II. AUG–BAR. [Motto.]

Philadelphia: Printed by Thomas Dobson, at the Stone House, No. 41, South Second Street. M.DCC.XCVIII. [1790.] [Copy-right secured according to law.] pp. (2), 799, (1), 60 plates, (32–91). 4to.

33678   —— ENCYCLOPÆDIA; OR, A DICTIONARY OF ARTS, SCIENCES, AND MISCELLANEOUS LITERATURE; . . . VOL. III. BAR–BZO. [Motto.]

Philadelphia: Printed by Thomas Dobson, at the Stone House, No. 41, South Second Street. M.DCC.XCVIII. [1791.] [Copy-right secured according to law.] pp. (2), 806, 20 plates (92–111). 4to.

ENCYCLOPÆDIA, continued.

33679 —— Encyclopædia; or, a dictionary of arts, sciences, and miscellaneous literature; . . . Vol. iv. Caa–Cic. [Motto.]

Philadelphia: Printed by Thomas Dobson, at the Stone House, No. 41, South Second Street. M.DCC.XCVIII. [1791.] [Copy-right secured according to law.] pp. (2), 793, 26 plates (112–137). 4to.

33680 —— Encyclopædia; or, a dictionary of arts, sciences, and miscellaneous literature; . . . Vol. v. Cic–Dia. [Motto.]

Philadelphia: Printed by Thomas Dobson, at the Stone House, No. 41, South Second Street. M.DCC.XCVIII. [1792.] [Copy-right secured according to law.] pp. (2), 807, (1), 24 plates (138–161). 4to.

33681 —— Encyclopædia; or, a dictionary of arts, sciences, and miscellaneous literature; . . . Vol. vi. Dia–Eth. [Motto.]

Philadelphia: Printed by Thomas Dobson, at the Stone House, No. 41, South Second Street. M.DCC.XCVIII. [1792.] [Copy-right secured according to law.] pp. (2), 794, 22 plates (162–183). 4to.

33682 —— Encyclopædia; or, a dictionary of arts, sciences, and miscellaneous literature; . . . Vol. vii. Etm–Goa. [Motto.]

Philadelphia: Printed by Thomas Dobson, at the Stone House, No. 41, South Second Street. M.DCC.XCVIII. [1792.] [Copy-right secured according to law.] pp. (2), 797, (1), 38 plates (184–221). 4to.

33683 —— Encyclopædia; or, a dictionary of arts, sciences, and miscellaneous literature; . . . Vol. viii. Gob–Hyd. [Motto.]

Philadelphia: Printed by Thomas Dobson, at the Stone House, No. 41, South Second Street. M.DCC.XCVIII. [1793.] [Copy-right secured according to law.] pp. (2) 800, 18 plates (222–238). 4to.

33684 —— Encyclopædia; or, a dictionary of arts, sciences, and miscellaneous literature; . . . Vol. ix. Hyd–Les. [Motto.]

Philadelphia: Printed by Thomas Dobson, at the Stone House No. 41, South Second Street. M.DCC.XCVIII. [1793.] [Copy-right secured according to law.] pp. (2), 800, 31 plates (239–269). 4to.

33685 —— Encyclopædia; or, a dictionary of arts, sciences, and miscellaneous literature; . . . Vol. x. Les–Mec. [Motto.]

Philadelphia: Printed by Thomas Dobson, at the Stone House No. 41, South Second Street. M.DCC.XCVIII. [1793.] [Copy-right secured according to law.] pp. (2), (2), 788, (1), 22 plates (270–291). 4to.

"Philadelphia. October 1793. The tenth volume of the Encyclopædia is now presented to the public; but as it makes its appearance in an imperfect state, some account of the reason of that imperfection should be given. On the 8th of September last the Publisher had the misfortune of having his Printing-Office burnt down by a fire which broke out in the neighbourhood, and a great quantity of his printing material destroyed, and among other articles, the figures, with which he was printing the tables of logarithms, belonging to the present volume, were melted down by the violence of the fire. As a supply of these could not be immediately obtained he was under the necessity of publishing the volume without these tables; but hopes he shall be able to publish them in the next volume which is now in considerable forwardness."

ENCYCLOPÆDIA, continued.

33686   —— ENCYCLOPÆDIA; OR, A DICTIONARY OF ARTS, SCIENCES, AND MISCELLANEOUS LIT-
        ERATURE; . . . VOL. XI. MED–MID. [Motto.]
            Philadelphia: Printed by Thomas Dobson, at the Stone House No. 41, *South
            Second Street.* M.DCC.XCVIII. [1794.] [Copy-right secured according to law.]
            pp. (2), 814, 19 plates (292–310). 4to.

33687   —— ENCYCLOPÆDIA; OR, A DICTIONARY OF ARTS, SCIENCES, AND MISCELLANEOUS LIT-
        ERATURE; . . . VOL. XII. MIE–NEG. [Motto.]
            Philadelphia: Printed by Thomas Dobson, at the Stone House No. 41, *South
            Second Street.* M.DCC.XCVIII. [1794.] [Copy-right secured according to law.]
            pp. (2), 799, (1), 35 plates (311–345). 4to.

33688   —— ENCYCLOPÆDIA; OR, A DICTIONARY OF ARTS, SCIENCES AND MISCELLANEOUS LITERA-
        ERATURE; . . . VOL. XIII. NEH–PAS. [Motto.]
            Philadelphia: Printed by Thomas Dobson, at the Stone House No. 41, *South
            Second Street.* M.DCC.XCVIII. [1795.] [Copy-right secured according to law.]
            pp. (2), 799, (1), 32 plates (346–377). 4to.

33689   —— ENCYCLOPÆDIA; OR A DICTIONARY OF ARTS, SCIENCES, AND MISCELLANEOUS LIT-
        ERATURE; . . . VOL. XIV. PAS–PLA. [Motto.]
            Philadelphia: Printed by Thomas Dobson, at the Stone House No. 41, *South
            Second Street.* M.DCC.XCVIII. [1795.] [Copy-right secured according to law.]
            pp. (2), 797, (1), 16 plates (378–393). 4to.

33690   —— ENCYCLOPÆDIA; OR, A DICTIONARY OF ARTS, SCIENCES, AND MISCELLANEOUS LIT-
        ERATURE; . . . VOL. XV. PLA–RAN. [Motto.]
            Philadelphia: Printed by Thomas Dobson, at the Stone House No. 41, *South
            Second Street.* M.DCC.XCVIII. [1796.] [Copy-right secured according to law.]
            pp. (2), 799, (1), 41 plates (394–434). 4to.

        A vindication of the character of George Fox, from the account given
        of him on page 734 of this volume, was printed, by particular desire of
        the Society of Friends in Philadelphia, as an addenda to the third vol-
        ume of the Supplement to the Encyclopædia, in 1803.

33691   —— ENCYCLOPÆDIA; OR, A DICTIONARY OF ARTS, SCIENCES, AND MISCELLANEOUS LIT-
        ERATURE; . . . VOL. XVI. RAN–SCO. [Motto.]
            Philadelphia: Printed by Thomas Dobson, at the Stone House No. 41, *South
            Second Street.* M.DCC.XCVIII [1796.] [Copy-right secured according to law.]
            pp. (2), 799, (1), 12 plates (435–446). 4to.

33692   —— ENCYCLOPÆDIA; OR, A DICTIONARY OF ARTS, SCIENCES, AND MISCELLANEOUS LIT-
        ERATURE; . . . VOL. XVII. SCO–STR. [Motto.]
            Philadelphia; Printed by Thomas Dobson, at the Stone House No. 41, *South
            Second Street.* M.DCC.XCVIII [1797.] [Copy-right secured according to law.]
            pp. (2), 827, (1), 37 plates (447–483). 4to.

33693   —— ENCYCLOPÆDIA; OR, A DICTIONARY OF ARTS, SCIENCES, AND MISCELLANEOUS LIT-
        ERATURE; . . . VOL. XVIII. STR–ZYM. [Motto.]
            Philadelphia: Printed by Thomas Dobson, at the Stone House No. 41, *South
            Second Street.* M.DCC.XCVIII. [Copy-right secured according to law.] pp. (2),
            945, (2), (1), 59 plates (484–542). 4to.

33694   ENFIELD, WILLIAM   1741–1797
THE SPEAKER: OR, MISCELLANEOUS PIECES, SELECTED FROM THE BEST ENGLISH WRIT-
ERS, AND DISPOSED UNDER PROPER HEADS, WITH A VIEW TO FACILITATE THE
IMPROVEMENT OF YOUTH IN READING AND SPEAKING. A NEW EDITION, CORRECTED.
TO WHICH IS PREFIXED, AN ESSAY ON ELOCUTION. BY WILLIAM ENFIELD, LL. D.
LATE LECTURER ON THE BELLES LETTRES IN THE ACADEMY AT WARRINGTON.
[Three lines of Latin from] OVID.
> *Hudson: Printed by Ashbel Stoddard,* M,DCC,XCVIII. pp. 341. 12mo.
>   AAS. JCB.

33695   EPITOME [cut] OF THE TIMES; OR, HISTORICAL, POLITICAL, AND COMMERCIAL MIS-
CELLANY. [Motto.] VOL. I. No. 1. MONDAY, MARCH 26, [— No. 81. MONDAY,
DECEMBER 31, 1798.
> *Norfolk: Printed every Monday and Thursday, by Augustus C. Jordan, op-
posite the Post-Office;* . . . 1798. fol.

> The motto, from Suetonius, reads: "In civitate libera linguam men-
> temque liberas esse debere." Established as a semi-weekly, by Augustus
> C. Jordan, and continued by him to March 30, 1802 — the last number
> located. Beginning January 1, 1799, the title was shortened to *Epitome
> of the Times.* From 1799 to 1802, a weekly edition for the country, with-
> out title heading, was also published.

33696   ERRA PATER, pseudonym.
THE BOOK OF KNOWLEDGE, TREATING OF THE WISDOM OF THE ANCIENTS. IN FOUR
PARTS. I. SHEWING THE VARIOUS AND WONDERFUL OPERATION OF THE SIGNS AND
PLANETS, AND OTHER CELESTIAL CONSTELLATIONS, ON THE BODIES OF MEN, &C.
II. PROGNOSTICATIONS FOREVER NECESSARY TO KEEP THE BODY IN HEALTH: WITH
SEVERAL CHOICE RECEIPTS IN PHYSIC AND SURGERY. III. AN ABSTRACT OF THE
ART OF PHYSIOGNOMY AND PALMISTRY, TOGETHER WITH THE SIGNIFICATION OF
MOLES, AND THE INTERPRETATION OF DREAMS, &C. IV, THE FARMER'S CALENDAR,
CONTAINING, 1. PERPETUAL PROGNOSTICATIONS FOR WEATHER. 2. THE WHOLE
MYSTERY OF HUSBANDRY. 3. THE COMPLEAT EXPERIENCED FARRIER AND COW-
LEECH, &C. WRITTEN BY ERRA PATER, A JEW DOCTOR IN ASTRONOMY & PHYSIC,
BORN IN BETHANY, NEAR MOUNT OLIVE, IN JUDEA. MADE ENGLISH BY W. LILLY,
STUDENT IN PHYSIC AND ASTROLOGY. TO WHICH IS ADDED, THE TRUE FORM OF
ALL SORTS OF BILLS, BONDS, COUNTER BONDS, INDENTURES, LETTERS OF ATTORNEY
AND LICENCE, DEEDS OF GIFT, BILLS OF EXCHANGE, &C.
> *New-Haven:* 1798. pp. 117. 24mo.

33697   ERSKINE, RALPH   1685–1752
GOSPEL SONNETS OR SPIRITUAL SONGS. IN SIX PARTS. I. BELIEVER'S ESPOUSALS; 2.
BELIEVER'S JOINTURE; 3. BELIEVER'S RIDDLE; 4. BELIEVER'S LODGING; 5. BE-
LIEVER'S SOLILOQUY; 6. BELIEVER'S PRINCIPLES. CONCERNING CREATION AND
REDEMPTION — LAW AND GOSPEL — JUSTIFICATION AND SANCTIFICATION — FAITH
AND SENSE — HEAVEN AND EARTH. BY THE LATE REVEREND RALPH ERSKINE,
MINISTER OF THE GOSPEL AT DUNFERMLINE. SECOND AMERICAN EDITION FROM
THE TWENTY FOURTH ENGLISH EDITION. IN WHICH THE HOLY SCRIPTURES ARE
FULLY EXTENDED. AND TO WHICH IS NOW PREFIXED AN ACCOUNT OF THE AUTHOR'S
LIFE AND WRITINGS. MIRA CANAM, SED VERA CANAM.— BUCH. PSALM LXXVIII.
> *Printed at Worcester—at the Press of Isaiah Thomas, jun. for Isaiah Thomas,
sold at their respective Bookstores, and by Thomas and Andrews in Boston.—Feb.*
1798. pp. 360. 12mo.   AAS. HC. JCB. LOC. NL. NYPL.

33698   ERSKINE, THOMAS, baron   1750–1823
SPEECHES OF MESSRS. ERSKINE AND KYDD, ON A TRIAL FOR PUBLISHING PAINE'S AGE
OF REASON. WITH LORD KENYON'S CHARGE TO THE SPECIAL JURY. PUBLISHED
AT THE REQUEST OF SEVERAL CLERGYMEN.
> *Washington, (K.) Printed by Hunter and Beaumont.* 1798.

33699   ESSEX COUNTY. MASSACHUSETTS. MUSICAL ASSOCIATION.
THE CONSTITUTION OF THE ESSEX MUSICAL ASSOCIATION. ESTABLISHED 28TH MARCH,
1797.
Newburyport: Printed by Edmund M. Blunt, State Street.—1798. pp. 12.
12mo.   BA.

33700   EUGENIUS AND SELIMA; OR, THE FATAL EFFECTS OF PARENTAL TYRANNY. A MORAL
STORY.
West-Springfield: Sold at the Printing-Office. 1798. pp. 12. 12mo.   LOC.

33701   EVANGELICAL REFORMED CHURCH IN THE UNITED STATES OF AMERICA.
KIRCHEN-FORMULARIEN DER EVANGELISCH-REFORMIRTEN GEMEINEN. [Vignette.]
Germantaun: Gedruckt bey Michael Billmeyer. 1798. pp. 60. 16mo.   AAS.

33702   EVANS, THOMAS
AN ADDRESS TO THE PEOPLE OF VIRGINIA, RESPECTING THE ALIEN & SEDITION LAWS.
BY A CITIZEN OF THIS STATE. [Signed, a Fellow-citizen of Virginia.]
Richmond: Printed by Augustine Davis. 1798. pp. [63.] (1), [iv]. 8vo.
AAS. BA. JCB. LOC. VSL.

33703   EWING, JAMES   1744–1824
THE COLUMBIAN ALPHABET. BEING AN ATTEMPT TO NEW MODEL THE ENGLISH AL-
PHABET, IN SUCH MANNER AS TO MARK EVERY SIMPLE SOUND BY AN APPROPRIATE
CHARACTER, THEREBY RENDERING THE SPELLING AND PRONUNCIATION MORE DE-
TERMINATE AND CORRECT, AND THE ART OF READING AND WRITING MORE EASILY
ATTAINABLE. BY JAMES EWING.
Trenton: Printed by Matthias Day. M,DCC,XCVIII. pp. (2), 28, (2).
16mo.   BA. LOC.

On the fly leaf of the copy in the Boston Athenæum is written this in-
scription: To George Washington to whose name no titles are any
addition, this attempt to call the attention of his country men to a very
important improvement in their language, is respectfully presented by
his very humble Servant The Author.

33704   THE EXAMINER. TRUTH ITS GUIDE, AND LIBERTY ITS OBJECT. VOL. I. NUM. 1.
MONDAY, DECEMBER 3, [— NUM. 9. MONDAY, DECEMBER 31, 1798.]
Richmond: Printed by Meriwether Jones & John Dixon. 1798. fol.

Established, as a semi-weekly, by Meriwether Jones, and John Dixon,
and continuing the advertisements of *Dixon's Observatory.* In May,
1799, Dixon withdrew, and publication continued by Meriwether Jones.
In January, 1803, the title was shortened to *Examiner*, and in August,
the publication was made in the name of Skelton Jones, although his
name does not appear until in September, up to January, 1804, when
the paper was printed by William W. Worsley for S. Jones and himself.
The last number located is that for January 7, 1804.

33705   EXETER. NEW HAMPSHIRE. FIRE SOCIETY.
CONSTITUTION AND RULES OF THE FIRE-SOCIETY OF EXETER.
Exeter: Printed by H. Ranlet. [January 15] M,DCC,XCVIII. pp. 8. 16mo.
JCB.
Signed by twenty subscribers.

33706   *Caption title:* FACTS AND CALCULATIONS RESPECTING THE POPULATION AND TERRITORY
OF THE UNITED STATES OF AMERICA.
[*Without place or Printer.* 1798.] pp. 7, (1). 8vo.   LOC.

This title is on the verso of page 7, also.

33707 FARLEY & Goss' ALMANAC, OR VERMONT CALENDAR, FOR THE YEAR OF OUR LORD 1799: BEING THE THIRD AFTER BISSEXTILE, OR LEAP YEAR, AND TWENTY THIRD OF THE INDEPENDENCE OF UNITED COLUMBIA. CALCULATED FOR THE MERIDIAN OF PEACHAM, LATITUDE 44 DEG. 20 M. NORTH. . . .

> *Printed at Peacham, Vermont, by Farley & Goss.* [1798.] pp. (24). 12mo. LOC.

33708 THE FARMER'S ALMANACK, FOR THE YEAR OF OUR LORD, 1799: BEING THE THIRD AFTER BISSEXTILE, OR LEAP YEAR; AND THE TWENTY THIRD OF AMERICAN INDE-PENDENCE. ADAPTED TO THE STATE OF NEWHAMPSHIRE. CALCULATED FOR THE LATITUDE AND LONGITUDE OF PORTSMOUTH; BUT WILL SERVE, WITHOUT ESSENTIAL VARIATION, FOR THE ADJACENT STATES. CONTAINING, BESIDES THE ASTRONOMICAL CALCULATIONS, A CALENDAR FOR YOUNG FARMERS AND GARDENERS; AND A VARIETY OF OTHER MATTER, INSTRUCTIVE, USEFUL, AND ENTERTAINING. [Four lines from] THOMSON.

> *Printed at Concord, Newhampshire, by Moses Davis. Sold at his Office, whole-sale and retail.* [1798.] pp. 24. 12mo. AAS. NHHS. NYPL.

33709 THE FARMER'S ALMANACK, FOR THE YEAR OF OUR LORD 1799. BEING THE THIRD AFTER BISSEXTILE, OR LEAP YEAR. AND TWENTY THIRD OF THE INDEPENDENCE OF THE UNITED STATES OF AMERICA. FITTED TO THE LATITUDE AND LONGITUDE OF THE TOWN OF BOSTON, BUT WILL SERVE WITHOUT ESSENTIAL VARIATION FOR THE AD-JACENT STATES. [Cut] THE BUST OF THE LITTLE AUTHOR.

> *Massachusetts: Printed [by Nathaniel and John Coverly] for, and sold by the Booksellers.* [1798.] pp. (24). 12mo. LOC.

There is no difference, but the title page, from the Weatherwise Alma-nac, printed by the same printers this year.

33710 THE FARMER'S JOURNAL, & NEWTON ADVERTISER. VOL. II. NUMBER 102. WEDNES-DAY, JANUARY 3, [— VOL. III. No. 140. WEDNESDAY, OCTOBER 17, 1798.]

> *Newton: Printed and published by E. Hopkins & P. Smith.* 1798. fol.

The above is the last number located.

33711 THE FARMER'S LIBRARY. OR, VERMONT AND NEW YORK INTELLIGENCER. A REPUBLICAN PAPER. [Motto.] VOL. I. NUM. 8. TUESDAY, JANUARY 2, [— VOL. I. NUM. 21. TUESDAY, APRIL 3, 1798.]

> *Printed at Fairhaven, by Judah P. Spooner.* 1798. fol.

The above is the last number located.

33712 FARMER'S [cut] ORACLE. VOLUME I. NUMBER 49. TUESDAY, JANUARY 2, [— VOL-UME II. NUMBER 13. TUESDAY, APRIL 24, 1798.]

> *Troy: (State of New-York) Printed by Luther Pratt, & Co.* 1798. fol.

Discontinued probably about the above date, as the field was invaded in May by the *Northern Budget.*

33713 THE FARMERS' [cut] REGISTER. VOL. I. No. 1. WEDNESDAY, APRIL 18, [— No. XXXVII. WEDNESDAY, DECEMBER 26, 1798.]

> *Chambersburg: (Penn.) Printed and published every Wednesday, by Snowden & M'Corkle, in Market-Street, near the Bridge.* 1798. pp. 152. fol. HSP.

Paged. Established, as a weekly, by John M. Snowden and William M'Corkle, and continued by them to the end of the first volume in April, 1799, when they removed their press to Greensburg, Pennsylvania, and established there a weekly newspaper with the same title.

33714   FARMER'S REGISTER. VOL. I. NO. 1, SATURDAY, MARCH 17. [— VOL. I NO. 33, SATURDAY, OCTOBER 27, 1798.]

Conway. Printed and published by Theodore & A. H. Leonard. 1798. fol.

Established, as a weekly, by Theodore and A. Hayden Leonard. In July, the title was changed to *The Farmers' Register*; and, with the issue for September 8th, the junior partner withdrew. The above is the last number located.

33715   THE FARMER'S WEEKLY MUSEUM: NEWHAMPSHIRE AND VERMONT JOURNAL. [Motto.] VOL. V. NO. 248. TUESDAY, JANUARY 2, [— VOL. VI. NO. 300. MONDAY, DECEMBER 31, 1798.]

Printed at Walpole, Newhampshire, by David Carlisle, in the Main Street. . . . 1798. fol.   AAS.

With the issue for February 20th, Isaiah Thomas resumed proprietorship, the imprint reading: Printed by David Carlisle for Isaiah Thomas, and this was changed, with the issue for May 29th, when Alexander Thomas was admitted to partnership, to "Thomas & Thomas."

33716   FARRAR, STEPHEN   1738–1809

A SERMON DELIVERED AT TOWNSEND (MASSACHUSETTS) NOVEMBER 15TH, AT THE INTERMENT OF THE REV. SAMUEL DIX, A. M. WHO DIED NOVEMBER 12TH, 1797, BY STEPHEN FARRAR, A. M. PASTOR OF THE CHURCH IN NEW-IPSWICH.

Amherst, Newhampshire: Printed by Samuel Preston. 1798.   BM.

33717   FAUGERES, MARGARETTA V. BLEECKER   1771–1801

AN ODE FOR THE 4TH OF JULY, 1798. DEDICATED TO THE FRIENDS OF LIBERTY AND INDEPENDENCE, BY MARGARETTA V. FAUGERES.

[New-York: 1798.] Broadside. fol.

33718   FAUST, BERNHARD CHRISTOPH   1755–1842

THE CATECHISM OF HEALTH; SELECTED FROM THE GERMAN OF DR. FAUST [by J. H. Basse]; AND CONSIDERABLY IMPROVED BY DR. GREGORY, OF EDINBURGH. PUBLISHED FOR THE USE OF THE CITIZENS OF THE UNITED STATES: AT THE RECOMMENDATION OF DR. RUSH, OF PHILADELPHIA; AND DR. WILLIAMSON, OF NORTH CAROLINA, NOW RESIDING IN NEW-YORK, &C.

New-York: Printed by R. Wilson, for Samuel Campbell, 124, Pearl-street. 1798. pp. xli, iv, 146. 12mo.   AAS. LOC. NYPL. 8GO.

33719   FAUSTUS, JOHANN

THE HISTORY OF DR. JOHN FAUSTUS, THE FAMOUS CONJURER, AND NECROMANCER. (AND SAID TO BE THE FIRST INVENTOR OF PRINTING.) WHEREIN ARE CONTAINED MANY WONDERFUL THINGS THAT HIMSELF HAD SEEN AND DONE IN THE EARTH AND AIR; WITH HIS BRINGING-UP, TRAVELS, AND LAST END. [Cut.] TRULY TRANSLATED FROM THE ORIGINAL COPIES.

Boston: Printed and sold at the Bible and Heart in Cornhill. [1798.] pp. 51. 8vo.   AAS.

Running title: THE FAMOUS HISTORY OF DOCTOR FAUSTUS.

33720   THE FAYETTE GAZETTE, AND UNION ADVERTISER. VOL. I. NO. 1. SATURDAY, JANUARY 13, [— NO. 51. FRIDAY, DECEMBER 28, 1798.]

Uniontown: Printed by Stewart and Mowry, near the Court-House. 1798. fol.

Established, as a weekly, by Jacob Stewart, and Charles Mowry, and continued by them into March, 1805, when it was merged with *The Genius of Liberty*. Only a few scattering numbers are known.

33721   FEDERAL [U.S. Arms] GALAXY [Motto.] VOL. II. No. 53. TUESDAY, JANUARY 2, [— No. 104. TUESDAY, DECEMBER 25, 1798.]

Published for Windham County, by Benjamin Smead, in Brattleborough, Vermont. 1798. fol.

AAS.

In June, the Printing-Office was in the "South lower room in the new building adjoining the City Bridge." In September, the cut of United States arms, was succeeded by a cut of the moon in its first quarter, up to November, when the whole cut was dropped.

33722   FEDERAL GAZETTE & BALTIMORE DAILY ADVERTISER. VOL. VI. No. 1298. MONDAY, JANUARY 1, [—VOL. VII. No. 1610. MONDAY, DECEMBER 31, 1798.]

Baltimore: Printed and sold by Yundt and Brown, No. 3, Calvert-Street, near the Court-House. 1798. fol.

33723   FEDERAL GAZETTE AND DAILY ADVERTISER. VOL. I. No. 1. MONDAY, JANUARY 1, [No. 63. MONDAY, MARCH 26, 1798.]

[Published] By Caleb P. Wayne, No. 17 Kilby Street, Boston. 1798. fol.

AAS. BA. MHS.

Established, as a daily, by Caleb P. Wayne. With the issue for March 8th, the title was changed to *Federal Gazette and General Advertiser*, and publication was made semi-weekly up to the issue for March 26th, 1798, when it was discontinued.

33724   FEDERAL OBSERVER. VOL. I. NUMB. 1. THURSDAY, NOVEMBER 22, [— NUMB. 6. THURSDAY, NOVEMBER 27, 1798.]

Portsmouth: Printed and published by Treadwell & Hart, at their Printing-Office opposite Mr. Greenleaf's Inn, Congress-Street. 1798. fol.

Established, as a weekly, by William Treadwell and Samuel G. Hart. With the issue for August 1, 1799, Hart withdrew. Beginning with the issue for May 22, 1800, publication was made in the name of W. Treadwell & Co. until discontinued, June 12, 1800.

33725   THE FEDERAL SPY. VOL. VI. No. 264. MONDAY, JANUARY 1, [VOL. VI. No. 52. TUESDAY, DECEMBER 25, 1798.]

Published by Francis Stebbins—Springfield—Massachusetts. 1798. fol.

33726   THE FEDERALIST: [U.S. Arms] OR, NEW-JERSEY GAZETTE. "ADAMS AND LIBERTY." VOL. I. No. 1. MONDAY EVENING, JULY 9, [No. 26. MONDAY EVENING, DECEMBER 31, 1798.]

Printed at Trenton, under the direction of G. Craft & W. Black, at their Office, in Second-Street, opposite J. Milnor's Store. 1798. fol.

Established by Gershom Craft, and William Black. "After the first side of No. 2, of the paper was struck off" Black sold his interest to Craft, who proudly announced in the issue of October 8, 1798, that "one thousand and eighty copies of the Federalist, are this week struck off, for the supply of subscribers." In 1799, Craft added to the imprint, "Printer of the Laws of the United States for the District of New-Jersey," and the Printing-Office was removed to Main-Street, until publication ceased with the issue for June 30, 1800. On July 8th, 1800, Craft consolidated the Federalist, with the rival publication, across the street, the two papers cleverly uniting their names, under joint proprietorship, as *The Federalist, & New-Jersey State Gazette*, with the serial volume and number of the latter.

33727   FELLOW CITIZENS. THE 2D SECTION OF THE 1ST ARTICLE OF THE CONSTITUTION OF THE UNITED STATES, WHICH IS IN THESE WORDS, SAYS, [Two columns. On rights of voters.] ANOTHER CITIZEN. CARLISLE, SEPTEMBER 29TH, 1798.

> *[Carlisle: Printed by George Kline, 1798.]* Broadside. fol.   HSP.

33728   FENN, lady ELEANOR FRERE   1743–1813
FABLES IN MONOSYLLABLES BY MRS. TEACHWELL. TO WHICH ARE ADDED MORALS IN DIALOGUES BETWEEN A MOTHER AND CHILDREN. [Six lines of French from] ROUSSEAU.

> *Philadelphia: Printed for Thomas Dobson, at the Stone House, No. 41 South Second Street.* 1798. pp. (60), frontispiece, 17 cuts in text; 39, frontispiece, 15 cuts in text. 12mo.   AAS. LOC.

> *Second title:* MORALS TO A SET OF FABLES, BY MRS. TEACHWELL. THE MORALS IN DIALOGUES BETWEEN A MOTHER AND CHILDREN. IN TWO SETS.

> *Philadelphia: Printed for Thomas Dobson, at the Stone House No. 41, South Second Street.* 1798. pp. 39, frontispiece, 15 cuts in text.

33729   FENNELL, JAMES   1776–1816
DESCRIPTION OF THE PRINCIPLES AND PLAN OF PROPOSED ESTABLISHMENTS OF SALT WORKS: FOR THE PURPOSE OF SUPPLYING THE UNITED STATES WITH HOME MADE SALT. BY JAMES FENNELL.

> *Philadelphia: Printed by J. Bioren.* 1798. pp. 12, [17–60], folded table. 8vo.   LOC.

33730   FENNING, DANIEL
THE READY RECKONER, OR, TRADER'S USEFUL ASSISTANT, ADAPTED TO THE USE OF ALL WHO DEAL BY WHOLESALE OR RETAIL. EXHIBITING AT ONE VIEW, THE AMOUNT OR VALUE OF ANY NUMBER OR QUANTITY OF GOODS OR MERCHANDIZE, FROM ONE UP TO TEN THOUSAND, AT THE VARIOUS PRICES FROM 1 FARTHING TO 1 POUND. TO WHICH ARE PREFIXED, I. A TABLE OF INTEREST AT SIX PER CENT. II. A TABLE OF THE WEIGHT & VALUE OF COINS, AS THEY PASS IN THE RESPECTIVE STATES OF THE UNION, WITH THEIR STERLING AND FEDERAL VALUE. III. A TABLE SHEWING THE AMOUNT OF CENTS, &C.

> *York: Printed by Salomon Myer [sic Mayer], for Mathew Carey, Philadelphia.* 1798. pp. 191. 8vo.   AAS. JCB. LOC. NYPL.

33731   FERNANDEZ, FELIPE
A NEW PRACTICAL GRAMMAR OF THE SPANISH LANGUAGE: IN FIVE PARTS. I. OF THE CHARACTER, SOUND, AND QUANTITY OF THE SPANISH LETTERS. II. OF THE VARIOUS SORTS AND CLASSES OF WORDS, THEIR DECLENSIONS AND PROPERTIES. III. THE SYNTAX; THE RULES OF WHICH ARE EXPLAINED IN A COPIOUS AND EXTENSIVE MANNER. IV. AN ENLARGED VOCABULARY; CONTAINING THE TERMS OF THE PARTS OF HUMAN BODY, &C.; OF COMMERCE, NAVIGATION, WAR, NATURAL HISTORY, AND THE VARIOUS ARTS AND TRADES. V. FAMILIAR PHRASES AND DIALOGUES; SELECT FABLES; WITH USEFUL EXAMPLES OF MERCANTILE CORRESPONDENCE—CAREFULLY COMPILED FROM THE BEST AUTHORS. THE WHOLE IN SPANISH AND ENGLISH, AND CALCULATED TO RENDER THE STUDY OF THE SPANISH LANGUAGE EASY, COMPREHENSIVE, AND ENTERTAINING. THE FIRST AMERICAN EDITION, CAREFULLY RE-PRINTED FROM THE SECOND LONDON, AND REVISED BY A GENTLEMAN IN THIS CITY. BY THE REV. DON FELIPE FERNANDEZ, A. M. A NATIVE OF SPAIN, AND FOUNDER OF THE ROYAL OECONOMICAL SOCIETY OF XEREZ DE LA FRONTERA.

> *Philadelphia: Printed by T. and W. Bradford, Booksellers, No. 8, South Front Street.* [1798] pp. viii, 356. 8vo.   AAS. JCB. LOC.

33732   FESSENDEN, CALEB PAGE
AN ORATION, DELIVERED AT CONWAY, BEFORE A RESPECTABLE NUMBER OF THE
INHABITANTS OF CONWAY, EATON AND BARTLETT, ON THE FOURTH DAY OF JULY
1798, BEING THE 21ST ANNIVERSARY OF AMERICAN INDEPENDENCE. BY CALEB
PAGE FESSENDEN. [Three lines from] SHAKESPEARE. [PUBLISHED AT THE RE-
QUEST OF THE COMMITTEE OF THE DAY.]
> *Printed at Fryeburg. [By Ezekiel Russell.]* 1798. pp. 16. 8vo.   AAS. BA. JCB.

33733   FESSENDEN, THOMAS GREEN   1771–1837
ORATION AT RUTLAND, VERMONT, JULY 4, 1798. TOGETHER WITH AN ODE ADAPTED
TO THAT OCCASION.
> *Printed at Rutland, by Josiah Fay.* 1798. pp. 31. 8vo.

33734   FIDELITY REWARDED: OR, THE HISTORY OF POLLY GRANVILLE.
> *Boston: Printed by Young and Minns.* 1796. pp. 98+ 12mo.   AAS.

33735   FINLAY'S AMERICAN NAVAL AND [cut] COMMERCIAL REGISTER. No. 190. FRIDAY,
JANUARY 4. [— No. 224. TUESDAY, MAY 1, 1798.]
> *Philadelphia: Printed (Tuesday and Friday) by Samuel Finlay, No. 16, Ches-*
> *nut Street.* 1798. fol.

The above is the last number located.

33736   FISKE, ABEL   1752–1802
Half-title: MR. FISKE'S DISCOURSE. TO WHICH IS ADDED, MR. BELL'S ORATION.
Title: A DISCOURSE, DELIVERED AT AMHERST, JUNE 25, 1798, BEFORE THE BE-
NEVOLENT LODGE OF FREE AND ACCEPTED MASONS. BY THE REV. ABEL FISKE,
OF WILTON. [One line from] ST. PAUL.
> *Printed at Amherst—by Samuel Preston.* 1798. pp. 20; 12. 8vo.   AAS. BM.

Second title: AN ORATION, DELIVERED AT AMHERST JUNE 25, A. L. 5798, BEFORE
THE BENEVOLENT LODGE OF FREE AND ACCEPTED MASONS, AT THE CELEBRATION
OF THE FESTIVAL OF ST. JOHN THE BAPTIST. BY BROTHER SAMUEL BELL.
> *Printed at Amherst—by Samuel Preston.* 1798. pp. 12.

33737   —— A SERMON, DELIVERED AUGUST 15, 1798, AT THE ORDINATION OF THE REV.
JACOB ABBOT, TO THE PASTORAL OFFICE OVER THE CHURCH AND SOCIETY IN AMP-
TON [*sic* HAMPTON]-FALLS. BY ABEL FISKE, A. M. PASTOR OF THE CHURCH IN
WILTON. PULISHED [*sic*] BY DESIRE.
> *Newburyport: Printed by Edmund M. Blunt.—State Street.* 1798. pp. (28).
8vo.   AAS. BA. BM. JCB. LOC. NYHS. UTS.

The error was corrected during printing. The American Antiquarian
Society has both forms.

33738   THE FIVE-HEADED MONSTER; OR, TALLEYRAND DISSECTED. A NEW SONG FOR THE
JOLLY TARS OF AMERICA. [Four line verses, with chorus. Tune, "Derry
Down".]
> *[Philadelphia?* 1798.]

33739   FLEET, THOMAS and JOHN
FLEETS' REGISTER, AND POCKET ALMANACK FOR THE YEAR OF OUR LORD 1799. BEING
THE THIRD AFTER LEAP YEAR, AND TWENTY-THIRD OF AMERICAN INDEPENDENCE,
WHICH BEGAN JULY 4TH, 1776. CALCULATED CHIEFLY FOR THE USE OF THE COM-
MONWEALTH OF MASSACHUSETTS, BOSTON, THE METROPOLIS, BEING IN LATITUDE
42 DEG. 23 MIN. NORTH, AND 70 DEG. 58, 53 WEST LONG. 348 MILES N. E. OF PHILA-
DELPHIA.
> *Boston: Printed and Sold by T. & J. Fleet, at the Bible and Heart in Corn-*
> *hill.* [1798.] pp. (20), (147). 24mo.   AAS. BA. BM. HC. LOC. MHS. NYPL.

33740 FLETCHER, Ebenezer   1762–1831

A Narrative of the captivity and sufferings of mr. Ebenezer Fletcher, of Newipswich, who was wounded at Hubbarston [*sic*], in the year 1777, and taken prisoner by the British, and, after recovering a little from his wounds, made his excape [*sic*] from them, and returned back to Newipswich. Written by himself.

> *Printed by Samuel Preston, Amherst.* 1798. pp. 26. 12mo.   NYPL.

> Reprinted, with notes, by C. I. Bushnell, in New York, in 1866; and, in his "Crumbs for Antiquarians." Vol. 2.

33741 FLORIAN, Jean Pierre Claris de   1755–1794

Galatea. A pastoral romance; imitated from Cervantes. By m. de Florian. Translated into English. To which is added Amelia, or the faithless Briton: an original American novel, founded upon recent facts. Amelia, or malevolence defeated [by a Lady of Massachusetts]: and miss Seward's Monody on major André. Embellished with engravings.

> *Boston: Printed for and sold by W. Spotswood, and C. P. Wayne.* 1798. pp. 28; 94, 4 plates; 61, frontispiece; 22. 12mo.   NYPL.

33742 FOLWELL, Richard

Short history of the yellow fever, that broke out in the city of Philadelphia, in July, 1797: with a list of the dead; of the donations for the relief of the poor, and a variety of other interesting particulars. Second edition.

> *Philadelphia: Printed by Richard Folwell, No. 33, Carter's-Alley.* 1798. pp. (64), (16). 8vo.   AAS. BA. JCB. LOC. NYHS. NYPL.

> Also included in the Select pamphlets collected and issued in a volume, by Mathew Carey, in 1799.

33743 FORSYTH, William

A Sermon, preached at Danville, before the fraternity of Free and Accepted Masons, of Harmony Lodge, at the celebration of the festival of St. John the baptist, June 25, 1798. By William Forsyth, a. m. [One line from] Thompson [*sic*.]

> *Printed at Peacham, Vermont, by Farley & Goss.* 1798. pp. 24. 8vo. AAS. BM.

33744 THE FORTUNATE discovery: or, the history of Henry Villars. By a Young lady of the State of New-York.

> *New-York: Printed by R. Wilson, for Samuel Campbell, 124, Pearl-Street.* 1798. pp. (2), (21), 180. 12mo.   AAS. LOC. NYPL.

33745 FORWARD, Justus   1730–1814

Controversial letters, respecting church communion and discipline. By Justus Forward, and M. Phelps.

> *Northampton: Printed by William Butler.* 1798. pp. 132. 8vo.

33746 FOSS, John

A Journal of the captivity and sufferings of John Foss; several years a prisoner at Algiers: together with some account of the treatment of Christian slaves when sick: — and observations on the manners and customs of the Algerines. [Eight lines of verse.] Published according to Act of Congress.

> *Newburyport: Printed by Angier March, Middle-Street.* [1798.] 12mo.

> 137th Massachusetts District Copyright, issued to Angier March, as Proprietor, 22 January, 1798. An edition of one thousand copies was sold in a few months; and, in November, a second edition, greatly enlarged and corrected, was published, as below:

33747   FOSS, JOHN, continued.
—— — A JOURNAL, OF THE CAPTIVITY AND SUFFERINGS OF JOHN FOSS; SEVERAL
YEARS A PRISONER AT ALGIERS: TOGETHER WITH SOME ACCOUNT OF THE TREAT-
MENT OF CHRISTIAN SLAVES WHEN SICK: — AND OBSERVATIONS OF THE MANNERS
AND CUSTOMS OF THE ALGERINES. [Eight lines of verse.] SECOND EDITION. PUB-
LISHED ACCORDING TO ACT OF CONGRESS.
    Newburyport: Printed by Angier March, Middle-Street. [1798.] pp. 189.
12mo.   AAS. BM. BU. LOC. NYPL.

    Second title: THE ALGERINE SLAVES, A POEM. BY A CITIZEN OF NEWBURYPORT.
[Three lines of verse.]
    Newburyport: Printed by Angier March, Middle-Street. 1798. pp. (2), [177]-
189.

    Signed, Juvenis. Sept. 1798.

33748   FOSTER, HANNAH WEBSTER   1759–1840
    THE BOARDING SCHOOL; OR, LESSONS OF A PRECEPTRESS TO HER PUPILS: CONSISTING
OF INFORMATION, INSTRUCTION, AND ADVICE, CALCULATED TO IMPROVE THE MAN-
NERS, AND FORM THE CHARACTER OF YOUNG LADIES. TO WHICH IS ADDED, A COL-
LECTION OF LETTERS, WRITTEN BY THE PUPILS, TO THEIR INSTRUCTOR, THEIR
FRIENDS, AND EACH OTHER. BY A LADY OF MASSACHUSETTS, AUTHOR OF THE
COQUETTE. PUBLISHED ACCORDING TO ACT OF CONGRESS.
    *Printed at Boston, by I. Thomas and E. T. Andrews. Sold by them, by C.
Bingham, and the other Booksellers in Boston; by I. Thomas, Worcester; by Thomas,
Andrews & Penniman, Albany; and by Thomas, Andrews & Butler, Baltimore —
June, 1798.* pp. 252. 12mo.   AAS. JCB. LOC. NYPL.

    149th Massachusetts District Copyright, issued to Caleb Bingham, as
Proprietor, 25 June, 1798.

33749   FOSTER, JOEL   1755–1812
    THE OFFICE OF THE HIGH PRIEST ILLUSTRATED AND APPLIED TO THE CHRISTIAN MIN-
ISTRY. A SERMON, DELIVERED AT THE ORDINATION OF THE REV. JOHN JACKSON,
IN GILL, JANUARY 10TH, 1798. BY JOEL FOSTER, A.M. PASTOR OF THE CONGRE-
GATIONAL CHURCH AND SOCIETY IN NEWSALEM. [Printer's mark.]
    Printed at Greenfield, Massachusetts, by Thomas Dickman. 1798. pp. 20+.
8vo.   JCB.

33750   THE FOUNDLING, OR THE HISTORY OF LUCIUS STANHOPE. PRICE FOUR CENTS.
    Boston: Printed and sold by John W. Folsom, No. 30, Union-Street. 1798.
32mo.

33751   FOWLER, ABRAHAM   1745–1815
    [PRIVATE SOCIETIES, FOR GOOD DESIGNS, WARRANTED BY SCRIPTURE AND REASON.]
A SERMON, DELIVERED AT THE INSTALLATION OF HARMONY LODGE OF FREE AND
ACCEPTED MASONS AT SALEM, IN WATERBURY, DECEM. 27, 1797. TO WHICH IS
ADDED, A CHARGE, GIVEN BY JESSE BEACH, ESQ. H. P. . . .
    New-Haven: Printed by George Bunce. 1798. pp. 32. 8vo.   CHS. YC.
    The author was not a mason.

33752   FOWLER, ANDREW   1760–1850
    THE LESSONS OF THE PROTESTANT EPISCOPAL CHURCH, IN THE UNITED STATES OF
AMERICA; SELECTED FROM THE HOLY SCRIPTURES: WITH AN EXPOSITION OF ALL
THE SUNDAYS AND PRINCIPAL HOLY DAYS THROUGHOUT THE YEAR. BY ANDREW
FOWLER, A.M.
    New-Brunswick, New-Jersey: Printed for the Compiler, by A. Blauvelt. — —
1798. — — *(Copy right secured.)* pp. 501. 24mo.   JCB. LOC.

33753   FRANCE. DIRECTORY.
THE PLAN OF THE INVASION OF ENGLAND AND IRELAND, BY THE COMBINED NAVAL AND MILITARY FORCE OF FRANCE, SPAIN, AND HOLLAND. SHEWING THE SEVERAL POINTS OF JUNCTION OF THE COMBINED FLEETS, THE STRENGTH OF EACH SQUADRON, THE SEVERAL ROUTES TO THEIR GRAND RENDEZVOUS OFF BREST; ALSO THE SEVERAL PLACES OF DEBARKATION BOTH IN ENGLAND AND IRELAND; LIKEWISE THE STATIONS AND STRENGTH OF THE SEVERAL FLEETS IN EUROPE, ACCORDING TO THE MOST ACCURATE INFORMATION. TO WHICH IS ANNEXED, THE LETTER ACCOMPANYING THE PLAN TO PHILADELPHIA FROM EUROPE. ALSO, THE INSTRUCTIONS BY THE EXECUTIVE DIRECTORY TO THE COMMANDER IN CHIEF GENERAL BUONAPARTE; WITH COMMENTS AND EXPLANATIONS.
Philadelphia: Printed by James Carey, No. 16, Chesnut-Street. 1798.

33754   FRANCISCO XAVIER, saint   1506–1552
THE LIFE OF FRANCIS XAVIER, APOSTLE OF THE INDIES. . . .
Philadelphia: Printed by Hogan & McElroy, for Alexander Brodie. January, 1798. pp. 192, portrait. 12mo.   AAS. NYPL.

33755   FRANKLIN, BENJAMIN   1706–1790
THE LIFE OF DOCTOR BENJAMIN FRANKLIN, WRITTEN BY HIMSELF: WITH ESSAYS, HUMOROUS, MORAL, AND LITERARY, CHIEFLY IN THE MANNER OF THE SPECTATOR. THE SEVENTH AMERICAN EDITION.
New-London: Printed for Charles Holt. 1798. pp. 200, (4), portrait. 12mo.   AAS. JCB. LOC. NYPL.

33756   —— THE WORKS OF THE LATE DR. BENJAMIN FRANKLIN. CONSISTING OF HIS LIFE WRITTEN BY HIMSELF. TOGETHER WITH ESSAYS HUMOROUS, MORAL AND LITERARY, CHIEFLY IN THE MANNER OF THE SPECTATOR.
Charlestown: Printed by John Lamson, for the principal Booksellers in Boston. 1796. pp. 300, portrait. 16mo.   AAS. BM. JCB. LOC. NYPL.
Includes the continuation of Franklin's Life by Dr. Henry Stueber.

33757   —— — THE WORKS OF THE LATE DR. BENJAMIN FRANKLIN: CONSISTING OF HIS LIFE, WRITTEN BY HIMSELF. TOGETHER WITH ESSAYS, HUMOROUS, MORAL, AND LITERARY, CHIEFLY IN THE MANNER OF THE SPECTATOR.
Printed and sold by J. Lyon, Fair Haven, Vermont. 1798. pp. 254, (2). 16mo.   AAS. JCB.

33758   —— — THE WORKS OF THE LATE DR. BENJAMIN FRANKLIN; CONSISTING OF HIS LIFE, WRITTEN BY HIMSELF: TOGETHER WITH ESSAYS, HUMOROUS, MORAL, AND LITERARY, CHIEFLY IN THE MANNER OF THE SPECTATOR.
New-York: Printed and sold by John Tiebout, No. 358 Pearl-Street. 1798. 2 vols. in one. pp. 184; 104, portrait. 16mo.   AAS. NYPL.

33759   THE FRANKLIN REPOSITORY. VOL. II. No. 38. TOTAL NO. 90. THURSDAY, JANUARY 4, [— VOL. III. No. 37. TOTAL NO. 141. THURSDAY, DECEMBER 27, 1798.]
Chambersburg: Published by Robert Harper. 1798. fol.

33760   FRASER, DONALD
A COLLECTION OF SELECT BIOGRAPHY: OR, THE BULWARK OF TRUTH: BEING A SKETCH OF THE LIVES AND TESTIMONIES OF MANY EMINENT LAYMEN, IN DIFFERENT COUNTRIES, WHO HAVE PROFESSED THEIR BELIEF IN, AND ATTACHMENT TO THE CHRISTIAN RELIGION,— WHETHER DISTINGUISHED AS STATESMEN, PATRIOTS, PHILOSOPHERS, &C.—TO WHICH ARE PREFIXED TWO LETTERS TO THOMAS PAINE, CONTAINING SOME IMPORTANT QUERIES AND REMARKS RELATIVE TO THE PROBABLE TENDENCY OF HIS AGE OF REASON. [Six lines of verse from] DRYDEN. BY D. FRASER: AUTHOR OF THE YOUNG GENTLEMAN AND LADY'S ASSISTANT, &C.
New-York: Printed for the Author, at the Literary Printing-Office. 1798. [*Copy-right secured.*] pp. vi, (1), [155], (9). 12mo.   AAS. NYPL.
Contains a nine page list of subscribers names.

33761   FREE AND ACCEPTED MASONS. GRAND ROYAL ARCH CHAPTER.
CONSTITUTION OF THE ROYAL ARCH CHAPTER, OF THE NORTHERN STATES OF AMERICA.
> *Hartford: Printed by br. Elisha Babcock.* 1798. pp. 12. 16mo.   AAS.

33762   FREE AND ACCEPTED MASONS. GRAND LODGE OF VERMONT.
THE CONSTITUTION, TOGETHER WITH THE BY-LAWS AND ORDINANCES OF THE GRAND LODGE OF VERMONT.
> *Printed in Bennington, by brother Anthony Haswell, A. L.* 5798. [1798.] pp. 8. 8vo.

33763   FREE AND ACCEPTED MASONS. GRAND LODGE OF VIRGINIA.
PROCEEDINGS OF THE GRAND LODGE OF VIRGINIA: HELD AT THE MASON'S HALL, IN THE CITY OF RICHMOND, ON MONDAY, THE 10TH DAY OF DECEMBER, A. L. 5798 — A. D. 1798
> *Richmond: Printed by T. Niconson* [*sic*] [1798.] pp. (36). 12mo.   LOC.

33764   FREE AND ACCEPTED MASONS. ROYAL ARCH CHAPTER.
NOTICE OF MEETING OF THE ROYAL CHAPTER OF ST. JOHN OF JERUSALEM, COMMONLY CALLED THE LODGE OF ROYAL ARCH SUPER EXCELLENT MASONS, NEWBURYPORT, [JANUARY 8, 5798] [Colophon:]
> [*Newburyport:*] *Printed by John Mycall.* [1798.] Broadside.   AAS.

33765   FREE AND ACCEPTED MASONS. LA SAGESSE. No. 2660.
TABLEAU DES F. F. QUI COMPOSENT LA LOGE PROVINCIALE FRANCAISE, SOUS LE TITRE DISTINCTIF DE LA SAGESSE: A L'ORIENT DE PORTSMOUTH, EN VIRGINIE, ETAT DE L'AMERIQUE SEPTENTRIONALE, A L'EPOQUE DE LA ST. JEAN, 5798.
> *Norfolk: Imprime par Willett & O'Conner.* 1798.

33766   FREEMAN'S JOURNAL. [Motto.] VOL. II. NUMBER 29. SATURDAY, JANUARY 6, [— VOL. III. NUMBER 28. SATURDAY, DECEMBER 29, 1798.]
> *Cincinnati: Printed by S. Freeman, and Son.* 1798. fol.

Before October, Samuel Freeman withdrew, and publication was continued in the name of his son, Edmund Freeman.

33767   FRIENDS, SOCIETY OF.
THE EPISTLE FROM THE YEARLY MEETING, HELD IN LONDON, BY ADJOURNMENTS, FROM THE 21ST TO THE 29TH OF THE FIFTH MONTH, 1798, INCLUSIVE; TO THE QUARTERLY AND MONTHLY MEETING OF FRIENDS IN GREAT BRITAIN, IRELAND, AND ELSEWHERE.
> [*Philadelphia:* 1798.] pp. [2.] fol.   AAS.

33768   —— A TESTIMONY OF THE MONTHLY MEETING OF FRIENDS, AT PYRMONT IN WESTPHALIA, GERMANY, CONCERNING JOHN PEMBERTON, OF PHILADELPHIA IN NORTH AMERICA: WITH HIS EPISTLE TO THE INHABITANTS OF AMSTERDAM. [AND, AN APPENDIX, BY THOMAS WILKINSON.] [Two lines from] NUMB. xxiii, 10.
> *Philadelphia: Printed by Henry Tuckniss.* 1798. pp. 36. 12mo.   JCB.

Reprinted in London, and Dublin, in 1798.

33769   FRIENDS AND FELLOW CITIZENS! TOMORROW WILL BE AN IMPORTANT DAY INDEED; ON YOUR CONDUCT WILL DEPEND WHETHER OR NOT WE ARE TO BE OVERWHELMED, IN THE LANGUAGE HELD OUT BY THE PARTY "WITH THE IMPETUOSITY OF THE VICTORIOUS BUONAPARTE." [Advocating the re-election of Benjamin R. Morgan as senator.] A PENNSYLVANIAN.
> [*Philadelphia: February 21st,* 1798.] Broadside. 4to.   HSP.

33770   FROTHINGHAM'S LONG-ISLAND HERALD. "EYE NATURE'S WALKS, SHOOT FOLLY AS IT FLIES,—AND CATCH THE MANNERS LIVING AS THEY RISE." VOL. VI. NUMB. 267. MONDAY, JANUARY 1, [—VOL. VII. NUMB. 319. MONDAY, DECEMBER 31, 1798.]

     Sag-Harbor: Printed by David Frothingham. 1798. fol.

33771   FULLING, THOMAS

THE ASTRONOMICAL REPOSITORY, OR THE FAMILY CALENDAR, FOR THE YEAR OF OUR LORD, 1799, CALCULATED FOR THE TOWN OF BOSTON, BUT WILL SERVE FOR THE NEIGHBORING STATES; CONTAINING EVERY THING NECESSARY FOR AN ALMANACK. BY THOMAS FULLING, A. M.

     Boston: Printed and sold at Edes' Printing-Office, Kilby-Street. [1798.] pp. (24). 12mo.

33772   FURLONG, LAWRENCE

THE AMERICAN COAST PILOT; CONTAINING THE COURSES AND DISTANCES BETWEEN THE PRINCIPAL HARBOURS, CAPES AND HEADLANDS, FROM PASSAMAQUODDY THROUGH THE GULPH OF FLORIDA, WITH DIRECTIONS FOR SAILING INTO THE SAME, DESCRIBING THE SOUNDINGS, BEARINGS OF THE LIGHT-HOUSES AND BEACONS FROM THE ROCKS, SHOALS, LEDGES, &C. TOGETHER WITH THE COURSES AND DISTANCES FROM CAPE-COD AND CAPE-ANN TO GEORGE'S-BANK, THROUGH THE SOUTH AND EAST CHANNELS, AND THE SETTING OF THE CURRENTS, WITH THE LATITUDES AND LONGITUDES OF THE PRINCIPAL HARBOURS ON THE COAST. TOGETHER WITH A TIDE TABLE. BY CAPT. LAWRENCE FURLONG. CORRECTED AND IMPROVED BY THE MOST EXPERI- ENCED PILOTS IN THE UNITED STATES— ALSO, INFORMATION TO MASTERS OF VES- SELS, WHEREIN THE MANNER OF TRANSACTING BUSINESS AT THE CUSTOM-HOUSES IS FULLY ELUCIDATED. SECOND EDITION, LARGELY IMPROVED. PUBLISHED ACCORDING TO ACT OF CONGRESS.

     Newburyport (Massachusetts): Printed by Edmund M. Blunt, (Proprietor.) Sold by all the Booksellers and Ship-chandlers in the United States.—1798. pp. (1), 172, (2), (2), (2), (2), [177]–239, (1). 8vo.   AAS. DEGL. JCB. LOC. NYPL.

     147th Massachusetts District Copyright, issued to Edmund March Blunt, as Proprietor, 22 June, 1798.

33773   GALLAGHER, S. F.

AN ORATION ON THE ANNIVERSARY OF THE ORPHAN ESTABLISHMENT, IN CHARLESTON, SOUTH-CAROLINA. DELIVERED BY S. F. GALLAGHER, ON THE 18TH OCTOBER, 1798, PUBLISHED AT THE REQUEST OF THE COMMISSIONERS OF THE ORPHAN HOUSE. [Monogram.]

     Printed by W. P. Young & T. C. Cox, Charleston. 1798. pp. 23. 8vo.   CLS.

33774   —— A SERMON PREACHED BY THE REV. MR. S. F. GALLAGHER, ON THE 9TH OF MAY, 1798, OBSERVED AS A DAY OF FASTING AND PRAYER, TO IMPLORE THE DIVINE AID AND PROTECTION IN FAVOR OF THE UNITED STATES.

     Charleston: Printed for Bailey, Waller & Bailey, Broad-street. 1798.

33775   GALLATIN, ABRAHAM ALBERT ALPHONSE   1761–1849

THE SPEECH OF ALBERT GALLATIN, DELIVERED IN THE HOUSE OF REPRESENTATIVES OF THE UNITED STATES, ON THE FIRST DAY OF MARCH, 1798, UPON THE FOREIGN INTERCOURSE BILL.

     [Philadelphia: Printed by Richard Folwell, 1798.] pp. (28). 8vo.

                     AAS. BA. HSP. JCB. MHS. NYHS. NYPL.

33776   —— — A CORRECT COPY OF THE SPEECH OF ALBERT GALLATIN, DELIVERED IN THE HOUSE OF REPRESENTATIVES OF THE UNITED STATES ON THE FIRST [of March] INSTANT UPON THE FOREIGN INTERCOURSE BILL: TO WHICH IS ADDED, A NOTE, COMPARING THE FUNDING SYSTEM OF THE UNITED STATES, WITH THAT OF GREAT- BRITAIN.

     Philadelphia: Printed by B. F. Bache, 1798.

33777   GALLATIN, ABRAHAM ALBERT ALPHONSE, continued.
—— — THE SPEECH OF ALBERT GALLATIN, DELIVERED IN THE HOUSE OF REPRE-
SENTATIVES OF THE UNITED STATES, ON THE FIRST OF MARCH, 1798, UPON THE
FOREIGN INTERCOURSE BILL. SECOND EDITION. WITH AN APPENDIX.

Philadelphia: Printed by Richard Folwell, No. 33, Carter's-Alley. 1798. pp.
(48). 8vo.   AAS. BA. HC. HSP. JCB. ICP. LOC. MHS. NYHS. NYPL.

Published April 14, 1798. "Printed on large letter, good paper, and
contains an appendix never before published."

33778   THE GAMUT, OR SCALE OF MUSIC, ADAPTED FOR THE USE OF BEGINNERS IN PSALMODY.
Greenfield: Printed by Thomas Dickman. 1798.

"By the gross, dozen or single."

33779   GARDINER, JOHN SYLVESTER JOHN   1765–1830
REMARKS ON THE JACOBINIAD: REVISED AND CORRECTED BY THE AUTHOR. PART
SECOND. [Eight lines of verse.]
Printed at Boston. 1798. pp. xi, (1), 10–56. 12mo.
AAS. BA. HSP. JCB. LOC. MHS. NYPL.

The first part was printed at Boston in 1795. The Advertisement states
that the Editors purchased the copyright from the Proprietor of the
Federal Orrery, and at the solicitation of many literary gentlemen, re-
published this second part corrected and enlarged from the original
manuscript. The long Dedication to Thomas Jefferson was sent by an
unknown hand and had never before been published. The Ode ["Benjamin's feast,"] at the end, though it had appeared in the Gazette of the
United States, was, as it celebrated a domestic occurrence, subjoined
by particular desire.

33780   GAZETTE FRANCAISE. No. 285. LUNDI, 1 JANVIER, [— No. 436. LUNDI, 31 DE-
CEMBRE, 1798.]
Imprimee par Claude Parisot a New-York, Pearl-Street, No. 51. 1798. 4to.
HC.

33781   GAZETTE OF THE UNITED STATES, AND PHILADELPHIA DAILY ADVERTISER. VOL.
NUMBER 1656. MONDAY, JANUARY 1, [—VOL. XIV. NUMBER 1961. MONDAY,
DECEMBER 31, 1798.]
[Philadelphia: Published] By John Fenno, No. 119, Chesnut Street. 1798.
fol.   AAS. BA. HSP. LCP. LOC.

John Fenno died from yellow fever, September 14th, and publication
was continued from September 17th, in the name of his son, John Ward
Fenno.

33782   THE GENERAL MAGAZINE, AND IMPARTIAL REVIEW OF KNOWLEDGE, AND ENTER-
TAINMENT, FOR JUNE, [— AUGUST,] 1798. VOLUME THE FIRST. [Seal.]
*Baltimore: Printed by A. Hanna, & H. Greene, No. 27, Market-street, next
door to the Vendue Store.* 1798. pp. (2), 112, 2 plates. 8vo. AAS. LOC. NYHS. NYPL.

33783   GENERAL REMARKS ON THE PROCEEDINGS LATELY HAD IN THE ADJACENT COUNTRY,
RELATIVE TO INFIDELITY: COMPREHENDING THE CONDUCT OF THOSE PERSONS WHO
SIGNED AN ADDRESS TO THE FORMER EDITOR OF THE MIRROR; THE WRITINGS OF
D. N. THE CONDUCT OF THE GOSHEN PRINTER; TOGETHER WITH SOME GENERAL
OBSERVATIONS ON THE CONSEQUENCES OF PERSECUTION.
Newburgh: Printed by David Denniston, 1798. 8vo.   LOC.

AUCTION
VALUES

33784   THE GENIUS OF LIBERTY. VOL. I. NO. 1. THURSDAY, MAY 24, [— No. 32. THURS-
DAY, DECEMBER 27, 1798.]

*Morris-Town: Printed and published by Jacob Mann, nearly opposite the
Academy. 1798.* fol.

Established, as a weekly, by Jacob Mann, in continuation of the *Morris
County Gazette*, and continued by him to the issue for 30 April, 1801,
when he disposed of his interests to Henry P. Russell, who continued
publication into the year 1808, changing its title, some time in 1806, to
The Genius of Liberty, and Morris Advertiser. Russell transferred
publication, in 1808, to Charles Russell, and about the same time the sub-
title was dropped. Before June, 1810, Henry P. Russell resumed publication, and in August of the same year the size of the paper was reduced
to quarto, this arrangement continuing until publication ceased with
the issue for July 30, 1811. Being succeeded by the *Morris-Town Herald*.

33785   THE GENIUS OF LIBERTY; AND FREDERICKSBURG & FALMOUTH ADVERTISER. VOL. I.
NO. 12. FRIDAY, JANUARY 5, [—VOL. II. NO. 63. FRIDAY, DECEMBER 28, 1798.]

Fredericksburg, (Va.) Printed by Mercer & Carter. 1798. fol.

33786   GENLIS, STÉPHANIE FÉLICITÉ BRULART DUCREST DE ST. AUBIN, comtesse DE
SYLVAN. THE SHEPHERD TWAIN. A NEW SONG. COMPOSED BY R. TAYLOR. THE
WORDS TAKEN FROM "THE KNIGHTS OF THE SWAN." WRITTEN BY THE COUNTESS
DE GENLIS.

Philadelphia: Published by B. Carr, at his Repository, Market Street. 1798.

33787   GEORGE, DANIEL

THE FARMERS' ALMANACK, FOR THE YEAR OF OUR LORD 1799: BEING THE THIRD
YEAR AFTER BISSEXTILE, OR LEAP YEAR: AND THE TWENTY THIRD OF AMERICAN
INDEPENDENCE. ADAPTED TO THE DISTRICT OF MAINE. CALCULATED FOR THE
MERIDIAN OF PORTLAND. LAT. 43 DEG. 43 MIN. NORTH.

Printed at Portland, by Baker & George. [1798.] pp. (36). 12mo. AAS. HC.

33788   THE GEORGETOWN GAZETTE. VOL. I. NO. 1. TUESDAY, MAY 8, [— No. 52. FRI-
DAY, DECEMBER 28, 1798.]

*Georgetown, (S. C.)—Printed every Tuesday [and Friday] by Elliott & Burd,
at five dollars per ann. payable half yearly. 1798.* fol.   CLS.

Established, as a weekly, and semi-weekly, by Robert Elliott, and John
Burd, and continued by them to the end of the year 1799, when Elliott withdrew, "as the income from the paper was not sufficient to
compensate two editors." With the issue for 7 September, 1798, publication was made semi-weekly, changing again to weekly 2 January,
1799, and back again to semi-weekly. 1 January, 1800, when John
Burd became sole publisher up to his death, 23 October, 1801. With
the issue for 28 October, Claudius Beleurgey became printer and publisher, up to the issue for 5 December, 1801, when he withdrew and for
a short time the paper was printed for the heirs of the late John Burd.
In 1802, the Gazette was printed by Andrew M'Farlan up to his death
in June, 1806; and, on 8 October, it was purchased, and published, by
Francis M. Baxter, as the *Georgetown Gazette, and Commercial Advertiser*, certainly up to 12 December, 1810; then followed, apparently, a
suspension of publication, until early in the year 1813, Thomas Tolman
continued, without change in volume numbering, the *Carolina American, and Georgetown Gazette*, of which only two numbers, in April, have
been located. In April, 1814, it was published by Edward B. Cooke, as
the *Georgetown Gazette;* and, in June, 1816, by Eleazer Waterman, as,
The Georgetown Gazette, and Mercantile Advertiser, up to 28 June, 1817,
when publication was discontinued. In October, 1817, Waterman established, in continuation, the *Winyaw Intelligencer*.

33789   GEORGIA. State.

ACTS OF THE GENERAL ASSEMBLY OF THE STATE OF GEORGIA: PASSED AT LOUIS-
VILLE, IN JANUARY AND FEBRUARY, 1798.

> *Augusta: Printed by A. M'Millan, Printer to the State.* 1798. pp. 28. fol.
> DeRGL.

33790   —— THE CONSTITUTION OF THE STATE OF GEORGIA. AS REVISED, AMENDED AND
COMPILED, BY THE CONVENTION OF THE STATE, AT LOUISVILLE, ON THE THIRTIETH
DAY OF MAY, M,DCC,XCVIII.

> *Louisville: Printed by A. M'Millan, Printer to the State.* M,DCC,XCVIII.
> pp. [24.] 8vo.   AAS. LOC.

33791   GEORGIA. THE AUGUSTA CHRONICLE AND GAZETTE OF THE STATE. [Motto.] VOL.
XII. No. 587. SATURDAY, JANUARY 6, [— VOL. XIII. No. 638. SATURDAY, DE-
CEMBER 29, 1798.]

> *Augusta: Printed by John E. Smith, Printer to the State.* 1798. fol.   GHS.

33792   GEORGIA GAZETTE. (No. 741). FRIDAY, JANUARY 5, [— No. 792. THURSDAY, DE-
CEMBER 27. 1798.]

> *Savannah: Printed by M. Johnson and Co.* 1798. fol.

Beginning July 12th, publication was made on Thursdays.

33793   DIE GERMANTAUNER ZEITUNG. NUM 390. DIENSTAG, DEN 3 JANUAR, [— NUM.
442. DIENSTAG, DEN 26 DECEMBER, 1798.]

> *Diese Zeitung wird wochentlich Dienstag Nachmittags herausgegeben von
> Michael Billmeyer, Buchdrucker, zu Germantaun,* . . . 1798. 4to.

33794   GIBSON, JAMES

ATLAS MINIMUS: OR, A NEW SET OF POCKET MAPS, OF VARIOUS EMPIRES, KINGDOMS
AND STATES, WITH GEOGRAPHICAL EXTRACTS RELATIVE TO EACH. DRAWN AND
ENGRAVED, BY J. GIBSON, FROM THE BEST AUTHORITIES. A NEW EDITION, REVISED,
CORRECTED AND IMPROVED.

> *Philadelphia: Printed for Mathew Carey, No.* 118, *Market-Street.* April 14,
> 1798. pp. (90), 41 maps. sq. 24mo.   AAS.

33795   GIBSON, ROBERT

A TREATISE OF PRACTICAL SURVEYING; WHICH IS DEMONSTRATED FROM ITS FIRST
PRINCIPLES. WHEREIN EVERY THING THAT IS USEFUL AND CURIOUS IN THAT ART,
IS FULLY CONSIDERED & EXPLAINED. PARTICULARLY THREE NEW AND VERY CON-
CISE METHODS FOR DETERMINING THE ARREAS OF RIGHT-LINED FIGURES ARITH-
METICALLY, OR BY CALCULATION, AS WELL AS THE GEOMETRICAL ONES HERETOFORE
TREATED OF. THE WHOLE ILLUSTRATED WITH COPPER-PLATES. THE EIGHTH
EDITION. BY ROBERT GIBSON, TEACHER OF THE MATHEMATICS. WITH ALTERA-
TIONS AND AMENDMENTS, ADAPTED TO THE USE OF AMERICAN SURVEYORS.

> *New-York: Printed by William A. Davis & Co. for Gaine & Ten Eyck, T.
> Allen, S. Campbell, E. Duykinck & Co. N. Judah, T. & J. Swords, B. Gomez, New
> York; M. Carey, Philadelphia, and C. R. & G. Webster, Albany.* 1798. pp. 452.
> 13 plates. 8vo.   AAS.

AUCTION
VALUES

33796   GIFFORD, John, assumed name of John Richards Greene   1758–1818
The History of France; from the earliest times, to the complete establishment of the Republic. The ancient part, and modern, down to the
commencement of the Revolution, from the French of Velly, Villaret,
Garnier, Mezeray, Daniel, and other eminent historians: with notes
critical and explanatory. By John Gifford, esq. The Revolutionary part,
collected from the best English and French authorities, by William
Duane. Vol. iv.
> *Philadelphia: Printed by Stewart and Rowson, No. 9, Cherry-Street.* 1798.
> pp. (2), 589, (6), 11 plates, map, plan. 4to.   AAS. LOC.

> The first volume was published in 1796, and the second and third vol-
> umes in 1797.

33797   —— A Residence in France, during the years 1792, 1793, 1794. and 1795;
described in a series of letters from an English lady: with general and
incidental remarks on the French character and manners. Prepared for
the press by John Gifford, esq. author of the History of France, Letter
to lord Lauderdale, Letter to the hon. T. Erskine, &c. First American
edition. [One line of French from] Du Belloy.
> *Elizabeth-Town: Printed by Shepard Kollock for Cornelius Davis, No. 94,
> Water-Street, New-York.* 1798. pp. 517. 8vo.   AAS. JCB. LOC. NYPL.

33798   GILDERSLEEVE, Cyrus   1769–1838
A Century sermon, delivered at Midway, January 1st, 1797. A copy of which
being requested, by the selectmen of the Society, in order to be printed,
was handed to them by the Author. The rev. Cyrus Gildersleeve, a. m.
pastor. [Two lines from] Psalms 83,1.
> *Savannah: Printed by Seymour & Woolhopter, on the Bay.* [1798.] pp. 32;
> 23. 16mo.   DeRGL. LOC. NYPL.

> *Second title:* A New-year sermon, delivered at Midway, January 1st, 1798.
> A copy of which being requested, by the selectmen of the Society, that
> it might be printed, with the Century sermon, was handed to them by
> the Author. The rev. Cyrus Gildersleeve, a. m. pastor. . . .
>> *Savannah: Printed by Seymour & Woolhopter, on the Bay.* [1798.] pp. 23.

33799   GILLIES, John   1712–1796
Memoirs of the life of the reverend George Whitefield, m. a. late chaplain to the right honorable the countess of Huntingdon: in which every
circumstance worthy of notice, both in his private and public character,
is recorded. Faithfully selected from his original papers, journals and
letters. Illustrated by a variety of interesting and entertaining anecdotes, from the best authorities. With a particular account of his
death and funeral: and extracts from the sermons, which were preached
on that occasion. Compiled by the rev. John Gillies, d. d. To which is
now added, an extract from mr. Whitefield's tracts. [Nine lines of Scripture texts.]
> *New-London, (Conn.) Printed by S. Green, for Cornelius Davis, N. York.*
> 1798. pp. xii, 275. 12mo.   AAS. BM. JCB. LOC. NL. NPYL.

33800   GIRARDIN, Louis Hue   1771–1825
Caption title: Education. . . .
> [*Signed, and dated:* L. H. Girardin. Dumfries, July 21st, 1798.] pp. (4).
> 4to.   NYPL.
> Circular, of the formation of a school at Dumfries, Virginia, for teaching
> languages and other subjects belonging to a course of liberal education.

33801   GISBORNE, THOMAS   1758–1846
AN ENQUIRY INTO THE DUTIES OF THE FEMALE SEX. BY THOMAS GISBORNE, M. A.
London, Printed, Philadelphia, Re-printed and sold by James Humphreys, North Third-Street. 1798. pp. (2), (2), (2), 312. 12mo.   AAS.

33802   GODDARD, JOSIAH
A NEW AND BEAUTIFUL COLLECTION OF HYMNS AND SPIRITUAL SONGS : SELECTED FROM
ALL AUTHORS THAT ARE ENTERTAINING, SPIRITUAL, AND DIVINE; FOR THE USE OF
CHURCHES, RELIGIOUS SOCIETIES AND CHRISTIAN CONFERENCES; AND IN PARTICULAR
FOR THE COMFORT AND EDIFICATION OF PRIVATE CHRISTIANS, FOR WHICH IT IS
MOSTLY DESIGNED. BY JOSIAH GODDARD. [Three lines of Scripture texts.] PUB-
LISHED ACCORDING TO ACT OF CONGRESS.
Conway: Printed by Theodore Leonard, for the Author. M,DCC,XCVIII.
pp. 396, (12). 12mo.   AAS. NYPL.

33803   GOETHE, JOHANN WOLFGANG VON   1749–1832
WERTER AND CHARLOTTE. THE SORROWS OF WERTER. A GERMAN STORY. TO WHICH
IS ANNEXED, THE LETTERS OF CHARLOTTE TO A FEMALE FRIEND, DURING HER
CONNECTION WITH WERTER. [By W. James.] THE WHOLE OF BOTH WORKS COM-
PLETE IN ONE VOLUME.
*Boston: For Thomas and Andrews. Sold at their Bookstore No. 45 Newbury-
Street; by I. Thomas, Worcester; by Thomas, Andrews and Penniman, Albany;
and by Thomas, Andrews, and Butler, Baltimore. October,* 1798. *Printing-Office,
No. 20 Union-Street.* pp. 147; [cxlix] — 284. 12mo.   AAS. HEH.

The Authorship of the "Letters of Charlotte" was divulged in a letter
to Cadell, the Scotch publisher, from W. James, now in the W. A. Speck
collection at Yale University.

33804   GOETZ, JOHANN NEPOMUCK
MORALPHILSOPHISCHE REDE ÜBER AUFRECHTERHALTUNG DES STAATES. VON JOHANN
GÖTZ, VORMALIGEM PROFESSOR UND PREDIGER AN DER KAISERL. KÖNIGL. ACA-
DEMIE ZU WIENERISCH NEUSTADT.
Philadelphia: Gedruckt bey H. Schweitzer. 1798. pp. 22. 8vo.

33805   GOLDSMITH, OLIVER   1728–1774
DR. GOLDSMITH'S ROMAN HISTORY, ABRIDGED BY HIMSELF. FOR THE USE OF SCHOOLS.
*Philadelphia: Printed for Thomas Dobson, at the Stone House No. 41, S.
Second-Street.* 1798. pp. 327. 12mo.   AAS. JCB.

33806   GOODFELLOW, ROBIN, pseudonym.
POOR ROBIN'S ALMANAC FOR THE YEAR 1799. BY ROBIN GOODFELLOW.
Philadelphia: Printed and sold by John M'Culloch. [1798.]   LOC.

33807   GOODRICH, JOHN   1753–1800
THE CIVIL AND EXECUTIVE OFFICERS' ASSISTANT; CONTAINING THE FORMS OF BONDS,
BILLS, DEEDS, LETTERS OF ATTORNEY, POLICIES OF INSURANCE, RELEASES, WILLS
WRITS, PLEAS, OFFICERS RETURNS, AND JUSTICES RECORDS OF COURRT [*sic*]. WITH
THE POWER AND DUTY OF JUSTICES OF THE PEACE, AS CONTAINED IN THE LAWS OF
THE STATE OF CONNECTICUT, AND EXHIBITING THE DUTY AND PROVINCE OF SELECT-
MEN, CONSTABLES, GRAND-JURORS, &C. WITH AN APPENDIX, CONTAINING A CON-
CISE MODE OF CASTING INTEREST, KEEPING TOWN ACCOMPTS, AND TRANSACTING
PUBLIC BUSINESS WITH FACILITY AND ACCURACY. BY JOHN GOODRICH, ESQ. THE
SECOND EDITION, REVISED, CORRECTED, AND CONSIDERABLY ENLARGED. PUBLISHED
ACCORDING TO ACT OF CONGRESS.
Hartford: Printed by Hudson & Goodwin. M,DCC,XCVIII. pg. xii, 239.
12mo.   AAS. NYPL. YC.

AUCTION
VALUES

33808   THE GOSHEN REPOSITORY. "WHILE DECENCY AND CANDOUR GUIDE THE PEN —
OUR PRESS SHALL SCORN THE IMPERIOUS FROWN OF MEN." VOL. IX. NUMBER 468.
TUESDAY, JANUARY 2, [VOL. X. NUMBER 517. TUESDAY, DECEMBER 25, 1798.]

> *Published every Tuesday, by John G. & William Hurtin, in Goshen, (Orange
> County) . . . 1798. fol.*

After April, publication was made in the name of John G. Hurtin, only.

33809   THE GOSPORT TRAGEDY OR THE PERJURED SHIP CARPENTER. TO WHICH IS ADDED,
BONNY WULLY. A SCOTCH BALLAD. [Woodcut.]

> *New-York: Printed for the Hawkers.*—1798. pp. 8. 16mo.   **AAS.**

33810   GOUGH, JOHN   1721–1791
PRACTICAL ARITHMETICK. IN FOUR BOOKS. I. WHOLE NUMBERS, WEIGHTS AND MEAS-
SURES. II. FRACTIONS, VULGAR AND DECIMAL. III. MERCANTILE ARITHMETICK.
IV. EXTRACTION OF ROOTS, PROGRESSIONS, &C. EXTRACTED FROM THE LARGE AND
ENTIRE TREATISE, AND ADAPTED TO THE COMMERCE OF IRELAND, AS WELL AS THAT
OF GREAT-BRITAIN. FOR THE USE OF SCHOOLS. BY JOHN GOUGH, AUTHOR OF THE
PRACTICAL ENGLISH GRAMMAR. CAREFULLY REVISED BY THOMAS TELFAIR, PHIL-
OMATH. AND NOW FITTED TO THE COMMERCE OF AMERICA. WITH AN APPENDIX
OF ALGEBRA, BY THE LATE W. ATDINSON, OF BELFAST. [Double rule.]

> *Dublin: Printed:—Wilmington: Re-printed, and sold, by Peter Brynberg.*
> M,DCC,XCVIII. pp. 359. 12mo.   **LOC.**

33811   GOULD, JAMES   1770–1838
AN ORATION PRONOUNCED AT LITCHFIELD, ON THE ANNIVERSARY OF THE INDEPEND-
ENCE OF THE UNITED STATES OF AMERICA, IN THE YEAR M,DCC,XCVIII. BY
JAMES GOULD. [Printer's mark.]

> *[Litchfield:] Printed by T. Collier.* [1798.] pp. 32. 8vo.
>   **AAS. BA. CHS. LOC. NYPL. YC.**

"Most of the following pages were written in the year 1795, and pronounced on the anniversary of American independence, before the Cincinnati of Connecticut, at New-Haven."

33812   GRAY, ROBERT   1761–1822
A DISCOURSE DELIVERED IN DOVER NOVEMBER 15TH, 1798, A DAY OBSERVED AS
AN ANNIVERSARY THANKSGIVING. BY ROBERT GRAY, A. B. PASTOR OF THE CHURCH
OF CHRIST IN DOVER.

> *Dover: Printed by Samuel Bragg, jun. for the Subscribers.* 1798. pp. (2),
> 21. 8vo.   **BM. CLA. HC.**

33813   —— A SERMON DELIVERED AT HOPKINTON, BEFORE THE HON. GENERAL COURT OF
THE STATE OF NEW-HAMPSHIRE, AT THE ANNUAL ELECTION, HOLDEN ON THE FIRST
WEDNESDAY IN JUNE, 1798. BY ROBERT GRAY, A. B. PASTOR OF THE CHURCH OF
CHRIST IN DOVER.

> *Dover: Printed by Samuel Bragg, jun. for the General Court.* [1798.] pp.
> 29. 8vo.   **BM. JCB. LOC. NYHS. NYPL.**

Printed in an edition of five hundred and fifty copies.

33814   GREAT BRITAIN.
OFFICIAL ACCOUNT OF A GLORIOUS VICTORY. . . . ☞ BY THE FOREGOING ACCOUNT
IT APPEARS THAT THE GALLANT NELSON HAS RETURNED THE BRIBE MONEY WHICH
SOME OF THE BOSTON EDITORS LATELY MADE HIM RECEIVE FROM HIS ADVERSARY.
[Colophon:]

> *Baltimore, November 20, 1798.* Broadside.   **EI.**

33815   [Cut.] THE GRECIAN DAUGHTER, OR AN EXAMPLE OF A VIRTUOUS WIFE, WHO FED HER FATHER WITH HER OWN MILK.

Windsor: Printed [by Alden Spooner] for the flying Booksellers. [1798.] Broadside. fol.

33816   GREEN, ASHBEL.   1762–1848
OBEDIENCE TO THE LAW OF GOD, THE SURE AND INDISPENSABLE DEFENCE OF NATIONS. A DISCOURSE, DELIVERED IN THE SECOND PRESBYTERIAN CHURCH, IN THE CITY OF PHILADELPHIA, MAY 9TH, 1798, BEING THE DAY APPOINTED BY THE PRESIDENT OF THE UNITED STATES, TO BE OBSERVED AS A SEASON FOR SOLEMN HUMILIATION, FASTING AND PRAYER. BY ASHBEL GREEN, D.D. PASTOR OF THE AFORESAID CHURCH.

Philadelphia: Printed by John Ormrod, No. 41, Chesnut-Street. [1798.] pp. (51). 8vo.   AAS. CLA. HSP. JCB. LOC. MHS. NYPL. PU.

33817   GREEN, SAMUEL
GREEN'S ALMANACK AND REGISTER, FOR THE YEAR OF OUR LORD, 1799; BEING THE TWENTY-THIRD OF THE INDEPENDENCE OF THE UNITED STATES.

New-London: Printed and sold by Samuel Green. [1798.] pp. (131), (1). 24mo.   AAS. CHS. JCB. LOC. NYPL. YC.

33818   GREEN, THOMAS   1761–1814
GOSPEL MINISTERS, THE WORKMANSHIP OF JESUS CHRIST. A SERMON, DELIVERED IN THE BAPTIST MEETING-HOUSE AT REEDFIELD, AUGUST THE 8TH, 1798. AT THE ORDINATION OF MR. JAMES MURPHY, TO THE OFFICE OF AN EVANGELIST. BY THOMAS GREEN, V. D. M. PASTOR OF THE BAPTIST CHURCH, NORTH YARMOUTH, MAINE.

Portland, Maine: Printed by B. Titcomb. 1798. pp. 28. 8vo.   JCB. NYPL.

33819   THE GREEN MOUNTAIN PATRIOT. "INTELLIGENCE IS THE LIFE OF LIBERTY."— DAWES. VOL. I. No. 1. FRIDAY, FEBRUARY 23, [— No. 45. FRIDAY, DECEMBER 28, 1798.]

Printed at Peacham, Vermont, by Farley & Goss, . . . 1798. fol.   AAS.

Established, as a weekly, by Amos Farley, and Samuel Goss, and continued by them to the issue for 23 April, 1801, when the partnership was dissolved, and Samuel Goss became sole publisher up to 26 May, 1807, when publication was discontinued, and Goss removed to Montpelier. In August, 1809, Goss resumed publication of the Patriot, and continued it in connection with "The Watchman," at Montpelier, certainly to the issue for 27 January, 1810—the last, and only number located. The American Antiquarian Society possesses a nearly complete file of this paper.

33820   GREENFIELD GAZETTE. AN IMPARTIAL REGISTER OF THE TIMES. No. 50 OF VOL. VI. WHOLE NO. 310. WEDNESDAY, JANUARY 3, [— No. 50 OF VOL. VII. WHOLE NO. 362. MONDAY, DECEMBER 31, 1798.]

Printed and published on Mondays by Thomas Dickman at Greenfield, (Massachusetts). 1798. fol.   AAS.

With the issue for August 13th, Dickman disposed of his interests to Francis Barker, who enlarged the paper, and with the issue for September 1st, changed the sub-title to "A Register of genuine Federalism."

33821   GREENLEAF'S NEW YORK JOURNAL & PATRIOTIC REGISTER. [Motto.] VOL. LII. NUMB. 1. TOTAL NUMB. 3255. WEDNESDAY, JANUARY 3, [— NUMB. 80. TOTAL NUMB. 3338. SATURDAY, DECEMBER 29, 1798.]

New-York—Printed and published (on Wednesdays and Saturdays) by Thomas Greenleaf, at his Printing Office, No. 54, Wall-Street. . . . 1798. fol. AAS. NYHS.

Thomas Greenleaf died, from yellow fever, September 14th, and publication was suspended from September 16th, to November 7th, on which date it was resumed by his widow, Ann Greenleaf.

33823 GRIFFITH, John
THE GENTLEMAN & LADY'S COMPANION; CONTAINING, THE NEWEST [IX] COTILLIONS AND [XXXI] COUNTRY DANCES; TO WHICH ARE ADDED, INSTANCES OF ILL MANNERS, TO BE CAREFULLY AVOIDED BY YOUTH OF BOTH SEXES. [Three lines from] 2 SAM. VI. 14. SECOND EDITION.

Stonington-Port. Printed by Samuel Trumbull, for John Trumbull, Printer, Norwich. 1798. pp. 23. 24mo.　　　　　　　　　　　　AAS. JCB. LOC.

33824 GRIMKE, John Faucherand　　　　　　　　　　　　1752–1819
CHARGE, DELIVERED TO THE GRAND JURIES OF BEAUFORT AND ORANGEBURGH DISTRICTS, BY THE HONORABLE J. F. GRIMKE, ONE OF THE ASSOCIATE JUDGES OF THE STATE OF SOUTH-CAROLINA, NOVEMBER TERM, 1798.

Charleston: Printed by Benjamin F. Timothy. MDCCXCVIII. pp. (2), 21. 8vo.　　　　　　　　　　　　　　　　　　　　　　　　LOC.

33825 GRISWOLD, Alexander Viets　　　　　　　　　　　　1766–1843
A DISCOURSE DELIVERED AT LITCHFIELD, IN THE SOCIETY OF NORTHFIELD, ON THE 12TH DAY OF MARCH, 1797; OCCASIONED BY THE DEATH OF MRS. LUCY BLAKSLEE, [*sic*] THE WIFE OF MR. DAVID BLAKSLEE [*sic.*] BY ALEXANDER V. GRISWOLD.

Printed at Litchfield, by T. Collier. [1797.] pp. 18. 8vo.　　CHS. LHS.

33826 —— A DISCOURSE, DELIVERED BEFORE THE AURORA LODGE OF FREE MASONS, AT HARWINTON, JUNE 27, 1797. BY ALEXANDER V. GRISWOLD, RECTOR OF ST. MATTHEW'S CHURCH IN PLYMOUTH. [Ornament.]

Hartford: Printed by Hudson & Goodwin. M,DCC,XCVIII. pp. 20. 8vo. AAS.

33827 —— A SHORT SKETCH, OF THE LIFE OF MR. LENT MUNSON. "HONOR AND SHAME FROM NO CONDITION RISE; ACT WELL YOUR PART;—THERE ALL THE HONOR LIES."

Litchfield: Printed by Thomas Collier. [1797.] pp. 8. 8vo.

33828 GRISWOLD, Stanley　　　　　　　　　　　　　　1763–1815
A STATEMENT OF THE SINGULAR MANNER OF PROCEEDING OF THE REV. ASSOCIATION, OF THE SOUTH PART OF LITCHFIELD COUNTY, IN AN ECCLESIASTICAL PROSECUTION BY THEM INSTITUTED AGAINST THE REV. STANLEY GRISWOLD, PASTOR OF THE FIRST CHURCH OF CHRIST IN NEW-MILFORD; WHO, WITHOUT BEING HEARD IN HIS OWN DEFENCE, WAS BY THEM SENTENCED TO AN EXCLUSION FROM THEIR ASSOCIATE COMMUNION. "AWAY WITH THIS MAN." BIBLE. TOGETHER WITH A SUBSEQUENT ADDRESS TO SAID ASSOCIATION, BY NEHEMIAH STRONG, ESQ. OF SAID NEW-MILFORD, LATE PROFESSOR OF NATURAL PHILOSOPHY, &C. AT YALE COLLEGE. TO WHICH IS ADDED A SHORT APPENDIX.

Hartford: Printed by Elisha Babcock. 1798. pp. [32.] 8vo.
AAS. LOC. MHS. UTS. YC.

33829 GUARDIAN; OR, NEW-BRUNSWICK ADVERTISER. NUM. 10 OF VOL. VI. WHOLE NUM. 270. TUESDAY, JANUARY 2, [— NUM. 9 OF VOL. VII. WHOLE NUM. 321. TUESDAY, DECEMBER 25, 1798.]

New-Brunswick, New-Jersey: Printed by Abraham Blauvelt, in Albany-Street. 1798. fol.　　　　　　　　　　　　　　　　　　　　　　AAS.

33830 THE GUARDIAN OF FREEDOM. WITH IMPARTIALITY FOR OUR GUIDE WE STUDY TO
BE USEFUL. NO. 1 OF VOL. I. THURSDAY, MAY 17, [— NO. 33 OF VOL. I. THURS-
DAY, DECEMBER 27, 1798.]
> *Frankfort, (Kentucky): Printed by John Bradford & Son, at the Capitol.*
> 1798. fol.

> Established, as a weekly, by John Bradford, and James M. Bradford,
> and continued by them into September, 1799, when John Bradford with-
> drew, and James M. Bradford continued publication, with a new serial
> numbering, to 25 January, 1804, when he sold his interests to Thomas
> Anderson whom he had chosen as his successor. Without making any
> issue, Anderson disposed of the establishment to Elijah Conway Berry,
> who continued publication certainly to 25 March, 1805 — the last
> number located.

33831 HAHN, JOHN
OBSERVATIONS AND EXPERIMENTS ON THE USE OF ENEMATA, AND THE EXTERNAL
APPLICATION OF MEDICINES TO THE HUMAN BODY; BEING AN INAUGURAL THESIS,
SUBMITTED TO THE EXAMINATION OF THE REV. JOHN EWING, S. T. P. PROVOST, THE
TRUSTEES, AND MEDICAL FACULTY OF THE UNIVERSITY OF PENNSYLVANIA, ON THE
22D DAY OF MAY, 1798, FOR THE DEGREE OF DOCTOR OF MEDICINE. BY JOHN
HAHN, OF PENNSYLVANIA, HONORARY MEMBER OF THE PHILADELPHIA MEDICAL
AND CHEMICAL SOCIETIES.
> *Philadelphia: Printed by Stephen C. Ustick, 1798.* pp. (2), 30. 8vo.
> AAS. LOC. SGO.

33832 HAIL PATRIOTS ALL. A NEW PATRIOTIC SONG.
> *Boston: Printed & sold by P. A. von Hagen jun. and Co. at their Musical
> Magazine, No. 62. Newbury Street.* 1798.

33833 HALL'S WILMINGTON GAZETTE. VOL. II. NO. 53. THURSDAY, JANUARY 4, [NO. 104.
THURSDAY, DECEMBER 27, 1798.]
> *Wilmington, N. C. Printed by Allmand Hall.* 1798. fol.

> Beginning in January, 1799, the title was changed to *The Wilmington
> Gazette;* enlarged, and printed twice a week.

33834 HALYBURTON, THOMAS   1674–1712
NATURAL RELIGION INSUFFICIENT, AND REVEALED NECESSARY, TO MAN'S HAPPINESS
IN HIS PRESENT STATE: OR, A RATIONAL ENQUIRY INTO THE PRINCIPLES OF THE
MODERN DEISTS; WHERIN IS LARGELY DISCOVERED THEIR UTTER INSUFFICIENCY TO
ANSWER THE GREAT ENDS OF RELIGION, AND THE WEAKNESS OF THEIR PLEADINGS
FOR THE SUFFICIENCY OF NATURE'S LIGHT TO ETERNAL HAPPINESS: AND PARTIC-
ULARLY THE WRITINGS OF THE LATE LEARNED LORD HERBERT, THE GREAT PATRON
OF DEISM, TO WIT, HIS BOOKS DE VERITATE, DE RELIGIONE GENTILIUM, AND
RELIGIO LAICI, IN SO FAR AS THEY ASSERT NATURE'S LIGHT ABLE TO CONDUCT US
TO FUTURE BLESSEDNESS ARE CONSIDERED, AND FULLY ANSWERED. TO WHICH IS
ADDED AN ESSAY ON THE TRUE GROUND OF FAITH. BY THE LATE REVEREND MR.
THOMAS HALYBURTON, PROFESSOR OF DIVINITY IN THE UNIVERSITY OF ST. AN-
DREWS. [Six lines of quotations.]
> *Philadelphia: Printed by Hogan & M'Elroy, No. 1, North Third-Street, and
> sold by A. Cunningham, Washington, (Penn.) A. M'Donald, Northumberland; C.
> Davis, New-York; and by J. M'Culloch, and the Publishers, Philadelphia.* 1798.
> pp. xxiv, (41)–464. 8vo.
> AAS. JCB.

> Preface signed James Hog. Corrected by the Rev. Dr. Charles Nisbet,
> President of Dickinson College. Contains, a four-page list of Subscribers'
> names.

33835   HAMILTON, JOSEPH
OCCASIONAL OBSERVATIONS ON THE SMALL-POX, OR THE TRAVELLER'S POCKET-DOCTOR.
BY JOSEPH HAMILTON, PHYSICIAN.
New-York: 1798.
70th New York District Copyright, issued to Joseph Hamilton, as Author, 3 December, 1798.

33836   HAMPSHIRE GAZETTE. VOL. XII. NUMB. 592. WEDNESDAY, JANUARY 3, [VOL. XIII. NUMB. 643. WEDNESDAY, DECEMBER 26, 1798.]
Printed at Northampton (Massachusetts,) by William Butler. 1798. fol.   MHS.

33837   HAENDEL, GEORG FRIEDRICH   1685–1759
HANDEL'S WATER MUSIC.
New-York: [1798.]

33838   HARPER, ROBERT GOODLOE   1765–1825
Half-title: A LETTER FROM ROBERT G. HARPER, OF SOUTH CAROLINA, TO ONE OF HIS CONSTITUENTS.
Title: A SHORT ACCOUNT OF THE PRINCIPAL PROCEEDINGS OF CONGRESS, IN THE LATE SESSION, AND A SKETCH OF THE STATE OF AFFAIRS BETWEEN THE UNITED STATES AND FRANCE IN JULY, 1798: IN A LETTER FROM ROBERT GOODLOE HARPER, OF SOUTH CAROLINA, TO ONE OF HIS CONSTITUENTS.
Philadelphia: Published by William Cobbett. August, 1798. pp. [22.] 8vo.
Reprinted in London in 1798.   AAS. BA. CLS. HC. JCB. LCP. LOC. MHS. NYPL. PU.

33839   —— MR. HARPER'S SPEECH ON THE FOREIGN INTERCOURSE BILL, IN REPLY TO MR. NICHOLAS AND MR. GALLATIN. DELIVERED IN THE COMMITTEE OF THE WHOLE OF THE HOUSE OF REPRESENTATIVES OF THE UNITED STATES, ON FRIDAY THE SECOND OF MARCH, 1798.
[Philadelphia: 1798.] pp. (43). 8vo·
          AAS. BM. CLS. HC. HSP. JCB. LCP. LOC. MHS. NYHS. NYPL. PU.

33840   —— — MR. HARPER'S SPEECH ON THE FOREIGN INTERCOURSE BILL, IN REPLY TO MR. NICHOLAS AND MR. GALLATIN. DELIVERED IN THE COMMITTEE OF THE WHOLE OF THE HOUSE OF REPRESENTATIVES OF THE UNITED STATES, ON FRIDAY THE SECOND OF MARCH, 1798.
[Philadelphia: Printed by Richard Folwell. 1798.] pp. 57. 8vo.
Reprinted in London this year.   AAS. JCB. LOC. NYPL.

33841   —— OBSERVATIONS ON THE DISPUTE BETWEEN THE UNITED STATES AND FRANCE: ADDRESSED BY ROBERT G. HARPER, ESQ. OF SOUTH CAROLINA, TO HIS CONSTITUENTS, IN MAY, 1797. WITH A PREFACE AND APPENDIX BY THE AUTHOR. THIRD AMERICAN EDITION. IT HAS PASSED THROUGH FIVE EDITIONS IN ENGLAND.
Philadelphia: Published by William Cobbett, opposite Christ Church. May, 1798. [Copy right secured according to law.] pp. 96. 8vo.   BA. HC. JCB. LOC. NYPL.

33842   —— — OBSERVATIONS ON THE DISPUTE BETWEEN THE UNITED STATES & FRANCE. ADDRESSED BY ROBERT GOODLOE HARPER, OF SOUTH-CAROLINA, TO HIS CONSTITUENTS, IN MAY, 1797. FOURTH AMERICAN EDITION. TO WHICH IS ANNEXED, HIS SPEECH, IN CONGRESS [*sic*], ON THE FOREIGN INTERCOURSE BILL, IN REPLY TO MR. NICHOLAS, MR. GALLATIN, AND OTHERS, DELIVERED MARCH 2, 1798.
Boston: Printed for the Subscribers, April, 1798. pp. 96. 8vo.
          AAS. BA. HC. JCB. MHS.
The following printed notice is inserted: "This excellent book is published at the expense of a few honest Americans, who wish to have the truth made known. You are requested to peruse it, and to communicate it wherever you think it will be candidly read and considered. Boston, April 1798.

33843   HARPER, ROBERT GOODLOE, continued.
—— —— OBSERVATIONS ON THE DISPUTE BETWEEN THE UNITED STATES &
FRANCE. ADDRESSED BY ROBERT GOODLOE HARPER, OF SOUTH-CAROLINA, TO HIS
CONSTITUENTS, IN MAY, 1797. FOURTH AMERICAN EDITION. TO WHICH IS ANNEXED,
HIS SPEECH, IN CONGRESS [*sic*], ON THE FOREIGN INTERCOURSE BILL, IN REPLY TO
• MR. NICHOLAS, MR. GALLATIN, AND OTHERS, DELIVERED MARCH 2, 1798.
> *Boston: Printed for the Subscribers, April,* 1798. pp. 151. 8vo.
> HSP. LOC. NL. NYHS. NYPL. PU.

This impression does not have the printed slip notice in the other Boston edition of this date.

33844   —— SPEECH OF ROBERT GOODLOE HARPER, ESQR., IN THE HOUSE OF REPRESENTA-
TIVES, MONDAY, THE 29TH DAY OF MAY, 1797, RELATIVE TO THE UNJUST, CRUEL,
INSOLENT AND PERFIDIOUS CONDUCT OF FRANCE TOWARDS THE UNITED STATES.
> *Philadelphia: Published by William Cobbett, opposite Christ Church. March,*
> 1798. pp. 44. 8vo.   AAS. HC. JCB. LOC. NYHS. PrPL.

33845   HARRIS, THADDEUS MASON   1768–1842
A DISCOURSE, DELIVERED AT THE PUBLIC CONSECRATION OF THE MERIDIAN SUN
LODGE IN BROOKFIELD, SEPTEMBER 12, A. L. 5798. BY THE REVEREND BROTHER
THADDEUS MASON HARRIS.
> *Brookfield (Massachusetts): Printed by E. Merriam & Co. December,* 1798.
> pp. 15. 8vo.   AAS. NYPL.

33846   —— A FEW NOTICES OF THE HISTORY OF FREE MASONRY IN SEVERAL PARTS OF
EUROPE, ASIA AND AFRICA.
> *Boston: Printed by Samuel Etheridge.* 1798. pp. [20]. 8vo. AAS. JCB. LOC. NYPL.

33847   —— A SERMON PREACHED IN MILTON ON THE MORNING, AND AT DORCHESTER IN
THE AFTERNOON OF THE 9TH OF MAY, 1798; BEING THE DAY RECOMMENDED BY
THE PRESIDENT OF THE UNITED STATES FOR SOLEMN HUMILIATION, FASTING, AND
PRAYER THROUGHOUT THE UNION. BY THADDEUS MASON HARRIS, MINISTER OF
THE RELIGIOUS SOCIETY IN DORCHESTER. [Two lines of French quotation.]
> *Boston: Printed by Samuel Etheridge, No. 22, Marlborough-Street.* 1798.
> pp. 24. 8vo.   AAS. BA. CLA. HC. HSP. JCB. LOC. MHS. NYPL. YC.

33848   HARRISON, RALPH   1748–1810
RUDIMENTS OF ENGLISH GRAMMAR; CONTAINING I. THE DIFFERENT KINDS, RELA-
TIONS, AND CHANGES OF WORDS. II. SYNTAX, OR THE RIGHT CONSTRUCTION OF
SENTENCES. WITH AN APPENDIX, COMPREHENDING A TABLE OF VERBS IRREGULARLY
INFLECTED; REMARKS ON SOME GRAMMATICAL FIGURES; RULES OF PUNCTUATION; A
PRAXIS ON THE GRAMMAR, AND EXAMPLES OF TRUE AND FALSE CONSTRUCTION. BY
MR. HARRISON. THE FIFTH AMERICAN EDITION. SCIENTIARUM JANITRIX GRAM-
MATICA.
> *Whitehall-Press: By William Young, for Matthew [sic] Carey, Bookseller,*
> *No.* 118, *High-street, Philadelphia.* 1798. pp. 120. 24mo.   AAS. JCB.

Used as a text-book in the University of Pennsylvania.

33849   —— —— A NEW EDITION, WITH CORRECTIONS AND ADDITIONS, BY A TEACHER OF
PHILADELPHIA, OF HARRISON'S RUDIMENTS OF ENGLISH GRAMMAR. CONTAINING
I. THE DIFFERENT KINDS, RELATIONS AND CHANGES OF WORDS. II. SYNTAX, OR
THE RIGHT CONSTRUCTION OF SENTENCES. WITH AN APPENDIX COMPREHENDING A
TABLE OF VERBS IRREGULARLY INFLECTED. REMARKS ON SOME GRAMMATICAL FIG-
URES, RULES OF PUNCTUATION, A PRAXIS ON THE GRAMMAR AND EXAMPLES OF TRUE
AND FALSE CONSTRUCTION. BY MR. HARRISON. SCIENTIARUM JANITRIX GRAM-
MATICA.
> *Philadelphia: Printed by Joseph and James Cruikshank.* 1798.

208th Pennsylvania District Copyright, issued to Ephraim Conrad, as
Proprietor, 30 May, 1798.

AUCTION
VALUES

33850　　HART, LEVI　　　　　　　　　　　　　　　　　　　　　1738–1808
　　　　THE RELIGIOUS IMPROVEMENT OF THE DEATH OF PIOUS MINISTERS, ATTEMPTED, IN A
　　　　DISCOURSE AT THE FUNERAL OF THE REVEREND TIMOTHY STONE, PASTOR OF THE
　　　　CHURCH AT GOSHEN IN LEBANON; WHO DIED, MAY 12TH, 1797, IN THE 56TH YEAR
　　　　OF HIS AGE, AND 30TH OF HIS MINISTRY. BY LEVI HART, A. M. PASTOR OF A CHURCH
　　　　IN PRESTON. "THEY MOURNED OVER HIM SAYING, ALAS, MY BROTHER." I KINGS
　　　　xiii. 30.
　　　　　　Printed in Norwich, (Connecticut,) by John Trumbull. M,DCC,XCVIII. pp.
　　　　(22). 8vo.　　　　　　　　　　　　　　　　　　　AAS. CHS. JCB. NYPL. YC.

33851　　HARTMANN, HENRICH
　　　　DIE WAHRE BRANTEWEIN-BRENNEREY; ODER, BRANTWEIN- GIN- UND CORDIAL-
　　　　MACHER-KUNST; WIE AUCH DIE ÄCHTE FÄRBE-KUNST, WIE MAN ALLE COULEUREN
　　　　AUF SEIDE, LEINEN UND WOLLE FÄRBEN KAN. [Ornament.]
　　　　　　York: Gedruckt bey Salomon Mäyer. 1797. 2 vols. in one. pp. (40); (30).
　　　　16mo.

　　　　179th Pennsylvania District Copyright, issued to Salomon Mayer, as
　　　　Proprietor, 19 May, 1797.

　　　　Second title: BESONDERE KUNST, AUF EINE LEICHTE UND WOHLSEILE ARTZ ZU FÄR-
　　　　BEN; ALLERLEY FARBE, SO WOHL AUF WOLLE, HALBWOLLE, LEINEN UND SEIDE.
　　　　FÜR DEN LAND UND STADTMANN. VON HENRICH HARTMANN, BERÜHMTEN SCHÖN-
　　　　FÄRBER. [Six stars. Ornament.]
　　　　　　York: Gedruckt bey Salomon Mäyer. 1797. pp. (30).

33852　　HARVARD UNIVERSITY.
　　　　HARVARD UNIVERSITY, IN CAMBRIDGE, COMMONWEALTH OF MASSACHUSETTS. THE
　　　　ORDER OF THE EXERCISES OF COMMENCEMENT, JULY 18TH, M,DCC,XCVIII. [Colo-
　　　　phon:]
　　　　　　[Printed by J. & T. Fleet.] [1798.] Broadside. fol.　　　　AAS. HC.

33853　　—— ILLUSTRISSIMO CRESCENTIO SUMNER, ARMIGERO, GUBERNATORI; HONORATISSIMO
　　　　MOSI GILL, ARMIGERO, VICE GUBERNATORI; CONSILARIIS ET SENATORIBUS REIPUB-
　　　　LICÆ MASSACHUSETTENSIS; REVERENDISQUE ECCLESIARUM IN OPPIDIS SEX VICINIS,
　　　　PRESBYTERIS, UNIVERSITATIS HARVARDIANÆ CURATORIBUS; REVERENDO JOSEPHO
　　　　WILLARD, S. T. D. LL. D. PRÆSIDI; [Four lines.] THESES HASCE, JUVENES IN ARTIBUS
　　　　INITIATI, [Forty-seven names.] HUMILLIMÈ DEDICANT. . . . HABITA IN COMITIIS
　　　　UNIVERSITATIS CANTABRIGIÆ, MASSACHUSETTENSIS, DIE JULII XVIII, ANNO SALUTIS
　　　　M,DCC,XCVIII. RERUMQUE PUBLICARUM FŒDERATARUM AMERICÆ SUMMÆ POTES-
　　　　TATIS XXIII. [Colophon:]
　　　　　　Bostoniæ: Typis Manning & Loring. [1798.] Broadside. fol.
　　　　　　　　　　　　　　　　　　　　　　　　　　AAS. EI. HC. MHS.

33854　　—— THE LAWS OF HARVARD COLLEGE. [Printers mark.]
　　　　　　Boston: Printed by John & Thomas Fleet, at the Bible & Heart, Cornhill.
　　　　MDCCXCVIII. pp. 1–36, (1), 37–66, (4), 67. 8vo.　　AAS. BA. BM. HC. JCB. NYPL.

33855　　HARWOOD, JOHN EDMUND.　　　　　　　　　　　　　1771–1809
　　　　ELLEN ARISE. A BALLAD. WRITTEN BY J. E. HARWOOD. COMPOSED BY B. CARR.
　　　　AS SUNG AT THE PHILADELPHIA AND NEW YORK THEATRES: BY MR. OLDMIXON AND
　　　　MR. HODGKINSON.
　　　　　　Philadelphia: Printed by B. Carr's Musical Repositories. 1798.

　　　　200th Pennsylvania District Copyright, issued to Benjamin Carr, as
　　　　Author and Proprietor, 22 January, 1798.

33856 HAVEN, SAMUEL 1727–1806
POETIC MISCELLANY, ON SUBJECTS MORAL AND RELIGIOUS. — FELIX QUI POTUIT COM-
MISCERE UTILE DULCI. HAPPY THE MAN WHO HAS THE ART, TO PLEASE THE TASTE,
AND MEND THE HEART.
Portsmouth, (*New-Hampshire*,) *Printed at the Oracle-Press, by Charles Peirce*
1798. pp. 23. 8vo. NYHS.

33857 —— THE VALIDITY OF PRESBYTERIAN ORDINATION, AND THE IMPORTANCE OF CANDOR
AND UNION AMONG CHRISTIANS OF DIFFERENT PERSUASIONS, WHO AGREE IN THE
ESSENTIALS OF CHRISTIANITY; ILLUSTRATED IN A DISCOURSE, DELIVERED AT THE
DUDLEIAN LECTURE OF HARVARD COLLEGE, SEPTEMBER 5, 1798. BY SAMUEL
HAVEN, D.D.
Boston: Printed by Manning & Loring. 1798. pp. [24.] 8vo.
AAS. BA. BM. HC. JCB. LOC. NYHS. NYPL.

33858 HAVERHILL FEDERAL GAZETTE. VOL. I. NO. 1. FRIDAY, OCTOBER 26, [— NO. 10.
FRIDAY, DECEMBER 28, 1798.]
Printed at Haverhill, (*Massachusetts*) *by Seth H. Moore & Chester Stebbins.*
1798. fol.
Established, as a weekly, in continuation of the *Impartial Herald*, by
Seth H. Moore, and Chester Stebbins, and continued by them to the
issue for November 27, 1799, when it was discontinued.

33859 HAWKESWORTH, JOHN 1725–1773
ALMORAN AND HAMET: AN ORIENTAL TALE. BY DR. HAWKESWORTH. INSTRUCT
AND PLEASE AT ONCE. HORACE.
*London Printed: Philadelphia Re-printed at the Southwark Office, No. 289,
South Front-Street,* M,DCC,XCVIII. pp. 157. 8vo. AAS.

33860 HAWKINS, JOSEPH 1772–
HAWKINS' VOYAGES TO THE COAST OF AFRICA, AND HIS TRAVELS IN THE INTERIOR OF
THAT COUNTRY DURING THE YEARS '94 AND '95, WITH A NARRATIVE OF THE UNHAPPY
FATE OF THE AUTHOR, WHOSE RESEARCH INTO THE PRODUCTIONS OF FOREIGN CLIMES
WERE TERMINATED BY A DEPRIVATION OF SIGHT, IN WHICH UNHAPPY SITUATION HE
RETURNED TO HIS NATIVE COUNTRY.
Boston: For sale by the Author, at the Sign of the Blue Bell, Marlboro'-Street.
1798.
"The first edition was published in Philadelphia, last winter."

33861 —— PHILANTHROPIC LOTTERY, BY ACT OF LEGISLATURE OF VERMONT, PASSED OCTO-
BER, 1798, FOR THE BENEFIT OF THE UNFORTUNATE MR. HAWKINS. SETH STONE,
MANAGER.
[*Burlington ?* 1798.] Broadside.

33862 HAWLES, SIR JOHN 1645–1716
THE ENGLISHMAN'S RIGHT, OR, A DIALOGUE BETWEEN A BARRISTER AT LAW AND A
JURYMAN; SHEWING, 1. THE ANTIQUITY. 2. THE EXCELLENT DESIGNED USE. 3.
THE OFFICE AND JUST PRIVILEGES OF JURIES BY THE LAW OF ENGLAND. (BEING
A CHOICE HELP FOR ALL WHO ARE QUALIFIED BY LAW, TO SERVE ON JURIES.) BY
SIR JOHN HAWLES, KNT. SOLICITOR GENERAL TO THE LATE KING WILLIAM. TO WHICH
IS PREFIXED, AN INTRODUCTORY ESSAY, ON THE MORAL DUTY OF A JUDGE. BY LORD
BACON. [Two lines of Latin from] PLIN. LIB. V. EPIST. 4.
Printed by John Thompson, of Philadelphia: for Alexander Brodie. 1798.
pp. [70.] 8vo. AAS. BM. JCB. LOC. NYPL.
Reprinted in "The Minor Library" in Philadelphia, in 1804.

33863   HAYDN, Franz Joseph   1732–1809
         Sonatina, composed by J. Haydn. Opera 71.

>   *Philadelphia: Printed and sold by G. Willig, No. 185 Market-Street. Price
>   62¼ cents.* [1798.] pp. 5. 4to.

33864   HAYNES, Lemuel   1753–1833
         The Influence of civil government on religion. A sermon delivered at Rut-
         land, West Parish, September 4, 1798, at the annual freemen's meeting.
         By Lemuel Haynes, pastor of a church in Rutland.

>   *Printed at Rutland, (Vermont) by John Walker, jun. for S. Williams.*
>   M,DCC,XCVIII. pp. 17. 8vo.

33865   HEATH, William   1737–1814
         Memoirs of major-general Heath: containing anecdotes, details of skirm-
         ishes, battles and other military events, during the Revolutionary war.
         Written by himself. Published according to Act of Congress.

>   *Printed at Boston, by I. Thomas and E. T. Andrews, Faust's Statue, No. 45
>   Newbury Street. Sold by them; by I. Thomas, Worcester; by Thomas, Andrews &
>   Penniman, Albany: by Thomas, Andrews & Butler, Baltimore; and by the Book-
>   sellers throughout the Continent. August, 1798.* pp. 388. 8vo.

                    AAS. BA. BM. HC. JCB. LCP. LOC. MHS. NL. NYHS. NYPL.

>   159th Massachusetts District Copyright, issued to William Heath, as
>   Author, 20th December, 1798. Reprinted in New York in 1901, and
>   1904.

33866   HEIDELBERG CATECHISM.
         Catechismus, oder Kurzer Unterricht Christlicher Lehre, für die ange-
         hende Jugend in der Chürfürstlichen Pfalz und andern Reformirten
         Orten zu gebrauchen: Samt der Haus-Tafel, mit und ohne Biblischem
         Sprüch-Büchlein. Alles zur Ehre und Lob Gottes. [Anhang zum Cate-
         chismo. Erste Wahrheits-Milch, für Säuglinge an Alter und Verstand.]

>   *Philadelphia: Gedruckt bey Henrich Schweitzer, in der Rees-Strasse, No. 85.*
>   1798. pp. 110. 24mo.   AAS.

33867   HELME, Elizabeth
         The History of Louisa, the lovely orphan; or, the cottage on the moor.
         Two volumes in one. [Seven lines of verse.] By mrs. Helme. Vol. i [— ii.]
         The ninth edition.

>   *Boston: Printed and sold by Samuel Etheridge.*—1798.—pp. (2), (2), 96,
>   frontispiece. 12mo.   AAS. JCB. LOC.

33868   HENRY, Matthew   1662–1714
         The Communicant's companion; or, instructions and helps, for the right re-
         ceiving of the Lord's Supper. By Matthew Henry, author of "Annotations
         on the Bible," &c. First American, from the twelfth London, edition.

>   *Leominster, Massachusetts: Printed by John Prentiss, & Co. for Robert B.
>   Thomas—Sterling.* 1798. pp. 347, [4.] 12mo.   AAS.

>   Contains, a four-page list of names of the Subscribers for re-printing
>   this work.

33869   THE HERALD of Liberty. "Man is man, and who is more?" Vol. i. No. 1. Mon-
         day, May 21, [— No. 33. Monday, December 31, 1798.]

>   *Washington, Pennsylvania: Printed by John Israel.* 1798. fol.

>   Established, as a weekly, by John Israel, and continued by him cer-
>   tainly to the issue for 14 September, 1801—the last issue located.

33870 HERALD OF THE UNITED STATES. NO. 39 OF VOL. VI. WHOLE NO. 300. SATURDAY, JANUARY 6, [— NO. 38 OF VOL. VII. WHOLE NO. 353. SATURDAY, DECEMBER 29, 1798.]

Warren: Published at the Post-Office, by Nathaniel Phillips, Printer to the State. 1798. pp. 1193–1400. fol.   AAS. HC.. JCB. RIHS.

33871 HERMIT OF THE FOREST. AND THE WANDERING INFANTS. PRICE FOUR CENTS.

Boston: Printed and sold by John W. Folsom, No. 30, Union-Street. 1798. 32mo.

33872 HERVEY, JAMES   1714–1758
MEDITATIONS AND CONTEMPLATIONS: IN TWO VOLUMES. CONTAINING VOLUME I. MEDITATIONS AMONG THE TOMBS. REFLECTIONS ON A FLOWER-GARDEN. A DISCANT ON CREATION. VOLUME II. CONTEMPLATIONS ON THE NIGHT. CONTEMPLATIONS ON THE STARRY HEAVENS. A WINTER-PIECE. BY JAMES HERVEY, A. M. LATE RECTOR OF WESTON-FAVELL IN NORTHAMPTONSHIRE. VOL. I. [— II.] FOURTH AMERICAN EDITION.

Printed at Exeter, by Henry Ranlet, for John West, Bookseller, No. 75, Cornhill, Boston. M,DCC,XCVIII. 2 vols. in one. pp. xvii, (1), 250; x, 256, (2). 12mo.   AAS.

33873 HETH, WILLIAM   1750–1807
AN INFALLIBLE CURE. FOR POLITICAL BLINDNESS, IF ADMINISTERED TO PATIENTS POSSESSING SOUND MINDS, HONEST HEARTS, AND INDEPENDENT CIRCUMSTANCES.

[Richmond: Printed by Thomas Nicolson. July, 1798.] pp. 38. 16mo.
BA. LOC.

33874 —— — AN INFALLIBLE CURE FOR POLITICAL BLINDNESS, IF ADMININSTERED [sic] TO PATIENTS POSSESSING SOUND MINDS, HONEST HEARTS, AND INDEPENDENT CIRCUMSTANCES.

[Richmond: Re-printed by Thomas Nicolson, October, 1798.] pp. 24. 16mo.

Consists of an Oration on the Progress of the United States to the present   LOC.
crisis, and duties in it. By Alexander Addison. pp. 4–22; and 3–21.
With title, and comments, by William Heth.

33875 HILLIARD, JOSEPH   –1843
THE RECIPROCAL DUTIES OF PASTOR AND PEOPLE, DELINEATED IN TWO DISCOURSES, DELIVER'D TO THE SECOND CHURCH AND SOCIETY IN BERWICK, OCTOBER 15TH, 1797. BY JOSEPH HILLIARD, A. M. PASTOR OF SAID CHURCH. PUBLISHED AT THE REQUEST OF THE HEARERS. [Double line.]

Printed at Dover, by Samuel Bragg, jun. for the Subscribers, 1798. pp. 34+ 8vo.   NYHS.

33876 HISTORY OF A LITTLE BOY FOUND UNDER A HAYCOCK. PRICE FOUR CENTS.

Boston: Printed and sold by John W. Folsom, No. 30, Union-Street. 1798. 32mo.

33877 A BEAUTIFUL LITTLE NOVEL. THE HISTORY OF CONSTANTIUS & PULCHERA, OR, CONSTANCY REWARDED. AN AMERICAN NOVEL. [Eight lines of verse.]

Portsmouth, N. H. Printed by Charles Peirce, No. 5, Daniel-street. 1798. pp. 102, (4). 12mo.   AAS. JCB.

Contains, a four-page list of books for sale by the Publisher.

33878 HISTORY OF LITTLE ANN AND LITTLE JAMES; TO WHICH IS ADDED, A PRESENT OF PICTURES. PRICE FOUR CENTS.

Boston: Printed and sold by John W. Folsom, No. 30, Union-Street. 1798. 32mo.

33879   THE HISTORY of the British Empire, from the year 1765, to the end of 1783. Containing an impartial history of the origin, progress, and termination of the American Revolution. By a Society of gentlemen. . . .
> *Philadelphia: Printed for R. Campbell & Co.* M,DCC,XCVIII. 2 vols. pp. 475; 452; 59. 2 portraits, Washington and Franklin. 8vo.   HC. JCB. LOC.

33880   THE HISTORY of the duchess of C------. From Adela and Theodore. Written by herself. To which is added, [Story of a Castilian, and] Edwin and Angelina, a ballad. [By Oliver Goldsmith.]
> *Printed at Northampton, by Andrew Wright, for Simeon Butler.*—1798. pp. 142, (1). 24mo.   AAS. HEH.

33881   HISTORY of Tommy Careless. Price four cents.
> *Boston: Printed and sold by John W. Folsom. No. 30, Union-Street.* 1798. 32mo.

33882   HISTORY of Tommy Gingerbread, who lived upon learning. Price four cents.
> *Boston: Printed and sold by John W. Folsom, No. 30, Union-Street.* 1798. 32mo.

33883   THE HIVE. Vol. i. No. 32. Wednesday, January 3, [No. 52. Wednesday, May 23, 1798.]
> *Printed by W. Hamilton, King street, Lancaster.* 1798. pp. (125)–(208). 4to.   LanHS.

> Discontinued at the above date. In June, 1803, Charles McDowell began the publication of a similar periodical, with the same title, which was also discontinued at the end of its second volume, in June, 1805.

33884   HOBBY, William J.
An Oration delivered at St. Paul's church, Augusta, on the fourth of July, one thousand seven hundred and ninety-eight, being the twenty-second anniversary of American independence. By William J. Hobby, esq.
> *Augusta Printed by John Erdman Smith.* 1798. pp. 24. 8vo.   LOC.

33885   DER HOCH-DEUTSCHE Americanische Calender, auf das Jahr 1799. Nach der Gnadenreichen Geburt unseres Herrn und Heylandes Jesu Christi, (welches ein gemeines Jahr von 365 Tagen ist.) [Eight lines.] Zum fünf-zehntenmal herausgegeben.
> *Germantaun, Gedruckt und zu finden bey Michael Billmeyer, u. s. w.* [Six lines.] [1798.] pp. (40). 4to.   AAS. LOC.

33886   HOCH-DEUTSCHES Reformirtes A B C und Namen-Büchlein, für Kinder, welche anfangen zu lernen.
> *Germantaun. Gedruckt und zu haben bey Peter Leibert.* 1798. pp. (32). 16mo.   JCB.

33887   HOFFMAN, Christian
Longevity: being an account of various persons, who have lived to an extraordinary age, with several curious particulars respecting their lives; the whole comprising an abridgement of longevity, as far as history extends in every quarter of the world, from the creation to the year 1792. Authenticated by referential notes from authors of veracity. By Christian Hoffman of New-York.
> *New-York: Printed by Jacob S. Mott, No. 7. Vesey-Street.*—1798.—[Copyright secured.] pp. 120. 12mo.   AAS. JCB. LOC. NYHS. NYPL.

> Contains, a six-page list of Subscribers' names, in double columns.

33888   HOLLINSHEAD, William   1748–1817
THE GOSPEL PREACHED TO EVERY CREATURE: A SERMON, DELIVERED ON WEDNESDAY, THE 21ST MARCH, 1798, BEFORE THE INCORPORATED BAPTIST CHURCH, IN CHARLESTON, SOUTH-CAROLINA: BEING THEIR CHARITY ANNIVERSARY FOR THE ASSISTANCE OF PIOUS YOUTH, IN AN EDUCATION FOR GOSPEL MINISTRY: AND PUBLISHED AT THEIR REQUEST. BY THE REV. WILLIAM HOLLINSHEAD, D. D. ONE OF THE MINISTERS OF THE INDEPENDENT, OR CONGREGATIONAL CHURCH IN CHARLESTON.

Charleston: Printed by W. P. Young, No. 43, Broad-Street. MDCCXCVIII. pp. 19. 8vo.
BM. JCB.

33889   HOLMES, ABIEL   1763–1837
THE LIFE OF EZRA STILES, D. D. LL. D. A FELLOW OF THE AMERICAN PHILOSOPHICAL SOCIETY; OF THE AMERICAN ACADEMY OF ARTS AND SCIENCES; OF THE CONNECTICUT SOCIETY OF ARTS AND SCIENCES; A CORRESPONDING MEMBER OF THE MASSACHUSETTS HISTORICAL SOCIETY; PROFESSOR OF ECCLESIASTICAL HISTORY; AND PRESIDENT OF YALE COLLEGE. BY ABIEL HOLMES, A. M. PASTOR OF THE FIRST CHURCH IN CAMBRIDGE. [Three lines of Latin quotation.] PUBLISHED ACCORDING TO ACT OF CONGRESS.

Boston: Printed by Thomas & Andrews, Faust's Statue, 45 Newbury Street. May, 1798. pp. 403, (1), portrait, drawn & engraved by S. Hill, Boston. 8vo.
AAS. BA. BM. BU. HC. JCB. LOC. NL. NYHS. NYPL. RIHS. YC.

150th Massachusetts District Copyright, issued to Abiel Holmes, as Author, 27 June, 1798.

33890   HOLT, CHARLES
A SHORT ACCOUNT OF THE YELLOW FEVER, AS IT APPEARED IN NEW-LONDON, IN AUGUST, SEPTEMBER, AND OCTOBER, 1798: WITH AN ACCURATE LIST OF THOSE WHO DIED OF THE DISEASE, THE DONATIONS, &C. &C. &C. BY CHARLES HOLT.

New-London: Printed by Charles Holt, at the Bee Office. 1798. pp. 24. 8vo.
SGO.

33891   —— — A SHORT ACCOUNT OF THE YELLOW FEVER, AS IT APPEARED IN NEW-LONDON IN AUGUST, SEPTEMBER, AND OCTOBER, 1798: WITH AN ACCURATE LIST OF THOSE WHO DIED OF THE DISEASE, THE DONATIONS, &C. &C. &C. THE SECOND EDITION.

New-London: Printed by Charles Holt. November, 1798.

33892   HOELTY. ——.
INVITATION TO JOY. [Song. Words.] BY HÖLTY.

New-York: [1798.]

33893   HOLYOKE, SAMUEL   1762–1820
EXETER: FOR THANKSGIVING BY SAMUEL HOLYOKE, A. B.

Exeter: Printed by Henry Ranlet. M,DCC,XCVIII. pp. 7. obl. 24mo. HC.

33894   HOMER, JONATHAN   1759–1843
Caption title: DESCRIPTION AND HISTORY OF NEWTON, IN THE COUNTY OF MIDDLESEX. BY THE REV. JONATHAN HOMER.

[Boston: Printed by Samuel Hall. 1798.] pp. 28. 8vo. NYPL.

Reprinted, with altered paging, from volume v. of the Collections of the Massachusetts Historical Society.

33895 HOPKINSON, JOSEPH 1770–1842
SONG [HAIL COLUMBIA!] ADAPTED TO THE PRESIDENT'S MARCH, SUNG AT THE THE-
ATRE BY MR. FOX, AT HIS BENEFIT. COMPOSED BY JOSEPH HOPKINSON, ESQ.
[Ornament.]
[Philadelphia:] Printed by J. Ormrod, 41, Chesnut-Street. [1798.] pp. 6.
8vo. AAS. BM. BU. NYHS. NYPL.

33896 —— — THE FAVORITE NEW FEDERAL SONG [cut of Eagle] ADAPTED TO THE PRES-
IDENT'S MARCH. SUNG BY MR. FOX—WRITTEN BY J. HOPKINSON, ESQ.
[Philadelphia: Published at Carr's Musical Repository. 1798.] pp.(2). 4to.

33897 —— — NEW FEDERAL SONG [HAIL COLUMBIA]; WRITTEN TO THE TUNE OF THE
'PRESIDENT'S MARCH' BY J. HOPKINSON, ESQ. AND SUNG BY MR. FOX, AT THE NEW
THEATRE WITH GREAT APPLAUSE, ORNAMENTED WITH A VERY ELEGANT PORTRAIT
OF THE PRESIDENT. (PRICE 25 CENTS.)
Philadelphia: Published at Carr's Musical Repository. 1798.

33898 —— — THE TRULY FEDERAL SONG HAIL COLUMBIA, (DEATH OR LIBERTY) TO THE
TUNE OF THE PRESIDENT'S MARCH, ADAPTED FOR THE VOICE, PIANO FORTE, VIOLIN,
GUITAR, CLARINET, HAUTBOY, GERMAN FLUTE, OR ANY OTHER INSTRUMENT.
*Boston: Published by P. A. von Hagen, jun. and Co's Musical Magazine, No.
62, Newbury-Street.* 1798.

33899 —— — HAIL COLUMBIA! HAPPY LAND. TO THE TUNE OF THE "PRESIDENT'S MARCH."
SUNG BY MR. FOX, AT THE NEW THEATRE, PHILADELPHIA.
Halifax: Printed by A. Hodge. May 21, 1798.

33900 —— — A NEW SONG. HAIL COLUMBIA! HAPPY LAND! [Four ten-line verses, with
chorus.]
Augusta: Printed by Peter Edes. June 18, 1798.

33901 —— — THE PRESIDENT'S MARCH. A FEDERAL SONG — [HAIL COLUMBIA, HAPPY
LAND . . .]
Alexandria: 1798.

33902 —— — THE PRESIDENT'S MARCH. A NEW FEDERAL SONG.
Philadelphia: Published by G. Willig, Marketstreet, No. 185. 4to.

33903 —— — THE TWO PATRIOTIC SONGS OF HAIL COLUMBIA, AND ADAMS AND LIBERTY
[By Thomas Paine], NOW SUNG WITH INCREASING APPLAUSE THROUGHOUT THE
UNITED STATES; TO WHICH IS ADDED THE FAVORITE SONG OF HEAVING THE LEAD.
[Walpole, New Hampshire. Printed by David Carlisle, 1798.] pp. (2). 4to.

33904 —— WHAT IS OUR SITUATION? AND WHAT OUR PROSPECTS? A FEW PAGES FOR
AMERICANS. BY AN AMERICAN.
[Philadelphia: 1798.] pp.(40). 8vo. AAS. BA. BM. CLS. JCB. LOC. NYPL.

33905 HORSFIELD, THOMAS
AN EXPERIMENTAL DISSERTATION ON THE RHUS VERNIX, RHUS RADICANS AND RHUS
GLABRUM; COMMONLY KNOWN IN PENNSYLVANIA BY THE NAMES OF POISON ASH,
POISON VINE AND COMMON SUMACH. BY THOMAS HORSFIELD, OF BETHLEHEM,
PENNSYLVANIA, MEMBER OF THE MEDICAL AND CHEMICAL SOCIETIES OF PHILA-
DELPHIA.
Philadelphia: Printed by Charles Cist, No. 104, North Second Street.
M,DCC,XCVIII. pp. vi, 88. 8vo. AAS. BM. LOC. SGO.
Reprinted in Caldwell, C. Medical theses. Vol. I. 1805.

33906 HOUGHTON, ASA
THE GENTLEMEN'S AND LADIES' DIARY: AND ALMANAC, WITH AN EPHEMERIS, FOR THE
YEAR OF THE CREATION, ACCORDING TO SACRED WRIT, 5761; AND OF THE CHRISTIAN
ERA 1799: BEING THE THIRD AFTER BISSEXTILE, OR LEAP YEAR, AND THE TWENTY-
THIRD YEAR OF THE INDEPENDENCE OF THE UNITED STATES OF AMERICA. CON-
TAINING, BESIDES MORE THAN USUAL ASTRONOMICAL CALCULATIONS, AS GREAT A
VARIETY OF INSTRUCTIVE, USEFUL AND ENTERTAINING MATTER AS ANY OTHER AL-
MANAC. FITTED TO THE LATITUDE AND LONGITUDE OF BOSTON, MASSACHUSETTS,
BUT WILL SERVE FOR THE ADJOINING STATES WITHOUT SENSIBLE VARIATION. BY
ASA HOUGHTON. [Five lines.]

*Printed by Cornelius Sturtevant: at Putney, Vermont. Sold by him at his
Printing-Office, and by most of the merchants in this and the adjacent States. Price
—7½ dollars per gross—75 cents per dozen—10 cents single.* [1798.] pp. (44).
12mo.
AAS. LOC.

33907 HOYT, EPAPHRAS   1765–1850
A TREATISE ON THE MILITARY ART, IN FOUR PARTS. CONTAINING: I. A COMPRE-
HENSIVE SYSTEM OF DISCIPLINE, FOR THE CAVALRY OF THE UNITED STATES;
ADAPTED TO THE PRINCIPLES OF BARON STEUBEN'S REGULATIONS FOR THE IN-
FANTRY, AND THE LATEST PRUSSIAN AND ENGLISH TREATISES ON CAVALRY. II. REG-
ULATIONS CONCERNING THE DUTY OF CAVALRY IN CAMP IN TIME OF WAR. III.
DIRECTIONS FOR THE CONDUCT OF PARTIZAN CORPS, WHETHER CAVALRY OR IN-
FANTRY, IN CARRYING ON THE PETITE GUERRE. IV. MAXIMS RELATING TO THE
MARCHING, ENCAMPING, AND OTHER GENERAL OPERATIONS OF AN ARMY IN THE
FIELD: COMPILED PRINCIPALLY FROM THE OBSERVATIONS OF EXPERIENCED OFFI-
CERS, AND THE MOST APPROVED WRITERS ON THE ART OF WAR. ILLUSTRATED WITH
PLATES: BY E. HOYT, AN OFFICER IN THE CAVALRY OF MASSACHUSETTS. VOL. I.
PART I. & II. [Motto from] VATTEL.

*Printed at Brattleborough, by Benjamin Smead, for the Author, sold by him
[at Deerfield], and by Russell & Ripley, Greenfield.* 1798. pp. v, 212, (2), 10 plates.
12mo.
AAS. BA. BM. JCB. LOC. NYPL.

157th Massachusetts District Copyright, issued to Epaphras Hoyt, as
Author, 15 November 1798. From the leaf of "Advertisement" it appears that the parts were also issued separately. "The propriety of
publishing and selling the first volume of this work, separate from the
second, will be obvious;—the first being calculated principally for the
discipline of the Cavalry — the second, containing rules for the management of Troops in the field . . . It is presumed that many would
wish to procure the first, who would not go to the expense of both."

33908 HUBARD JAMES THRUSTON
AN INAUGURAL DISSERTATION ON PUERPERAL FEVER, SUBMITTED TO THE EXAMINATION
OF THE REV. JOHN EWING, S. T. P. PROVOST, THE TRUSTEES, AND MEDICAL FACULTY,
OF THE UNIVERSITY OF PENNSYLVANIA, ON THE 22D DAY OF MAY, 1798. FOR THE
DEGREE OF DOCTOR OF MEDICINE. BY JAMES THRUSTON HUBARD, OF VIRGINIA,
HONORARY MEMBER OF THE MEDICAL SOCIETY OF PHILADELPHIA. [Three lines of
Latin from] SENECA.

Philadelphia: Printed by John Ormrod, No. 41, Chesnut-Street. [1798.] pp.
(4), 30. 8vo.
HEH. LCP. LOC. SGO.

33909 HUBBELL, SILAS
AN ORATION DELIVERED AT LANESBOROUGH — AT THE CELEBRATION OF AMERICAN
INDEPENDENCE ON THE FOURTH OF JULY 1798. BY SILAS HUBBELL.

Pittsfield: Printed by Holly & Smith. 1798.

33910   HUDSON. New York.

SIR, AT A MEETING OF A NUMBER OF GENTLEMEN OF THE CITY OF HUDSON, ON SAT-
URDAY EVENING THE 9TH INSTANT, IT WAS UNANIMOUSLY RESOLVED, TO CELEBRATE
THE ENSUING ANNIVERSARY OF AMERICAN INDEPENDENCE . . . [inviting Peter
Van Schaak, esq., Kinderhook, and his friends to be present. Signed, Rufus Backus,
and others. Hudson June 14th, 1798.]

[Hudson: Printed by Ashbel Stoddard. 1798.] Broadside. obl. 12mo.   NYPL.

33911   HUDSON GAZETTE. VOL. XIII. NUMB. 666. TUESDAY, JANUARY 2, [— VOL. XIV.
NUMB. 717. TUESDAY, DECEMBER 25, 1798.]

[Hudson:] Printed by Ashbel Stoddard. 1798. fol.

33912   THE HUMMING BIRD, OR HERALD OF TASTE. "IS THERE ANY THING WHEROF IT
MAY BE SAID, SEE, THIS IS NEW?" VOL. I. NO. 1. SATURDAY, MAY 12, [—NO. 5.
SATURDAY, JUNE 9, 1798.]

Newfield: Printed by L. Beach. 1798. fol.   AAS.

Established, as a weekly, by Lazarus Beach, and continued to June 9,
1798—the last, and only number located.

33913   THE HUMMING BIRD; OR, NEW AMERICAN SONGSTER.

Boston: Published by William Spotswood, No. 22 Marlboro Street. 1798.
frontispiece. 16mo.

33914   HUMPHREYS, DAVID   1752–1818

AN ESSAY ON THE LIFE OF THE HONORABLE MAJOR-GENERAL ISRAEL PUTNAM: AD-
DRESSED TO THE STATE SOCIETY OF THE CINCINNATI IN CONNECTICUT. BY COL.
DAVID HUMPHREYS.

Philadelphia: Printed for Robert Campbell & Co. 1798. pp. 125. 18mo.
NYPL. WL. YC.

33915   HUNTER, WILLIAM

THE OHIO NAVIGATOR. COMPRISING AN AMPLE ACCOUNT OF THAT BEAUTIFUL RIVER
FROM ITS HEAD TO ITS JUNCTION WITH THE MISSISSIPPI; THE SEVERAL TOWNS ON
ITS BANKS; ITS DIFFERENT PORTS AND HARBOURS; AND CONTAINING ACCURATE DI-
RECTIONS FOR ITS NAVIGATION, AS WELL IN TIMES OF HIGH FRESHES AS WHEN THE
WATER IS LOW. THE DESCRIPTION OF ITS ROCKS, RIFFLES, SHOALS AND CHANNELS;
THE DISTANCES FROM PLACE TO PLACE. TAKEN FROM THE JOURNALS OF GENTLE-
MEN OF OBSERVATION WHO HAVE FREQUENTLY NAVIGATED IT.

Washington (K). Printed by Hunter & Beaumont. 1798.

Compiled and published by the said William Hunter and William H.
Beaumont, Editors of The Palladium in Frankfort, and The Mirror in
Washington, Kentucky.

33916   —— — THE SECOND EDITION OF THE OHIO NAVIGATOR, COMPRISING AN AMPLE
ACCOUNT OF THAT BEAUTIFUL RIVER FROM ITS HEAD TO ITS JUNCTION WITH THE
MISSISSIPPI; THE SEVERAL TOWNS ON ITS BANKS; ITS DIFFERENT PORTS AND HAR-
BOURS; AND CONTAINING ACCURATE DIRECTIONS FOR ITS NAVIGATION, AS WELL IN
TIMES OF HIGH FRESHES AS WHEN THE WATER IS LOW. THE DESCRIPTION OF ITS
ROCKS, RIFFLES, SHOALS AND CHANNELS; THE DISTANCES FROM PLACE TO PLACE.
TAKEN FROM THE JOURNALS OF GENTLEMEN OF OBSERVATION WHO HAVE FRE-
QUENTLY NAVIGATED IT.

Washington (K.) Printed by Hunter and Beaumont. 1798.

☞ "The rapid sale of the first edition of this truly useful little work,
supercedes the necessity of any other recommendation than barely men-
tioning the fact." Kentucky District Copyright, issued to Hunter and
Beaumont, as Authors, 26 December, 1798.

The mystery surrounding the first two, unknown, editions of Zadok

HUNTER, William, continued.

Cramer's Ohio and Mississippi Navigator,–the Third corrected edition of which, issued at Pittsburgh, in 1802, is the first known,– is revealed by this hitherto unrecorded publication, upon which Cramer, legitimately, or surreptitiously, based his work. As original investigators, basing their work in the only true way upon the written journals of earlier navigators, the credit for the design, purpose, and practical use, of the Navigator belongs to William Hunter, and William H. Beaumont, of Kentucky, and not to Zadok Cramer, bookseller, of Pittsburgh, Pennsylvania. No existing copy of either edition is known—mute testimony to the great traffic, hardships, and disasters of the early western exodus by way of the Ohio River.

33917 THE HUNTINGTON Courier and Weekly Advertiser. Vol. I. No. 27. Tuesday, January 2, [— No. 35 ? Tuesday, February 27 ? 1798.]
Huntingdon, Pennsylvania. Published by Michael Duffey. 1798. fol.
Discontinued in February.

33918 HURLOTHRUMBO, doctor, pseudonym.
The Fortune-teller. By which young gentlemen and ladies may easily foretel a variety of important events that will happen both to themselves and their acquaintance. By the renowned doctor Hurlothrumbo, chief magician and astrologer to the king of the cuckows.
Boston: Printed and sold by John W. Folsom, No. 30, *Union-Street.* 1798.
pp. 60+ 64mo. 26 cuts in text. AAS.

33919 HUTCHINS, Gabriel
The United States Almanac, for the year of our Lord, 1799: being the third after leap-year, and the xxiiid of American independence, 'till 4th July; containing every thing that is useful or necessary in an almanac. Also, a variety of entertaining matter in prose and verse. By Gabriel Hutchins, mathematician.
Elizabeth-Town: Printed by Shepard Kollock, for Samuel Campbell, No. 124, *Pearl-Street, New-York.* [1798.] pp. (36). 12mo.

33920 HUTCHINS, John Nathan
Hutchins improved: being an Almanack and ephemeris of the motions of the sun and moon; the true places and aspects of the planets; the rising and setting of the sun; and the rising, setting, and southing of the moon, for the year of our Lord 1799: being the 3d after bissextile, or leap-year, and 23d year of American independence. 'till 4th July. Containing also, the lunations, conjunctions, eclipses, judgment of the weather, rising and setting of the planets, length of days and nights, courts, roads, &c. Together with useful tables, entertaining remarks, &c. &c. By John Nathan Hutchins, philom.
New-York: Printed and sold by H. Gaine, at his Printing-Office, at the Bible, in Pearl-Street. Where may be had, the New-York Pocket Almanack. [1798.] pp. [36.] 12mo. AAS. EI. LOC. NYHS. NYPL.

33921 IMPARTIAL [cut] Herald. Vol. I. No. 1. Friday, July 27, [— No. 13, Friday, October 19, 1798.]
Printed at Haverhill, (Massachusetts), by Angier March. 1798. fol.
Established, as a weekly, by Angier March. With the issue for October 19th, March disposed of his interests to Seth H. Moore, and Chester Stebbins, who established, on October 26th, in continuation, the *Haverhill Federal Gazette.*

33922 IMPARTIAL HERALD. VOL. I. NO. 30. WEDNESDAY, JANUARY 3, [— No. 57 ? MON-DAY, JULY 9, 1798.] No. 1. TUESDAY, JULY 17, [— No. 24. TUESDAY, DECEMBER 25, 1798.]

    Sheffield, Connecticut. Published by H. & O. Farnsworth. 1798. fol.

Beginning with the issue for July 17th, Havila, and Oliver Farnsworth were succeeded by Edward Gray, and Rescome D. Albro, as Gray & Albro, and a new numbering was begun with that issue. At the end of the year Albro withdrew from the firm, and publication continued by Edward Gray into June, 1799, when it was discontinued.

33923 THE INDEPENDENT [Mass. arms.] CHRONICLE: AND THE UNIVERSAL ADVERTISER. VOL. XXX. NUMBER 1750. FROM THURSDAY, DECEMBER 28, 1797—TO MONDAY, JANUARY 1, [— NUMBER 1855. FROM THURSDAY, DECEMBER 27, TO MONDAY, DECEMBER 31, 1798.]

    Boston—(Massachusetts)—Printed and published every Monday and Thursday, by Thomas Adams, at his Printing-Office, opposite the Court-House, Court-Street. 1798. fol.   **AAS. LOC. MHS.**

33924 —— [Arms.] THE CARRIERS, OF THE INDEPENDENT CHRONICLE TO THEIR PATRONS AND FRIENDS. . . .

    [Boston: Printed by Thomas Adams. January 1, 1798.] Broadside.   **HSP.**

33925 INDIANS. ONEIDAS.

    Caption title: AT A TREATY HELD WITH THE ONEIDA NATION OR TRIBE OF INDIANS, AT THEIR VILLAGE IN THE STATE OF NEW-YORK ON THE FIRST DAY OF JUNE IN THE YEAR ONE THOUSAND SEVEN HUNDRED AND NINETY-EIGHT, PRESENT JOSEPH HOPKINSON, COMMISSIONER APPOINTED UNDER THE AUTHORITY OF THE UNITED STATES TO HOLD THE TREATY: EGBERT BENSON, EZRA L'HOMMEDIEU AND JOHN TAYLOR, AGENTS FOR THE STATE OF NEW-YORK.

    [Without place or Printer. 1798.] pp. 3. 8vo.

33926 THE INSTRUCTIVE STORY OF INDUSTRY AND SLOTH. [etc.] ORNAMENTED WITH [eleven] CUTS.

    Hartford: Printed by John Babcock. 1798. pp. [31], frontispiece. 32mo. **AAS.**

33927 IVERNOIS, SIR FRANCIS D·   1757–1842

    AN ACCOUNT OF THE LATE REVOLUTION IN GENEVA: AND OF THE CONDUCT OF FRANCE TOWARDS THAT REPUBLIC, FROM OCTOBER, 1792, TO OCTOBER, 1794; IN A SERIES OF LETTERS, TO A CITIZEN OF PHILADELPHIA. VELUTI IN SPECULO. [Ornament.]

    Philadelphia: Published by Francis C. King, No. 42, Market-Street. 1798. Price 37½ cents. pp. vi, 76. 8vo.   **BM. NYHS.**

33928 —— REFLEXIONS SUR LA GUERRE. EN RÉPONSE AUX REFLEXIONS SUR LA PAIX. PAR M. D'IVERNOIS, AVEC REMARQUE, CITATION, &C. PAR J. ADAMS, PRESIDENT DES ETATS UNIES. D'ABORD ON MÉPRISAIT TROP LES ARMES FRANÇAISES: MAINTENANT ON LES REDOUTE AU—DELÀ MÊME DE LEURS FORCES. REFLEXIONS SUR LA PAIX, P. 8. [Ornament.]

    Philadelphia: Et se vend chez Francis C. King, Rue du Marché, No. 42. 1798. Prix 63 cents. pp. (2), 157. 8vo.   **NYHS.**

33929 —— *Half-title:* D'IVERNOIS ON THE DOWNFAL [*sic*] OF SWITZERLAND. [Dated, London, St. James' Place, 28th May, 1798.]

    [Without title-page. 1798.] pp. (20). 8vo.   **BA. LOC.**

33930 JACKSON, CHARLES 1775–1855
AN ORATION, DELIVERED BEFORE THE RIGHT WORSHIPFUL MASTER AND BRETHREN
OF ST. PETER'S LODGE, AT THE EPISCOPAL CHURCH IN NEWBURYPORT, MASSA-
CHUSETTS, ON THE FESTIVAL OF ST. JOHN THE BAPTIST; CELEBRATED JUNE 25,
5798. BY THE WORSHIPFUL BROTHER CHARLES JACKSON, P. M.

Newburyport: Printed by brother Angier March; A. L. 5798. [1798.] pp.
(24). 4to.   AAS. BA. BM. HC. JCB. LOC. MHS. NYPL.

33931 JANEWAY, JAMES 1636–1674
A TOKEN FOR CHILDREN, BEING AN EXACT ACCOUNT OF THE CONVERSION, HOLY AND
EXEMPLARY LIVES AND JOYFUL DEATHS, OF SEVERAL YOUNG CHILDREN. BY JAMES
JANEWAY, MINISTER OF THE GOSPEL. TO WHICH IS ADDED, A TOKEN FOR THE
CHILDREN OF NEWENGLAND, OR, SOME EXAMPLES OF CHILDREN, IN WHOM THE FEAR
OF GOD WAS REMARKABLY BUDDING BEFORE THEY DIED; IN SEVERAL PARTS OF
NEWENGLAND. PRESERVED AND PUBLISHED FOR THE ENCOURAGEMENT OF PIETY
IN OTHER CHILDREN. [By Cotton Mather.]

*Printed at Worcester, Massachusetts, by James R. Hutchins, for Nathaniel Ely,
jun. of Longmeadow.* MDCCXCV. pp. 188. 24mo.

A variant of my X : 28895.

33932 JARVIS, ABRAHAM 1739–1813
BISHOP JARVIS'S CHARGE TO THE CLERGY OF HIS DIOCESE. DELIVERED IMMEDIATELY
AFTER HIS CONSECRATION, IN TRINITY CHURCH, NEW-HAVEN, ON THE FESTIVAL OF
ST. LUKE, OCTOBER 18, 1797. TOGETHER WITH THE ADDRESS OF THE CONVENTION
OF THE PROTESTANT EPISCOPAL CHURCH, IN CONNECTICUT, TO THEIR BISHOP. AND
THE BISHOP'S ANSWER.

Printed at Newfield, By Lazarus Beach. 1798. pp. 29. 8vo.
  AAS. BA. JCB. LOC. YC.

33933 JARVIS, PETER
THE SUPPLICATIONS OF PETER JARVIS, WHO, FOR HIS FORMER SERVICES, BEGS A POR-
TION OF YOUR BOUNTY.

[Without place or Printer. 1798.] Broadside.   HSP.

33934 JEFFERSON, THOMAS 1743–1826
A SUPPLEMENTARY NOTE ON THE MOULD BOARD DESCRIBED IN A LETTER TO SIR JOHN
SINCLAIR, OF MARCH 23, 1798, INSERTED IN THE AMERICAN PHILOSOPHICAL
TRANSACTIONS, VOL. 4, AND IN MAESE'S DOMESTIC ENCYCLOPÆDIA VOCE PLOUGH.
[Thirty-seven lines, and diagram.] TH: JEFFERSON.

[Philadelphia: 1798.] Broadside. 4to.   LOC.

33935 JENKS, BENJAMIN 1646–1784
PRAYERS, AND OFFICES OF DEVOTION FOR FAMILIES, AND FOR PARTICULAR PERSONS,
UPON MOST OCCASIONS. BY BENJAMIN JENKS, LATE RECTOR OF HARLEY, IN SHROP-
SHIRE, AND CHAPLAIN TO THE RIGHT HONORABLE THE EARL OF BRADFORD. [Two
lines of Scripture texts.] TWENTY FOURTH EDITION.

Boston: From J. Bumstead's Printing-Office, Union-Street. 1798. pp. 270,
(5). 12mo.   AAS. JCB.

33936 JOHNSON, EBENEZER
A SHORT ACCOUNT OF A NORTHWEST VOYAGE, PERFORMED IN THE YEARS 1796, 1797
& 1798. BY EBENEZER JOHNSON. [Cut of ship.]

[Boston:] Massachusetts: Printed for the Author,—1798.—pp. 15. 8vo. AAS.

33937   JOHNSON, John Barent   1769–1803
The Dealings of God with Israel and America: a discourse, delivered on the fourth of July, 1798. By John B. Johnson, one of the ministers of the Reformed Dutch Church, in the city of Albany.

Albany: Printed by Charles R. & George Webster, at their Bookstore, in the White House, corner of State and Pearl-streets. MDCCXCVIII. pp. 21. 8vo.
         JCB. NYHS.

33938   THE JOHNSTOWN Gazette. Vol. iii. Numb. 130. Wednesday, January 3, [— Vol. iv. Numb. 181. Wednesday, December 26, 1798.]
Johnstown, (State of New-York:) Printed by Jacob Dockstader. 1798. fol.

Sometime this year, Dockstader disposed of his interests to David Holden and James Smith.

33939   JONES, Samuel   1735–1814
A Selection of Psalms and hymns done under the appointment of the Philadelphian Association. By Samuel Jones, d.d. and Burges Allison, a.m.
Philadelphia: 1798.

210th Pennsylvania District Copyright, issued to Samuel Jones, D. D. as Proprietor, 1 June, 1798.

33940   —— A Treatise of church discipline, and a Directory. Done by appointment of the Philadelphia Baptist Association. By Samuel Jones, d.d. [Three lines of Scripture texts.]
Philadelphia: Printed by S. C. Ustick, No. 79, North Third-Street. 1798. pp. 38. 12mo.   AAS. JCB. LOC. NYPL.

206th Pennsylvania District Copyright, issued to Samuel Jones, as Author, 24 April, 1798.

33941   JONES, Thomas
Der Triumph der Christlichen Liebe, der Hauptinhalt einer Predigt, welche . . . zu Reading in Berks County vorgetragen worden . . . den 24th Juny, 1798. Vor der Freimaurer Loge No. 62.
Reading: Gedruckt bey Jacob Schneider und Comp. 1798. 12mo.

33942   JOURNAL of the Times. Vol. i. No. 1. Wednesday, October 10, [— No. 12. Wednesday, December 26, 1798.]
Stonington Point, (Connecticut.) Printed by Samuel Trumbull. 1798. fol. chs.

Established by Samuel Trumbull, and continued by him to May, 1804. With the issue for January 2, 1799, the paper was enlarged from small to large folio. At the end of the first volume in October, 1799, the name was changed to *Impartial Journal*, under which name it appeared until publication ceased in May, 1804.

33943   JOVIAL songster. A collection of the most esteemed songs, sung at the American and English theatres. Fourth edition.
Baltimore: Printed for Henry S. Keatinge. 1798.

33944   K., S.
Plan for establishing a General Marine Society throughout the United States, and systems of regulations therein; written at sea, in the year 1794: now printed for the benefit of that institution, by the Author. [Eight lines of quotation.]
Philadelphia: Printed by John Fenno, No. 119, Chesnut Street. 1798. pp. (32). 8vo.   AAS. BA. JCB. LOC. NYHS. NYPL.

33945 KENDRICK, Ariel   1772–1856
A Brief reply to a pamphlet lately published bv S. Delanoe, (under the
fictitious name of Candor) in favour of universalism. Entitled, Miscellaneous thoughts on the doctrine of limited election and reprobation,
as it stands contrasted with Scripture and reason. By Ariel Kendrick,
minister of the Gospel, Woodstock, Vermont. [Motto.]

Printed at Hanover, New Hampshire, by Benjamin True. 1798. pp. 23.
8vo.   AAS.

33946 [U. S. Arms.] KENNEBECK Intelligencer. [Seal of District of Maine.] [Motto.]
Vol. iii. No. 110. Tuesday, January 2, [—Vol. iii. No. 155. Saturday, December 29, 1798.]

*[District of Maine.] Published by Peter Edes, near the Court-House, in Au-
gusta.* 1798. fol.   AAS.

33947 KENNEDY, Patrick
An Answer to Paine's Letter to general Washington: including some pages
of gratuitous counsel to mr. Erskine. Impices, ingratusque, audax scer-
arumque magister. By P. Kennedy, esq.

Philadelphia: Re-published by William Cobbett, opposite Christ-Church. Jan.
1798. pp. (2), (42). 8vo.   AAS. BA. LCP. LOC. MHS. NYHS. NYPL.

33948 KENRICK, William   1725–1779
The Whole duty of woman. A new edition. With considerable improvements. [Heavy line.]

London Printed: Reprinted at Litchfield, by T. Collier. [1798.] pp. 106.
24mo.

33949 —— — The Whole duty of woman. A new edition. With considerable improvements.

Philadelphia: Printed by J. Ormrod, No. 41, Chesnut-street. 1798. pp. 157,
frontispiece. 32mo.   AAS.

Consisting of selections from the English work, with this title, by William Kenrick.

33950 KENTUCKY. State.
Acts passed at the first session of the sixth General Assembly, for the
Commonwealth of Kentucky, begun and held in the capitol, in the town
of Frankfort, on . . . in the year of our Lord one thousand, seven hundred, and ninety-seven, and of the Commonwealth the fifth. Published
by authority.

Frankfort: 1798. 8vo.

33951 —— Acts of a local, or private nature, passed at the second session of the
sixth General Assembly for the Commonwealth of Kentucky: begun and
held at the capitol, in the town of Frankfort, on Monday the first day
of January, in the year of our Lord, one thousand seven hundred and
ninety-eight, and in the sixth year of the Commonwealth. Published by
authority.

Frankfort: Printed by John Bradford, Printer to the Commonwealth. [1798.]
pp. 87. 8vo.   MHS.

KENTUCKY. STATE, continued.

33952 —— LEGISLATURE OF KENTUCKY. IN THE HOUSE OF REPRESENTATIVES, NOVEMBER 10TH, 1798. . . . RESOLVED, THAT THE SEVERAL STATES COMPOSING THE UNITED STATES OF AMERICA, ARE NOT UNITED ON THE PRINCIPLE OF UNLIMITED SUBMISSION TO THEIR GENERAL GOVERNMENT. [Four columns.] APPROVED NOVEMBER 16TH, 1798. JAMES GARRARD, G. K. BY THE GOVERNOR, HARRY TOULMIN, SECRETARY OF STATE.

[Lexington: Printed by John Bradford, 1798.] Broadside. fol.   NYPL.

The type was rearranged in four quarto pages format for transmission to the governors of the other States, as follows:

33953 —— —— LEGISLATURE OF KENTUCKY. IN THE HOUSE OF REPRESENTATIVES, NOVEMBER 10TH, 1798. [Resolutions of State rights.] APPROVED NOVEMBER 16TH, 1798. JAMES GARRARD, G. K. BY THE GOVERNOR, HARRY TOULMIN, SECRETARY OF STATE.

[Lexington: Printed by John Bradford. 1798.] pp. (4). 4to.   HEH. MA.

33954 THE KENTUCKY ALMANAC, FOR THE YEAR OF OUR LORD, 1799. BEING THE THIRD AFTER BISSEXTILE, OR LEAP YEAR—THE 23D OF AMERICAN INDEPENDENCE—THE 11TH OF OUR FEDERAL GOVERNMENT—AND THE 8TH OF THIS COMMONWEALTH. CONTAINING THE LUNATIONS, CONJUNCTIONS, ECLIPSES, JUDGMENT OF THE WEATHER, REMARKABLE DAYS, LENGTH OF DAYS AND NIGHTS, TIME COURTS ARE HELD, &C. TOGETHER, WITH USEFUL TABLES, AND A VARIETY OF ENTERTAINING PIECES, IN PROSE AND VERSE. CALCULATED FOR THE LATITUDE OF 37° NORTH AND A MERIDIAN OF 15' WEST OF PHILADELPHIA; AND WILL SERVE, WITHOUT ANY SENSIBLE VARIATION, FOR THE NORTH WESTERN TERRITORY, ST. VINCENNES, STATE OF TENNESSEE, AND THE WESTERN PARTS OF VIRGINIA.

Lexington: Printed and sold (wholesale and retail) by John Bradford, on Main street. [1798.] pp. (32). 16mo.   AAS.

Contains, The Qnaker and clown. A curious description of a wonderful old man. A choice of a wife by cheese. Natural history of that most extraordinary sea-animal, called the Kraken. A calculation of the number of books, chapters, verses, letters, words &c. in the Bible. Anecdotes, etc.

33955 KENTUCKY [Arms] GAZETTE. VOL. XI. No. 589. WEDNESDAY, JANUARY 3, [—VOL. XII. No. 640. WEDNESDAY, DECEMBER 26, 1798.]

Lexington—Printed by John Bradford, Printer to the Commonwealth, on Main Street, price 15 s per ann. 1798. fol.

The cut represents the State Arms, oval in shape, with the motto, "United we stand, divided we fall." This was withdrawn when Bradford ceased to be State Printer, in 1799.

33956 THE KENTUCKY PRIMER: CONTAINING A VARIETY OF EASY LESSONS IN SPELLING AND READING, ADAPTED TO THE CAPACITIES OF CHILDREN. "TO TEACH THE YOUNG IDEA HOW TO SHOOT."

Washington (K). Printed by Hunter and Beaumont. 1798.

"☞ This first humble attempt to commence the manufacture of school books in this State they trust will meet with such encouragement as to warrant their perseverance in the establishment of an extensive manufactory of that useful article. They intend to put a Spelling-book to press very shortly, and will continue to print such other publications as may be in sufficient demand."

33957   THE KENTUCKY Spelling-book: or, young scholar's assistant. Containing a variety of easy lessons and tables, admirably adapted to facilitate the improvement of the young pupil in spelling and reading. A number of useful tables of words, with their explanation annexed, which will tend both to the amusement and information of the learner, and will unite the benefits of a pocket-dictionary to the usual advantages of a spelling-book. To which are added, extracts from some of the most approved English writers, in prose and verse, for the improvement of the scholar in the art of speaking.

Washington, (K). Printed by Hunter and Beaumont. 1798.

33958   THE KEY. Vol. i. No. 1. Saturday, January 13, [— No. 27. Saturday, July 14, 1798.]

Frederick Town: Printed weekly, by John D. Cary, at the Office of the Federal Gazette, in Market-Street. 1798. pp. 213, (3). 8vo.   BM. LOC. MdHS.

Established, as a weekly, by John D. Cary, and named in compliment to General John Ross Key. It was the first magazine published in Western Maryland, its publication beginning and ending as above.

33959   KING, Cyrus   1772–1817
An Oration pronounced at Biddeford on the fourth of July, 1798, the anniversary of American independence, 1798. At the request of the gentlemen of that and the adjoining town of Pepperellboro; by whose desire this hasty production is submitted to the public, by Cyrus King.

Printed by E. A. Jenks, Portland. [1798.] pp. 20. 8vo.   JCB. LOC.

33960   KING, Walter   1758–1815
St. Paul's manner of preaching, recommended for imitation, in a sermon delivered at the ordination of the Rev. Daniel Hall to the pastoral care of the church in Sag-Harbor, Long-Island: Sept. 21, 1797. By Walter King, a. m. pastor of the second church in Norwich, Connecticut.

Printed at Norwich: by Thomas Hubbard, M,DCC,XCVIII. pp. 30, (1). 8vo.   AAS. BM. CHS. JCB. MHS. NYPL. UTS. YC.

With an Appendix, giving a brief account of the town of Sag Harbor.

33961   KING, Walter, and others.   .
Circular letters, containing an invitation to the ministers and churches of every christian denomination in the United States, to unite in their endeavours to carry into execution the "humble attempt" of President Edwards, to promote explicit agreement and visible union of God's people, in extraordinary prayer, for the revival of religion and advancement of Christ's Kingdom on Earth. [Four lines from] Zechariah.

Concord: Printed by Geo. Hough. 1798. pp. (32). 8vo.   AAS. BA. JCB. NYPL.

33962   KINNE, Aaron   1744–1824
Alamoth. An address, delivered to the singing schools, in the first and second societies in Groton. By Aaron Kinne, a. m. [Two lines from] Psalm xcv.i. [Ornament.]

New-London:—Printed by S. Green. 1798. pp. 16. 8vo.

CHS. MHS. NYPL. UTS.

Reprinted in Brattleborough, Vermont, in 1812.

33963　KIRKLAND, John Thornton　　　　　　　　　　　　　　1770–1840
AN ORATION, DELIVERED, AT THE REQUEST OF P B K, IN THE CHAPEL OF HARVARD
COLLEGE, ON THE DAY OF THEIR ANNIVERSARY. JULY 19, 1798. BY JOHN THORN-
TON KIRKLAND. [Vignette.]
　　Boston: Printed by John Russell. 1798. pp. 24. 8vo.
　　　　　　　　　　　　　AAS. BA. BM. HC. JCB. LOC. MHS. NYHS. NYPL.

33964　——— A SERMON, DELIVERED AT THE INTERMENT OF THE REV. JEREMY BELKNAP, D. D.
MINISTER OF THE CHURCH IN FEDERAL STREET, BOSTON, JUNE 22, 1798. BY JOHN
THORNTON KIRKLAND, MINISTER OF THE NEW SOUTH CHURCH, BOSTON.
　　Boston: Printed by Manning & Loring. [1798.] pp.27. 8vo.
　　　　　　　　　　　　　AAS. BA. BM. HC. JCB. LOC. MHS.
　　[Title within ornamental border.] Character of the late Rev. Dr. Bel-
knap; from the Columbian Centinel. By Rev. John Eliot. pp. 22–26.
List of Dr. Belknap's publications, pp. 26–27.

33965　——— A SERMON, DELIVERED ON THE 9TH OF MAY, 1798. BEING THE DAY OF A NA-
TIONAL FAST, RECOMMENDED BY THE PRESIDENT OF THE UNITED STATES. BY JOHN
THORNTON KIRKLAND, MINISTER OF THE NEW SOUTH CHURCH, BOSTON.
　　Boston: Printed by John Russell, at his Office, Quaker-Lane. 1798. pp. (2),
23. 8vo.　　　AAS. BA. BM. CHS. CLA. HC. HSP. JCB. LOC. MHS. UTS.

33966　KLINE'S CARLISLE WEEKLY GAZETTE. VOL. XIII. NO. 622. WEDNESDAY JANUARY
3, [—VOL. XIV. NO. 673. WEDNESDAY, DECEMBER 26, 1798.]
　　Carlisle: (State of Pennsylvania) Printed by George Kline. 1798. fol.　AAS.

33967　KNOX, Henry　　　　　　　　　　　　　　　　　　1750–1806
FOR SALE, LOTS OR TRACTS OF LAND, OF ANY SIZE, AS MAY BEST SUIT THE PURCHASERS,
FROM 100 ACRES TO 1000 ACRES AND UPWARDS.
　　[Without place or Printer. 1798.] Broadside.　　　　　　BPL.

33968　KNOX, Vicesimus　　　　　　　　　　　　　　　　1752–1821
A COMPLETE LIBRARY. PROPOSALS FOR PUBLISHING IN THREE OCTAVO VOLUMES OF
ONE THOUSAND, DOUBLE COLUMN PAGES. EXTRACTS, ELEGANT, INSTRUCTIVE, AND
ENTERTAINING, IN PROSE AND VERSE; SELECTED FROM THE BEST MODERN AUTHORS,
AND DISPOSED UNDER PROPER HEADS: THE WHOLE FORMING A VALUABLE TREASURY
OF USEFUL AND ORNAMENTAL KNOWLEDGE. BY THE CELEBRATED DOCT. KNOX.
　　[New-York: Printed for Lee & Stokes, No. 25, Maiden-Lane. 1798.] pp.
(4). 8vo.　　　　　　　　　　　　　　　　　AAS.

33969　KNOXVILLE [cut of] THE GENIUS OF LIBERTY. REGISTER. THE PRESS IS THE CRADLE
OF SCIENCE, THE NURSE OF GENIUS, AND THE SHIELD OF LIBERTY. VOL. I. NUMBER
1. TUESDAY, JUNE 12, [— NUMBER 21. TUESDAY, OCTOBER 30, 1798.]
　　*Knoxville, (State of Tennessee) Printed (every Tuesday) by George Roulstone
& John R. Parrington.* 1798. fol.　　　　　　　　　AAS.
　　Established, as a weekly, by George Roulstone, and John Rivington
Parrington, in continuation of *Roulstone's Knoxville Gazette,* and con-
tinued by them to October 30, 1798—the last number located. The
paper was editorially and generally referred to, by its sub-title, as *The
Genius of Liberty.*

33970　KOTZWARA, Franz　　　　　　　　　　　　　　　　–1791
WHEN DELIA ON THE PLAIN APPEARS. COMPOSED BY KOTZWARA, AUTHOR OF THE
BATTLE OF PRAGUE.
　　*New-York: Published by George Gilbert at his Music Store, 177 Broadway,
Apollo's Head.* 1798.

33971   KYD, STEWART   –1811
A TREATISE ON THE LAW OF BILLS OF EXCHANGE AND PROMISSORY NOTES. BY STEWART
KYD, OF THE MIDDLE TEMPLE, ESQ. BARRISTER AT LAW. THE FIRST AMERICAN,
FROM THE THIRD LONDON, EDITION. WITH CONSIDERABLE ADDITIONS.
> *Boston: Printed by Manning & Loring, for S. Hall, W. Spotswood, J. White,*
> *Thomas & Andrews, D. West, E. Larkin, W. P. & L. Blake, and J. West.* 1798.
> pp. xii, 288. 12mo.   AAS. HC. JCB. LOC. NYPL.

33972   —— — A TREATISE ON THE LAW OF BILLS OF EXCHANGE AND PROMISSORY NOTES.
BY STEWART KYD, OF THE MIDDLE TEMPLE, ESQ. BARRISTER AT LAW. THE FIRST
AMERICAN, FROM THE THIRD LONDON, EDITION. WITH CONSIDERABLE ADDITIONS.
> *Boston: Printed by Manning & Loring, for David West. Sold at his Book-*
> *store, No. 56, Cornhill; by Ebenezer S. Thomas, Charleston, South-Carolina; and*
> *by Solomon Cottom & Co. Baltimore.* 1798. pp. xii, 288. 12mo   AAS.

33973   THE LADIES' PATRIOTIC SONG.
> *Boston: Printed & sold by P. A. von Hagen, jun. and Co. at their Musical*
> *Magazine, No. 62, Newbury Street.* 1798.

33974   LAMBERT, JOHN
A SHORT AND PRACTICAL ESSAY ON FARMING, BEING THE EXPERIENCE OF A FARMER
OF ABOUT SIXTY YEARS OF AGE, NEAR FORTY YEARS OF WHICH WERE SPENT IN ENG-
LAND, ESSEX COUNTY, ON LAND WHERE FARMING IS DONE IN THE GREATEST PER-
FECTION AND NEAR SEVEN YEARS ON THREE HUNDRED AND TWENTY ACRES OF WORN
OUT LAND IN PATTY GROVE AND ALLOWAY CREEK IN SALEM COUNTY, WEST JERSEY.
SHEWING THE MEANS WHEREBY THESE WORN OUT LANDS MAY BE IMPROVED AND
THAT THE MEANS ARE IN THE POWER OF ALMOST EVERY FARMER.
> *[Philadelphia ?* 1798.]

217th Pennsylvania District Copyright, issued to John Lambert, as
Author, 10 December, 1798.

33975   LANCASTER JOURNAL. VOL. IV. No. 33. SATURDAY, JANUARY 6, [—VOL. V. No. 32.
SATURDAY, DECEMBER 29, 1798.]
> *Lancaster: Printed by William Hamilton, at the German and English Print-*
> *ing-Office, Franklin's Head, King-Street, west of the Court-House, at the low price*
> *of two dollars per annum. . . . 1798. fol.*

33976   DAS LANDMANNS WOCHENBLATT. NUM. 1. DIENSTAG, FEBRUAR 27, [— NUM. 44.
DIENSTAG, DEZEMBER 25, 1798.]
> *Lancaster: Gedruckt bey William Hamilton und Conrad Wortmann.* 1798. fol.

Established, as a weekly, by William Hamilton, and Conrad Wortmann,
and publication discontinued at the end of the first year, in February,
1799, when it was succeeded by *Der Lancaster Wochenblatt.* No copies
are known.

33977   LANE, ISAAC
ANTHEM FOR ORDINATION. BY ISAAC LANE.
> *Northampton: Printed by Daniel Wright and Co.* 1797.   HC.

33978   LANGDON, JOHN
A CATALOGUE OF ENGLISH KITCHEN-GARDEN AND FANCY FLOWER SEEDS, IMPORTED IN
THE SNOW, HAZARD, FROM LONDON, AND FOR SALE AT THE STORE OF JOHN LANG-
DON, No. 6 FLETCHER-STREET, NEAR THE FLY-MARKET. WHOLESALE AND RETAIL.
. . . [Colophon:]
> *Printed by J. Buel, No. 74, William-Street, New-York.* [1798.] Broadside.
> fol.   NYPL.

33979   LANGDON, TIMOTHY   1758–1801
A SERMON, PREACHED AT DANBURY, NOVEMBER 8TH, A.D. 1798, BEING THE DAY OF
THE EXECUTION OF ANTHONY, A FREE NEGRO, PURSUANT TO SENTENCE OF DEATH
PASSED UPON HIM BY THE HON. SUPERIOR COURT, FOR THE CRIME OF A RAPE. BY
TIMOTHY LANGDON, A.M. PASTOR OF THE FIRST CHURCH IN DANBURY. [One line
from] ECCL.
> *Danbury: Printed and sold by Douglas & Nichols.* 1798. pp. [23.] 8vo.
>   AAS. CHS.

33980   LANMAN, JAMES   1767–1841
AN ORATION PRONOUNCED ON THE TWENTY-SECOND ANNIVERSARY OF AMERICAN IN-
DEPENDENCE, BEFORE THE CITIZENS OF NORWICH.
> *Norwich: Printed by John Trumbull.* 1798. pp. 22. 12mo.   NYHS.

33981   LANSINGBURGH GAZETTE. VOL. I. No. 1. TUESDAY, SEPTEMBER 18, [—No. 15.
TUESDAY, DECEMBER 25, 1798.]
> *[Lansingburgh:] Printed every Tuesday, by Gardiner Tracy, at the Printing-
> Office, in King's Street.* 1798. fol.

Established, as a weekly, in continuation of the *American Spy*, whose
advertising it carried on, by Gardiner Tracy, and continued by him to
14 October, 1806, when Luther Bliss was admitted to partnership under
the firm name of Tracy & Bliss, and this arrangement continued beyond
the period of this work.

33982   LARKIN, EBENEZER
CATALOGUE OF BOOKS, FOR SALE BY E. LARKIN, No. 47, CORNHILL, BOSTON. CON-
SISTING OF A GREAT VARIETY OF AUTHORS IN HISTORY, VOYAGES, TRAVELS, LIVES,
MEMOIRS, ANTIQUITIES, PHILOSOPHY, NOVELS, DIVINITY, LAW, PHYSIC, SURGERY,
CHEMISTRY, GEOGRAPHY, HUSBANDRY, NAVIGATION, ARTS, SCIENCES, ARCHITECTURE,
MISCELLANIES, POETRY, PLAYS, &C. &C.
> *Boston: Printed for E. Larkin.* 1798. pp. 56. 12mo.   AAS. HEH.

33983   LARKIN, SAMUEL
THE COLUMBIAN SONGSTER, AND FREEMASON'S POCKET COMPANION. A COLLECTION
OF THE NEWEST AND MOST SENTIMENTAL, CONVIVIAL, HUMOUROUS, SATIRICAL, PAS-
TORAL, HUNTING, SEA AND MASONIC SONGS, BEING THE LARGEST AND BEST COLLEC-
TION EVER PUBLISHED IN AMERICA. SELECTED BY S. LARKIN.
> *Portsmouth, New-Hampshire: Printed by J. Melcher, for S. Larkin, at the
> Portsmouth Book-Store.* 1798. pp. 216; 70, (2). 12mo.   LOC.
> *Second title:* THE FREE-MASON'S POCKET COMPANION. A COLLECTION OF MASONIC
> SONGS. SELECTED BY S. LARKIN.
> *Portsmouth.—New-Hampshire, Printed by J. Melcher, for S. Larkin,* 1798.
> pp. 70, (2).

33984   LATHROP, JOHN   1740–1816
A SERMON PREACHED AT THE CHURCH IN BRATTLE-STREET, BOSTON, THURSDAY,
SEPTEMBER 27, 1798. A DAY RELIGIOUSLY OBSERVED ON ACCOUNT OF THE EPIDEMIC
NOW PREVAILING IN THIS TOWN, AND SEVERAL OTHER SEAPORTS IN AMERICA. BY
JOHN LATHROP, D.D. PRINTED BY THE DESIRE OF MANY WHO HEARD IT.
> *Boston: Printed by Benjamin Edes, in Kilby-Street.* 1798. pp. [24,] [iv.]
> 8vo.   AAS. BA. BM. LOC. MHS.

33985   LATHROP, JOHN, JUNIOR   1772–1820
AN ORATION, PRONOUNCED ON THE 4TH DAY OF JULY, 1798, AT THE REQUEST OF A
NUMBER OF THE INHABITANTS OF DEDHAM AND ITS VICINITY, IN COMMEMORATION
OF THE ANNIVERSARY OF AMERICAN INDEPENDENCE. BY JOHN LATHROP, JUN.
[Cut of Eagle.]
> *Dedham: Printed at the Minerva Press.* 1798. pp. [19.] 8vo.
>   AAS. BA. BM. JCB. LOC. MHS. NYPL. UTS.

AUCTION
VALUES

33986   LATHROP, JOSEPH   1731–1820
A SERMON, ON THE DANGERS OF THE TIMES, FROM INFIDELITY AND IMMORALITY; AND ESPECIALLY FROM A LATELY DISCOVERED CONSPIRACY AGAINST RELIGION AND GOVERNMENT, DELIVERED AT WEST-SPRINGFIELD, AND AFTERWARD AT SPRINGFIELD. BY JOSEPH LATHROP, D. D.

> *Springfield: Printed by Francis Stebbins. September,* 1798. pp. [24.] 8vo.
> AAS. BA. BM. BU. CHS. JCB. LOC. NYPL. UTS. YC.

33987   LATROBE, BENJAMIN HENRY   1764–1826
AMERICAN COPPER-MINES. TO THE CHAIRMAN OF THE COMMITTEE OF COMMERCE AND MANUFACTURES, TO WHOM HAS BEEN REFERRED THE PETITION OF N. I. ROOSEVELT AND HIS ASSOCIATES, PRAYING FOR AN ACT OF INCORPORATION OF A MINE AND METAL COMPANY. [Signed, B. H. Latrobe.]

> *[Philadelphia:* 1798. pp. (8). 8vo.   AAS. BM.

33988   LATTA, JAMES   1732–1801
A DISCOURSE ON PSALMODY; IN WHICH IT IS CLEARLY SHEWN THAT IT IS THE DUTY OF CHRISTIANS TO TAKE THE PRINCIPAL SUBJECTS AND OCCASIONS OF THEIR PSALMS, HYMNS AND SPIRITUAL SONGS FROM THE GOSPEL OF CHRIST. WITH CORRECTIONS AND ADDITIONS. BY JAMES LATTA, A. M. MINISTER OF THE GOSPEL, AT CHESNUT-LEVEL.

> *Washington: Printed and sold by John Colerick, with permission of the Author.*
> 1798. pp. xii, 98. 12mo.   AAS. BM.

33989   LEAMING, JEREMIAH   1717–1804
DISSERTATIONS UPON VARIOUS SUBJECTS, WHICH MAY BE WELL WORTH THE ATTENTION OF EVERY CHRISTIAN; AND OF REAL SERVICE TO THE SINCERE INQUIRER AFTER TRUE RELIGION. BY JEREMIAH LEAMING, A. M. RECTOR OF CHRIST CHURCH IN STRATFORD. YE KNOW THE TRUTH; THE TRUTH SHALL MAKE YOU FREE. [Ornament.]

> *Re-printed by T. Collier, in Litchfield.* 1798. pp. 72. 8vo.   CLA.

33990   —— AN ESSAY ON CONVERSION. BY JEREMIAH LEAMING, LATE RECTOR OF CHRIST'S CHURCH, IN STRATFORD. WHEN THOU ART CONVERTED, STRENGTHEN THY BRETHREN. JESUS CHRIST.

> *Reprinted at Litchfield,* 1798, *from the 5th edition.* pp. 8. 12mo.   CHS.

33991   LEE, CHARLES   1758–1815
DEFENCE OF THE ALIEN AND SEDITION LAWS, SHEWING THEIR ENTIRE CONSISTENCY WITH THE CONSTITUTION OF THE UNITED STATES, AND THE PRINCIPLES OF OUR GOVERNMENT. ADDRESSED TO THE PEOPLE OF VIRGINIA. BY VIRGINIENSIS.

> *Philadelphia: Printed by John Ward Fenno.* M,DCC,XCVIII. pp. (47).
> 8vo.   BA. LOC.

33992   LENT, ADOLPH C.
AN INAUGURAL DISSERTATION, SHEWING IN WHAT MANNER PESTILENTIAL VAPOURS ACQUIRE THEIR ACID QUALITY, AND HOW THIS IS TO BE NEUTRALIZED AND DESTROYED BY ALKALIES, &C. &C. BY ADOLPH C. LENT, CITIZEN OF THE STATE OF NEW-YORK.

> *New-York: Printed by T. & J. Swords.* 1798. pp. 54. 8vo.   SGO.

33993   LESLIE, CHARLES   1650–1722
A SHORT AND EASY METHOD WITH THE DEISTS. ALSO, THE TRUTH OF CHRISTIANITY DEMONSTRATED. BY CHARLES LESLIE.

> *Lexington, (Ky.) Printed by John Bradford.* 1798.

33994   A LETTER FROM A FATHER TO HIS SON, IN ANSWER TO QUERIES RESPECTING THE STRUGGLES OF SIN IN THE MIND OF A BELIEVER; WHETHER HE BE IN A STATE OF GRACE, WHILE UNDER THE STRUGGLES AND COMBATS OF SIN. [Ornament.]

> *Newburyport: Printed by Angier March.* [1798.] pp. (18). 12mo.   AAS.

AUCTION VALUES

33995   LETTER TO THE MEMBERS OF THE ASSOCIATE REFORMED CHURCH, ILLUSTRATING THE ACTS OF SYNOD CONCERNING A SYNODICAL FUND.

New-York: 1798. pp. 24. 8vo.   JCB.

33996   A LETTER TO THOMAS PAINE, IN ANSWER TO HIS SCURRILOUS EPISTLE TO OUR LATE WORTHY PRESIDENT WASHINGTON.

Sag-Harbor: Printed by David Frothingham. 1798.

33997   LETTERS ON FREQUENT COMMUNION, ADDRESSED PARTICULARLY TO THE MEMBERS OF THE ASSOCIATE-REFORMED CHURCH IN NORTH-AMERICA. [Double line.]

New-York: Printed by T. & J. Swords, No. 99 Pearl-street.—1798.—pp. viii, 113. 8vo.   JCB.

33998   LEVANA GAZETTE: OR, ONONDAGA ADVERTISER. VOL. I. NUMB. 1. WEDNESDAY, JUNE 20, [— NUMB. 28. WEDNESDAY, DECEMBER 26, 1798.]

Scipio, (Onandago County, S. N. Y.) Printed by R. Delano. 1798. fol.

Established, as a weekly, by Roger Delano, and continued, probably, into the following year. Only a few scattering numbers are known. Levana, a small village, is given at the heading of local news, but Scipio is the place of publication.

33999   LEVI, DAVID   1740–1799
A DEFENCE OF THE OLD TESTAMENT, IN A SERIES OF LETTERS, ADDRESSED TO THOMAS PAINE, AUTHOR OF A BOOK INTITLED, "THE AGE OF REASON, PART THE SECOND, BEING AN INVESTIGATION OF TRUE AND FABULOUS THEOLOGY." BY DAVID LEVI, AUTHOR OF LETTERS TO DR. PRIESTLEY, IN ANSWER TO HIS TO THE JEWS, &C. &C. &C. [Two lines of Scripture texts.]

Philadelphia: Printed and sold by Hogan & M'Elroy, No. 222, South Third-street, a few doors below South street. 1798. pp. 207, (6), (2). 12mo.   AAS. JCB. NYPL.

Contains a six-page list of Subscribers' names, mostly from Carlisle.

34000   LEWIS, MATTHEW GREGORY   1775–1818
THE CASTLE SPECTRE: A DRAMA. IN FIVE ACTS. BY M. G. LEWIS, ESQ. M. P. AUTHOR OF "THE MONK," &C. NOW PERFORMING WITH UNBOUNDED APPLAUSE AT THE THEATRE IN BOSTON.

Printed at Boston. Sold [by David West] at the Bookstore, No. 56, Cornhill. [1798.] pp. 70. 12mo.   AAS.

34001   LEWIS, WILLIAM
OPINIONS OF WILLIAM LEWIS, AND WILLIAM RAWLE, ESQUIRES. ON THE RIGHTS OF THE CORPORATION OF THE CITY OF PHILADELPHIA TO THE SCHUYLKILL-FERRY, AND OF THE RIGHTS OF THE CORPORATION FOR ERECTING A PERMANENT BRIDGE OVER THAT RIVER.

Philadelphia: Printed by John Ward Fenno, No. 119, Chesnut-Street. 1798. pp. (18). 8vo.   AAS. LOC.

34002   LINLEY, THOMAS   1732–1795
STILL THE LARK FINDS REPOSE.

New-York: Printed and sold by George Gilbert, at his Music Store, 177 Broadway, Apollo's Head. 1798.

34003   LINN, WILLIAM   1752–1808
A DISCOURSE ON NATIONAL SINS: DELIVERED MAY 9, 1798; BEING THE DAY RECOM-
MENDED BY THE PRESIDENT OF THE UNITED STATES TO BE OBSERVED AS A DAY OF
GENERAL FAST. BY WILLIAM LINN, D. D. ONE OF THE MINISTERS OF THE REFORMED
DUTCH CHURCH IN THE CITY OF NEW-YORK.

New-York: Printed by T. & J. Swords, No, 99, Pearl-Street. 1798. pp. 37.
8vo.   AAS. BA. CHS. CLA. HC. HSP. JCB. LOC. NYHS. NYPL. PU. UTS. YC.

34004   LITTLE, WILLIAM
THE EASY INSTRUCTOR; OR, A NEW METHOD OF TEACHING SACRED HARMONY. CON-
TAINING, I. THE RUDIMENTS OF MUSIC ON AN IMPROVED PLAN, WHEREIN THE
NAMING AND TIMING OF THE NOTES ARE FAMILIARIZED TO THE WEAKEST CAPACITY.
II. A CHOICE COLLECTION OF PSALM TUNES AND ANTHEMS, FROM THE MOST CELE-
BRATED AUTHORS, WITH A NUMBER COMPOSED IN EUROPE AND AMERICA, ENTIRELY
NEW; SUITED TO ALL THE METRES SUNG IN THE DIFFERENT CHURCHES IN THE
UNITED STATES. PUBLISHED FOR THE USE OF SINGING SOCIETIES IN GENERAL, BUT
MORE PARTICULARLY FOR THOSE WHO HAVE NOT THE ADVANTAGE OF AN INSTRUCTOR.
BY WILLIAM LITTLE AND WILLIAM SMITH.

Philadelphia. 1798. pp. 74. obl. 12mo.

The advertisement, dated, August 15, 1798, states: They have been hon-
ored with upwards of three thousand subscribers before publication.
211th Pennsylvania District Copyright, issued to Edward Stammers and
William Little, as Proprietors, 15 June, 1798.

34005   THE LITTLE TRIFLER. A DRAMA. IN THREE PARTS.
Boston: 1798. frontispiece. 32mo.

34006   THE LITTLE VISITOR, BEING OBSERVATIONS OF TOMMY THOUGHTFUL. PRICE FOUR
CENTS.
Boston: Printed and sold by John W. Folsom, No. 30, Union-Street. 1798.
32mo.

34007   LIVINGSTON, EDWARD   1764–1836
SPEECH OF EDWARD LIVINGSTON, IN THE HOUSE OF REPRESENTATIVES OF THE UNITED
STATES, ON THE THIRD READING OF THE ALIEN BILL, JUNE 21, 1798.

*Albany: Printed by Barber & Southwick, and sold at their Book-Store, two
doors north of the City-Hall, Court-Street.* [1798.] pp. 20. 8vo.   JCB.

34008   —— — THE SPEECH OF EDWARD LIVINGSTON, ESQ. ON THE THIRD READING OF THE
ALIEN BILL. [Three heavy lines.]

Philadelphia: Printed by James Carey, No. 19, Carter's Alley. [1798.] pp.
16. 8vo.   BA. BM. JCB. LOC. NYPL.

Reprinted in Moore's American eloquence. Vol. 2.

34009   LIVINGSTON, JOHN HENRY   1746–1825
THE MARRIAGE OF A DECEASED WIFE'S SISTER INCESTUOUS. IN ANSWER TO "A LETTER
FROM A CITIZEN TO HIS FRIEND." [Two lines from] ISAIAH. [Signed, Eudoxious.]

New-York: Printed by T. & J. Swords, No. 99 Pearl-street. 1798. pp. 61.
8vo.
                                                                    NYPL.

34010   LOCHMAN, GEORG
AUF DIE EINWEISUNG DER DEUTSCHEN EVANGELISCH-LUTHERISCHEN SALEMS-KIRCHE
IN LIBANON. DEN DRITTEN JUNY, 1798.

Germantaun: Gedruckt bey Michael Billmeyer. 1798. pp. 8. 16mo.   AAS.

34011   LOGAN, GEORGE   1753–1821

AN ADDRESS ON THE NATURAL AND SOCIAL ORDER OF THE WORLD, AS INTENDED TO PRODUCE UNIVERSAL GOOD; DELIVERED BEFORE THE TAMMANY SOCIETY, AT THEIR ANNIVERSARY, ON THE 12TH OF MAY, 1798. FAIRE LE BIEN C'EST LE RECEVOIR. BY GEORGE LOGAN.

Philadelphia: Printed by Benjamin Franklin Bache. [1798.] pp. [12.] 8vo.
BM. HSP. LOC. NYPL.

34012   LONGWORTH, DAVID

LONGWORTH'S AMERICAN ALMANACK, NEW-YORK REGISTER, AND CITY DIRECTORY, FOR THE TWENTY-THIRD YEAR OF AMERICAN INDEPENDENCE. CONTAINING MOST THINGS USEFUL IN A WORK OF THE KIND. PRICE 5s. STITCHED—HALF BOUND 6.

New-York: Printed for the Publisher, by T. & J. Swords, No. 99 Pearl Street. —1798.—pp. (2), 86; (220). 16mo.   AAS. NYHS. NYPL.

Second title: ASTRONOMICAL CALCULATIONS FOR THE TWENTY-THIRD YEAR OF AMERICAN INDEPENDENCE, COMMENCING THE FOURTH OF JULY, A. D. 1798: BEING SECOND AFTER LEAP-YEAR, UNTIL THE FIRST OF JANUARY. CONTAINING THE RISING, SETTING, PLACES, AND ECLIPSES OF THE SUN AND MOON; THE RISING, SETTING, AND SOUTHING OF THE MOST CONSPICUOUS PLANETS AND FIXED STARS; THE EQUATION OF TIME; AND TIME OF HIGH WATER AT NEW-YORK, &C. ALSO, THE INCREASE, DECREASE, AND LENGTH OF DAYS; WITH THE FESTIVALS, &C. CALCULATED FOR THE LATITUDE AND MERIDIAN OF NEW-YORK. BY ABRAHAM SHOEMAKER.

[New-York:] From the Press of T. & J. Swords. [1798.] pp. (15).

34013   LORD, BENJAMIN   1693–1784

GOD GLORIFIED IN HIS WORKS OF PROVIDENCE AND GRACE. A REMARKABLE INSTANCE OF IT, IN THE VARIOUS AND SIGNAL DELIVERANCES, THAT EVIDENTLY APPEAR TO BE WROUGHT FOR MRS. MERCY WHEELER, OF PLAINFIELD: WHO WAS RESTORED FROM EXTREME IMPOTENCE, AND LONG CONFINEMENT. PUBLISHED AT THE DESIRE OF MANY. BY BENJAMIN LORD, A. M. THE THIRD EDITION.

Boston: Printed in the year 1743. *Hartford: Re-printed by Elisha Babcock.* 1798. pp. 59. 12mo.   AAS. NYPL.

Contains, The three warnings. A poem. pp. (4).

34014   —— — GOD GLORIFIED IN HIS WORKS OF PROVIDENCE AND GRACE: A REMARKABLE INSTANCE OF IT, IN THE VARIOUS AND SIGNAL DELIVERANCES WROUGHT FOR MISS MERCY WHEELER, OF PLAINFIELD, IN CONNECTICUT; LATELY RESTORED FROM EXTREME IMPOTENCE AND LONG CONFINEMENT. PUBLISHED AT THE DESIRE OF MANY. BY BENJAMIN LORD, A. M. PASTOR OF THE FIRST CHURCH IN NORWICH. THE THIRD [sixth] EDITION. [Seven lines of Scripture texts.]

New-London, Connecticut: Printed by Timothy Green, 1795 [1798.] pp. 40. 8vo.   AAS.

First printed in Boston, in two editions, in 1743; in a third edition in Boston, in 1744; in New London, in 1771; in New London, in 1795; and a colophon to this edition states: [The last part of this pamphlet, containing a sketch of Mrs. M. W. Case, written by Reverend Joel Benedict, of Plainfield, who preached her funeral sermon, in 1796, was printed by S. Green, in 1798.]

34015   LORD SAVE US, THE CONGRESS ARE FIGHTING! A NEW SONG: TUNE — "THE NIGHT BEFORE LARRY WAS STRETCH'D. [Thirteen eight-line verses, on the Lyon-Griswold imbroglio.]

[Alexandria: Printed by Thomas and Westcott, 1798.] Broadside. fol. LOC.

34016　LOUISIANA. Colony.
. . . BANDO DE BUEN GOBIERNO. [Spanish and French texts, in parallel columns. Dated, Enero de 1798.]
　　[Nueva Orleans: 1798.] pp. (12). 4to.　　　　　　NYPL.
　　Reproduced in facsimile.

34017　—— ORDRE DU ROI CONCERNANT LES DONS ET PRÊTS PATRIOTIQUE, AVEC LE DÉCRET À CONTINUATION. . . . 20 JUIN, 1798.
　　[Nouvelle Orleans: 1798.] pp. (4). fol.　　　　　NYPL.
　　Reproduced in facsimile.

34018　LOUVET DE COUVRAY, JEAN BAPTISTE　　　　　　1760–1797
AMELIA VERMONT; OR DIVORCE NECESSARY. TO WHICH ARE ADDED, THE AMOURS OF CURATE SEVIN. IN A SERIES OF LETTERS. TRANSLATED FROM THE FRENCH OF MR. LOUVET. BY M. NASH.
　　Hartford: Printed by Hudson and Goodwin, and Oliver D. & I. Cooke. 1798. pp. 300. 12mo.
　　Proposals for printing the above were made July 5, 1798.

34019　LOVE, CHRISTOPHER　　　　　　　　　　　　1618–1651
PROPHECIES OF THE REVEREND CHRISTOPHER LOVE; AND HIS LAST WORDS ON THE SCAFFOLD, WHO WAS BEHEADED AT TOWER HILL, LONDON, ON THE TWENTY-SECOND DAY OF AUGUST, 1651.
　　Augusta, (Kennebeck): Printed by Peter Edes. 1798.

34020　LOW, NATHANAEL　　　　　　　　　　　　　1740–1808
[Low's.] AN ASTRONOMICAL DIARY: OR ALMANACK, FOR THE YEAR OF CHRISTIAN ÆRA 1799. BEING THE THIRD AFTER BISSEXTILE, OR LEAP-YEAR. AND THE TWENTY THIRD OF THE INDEPENDENCE OF THE UNITED STATES OF AMERICA, WHICH BEGAN JULY 4TH, 1776. CONTAINING ALL THAT IS USUAL IN AN ALMANACK, AND A VARIETY OF OTHER MATTERS USEFUL AND ENTERTAINING. CALCULATED FOR THE MERIDIAN OF BOSTON IN AMERICA. LATITUDE 42 DEGREES 23 MINUTES NORTH. LONGITUDE 70 DEG. 37 MIN. 15 SEC. WEST FROM THE ROYAL OBSERVATORY AT GREENWICH, IN THE KINGDOM OF GREAT BRITAIN; AND 72 DEG. 57 MIN. 15 SEC. WEST OF THE RE-PUBLICAN OBSERVATORY AT PARIS, IN FRANCE. BUT WILL SERVE FOR ANY OF THE ADJACENT STATES. BY NATHANAEL LOW. [Six lines of verse.]
　　Boston: Printed and sold by John & Thomas Fleet, at the Bible and Heart, Cornhill. Where may be had their Register & Pocket Almanack, for 1799. [Copy rights secured.] [1798.] pp. [24.] 12mo.　　AAS. LOC. NYPL. YC.

34021　—— A SHEET ALMANACK, WITH LOW'S CALCULATIONS FOR THE YEAR 1799.
　　Boston: Printed and sold by T. & J, Fleet, at the Bible and Heart, in Corn-hill. [1798.] Broadside. fol.　　　　　　　　　　AAS.

34022　LOWELL, JOHN　　　　　　　　　　　　　1769–1840
AN ESSAY ON HEREDITARY TITLES, AND UNIVERSITY DEGREES; PARTICULARLY DOCTOR-ATES IN DIVINITY. BY A NEW-ENGLAND FARMER.
　　Boston: Printed by Manning & Loring, for Caleb Bingham, No. 44, Corn-hill. 1798. pp. 40. 8vo.　　　　　　AAS. BA. JCB. LCP. MHS.

34023　LUCAS, CHARLES　　　　　　　　　　　　　1769–1854
THE HISTORY OF JACK SMITH: OR, THE CASTLE OF SAINT DONATO. BY CHARLES LUCAS, A. M. AUTHOR OF THE INFERNAL QUIXOTE, &C. [One line of Latin from] HORACE'S ART OF POETRY.
　　Baltimore: Printed for Thomas, Andrews & Butler, by W. Pechin. 1798. pp. 291. 12mo.　　　　　　　　　　　　　　AAS.

34024   LUTHER, Martin   1483–1546
Der Kleine Catechismus des sel. d. Martin Luthers. Nebst den gewöhn-
lichen Morgen- Tisch- und Abend-Gebeten. Welchem die Ordnung des
Heils, in einem Liede, in kurzen Sätzen, in Frag und Antwort, und in
einer Tabelle: wie auch eine Zergliederung des Catechismus; das Wür-
tembürgische Kurze Kinder-Examen. Die Confirmation und des Heils,
Das Guldene A, B, C, der Kinder, und die Sieben Buss Psalmen, angehän-
get sind. Zum Gebrauch der Jungen und Alten.

         Philadelphia: Gedruckt bey H. Schweitzer. 1798. pp. 144. 12mo.

34025   Lynchburg Weekly Gazette. Vol. i Num. 1. Saturday, June 2, [— Num.
xxxi. Saturday, December 29, 1798.]

        [Lynchburg, Va.:] Printed by John Carter & Co. 1798. fol.

      Established, as a weekly, by John Carter & Company, and continued by
them into 1799, when John Carter alone continued publication into
May, 1801.

34026   Lynchburg Weekly Museum. Vol. i. No. 31. Monday, January 1, [— No. 52.
Saturday, May 26, 1798.]

        Lynchburg, (Va.) Printed by John Davis & Co. 1798. fol.

      Evidently discontinued at the above date, and succeeded in June by the
Lynchburg Weekly Gazette above.

34027   LYON, Abigail Blodget Stickney   1751–1808
Observations on Free Masonry: with a masonic vision. Addressed, by a Lady
in Worcester, to her female friend. [Nine lines of verse.]

        Printed at Worcester, by Leonard Worcester. 1798. pp. 14. 8vo.   AAS. HC.

34028   LYON, James
A Republican Magazine; or, repository of political truths. By James Lyon,
of Fairhaven, Vermont. [Four lines from] De Foe's Jure Divino. [Num-
bers 1 – 4. October 1, – December 15, 1798.]

        Printed and published at Fairhaven, (Vermont,) [by James Lyon.] M,DCC,-
XCVIII. pp. (2), 192. 8vo.   AAS. LOC. NYPL. YC.

      The successive numbers bear the heading: The scourge of aristocracy,
and repository of important political truths; and relates, almost entirely,
to the arrest, trial, conviction and imprisonment of his father, Matthew
Lyon, for an alleged violation of the alien and sedition laws, passed in
the administration of John Adams.

34029   LYON, Matthew   1746–1822
Capt. John Wood's Lottery—assigned to Col. Matthew Lyon. The honorable
the General Assembly of the State of Vermont having by their Act,
passed the 9th of March 1797 given liberty to John Wood to raise by
lottery the sum of five hundred dollars, to reimburse him for services
rendered the public, before the existence of said State, the managers
. . . present the following scheme to the public. . . .

        [Fairhaven: Printed by James Lyon. 1798.] Broadside.

34030   MACANULTY, Barnard B.
Salem, December, 1798. Proposals for printing by subscription a Treatise
on the plague and yellow fever. By James Tytler.

        [Salem: Printed by Joshua Cushing. 1798.] Broadside.   EI.

34031 MACCLINTOCK, Samuel   1732–1804
THE CHOICE: A DISCOURSE, OCCASIONED BY THE PRESENT SEVERE DROUGHT; THE
MORTAL FEVER WHICH PREVAILS IN PORTSMOUTH, IN THIS NEAR VICINITY, AND IN
MANY OF OUR CAPITAL, SEA-PORT TOWNS; AND THE THREATENING PROSPECT OF A
CALAMITOUS WAR WITH A POWERFUL NATION. DELIVERED AT GREENLAND, SEPT.
9, 1798. BY SAMUEL MACCLINTOCK, D. D.

Boston: Printed for Thomas Adams, Court-Street. 1798. pp. 21. 8vo.

AAS. BA. BM. JCB. LOC. MHS. NYHS.

34032 M'CORKLE, Samuel Eusebius   1746–1811
A DISCOURSE, ON THE DOCTRINE AND DUTY OF KEEPING THE SABBATH. BY SAMUEL
E. M'CORKLE, D.D. PASTOR OF THE CHURCH AT THYATIRA NEAR SALISBURY, ROWAN
COUNTY, NORTH-CAROLINA.

Salisbury: Printed by John M. Slump, at Michael Brown's English and German Printing-Office. MDCCXCVIII. pp. 36, (2). 8vo.   PU.

34033 —— THE WORK OF GOD FOR THE FRENCH REPUBLIC, AND THEN HER REFORMATION
OR RUIN; OR, THE NOVEL AND USEFUL EXPERIMENT OF NATIONAL DEISM, TO US AND
ALL FUTURE AGES. BY SAMUEL E. M'CORKLE, D.D. PASTOR OF THE CHURCH AT
THYATIRA ROWAN COUNTY, N. C. IN A DISCOURSE DELIVERED AT THYATIRA AND
IN SALISBURY ON THE FAST-DAY APPOINTED BY THE PRESIDENT, MAY 9, 1798.

Salisbury: Printed by Francis Coupee. M.DCC.XCVIII. pp. (2), 45. 12mo.
LOC.

34034 M'CULLOCH, John
M'CULLOCH'S POCKET ALMANAC, FOR THE YEAR 1799. BEING THE THIRD AFTER
LEAP-YEAR, AND 23–24 OF AMERICAN INDEPENDENCE. [Twelve lines.]

Philadelphia: Printed and sold by J. M'Culloch, No. 1, North Third-Street.
[1798.] pp. (32). 32mo.
AAS.

34035 M'FARLAND, Asa   1769–1827
THE DUTY OF A PEOPLE TO STRENGHTEN THE HANDS OF THEIR MINISTER, ON ACCOUNT
OF HUMAN IMPERFECTION, AND THE IMPORTANCE OF THE MINISTERIAL OFFICE:
ILLUSTRATED IN A SERMON, DELIVERED AT CONCORD, BY ASA M'FARLAND, A. M.
PASTOR OF THE CHURCH IN CONCORD, ON THE 11TH DAY OF MARCH, 1798, THE
NEXT SABBATH AFTER HIS ORDINATION TO THE WORK OF THE MINISTRY. NOW
PUBLISHED, FROM THE PRESS, IN COMPLIANCE WITH THE DESIRE OF MANY OF THE
HEARERS.

Concord: Printed and sold by Moses Davis. MDCCXCVIII. pp. 32. 8vo.
AAS. JCB.

34036 —— A SERMON, DELIVERED AT CONCORD, NEW-HAMPSHIRE, ON THE DAY OF ANNUAL
THANKSGIVING, NOVEMBER 15, 1798. BY ASA M'FARLAND, A. M. PASTOR OF THE
CHURCH IN CONCORD. NOW PUBLISHED, FROM THE PRESS, BY DESIRE.

Printed at Concord, by George Hough. Sold at his Office — Price 12½ *cents.*
[1798.] pp. (24). 8vo.   AAS. CLA. JCB. LOC. NHHS.

34037 MACGOWAN, John   1726–1780
THE LIFE OF JOSEPH, THE SON OF ISRAEL. IN EIGHT BOOKS. CHIEFLY DESIGNED TO
ALLURE YOUNG MINDS TO A LOVE OF THE SACRED SCRIPTURES. BY JOHN MACGOWAN.

Carlisle: Printed by George Kline. 1796.

34038 M'KEAN, Thomas   1734–1817
OPINION OF CHIEF JUSTICE M'KEAN. "THE CHIEF JUSTICE OF PENNSYLVANIA IS
REQUESTED TO ANSWER THE FOLLOWING QUERIES, AT THE PARTICULAR DESIRE OF
THE JUDGES OF THE ELECTION FOR THE TOWNSHIP OF THE NORTHERN LIBERTIES,
THE DISTRICT OF SOUTHWARK AND THE TOWNSHIPS OF MOYAMENSING AND PAS-
SYUNK." [Two columns.] THOMAS M'KEAN.

[Philadelphia: 1798.] Broadside. fol.
HSP.

34039 McKEEN, Joseph 1757–1807
Two discourses, delivered at Beverly, on the day of the national fast, May 9, 1798. By Joseph M'Keen, a.m. minister of the first parish in Beverly. [Ornament.]
> *Printed by Thomas C. Cushing, Essex Street, Salem.* 1798. pp. (31.) 8vo.
> AAS. BA. CLA. EI. HC. JCB. LOC. NYPL. UTS. YC.

34040 M'MANUS, Charles, and others.
A Correct account of the trials of Charles M'Manus, John Hauer, Elizabeth Hauer, Patrick Donagan, Francis Cox, and others; at Harrisburgh — June oyer and terminer, 1798. For the murder of Francis Shitz, on the night of the 28th December, 1797, at Heidelberg Township, Dauphin County, in the Commonwealth of Pennsylvania. Containing the whole evidence, and the substance of all the law arguments in those celebrated trials.
> *Printed at Harrisburgh, by John Wyeth.* 1798. [Entered according to law.]
> pp. [160], (2), [161]–[163.] 8vo. BA. BM. JCB. LOC. NYPL.

34041 MACPHERSON, John
Lectures on moral philosophy. By John Macpherson.
> *Philadelphia: Printed by Zachariah Poulson, junior, No. 30, North Fourth-Street, near the University.* 1798. pp. (36). 12mo. BA.

34042 MAGAW, Samuel 1740–1812
A Discourse delivered in Christ-Church and St. Peter's, Philadelphia; on Sunday, December 17, 1797; having a reference to the decease, a few days before, of mrs. Mary White, consort of the right rev. William White, d.d. bishop of the Protestant Episcopal Church, in Pennsylvania, by Samuel Magaw, d.d. rector of St. Paul's Church.
> *Philadelphia: Printed at the request of the church wardens, by Ormrod & Conrad, No. 41, Chesnut Street.* 1798. pp. (28), (1). 8vo. AAS. LOC.

34043 MANN, James 1759–1832
An Oration, addressed to the fraternity of the Free Masons, in the presence of a large concourse of people, on the tenth of October, in Wrentham, at a public installation of the officers of Montgomery Lodge, which usually convene at Franklin. By r. w. James Mann.
> *Printed at Wrentham, Massachusetts, by Nathaniel Heaton, jun.* M,DCC,-
> XCVIII. pp. (32). 8vo. AAS. BA. JCB.

34044 MARBLEHEAD. Massachusetts. Marine Society.
Laws and regulations of the Marine Society of Marblehead, as revised and agreed upon October 5, 1798.
> *Boston: Printed by Thomas Adams.* [1798.] pp. 14+ 16mo. HC.

34045 MARMONTEL, Jean François 1723–1799
The Widow of the village: or, the adventures of innocence; a moral tale, by the celebrated Marmontel. Translated from the original French, by mr. [Robert] Heron. To which is added, The error of a good father.
> *Suffield: Printed by H. & O. Farnsworth.* 1798. pp. 108. 12mo. AAS. NYPL.

34046 MARSH, Ebenezer Grant 1777–1803
An Oration, delivered before the P B K Society, at their anniversary meeting in New-Haven, on the fifth of December A. D. 1797. By Ebenezer Grant Marsh.
> *Hartford: Printed by Hudson & Goodwin.* 1798. pp. 32. 8vo.
> AAS. BA. BM. HC. JCB. LOC. MHS. NYPL. UTS. YC.

34047 MARSH, EBENEZER GRANT. continued.
—— AN ORATION, ON THE TRUTH OF THE MOSAIC HISTORY OF THE CREATION; DE-
LIVERED AT NEW-HAVEN, ON THE PUBLIC COMMENCEMENT, SEPTEMBER A. D. 1798.
BY EBENEZER GRANT MARSH. [Ornament.]
Hartford: Printed by Hudson and Goodwin. 1798. pp. 59. 8vo.
"[Copy right secured.]" AAS. BA. BM. HC. JCB. LOC. MHS. NYPL. UTS. YC.

34048 MARSHALL, HUMPHREY 1756–1841
THE ALIENS: A PATRIOTIC POEM, BY H. MARSHALL, A SENATOR OF THE UNITED
STATES. OCCASIONED BY THE ALIEN BILL, NOW BEFORE THE SENATE, MAY 15TH,
1798. COPYRIGHT SECURED.
Philadelphia: Printed for the Author. 1798. pp. (24). 8vo. BU. LOC.
Reprinted in Metuchen, New-Jersey, in 1925.

34049 MARSHALL, WILLIAM 1735–1808
THE CHILD'S CATECHISM; OR, A NEW HELP FOR INSTRUCTING THE RISING GENERATION
IN THE FIRST PRINCIPLES OF THE ORACLES OF GOD. BY THE REV. WILLIAM
MARSHALL, A. M. MINISTER OF THE GOSPEL IN PHILADELPHIA, AND THOMAS BEV-
ERIDGE, MINISTER OF THE GOSPEL AT CAMBRIDGE. SECOND EDITION.—TO WHICH
IS PREFIXED, AN EARNEST ADDRESS TO PARENTS; AND TO THE WHOLE IS ADDED,
AN EXPLANATION OF SOME TERMS IN RELIGION.
*Philadelphia: Printed for David Hogan, in George-street, 3d door below South-
street.* 1798.

34050 MARTIN, ALEXANDER 1740–1807
A NEW SCENE INTERESTING TO THE CITIZENS OF THE UNITED STATES OF AMERICA,
ADDITIONAL TO THE HISTORICAL PLAY OF COLUMBUS, BY A SENATOR OF THE UNITED
STATES. MAGNUS AB INTEGRO SEC'LORUM NASCITUR ORDO.—VIR. LATELY PER-
FORMED WITH APPLAUSE AT THE NEW THEATRE IN PHILADELPHIA.
[Philadelphia:] Printed by Benj. Franklin Bache. M.DCCXCVIII. pp. 12.
12mo.
BA.

34051 —— — A NEW SCENE INTERESTING TO THE CITIZENS OF THE UNITED STATES OF
AMERICA, ADDITIONAL TO THE HISTORICAL PLAY OF COLUMBUS, BY ALEXANDER
MARTIN, L. L. D. LATE GOVERNOR OF THE STATE OF NORTH-CAROLINA, AND NOW
SENATOR OF THE UNITED STATES THEREFROM. [One line of Latin from] VIR.
[LATELY PERFORMED WITH APPLAUSE AT THE NEW THEATRE IN PHILADELPHIA.]
*Philadelphia: Printed [by Benjamin Franklin Bache] for Thomas Condie,
No. 20, Carter's-Alley.* 1798. pp. [8.] 8vo. BU. LOC.

34052 MARTINET, JOHANNES FLORENTIUS 1729–1795
THE CATECHISM OF NATURE. FOR THE USE OF CHILDREN. BY DOCTOR MARTINET,
PROFESSOR OF PHILOSOPHY AT ZUTPHEN. TRANSLATED FROM THE DUTCH. [By
John Hall.] READ NATURE—NATURE IS A FRIEND TO TRUTH. YOUNG.
Boston: Printed by Samuel Etheridge, for David West, No. 36, Cornhill.
1798. pp. 108. 18mo.
AAS.

34053 —— — THE CATECHISM OF NATURE. FOR THE USE OF CHILDREN. BY DR. MAR-
TINET, PROFESSOR OF PHILOSOPHY AT ZUTPHEN. TRANSLATED FROM THE DUTCH.
[By John Hall.]
London printed: Reprinted at Litchfield, by T. Collier. [1798.] pp. 105.
24mo.
CHS.

34054 MARYLAND. STATE.
LAWS OF MARYLAND, MADE AND PASSED AT A SESSION OF ASSEMBLY, BEGUN AND HELD
AT THE CITY OF ANNAPOLIS ON MONDAY THE SIXTH OF NOVEMBER, IN THE YEAR
OF OUR LORD ONE THOUSAND SEVEN HUNDRED AND NINETY-SEVEN.
Annapolis: Printed by Frederick Green, Printer to the State. [1798.] pp.
[134.] fol.
LOC.

MARYLAND. State, continued.

34055 —— Votes and proceedings of the House of Delegates of the State of Maryland. November session, 1797. Being the first session of this Assembly, [— 21 January. 1798.]
[Annapolis: Printed by Frederick Green, 1798.] pp. 149. fol.   LOC.

34056 —— Votes and proceedings of the Senate of the State of Maryland. November session, 1796. Being the first session of the fifth Senate. [— 31 December, 1797.]
[Annapolis: Printed by Frederick Green, 1798.] pp. 59. fol.   LOC.

34057 —— Votes and proceedings of the Senate of the State of Maryland. November session, 1797. Being the second session of the fifth Senate. [— 21 January, 1798.]
[Annapolis: Printed by Frederick Green, 1798.] pp. 70. fol.   LOC.

34058 THE MARYLAND Gazette. liiid. year. No. 2660. Thursday, January 4, [— livth. year. No. 2711. Thursday, December 27, 1798.]
Annapolis: Printed by Frederick and Samuel Green. 1798. fol.

34059 THE MARYLAND Herald and Eastern Shore Intelligencer. Vol. viii. No. 395. Tuesday, January 2, [—Vol. ixth. No. 446. Tuesday, December 25, 1798.]
Easton: Printed by James Cowan. 1798. fol.   mdhs.

34060 THE MARYLAND Herald, and Elizabeth-Town Advertiser. Vol. i. No. 45. Thursday, January 4, [—Vol. ii. No. 96. Thursday, December 27, 1798.]
Elizabeth (Hager's) Town: Printed (every Thursday) by Thomas Grieves, near the Court-House. 1798. fol.   mdhs.

34061 MASON, John   1646–1694
Remains of the Rev. John Mason, a. m. late rector of Water-Stratford in the County of Bucks. Containing, a variety of devout and useful sayings, on divers subjects, digested under proper heads; religious observations; serious advice to youth, occasional reflections, &c. and christian letters. First American edition. [Double line.]
Norwich: Printed and sold by John Sterry. Sold also, by I. Beers, New-haven; Hudson and Goodwin, Hartford; Carter and Wilkinson, Providence; and by J. Richardson, New-port. 1798. pp. viii, 184. 24mo.   AAS. NYPL.

34062 MASON, John Mitchell   1770–1829
Letters on frequent communion, addressed particularly to the members of the Associate-Reformed Church in North-America.
New-York: Printed by T. & J. Swords, No. 99 Pearl-Street. 1798. pp. viii, 113. 8vo.   BM. JCB.

34063 MASSACHUSETTS. State.
[Arms.] Acts and laws, passed by the General Court of Massachusetts: begun and held at Boston, in the County of Suffolk, on Wednesday. the tenth day of January, Anno Domini, 1798. [Colophon:]
Boston: Printed by Young & Minns, Printers to the State. [1798.] pp. 155–206. fol.   AAS. JCB. LOC. NYPL.

34064 —— — [Arms.] Acts and laws, passed by the General Court of Massachusetts: at the session begun and held at Boston, in the County of Suffolk, on Wednesday, the thirteenth day of May, and ended on Friday, the twenty-ninth day of June, Anno Domini, 1798. [Colophon:] .
Boston: Printed by Young & Minns, Printers to the State. [1798.] pp. 207–136 [sic 236.] fol.   AAS. LOC. NYPL.

MASSACHUSETTS. State, continued.

34065 —— COMMONWEALTH OF MASSACHUSETTS. IN THE HOUSE OF REPRESENTATIVES, FEBRUARY 12TH, 1798. ON THE MEMORIAL OF THE DELEGATES OF THE TOWNS OF TEMPLETON, BARRE, PETERSHAM, ATHOL, WINCHENDON, HUBBARDSTON, OAKHAM, WARWICK, GERRY, GARDNER AND ROYALSTON, PRAYING, FOR A DIVISION OF THE COUNTY OF WORCESTER; [Resolution, to have the several towns vote on the division of the County into two Counties, on the first Monday in April,] MARCH 3D, 1798. APPROVED, INCREASE SUMNER. TRUE COPY, ATTEST, JOHN AVERY, SECRETARY.

[Boston: Printed by Young & Minns. 1798.] Broadside. fol.   AAS.

34066 —— COMMONWEALTH OF [Arms] MASSACHUSETTS. IN THE HOUSE OF REPRESENTATIVES, JUNE 28, 1798. WHEREAS IT IS HIGHLY EXPEDIENT THAT EVERY CONSTITUTIONAL BARRIER SHOULD BE OPPOSED TO THE INTRODUCTION OF FOREIGN INFLUENCE INTO OUR NATIONAL COUNCILS, AND THAT THE CONSTITUTION OF THE UNITED STATES SHOULD BE SO AMENDED AS TO EFFECT AND SECURE, IN THE BEST MANNER, THE GREAT OBJECTS FOR WHICH IT WAS DESIGNED: [Proposing a constitutional amendment that no one not a natural born citizen shall be eligible for election as president, vice-president, senator, or representative in Congress.] JUNE 29TH, 1798. APPROVED. INCREASE SUMNER.

[Boston: Printed by Young & Minns. 1798.] pp. (2). fol.   NYPL.

34067 —— COMMONWEALTH OF [Arms] MASSACHUSETTS. IN THE YEAR OF OUR LORD ONE THOUSAND SEVEN HUNDRED AND NINETY-EIGHT. AN ACT IN ADDITION TO THE SEVERAL LAWS REGULATING ELECTIONS. [Thirty-six lines.] JUNE 29, 1798. BY THE GOVERNOR APPROVED. INCREASE SUMNER. ATTEST, JOHN AVERY, SECRETARY. [Colophon:]

Boston: Printed by Young & Minns. [1798.] Broadside. fol. AAS. EI. MHS.

34068 —— COMMONWEALTH OF MASSACHUSETTS. IN THE YEAR OF OUR LORD, 1798. AN ACT TO PREVENT PROFANE CURSING AND SWEARING.

[Boston: Printed by Young & Minns. 1798.] Broadside. fol.

34069 —— [Arms.] COMMONWEALTH OF MASSACHUSETTS. BY HIS EXCELLENCY INCREASE SUMNER, ESQ. GOVERNOR OF THE COMMONWEALTH OF MASSACHUSETTS. A PROCLAMATION FOR A DAY OF FASTING AND PRAYER . . . THURSDAY THE FIFTH OF APRIL NEXT . . . GIVEN AT THE COUNCIL CHAMBER IN BOSTON, THIS FIRST DAY OF MARCH, IN THE YEAR OF OUR LORD, ONE THOUSAND SEVEN HUNDRED AND NINETY-EIGHT, AND IN THE TWENTY-SECOND YEAR OF THE INDEPENDENCE OF THE UNITED STATES OF AMERICA. INCREASE SUMNER. BY HIS EXCELLENCY'S COMMAND, WITH ADVICE AND CONSENT OF THE COUNCIL, JOHN AVERY, SECRETARY. GOD SAVE THE COMMONWEALTH OF MASSACHUSETTS!

[Boston: Printed by Young & Minns. 1798.] Broadside. fol.   AAS. MHS.

34070 —— [Arms.] COMMONWEALTH OF MASSACHUSETTS. BY HIS EXCELLENCY INCREASE SUMNER, ESQ. GOVERNOR OF THE COMMONWEALTH OF MASSACHUSETTS. A PROCLAMATION FOR A DAY OF PUBLIC THANKSGIVING. . . . THURSDAY, THE TWENTY-NINTH OF NOVEMBER NEXT, . . . GIVEN AT THE COUNCIL CHAMBER IN BOSTON, THIS TWENTY-THIRD DAY OF OCTOBER, IN THE YEAR OF OUR LORD, ONE THOUSAND, SEVEN HUNDRED AND NINETY-EIGHT, AND IN THE TWENTY-THIRD YEAR OF THE INDEPENDENCE OF THE UNITED STATES OF AMERICA. INCREASE SUMNER. . . . GOD SAVE THE COMMONWEALTH OF MASSACHUSETTS!

[Boston: Printed by Young & Minns. 1798.] Broadside. fol. AAS. LOC. MHS.

34071 —— REPORT OF THE COMMITTEE ON THE JUDICIAL REFORM, MADE TO THE LEGISLATURE OF MASSACHUSETTS JUNE 21, 1798. [Colophon:]

[Boston:] Printed by Young and Minns, State Printers. [1798.] pp. 32. 8vo.

AAS. HC. LOC. MHS. NYPL.

MASSACHUSETTS. State, continued.

34072 —— [Arms.] Resolves, &c. of the General Court of Massachusetts. Begun and held at Boston, on Wednesday, the thirty-first day of May, Anno Domini 1797, and continued by adjournment to March 3, 1798. [Colophon:]
     Boston: Printed by Young & Minns, Printers to the State. [1798.] pp. (31)– 76. fol.   AAS. LOC. NYPL.

34073 —— —— Resolves of the General Court of the Commonwealth of Massachusetts. Together with the governor's communications, &c. to the Court. Begun and held at Boston, in the County of Suffolk, on Wednesday, the thirtieth day of May, Anno Domini—m,dcc,xcviii. [—29 June, 1798.] [Arms.]
     Boston: Printed by Young and Minns, Printers to the honorable the General Court. [1798.] pp. 36. fol.   AAS. LOC. NYPL.

34074 —— Tax, for the year 1798. [Arms.] Commonwealth of Massachusetts. In the year of our Lord, one thousand, seven hundred and ninety-eight. An Act to apportion and assess a tax of one hundred and thirty-three thousand, three hundred and eighty-one dollars and fifty-three cents, and providing for the reimbursement of eighteen thousand, five hundred and sixty dollars, paid out of the public treasury, to the members of the House of Representatives for their attendance the two last sessions of the General Court.
     [Boston: Printed by Young and Minns. 1798.] pp. 20. fol.
     AAS. HSP. LOC. NYHS.

34075 —— —— Tax for the year 1798. [Arms.] Commonwealth of Massachusetts. Peleg Coffin, esquire, treasurer and receiver-general of said Commonwealth. To the selectmen and assessors of the   of   Given under my hand and seal, at Boston, the   day of   in the year of our Lord, one thousand seven hundred and ninety-eight.
     [Boston: Printed by Young and Minns. 1798.] Broadside. fol.   AAS.

34076 —— Constitution of the State of Massachusetts and that of the United States ordered by the General Court for the use of the members.
     Boston: Printed by Young and Minns. 1798. 16mo.

34077 —— State of [cut] Massachusetts. The Board of Commissioners, appointed for the State of Massachusetts, pursuant to an Act of the United States, passed on the ninth day of July . . . 1798.
     [Boston: Printed by Young and Minns. 1798.] Broadside.   MA.

34078 —— Notice to assessors relative to valuation of property. (With U. S. Act of 1798).
     [Boston? 1798.] pp. 35, 2 tables. 8vo.

34079 —— Massachusetts District. Supervisor's Office. Boston, May 31st, 1798. A Table or list of the different rates of stamp duties upon stamped paper. . . .
     [Boston: Printed by Young and Minns. 1798.] Broadside.   EI.

34080 —— Division orders of the 2d Division, Massachusetts militia, concerning court martial of Capt. Abel Boardman, Lt. David Wells and Capt. Ithamar Emerson, issued by Maj. general Stephen Abbot. Salem. Mar. 1, 1798.
     [Salem: Printed by Thomas C. Cushing. 1798.] Broadside.   EI. NYHS.

34081 —— General orders. Headquarters, Roxbury, May 1, 1798. . . . Signed, William Donnison, adjutant general.
     Boston: Printed by Young and Minns. 1798.   AAS. NYHS.

34082 MASSACHUSETTS HISTORICAL SOCIETY.
COLLECTIONS OF THE MASSACHUSETTS HISTORICAL SOCIETY, FOR THE YEAR M,DCC,-
XCVIII. [VOL. V.] [Ornamental line. Vignette.]
Printed by Samuel Hall, No. 53, Cornhill, Boston. 1798. pp. 290, (2). 8vo.
Reprinted in Boston, in 1816.　　　AAS. BA. BM. LOC. NL. NYPL.

34083 MASSACHUSETTS [Arms] MERCURY. No. 1 OF VOL. XI. TUESDAY, JANUARY 2,
[— No. 52 OF VOL XII. FRIDAY, DECEMBER 28, 1798.]
*Boston: Printed by Young and Minns, Printers to the honorable the General
Court.* 1798. fol.　　　AAS. BA. MHS.

34084 MASSACHUSETTS SOCIETY FOR PROMOTING AGRICULTURE.
ON THE CULTURE OF POTATOES: EXTRACTED FROM COMMUNICATIONS MADE TO THE
BOARD OF AGRICULTURE IN GREAT BRITAIN. PUBLISHED BY ORDER OF THE
TRUSTEES OF THE MASSACHUSETTS SOCIETY FOR PROMOTING AGRICULTURE. [Four
lines from] SWIFT.
*Boston: Printed by Young & Minns, Printers to the State and to the Agricultural
Society.* MDCCXCVIII. pp. 25. 8vo.　　　AAS. BA. BM. HC. JCB. LOC.

34085 MAXCY, JONATHAN　　　　　　　　　　　　　　1768–1820
AN ADDRESS, DELIVERED TO THE GRADUATES OF RHODE-ISLAND COLLEGE, AT THE
ANNIVERSARY COMMENCEMENT, IN THE BAPTIST MEETING-HOUSE IN PROVIDENCE,
SEPTEMBER 5, A. D. 1798. BY JONATHAN MAXCY, A. M. PRESIDENT OF RHODE-
ISLAND COLLEGE.
Providence: Printed by Carter and Wilkinson. [1798.] pp. (12). 8vo.
AAS. JCB. LOC. NYPL. RIHS.

34086 —— A SERMON, DELIVERED IN THE BAPTIST MEETING HOUSE IN PROVIDENCE, ON
LORD'S DAY AFTERNOON, OCTOBER 14, A. D. 1798. OCCASIONED BY THE DEATH
OF WELCOME ARNOLD, ESQ.; ONE OF THE TRUSTEES OF RHODE-ISLAND COLLEGE,
AND MEMBER OF THE GENERAL ASSEMBLY OF THIS STATE, WHO DEPARTED THIS
LIFE SEPTEMBER 29, 1798, IN THE 54TH YEAR OF HIS AGE. BY JONATHAN MAXCY,
A. M. PRESIDENT OF RHODE-ISLAND COLLEGE.
Providence: Printed by Carter and Wilkinson. 1798. pp. 15. 8vo.
BU. JCB. RIHS.

34087 MAY I NEVER BE MARRIED. A FAVORITE SONG.
New-York: Printed by G. Gilfert, No. 177 Broadway. [1798.] pp. (2). 4to.
LOC.

34088 MEANWELL, NANCY, pseudonym.
THE HISTORY OF A DOLL; CONTAINING ITS ORIGIN AND PROGRESS THROUGH LIFE.
WITH THE VARIOUS CALAMITIES THAT BEFEL IT. BY MISS NANCY MEANWELL.
Boston: Printed and sold by John W. Folsom, No. 30, Union-Street. 1798.
pp. 29, (1), frontispiece, and 9 cuts in text. 32mo.　　　AAS.

34089 THE MEDICAL REPOSITORY. CONDUCTED BY S. L. MITCHELL, E. MILLER, AND ELIHU
H. SMITH. VOL. II. [JANUARY – OCTOBER, 1798.]
*New-York: Printed by T. & J. Swords, Printers to the Faculty of Physic of
Columbia College, No. 99 Pearl-Street.* 1798. 8vo. AAS. BA. LCP. LOC. NYPL. SGO. YC.
After the second volume, Elihu H. Smith's name was dropped.
Vol. I. No. IV. 62d New York District Copyright, issued to Samuel
Latham Mitchel, Edward Miller, andElihu Hubbard Smith, as Proprie-
tors, 1 May, 1798.
Vol. II. No. I. 65th New York District Copyright (to same) 3 August,
1798. Vol. II. No. II. 73d New York District Copyright, issued to
Samuel Latham Mitchel, and Edward Miller, as Proprietors, 15 Decem-
ber 1798.
Reprinted in New York, in 1800, and in 1805.

34090 THE MEDLEY OR NEWBEDFORD MARINE JOURNAL. NUMBER 10 OF VOLUME VI.
WHOLE NUMBER 269. FRIDAY, JANUARY 5, [— NUMBER 10 OF VOLUME VII.
WHOLE NUMBER 322. FRIDAY, DECEMBER 28, 1798.]
> *Newbedford (Massachusetts): Printed and published by John Spooner, at his
> Office, corner of Union & Sixth Streets.* 1798. fol.   AAS.

34091 MELLEN, HENRY   1757–1809
SKETCHES OF MASONIC HISTORY, IN AN ORATION DELIVERED JULY 25TH, A. L. 5798,
AT SAINT JOHN'S CHAPEL, PORTSMOUTH, BEFORE THE GRAND LODGE OF NEW-
HAMPSHIRE, ACCOMPANIED BY ST. JOHN'S LODGE, AT THE INSTALLATION OF NATH-
ANIEL ADAMS, ESQ. GRAND MASTER. BY HENRY MELLEN, ESQ. [Three lines of
quotations.]
> *Portsmouth:—New-Hampshire, Printed by John Melcher,* 1798. pp. (19). 4to.
>   LOC.

34092 MELVILLE, DANIEL C.
MISCELLANEOUS EXTRACTS IN PROSE AND VERSE. CALCULATED FOR THE AMUSEMENT
OF THE HUMEROUS [*sic*] AND GAY, AS WELL AS FOR THE INSTRUCTION AND SERVICE
OF THE ENQUIRING AND BUSY WORLD. TO WHICH ARE ADDED, A NUMBER OF IM-
PORTANT QUESTIONS; WHICH QUESTIONS, WHOEVER WILL EFFECTUALLY AND SATIS-
FACTORILY ANSWER, SHALL BE ENTITLED TO ONE HUNDRED DOLLARS REWARD ON
DEMAND, FROM DAN. C. MELVILLE.
> *New-Haven: Printed in the year* 1798. pp. [36.] 12mo.   AAS.

34093 A MEMORIAL ON THE PRACTICABILITY OF GROWING VINEYARDS IN THE STATE OF
SOUTH-CAROLINA. READ BY THE AUTHOR TO THE AGRICULTURAL SOCIETY AT THEIR
EXTRA MEETING ON WEDNESDAY, THE 7TH OF NOVEMBER, 1798, AND PUBLISHED
UNDER THEIR PATRONAGE.
> *Printed by W. P. Young and T. C. Cox, Charleston.* 1798. pp. (2), 21. 8vo.
>   CLS. HSP.

34094 MENDON. MASSACHUSETTS. MENDON ASSOCIATION.
EVIDENCES OF REVEALED RELIGION. BY MENDON ASSOCIATION. (MASSACHUSETTS).
> *Printed at Northampton, by William Butler.* 1798. pp. 252. 12mo.
>   AAS. BM. FL. JCB. LOC. NYPL.

34095 MERCANTILE [cut] ADVERTISER. OPEN TO ALL PARTIES, BUT INFLUENCED BY NONE.
No. 1970. TUESDAY, NOVEMBER 13. [— No. 2011. MONDAY, DECEMBER 31, 1798.]
> *Printed and published by John Crooks, for the Proprietor, No. 68 Pine-Street,
> New-York.* 1798. fol.

In continuation of the *Diary and Mercantile Advertiser.*

34096 THE MERCHANTS' DAILY ADVERTISER. VOL. III. No. 300. MONDAY, JANUARY 1,
[— VOL. III. No. 454. SATURDAY, JUNE 30, 1798.]
> *[Philadelphia: Published] By Thomas Bradford, No. 8, South Front-Street.*
> 1798. fol.   AAS. HC. HSP.

Thomas Bradford was succeeded as publisher by his son, Samuel F. Bradford, June 4th, who discontinued publication June 30th; and, on July
2d, established, in continuation, *The True American and commercial advertiser.*

34097 THE MERCHANT'S VADE MECUM; BEING A GENERAL ABSTRACT OF THE REVENUE LAWS;
A COMPILATION OF OATHS AND FORMS NECESSARY TO BE OBSERVED IN TRANSACTIONS
AT THE CUSTOM-HOUSE; INFORMATION RELATIVE TO DRAWBACKS; ABSTRACT OF STAMP
DUTIES; LIST OF DUTIES PAYABLE ON GOODS, WARES AND MERCHANDIZE IMPORTED
INTO THE UNITED STATES; TONNAGE, &C. &C. PUBLISHED UNDER THE INSPECTION
OF THE INSPECTOR OF REVENUE, FOR THE DISTICT OF ALEXANDRIA.
> *Alexandria: Printed by Thomas & Westcott.* 1798.

34098   DAS MERKWÜRDIGE LEBEN, KRANKHEIT, TOD UND BEGRÄBNISS DER FRANZÖSI-
SCHEN FREYHEIT UND GLEICHHEIT SAMT DER LETZTEN REDE BEYM BEGRÄBNISS
DERSELBEN ETC. HERAUSGEGEBEN VON EINEM EHRLICHEN DEUTSCHEN.
> *Lancaster: Gedruckt bey Johann Albrecht u. Comp.* 1798.

34099   MERRILL, PHINEHAS
THE SCHOLAR'S GUIDE TO ARITHMETIC; BEING A COLLECTION OF THE MOST USEFUL
RULES, VIZ. NOTATION, ADDITION, SUBTRACTION, MULTIPLICATION, DIVISION, REDUC-
TION, RULE OF THREE, PRACTICE, INTEREST, BARTER, LOSS AND GAIN, TARE AND
TRETT, FELLOW-SHIP, ALLIGATION, DOUBLE RULE OF THREE, VULGAR FRACTIONS,
DECIMAL FRACTIONS, INTEREST BY DECIMALS, EXTRACTION OF THE SQUARE & CUBE
ROOTS, POSITION, PROGRESSION, DUODECIMALS, OR CROSS MULTIPLICATION. TO WHICH
IS ADDED, A SHORT TREATISE ON MENSURATION OF PLANES AND SOLIDS; WITH A SUF-
FICIENT NUMBER OF PRACTICAL QUESTIONS AT THE END OF EACH RULE. DESIGNED
FOR THE USE OF SCHOOLS. BY PHINEHAS MERRILL. THE THIRD EDITION, CORRECTED
AND IMPROVED BY THE AUTHOR. PUBLISHED ACCORDING TO ACT OF CONGRESS.
> *Portsmouth, New-Hampshire:—Printed by Charles Peirce (Proprietor of the
work) and sold by him, wholesale or retail, at the Columbian Book-Store, No. 5,
Daniel-Street, Portsmouth.* 1798.   pp. 103, (1).   8vo.   AAS.

34100   THE MERRY COMPANION: CONTAINING TWENTY-SIX OF THE NEWEST AND MOST AP-
PROVED SONGS, SUNG AT THE THEATRES IN BOSTON, AND OTHER GENTEEL PLACES
OF AMUSEMENT.
> *Boston: Printed and sold by J. White, near Charles River Bridge.* 1798. 16mo.

34101   THE MERRY FELLOW'S COMPANION: CONTAINING MATTER HUMOROUS, WITTY AND
ENTERTAINING.
> *Wiscasset, (District of Maine). Printed ? by Henry Hoskins & John W. Scott.*
> 1798.

34102   METHODIST EPISCOPAL CHURCH IN AMERICA.
THE DOCTRINES AND DISCIPLINE OF THE METHODIST EPISCOPAL CHURCH, IN AMERICA.
WITH EXPLANATORY NOTES, BY THOMAS COKE AND FRANCIS ASBURY. THE TENTH
EDITION.
> *Philadelphia: Printed by Henry Tuckniss. Sold by John Dickins, No. 41,
Market-street, between Front and Second-streets, and by the Methodist ministers and
preachers throughout the United States.* 1798.   pp. (187), (3). 12mo.   BM.

> The last page of contents is wrongly numbered 169.

34103   —— MINUTES TAKEN AT THE SEVERAL CONFERENCES OF THE METHODIST EPISCOPAL
CHURCH IN AMERICA, FOR THE YEAR 1798.
> *Philadelphia: Printed by William W. Woodward, No. 17, Chesnut, near Front
Street.* [1798.] [Price eight pence.] pp. [20.] 12mo.   AAS.

34104   —— A POCKET HYMN-BOOK, DESIGNED AS A CONSTANT COMPANION FOR THE PIOUS.
COLLECTED FROM VARIOUS AUTHORS. THE TWENTY-SECOND EDITION. PSALM CIV.
33. [Three lines.]
> *Philadelphia: Printed by Henry Tuckniss, No. 25, Church-Alley. And sold by
John Dickins, No. 41, Market-Street, between Front and Second-Streets.* 1798. [Price
half a dollar.] pp. (2), 285, (13). 24mo.   LOC.

34105   THE METHODIST MAGAZINE, FOR THE YEAR 1798. CONTAINING, ORIGINAL SERMONS,
EXPERIENCES, LETTERS, AND OTHER RELIGIOUS PIECES; TOGETHER WITH INSTRUCT-
IVE AND USEFUL EXTRACTS, FROM DIFFERENT AUTHORS. VOLUME II.
> *Philadelphia: Printed by Henry Tuckniss: Sold by John Dickins, No. 50,
North Second Street, Philadelphia, and by the Methodist ministers and preachers
throughout the United States.* [1798.] pp. 384+ 8vo.   AAS. LCP. NYHS.

34106　　MIDDLESEX COUNTY. MASSACHUSETTS. MIDDLESEX CANAL.
AT A MEETING OF THE MIDDLESEX-CANAL CORPORATION, HELD AT CHARLESTOWN, ON
THE 16TH DAY OF OCTOBER, 1798.

　　[Boston: 1798.] Broadside.

34107　　MIDDLESEX GAZETTE. VOL. XIII. NUMB. 633. FRIDAY, JANUARY 5, [— VOL. XIV.
NUMB. 684. FRIDAY, DECEMBER 28, 1798.]

　　*Middletown—(Connecticut)—Printed and published every Friday, by T. Dun-
ning.* 1798. fol.　　　　　　　　　　　　　　　　　　　　　　AAS. CHS.

34108　　MIDDLETON, ERASMUS　　　　　　　　　　　　　　　1739–1805
EVANGELICAL BIOGRAPHY: OR, AN HISTORICAL ACCOUNT OF THE LIVES AND DEATHS
OF SOME EMINENT MEN OF VARIOUS COUNTRIES, AND OF VARIOUS DENOMINATIONS
IN THE PROTESTANT CHURCH. EXHIBITING THE UNITY OF THEIR FAITH AND EXPE-
RIENCE IN THEIR SEVERAL AGES, COUNTRIES, AND PROFESSIONS; AND ILLUSTRATING
THE POWER OF DIVINE GRACE IN THEIR VERY REMARKABLE HOLY-LIVING AND DY-
ING. CHIEFLY SELECTED FROM THE WORKS OF THE REV. ERASMUS MIDDLETON, OF
KING'S COLLEGE, CAMBRIDGE.

　　Philadelphia: Printed and sold by John McCulloch, No. 1. *North Third-Street.*
M,DCC,XCVIII. pp. 455, (1). 12mo.　　　　　　　　　　　　　AAS. JCB.

　　Contains, a four-page list of Subscribers' names.

34109　　MILLER, SAMUEL.　　　　　　　　　　　　　　　　1769–1850
A SERMON, DELIVERED MAY 9, 1798, RECOMMENDED, BY THE PRESIDENT OF THE
UNITED STATES, TO BE OBSERVED AS A DAY OF GENERAL HUMILIATION, FASTING,
AND PRAYER. BY SAMUEL MILLER, A.M. ONE OF THE MINISTERS OF THE UNITED
PRESBYTERIAN CHURCHES IN THE CITY OF NEW-YORK.

　　New-York: Printed by T. & J. Swords. 1798. pp. 46. 8vo.
　　　　　　　　　AAS. BA. CHS. CLA. HC. JCB. LOC. MHS. NYHS. NYPL. UTS.

34110　　—— NEW-YORK, FEBRUARY 10, 1798. SIR, I HAVE, FOR SOME MONTHS PAST, DEVO-
TED MY LEISURE HOURS TO THE COLLECTION OF MATERIALS, WITH A VIEW TO
WRITING AN HISTORY OF NEW-YORK. . . . SAMUEL MILLER. QUERIES, &C.
. . .

　　[New-York: 1798.] pp. (2). fol.　　　　　　　　　　　　　　LOC.

34111　　MILNS, WILLIAM　　　　　　　　　　　　　　　　　1761–1801
ALL IN A BUSTLE: OR, THE NEW HOUSE. A COMIC PRELUDE, WRITTEN FOR THE
OPENING OF THE NEW THEATRE IN NEW-YORK. BY WILLIAM MILNS: AUTHOR OF
THE COMET, &C. &C.

　　New-York: Printed at the Literary Printing-Office, No. 29 *Gold-Street.* [Copy-
right secured.] 1798. pp. 18. 12mo.　　　　　　　　　　　　　HEH.

34112　　—— *Engraved title:* THE COLUMBIAN LIBRARY CONTAINING A CLASSICAL SELECTION
OF BRITISH LITERATURE. VOL. II. [Vignette.]
　　New-York: Printed & published by W. Milns, No. 29 *Gold St.* 1797.

Title: SELECTION OF FABLES FROM THE BEST ENGLISH WRITERS, CONTAINING THE
LARGEST COLLECTION EVER PUBLISHED; SELECTED FROM DRYDEN, SWIFT, WILKIE,
WHITEHEAD, COTTON, MERRICK, SHENITONE [*sic*], GARRICK, SMART; SOMERVILLE,
PETER PINDAR, &C. &C. &C. INCLUDING ALL THE FABLES OF GAY AND MOORE.
　　New-York: Printed for the Editor. 1798. pp. vii, 184; 131. 16mo.
　　　　　　　　　　　　　　　　　　　　　AAS. BM. LOC.

34113   MILNS, WILLIAM, continued.
—— THE FEDERAL CONSTITUTION & LIBERTY FOREVER. A NEW PATRIOTIC SONG WRITTEN BY MR. MILNS & SUNG WITH GREAT APPLAUSE BY MR. WILLIAMSON. THE MUSIC ADAPTED BY MR. HEWITT.
New-York: Printed & sold at J. Hewitt's Musical Repository. [1798.] pp.(2). 4to.

34114   —— WHEN THE OLD HEATHEN GODS IN DEBATE FIRST ASSEMBLED.
Boston: Published by P. A. von Hagen jun. and Co's Musical Magazine, No. 62 Newbury-Street. 1798.

34115   —— — WHEN THE OLD HEATHEN GODS. SUNG BY MR. WILLIAMSON IN THE FARCE OF FLASH IN THE PAN. THE WORDS BY MR. MILNS. MUSIC BY J. HEWITT.
New York. Printed & sold by J. Hewitt at his Musical Repository, No. 131 William St. Sold also by B. Carr, Philadelphia & J. Carr, Baltimore. [1798.] pp. (2). 4to.
        HSP.

34116   MILTON, JOHN GARDINER
A BRIEF CONSIDERATION OF THE IMPORTANT SERVICES, AND DISTINGUISHED VIRTUES AND TALENTS, WHICH RECOMMEND MR. ADAMS FOR THE PRESIDENCY OF THE UNITED STATES.
Boston: Printed by Manning & Loring, and to be sold by Joseph Nancrede, at No. 49 Marlbro' Street. 1796. pp. 31, (1). 16mo.
        BA.

34117   THE MINERVA. VOLUME II. NUMBER 65. THURSDAY, JANUARY 4, [— VOL. III. No. 116. THURSDAY, DECEMBER 27, 1798.]
Dedham (Massachusetts). Printed and published by Herman Mann, about 60 rods east of the Court-House. 1798. fol.
        AAS.

From March 8th, to September 20th, James H. Adams was associated with Mann in its publication. With the issue for January 3, 1799, the title was changed to *Columbian Minerva.*

34118   MINOT, GEORGE RICHARDS   1758–1802
CONTINUATION OF THE HISTORY OF THE PROVINCE OF MASSACHUSETTS BAY, FROM THE YEAR 1748 [— 1765], WITH AN INTRODUCTORY SKETCH OF EVENTS FROM ITS ORIGINAL SETTLEMENT. BY GEORGE RICHARDS MINOT, FELLOW OF THE AMERICAN ACADEMY OF ARTS AND SCIENCES, AND MEMBER OF THE MASSACHUSETTS HISTORICAL SOCIETY. VOL. I.
Boston: Printed by Manning & Loring, February, 1798. pp. 304. 8vo.
        AAS. BA. BM. HC. JCB. LOC. MHS. NL. NYHS. NYPL.
138th Massachusetts District Copyright, issued to George Richards Minot, as Author, 31 January, 1798. The second volume was published in 1803.

34119   THE MIRROR. VOL. VI. No. 270. TUESDAY, JANUARY 2, [— VOL. VII. NUMB. 322. MONDAY, DECEMBER 31, 1798.]
Published by Moses Davis, Concord, [Newhampshire.] 1798. fol.   AAS.
In October, the day of publication was changed to Monday.

34120   THE MIRROR. VOL. I. No. 14. MONDAY, JANUARY 1, [— VOL. II. No. 14. MONDAY, DECEMBER 31, 1798.]
Newburgh, [N. Y.] Published by Philip Van Horne. 1798. fol.
In November, Van Horne disposed of his interests to Joseph W. Barber, who continued publication.

34121   THE MIRROR. FIRM, FREE, AND TEMPERATE. VOL. I. No. 17. SATURDAY, JANUARY 6, [— VOL. II. No. 16. SATURDAY, DECEMBER 29, 1798.]

Washington, (K.) Printed and published (weekly) by Hunter & Beaumont. . . . 1798. fol.   UOC.

In August, the firm established at Frankfort, The Palladium, which William Hunter conducted there, while William H. Beaumont conducted The Mirror, at Washington.

34122   THE MOHAWK MERCURY. VOL. IV. No. 160. TUESDAY, JANUARY 2, [— No. 172? TUESDAY, MARCH 27? 1798.]

Schenectady, (on the banks of the Mohawk). Printed by Cornelius P. Wyckoff, corner of State and Washington Streets. 1798. fol.   AAS.

Discontinued at about the above date. And succeeded, in January, 1799, by the *Schenectady Gazette.*

34123   MONITEUR DE LA LOUISIANE. No 64. SAMEDI, 6 JANVIER, [— No. 115. SAMEDI, 29 DÉCEMBRE, 1798.]

Nouvelle Orleans: 1798. 4to.

34124   THE MONITOR. VOL. 14. No. 656. WEDNESDAY, FEBRUARY 28, [—VOL. 14. NUMB. 698. WEDNESDAY, DECEMBER 26, 1798.]

Litchfield, (Connecticut): Printed by Thomas Collier. 1798. fol.

In continuation of *Weekly Monitor.*

34125   THE MONITOR OF MIFFLIN & HUNTINGDON. VOL. I. No. 1. NOVEMBER 3, [— No. 9, DECEMBER 29, 1798.]

Lewiston, Pennsylvania. Published by John Doyle. 1798. fol.

Established, as a weekly, by Joseph Doyle, and only known through a single issue for December 22, 1798.

34126   MONTOLIEU, ISABELLE   1751–1832
CAROLINE OF LICHTFIELD; A NOVEL. TRANSLATED FROM THE FRENCH BY THOMAS HOLCROFT. THE FIRST AMERICAN EDITION. IN TWO VOLUMES. VOL. I. [— II.] [Four lines of French from] VOLTAIRE.

London, Printed: New-York, Re-printed by J. S. Mott for Evert Duyckinck & Co. 1798. 2 vols. in one. pp. 144; 153. 12mo.   AAS. NYPL.

By, more correctly, Jeanne Isabelle Pauline Polier de Botteu de Crousaz, baronne de Montolieu.

34127   MOORE, ALPHEUS
AN ORATION, PRONOUNCED AT WESTMORELAND, ON THE ANNIVERSARY OF AMERICAN INDEPENDENCE; JULY 4TH, 1798. BY ALPHEUS MOORE.

Walpole, Newhampshire: Printed by David Carlisle, for Thomas & Thomas. 1798. pp. 13. 4to.   AAS. BA.

34128   MOORE, EDWARD   1712–1757
FABLES FOR THE FEMALE SEX. BY MR. EDWARD MOORE, AUTHOR OF THE WORLD, &C. [Vignette.]

—Reprinted at Litchfield, by T. Collier.—[1798.] pp. 120. 24mo.   AAS.

34129 MOORE, JOHN   1730–1802
EDWARD. VARIOUS VIEWS OF HUMAN NATURE, TAKEN FROM LIFE AND MANNERS, CHIEFLY IN ENGLAND. [Three lines of Latin from] JUV. BY JOHN MOORE, M.D. AUTHOR OF TRAVELS THROUGH FRANCE AND ITALY, ZELUCO, &c. IN TWO VOLUMES. VOLUME I. [— II.]

> *Mount-Pleasant: County of West-Chester. Printed by W. Durell, for J. Harrisson, C. Davis, E. Duycinck [sic] & Co. W. Milns, A. Somerville, R. Macgill. Gaine & Teneyck, Spencer & Webb, Thomas, Andrews & Penniman, and Carter & Wilkinson. 1798. 2 vols.* pp. 285; 284, (1). 12mo.   AAS. LOC. NYPL.

In unbound copies of Vol. II. is inserted a duplicate title-page, correcting the error of making the year of publication 1789.

34130 MOORE, JOHN HAMILTON   –1807
THE YOUNG GENTLEMAN AND LADY'S MONITOR, AND ENGLISH TEACHER'S ASSISTANT: BEING A COLLECTION OF SELECT PIECES FROM OUR BEST MODERN WRITERS: CALCULATED TO ERADICATE VULGAR PREJUDICES AND RUSTICITY OF MANNERS; IMPROVE THE UNDERSTANDING; RECTIFY THE WILL; PURIFY THE PASSIONS; DIRECT THE MINDS OF YOUTH TO THE PURSUIT OF PROPER OBJECTS; AND TO FACILITATE THEIR READING, WRITING, AND SPEAKING THE ENGLISH LANGUAGE, WITH ELEGANCE AND PROPRIETY. PARTICULARLY ADAPTED FOR THE USE OF OUR EMINENT SCHOOLS AND ACADEMIES, AS WELL AS PRIVATE PERSONS, WHO HAVE NOT AN OPPORTUNITY OF PERUSING THE WORKS OF THOSE CELEBRATED AUTHORS, FROM WHENCE THIS COLLECTION IS MADE. BY J. HAMILTON MOORE. AUTHOR OF THE PRACTICAL NAVIGATOR, AND SEAMAN'S NEW DAILY ASSISTANT.

> *New-York: Printed and sold by Gaine & Ten Eyck, in Pearl-Street.* 1798.

34131 MOORE, THOMAS, pseudonym.
GAINE'S NEW-YORK POCKET ALMANACK, FOR THE YEAR 1799: BEING THE 3D AFTER LEAP-YEAR, AND 23D OF AMERICAN INDEPENDENCE, 'TILL 4TH JULY. CALCULATED FOR THIS AND THE NEIGHBOURING STATES. [Thirteen lines.] BY THOMAS MOORE, PHILO.

> *New-York: Printed by H. Gaine, at the Bible, in Pearl-Street.* [1798.] pp. (96). 32mo.   AAS. NYHS. NYPL.

34132 MOORE, ZEPHANIAH SWIFT   1770–1823
SKETCHES OF THE RECIPROCAL DUTIES OF A CHRISTIAN PASTOR AND PEOPLE. A SERMON, DELIVERED AT LEICESTER, MASSACHUSETTS, JANUARY 21, 1798. BY ZEPHANIAH SWIFT MOORE, A.M. PASTOR OF THE CONGREGATIONAL CHURCH IN LEICESTER. PUBLISHED BY REQUEST OF THE HEARERS.

> *Printed at Worcester, by Leonard Worcester.* 1798. pp 48. 8vo.
>   AAS. BM. JCB NYPL.

34133 MORE, HANNAH   1745–1833
THE FORTUNE TELLER.

> *Caption title:* TAWNEY RACHEL; OR, THE FORTUNE TELLER: WITH SOME ACCOUNT OF DREAMS, OMENS, AND CONJURERS. [Vignette.]

> *Published by B. Johnson, No. 247 Market-Street, Philadelphia.* [1798.] pp. (2), 36. 24mo.   LOC.

34134 —— THE HISTORY OF TOM WHITE, THE POSTILLON.

> *Published by B. Johnson, No. 247, Market-Street, Philadelphia.* [1798.] pp. (2), 36. 24mo.

34135　MORE, Sarah　　　　　　　　　　　　　　　　　　　　　　　　　　　–1817
THE CHEAPSIDE APPRENTICE. [Vignette.]
　　　　Published by B. Johnson, No. 247 Market St. Philadelphia. [1798.] pp. (2),
36. 24mo.　　　　　　　　　　　　　　　　　　　　　　　　　　　LOC.

34136　—— *Caption title:* THE HUBBUB; OR, THE HISTORY OF FARMER RUSSEL, THE HARD-
HEARTED OVERSEER.
　　　　[Philadelphia: Published by B. Johnson, No. 247 Market St. [1798.] pp.
35, (1), frontispiece. 24mo.　　　　　　　　　　　　　　　　　LOC.

34137　MOREAU DE ST. MERY, Medéric Louis Elie　　　　　　　　　1750–1819
DESCRIPTION TOPOGRAPHIQUE, PHYSIQUE, CIVILE, POLITIQUE ET HISTORIQUE DE LA
PARTIE FRANÇAISE DE L'ISLE SAINT-DOMINIGUE. AVEC DES OBSERVATIONS GÉN-
ÉRALES SUR SA POPULATION, SUR LE CARACTÈRE & LES MOEURS DE SES DIVERS
HABITANS; SUR SON CLIMAT, SA CULTURE, SES PRODUCTIONS, SON ADMINISTRATION, &C.
PAR M. L. E. MOREAU DE SAINT-MERY. TOME II.
　　　　a Philadelphie, chez l'Auteur; Paris, chez Dupont; . . . 1798. pp. viii,
856, map, table, 4to.　　　　　　　　　　　　　　　　　BM. HC. NYPL.

34138　—— A TOPOGRAPHICAL AND POLITICAL DESCRIPTION OF THE SPANISH PART OF SAINT-
DOMINGO; CONTAINING, GENERAL OBSERVATIONS ON THE CLIMATE, POPULATION, AND
PRODUCTIONS; ON THE CHARACTER AND MANNERS OF THE INHABITANTS; WITH AN
ACCOUNT OF THE SEVERAL BRANCHES OF THE GOVERNMENT. BY M. L. E. MOREAU DE
SAINT-MERY. MEMBER OF THE PHILOSOPHICAL SOCIETY OF PHILADELPHIA, &C.
TRANSLATED FROM THE FRENCH BY WILLIAM COBBETT. VOL. I. [— II.]
　　　　*Philadelphia: Printed and sold by the Author, Printer and Bookseller, No.
84, South Front-Street.* 1798. 2 vols. pp. 8, (liv), 314; 318, (1). 8vo.
　　　　　　　　　　　　　　　　　　　　AAS. JCB. LOC. NYHS.
Same as the edition of 1796, with new title pages.
On June 17, 1798, this enterprising and scholarly publisher, a native of
Port Royal, who had added lustre to his profession during his brief resi-
dence in this country, announced that having nearly completed the second volume of the Voyage to China, by Van Braam, of which he is the
Editor; and of his second volume of the French part of St. Domingo,
now offers for sale: 1st. A complete printing-office, where works in
French and English may be undertaken at the same time. 2. 300 of one
thousand copies of Description of the French part of St. Domingo. (The
first volume of which is already printed and published in Dutch in Haar-
lem.) 3. 300 copies of Description of the Spanish part of St. Domingo.
4. 500 copies of the English translation of Description of the Spanish
part (with the Copyright). 5. Some copies of the Atlas of St. Domingo.
6. 300 copies of one thousand of his Epitome of the Sciences (with the
Copyright). 7. 300 copies of the last translated into English (with the
Copyright). 8. 150 copies of Nouvelles Etrennes spirituelles.

34139　MORISON, William　　　　　　　　　　　　　　　　　　　1748–1818
A SERMON, DELIVERED JUNE 28, 1797, AT THE INSTALMENT OF THE REVEREND JOHN
BODDILY, TO THE PASTORAL CARE OF THE 2D. PRESBYTERIAN SOCIETY IN NEWBURY-
PORT. BY WILLIAM MORISON, V. D. M. PASTOR OF A PRESBYTERIAN CHURCH IN
LONDONDERRY.
　　　　Newburyport: Printed by Edmund M. Blunt—State-Street. 1798. pp. [23.]
8vo.　　　　　　　　　　　　　　　　　　　　AAS. BA. JCB. LOC.

34140　MORRIS, James.　　　　　　　　　　　　　　　　　　　　1752–1820
MR. MORRIS'S FAREWELL ADDRESS TO HIS PUPILS, DELIVERED AT LITCHFIELD, (SOUTH-
FARMS,) AT THE CLOSE OF HIS SCHOOL, MARCH 9TH, 1797. PUBLISHED BY THEIR
REQUEST. "TIS VIRTUE, NOT ROLLING SUNS, THE MIND MATURES." YOUNG.
　　　　Litchfield: Printed by T. Collier. [1797.] pp. 18. 12mo.　　　LHS.

34141   MORRIS, THOMAS   1732–180–
QUASHY, OR THE COAL-BLACK MAID. [A poem.]
[Philadelphia: Printed by James Humphreys, No. 74, North Third-street.
1798.] pp. [13], (1). 8vo.   LOC.

34142   MORRIS COUNTY GAZETTE. [Motto.] VOL. I. NO. 33. TUESDAY, JANUARY 2, [—
VOL. I. NO. 52. TUESDAY, MAY 15, 1798.]
Morris-Town: Printed and published by Jacob Mann. 1798. fol.

With the issue for January 2nd, Caleb Russell disposed of his interests
to Jacob Mann, who continued publication to the end of the first volume,
as above; and, on May 24th, established in continuation, *The Genius of
Liberty.*

34143   MORSE, JEDIDIAH   1761–1826
AN ABRIDGMENT OF THE AMERICAN GAZETTEER. EXHIBITING, IN ALPHABETICAL
ORDER, A COMPENDIOUS ACCOUNT OF THE STATES, PROVINCES, COUNTIES, CITIES,
TOWNS, VILLAGES, RIVERS, BAYS, HARBOURS, GULFS, SOUNDS, CAPES, MOUNTAINS,
FORTS, INDIAN TRIBES, & NEW DISCOVERIES, ON THE AMERICAN CONTINENT, AND ITS
APPENDANT ISLANDS; PARTICULARLY THE WEST INDIES. DESCRIBING THE EXTENT,
BOUNDARIES. POPULATION. GOVERNMENT, PRODUCTIONS, COMMERCE, MANUFACTURES,
CURIOSITIES. &C. OF SEVERAL COUNTRIES, AND OF THEIR IMPORTANT CIVIL DIVISIONS
— AND THE LONGITUDE AND LATITUDE, THE BEARINGS AND DISTANCES, FROM NOTED
PLACES, OF THE CITIES, TOWNS, AND VILLAGES. TO WHICH IS ANNEXED AN ACCURATE
TABLE OF ALL THE POST-OFFICES IN THE UNITED STATES. BY JEDIDIAH MORSE, D.D.
AUTHOR OF THE AMERICAN UNIVERSAL GEOGRAPHY — FELLOW OF THE AMERICAN
ACADEMY OF ARTS AND SCIENCES—AND MEMBER OF THE MASSACHUSETTS HISTOR-
ICAL SOCIETY. ILLUSTRATED WITH A MAP OF NORTH AMERICA. ABRIDGED BY
THE AUTHOR. PUBLISHED ACCORDING TO ACT OF CONGRESS.
*Printed at Boston by Thomas and Andrews, sold by them, by E. Larkin, and
other Booksellers, in Boston; by I. Thomas, Worcester; by Thomas, Andrews & Pen-
niman, Albany; and by Thomas, Andrews & Butler, Baltimore.—June,* 1798. pp.
388, map. 12mo.   AAS. BA. BM. HC. JCB. MHS. NYPL.

148th Massachusetts District. Copyright, issued to Jedidiah Morse, and
Thomas and Andrews, as proprietors, 24 June, 1798.

34144   —— THE CHARACTER AND REWARD OF A GOOD AND FAITHFUL SERVANT ILLUSTRATED
IN A SERMON, DELIVERED AT CHARLESTOWN, APRIL 29, 1798, THE LORD'S DAY,
FOLLOWING THE DEATH AND INTERMENT OF THE HONORABLE JAMES RUSSELL, ESQ.
WHO DIED APRIL 24TH, AGED 83 YEARS. BY JEDIDIAH MORSE, D.D. MINISTER OF
THE CONGREGATION IN CHARLESTOWN. [Ornament.]
Printed by Samuel Hall, No. 53, Cornhill, Boston. 1798. pp. [21.] 8vo.
         AAS. BA. BM, CHS. HC. JCB. LOC. MHS. NYHS. NYPL.

34145   —— ELEMENTS OF GEOGRAPHY; CONTAINING A SHORT AND COMPREHENSIVE VIEW INTO
ASTRONOMICAL GEOGRAPHY, PHYSICAL OR NATURAL GEOGRAPHY, AND POLITICAL
GEOGRAPHY, ON A NEW PLAN, WHICH IS ADAPTED TO THE CAPACITIES OF CHILDREN
AND YOUTH; AND DESIGNED, FROM ITS CHEAPNESS, FOR A READING AND CLASSICAL
BOOK, IN COMMON SCHOOLS, AND AS A USEFUL WINTER EVENING'S ENTERTAINMENT
FOR YOUNG PEOPLE IN PRIVATE FAMILIES. ILLUSTRATED WITH A NEAT MAP OF
THE UNITED STATES, AND A WHOLE BEAUTIFUL CHART OF THE WORLD. THIRD EDI-
TION. IMPROVED BY JEDIDIAH MORSE, D.D. AUTHOR OF AMERICAN UNIVERSAL
GEOGRAPHY, AMERICAN GAZETTEER, &C. &C.
Printed at Boston by Isaiah Thomas and Ebenezer T. Andrews, Feb. 1798.
pp. 143, 2 maps. 12mo.

"Two editions amounting to nearly eight thousand copies sold in two
years in this country, besides a handsome edition in England."

AUCTION
VALUES

MORSE, JEDIDIAH, continued.

34146 —— GEOGRAPHY MADE EASY: BEING AN ABRIDGMENT OF THE AMERICAN UNIVERSAL GEOGRAPHY. CONTAINING ASTRONOMICAL GEOGRAPHY; DISCOVERY AND GENERAL DESCRIPTION OF AMERICA; GENERAL VIEW OF THE UNITED STATES; PARTICULAR ACCOUNTS OF THE UNITED STATES OF AMERICA, AND OF ALL THE KINGDOMS, STATES AND REPUBLICS IN THE KNOWN WORLD. IN REGARD TO THEIR BOUNDARIES, EXTENT, RIVERS, LAKES, MOUNTAINS, PRODUCTIONS, POPULATION, CHARACTER, GOVERNMENT, TRADE, MANUFACTURES, CURIOSITIES, HISTORY, &C. TO WHICH IS ADDED, AN IMPROVED CHRONOLOGICAL TABLE OF REMARKABLE EVENTS, FROM THE CREATION TO THE PRESENT TIME. ILLUSTRATED WITH A MAP OF THE WORLD, AND A MAP OF NORTH AMERICA. CALCULATED PARTICULARLY FOR THE USE AND IMPROVEMENT OF SCHOOLS AND ACADEMIES IN THE UNITED STATES OF AMERICA. BY JEDIDIAH MORSE, D. D. MINISTER OF THE CONGREGATION IN CHARLESTOWN, MASSACHUSETTS — AUTHOR OF THE AMERICAN UNIVERSAL GEOGRAPHY, AND THE AMERICAN GAZETTEER. SIXTH EDITION, CORRECTED BY THE AUTHOR. PUBLISHED ACCORDING TO ACT OF CONGRESS. [Five lines of quotations.]

Printed at Boston, by I. Thomas and E. T. Andrews, Faust's Statue, No. 45. Newbury Street. Sold by said Thomas & Andrews, and other Booksellers in Boston; I. Thomas, Worcester; S. Campbell, New-York; Thomas, Andrews & Penniman, Albany; M. Carey, Philadelphia; and Thomas, Andrews & Butler, Baltimore.—1798. pp. 432, 2 maps. 12mo.   **AAS. BA. JCB.**

34147 —— THE HISTORY OF AMERICA, IN TWO BOOKS. CONTAINING, I. A GENERAL HISTORY OF AMERICA. II. A CONCISE HISTORY OF THE LATE REVOLUTION. EXTRACTED FROM THE AMERICAN EDITION OF THE ENCYCLOPÆDIA, THE THIRD EDITION.

Philadelphia: Printed by Thomas Dobson, at the Stone-House, South Second-Street. M.DCC.XCVIII. pp. iv, 356, 2 maps. 12mo.   **AAS. JCB. LCP. LOC.**

34148 —— A SERMON, DELIVERED AT THE NEW NORTH CHURCH IN BOSTON, IN THE MORNING, AND IN THE AFTERNOON AT CHARLESTOWN, MAY 9TH, 1798, BEING THE DAY RECOMMENDED BY JOHN ADAMS, PRESIDENT OF THE UNITED STATES OF AMERICA, FOR SOLEMN HUMILIATION, FASTING AND PRAYER. [Ornament.] BY JEDIDIAH MORSE. D. D. MINISTER OF THE CONGREGATION IN CHARLESTOWN. PUBLISHED AT THE REQUEST OF A NUMBER OF THE HEARERS, IN BOTH CONGREGATIONS. [Ornament.]

Printed by Samuel Hall, No. 53, Cornhill, Boston. 1798. pp. [29.] 8vo.
    AAS. BA. BM. CHS. CLA. HC. HSP. JCB. LOC. MHS. NYHS. NYPL. UTS. YC.

34149 —— —— A SERMON, DELIVERED AT THE NEW NORTH CHURCH IN BOSTON, IN THE MORNING, AND IN THE AFTERNOON AT CHARLESTOWN, MAY 9TH, 1798, BEING THE DAY RECOMMENDED BY JOHN ADAMS, PRESIDENT OF THE UNITED STATES OF AMERICA, FOR SOLEMN HUMILIATION, FASTING AND PRAYER. [Second edition.]

Printed by Samuel Hall, Boston. 1798. pp. 30. 8vo.

34150 —— A SERMON DELIVERED BEFORE THE GRAND LODGE OF FREE AND ACCEPTED MASONS OF THE COMMONWEALTH OF MASSACHUSETTS, AT A PUBLIC INSTALLATION OF THE OFFICERS OF THE CORINTHIAN LODGE, AT CONCORD, IN THE COUNTY OF MIDDLESEX, JUNE 25TH, 1798. BY JEDEDIAH [*sic*] MORSE, D. D. MINISTER OF THE CONGREGATION IN CHARLESTOWN.

Leominster, Massachusetts, Printed by brother Charles & John Prentiss.—1798. pp. 24, 8. 8vo.   **AAS. BA. BM. HC. JCB. LOC. NYPL. UTS.**

Second title: REV. BROTHER RIPLEY'S PRAYER AT THE FOREGOING INSTALLATION. pp. 8.

"I consent to its publication in company with Doctor Morse's excellent discourse, in deference to the opinion and polite attention of the Lodge. . . . Ezra Ripley."

34151   MORSE, JEDIDIAH, continued.
—— A SERMON, PREACHED AT CHARLESTOWN, NOVEMBER 29, 1798, ON THE ANNI-
VERSARY THANKSGIVING IN MASSACHUSETTS. WITH AN APPENDIX, DESIGNED TO
ILLUSTRATE SOME PARTS OF THE DISCOURSE; EXHIBITING PROOFS OF THE EARLY
EXISTENCE, PROGRESS, AND DELETERIOUS EFFECTS OF FRENCH INTRIGUE AND IN-
FLUENCE IN THE UNITED STATES. BY JEDIDIAH MORSE, D. D. PASTOR OF THE
CHURCH IN CHARLESTOWN. PUBLISHED BY REQUEST.

Printed by Samuel Hall, No. 53, Cornhill, Boston. December, 1798. pp. 74.
8vo.   NYPL.

34152   —— — A SERMON, PREACHED AT CHARLESTOWN, NOVEMBER 29, 1798, ON THE ANNI-
VERSARY THANKSGIVING IN MASSACHUSETTS. WITH AN APPENDIX, DESIGNED TO
ILLUSTRATE SOME PARTS OF THE DISCOURSE; EXHIBITING PROOFS OF THE EARLY
EXISTENCE, PROGRESS, AND DELETERIOUS EFFECTS OF FRENCH INTRIGUE AND IN-
FLUENCE IN THE UNITED STATES. BY JEDIDIAH MORSE, D. D. PASTOR OF THE
CHURCH IN CHARLESTOWN. PUBLISHED BY REQUEST.

Printed by Samuel Hall, No. 53, Cornhill, Boston. December, 1798. pp. 74,
(6). 8vo.   AAS. BA. BM. CHS. CLA. HC. HSP. JCB. LOC. MHS. NYPL. UTS. YC.

"The appended six pages were a part of the second edition of this sermon, and were printed in this manner, for the benefit of the purchasers
of the first edition. Feb. 18, 1799."

34153   MORTON, THOMAS   1764–1838
A CURE FOR THE HEART-ACHE. A COMEDY, IN FIVE ACTS. AS PERFORMED AT THE
THEATRE-ROYAL, COVENT-GARDEN. AND BY THE OLD AMERICAN COMPANY, NEW-
YORK, WITH UNIVERSAL APPLAUSE. BY THOMAS MORTON, ESQ. AUTHOR OF CO-
LUMBUS, ZORINSKI, WAY TO GET MARRIED, AND CHILDREN IN THE WOOD. FIRST
AMERICAN EDITION.

New-York: Printed and sold by R. Wilson, No. 149, Pearl-Street. 1798.
pp. 60. 12mo.   AAS.

34154   MOSHEIM, JOHANN LORENZ VON   1694–1755
AN ECCLESIASTICAL HISTORY, ANCIENT AND MODERN, FROM THE BIRTH OF CHRIST, TO
THE BEGINNING OF THE PRESENT CENTURY: IN WHICH THE RISE, PROGRESS, AND
VARIATIONS OF CHURCH POWER ARE CONSIDERED IN THEIR CONNEXION WITH THE
STATE OF LEARNING AND PHILOSOPHY, AND THE POLITICAL HISTORY OF EUROPE
DURING THAT PERIOD. BY THE LATE LEARNED JOHN LAWRENCE MOSHEIM, D. D.
AND CHANCELLOR OF THE UNIVERSITY OF GÖTTINGEN. TRANSLATED FROM THE
ORIGINAL LATIN, AND ACCOMPANIED WITH NOTES AND CHRONOLOGICAL TABLES, BY
ARCHIBALD MACLAINE, D. D. IN SIX VOLUMES. TO THE WHOLE IS ADDED AN ACCU-
RATE INDEX. FIRST AMERICAN EDITION. VOLUME II. [— VI.]

Philadelphia: Printed by Stephen C. Ustick, No. 79, North Third-Street,
1798. 5 vols. pp. (2), (2), 571; (2), (2), 456; (2), (2), 510; (2), (2), 496; (2), (2),
387, 8, (18). 8vo.   AAS. LOC.

Contains an eight page Vindication of the Quakers. And an eighteen
page list of subscribers. A peculiarity of the printing of this edition is
that it comes very near to not containing a single divided word at the
end of a line in the whole six volumes.

34155   MOTT, SAMUEL

AN ALMANACK AND EPHEMERIS, FOR THE YEAR OF OUR LORD, 1799. BEING THE 3D AFTER BISSEXTILE OR LEAP YEAR; OF AMERICAN INDEPENDENCE (WHICH WAS DECLARED THE 4TH OF JULY, 1776) PART OF THE 23D AND 24TH YEARS: CALCULATED FOR A LATITUDE OF 42, NORTH, AND FOR A MERIDIAN 5 HOURS WEST OF THE ROYAL OBSERVATORY AT GREENWICH. BY SAMUEL MOTT, MATHEMATICIAN.

State of New York: Poughkeepsie, Printed and sold by Power and Southwick, near the Court House. Wholesale and Retail. [1798.] pp. (36). 12mo.   AAS.

Contains, Officers of the government of the State, and Counties of New York. Revenue laws of the United States. Singular anecdote of a diver, etc.

34156   THE MOUNT-PLEASANT REGISTER.

Mount-Pleasant, New-York: Printed by William Durell. 1798. fol.

Established, as a weekly, by William Durell, and only known from references, in the "American Citizen," of April, 1800, which state: that William Durell, late editor of the "Mount-Pleasant Register," who was convicted, on April 3, 1800, for a libellous communication, against President John Adams, printed June 19, 1798, in his Register, and sentenced to four months imprisonment, and to pay a fine of fifty dollars, for publishing sedition; and, on May 5, 1800, "The President of the United States has been pleased to remit the fine and imprisonment of William Durell, late Printer of the *Mount-Pleasant Register*."

34157   MUIR, JAMES   1757–1820

A SERMON PREACHED IN THE PRESBYTERIAN CHURCH IN ALEXANDRIA, ON THE 9TH OF MAY, 1798, BEING THE DAY APPOINTED FOR A GENERAL FAST. BY THE REVD. DOCTOR JAMES MUIR.

Philadelphia: Published by William Cobbett. May 9, 1798. pp. 14. 8vo.   BA.

34158   MUNFORD, ROBERT

A COLLECTION OF PLAYS AND POEMS, BY THE LATE COL. ROBERT MUNFORD, OF MECKLENBURG COUNTY, IN THE STATE OF VIRGINIA. NOW FIRST PUBLISHED TOGETHER. [Edited, with Preface, by William Munford.]

Petersburg: Printed by William Prentis. M,DCC,XCVIII. pp. 206 [*sic* 188.] 8vo.   BU. JCB. LOC. VSL.

Pages 169–188 misnumbered 187–206. Contains, The Candidates; or, the humours of a Virginia election. — The Patriots. A comedy in five acts.— The first book of Ovid's Metamorphoses translated. — Miscellaneous poems: The Ram, a comic poem. — Letter from the Devil to his son.—Answer to the Winter piece.— Colin and Celia, a pastoral poem. —A Dream.—A patriotic song.

34159   MUNFORD, WILLIAM   1775–1825

POEMS, AND COMPOSITIONS IN PROSE ON SEVERAL OCCASIONS. BY WILLIAM MUNFORD, OF THE COUNTY OF MECKLENBURG, AND STATE OF VIRGINIA. [One line from] POPE'S ESSAY ON CRITICISM.

Richmond: Printed by Samuel Pleasants, junr. 1798. pp. (2), 189, (1). 8vo.   AAS. BU. JCB. LOC. VSL.

12th Virginia District Copyright, issued to William Munford, as Author, 29 October, 1798. Contains, Almoran and Hamet, a tragedy.—A Poem on the defeat of Gen. St. Clair, Nov. 4, 1792, or a lamentation for the death of the patriots who fell on that unfortunate day.—Oration on the subject of American independence, spoken at Williamsburg, on 4th of July 1793. — The Political contest. — An Address to the people of the County of Mecklenburg on calling a Convention to devise amendments to the Constitution of Virginia in 1797.

34160   MURDOCK, John
> The Politicians; or, a state of things. A dramatic piece. Written by an American, and a Citizen of Philadelphia.
>> *Philadelphia: Printed for the Author.* 1798. pp. 37. 8vo.   BU. HSP. LOC.
>
> In the copies belonging to the Historical Society of Pennsylvania, and Library of Congress, the last two lines of the title have been blotted out with ink. And a manuscript note in the last mentioned reads: "by Jno. Murdock Hair Dresser No. 57 Walnut Street."

34161   MURRAY, John   1741–1815
> Universalism vindicated: being the substance of some observations on the revelation of the unbounded love of God, made to the patriarch, in the field of Padanaram. Genesis, xxviii. 14. And confirmed by the joint suffrages of the prophets and apostles. Delivered some time since to the people who stately worship the only wise God our Saviour, in the meeting house in Middle Street, corner of Bennet Street. By John Murray. Published at the request of the congregation. i John iii. 10. – – Hereby perceive we the love of God, because He laid down His life for us. i John iv. 10. – – Herein is love, not that we loved God, but that He loved us, and sent His Son to be the propitiation for our sins. Romans viii. 32. – – He that spared not His own Son, but delivered Him up for us all, how shall He not with Him also, freely give us all things.
>> *Charlestown: Printed by F. Lamson, for the Author, and sold by J. W. Folsom, in Union Street, Boston, J. White, in Court Street, and at various other places in town and country.* [1798.] pp. xvi, 96, (1). 8vo.   BA. BM. HC. NYPL.

34162   MURRAY, Judith Sargent Stevens   1751–1820
> The Gleaner. A miscellaneous production. In three volumes. By Constantia. [Four lines of verse.] Vol. i. [— iii.] Published according to Act of Congress.
>> *Printed at Boston, by I. Thomas and E. T. Andrews, Faust's Statue, No. 45, Newbury-Street.* Feb. 1798. 3 vols. pp. 348; 321; 328. 12mo.
>>   AAS. BA. BM. HC. JCB. LCP. LOC. NYPL.
>
> Dedicated to John Adams, L. L. D. Contains a representative list of Subscribers' names. 141st Massachusetts District Copyright, issued to Judith Sargent Murray, as Author, 22 March, 1798.

34163   MURRAY, Lindley   1745–1826
> English exercises adapted to the Grammar lately published by L. Murray; consisting of exemplifications of the parts of speech; instances of false orthography; violations of the rules of syntax; defects in punctuation; and violations of the rules respecting perspicuity and accuracy. Designed for the benefit of private learners as well as for the use of schools. By Lindley Murray.
>> *New-York:* 1798.
>
> 71st New York District Copyright, issued to John Murray, junior, as Proprietor, 4 December, 1798.

34164   —— English grammar, adapted to the different classes of learners. With an appendix, containing rules and observations for assisting the more advanced students to write with perspicuity and accuracy. By Lindley Murray.
>> *New-York:* 1798.
>
> 72d New York District Copyright, issued to John Murray, junior, as Proprietor, 4 December, 1798.

34165 NANCREDE, PAUL JOSEPH GUERARD DE   1760–1841
BOOKS: — IMPORTATION OF MAY, 1798. JOSEPH NANCREDE'S CATALOGUE OF BOOKS,
JUST IMPORTED FROM LONDON, FOR SALE, WHOLESALE AND RETAIL, AT HIS BOOK-
STORE, No. 49, MARLBRO'-STREET, BOSTON: CONSISTING PRINCIPALLY OF A VARIETY
OF PUBLICATIONS IN DIVINITY, LAW, PHYSIC, CHEMISTRY, GEOGRAPHY, VOYAGES,
MISCELLANIES, NOVELS, ARTS AND SCIENCES, GEOGRAPHY, UNIVERSAL HISTORY, NAVI-
GATION, ASTRONOMY, MATHEMATICS, TRADE AND MANUFACTURES, BOOK-KEEPING, &C.
[Fifteen lines.]
> *Boston, June, 1798. pp. 84. 12mo.*   AAS.

34166 THE FAVORITE SONG OF NANCY OR THE SAILORS JOURNAL. AS SUNG BY MR. WILL-
IAMSON, AT THE HAY-MARKET THEATRE, BOSTON, WITH UNIVERSAL APPLAUSE.
> *Boston. Printed by Thomas & Andrews, Newbury Street. Price 25 cents.*
[1798.] pp. 3. 4to.   AAS.

34167 NAUTICAL SONGSTER OR SEAMAN'S COMPANION. TO INCREASE THE JOYS OF SATUR-
DAY NIGHT: A COLLECTION OF THE NEWEST AND MOST APPROVED SONGS, INTER-
SPERSED WITH MANY ORIGINALS.
> *Baltimore: Printed for Henry S. Keatinge. 1798. pp. 64, frontispiece.*
16mo.   JCB. LOC.

34168 NELSON, JOHN   1738–1766
A LETTER TO THE PROTESTANT - DISSENTERS IN THE PARISH OF BALLYKELLY, IN
IRELAND; OCCASIONED BY THEIR OBJECTIONS AGAINST THEIR LATE MINISTER. IN
THIS LETTER THERE IS AN ATTEMPT, UPON SCRIPTURAL AND PROTESTANT PRINCIPLES,
TO SHOW WHAT REGARD IS DUE TO HUMAN ARTICLES OF FAITH; AND ALSO, TO EX-
PLAIN SEVERAL PARTICULARS RELATIVE TO THE DOCTRINES OF ORIGINAL SIN AND
ELECTION, &C. BY JOHN NELSON, THEIR LATE PASTOR. [Eleven lines of quota-
tions.] THE SECOND AMERICAN EDITION.
> *Newburyport: Printed by Angier March, MDCCXCVIII. pp. 209. 12mo.*
AAS. NYPL.

34169 DER NEUE GEMEINNÜTZIGE LANDWIRTHSCHAFTS CALENDER, AUF DAS JAHR, NACH
DER HEILBRINGENDEN GEBURT UNSERS HERRN JESU CHRISTI, 1799. WELCHES
EIN GEMEINES JAHR VON 365 TAGEN IST. [Nine lines.] ZUM ZWÖLFTENMAL HER-
AUSGEGEBEN.
> *Lancäster: Gedruckt und zu haben bey Johann Albrecht und Comp. in der*
> *neuen Buchdruckerey, in der Prinz-Strasse, das 2te Haus nördlich vom Gefängniss.*
[1798.] pp. (42). 4to.   AAS. LOC.

> The cover gives a full-page woodcut of a farming scene, and the title
> as: Neuer Lancästerscher Calender. 1799.

34170 DER NEUE HOCH-DEUTSCHE AMERICANISCHE CALENDER AUF DAS JAHR CHRISTI 1799.
> *Baltimore: Gedruckt und zu finden bey Samuel Saur. [1798.] pp. 40. 4to.*

34171 DER NEUE NORD-AMERICANISCHE STADT UND LAND CALENDER. AUF DAS JAHR
UNSERS HEYLANDES JESU CHRISTI 1799. ZUM SECHSTENMAL HERAUSGEGEBEN.
> *Hägerstown, Maryland. Gedruckt bey Johann Gruber. [1798.] 4to.*

34172 DER NEUE UNPARTHEYISCHE BALTIMORE [cut] BOTE UND MÄRYLÄNDER STAATS-
REGISTER. JANUAR, [— DEZEMBER, 1798.]
> *Diese Zeitung herausgegeben von Samuel Saur in Baltimore. 1798. 4to.*

34173 NEUE UNPARTHEYISCHE READINGER ZEITUNG UND ANZEIGS-NACHRICHTEN. MITT-
WOCH, DEN 3 JANUAR, [— MITTWOCH, DEN 26 DEZEMBER, 1798.]
> *Reading: Gedruckt bey Gottlob Jungmann und Comp. 1798. fol.*

34174 NEUER HAUSWIRTHSCHAFTS CALENDER, AUF DAS JAHR, NACH DER HEILBRINGENDEN
GEBURT UNSERS HERRN UND HEYLANDES JESU CHRISTI, 1799. WELCHES EIN
GEMEIN-JAHR VON 365 TAGEN IST. [Six lines.] ZUM ERSTENMAL HERAUSGEGEBEN.

Philadelphia: Gedruckt und zu haben bey Henrich Schweitzer, an der südwest-
lichen Ecke der Rees- und Vierten-Strasse. [1798.] pp. (40). 4to.

34175 NEUER HAUSWIRTHSCHAFTS CALENDER, AUF DAS GNADENREICHE JAHR NACH DER
HEILBRINGENDEN GEBURT UNSERS HERRN UND HEYLANDES JESU CHRISTI, 1799.
WELCHES EIN GEMEIN-JAHR VON 365 TAGEN IST. [Six lines.] ZUM ZWEYTENMAL
HERAUSGEGEBEN.

Reading: Gedruckt und zu haben by Gottlob Jungmann und Comp. in der
Deutsch- und Englischen Buchdruckerey, in der Callowhill-Strasse, süd von dem
Courthaus. [1798.] pp. (44). 4to.   AAS. LOC.

The cover gives a full-page woodcut of a südwestlicher Prospect von
Reading.

34176 NEUER UNPARTHEYISCHER EASTONER BOTHE, UND NORTHAMPTONER KUNDSCHAFTER.
NUM. 224. DIENSTAG, DEN 2 JANUAR, [— NUM. 275. DIENSTAG, DEN 25 DEZEM-
BER, 1798.]

Diese Zeitung wird alle Dienstag morgen herausgegeben von Jacob Weygandt
und Sohn, in der Neuen Buchdruckerey zu Easton . . . 1798. fol.

34177 THE NEW COMPLETE LETTER WRITER; OR, THE ART OF CORRESPONDENCE. CONTAINING
LETTERS ON THE FOLLOWING SUBJECTS: BUSINESS, FRIENDSHIP, LOVE AND MARRI-
AGE, COURTSHIP, POLITENESS, ECONOMY, AFFECTION, AMUSEMENT, DUTY, ADVICE,
RELIGION, &C. COMPOSED BY WRITERS EMINENT FOR PERSPICUITY AND ELEGANCE
OF EXPRESSION. TO WHICH ARE ADDED, MORAL MAXIMS AND REFLECTIONS BY THE
LATE DUKE DE LA ROCHEFOUCAULT. LIKEWISE FORMS OF MESSAGE CARDS, AND
INSTRUCTIONS HOW TO ADDRESS PERSONS OF ALL RANKS IN THE UNITED STATES.

Printed at Boston, by Samuel Etheridge, for Daniel Brewer, sold by him in
Taunton, and by D. West, and Thomas & Andrews, in Boston. April, 1798. pp. 228.
nar. 8vo.   JCB.

34178 NEW ENGLAND MISSISSIPPI LAND COMPANY.

Heading: XXIII ARTICLES OF ASSOCIATION AND AGREEMENT, CONSTITUTING THE NEW-
ENGLAND MISSISSIPPI LAND COMPANY, AS AMENDED MARCH 12, 1798.

[*Boston:* 1798.] pp. 9. 8vo.   AAS. DeRGL. YC.

34179 —— MEMORIAL. [To the President of the United States.]

[*Boston:* 1798.] pp. 19. 8vo.   BA. DeRGL. JCB.

34180 THE NEW-ENGLAND PRIMER AMENDED AND IMPROVED; BY THE AUTHOR OF THE
GRAMMATICAL INSTITUTE [NOAH WEBSTER, JUNIOR.] CONTAINING BESIDES WHAT
IS USUALLY PUT IN A PRIMER, A LARGE NUMBER OF MORAL AND ENTERTAINING
LESSONS FOR CHILDREN; PROVERBS AND MAXIMS; A RELIGIOUS DIALOGUE; A VARIETY
OF ENTERTAINING STORIES. ADORN'D WITH EMBLEMATICAL ENGRAVINGS, SPIRITUAL
SONGS, &C. &C. &C.

Hartford: Printed and sold by Elisha Babcock. 1798.

34181 —— THE NEW-ENGLAND PRIMER IMPROVED, AND ARRANGED AS A FIRST BOOK FOR
CHILDREN. WITH THE ASSEMBLY OF DIVINES CATECHISM.

Baltimore: Printed for Henry S. Keatinge. 1798.   AAS.

34182 —— THE NEW-ENGLAND PRIMER, OR, AN EASY AND PLEASANT GUIDE TO THE ART
OF READING. ADORN'D WITH CUTTS. TO WHICH ARE ADDED, THE ASSEMBLY OF
DIVINES' CATECHISM.

Boston: Printed and sold by J. White, near Charles-River Bridge. [1798.]
pp. (96). 24mo.   BU.

AUCTION
VALUES

THE NEW-ENGLAND PRIMER, continued.

34183   —— THE NEW-ENGLAND PRIMER ENLARGED: OR, AN EASY AND PLEASANT GUIDE TO THE ART OF READING. ADORN'D WITH CUTS. TO WHICH ARE ADDED, THE ASSEMBLY OF DIVINES CATECHISM., &C.

     Boston: Printed by E. Draper, for James White, at Franklin's Head, Court-Street. 1798. pp. (80). 32mo.   AAS. HC. NYPL. PLA.

34184   —— THE NEW-ENGLAND PRIMER, (ENLARGED AND MUCH IMPROVED), FOR THE MORE EASY ATTAINING THE TRUE READING OF ENGLISH. ADORNED WITH CUTS. TO WHICH IS ADDED, THE ASSEMBLY'S CATECHISM.

     Carlisle: Printed by George Kline, for A. Loudon. [April 13, 1796.]

34185   —— THE AMERICAN PRIMER. IMPROVED. OR, AN EASY AND PLEASANT GUIDE TO THE ART OF READING. ADORNED WITH CUTS. TO WHICH IS ADDED, THE ASSEMBLY OF DIVINES' CATECHISM.

     Medford: Printed and sold by Nathaniel Coverly [junior.] 1798. (*Price six pence.*) pp. [64.] 32mo.   AAS. LOC.

34186   —— THE NEW-ENGLAND PRIMER, FOR THE MORE EASY ATTAINING THE TRUE READING OF ENGLISH. TO WHICH IS ADDED, THE ASSEMBLY OF DIVINES SHORTER CATECHISM. ALSO SOME SHORT AND EASY QUESTIONS FOR CHILDREN, &C.

     New-York: Printed and sold by J. Harrisson, at his book-store and printing-office, No. 3, Peck-Slip. 1796. pp. (80), frontispiece of George Washington, EsqQ and cuts. 32mo.

34187   —— THE NEW-ENGLAND PRIMER; IMPROVED, FOR THE MORE EASY ATTAINING THE TRUE READING OF ENGLISH. TO WHICH IS ADDED, THE ASSEMBLY OF DIVINE'S CATECHISM. [Double line.]

     Springfield, Printed by Edward Gray. M,DCC,XCV. pp. (60). 32mo.   AAS.

34188   —— THE NEW-ENGLAND PRIMER, IMPROVED. FOR THE MORE EASY ATTAINING THE TRUE READING OF ENGLISH. TO WHICH IS ADDED, THE ASSEMBLY OF DIVINES CATECHISM. [Ornament.]

     Suffield: Printed by H. & O. Farnsworth. 1798. pp. (80). 32mo.   HEH.

34189   —— — THE NEW-ENGLAND PRIMER, IMPROVED. FOR THE MORE EASY ATTAINING, THE TRUE READING OF ENGLISH. TO WHICH IS ADDED, THE ASSEMBLY OF DIVINES CATECHISM.

     Suffield: Printed by H. & O. Farnsworth, for Oliver D. & I. Cooke. 1798. pp. (80). 32mo.

34190   —— THE NEW-ENGLAND PRIMER, IMPROVED FOR THE MORE EASY ATTAINING THE TRUE READING OF ENGLISH. TO WHICH IS ADDED, THE ASSEMBLY OF DIVINE'S CATECHISM.

     Suffield: Printed by Gray & Albro, for Henry Dwier, Hartford, ten rods north of the Court-House. 1798. pp. (64). 32mo.

34191   THE NEW GARDENER'S CALENDAR, OR EVERY MAN A COMPLETE GARDENER: CONTAINING, ALL THE NECESSARY INFORMATION RELATING TO GARDENS, ORCHARDS, &C. GRAFTING, TRANSPLANTING, &C. DESTROYING VERMIN, JUDGING THE WEATHER, MANAGING BEES, &C. &C.

     New-London: Sold by Charles Holt. May 9, 1798.

34192   NEW HAMPSHIRE. State.
THE BOARD OF COMMISSIONERS APPOINTED IN THE STATE OF NEW-HAMPSHIRE, IN
PURSUANCE OF AN ACT OF CONGRESS PASSED ON THE 9TH DAY OF JULY, 1798, EN-
TITLED "AN ACT TO PROVIDE FOR THE VALUATION OF LANDS AND DWELLING-
HOUSES, AND THE ENUMERATION OF SLAVES WITHIN THE UNITED STATES." [Form
of appointment of district assessors.] GIVEN UNDER OUR HANDS AND SEALS AT
THIS DAY OF   1798.

    [Exeter: Printed by Henry Ranlet ? 1798.] Broadside. fol.   LOC. NYPL.

34193   —— A JOURNAL OF THE PROCEEDINGS OF THE HON. HOUSE OF REPRESENTATIVES OF
THE STATE OF NEW-HAMPSHIRE, AT THEIR SESSION BEGUN AND HOLDEN AT PORTS-
MOUTH, NOVEMBER, 1797. [— 21 DECEMBER, 1797.] [Arms.]

    *State of New-Hampshire, Portsmouth: Printed by John Melcher, Printer to
the State,* 1798. pp. 127. 8vo.   AAS. LOC. NYPL.

34194   —— A JOURNAL OF THE PROCEEDINGS OF THE HONORABLE SENATE OF THE STATE OF
NEW-HAMPSHIRE, AT A SESSION OF THE GENERAL-COURT, HOLDEN AT PORTSMOUTH,
NOV. 1797. [— 21 DECEMBER, 1797.] [Arms.]

    *State of New-Hampshire: Portsmouth: Printed by John Melcher, Printer to
the State,* 1798. pp. 80. 8vo.   AAS. LOC. NYPL.

34195   —— A JOURNAL OF THE PROCEEDINGS OF THE HON. HOUSE OF REPRESENTATIVES OF
THE STATE OF NEW-HAMPSHIRE, AT THEIR SESSION BEGUN AND HOLDEN AT HOP-
KINTON THE 1ST WEDNESDAY IN JUNE, 1798. [—20 JUNE 1798.] [Arms.]

    *State of New-Hampshire: Portsmouth: Printed by John Melcher, Printer to
the State.* 1798. pp. 76. 8vo.   AAS. LOC. NYPL.

34196   —— A JOURNAL OF THE PROCEEDINGS OF THE HONORABLE SENATE OF THE STATE OF
NEW-HAMPSHIRE, AT THEIR SESSION BEGUN AND HOLDEN AT HOPKINTON THE 1ST
WEDNESDAY IN JUNE, 1798. [— 20 JUNE, 1798.] [Arms.]

    *State of New-Hampshire: Portsmouth: Printed by John Melcher, Printer to
the State,* 1798.   AAS. LOC.

34197   THE NEW HAMPSHIRE GAZETTE. — OUR COUNTRY'S GOOD OUR CONSTANT AIM.
VOL. xlii. NUMB. 2145. WEDNESDAY, JANUARY 3, [— VOL. xliii. NUMB. 2195.
WEDNESDAY, DECEMBER 26, 1798.]

    *Portsmouth: (New-Hampshire)—Published every Wednesday morning by John
Melcher, Printer to the State, at his Office, corner of Market-Street.* 1798. fol.

A Gazette Extraordinary was issued April 19th. In June, Tuesday was
the day of publication, which was changed to Wednesday, in November.
The motto was altered, in September, to *My* Country's good *shall be my*
constant aim.

34198   NEW HOLIDAY PRESENT. PRICE FOUR CENTS.

    Boston: Printed and sold by John W. Folsom, No. 30, Union-Street. 1798.
32mo.

34199   NEW JERSEY. State.
ACTS OF THE TWENTY-SECOND GENERAL ASSEMBLY OF THE STATE OF NEW-JERSEY.
AT A SESSION BEGUN AT TRENTON ON THE TWENTY-FOURTH DAY OF OCTOBER, SEVEN-
TEEN HUNDRED AND NINETY-SEVEN, AND CONTINUED BY ADJOURNMENTS. BEING
THE SECOND SITTING. [Arms.]

    Trenton: Printed by Matthias Day, Printer to the State. M,DCC,XCVIII. pp.
(2), (259)–412. fol.   LOC.

NEW JERSEY. STATE, continued.

34200 —— STATE OF NEW-JERSEY. AN ACT INCORPORATING THE INHABITANTS OF TOWN-
SHIPS, DESIGNATING THEIR POWERS, AND REGULATING THEIR MEETINGS. PASSED
AT TRENTON, FEBRUARY 21, 1798.
[Trenton: Printed by Matthias Day, 1798.] pp. (14). fol.   LOC.

34201 —— STATE OF NEW-JERSEY. AN ACT, RESPECTING SLAVES. PASSED AT TRENTON,
MARCH 14, 1798. [Colophon:]
[Trenton: Printed by G. Craft.] [1798.] pp. [16.] 8vo.   NYPL.

34202 —— VOTES AND PROCEEDINGS OF THE TWENTY-SECOND GENERAL ASSEMBLY OF THE
STATE OF NEW-JERSEY, AT A SESSION BEGUN AT TRENTON ON THE TWENTY-FOURTH
DAY OF OCTOBER, SEVENTEEN HUNDRED NINETY-SEVEN, AND CONTINUED BY AD-
JOURNMENTS. [— 16 March, 1798.] BEING THE SECOND SITTING.
Trenton: Printed by Matthias Day, Printer to the State. M,DCC,XCVII.
[1798.] pp. 72. fol.   JCB. LOC.

34203 THE NEW-JERSEY [cut] JOURNAL. VOL. XV. No. 743. TUESDAY, JANUARY 2,
[— VOL. XVI. No. 793. TUESDAY, DECEMBER 25, 1798.]
*Elizabeth-Town: Printed and published by Shepard Kollock, every Tuesday, at
two dollars per annum . . . 1798. fol.*

With the issue for August 21st, the title was shortened to *New-Jersey
Journal.*

34204 THE NEW-WINDSOR GAZETTE. VOL. I. No. 8. TUESDAY, JANUARY 2, [— VOL. II
No. 7. TUESDAY, DECEMBER 25, 1798.]
New-Windsor, [N. Y.] Printed by Jacob Schultz & Abraham Lott. 1798. fol.

34205 NEW YORK. STATE.
AN ACT FOR THE BENEFIT OF INSOLVENT DEBTORS . . . [Colophon:]
[Albany:] Printed by Loring Andrews & Co. Printers to the State. [1798.]
JCB.

34206 —— — AN ACT FOR THE BENEFIT OF INSOLVENT DEBTORS AND THEIR CREDITORS.
. . . STATE OF NEW-YORK, IN ASSEMBLY, MARCH 31ST, 1798: THIS BILL HAVING
BEEN READ THE THIRD TIME, RESOLVED — THAT THE BILL DO PASS. BY ORDER OF
THE ASSEMBLY, DIRCK TEN BROECK, SPEAKER. [Colophon:]
[New-York:] George F. Hopkins, Printer. [1798.] pp. 16. 8vo. JCB. LOC.

34207 —— AN ACT TO AMEND AN ACT ENTITLED AN ACT TO REGULATE HIGHWAYS, [PASSED
AT THE LATE SESSION OF THE LEGISLATURE.]
Albany: Printed by Loring Andrews & Co. 1798.

34208 —— AN ACT TO INCORPORATE THE INHABITANTS OF THAT PART OF THE TOWN OF
SCHENECTADY THEREIN MENTIONED; OF WHICH THE FOLLOWING IS A COPY, IS NOW
BEFORE THE HONOURABLE THE HOUSE OF ASSEMBLY, OF THIS STATE, FEBRUARY
9TH, 1798.
Albany: Printed by C. R. & G. Webster, [1798.] pp. 14. 4to.

34209 —— AN INDEX TO THE LAWS OF THE 20TH AND 21ST SESSION OF THE LEGISLATURE
OF THE STATE OF NEW-YORK.
Albany: Printed by Loring Andrews & Co. 1798.

34210 —— JOURNAL OF THE ASSEMBLY OF THE STATE OF NEW-YORK; AT THEIR TWENTY-
FIRST SESSION, BEGAN AND HELD AT THE CITY OF ALBANY, THE SECOND DAY OF
JANUARY, 1798. [— 6 APRIL, 1798.] [Arms.]
Albany: Printed by Loring Andrews & Co. Printers to the State. [1798.] pp.
(339). fol.   HC. LOC. NYPL.

NEW YORK. STATE, continued.

34211 —— JOURNAL OF THE SENATE OF THE STATE OF NEW-YORK; AT THEIR TWENTY-FIRST SESSION, BEGAN AND HELD AT THE CITY OF ALBANY, THE SECOND DAY OF JANUARY, 1798. [— 6 APRIL, 1798.]]Arms.]

Albany: Printed by Loring Andrews & Co. Printers to the State. [1798.] pp. (144). fol. AAS. LOC. NYPL.

34212 —— JOURNAL OF THE ASSEMBLY OF THE STATE OF NEW-YORK; AT THEIR TWENTY-SECOND SESSION, BEGAN AND HELD AT THE CITY OF ALBANY, THE NINTH DAY OF AUGUST, 1798. [— 27 AUGUST, 1798.] [Arms.]

Albany: Printed by Loring Andrews & Co. Printers to the State. [1798.] pp. [39.] fol. LOC.

34213 —— JOURNAL OF THE SENATE OF THE STATE OF NEW-YORK; AT THEIR TWENTY-SECOND SESSION, BEGAN AND HELD AT THE CITY OF ALBANY, THE NINTH DAY OF AUGUST, 1798. [— 27 AUGUST, 1798.] [Arms.]

Albany: Printed by Loring Andrews & Co. Printers to the State. [1798.] pp. [26.] fol. AAS. LOC. NYPL.

34214 —— LAWS OF THE STATE OF NEW-YORK, COMPRISING THE CONSTITUTION, AND THE ACTS OF THE LEGISLATURE, SINCE THE REVOLUTION, FROM THE FIRST TO THE TWENTIETH SESSION, INCLUSIVE. [Arms,] IN THREE VOLUMES. VOLUME I. [16 MARCH 1778 – 21 APRIL 1787.] SECOND EDITION. [Three lines of Latin quotations.]

*New-York.—Printed by Thomas Greenleaf—*M,DCC,XCVIII. pp. (2), (2), 507. 8vo. AAS. NYHS.

34215 —— LAWS OF THE STATE OF NEW-YORK, PASSED AT THE TWENTY-FIRST SESSION OF THE LEGISLATURE, BEGUN AND HELD AT THE CITY OF ALBANY, THE SECOND DAY OF JANUARY, 1798. [Arms.]

Albany: Printed by Loring Andrews & Co. Privters to the State. 1798. pp. (2), (243)–535, (4), (1). 8vo. AAS. LOC.

34216 —— LAWS OF THE STATE OF NEW-YORK, PASSED AT THE TWENTY-SECOND SESSION OF THE LEGISLATURE, BEGUN AND HELD AT THE CITY OF ALBANY, THE NINTH DAY OF AUGUST, 1798. [Arms.]

Albany: Printed by Loring Andrews & Co. Printers to the State. 1798. pp. (2), (539)–552. 8vo. LOC.

34217 —— SPEECH OF HIS EXCELLENCY JOHN JAY, ESQ. GOVERNOR OF THE STATE OF NEW-YORK, TO THE TWO HOUSES OF THE LEGISLATURE, AT THE OPENING OF THE SESSION, AT ALBANY, TUESDAY, JANUARY 2D, 1798. . . . JOHN JAY. [Colophon:]

Albany: Printed by C. R. & G. Webster. [1798.] pp. (4). 4to. NYPL.

34218 —— STATEMENT OF THE FUNDS OF THE STATE OF NEW-YORK; AND OF THE ANNUAL REVENUE THEREOF; AND ALSO OF THE RECEIPTS AND PAYMENTS IN THE YEAR 1797: TOGETHER WITH THE TREASURER'S ACCOUNT.

Albany: Printed by Loring Andrews & Co. Printers to the State. 1798. pp. [16.] 8vo. AAS. JCB. NYHS.

34219 —— *Heading:* WHEREAS THE STATE OF NEW YORK, DOES NOT ACKNOWLEDGE THE CLAIM OF CONNECTICUT TO ANY LANDS IN THIS STATE, AND WHEREAS, THIS STATE HAS FULL CONFIDENCE IN THE IMPARTIALITY, KNOWLEDGE AND INTEGRITY OF THE JUDICIARY OF THE UNITED STATES IN REGARD TO ANY SUIT COMMENCED . . . THEREFORE, RESOLVED, THAT IT WOULD BE IMPROPER FOR THIS STATE TO APPOINT COMMISSIONERS TO CONFER WITH THE COMMISSIONERS OF CONNECTICUT. . . . DATED, ALBANY, FEBRUARY 16, 1798.]

[Albany: Printed by Loring Andrews. 1798.] Broadside. 12mo.

AUCTION VALUES

34220   NEW YORK. STATE. COURT OF ERRORS.
REPORT OF THE CASE IN THE COURT OF ERRORS FOR THE STATE OF NEW-YORK, BETWEEN ISAAC GOUVERNEUR AND PETER KEMBLE, PLAINTIFFS IN ERROR, AND LOUIS LE GUEN, DEFENDANT IN ERROR.
     Albany: Printed by Charles R. & George Webster. 1798. pp. 135, folded table. 8vo.   NYHS. NYPL.

34221   NEW YORK. SOCIETY FOR AGRICULTURE, ARTS AND MANUFACTURES.
TRANSACTIONS OF THE SOCIETY, INSTITUTED IN THE STATE OF NEW-YORK, FOR THE PROMOTION OF AGRICULTURE, ARTS AND MANUFACTURES. PART III. PUBLISHED BY ORDER OF THE SOCIETY.
     Albany: Printed by Loring Andrews, Printer to the State. M,DCC,XCVIII. pp. xli, 126, (3). 4to.   AAS. BA. BM. HC. MHS. NYHS.

34222   NEW YORK. CITY.
TO THE INHABITANTS. [Notification that the tax on houses, etc. authorized by Act of Congress of 14th July, 1798, is due.]
     [New-York: 1798.] Broadside. 4to.

34223   NEW YORK. CITY. BAPTIST ASSOCIATION.
MINUTES OF THE NEW YORK BAPTIST ASSOCIATION. HELD IN THE CITY OF NEW YORK, MAY 23RD, 1798.
     [New-York: 1798.] pp. 10. 4to.

34224   NEW YORK. CITY. GENERAL SOCIETY OF MECHANICS AND TRADESMEN.
THE CHARTER AND BYE-LAWS OF THE GENERAL SOCIETY OF MECHANICS AND TRADESMEN OF THE CITY OF NEW-YORK. ALSO—THE RULES OF ORDER, WITH A CATALOGUE OF MEMBERS' NAMES. PUBLISHED BY ORDER OF THE SOCIETY.
     New-York: Printed by Geo: Forman, No. 64 Water-Street, between Coenties and the Old-Slip. 1798. pp. 24. 8vo.   JCB. NYPL.

34225   NEW YORK. CITY. MUTUAL ASSURANCE COMPANY.
AN ACT TO INCORPORATE THE MUTUAL ASSURANCE COMPANY OF THE CITY OF NEW-YORK, PASSED THE 23D DAY OF MARCH, 1798. TOGETHER WITH THE BYE-LAWS, RULES AND REGULATIONS FOR MANAGING THE AFFAIRS OF SAID COMPANY.
     New-York: Printed by James Oram, No. 33 Liberty-Street. 1798. pp. (24). 12mo.   NYHS. NYPL.

34226   NEW YORK. CITY. NEW YORK INSURANCE COMPANY.
AN ACT TO INCORPORATE THE STOCKHOLDERS OF THE NEW-YORK INSURANCE COMPANY. (PASSED 2D APRIL, 1798.) [Ornament, between two double lines.]
     Printed at New-York, by James Oram, No. 33 Liberty-Street.—1798.—pp. 15. 8vo.   NYHS.

34227   NEW YORK. CITY. WASHINGTON MILITARY SOCIETY.
THE CONSTITUTION AND BYE-LAWS OF THE NEW YORK WASHINGTON MILITARY SOCIETY. PUBLISHED BY THE ORDER OF THE SOCIETY, 22D MAY, 1798.
     New-York: Printed by John Tiebout. 1798. pp. 14. 16mo.   LOC.

34228   THE NEW-YORK GAZETTE AND GENERAL ADVERTISER. NUMB. 2845. MONDAY, JANUARY 1, [— NUMB. 3156. MONDAY, DECEMBER 31, 1798.]
     Published (daily) by M'Lean & Lang, Franklin's Head, No. 116, Pearl-Street. 1798. fol.

     Archibald M'Lean died September 22d, but by arrangement with his widow the firm name was continued.

AUCTION
VALUES

34229   NEWARK [cut] GAZETTE. VOLUME I. NUMBER 9. TUESDAY, JANUARY 2, [— VOL-UME II. No. 8. NUMBER 60. TUESDAY, DECEMBER 25, 1798.]
> *[Newark:] Printed by John Woods, for the Proprietors.* 1798. fol.   AAS.

With the issue for February 6th, John H. Williams began printing for the Proprietors, and Woods' connection ceased.

34230   THE NEWBERN GAZETTE. VOL. I. NUMB. 1. SATURDAY, APRIL 7, [— NUMB. 39. SATURDAY, DECEMBER 29, 1798.]
> *Newbern, (North-Carolina:) Printed for John C. Osborn & Co.* 1798. fol.

Established, as a weekly, by John C. Osborn and Company, and continued by them into 1800, when they were succeeded by John S. Pasteur as publisher. In 1801 the title was altered to *The Newbern Gazette, And political and miscellaneous register,* dropping the sub-title in 1804. No issue of the Gazette has been located after March, 1804.

34231   THE NEWBURYPORT HERALD AND COUNTRY GAZETTE. No. 19 OF VOL. I. TUES-DAY, JANUARY 2, [— No. 18 OF VOL. II. FRIDAY, DECEMBER 28, 1798.]
> *Published on Tuesdays and Fridays, by Angier March, at his Office, Middle-Street.* 1798. fol.   AAS.

34232   —— TO THE PATRONS OF THE NEWBURYPORT HERALD, &C. IT IS A CUSTOM TO APPEAR AND WISH YOU ALL A HAPPY YEAR: . . .
> *[Newburyport: Printed by Angier March, January 1, 1798.]* Broadside.   EI.

34233   THE NEWPORT MERCURY. No. 1863. TUESDAY, JANUARY 2, [— No. 1914. TUES-DAY, DECEMBER 25, 1798.]
> *Newport (Rhode Island) Published by Henry Barber, near the State-House.* 1798. fol.   AAS. LOC. NHS. RIHS. RL.

34234   NEWTON, JOHN   1725–1807
A VIEW OF ECCLESIASTICAL HISTORY. BY JOHN NEWTON.
> *Boston: Printed for Joseph Bumstead, Printer and Bookseller, No. 20, Union-Street.* [1798] pp. xviii, 320. 12mo.   AAS.

34235   NICHOLAS, GEORGE   1755–1799
A LETTER FROM GEORGE NICHOLAS, OF KENTUCKY, TO HIS FRIEND, IN VIRGINIA [Thomas Jefferson]. JUSTIFYING THE CONDUCT OF THE CITIZENS OF KENTUCKY, AS TO SOME OF THE LATE MEASURES OF THE GENERAL GOVERNMENT; AND CORRECTING CERTAIN FALSE STATEMENTS, WHICH HAVE BEEN MADE IN THE DIFFERENT STATES. OF THE VIEWS AND ACTIONS OF THE PEOPLE OF KENTUCKY.
> *Lexington: Printed by John Bradford, on Main-Street.* 1798. pp. (42). 8vo.   AAS. BA. LOC. NYPL.

34236   THE NIGHT WAS DARK.
> *Boston: Published by P. A. von Hagen jun. and Co's Musical Magazine, No. 62, Newbury-Street.* 1798.

34237   THE NIGHTINGALE; OR CHARMS OF MELODY.
> *Baltimore: Printed for Henry S. Keatinge.* 1798.

34238   THE NORFOLK HERALD, & PUBLIC ADVERTISER. VOL. 4. No. 364. MONDAY, JAN-UARY 1, [— VOL. 6. No. 517. SATURDAY, DECEMBER 29, 1798.]
> *Norfolk: Published on Mondays, Thursdays, and Saturdays, by Willett and O'Connor, near the Market.* 1798. fol.   LOC.

Beginning January 9th, Tuesday was substituted for Monday, as one of the days of publication. The sub-title was dropped after February 17th. The issue for April 16th, containing the full text of the "Letters of credence and full powers to the envoys to France," is headed, "The Norfolk Herald, Anticipated."

34239   NORMAN, JOHN   1748–1817
THE AMERICAN PILOT, CONTAINING THE NAVIGATION OF THE SEA COAST OF NORTH
AMERICA, FROM THE STREIGHTS OF BELLE ISLE TO CAYENNE, INCLUDING THE ISLAND
AND BANKS OF NEWFOUNDLAND, THE WEST-INDIA-ISLANDS, AND ALL THE ISLANDS ON
THE COAST; WITH PARTICULAR DIRECTIONS FOR SAILING TO AND ENTERING THE PRIN-
CIPAL HARBOURS, RIVERS, &C. DESCRIBING ALSO THE CAPES, HEADLANDS, RIVERS,
BAYS, ROADS, HAVENS, HARBOURS, STRAITS, ROCKS, SANDS, SHOALS, BANKS, DEPTHS
OF WATER AND ANCHORAGE; SHEWING THE COURSES AND DISTANCES FROM ONE
PLACE TO ANOTHER, THE EBBING OF THE SEA, THE SETTING OF THE TIDE AND CUR-
RENTS, &C. WITH MANY OTHER THINGS NECESSARY TO BE KNOWN IN NAVIGATION;
LIKEWISE NECESSARY DIRECTIONS FOR THOSE WHO ARE NOT FULLY ACQUAINTED
WITH THE USE OF CHARTS.
> *Boston: Published by William Norman, at his Book Store, No. 75, Newbury-
Street, nearly opposite the Sign of the Lamb.* 1798. pp. 6, 9 maps. fol.

34240   NORTH CAROLINA. STATE.
JOURNAL OF THE HOUSE OF COMMONS OF THE GENERAL ASSEMBLY OF NORTH-CARO-
LINA. NOVEMBER, AND DECEMBER SESSION, 1796. [Colophon:]
> *Edenton: Printed by Hodge & Wills, Printers to the State.* [1797.] pp. 54.
fol.   NCSL.

34241   —— JOURNAL OF THE SENATE OF THE GENERAL ASSEMBLY OF NORTH-CAROLINA.
NOVEMBER, AND DECEMBER SESSION, 1796. [Colophon:]
> *Edenton: Printed by Hodge & Wills, Printers to the State.* [1797.] pp. 47.
fol.   NCSL.

34242   —— JOURNAL OF THE HOUSE OF COMMONS OF THE GENERAL ASSEMBLY OF NORTH-
CAROLINA. NOVEMBER, AND DECEMBER SESSION, 1797. [Colophon:]
> *Halifax: Printed by Abraham Hodge, Printer to the State.* [1798.] pp. 56.
fol.   NCSL.

34243   —— JOURNAL OF THE SENATE OF THE GENERAL ASSEMBLY OF NORTH-CAROLINA.
NOVEMBER, AND DECEMBER SESSION. 1797. [Colophon:]
> *Halifax: Printed by Abraham Hodge, Printer to the State.* [1798.] pp. 44.
fol.   LOC. NCSL.

34244   —— JOURNAL OF THE HOUSE OF COMMONS OF THE GENERAL ASSEMBLY OF NORTH-
CAROLINA. NOVEMBER SESSION. 1798.
> *[Wilmington: Printed by A. Hall, Printer to the State.* 1798.] pp. 58. fol.
                     NCSL.

34245   —— JOURNAL OF THE SENATE OF THE GENERAL ASSEMBLY OF NORTH-CAROLINA.
NOVEMBER SESSION. 1798. [Colophon:]
> *Wilmington, (N. C.) Printed by A. Hall, Printer to the State.* [1798.] pp. 79.
fol.   LOC. NCSL.

34246   —— LAWS OF NORTH - CAROLINA. NOVEMBER, AND DECEMBER SESSION. 1797.
[Colophon:]
> *Halifax: Printed by Abraham Hodge, Printer to the State.* [1798.] pp. 25,
(1). fol.   LOC. NCSL. NCU. NYPL.

34247   —— LAWS OF NORTH-CAROLINA. NOVEMBER SESSION. 1798. [Colophon:]
> *Wilmington. A. Hall, Printer to the State.* [1798.] pp. 58. fol.   NCSL. NCU.

34248   THE NORTH-CAROLINA ALMANACK FOR THE YEAR OF OUR LORD, 1799: AND OF
AMERICAN INDEPENDENCE, 23-24. BEING THE 3D AFTER LEAP YEAR. CALCULATED
FOR THE MERIDIAN OF NEWBERN, 35 DEG. 4 MIN. NORTH LAT. 2 DEG. 6½ MIN.
LONG. WEST FROM PHILADELPHIA.
> *Newbern: Printed for John C. Osborn & Co.* [1798.]

34249   NORTH CAROLINA ALMANAC FOR THE YEAR, 1799.

Salisbury: Printed and sold by Francis Coupee. [1798.]   LOC.

34250   THE NORTH-CAROLINA JOURNAL. No. 285. MONDAY, JANUARY 1, [— No. 337. MONDAY, DECEMBER 31, 1798.]

Halifax: Printed by Abraham Hodge, Joint Printer to the State with H. Wills. 1798. fol.   HSP. LOC.

Beginning January 15th, Hodge became Printer to the State.

34251   THE NORTH-CAROLINA MERCURY, AND SALISBURY ADVERTISER. VOL. I. No. 1. SATURDAY, MAY 26, [— No. 32. SATURDAY, DECEMBER 29, 1798.]

Salisbury: Published by Francis Coupee. 1798. fol.

Established, as a weekly, by Francis Coupee, and continued by him to August 13, 1801 — the last number located.

34252   THE NORTH-CAROLINA MINERVA, AND FAYETTEVILLE ADVERTISER. VOL. II. NUMB. 95. TUESDAY, JANUARY 2, [—VOL. III. NUMB. 147. TUESDAY, DECEMBER 29, 1798.]

Fayetteville: Published every Tuesday by Hodge & Boylan. 1798. fol.

34253   NORTHERN [cut] BUDGET. [Motto.] VOL. I. No. 29. TUESDAY, JANUARY 2, [—No. 47. TUESDAY, MAY 8, 1798.]

Lansingburgh: Published by Robert Moffitt & Co. 1798. fol.

The Printing-Office was removed to Troy, and publication continued there as follows:

34254   NORTHERN [cut] BUDGET. [Motto.] VOL. I. NUMBER 48. TUESDAY, MAY 15, [— VOL. II. NUMBER 81. TUESDAY, DECEMBER 25, 1798.]

Troy: Published every Tuesday, at Franklin's Head, by Robert Moffitt & Co. at two dollars per annum. 1798. fol.   AAS.

Extra numbers were printed on July 3d, and October 9th.

34255   NORTHERN [cut] CENTINEL. VOL. I. No. 1. MONDAY, JANUARY 1, [— No. 52. TUESDAY, DECEMBER 25, 1798.]

Salem, Washington County, State of New-York: Published every Tuesday by Henry Dodd. Subscriptions for this paper are received by the publisher hereof, in the house formerly occupied by Thomas Barrow, a few rods north of the Court-House. 1798. fol.   AAS.

The cut is a representation of a marching sentinel, saying "All is well." Surrounded by a scroll on which are the sentiments, "La Nuit est passé. Watch for the Republic." Which had formerly been used by the *Washington Patrol*, published at Salem.

Established, as a weekly, by Henry Dodd, with St. John Honeywood as Editor. Honeywood died 1 September, 1798, and Dodd continued publication certainly into the year 1800. In May, 1804, it was succeeded by *The Northern Post.*

34256   THE NORTHERN LIBERTIES AND DAILY ADVERTISER.

Philadelphia: Printed by Bernard Scheffler & Co. 1798.

A short-lived newspaper, devoted to the interests of that part of Philadelphia locally known as the Township of Northern Liberties, established early this year, of which no copies are known.

AUCTION
VALUES

34257   NORTH WEST TERRITORY.
LAWS OF THE TERRITORY OF THE UNITED STATES NORTH WEST OF THE RIVER OHIO. ADOPTED AND PUBLISHED AT A SESSION OF THE LEGISLATURE BEGUN IN THE TOWN OF CINCINNATI, COUNTY OF HAMILTON AND TERRITORY AFORESAID UPON THE 23D DAY OF APRIL IN THE YEAR OF OUR LORD 1798 AND CONTINUED BY ADJOURNMENT TO THE SEVENTH DAY OF MAY IN THE SAME YEAR. BY AUTHORITY.
> *Cincinnati: Printed and sold by Edmund Freeman.* M,DCC,XCVIII. pp. [32.] 4to.   LOC. NYPL.

Reprinted in facsimile.

34258   NORTON, ELIJAH
THE IMPOSSIBILITY OF SINNERS' COMING TO CHRIST, WITHOUT THE ALMIGHTY DRAW- ING OF GOD THE FATHER, ILLUSTRATED AND PROVED IN A DISCOURSE, PREACHED AT ROYALTON, FROM JOHN VI. 44. AND V. 40. MADE PUBLIC BY REQUEST OF THE HEARERS — WITH SOME ADDITIONS AND ENLARGEMENT. BY ELIJAH NORTON OF WOODSTOCK. [Two lines from] JEHOVAH.
> *Printed at Suffield, by H. & O. Farnsworth, for the Author.* M,DCC,XCVIII. pp. (48). 8vo.   AAS. JCB.

34259   NORWICH. CONNECTICUT. MUTUAL INSURANCE COMPANY.
[Engraving of fire engine in action by E. Tisdale.] INSURANCE POLICY OF THE NOR- WICH MUTUAL ASSURANCE COMPANY. . . . [Colophon:]
> *Norwich: Printed by Thomas Hubbard.* 1798. Broadside. fol.

34260   THE NORWICH PACKET. VOL. XXV. No. 1243. TUESDAY, JANUARY 2, [— VOL. XXVI. No. 1294. WEDNESDAY, DECEMBER 26, 1798.]
> *Norwich (Connecticut). Published by John Trumbull, a few rods west of the Meeting-House.* 1798. fol.

In November, the day of publication was changed to Wednesday.

34261   NOTES UPON SCRIPTURE TEXTS, NO. I, VIZ. I. THE SCRIPTURE WARNING, AND SIGNS OF THE LAST TIMES, TOUCHED UPON IN A SHORT DISCOURSE FROM EZEK. VII. 12. II. NOTES ON THE PARABLE OF THE TEN VIRGINS. NOTES ON ISAIAH LXVI. 5. BY A PLAIN, SINGULAR MAN, WHO PROFESSES TO BELIEVE THE PROPHECIES AND DOCTRINES OF THE BIBLE. — THESE ARE THE BEGINNINGS OF SORROWS. — THE GREAT DAY OF THE LORD IS NEAR. — IT IS NEAR AND HASTENETH GREATLY. — A DAY OF DARKNESS, AND OF GLOOMINESS. BIBLE.
> *Boston: From the Printing-Office in Union-Street November,* 1798. pp. (24). 12mo.   BA.

34262   O COME AWAY MY SOLDIER BONNY. SUNG BY MRS. WARREL OF THE NEW THEATRE WITH UNIVERSAL APPLAUSE. IN THE OPERA OF THE RIVAL SOLDIERS.
> *Philadelphia: Published by G. Willig, No. 185, Market Street.* [1798.] pp. (2). 4to.

34263   O HAD IT BEEN MY HAPPY LOT.
> *Boston: Published by P. A. von Hagen, jun. & Co's Musical Magazine, No. 62, Newbury-Street.* 1798.

34264   OBSERVATIONS ON THE INFLUENCE OF THE MOON ON CLIMATE, AND THE ANIMAL ECONOMY: WITH A PROPER METHOD OF TREATING DISEASES, WHEN UNDER THE POWER OF THAT LUMINARY.
> *Philadelphia: Printed by Richard Folwell, No. 33, Carter's-Alley.* M.DCC.- XCVIII. pp. (24). 8vo.   AAS.

Preface signed, Y. Philadelphia, July 31, 1795.

34265   THE OBSERVATORY; OR, A VIEW OF THE TIMES. VOL. I. NO. 53. MONDAY, JANU-
ARY 1, [— VOL. II. NO. 125. MONDAY, SEPTEMBER 10, 1798.]
> *Richmond: Printed Mondays and Thursdays, by John Dixon.* 1798. fol.

> With the issue for September 13th, the title was changed to *Dixon's Ob-
> servatory.*

34266   OGDEN, DAVID B.
AN ORATION DELIVERED ON THE FOURTH OF JULY, 1798. TO A NUMEROUS AUDIENCE,
ASSEMBLED IN THE PRESBYTERIAN CHURCH OF NEWARK, TO CELEBRATE THE
TWENTY-SECOND ANNIVERSARY OF AMERICAN INDEPENDENCE. [Ornament.] BY
DAVID B. OGDEN, ESQUIRE, APPOINTED BY THE ASSOCIATION OF YOUNG MEN OF
NEWARK. [Ornament.] PUBLISHED BY PARTICULAR REQUEST. [Double line.]
> *Newark—Printed by Jacob Halsey, & Co.—*1798. pp. 12. 12mo.   NYHS.

34267   OGDEN, JOHN COSINS   1751–1800
AN APPEAL TO THE CANDID, UPON THE PRESENT STATE OF RELIGION AND POLITICS IN
CONNECTICUT.
> *[Litchfield? Printed by Thomas Collier.* 1798.] .pp. 23, [*sic* 24.] 12mo.
> > BA. LOC. NYHS. NYPL. YC.

> A criticism of the lack of freedom shown to Episcopal students in Yale
> College.

34268   OGDEN, UZAL   1744–1822
[Double line.] A LETTER FROM THE REV. UZAL OGDEN, RECTOR OF TRINITY CHURCH
IN NEWARK, TO THE SEVERAL CONGREGATIONS OF THE PROTESTANT EPISCOPAL
CHURCH IN THE STATE OF NEW-JERSEY. [Double line.]
> *[Newark: Printed by Pennington and Dodge.* 1798.] pp. 7. 8vo.   NYHS.

34269   OGILVIE, JAMES   1760–1820
A SPEECH DELIVERED IN ESSEX COUNTY IN SUPPORT OF A MEMORIAL, PRESENTED
TO THE CITIZENS OF THAT COUNTY AND NOW LAID BEFORE THE ASSEMBLY, ON THE
SUBJECT OF THE ALIEN AND SEDITION ACTS; BY JAMES OGILVIE. [Ornament.]
> *Richmond: Printed by Jones & Dixon, Printers to the Commonwealth.* M,DCC,-
> XCVIII. pp. [12.] 8vo.   LOC.

34270   O'KELLY, JOHN
THE PRECEPTOR'S GUIDE: WITH A KEY. BY JOHN O'KELLY. IN TWO VOLUMES.
> Proposals for printing the above were made in the Georgia Gazette from
> May 16 – June 8, 1798.

34271   OLIVER, PETER
THE ADOPTED SON. A COMEDY IN FIVE ACTS.
> *Boston:* 1798.

> 145th Massachusetts District Copyright, issued to Peter Oliver, as Au-
> thor, 21 May. 1798.

34272   ONONDAGA. NEW YORK. SALT SPRINGS.
ANNUAL REPORT OF THE SUPERINTENDENT OF THE ONONDAGA SALT SPRINGS, . . .
1798.
> *[Albany: Printed by Loring Andrews?* 1798.] 8vo.

34273   ONTARIO GAZETTE. VOL. II. NO. 1. TUESDAY, APRIL 10, [— NO. 38. TUESDAY,
DECEMBER 25, 1798.]
> *Canandaigua: Published by Lucius Cary.* 1798. fol.

> Established, as a weekly, with a continuous numbering to the Ontario
> Gazette which he had been publishing at Geneva, by Lucius Cary, and
> continued by him to April, 1803, when he sold his interests to the
> Proprietors of the *Western Repository, & Genesee Advertiser.*

34274   THE ORACLE OF DAUPHIN. AND HARRISBURGH ADVERTISER. VOL. VI. No. 12. WEDNESDAY, JANUARY 3, [—VOL. VII. No. 11. WEDNESDAY, DECEMBER 26, 1798.]
Harrisburgh: Published by John Wyeth. 1798. fol.

34275   THE ORACLE OF THE DAY. [Motto.] No. 12 OF VOL. VIII. SATURDAY, JANUARY 6, [—No. 11 OF VOL. IX. SATURDAY, DECEMBER 29, 1798.]
Printed and published every Saturday morning, by Charles Peirce, No. 5, Daniel-Street, Portsmouth, New-Hampshire . . . 1798. fol.   AAS.

34276   ORAM'S NEW-YORK PRICE CURRENT, AND MARINE REGISTER. No. 107. SATURDAY, JANUARY 6, [— No. 158. SATURDAY, DECEMBER 29, 1798.]
New-York: Published weekly by James Oram. 1798. 4to.   NYHS.

34277   AN ORATION COMMEMORATIVE OF AMERICAN INDEPENDENCE, INTENDED TO HAVE BEEN DELIVERED AT LEXINGTON ON THE FOURTH DAY OF JULY, 1798. [Two columns.]
[Boston? 1798.] pp. (2). fol.   JCB.

34278   AN ORATION DELIVERED AT WASHINGTON, PENNSYLVANIA, ON THE GENERAL FAST, MAY 9TH, 1798.
Washington, Pennsylvania. Printed by John Colerick. 1798.

34279   ORIENTAL [cut] TRUMPET. VOL. 2. No. 56. THURSDAY, JANUARY 4, [—VOL. 2. No. 107. THURSDAY, DECEMBER 27, 1798.]
Portland —(Dist. of Maine)— Published by John Rand, at his Office in Middle-Street, near the head of Fish-Street. 1798. fol.   AAS.

With the issue for April 25th, William Burdick was admitted to partnership, as Rand and Burdick. And the title was enlarged to *Oriental Trumpet, or, the town and country gazette.* Devoted to public affairs, to trade, to husbandry, to literature, and all the other branches of useful information.

34280   ORR, HECTOR   1770–1855
A HISTORY OF FREE MASONRY; AND THE DUTIES INCUMBENT ON THE CRAFT; CONSIDERED IN A DISCOURSE BEFORE THE MEMBERS OF FELLOWSHIP LODGE, IN BRIDGEWATER, AT THEIR FIRST REGULAR MEETING, JUNE 30TH, A. L. 5797. BY HECTOR ORR, R. W. M, ELECT. [One line Latin quotation.]
Boston: Printed by Samuel Etheridge. 1798. pp. [32.] 8vo.
     AAS. HC. JCB. LOC. MHS. NYPL.

34281   ORR, WILLIAM   1766–1797
THE TRIAL OF WILLIAM ORR, AT CARRICKFERGUS ASSIZES, FOR BEING AN UNITED IRISHMAN; WITH HIS DYING DECLARATION, &C, &C. &C. [Triple lines.]
Philadelphia: Printed by J. Carey, No. 19, Carter's Alley, for G. Douglas, No. 2, South Third-Street. 1798. pp. 20. 8vo.   NYHS.

34282   OSBORN, SELLECK   1783–1826
AN ORATION, DELIVERED AT NEWBURGH, IN THE STATE OF NEW-YORK, ON THE 4TH OF JULY, 1798. BY SELLECK OSBORN.
[Newburgh: Printed by Philip Van Horne. 1798.] 12mo.   NYHS.

34283   OSGOOD, DAVID   1747–1822
THE SIGNAL ADVANTAGES DERIVED TO THE NATIONS OF CHRISTENDOM FROM THEIR RELIGION, ILLUSTRATED IN A DISCOURSE DELIVERED BEFORE THE ANNUAL CONVENTION OF THE CONGREGATIONAL MINISTERS OF MASSACHUSETTS, IN BOSTON, MAY 31, 1798. BY DAVID OSGOOD, D.D. PASTOR OF THE CHURCH IN MEDFORD. [Ornament.]
Printed by Samuel Hall, No. 53 Cornhill, Boston. 1798. pp. [32.] 8vo.
     AAS. BA. BM. HC. JCB. LOC. MHS. NYHS. NYPL.
Harvard College Library has copies in both quarto and octavo.

34284 OSGOOD, DAVID, continued.
—— SOME FACTS EVINCIVE OF THE ATHEISTICAL, ANARCHIAL, AND IN OTHER RESPECTS, IMMORAL PRINCIPLES OF THE FRENCH REPUBLICANS, STATED IN A SERMON, DELIVERED ON THE 9TH OF MAY, 1798, THE DAY RECOMMENDED BY THE PRESIDENT OF THE UNITED STATES FOR SOLEMN HUMILIATION, FASTING, AND PRAYER. BY DAVID OSGOOD, D. D. MINISTER OF THE CHURCH IN MEDFORD. [Ornament.]
Printed by Samuel Hall, No. 53, Cornhill, Boston. 1798. pp. [27.] 8vo.
AAS. BA. BM. CLA. HC. HSP. JCB. LOC. MHS. NYHS. NYPL. UTS. YC.

34285 OTIS, HARRISON GRAY 1765–1848
LETTER, FROM THE HON. HARRISON G. OTIS, TO THE HON. WILLIAM HEATH, AS CHAIRMAN OF THE ROXBURY COMMITTEE FOR PETITIONING CONGRESS AGAINST PERMITTING MERCHANT VESSELS TO ARM.
Boston: Printed by John Russell, at his Office, Quaker-Lane, near Water-Str. April 1798. pp. (30). 8vo.
AAS. BA. BM. HC. LOC. MHS.

34286 OTSEGO HERALD: OR, WESTERN ADVERTISER. [Motto.] VOL. III. NUMB. 145. THURSDAY, JANUARY 4, [— VOL. IV. NUMB. 196. THURSDAY, DECEMBER 27, 1798.]
Cooperstown: Printed and published by Elihu Phinney, first door east of the Court-House. 1798. fol.

34287 OUR COUNTRY IS OUR SHIP. A NEW PATRIOTIC SONG.
Boston: Printed & sold by P. A. von Hagen jun. and Co. at their Musical Magazine, No. 62, Newbury Street. 1798.

34288 PACKARD, HEZEKIAH 1761–1849
PACKARD'S CATECHISM. CONTAINING THE FIRST PRINCIPLES OF RELIGIOUS AND SOCIAL DUTIES. ADAPTED TO THE CAPACITIES OF CHILDREN AND YOUTH, AND BENEFICIAL TO HEADS OF FAMILIES.
Amherst, Newhampshire. Printed by Samuel Preston. 1798.

34289 —— A SERMON AT THE FUNERAL OF MISS POLLY VARNUM, ELDEST CHILD OF PARKER VARNUM, ESQ. OF DRACUTT; PREACHED AUGUST 19, 1798. BY HEZEKIAH PACKARD. MINISTER OF CHELMSFORD.
Printed at Amherst — by Samuel Preston. Sept. 1798. pp. 19. 8vo. AAS.

34290 PADDY'S RESOURCE. BEING A SELECT COLLECTION OF ORIGINAL AND MODERN PATRIOTIC SONGS: COMPILED FOR THE USE OF THE PEOPLE OF IRELAND. TO WHICH IS ADDED, ARTHUR O'CONNOR'S ADDRESS. FROM THE LATEST EDITION—WITH CORRECTIONS.
New-York: Printed by R. Wilson, 149, Pearl-Street; at the request of a number of Hibernians in this country, who were desirous of having copies of them. 1798. pp. (2), (2), [48.] 12mo.
JCB. LOC.

34291 PAGE, JOHN 1744–1808
TO THE CITIZENS OF ACCOMACK, NORTHAMPTON, ELIZABETH-CITY, WARWICK AND YORK. FRIENDS AND FELLOW-CITIZENS, AS I HAD THE HONOR OF BEING TWICE ELECTED YOUR REPRESENTATIVE WITHOUT OPPOSITION, WHEN YOUR COUNTIES WERE ADDED TO GLOUCESTER AND MATHEWS TO COMPOSE A NEW DISTRICT, AND I HAD BEEN TWICE ELECTED BY THE TEN COUNTIES OF THE FIRST DISTRICT IN WHICH GLOUCESTER (MY NATIVE COUNTY) HAD BEEN PLACED: [Again offering his services as a Representative.] JOHN PAGE. ROSEWELL, NOVEMBER 16, 1798.
[Philadelphia? 1798.] Broadside. fol. LOC.

34292 PAINE, THOMAS 1737–1809
LETTER TO THE PEOPLE OF FRANCE, AND THE FRENCH ARMIES, ON THE EVENT OF THE 18TH FRUCTIDOR—SEP. 4—AND ITS CONSEQUENCES. BY THOMAS PAINE.
Paris: Printed at the Printing-Office of the Social-Circle, 1797. New-York: Reprinted at the Argus-Office. 1798. pp. 28. 8vo.
BA. JCB. LOC. NYHS.

34293   PAINE, Thomas, afterwards Robert Treat, junior   1773–1811
ADAMS & LIBERTY, THE BOSTON PATRIOTIC SONG. WRITTEN BY THOMAS PAINE, A. M.

> *Boston: Printed by I. Thomas and E. T. Andrews, 1798. obl. 4to.*   AAS.

"The above song is set to music, as was lately, (Friday, May 25, 1798,) sung at the Massachusetts Charitable Fire Society with the most unbounded applause."

34294   —— — ADAMS & LIBERTY, THE BOSTON PATRIOTIC SONG. WRITTEN BY THOMAS PAINE, A. M. SECOND EDITION.

> *Boston: Printed by I. Thomas and E. T. Andrews, 1798. obl. 4to.*

34295   —— — ADAMS & LIBERTY. THE BOSTON PATRIOTIC SONG. WRITTEN BY THOMAS PAINE, A. M.

> *[Boston: 1798.] Broadside.*

34296   —— — [Cut] ADAMS AND LIBERTY. THE BOSTON PATRIOTIC SONG. TUNE, "ANACREON IN HEAVEN." [Colophon:]

> *Printed and sold by J. White, near Charles-river Bridge, Boston.* [1798.]
Broadside.   AAS. HSP.

34297   —— — ADAMS AND LIBERTY. A PATRIOTIC SONG. WRITTEN BY THOMAS PAINE, A. M. OF BOSTON: [Nine nine-line verses. Ye sons of Columbia, who bravely have fought, . . .]

> *Concord: Printed by George Hough, 1798. Broadside.*

34298   —— — ADAMS AND LIBERTY. THE BOSTON PATRIOTIC SONG. WRITTEN BY THOMAS PAINE, A. M. [Nine nine-line verses, with music.]

> *[Portsmouth: Printed by John Melcher, 1798.] pp. (2), 4to.*   BU.

34299   —— — ADAMS AND LIBERTY. WRITTEN BY THOMAS PAINE, A. M. [Colophon:]

> *Printed and sold at the Bible and Heart, Salem.* [1798.] Broadside.   EI.

34300   —— ADAMS AND WASHINGTON. A NEW PATRIOTIC SONG. THE MUSIC COMPOSED BY P. A. VON HAGEN JR.

> *Boston: Printed & sold by P. A. von Hagen jun. & Co. at their Musical Magazine No. 62 Newbury Street.* [1798.] pp. (2).   HC.

34301   —— DEDICATORY ADDRESS; SPOKEN BY MR. HODGKINSON, OCTOBER 29, 1798, AT THE OPENING OF THE NEW FEDERAL THEATRE IN BOSTON.

> *[Boston: 1798.] 8vo.*

34302   —— THE GREEN MOUNTAIN FARMER, OR WASHINGTON AND VICTORY. A NEW PATRIOTIC SONG. WRITTEN BY THOMAS PAINE, A. M. THE MUSIC AND ACCOMPANIMENTS BY THE CELEBRATED SHIELD. [Copyright secured according to law.]

> *Boston, Printed & sold by Messrs. Lindley and Moore, No. 19, Marlborough-Street.* [1798.] pp. (2). 4to.

155th Massachusetts District Copyright, issued to Thomas Paine, Francis Linley, and John Moore, as Proprietors, 27 October, 1798.

34303   THE PALLADIUM: A LITERARY AND POLITICAL WEEKLY REPOSITORY. BY HUNTER AND BEAUMONT. VOL. I. NO. 1. TUESDAY, AUGUST 7, [— NO. 21. TUESDAY, DE-CEMBER 25, 1798.]

     ☞ *Frankfort: Printed and published (weekly) by Hunter & Beaumont.— Subscriptions and advertisements are received by the respective postmasters throughout the State. 1798. fol.*   KSL. UOC. WHS.

Established, as a weekly, by William Hunter, and William H. Beaumont, who were also the printers and publishers of The Mirror, at Washington, Kentucky. The two publications being carried on by Hunter at Frankfort, and Beaumont at Washington, until the end of December, 1799, when the partnership was dissolved, and The Mirror ceased publication. With the issue for 11 December, 1798, "Printers to the Commonwealth" was added to the imprint. William Hunter continued publication of *The Palladium* into September, 1809, when he disposed of his interests, by sale, to Robert Johnston and George Washington Pleasants, who continued publication to the death of the latter, 8 April, 1812, aged 23 years, whose interests were continued into the year 1814, when Joseph Buchanan was admitted to partnership, as Johnston and Buchanan, and the title altered to *Kentucky Palladium*, with a new serial numbering, but also continuing the old. In 1816, the paper was purchased and published by G. E. & J. B. Russell, and continued certainly to the issue for 6 September, 1816 — the last number located — and, perhaps, into the year 1826, or later.

34304   PALMER, STEPHEN   1766–1821
A SERMON, OCCASIONED BY THE DEATH OF MR. JEREMIAH FULLER, WHO DIED APRIL 19, 1798. ÆT. 25. DELIVERED THE LORD'S DAY AFTER HIS INTERMENT. BY STEPHEN PALMER, A. M. MINISTER OF THE FIRST PARISH, IN NEEDHAM.

     Dedham: Printed by Mann and Adams. 1798. pp. [27.] 8vo.
                                       AAS. JCB. LOC. MHS.

34305   PANTHER, ABRAHAM
A VERY SURPRISING NARRATIVE OF [a] YOUNG WOMAN WHO WAS DISCOVERED IN A ROCKY CAVE, AFTER HAVING BEEN TAKEN BY THE SAVAGE INDIANS OF THE WILDERNESS, IN THE YEAR 1777, AND SEEING NO HUMAN BEING FOR THE SPACE OF NINE YEARS. IN A LETTER FROM A GENTLEMAN TO HIS FRIEND. [Heavy lines.]

     Printed and sold [by Peter Edes] at the Printing Office in Augusta. [1798.] pp. 12. 12mo.

34306   PARISH, ELIJAH   1762–1825
THE EXCELLENCE OF THE GOSPEL VISIBLE IN THE WRETCHEDNESS OF PAGANISM. A DISCOURSE DELIVERED DECEMBER 20, 1797, BEING THE TENTH ANNIVERSARY OF HIS ORDINATION. BY ELIJAH PARISH, A. M. MINISTER OF THE CONGREGATION IN BYFIELD. [Ornament.]

     Printed by A. March, Newburyport. Jan. 1798. pp. (28). 8vo.
                           AAS. BA. BM. JCB. MHS. NYPL.

34307   PARISMAS, THOMAS
THE HISTORY OF CAPT. THOMAS PARISMAS, CONTAINING A PARTICULAR ACCOUNT OF THE CRUEL AND BARBAROUS TREATMENT OF A YOUNG LADY, WHO WAS THE WIFE OF MR. JAMES NEGOTIO, AN ENGLISH MERCHANT, IN THE EAST-INDIES. THE HISTORY OF THIS INNOCENT AND UNFORTUNATE LADY, IS ALLOWED BY ALL THOSE WHO HAVE PERUSED IT, TO BE ONE OF THE MOST STRIKING ACCOUNTS, THAT EVER APPEARED IN PRINT . . . TO WHICH IS ADDED, THE REMARKABLE AND ENTERTAINING STORY OF ALCANDER AND ROSILLA.

     Medford, (Massachusetts.) Printed and sold by Nathaniel Coverly. 1798. pp. 34; 21; 5, frontispiece. 12mo.   LOC.

Contains, also, The Fatal effects of seduction: exemplified in a letter, from the reformed Edmund to his friend. By Thomas Bellamy. pp. 5.

34308   PARKHURST, Jabez
An Oration, delivered on the fourth of July, 1798, in the Presbyterian
church, at Newark, before a numerous audience, assembled to celebrate
the twenty-second anniversary of American independence. By capt. Jabez
Parkhurst. Published at the request of the citizens of the town.
Newark: Printed by Pennington and Dodge. M,DCC,XCVIII. pp. 12.
12mo.   NYHS.

34309   THE PARLOUR preacher: a pack of cards for all who are determined to win
Christ.
Newburyport: Printed by Angier March. 1798.

34310   PARRINGTON, John Rivington
A Map and Description of the State of Tennessee. By John Rivington Par-
rington.
Knoxville: Printed ? by George Roulstone, & John R. Parrington. 1798.
Two columns of the "Knoxville Register," for August 14, 1798, are given
up to a plea for assistance in the publication of this work.

34311   PASCALIS-OUVIÈRE, Alexandre Felix   1750–1840
An Account of the contagious epidemic yellow fever, which prevailed in
Philadelphia in the summer and autumn of 1797; comprising the questions
of its causes and domestic origin, characters, medical treatment, and
preventives. By Felix Pascalis Ouvière, m. d. corresponding member of the
Medical Society of Connecticut and resident member of the Philadelphia
Academy of Medicine. [Eight lines of Latin from] Wannsweiten Comm: in
Boeth:Aphor: 1412 de Morb:spid.
*Philadelphia: From the Press of Snowden & McCorkle, No. 47, North Fourth-
Street.* 1798. pp. viii, 182, portrait. 8vo.   LCP. LOC. SGO.
203d Pennsylvania District Copyright, issued to Felix Pascalis Ouvière,
M. D. as Author, 8 February, 1798.

34312   THE PATH to happiness, explored and illustrated. By an anonymous author.
A Plea for peace and union, among the members of the church of Christ.
And a Word in season, designed to encourage the Missionary Society. By
the rev. T. Haweis, l. l. b. & m. d.
Newark. Printed by Pennington & Dodge, for Cornelius Davis, New-York.
1798. pp. 92; 38; 22. 12mo.   AAS. JCB. NYPL.

34313   THE PATRIOT, a poem. [Double line.] The duration and advantages of a free
government, depend on the wisdom and virtue of "THE PEOPLE." [Double
line.] By a Mechanic of Charlestown.
Charlestown: Printed [by John Lamson] for the Author. 1798. pp. 24.
12mo.   BU.

34314   THE PATRIOTIC songster for July 4th, 1798. (Addressed to the volunteers
of Baltimore.) Containing all the late patriotic songs that have been
published.
*Baltimore: Printed and sold at S. Sower's Printing Office, No. 67, Market
Street, at his Book-Store in Fayette-Street, and at Thomas, Andrews and Butler's
Bookstore.* (Price eleven-pence). 1798.

34315   PAUL, Jeremiah
A Collection of copies for writing alphabetically arranged. [Two lines
from] Thomson.
[Philadelphia: 1798.]
215th Pennsylvania District Copyright, issued to Jeremiah Paul, as Proprietor, 23 July, 1798.

34316 PAYNE, JOHN
A NEW AND COMPLETE SYSTEM OF UNIVERSAL GEOGRAPHY; DESCRIBING ASIA, AFRICA,
EUROPE AND AMERICA; WITH THEIR SUBDIVISIONS OF REPUBLICS, STATES, EMPIRES,
AND KINGDOMS; EXTENT, BOUNDARIES AND REMARKABLE APPEARANCES OF EACH
COUNTRY, CITIES, TOWNS, AND CURIOSITIES, OF NATURE AND ART, ALSO GIVING A
GENERAL ACCOUNT OF THE FOSSIL AND VEGETABLE PRODUCTIONS OF THE EARTH.
THE HISTORY OF MAN, IN ALL CLIMATES, REGIONS, AND CONDITIONS . . . TO WHICH
IS ADDED, A VIEW OF ASTRONOMY, AS CONNECTED WITH GEOGRAPHY; OF THE
PLANETARY SYSTEM . . . AND OF THE UNIVERSE IN GENERAL. WITH A COPIOUS
INDEX . . . TO EACH VOLUME . . . BY JOHN PAYNE, WITH ADDITIONS, . . .
BY JAMES HARDIE. IN FOUR VOLUMES. VOL. I.

*New-York: Printed for and sold by John Low, Book-seller, at the Shakespeare-
Head, No. 332 Water-Street. 1798. pp. xlviii, 518, ii. 8vo.* · BA. LOC. NYPL.

First published in twenty-eight numbers — the first, with an elegant
painted plate, and a chart elegantly engraved by Rollinson — each to
contain eighty pages, large octavo, with one or more maps or engravings,
a number every fortnight.

34317 PEASE, SETH   1764–1819
A MAP OF THE CONNECTICUT WESTERN RESERVE, FROM ACTUAL SURVEY. BY SETH
PEASE.

Engraved and printed for the Author by Amos Doolittle, Newhaven, 1798.
19x32½.

34318 PEDEN, ALEXANDER   1626–1686
THE LORD'S TRUMPET SOUNDING AN ALARM AGAINST SCOTLAND, BY A WARNING OF A
BLOODY SWORD. BEING THE SUBSTANCE OF A PREFACE AND TWO PROPHETICAL SER-
MONS PREACHED AT GLENLUCE, ANNO 1682, BY THAT GREAT SCOTS PROPHET MR.
ALEXANDER PEDEN, LATE MINISTER OF THE GOSPEL AT GLENLUCE. [Twelve lines
of Scripture texts.]

*Printed at Newry. Re-printed at Newburyport [by Angier March] for Alex-
ander Walker, [Warren Lane.]* 1798. pp. (42). 8vo.   AAS.

34319 PEMBROKE. NEW HAMPSHIRE. CHURCHES.
A PLAN OF UNION, AGREED ON, AND ADOPTED, BY THE PRESBYTERIAN AND CONGRE-
GATIONAL CHURCHES IN PEMBROKE, JUNE – 1797. THAT THEY ALL MAY BE ONE.
JESUS CHRIST. THAT YE BE PERFECTLY JOINED TOGETHER IN ONE MIND; AND
SPEAK THE SAME THINGS. ST. PAUL.

Concord: Printed by George Hough. March—1798. pp. (8). 24mo.   BA.

34320 PENN, JAMES   1727–1800
THE FARMER'S DAUGHTER OF ESSEX. CONTAINING AN ACCOUNT OF HER DISTRESS,
WONDERFUL ADVENTURES, MANNER OF BEING COURTED, AND SEDUCED BY A NOBLE-
MAN IN LONDON, WHO AFTER LIVING WITH HER SOME YEARS, PARTED IN THE MOST
DISHONORABLE MANNER.—WITH AN ACCOUNT OF HER MEETING HIM A SECOND TIME,
AND MANY PARTICULAR OCCURRENCES THAT HAPPENED DURING THE REMAINDER OF
THEIR LIVES. WRITTEN BY HERSELF.

New-York: Printed by Jacob S. Mott. 1798. pp. (96). 12mo.   AAS. JCB. LOC.

Contains, also, Collin and Celia. A story founded on fact. pp. 92–96.

34321 PENNSYLVANIA. STATE.
AN ACT OF THE LEGISLATURE OF PENNSYLVANIA AND A PATENT TO INCORPORATE A
COMPANY FOR ERECTING A PERMANENT BRIDGE OVER THE RIVER SCHUYLKILL.

Philadelphia: Printed by John Fenno, No. 119 Chesnut-Street, [1798.] pp.
(21). 8vo.
                                                           LOC. MHS.

PENNSYLVANIA. STATE, continued.

34322 —— AN ACT TO ENABLE THE GOVERNOR OF THIS COMMONWEALTH TO INCORPORATE A COMPANY FOR THE PURPOSE OF IMPROVING THE NAVIGATION OF THE RIVER LEHIGH. . . . APPROVED FEBRUARY 27, 1798. THOMAS MIFFLIN, GOVERNOR OF THE COMMONWEALTH OF PENNSYLVANIA.
[Philadelphia: Printed by Hall and Sellers, 1798.] pp. (15). 8vo.   LOC.

34323 —— ACTS OF THE GENERAL ASSEMBLY OF THE COMMONWEALTH OF PENNSYLVANIA, PASSED AT A SESSION, WHICH WAS BEGUN AND HELD AT THE CITY OF PHILADELPHIA ON TUESDAY, THE FIFTH DAY OF DECEMBER, IN THE YEAR ONE THOUSAND SEVEN HUNDRED AND NINETY-SEVEN, AND OF THE INDEPENDENCE OF THE UNITED STATES OF AMERICA THE TWENTY-SECOND. [— 5 APRIL, 1798.] PUBLISHED BY AUTHORITY.
Philadelphia: Printed by Hall and Sellers, No. 51, Market-Street. M.DCC.-XCVIII. pp. (2), (189)–316. fol.   LOC.

34324 —— A COMPILATION OF THE HEALTH-LAWS OF THE STATE OF PENNSYLVANIA.
Philadelphia: Printed by Zachariah Poulson, junior, No. 106, Chesnut-Street, nearly opposite the Bank of North America. 1798. pp. (56). 8vo.
AAS. JCB. LOC. MHS. SGO.

34325 —— A FURTHER SUPPLEMENT TO THE ACT ENTITLED "AN ACT FOR MAKING AN ARTIFICIAL ROAD FROM THE CITY OF PHILADELPHIA TO THE BOROUGH OF LANCASTER, "FOR THE MORE EFFECTUAL PREVENTING EVASIONS OF THE SALUTARY REGULATIONS INTENDED IN AND BY THE ACT FOR MAKING AN ARTIFICIAL ROAD FROM THE CITY OF PHILADELPHIA TO THE BOROUGH OF LANCASTER." . . . APPROVED, APRIL 4TH, 1798. THOMAS MIFFLIN, GOVERNOR OF THE COMMONWEALTH OF PENNSYLVANIA. . . .
[Philadelphia: 1798.] Broadside. fol.   HSP.

34326 —— JOURNAL OF THE FIRST SESSION OF THE EIGHTH HOUSE OF REPRESENTATIVES OF THE COMMONWEALTH OF PENNSYLVANIA, 1797–98.
Philadelphia: 1798. pp. 398. fol.

34327 —— TAGEBUCH DES ACHTEN HAUSES DER REPRÄSENTANTEN DER REPUBLIK PENNSYLVANIEN.
Lancaster: Gedruckt bey Albrecht und Lahn. 1798.

34328 —— — TAGEBUCH DES ACHTEN HAUSES DER REPRÄSENTANTEN DER REPUBLIK PENNSYLVANIEN.
Lancaster: Gedruckt bey Johann Albrecht u. Comp. 1798.

34329 —— JOURNAL OF THE SENATE OF THE COMMONWEALTH OF PENNSYLVANIA. COMMENCING ON TUESDAY, THE FIFTH DAY OF DECEMBER, IN THE YEAR OF OUR LORD ONE THOUSAND SEVEN HUNDRED AND NINETY-SEVEN, AND OF THE INDEPENDENCE OF THE UNITED STATES OF AMERICA THE TWENTY-SECOND. [— 5 APRIL, 1798.]
Philadelphia: Printed by Zachariah Poulson, junior, number eighty, Chesnut-Street. 1797. [1798.] pp. 278. fol.   LOC.

34330 —— TAGEBUCH DES SENATS DER REPUBLIK PENNSYLVANIEN. 1797–1798.
Germantown: Gedruckt bey Michael Billmeyer. 1798.

34331 —— LAWS OF THE COMMONWEALTH OF PENNSYLVANIA, FROM THE SECOND DAY OF OCTOBER, ONE THOUSAND SEVEN HUNDRED AND EIGHTY-ONE, TO THE SECOND DAY OF OCTOBER, ONE THOUSAND SEVEN HUNDRED AND NINETY. REPUBLISHED, UNDER THE AUTHORITY OF THE LEGISLATURE, BY ALEXANDER JAMES DALLAS. VOL. II.
Philadelphia: Printed by Hall and Sellers. MDCCXCVIII. pp. (2), (2), (2), [ix], [817], [iii], (33), fol.   AAS. HC. HSP. LOC. NYHS.
Volume one was published in Philadelphia in 1797. The third volume in Philadelphia in 1795. And the fourth volume in Lancaster in 1801.

PENNSYLVANIA. STATE, continued.

34332 —— LETTER FROM THE SECRETARY OF THE COMMONWEALTH OF PENNSYLVANIA, BY DIRECTION OF THE GOVERNOR, RELATIVE TO THE LATE MALIGNANT FEVER; AND REPORT OF THE BOARD OF MANAGERS, OF THE MARINE AND CITY HOSPITALS, IN REPLY.

Philadelphia: Printed by Thomas and Samuel F. Bradford, No. 8, South Front Street. 1798. pp. 16. 8vo. AAS. BM. LOC. NYPL. 8GO.

34333 —— RECEIPTS AND EXPENDITURES IN THE TREASURY OF PENNSYLVANIA, FROM THE FIRST OF JANUARY TO THE THIRTY-FIRST OF DECEMBER, 1797, BOTH DAYS INCLUSIVE. [Ornament.]

Philadelphia: Printed by Zachariah Poulson, junior, number eighty Chesnut-Street. 1798. pp. [62.] fol. LOC.

34334 —— REPORT OF THE REGISTER-GENERAL OF THE STATE OF THE FINANCES OF PENNSYLVANIA, FOR THE YEAR 1797. [Ornament.]

Philadelphia: Printed by Zachariah Poulson, junior, number eighty, Chesnut-Street. 1798. pp. (19). fol. LOC.

34335 —— THE REPRESENTATION AND PETITION OF DIVERS RELIGIOUS DENOMINATIONS OF THE CITY OF PHILADELPHIA, TO THE LEGISLATURE OF THE STATE OF PENNSYLVANIA.

Philadelphia: Printed by R. Aitkin. 1798. pp. 16. 8vo.

34336 THE PENNSYLVANIA GAZETTE. NUMBER 3520. WEDNESDAY, JANUARY 3, [—NUMBER 3571. WEDNESDAY, DECEMBER 27, 1798.]

Philadelphia: Printed by Hall and Sellers, at the New Printing-Office, near the Market. 1798. fol. AAS. HC. LCP.

34337 THE PENNSYLVANIA HERALD, AND YORK GENERAL ADVERTISER. VOL. IX. No. 48. TOTAL NO. 464. WEDNESDAY, JANUARY 3, [— VOL. X. No. 47. TOTAL No. 515. WEDNESDAY, DECEMBER 26, 1798.]

York: Printed every Wednesday, by John Edie. 1798. fol. YHS.

34338 DIE PENNSYLVANISCHE CORRESPONDENZ. NUM. 25, DIENSTAG, JANUAR 2, [—NUM. 58. FREITAG, APRIL 27, 1798.]

Philadelphia: Gedruckt bey Henrich Schweitzer, corner Vierte und Rees-Strasse. 1798. fol.

How much, if any, longer after the above date publication was continued is not known, and the paper was apparently consolidated with the *Philadelphische Correspondenz.*

34339 DIE PENNSYLVANISCHE WOCHENSCHRIFT. JANUAR [— DEZEMBER, 1798.]

Hanover, York County, Pennsylvania. Gedruckt bey Stellingius & Lepper. 1798. fol.

34340 PENNSYLVANISCHER KALENDER AUF DAS 1799STE JAHR CHRISTI.

York, York Co.: Gedruckt bey Salomon Mayer. 1798. 4to. LOC.

34341 PEPPER, HENRY

JUVENILE ESSAYS; OR, A COLLECTION OF POEMS: INSCRIBED TO MY VALUED FRIEND, HENRY MacNEALE KENNEDY. BY HENRY PEPPER. [One line of French from] MOL.

Philadelphia: Printed by Richard Folwell, No. 33, Carter's-Alley. [1798.] pp. 75, (1). 8vo. AAS. BU.

34342 PERCIVAL, Thomas
MORAL AND LITERARY DISSERTATIONS; CHIEFLY INTENDED AS THE SEQUEL TO A FATHER'S INSTRUCTIONS. THE SECOND EDITION, REVISED, AND MUCH ENLARGED; BY THOMAS PERCIVAL, M.D. F.R.S. AND A.S. LOND. F.R.S. AND R.M.S. EDINB. MEMBER OF THE ROYAL SOCIETY OF MEDICINE AT PARIS; OF THE ROYAL SOCIETY OF AGRICULTURE AT LYONS; AND OF THE AMERICAN PHILOSOPHICAL SOCIETY AT PHILADELPHIA, &C. &C.

Philadelphia: Printed by Thomas Dobson, at the Stone House, South Second-Street. MDCCXCVIII. pp. xii, 204, (1). 12mo.   AAS.

34343 PERRY, William
THE ONLY SURE GUIDE TO THE ENGLISH TONGUE: OR, NEW PRONOUNCING SPELLING BOOK. UPON THE SAME PLAN AS PERRY'S ROYAL STANDARD ENGLISH DICTIONARY, NOW MADE USE OF IN ALL THE CELEBRATED SCHOOLS IN GREATBRITAIN, IRELAND AND AMERICA. TO WHICH IS ADDED, A GRAMMAR OF THE ENGLISH LANGUAGE; AND, A SELECT NUMBER OF MORAL TALES AND FABLES, FOR THE INSTRUCTION OF YOUTH. WITH AN APPENDIX. CONTAINING, DIRECTIONS FOR THE DIFFERENT SOUNDS OF THE CONSONANTS BEFORE ALL THE VOWELS, WITH EVERY EXCEPTION THAT IS TO BE MET WITH IN OUR LANGUAGE, FROM SUCH GENERAL RULES: ALSO, A COMPLETE LIST OF ALL THE WORDS IN WHICH E FINAL DOES NOT LENGTHEN THE SYLLABLE: LIKEWISE, SEVERAL VALUABLE APHORISMS RESPECTING THE SOUNDS OF THE VOWELS IN THE LAST SYLLABLE OF WORDS ENDING WITH E. AND, A COMPLETE LIST OF ALL THE WORDS IN THE ENGLISH LANGUAGE, WHICH, THOUGH WRITTEN DIFFERENTLY HAVE A SIMILARITY OF SOUND.— OF THOSE SUBSTANTIVES AND VERBS, OF THE SAME ORTHOGRAPHY, BUT OF DIFFERENT ACCENT. — OF THOSE SUBSTANTIVES AND VERBS, WHICH VARY IN THEIR SOUND EITHER BY A DIFFERENT CONSONANT, OR BY CHANGING THE HARD SOUND OF THAT CONSONANT INTO THE SOFT SOUND.—OF THOSE ADJECTIVES AND VERBS ALIKE IN ORTHOGRAPHY, BUT DIFFERENTLY ACCENTED.— OF THE SUBSTANTIVES AND ADJECTIVES CHANGING THE SEAT OF THE ACCENT. BY W. PERRY, LECTURER ON THE ENGLISH LANGUAGE, IN THE ACADEMY, EDINBURGH. ELEVENTH WORCESTER EDITION. ILLUSTRATED WITH [twelve] CUTS. CAREFULLY REVISED BY PERRY'S ROYAL STANDARD ENGLISH DICTIONARY, BY ISAIAH THOMAS. AND CORRECTED OF THE NUMEROUS ERRORS, WHICH ARE IN ALL OTHER EDITIONS BOTH BRITISH AND AMERICAN.

Printed at Worcester, Massachusetts, by Isaiah Thomas, jun. Sold wholesale and retail at his Bookstore in Worcester, sold also at the Worcester Bookstore, and by Thomas and Andrews, and other Booksellers in Boston. MDCCXCVIII. pp. 180, frontispiece. 12mo.   AAS. LOC.

34344 PETTIBONE, Augustus   1766–1847
AN ORATION, PRONOUNCED AT NORFOLK, ON THE ANNIVERSARY OF AMERICAN INDEPENDENCE, FOURTH OF JULY, 1798. BY AUGUSTUS PETTIBONE. PUBLISHED BY REQUEST. [Printer's mark.]

Printed at Litchfield, by T. Collier, 1798. pp. 16. 8vo.   CHS.

34345 THE PHENIX. VOL. III. No. 1. WEDNESDAY, MARCH 14, [— VOL. III. No. 42. WEDNESDAY, DECEMBER 26, 1798.]

Staunton (Virginia). Published every Wednesday by John Wise, on the Main Street, three doors above the Rising-Sun Tavern. 1798. fol.

In continuation of the *Virginia Gazette, and Staunton Weekly Advertiser.*

34346 THE PHENIX; OR WINDHAM HERALD. VOL. VII. NUMB. 357. THURSDAY, JANUARY 4, [— VOL. VII. NUMB. 371. THURSDAY, APRIL 12, 1798.]

Windham, Connecticut: Printed by John Byrne, north of the Court House. 1798. fol.   AAS. CHS. NYHS.

With the issue for April 19th, the first part of the title was dropped, and the paper continued as the *Windham Herald.*

34347   PHILADELPHIA. Pennsylvania.
THE ORDINANCES OF THE CITY OF PHILADELPHIA. TO WHICH ARE PREFIXED, THE
ACT OF INCORPORATION, AND THE SEVERAL SUPPLEMENTS THERETO; TOGETHER
WITH THE ADDRESS OF GEORGE WASHINGTON, LATE PRESIDENT OF THE UNITED
STATES, TO HIS FELLOW CITIZENS.
Philadelphia: Printed by Zachariah Poulson, junior. 1798. pp. 166. 8vo.
AAS. MHS. NYPL.

34348   —— *Caption title:* A COMMUNICATION FROM THE JOINT COMMITTEE OF THE SELECT
AND COMMON COUNCILS, APPOINTED TO SUPERINTEND THE CITY INTEREST IN THE
BRIDGE AND FERRY OVER SCHUYLKILL, AT THE WEST END OF HIGH-STREET.
Philadelphia: July 30th, 1798. pp. 7. 8vo.   NYPL.

34349   —— *Caption title:* . . . REPORT OF THE COMMITTEE OF THE COMMON COUNCIL, ON
THE CITY DEBTS AND EXPENDITURES, AND ON THE CITY CREDITS AND RESOURCES.
[Philadelphia:] Printed by Z. Poulson, jun. Feb. 15, 1798. pp. 12. fol. NYPL.

34350   —— REPORT OF THE JOINT COMMITTEE OF THE SELECT AND COMMON COUNCILS, ON
THE SUBJECT OF BRINGING WATER TO THE CITY. [Ornament.]
*Philadelphia: Printed by Zachariah Poulson, junior. number eighty, Ches-
nut-Street.* 1798. pp. (12). 8vo.   AAS. JCB. MHS. NYPL.

34351   PHILADELPHIA. Associated Independent Troop of Volunteers.
ARTICLES, OR BY-LAWS, FOR THE GOVERNMENT OF THE ASSOCIATED INDEPENDENT
PHILADELPHIA TROOP OF VOLUNTEER GREENS, ORIGINALLY SETTLED . . . JULY,
1794. . . .
Philadelphia: Printed by Henry Tuckniss. 1798. pp. 8, (2). 8vo.

34352   PHILADELPHIA. Pennsylvania. Academy of Medicine.
PROOFS OF THE ORIGIN OF THE YELLOW FEVER, IN PHILADELPHIA & KENSINGTON,
IN THE YEAR 1797, FROM DOMESTIC EXHALATION; AND FROM THE FOUL AIR OF THE
SNOW NAVIGATION, FROM MARSEILLES: AND FROM THAT OF THE SHIP HULDAH,
FROM HAMBURGH, IN TWO LETTERS, ADDRESSED TO THE GOVERNOR OF THE COM-
MONWEALTH OF PENNSYLVANIA, BY THE ACADEMY OF MEDICINE OF PHILADELPHIA.
*Philadelphia: Printed by Thomas & Samuel F. Bradford, No. 8. South Front
Street.* 1798. pp. (2), (2), (49). 8vo.   AAS. BM. HC. JCB. LOC. NYPL. SGO.

34353   PHILADELPHIA. Pennsylvania. Baptist Association.
MINUTES OF THE PHILADELPHIA BAPTIST ASSOCIATION, HELD AT NEW MILLS, BUR-
LINGTON COUNTY, STATE OF NEW JERSEY, OCTOBER 2D, 3D, AND 4TH, 1798.
Bedminster, Bucks County, Printed by Stephen C. Ustick. 1798. pp. 8. 4to.
BU. LOC.

34354   PHILADELPHIA. Pennsylvania. Churches.
AN ACCOUNT OF THE BAPTISMS AND BURIALS IN THE UNITED CHURCHES OF CHRIST
CHURCH AND ST. PETER'S.
Philadelphia: 1797. Broadside. fol.   LCP.

34355   PHILADELPHIA. Pennsylvania. College of Physicians.
FACTS AND OBSERVATIONS RELATIVE TO THE NATURE AND ORIGIN OF THE PESTILEN-
TIAL FEVER, WHICH PREVAILED IN THIS CITY, IN 1793, 1797, AND 1798. BY THE
COLLEGE OF PHYSICIANS OF PHILADELPHIA.
*Philadelphia: Printed for Thomas Dobson, at the Stone House, No. 41, South
Second Street.* 1798. pp. 52. 8vo.   AAS. BM. HC. JCB. LOC. MHS. NYPL. SGO.
Reprinted in London this year, and in 1799. "Additional Facts and
observations," were published in 1806.

34356   —— PROCEEDINGS OF THE COLLEGE OF PHYSICIANS OF PHILADELPHIA, RELATIVE TO
THE PREVENTION OF THE INTRODUCTION AND SPREADING OF CONTAGIOUS DISEASES.
*Philadelphia: Printed by Thomas Dobson, at the Stone-House, No. 41, South
Second Street.* 1798. pp. (4), (37). 8vo.   AAS. BM. JCB. LOC. NYPL. SGO.

34357   PHILADELPHIA. PENNSYLVANIA. LIBRARY COMPANY.
FOURTH SUPPLEMENT TO THE CATALOGUE OF BOOKS, BELONGING TO THE LIBRARY COMPANY OF PHILADELPHIA. TO WHICH IS ADDED, A CATALOGUE OF THE BOOKS THAT ARE NOT TO BE TAKEN OUT OF THE LIBRARY, AND OF THOSE THAT ARE TO GO OUT UNDER CERTAIN RESTRICTIONS. COMMUNITER BONA PROFUNDERE DEORUM EST.
—*Philadelphia:—Printed by Zachariah Poulson, junior, Librarian, No.* 106, *Chesnut-Street, nearly opposite to the Bank of North America. November* 30, 1798. pp. 40, 8. 8vo.   NYPL.

34358   PHILADELPHIA. PENNSYLVANIA. POST-OFFICE.
POST-OFFICE, PHILADELPHIA, 22D MAY, 1798. ESTABLISHMENT OF THE MAILS. . . . THE TIMES AT WHICH LETTERS MUST BE LEFT AT THE OFFICE TO ENSURE THEIR GOING IN THE MAIL OF THE DAY. . . .
[Philadelphia: 1798.] Broadside. fol.

34359   PHILADELPHIA. PENNSYLVANIA. ST. PAUL'S CHURCH.
ARTICLES OF AGREEMENT &c. FOR RAISING A SUM OF MONEY, TO PURCHASE A LOT OF GROUND, AND ERECTING THEREON A CHURCH (SINCE KNOWN BY THE NAME OF ST. PAUL'S CHURCH) IN THE CITY OF PHILADELPHIA.
Philadelphia: Printed by John Ormrod. 1798. pp. 16. 8vo.

34360   PHILADELPHIA. PENNSYLVANIA. SCHUYLKILL RIVER BRIDGE.
CALCULATION, SHEWING IN WHAT TIME A PERMANENT BRIDGE OVER THE RIVER SCHUYLKILL, SUPPOSED TO COST TWO HUNDRED THOUSAND DOLLARS, MAY BE BUILT AND REDEEMED FROM THE ESTIMATED COMBINED PRODUCT OF DUTIES ON SALES AT AUCTION WITHIN THE CITY OF PHILADELPHIA AND THE PRODUCT OF BRIDGE TOLL, CONTEMPLATING A LOAN TO BE OBTAINED ON THE CREDIT OF SAID COMBINED PRODUCT, SO AS TO ACQUIRE THE OBJECT OF HAVING NOT ONLY A PERMANENT BUT A FREE BRIDGE WHEN REDEEMED.
[Philadelphia: Printed by Z. Poulson, jun. January 8, 1798.] pp. (3). fol.
                HSP. LOC.

34361   ——— CALCULATION SHEWING THAT WITHIN A CERTAIN PERIOD OF TIME, A BRIDGE, SUPPOSED TO COST TWO HUNDRED THOUSAND DOLLARS, MAY BE ERECTED AND COMPLEATED WITHOUT A LOAN AND THE CONSEQUENT INCREASE OF EXPENCE IN THE ARTICLE OF INTEREST. — ALSO, WHAT PROPORTION OF THE ABOVE SUM THE CITY AND SUBURBS WILL PAY TOWARDS THE ERECTION OF SAID BRIDGE.
[Philadelphia:] [Printed by Z. Poulson, jun. Jan. 8, 1798. pp. (3). fol. HSP.

34362   THE PHILADELPHIA GAZETTE & UNIVERSAL DAILY ADVERTISER. [Motto.] VOL. XV. No. 2378. MONDAY, JANUARY 1, [— No. 3185. MONDAY, DECEMBER 31, 1798.]
[Philadelphia: Published.] By A. Brown, No. 29, *Chesnut-Street.* 1798. fol.
                BM. HSP. LCP. WHS.

Although the mortality in the Office from yellow fever was great, by extraordinary effort the Publisher continued publication throughout the epidemic — the only newspaper in Philadelphia which did so.

34363   ——— VERY IMPORTANT. OFFICE OF THE PHILADELPHIA GAZETTE. JUNE 18, 1798. 8 O'CLOCK, P. M. THE FOLLOWING WAS THIS MOMENT HANDED TO ME BY A GENTLEMAN FROM NEW-YORK. A. BROWN. [Announcing the arrival of Mr. Marshall, one of our envoys, from Paris, with their reply to Talleyrand.] J. LANG. (ONE OF THE EDITORS OF THE NEW-YORK GAZETTE.)
[Philadelphia: Printed by A. Brown, 1798.] Broadside. 4to.   LOC.

34364   THE PHILADELPHIA MINERVA. — UTILE DULCI — No. 49, OF VOL. III. WHOLE
NO. 153. SATURDAY, JANUARY 6, [— No. 28 OF VOL. IV. WHOLE NO. 179 ? SAT-
URDAY, JULY 7, 1798.]

> *Printed and published by William T. Palmer, No. 18, North Third-Street,
Philadelphia. 1798. 4to.*   WHS.

> Purchased in July by Samuel F. Bradford, and issued by him as, *The
Dessert to the True American,* as a supplement to that paper.

34365   THE PHILADELPHIA MONTHLY MAGAZINE, OR, UNIVERSAL REPOSITORY OF KNOWL-
EDGE AND ENTERTAINMENT: CONSISTING OF ORIGINAL PIECES, AND SELECTIONS FROM
PERFORMANCES OF MERIT, FOREIGN AND DOMESTIC. CALCULATED TO DISSEMINATE
USEFUL KNOWLEDGE AMONG ALL RANKS OF PEOPLE, AT A SMALL EXPENSE. VOLUME
FIRST, FOR [JANUARY – JUNE] 1798.

> *Philadelphia: Printed for Thomas Condie, Stationer, No. 20, Carter's-Alley.
Where orders, and literary communications (post paid) will be thankfully received,
and punctually acknowledged.* [1798.] pp. (xi,) (15)–358, 4 plates. 8vo.
> AAS. BA. HC. HSP. JCB. LCP. LOC. NYHS. NYPL. SGO. WHS.

> Contains, Memoir of George Washington, esq., late president of the
United States, compiled by Thomas Condie. With portrait, by Houston, sc.

34366   —— THE PHILADELPHIA MONTHLY MAGAZINE, OR, UNIVERSAL REPOSITORY OF
KNOWLEDGE AND ENTERTAINMENT: CONSISTING OF ORIGINAL PIECES, AND SELEC-
TIONS FROM PERFORMANCES OF MERIT, FOREIGN AND DOMESTIC. CALCULATED TO
DISSEMINATE USEFUL KNOWLEDGE AMONG ALL RANKS OF PEOPLE, AT A SMALL EX-
PENSE. EMBELLISHED WITH ELEGANT ENGRAVINGS. VOLUME SECOND, FOR [JULY
– SEPTEMBER] 1798.

> *Philadelphia: Printed for Thomas Condie, Stationer, No. 20, Carter's-Alley,
Where orders and literary communications (post paid) will be thankfully received.
and punctually acknowledged.* [1798.] pp. 167, (1). 8vo.   AAS. JCB.

34367   THE PHILADELPHIA PRICE-CURRENT, AND MARKET-DAY ADVERTISER. MARCH –
SEPTEMBER, 1798.

> *Philadelphia: Printed, every Wednesday and Saturday morning, by James
Humphreys, 1798. 4to.*

> Established, as a semi-weekly, by James Humphreys, and continued by
him "with great encouragement" for about six months, when publication
was suspended on account of the yellow fever, and was not resumed.
No copies have been located. On March 17, 1798, Joseph N. Russell,
formerly printer at Boston, and Wiscasset, Maine, also issued proposals
for printing in Philadelphia, the *Philadelphia Price Current and Nautical Recorder* which, apparently, never reached the state of publication.

34368   PHILADELPHISCHE [cut] CORRESPONDENZ. ALTE NUM. 658. NUM. 1. DIENSTAG,
DEN 1 MAY, [— NUM. 28. ALTE NUM. 684. DIENSTAG, DEN 25 DECEMBER, 1798.]

> *Alle Dienstag herausgegeben von Henrich und Joseph K. Kammerer, jun. für
anderthalb Thaler des Jahres.* 1798. fol.   HSP.

> In continuation of Steiner and Kämmerer's *Philadelphische Correspon-
denz,* which suspended publication in October, 1797. Publication was
again suspended from 18 September, to 13 November, of this year, owing
to the death of Henrich Kämmerer, junior, from yellow fever, and when
resumed at the latter date, it was published by Joseph R. Kämmerer
und Comp.

34369   PHILADELPHISCHES MAGAZIN ODER UNTERHALTENDER GESELLSCHAFTER FÜR DIE
DEUTSCHEN IN AMERIKA. MAY, 1798.

> *Philadelphia: H. u. J. R. Kammerer.* 1798. pp. 48. 4to.   HSP.

34370   PHILANTHROPOS, pseudonym.
NEGRO SLAVERY DEFENDED BY THE WORD OF GOD. BY PHILANTHROPOS.

> [*New-York ?* 1798.]

34371   PHILLIPS, CATHERINE PAYTON   1727–1794
MEMOIRS OF THE LIFE OF CATHERINE PHILLIPS: TO WHICH ARE ADDED SOME OF
HER EPISTLES.

> *Philadelphia: Printed by Budd and Bartram, for Robert Johnson and Co.
No. 147 High Street.* 1798. pp. 384. 12mo.   AAS. NYPL.

34372   PHILLIPS, JOHN
AN APPEAL TO MATTER OF FACT & COMMON SENSE, RECOMMENDED TO THE SERIOUS
CONIDERATION [*sic*] OF THE INHABITANTS OF CHARLESTON, SOUTH CAROLINA, &C.
TO WHICH IS AFFIXED, A LETTER TO THE ****. BY JOHN PHILLIPS. [Quotations.]

> *New-York: Printed by T. Kirk, No.* 112, *Chatham-Street.* 1798. pp. 31, (1).
8vo.   AAS. LOC.

34373   —— FAMILIAR DIALOGUES ON DANCING, BETWEEN A MINISTER AND A DANCER; TAKEN
FROM MATTER OF FACT WITH AN APPENDIX CONTAINING SOME EXTRACTS FROM THE
WRITINGS OF PIOUS AND EMINENT MEN AGAINST THE ENTERTAINMENTS OF THE
STAGE, AND OTHER VAIN AMUSEMENTS RECOMMENDED TO THE PERUSAL OF CHRIST-
IANS OF EVERY DENOMINATION. BY JOHN PHILLIPS. [Quotations.]

> *New-York: Printed by T. Kirk, No.* 112, *Chatham-Street.* 1798. pp. 39.
8vo.   AAS. LOC.

34374   —— A SHORT TREATISE ON DIVINE PRESCIENCE, TO WHICH IS AFFIXED, A LETTER, ON
THE SUBJECT OF GUILE, ADDRESSED TO THE REV. MR. S – – H. TOGETHER WITH
REMARKS ON A CONVERSATION BETWEEN THE REV. BISHOP C – – KE, AND THE AU-
THOR, AND SOME STRICTURES ON A SERMON PREACHED BY THE REV. BISHOP A–B–
Y, AT CHARLESTON, SOUTH CAROLINA. [Quotations.] BY JOHN PHILLIPS.

> *New-York: Printed for the Author.* 1798. pp. 49. 8vo.   AAS. LOC.

34375   PHILODEMOS, pseudonym.
AN ENQUIRY WHETHER THE ACT OF CONGRESS, "IN ADDITION TO THE ACT, ENTITLED
AN ACT, FOR THE PUNISHMENT OF CERTAIN CRIMES AGAINST THE UNITED STATES"
GENERALLY CALLED THE SEDITION BILL, IS UNCONSTITUTIONAL OR NOT. [Signed,
Philodemos.]

> *Richmond: Printed by S. Pleasants, jun.* Nov. 1798. pp. 15. 8vo. AAS. LOC.

34376   PHILOMATHES, pseudonym.
FRANKLIN'S LEGACY: OR, THE NEW-YORK AND VERMONT ALMANACK, FOR THE YEAR
OF OUR LORD, 1799; BEING THE 3D AFTER BISSEXTILE, OR LEAP-YEAR, AND THE 23D
OF AMERICAN INDEPENDENCE, UNTIL THE FOURTH OF JULY. CALCULATED FOR THE
MERIDIAN OF TROY, LATITUDE 42 DEGREES AND 48 MINUTES NORTH — AND, FROM
THE ENGLISH OBSERVATORY, 73 DEGREES AND 8 MINUTES WEST LONGITUDE. CON-
TAINING, ALSO, THE LUNATIONS, CONJUNCTIONS, ECLIPSES, JUDGMENT OF THE
WEATHER, RISING AND SETTING OF THE PLANETS, LENGTH OF DAYS AND NIGHTS,
COURTS, &C. TOGETHER WITH USEFUL TABLES, AND A GREAT VARIETY OF INSTRUCT-
ING AND ENTERTAINING PIECES. BY PHILOMATHES, A. M.

> *Troy: Printed by R. Moffitt & Co. and sold by them at their Office, a few doors
north of Peirce's Inn, by the gross, dozen or single; by Mr. David Buel, in Troy;
and by John Shaw, bookbinder, Lansingburgh.* ☞ *Great allowance made to those
who buy a quantity.* [1798.] pp. (36). 12mo.   AAS.

34377   A PHYSICAL ENQUIRY INTO THE ORIGIN AND CAUSES OF THE PESTILENTIAL FEVERS. HOW WONDROUS ARE THY WORKS DISPLAY'D GREAT GOD, AND HOW MYSTERIOUS MADE ARE ALL THY WAYS—IN EV'RY CLIME THY HAND EXTENDS TO ACTS SUBLIME! THE AUTHOR.

New-York: Printed by J. Tiebout, for Thomas B. Jansen, Bookseller and Stationer, No. 344 Water-Street, near the New-Slip. 1798. (Copy right secured in America, Great Britain and Ireland.)   LOC.

69th New York District Copyright, issued to Thomas B. Jansen, as Proprietor, 23 November, 1798.

34378   PICKERING, TIMOTHY   1715–1829
FROM TIMOTHY PICKERING, TO P. JOHNSTON, ESQ. OF PRINCE EDWARD COUNTY, VIRGINIA. . . .

Trenton, Printed by Matthias Day. Sept. 29, 1798. Broadside.   EI.

34379   PIERCE, JOHN   1773–1849
ON THE MYSTERY OF GODLINESS. A DISCOURSE DELIVERED AT MEDFIELD, ON THE SECOND SABBATH IN OCTOBER, 1797. AND TO A FEW OTHER SOCIETIES. BY JOHN PIERCE, MINISTER OF BROOKLINE. [Three lines from] DEUT. XXIX. 29.

Dedham: Printed by Mann and Adams. 1798. pp. (22). 8vo.
            AAS. BA. JCB. NYPL.

34380   PIKE, NICHOLAS   1743–1819
THE NEW COMPLETE SYSTEM OF ARITHMETIC, COMPOSED FOR THE USE OF THE CITIZENS OF THE UNITED STATES. BY NICOLAS [sic] PIKE, A. M. MEMBER OF THE AMERICAN ACADEMY OF ARTS AND SCIENCES. ABRIDGED FOR THE USE OF SCHOOLS. THE THIRD EDITION, CORRECTED AND ENLARGED.

Printed at Worcester, Massachusetts, at the Press of Isaiah Thomas, by Leonard Worcester, for said Thomas. Sold at his Bookstores in Worcester & Walpole; by said Thomas & Andrews, in Boston; and by the Booksellers in the United States. 1798. pp. 352. 12mo.
            AAS. BM. JCB. LOC.

34381   PINCHARD, MRS. ——
DRAMATIC DIALOGUES FOR THE USE OF YOUNG PERSONS. EMBELLISHED WITH SIX COPPER PLATE ENGRAVINGS. BY THE AUTHOR OF THE BLIND CHILD.

Boston: Printed for William Spotswood, No. 22, Marlborough-Street. 1798. 6 plates. 24mo.

34382   PINCKNEY, CHARLES   1758–1824
CHARLESTON, JULY 24, 1798. DEAR SIR, IT IS WITH GREAT CONCERN I FIND, IT HAS BECOME MY DUTY TO TRANSMIT TO YOU, A VERY DIFFERENT STATE OF OUR PUBLIC AFFAIRS, FROM THAT, WHICH, AT OUR LAST MEETING, WE ALL HOPED WOULD HAVE BEEN PRODUCED BY THE EXPECTED FAVORABLE RECEPTION OF OUR ENVOYS, AND THE HONORABLE ADJUSTMENT OF OUR DIFFERENCES WITH THE FRENCH REPUBLIC. . . . CHARLES PINCKNEY.

[Charleston: 1798.] Broadside. fol.   LOC.

34383   PITT, C. I.
THE POOR BLIND GIRL. A FAVORITE PATHETIC BALLAD. WRITTEN BY C. I. PITT. MUSIC BY V. DE CLEVE.

New-York: [1798.]   JCB.

34384   THE PITTSBURGH GAZETTE. VOL. 12. NO, 592. SATURDAY, JANUARY 6, [— VOL. 13. NO. 642. SATURDAY, DECEMBER 29, 1798.]

Pittsburgh: Printed by John Scull, in Front Street, next door to the corner of Market Street. 1798. fol.

34385 A PLAIN ACCOUNT OF THE ORDINANCE OF BAPTISM: IN WHICH ALL THE TEXTS IN THE NEW-TESTAMENT RELATING TO IT, ARE PROVED; AND THE WHOLE DOCTRINE CONCERNING IT DRAWN FROM THEM ALONE. IN A COURSE OF LETTERS TO THE RIGHT REV. DOCTOR BENJAMIN HOADLY, LATE LORD BISHOP OF WINCHESTER; AUTHOR OF THE PLAIN ACCOUNT OF THE LORD'S SUPPER. . . . FIRST BALLSTON EDITION.

London printed: Ballston: – – Re-printed by I. & W. Child. Sold at their Printing-Office, nearly opposite the Court-House. 1798. pp. 84. 12mo.   JCB.

34386 PLEASANTS, Mrs. ———
MRS. PLEASANT'S STORY BOOK. COMPOSED FOR THE AMUSEMENT OF HER LITTLE FAMILY: TO WHICH ARE ADDED, INSTRUCTIONS FOR THE PROPER APPLICATION OF THEM.

Philadelphia: Printed for David Hogan, in George-street, 3d door below South-street. 1798.

34387 THE POCKET MISCELLANY. IN PROSE AND VERSE. [Ornament.]

Philadelphia: Printed for Mathew Carey. 1798. pp. (2), (282). 16mo.
AAS. LOC.

34388 POETIC MISCELLANY, ON SUBJECTS MORAL AND RELIGIOUS.

Portsmouth, N. H.: Printed and sold by Charles Peirce. 1798.

34389 THE POLITE LADY; OR, A COURSE OF FEMALE EDUCATION; IN A SERIES OF LETTERS, FROM A MOTHER TO HER DAUGHTER. [Two lines from] POPE. FIRST AMERICAN EDITION.

Philadelphia: Printed for Mathew Carey. 1798. pp. 271, (4). 12mo.
AAS. JCB. LOC.

First printed in London in 1760. Letters signed Portia; the replies, Sophia.

34390 A POLITICAL ADDRESS, LATELY DELIVERED IN KENTUCKY, AND VARIOUS OTHER PARTS, BY A VIRGINIAN, DURING HIS TRAVELS TO THE WESTERN COUNTRY; AND WHICH, FROM NUMEROUS SOLICITATIONS, THE AUTHOR HAS BEEN PREVAILED UPON TO OFFER THE PUBLIC THROUGH THE MEDIUM OF THE PRESS. THIS PUBLICATION IS DESIGNED TO DISSEMINATE FACTS, ERADICATE ERROR, AND SPREAD THE GLEAMS OF TRUTH BEFORE THE PUBLIC.

"Just received, and for sale at most of the Stores in Hagers-Town, Maryland, October 1, 1798,"

34391 THE POLITICAL FOCUS. VOL. I. No. 1. THURSDAY, JULY 5, [— No. 26. THURSDAY, DECEMBER 27, 1798.]

Published every Thursday by Charles & John Prentiss, in Leominster, (Massachusetts). 1798. fol.   AAS.

Established, as a weekly, by Charles, and John Prentiss. With the issue for February 28, 1799, John Prentiss withdrew, and publication was continued certainly to December 5, 1799 — the last number located.

34392 THE POLITICAL REPOSITORY: OR, FARMER'S JOURNAL. "UTILE DULCI" — "WE BLEND THE SWEET WITH THE USEFUL" — HORACE. VOL. I. No. 1. TUESDAY, AUGUST 14, [— No. 20. TUESDAY, DECEMBER 25, 1798.]

Printed at Brookfield, Massachusetts, by Ebenezer Merriam & Co. . . . 1798. fol.   AAS.

Established, as a weekly, by Ebenezer Merriam and Company, and continued by them to the issue for May 4, 1802, when it was discontinued.

34393 POMMEREUL, Francois René Jean de   1745–1823
CAMPAIGN OF GENERAL BUONAPARTE IN ITALY, DURING THE FOURTH AND FIFTH
YEARS [1796–1797] OF THE FRENCH REPUBLIC. BY A GENERAL OFFICER. [Copy
right secured according to law.]
*New-York: Printed [by Thomas Greenleaf] at the Argus Office [for Hocquet
Caritat.] M,DCC,XCVIII. pp. 304. 8vo.*   AAS. BA. JCB. NYPL.

63d New York District Copyright, issued to Thomas Greenleaf, as Proprietor, 1 June, 1798.

"I came to this country the middle of last March, with no other recommendation than a love of literature. I had caught the bliss of publication in England, which will ever constitute my supreme felicity.
By a concurrence of circumstances the Campaign of General Buonaparte
in Italy, was given me to translate, and how I have executed it the world
is to determine: the book is now before it, and I lie exposed to every
blast of criticism and gale of censure." — John Davis.

34394 POOR ROBIN, pseudonym.
[No. 1.] THE FARMER'S, MERCHANT'S AND MECHANIC'S ALMANACK: OR, THE REG-
ISTER OF MAINE. FOR THE YEAR OF OUR LORD, 1799: BEING THE THIRD AFTER
BISSEXTILE, OR LEAP YEAR, AND THE TWENTY THIRD OF AMERICAN INDEPENDENCE.
FITTED TO THE LATITUDE AND LONGITUDE OF PORTLAND. CONTAINING, BESIDES
THE USUAL ASTRONOMICAL CALCULATIONS, COURT CALENDAR, TABLES, &C. A FAR-
MER'S CALENDAR FOR EVERY MONTH IN THE YEAR — AND A GREATER VARIETY AND
LARGER QUANTITY THAN ANY ALMANACK EVER PUBLISHED IN MAINE — OF MATTERS
USEFUL, ENTERTAINING, AND CURIOUS. [Four lines of verse from] THOMPSON [sic]
[Cut of eagle, E. A. J.]
*Printed by Elezer A. Jenks, Portland. Sold at his Office, in Middlestreet
wholesale & retail—Sold also at the several Bookstores and various places in town &
country. [1798.] pp. (36). 12mo.*   AAS.

Preface signed Poor Robin. Contains, Adams and Liberty: a patriotic
song.—By Thomas Paine. A. M. Ministers of religious societies in Maine.
Justices of the Peace in Maine. Attornies at law, in the District of
Maine. Stamp duties, Routes of the public mails in Maine. Roads.

34395 —— JENKS' SHEET ALMANACK, FOR THE YEAR OF OUR LORD, 1799.
Printed by Elezer A. Jenks, Portland. 1798. Broadside. fol.

34396 POOR WILL'S ALMANACK, FOR THE YEAR OF OUR LORD 1799: BEING THE THIRD
AFTER BISSEXTILE OR LEAP-YEAR. [Sixteen lines.]
*Philadelphia: Printed for, and sold by, Joseph and James Cruikshank, No.
87, High-Street. [1798.] pp. (36). 12mo.*   AAS. HSP. LOC.

34397 POOR WILL'S POCKET ALMANACK, FOR THE YEAR 1799; BEING THE THIRD AFTER
BISSEXTILE OR LEAP-YEAR. [Eighteen lines.]
*Philadelphia: Printed for, and sold by, Joseph & James Cruikshank, No. 87,
High-Street. [1798.] pp. [48] interleaved. 32mo.*   AAS. HSP. LOC. NYPL.

34398 POPE, ALEXANDER   1688–1744
AN ESSAY ON MAN. IN FOUR EPISTLES. BY ALEXANDER POPE, ESQ. ENLARGED AND
IMPROVED BY THE AUTHOR.
Printed at Peacham, Vermont, by Farley & Goss. 1798. pp. 44. 8vo.

34399 PORCUPINE'S [cut] GAZETTE. VOL. II. No. 258. MONDAY, JANUARY 1, [— VOL. III.
No. 567. MONDAY, DECEMBER 31, 1798.]
*Philadelphia: Published every evening, by William Cobbett, opposite Christ
Church. 1798. fol.*   AAS. HSP. LCP. LOC. MdHS. NYHS. NYPL. PSL.

PORCUPINE'S Gazette, continued.

34400 —— The Carriers of Porcupine's Gazette, to its friends; on the commencement of the year 1798. [Two columns.]

　　[Philadelphia: Printed by William Cobbett, 1798.] Broadside. fol.

34401 PORTER, Eliphalet　　　　　　　　　　　　1758–1833
A Discourse, delivered at Brookline, in the morning, and at the first parish in Roxbury, in the afternoon, on the 9th of May, 1798, being the day recommended by John Adams, President of the United States, for solemn humiliation, fasting & prayer, throughout the Union. By Eliphalet Porter, minister of the first religious society in Roxbury. Published at the desire of many of the hearers in both congregations.

　　Boston: Printed by John Russell, at his office, Quaker-Lane. 1798. pp. 36.
8vo.　　　　　　　　　AAS. BA. BM. CHS. HC. JCB. LOC. MHS. NYPL. UTS. YC.

34402 PORTER, Nathaniel　　　　　　　　　　　　1745–1837
The Friendly monitor. Being two sermons, from II Peter, 2. 3. By Nathaniel Porter, of Conway.

　　Concord: Printed and sold by Moses Davis. 1798.

34403 PORTLAND. District of Maine. Marine Society.
Laws of the Marine Society, instituted at Portland, and incorporated by the General Court, February, 1796.

　　Portland: Printed by Baker & George. 1798. pp. 14. 16mo.　　　MEHS.

34404 PORTLAND Gazette. Vol. I. No. 1. Monday, April 16, [— No. 38. Monday, December 31, 1798.]

　　*Published by Elezer Alley Jenks, Portland, District of Maine, Massachusetts.
1798.* fol.

　　Established, as a weekly, by Elezer Alley Jenks. With the issue for April 29, 1799, the title was changed to *Jenks' Portland Gazette*, and to this title was added, with the issue for September 27, 1802, the words "Maine Advertiser." This sub-title was dropped with the issue for October 31, 1803. And, with the issue for March 18, 1805, the title was shortened to *Portland Gazette*. With the issue for July 16, 1805, Jenks disposed of his interests to Isaac Adams, and William Jenks, junior, who changed the title to *Portland Gazette, and Maine Advertizer*, with the issue for July 23, 1805. With the issue for July 14, 1806, William Jenks, junior withdrew, and publication was continued by Isaac Adams to the issue for September 12, 1808, when he disposed of his interests to Arthur Shirley. With the issue for October 26, 1812, the spelling was changed to "Advertiser" in the sub-title. With the issue for September 19, 1814, Joshua Shirley was admitted to partnership as A. & J. Shirley, until 1819, when Joshua Shirley withdrew. With the issue for April 7, 1818, the title was shortened to *Portland Gazette*, and was so continued, by Arthur Shirley, beyond the period of this work.

34405 POTE, Jeremy
A Narrative containing strictures on the life of Jeremy Pote, of Falmouth, in the District of Maine: taken mostly from his own mouth, and by him examined.

　　Portland: Printed by Baker & George ? 1798.

34406   THE POTOMAK GUARDIAN, & BERKELEY ADVERTISER. VOL. VIII. NO. 371. THURS-
DAY, JANUARY 4, [— VOL, IX. No. 421. WEDNESDAY, DECEMBER 26, 1798.]

     *Martinsburg, Virginia: Printed and published every Thursday [Wednes-
day], by N. Willis, Burke-Street.* 1798. fol.

     In February, the title was shortened to *The Potomak Guardian,* and from
February – August, publication was made in the name of Willis & [Isaac]
Baldwin.

34407   POTTER, ISAIAH   1746–1817
THE YOUNG MEN ARE DEAD! SUDDEN UNTIMELY DEATH A SERIOUS LESSON OF IN-
STRUCTION TO THE LIVING. A SERMON, PREACHED ON ACCOUNT OF THE DEATH OF
ERASTUS CHAMBERLAIN AND REUBEN CURRIER, WHO WERE DROWNED ON THE 16
OF APRIL, 1798. BY THE REV. ISAIAH POTTER, OF LEBANON, NEW-HAMPSHIRE.
[Two lines from] ELIHU.

     Printed at Hanover, New-Hampshire, by Benjamin True. 1798. pp. [16.]
8vo.
                                              AAS. CLA.

     The author was a companion of the young men when the canoe was
upset.

34408   THE POUGHKEEPSIE JOURNAL. TOTAL NUM. 650. TUESDAY, JANUARY 2, [—TOTAL
NUM. 701. TUESDAY, DECEMBER 25, 1798.]

     *Poughkeepsie, Dutchess County—Published by Nicholas Power, at the Post-
Office.* 1798. fol.

     With the issue for March 27th, Henry Collins Southwick was admitted
to partnership, as Power and Southwick.

34409   POWNALL, MARY A. WRIGHTEN   –1796
JEMMY OF THE GLEN. WORDS AND MUSIC BY THE LATE MRS. POWNALL.

     Baltimore: Published and for sale at J. Carr's Music Store, Gay Street.
1798. pp. (2). 4to.
                                              LOC.

34410   PRESBYTERIAN CHURCH IN THE UNITED STATES OF AMERICA.
ACTS AND PROCEEDINGS OF THE GENERAL ASSEMBLY OF THE PRESBYTERIAN CHURCH
IN THE UNITED STATES OF AMERICA, MAY 17TH, 1798.

     Philadelphia: 1798. pp. [16], xii, (4). 8vo.

     Contains, A List of the Synods, Presbyteries, Licentiates, and Congre-
gations, in 1798. Reprinted in Philadelphia in 1803.

34411   PRICE, ISAAC
THE JERSEY MAN'S COMMON SENSE.

     Morris Town: Printed by E. Cooper & Co. 1798.

34412   PRIDEAUX, HUMPHREY   1648–1724
THE TRUE NATURE OF IMPOSTURE FULLY DISPLAYED IN THE LIFE OF MAHOMET. BY
HUMPHREY PRIDEAUX, D. D. DEAN OF NORWICK [sic.] FIRST AMERICAN EDITION.
     Fairhaven: Printed by James Lyon. 1798. pp. (108); (84). 12mo.
                                         JCB. LOC. NYPL.

     Second title: HISTORY OF TWO CELEBRATED THEBANS PELOPIDAS AND EPAMINON-
DAS. [By John Blair Linn.] pp. (84).

34413   PRIESTLEY, JOSEPH   1733–1804
EXTRACTS FROM A CATECHISM, IN WHICH THE PLAINNESS AND SIMPLICITY OF DOCTOR
WATTS ARE IMITATED: AND FROM WHICH THE TECHNICAL TERMS OF PARTICULAR
SYSTEMS ARE EXCLUDED.

     Boston: Printed and sold by Samuel Hall, in Cornhill. 1798. pp. 22. 24mo.
                                              AAS.

34414   PRINCE, JOHN   1751–1836
A DISCOURSE, DELIVERED AT SALEM, ON THE DAY OF THE NATIONAL FAST. MAY 9,
1798; APPOINTED BY PRESIDENT ADAMS, ON ACCOUNT OF THE DIFFICULTIES SUB-
SISTING BETWEEN THE UNITED STATES AND FRANCE. BY JOHN PRINCE, L. L. D.
MINISTER OF THE FIRST CONGREGATIONAL SOCIETY IN SALEM. [Ornament.]
Printed by Thomas C. Cushing, Essex Street, Salem. 1798. pp. [44.] 8vo.
AAS. BA. EI. HC. HSP. JCB. LOC. MHS. NYPL. YC.

34415   —— — A DISCOURSE, DELIVERED AT SALEM, ON THE DAY OF THE NATIONAL FAST,
MAY 9, 1798; APPOINTED BY PRESIDENT ADAMS, ON ACCOUNT OF THE DIFFICULTIES
SUBSISTING BETWEEN THE UNITED STATES AND FRANCE. BY JOHN PRINCE, LL. D.
MINISTER OF THE FIRST CONGREGATIONAL SOCIETY IN SALEM. SECOND EDITION.
Printed by Thomas C. Cushing, Essex-Street, Salem. 1798. pp. (2), (2), [30].
8vo.   AAS. BA. BM. CLA. EI. HC. JCB. LOC. MHS.

34416   —— — A DISCOURSE, DELIVERED AT SALEM, ON THE DAY OF THE NATIONAL FAST,
MAY 9, 1798; APPOINTED BY PRESIDENT ADAMS, ON ACCOUNT OF THE DIFFICULTIES
SUBSISTING BETWEEN THE UNITED STATES AND FRANCE. BY JOHN PRINCE, LL. D.
MINISTER OF THE FIRST CONGREGATIONAL SOCIETY IN SALEM. THIRD EDITION.
Printed by Thomas C. Cushing, Essex-Street, Salem. 1798. pp. 30. 8vo.
HC. MHS.

34417   THE PRINCE OF BRITTANY: AN HISTORICAL NOVEL. TO WHICH ARE ADDED, EDWARD
AND MATILDA, MIRANDA, — CHARIESSA, AND LEONTINE.
New-York: Printed and sold by John Harrisson, 1798. pp. 144. 12mo.

34418   PRIOLEAU, PHILIP GENDRON
AN INAUGURAL DISSERTATION ON THE USE OF THE NITRIC AND OXIGENATED MURIATIC
ACIDS, IN SOME DISEASES. SUBMITTED TO THE EXAMINATION OF THE REV. JOHN
EWING, S. T. P. PROVOST; THE TRUSTEES AND MEDICAL FACULTY OF THE UNIVERSITY
OF PENNSYLVANIA, ON THE TWENTY-SECOND DAY OF MAY, 1798. FOR THE DEGREE
OF DOCTOR OF MEDICINE. BY PHILIP GENDRON PRIOLEAU, A. B. OF CHARLESTON,
SOUTH CAROLINA — HONORARY MEMBER OF THE PHILADELPHIA MEDICAL AND
CHEMICAL SOCIETIES. [One line of Latin.]
Philadelphia: Printed by John Bioren. MDCCXCVIII. pp. (72). 8vo.
Reprinted in Caldwell, T. Medical theses. Vol. 1. 1805.   AAS. HEH. JCB. LOC. NYPL.

34419   PROTESTANT EPISCOPAL CHURCH IN NEW JERSEY.
PROCEEDINGS OF A CONVENTION OF THE PROTESTANT EPISCOPAL CHURCH, IN THE
STATE OF NEW-JERSEY. HELD AT NEWARK, JUNE THE 6TH, AND 7TH, AND, BY
ADJOURNMENT, AT NEW-BRUNSWICK, AUGUST THE 15TH AND 16TH, 1798.
*—Newark—New-Jersey—Printed by Jacob Halsey and Co. at the Office of the
Gazette—*1798. pp. (12). 8vo.   AAS. LOC. NYHS.

34420   PROTESTANT EPISCOPAL CHURCH IN THE UNITED STATES OF AMERICA.
THE BOOK OF COMMON PRAYER, AND ADMINISTRATION OF THE SACRAMENTS AND OTHER
RITES AND CEREMONIES OF THE CHURCH, ACCORDING TO THE USE OF THE PROTEST-
ANT EPISCOPAL CHURCH OF THE UNITED STATES OF AMERICA: TOGETHER WITH
THE PSALTER OR PSALMS OF DAVID.
*New York: By Direction of the General Convention. Printed by Hugh Gaine,
at the Bible, Pearl-Street.* M,DCC,XCVIII. pp. 2, (4), 350. 12mo.   AAS. HEH.

Second title: THE WHOLE BOOK OF PSALMS, IN METRE; WITH HYMNS SUITED TO THE
FEASTS AND FASTS OF THE CHURCH, AND OTHER OCCASIONS OF PUBLIC WORSHIP.
*New-York: By direction of the General Convention, Printed by Hugh Gaine,
at the Bible, Pearl-Street.* M,DCC,XCVIII.

34421 PROUD, ROBERT   1728–1813
THE HISTORY OF PENNSYLVANIA, IN NORTH AMERICA, FROM THE ORIGINAL INSTITU-
TION AND SETTLEMENT OF THAT PROVINCE, UNDER THE FIRST PROPRIETOR AND
GOVERNOR WILLIAM PENN, IN 1681, TILL AFTER THE YEAR 1742; WITH AN INTRO-
DUCTION, RESPECTING THE LIFE OF W. PENN, PRIOR TO THE GRANT OF THE
PROVINCE, AND THE RELIGIOUS SOCIETY OF THE PEOPLE CALLED QUAKERS: —
WITH THE FIRST RISE OF THE NEIGHBORING COLONIES, MORE PARTICULARLY OF
WEST-NEW-JERSEY, AND THE SETTLEMENT OF THE DUTCH AND SWEDES ON DELA-
WARE. TO WHICH IS ADDED, A BRIEF DESCRIPTION OF THE SAID PROVINCE, AND
OF THE GENERAL STATE, IN WHICH IT FLOURISHED, PRINCIPALLY BETWEEN THE
YEARS 1760 AND 1770. THE WHOLE INCLUDING A VARIETY OF THINGS, USEFUL AND
INTERESTING TO BE KNOWN, RESPECTING THAT COUNTRY IN EARLY TIME, &C. WITH
AN APPENDIX. WRITTEN PRINCIPALLY BETWEEN THE YEARS 1776 AND 1780, BY
ROBERT PROUD. [Four lines of quotations.] VOLUME II.
> *Philadelphia: Printed and sold by Zachariah Poulson, junior, No. 106 Chesnut
> Street, nearly opposite to the Bank of North America.* 1798. pp. 373, 146, map.
> 8vo.   BA. BM. HC. HSP. JCB. LOC. MHS. NL. NYHS. NYPL.

34422 PROUDFIT, ALEXANDER MONCRIEF   1770–1843
A SERMON, PREACHED BEFORE THE NORTHERN MISSIONARY SOCIETY IN THE STATE
OF NEW-YORK, AT THEIR FIRST ANNUAL MEETING IN TROY, FEBRUARY 8; AND BY
PARTICULAR REQUEST, IN ALBANY, MARCH 6, 1798, AT A SPECIAL MEETING OF THE
SOCIETY. BY ALEXANDER PROUDFIT, ONE OF THE MINISTERS OF THE ASSOCIATE
REFORMED CONGREGATION, IN SALEM.
> *Albany: Printed by Loring, Andrews & Co.* 1798. pp. [38.] errata. 8vo.
>   AAS. BA. BM. JCB. NYHS. NYPL.

34423 PROVIDENCE. RHODE ISLAND. ASSOCIATION OF MERCHANICS AND MANUFACTURERS.
THE CHARTER, ARTICLES OF AGREEMENT, BYE-LAWS, RULES AND REGULATIONS OF
THE PROVIDENCE ASSOCIATION OF MECHANICS AND MANUFACTURERS. ALSO, A
CATALOGUE OF THE NAMES OF THE MEMBERS. PUBLISHED BY ORDER OF THE
ASSOCIATION.
> *Providence: Printed by Bennett Wheeler.* 1798. pp. 40. 8vo.
>   JCB. NYHS. NYPL. RIHS.

34424 PROVIDENCE. RHODE ISLAND. BENEFICENT CONGREGATIONAL CHURCH.
A SHORT CATECHISM, PARTICULARLY DESIGNED FOR THE INSTRUCTION OF THE CHIL-
DREN, OF THE BENEFICENT CONGREGATIONAL CHURCH OF CHRIST, IN PROVIDENCE.
. . .
> *Providence: Printed by B. Wheeler, and sold at his book store.* 1798. pp. 36.
> 24mo.   RIHS.

34425 THE PROVIDENCE GAZETTE. VOL. XXXV. NO. 1775. SATURDAY, JANUARY 6, [—
NO. 1826. SATURDAY, DECEMBER 29, 1798.]
> *[Providence:] Printed by Carter and Wilkinson, at the Post-Office, opposite
> the Market.* 1798. fol.   AAS. BU. JCB. LOC. RL. RIHS.

The issue for Saturday evening, December 15th, is a broadside of the
President's Speech.

34426 PUCKLE, JAMES   1667–1724
A GREY-CAP FOR A GREEN-HEAD. IN A DIALOGUE BETWEEN FATHER AND SON. THE
FIRST AMERICAN EDITION, FROM THE FOURTH BRITISH EDITION.
> *Philadelphia: Printed by and for Samuel Longcope, No. 147, Spruce Street.*
> M.DCC.XCVIII. pp. (2), (2), [13] – 159. 12mo.   AAS. JCB. LOC.

The first two leaves and the last two leaves are printed on a different
colored paper than the rest of the text, and probably indicate a sub-
stitution for the original printing. With a list of Subscribers' names.

34427   PUTNAM, Aaron   1734–1813
A Sermon upon the being of God, and the mediation of Christ. By Aaron Putnam, a.m. pastor of the first church of Christ, in Pomfret. [Printer's mark.]
New-London: Printed by Samuel Green. 1798. pp.[–16–] 8vo. AAS. BM. JCB.

34428   PUTNEY Argus. Guided by truth, we aim at impartiality. No. 42 of vol. II. Whole no. 94. Saturday, November 3, [— No. 50 of vol. II. Whole no. 102. Tuesday, December 25, 1798.]
Published every Saturday, [Tuesday] by Cornelius Sturtevant, at Putney, Vermont. 1798. fol.   AAS.
In continuation of *The Argus.*

34429   QUINCY, Josiah.   1772–1864
An Oration, pronounced July 4, 1798, at the request of the inhabitants of the town of Boston, in commemoration of the anniversary of American independence. By Josiah Quincy. [Seven lines from] J. Quincy, jun. [Printer's mark.]
Boston; Printed by John Russell. 1798. pp. 31. 8vo.
       AAS. BM. HC. JCB. LOC. MHS. NYPL. UTS.

34430   —— — An Oration, pronounced July 4, 1798, at the request of the inhabitants of the town of Boston, in commemoration of the anniversary of American independence. By Josiah Quincy. [Seven lines from] J. Quincy, jun. Second edition.
Boston: Printed by John Russell. 1798. pp. 31. 8vo.
       BA. BM. JCB. LOC. MHS. NYPL.

34431   —— — An Oration, pronounced, July 4, 1798, at the request of the inhabitants of the town of Boston, in commemoration of the anniversary of American independence. By Josiah Quincy. [Seven lines from] J. Quincy, jun.
Boston; printed; Philadelphia: Re-printed, by John Fenno, No. 119, Chesnut-Street. 1798. pp. 21. 8vo.   BA. JCB. LOC.

34432   RAMSAY, Allan   1685–1758
The Gentle shepherd: a Scots pastoral comedy, by Allan Ramsay. A new edition, with the songs; carefully corrected. [Four lines of verse from] Spencer, p. 1113.
Philadelphia: Printed and sold by Peter Stewart, No. 34, South Second-Street. 1798. pp. 72. 12mo.   AAS.

34433   RANLET, Henry
Ranlet's New-Hampshire and Massachusetts Almanack, for the year of christian æra, 1799. Being the third after bissextile or leap year, and the twenty-third of American independence. Calculated for the meridian of Boston, lat. 42 deg. 25 min. north, but, with little variation will serve the adjacent States. Containing, [Fourteen lines in two columns. Four lines of verse.]
Printed at Exeter, by H. Ranlet, and sold at his Book Store, Water Street, by the hundred, dozen, or single. Where every kind of printing, in its modern perfection, is done on moderate terms. 1798. pp. (24). 12mo.   AAS. NHHS.

34434   RANLET'S Federal Miscellany. Vol. i. No. 1. Wednesday, December 5, [— No. 4. Wednesday, December 26, 1798.]
Exeter (New-Hampshire) Printed and published by Henry Ranlet. 1798. fol.
Established, as a weekly, by Henry Ranlet. With the issue for January 16, 1799, the title was changed to *Exeter Federal Miscellany.* And, with the issue for October 1, 1799, this was altered to *Political Banquet, and Farmer's Feast,* — the issue for October 8th, 1799, is the last number located.

34435   READING. PENNSYLVANIA. THEATRE.
[Play bill of] THE MORAL AND HISTORICAL PLAY OF GEORGE BARNWELL, OR THE
LONDON MERCHANT . . .
> *[Reading: Printed by Jacob Schneider. 1798.]* Broadside.   NYPL.

> Reproduced in J. P. Nolan's Printing in Reading, 1930. pages 53–55.

34436   REDFIELD, LEVI   1745–
A SUCCINCT ACCOUNT OF SOME MEMORABLE EVENTS AND REMARKABLE OCCURRENCES
IN THE LIFE OF LEVI REDFIELD, LATE OF CONNECTICUT, NOW RESIDING IN BRAT-
TLEBORO' VER. WRITTEN BY HIMSELF. [One line from] SHAKESPEARE.
> *Printed for the Author. Brattleborough: From the Press of B. Smead.* 1798.
> pp. 12. 12mo.   HEH.

34437   THE RELIGIOUS MONITOR, OR THEOLOGICAL SCALES. VOL. I. No. 1. SATURDAY,
APRIL 7, [— No. 13. SATURDAY, SEPTEMBER 22, 1798.]
> *Danbury, Connecticut: Printed by Douglas & Nichols,* 1798. 8vo. AAS. NYPL.

> Established, as a fortnightly publication, of eight pages, by Nathan
> Douglas and Stiles Nichols, and continued into September, as above.

34438   REMARKABLE PROPHECY, FOUND ENGRAVED ON A STONE UNDER AN OLD WALL IN
FRANCE WHERE IT HAD LAIN SIX HUNDRED YEARS.
> *Portsmouth, N. H.: Printed and sold by Charles Peirce.* 1798.

34439   A REPLY TO AN ADDRESS: WRITTEN BY THE GREAT I, ADDRESSED TO THE "INFLUEN-
TIAL" CHARACTERS OF BRIMFIELD: UNDER THE APPELLATION OF "MY INFLUENTIAL
NEIGHBOURS, SELECTMEN AND COMMITTEES OF BRIMFIELD." "WHAT A WISE MAN
IS THIS I!—HE FORESEES ALL EVILS, AND TELLS WHEN AND HOW THEY WILL HAP-
PEN."
> *[Worcester:] Printed [by Leonard Worcester] at the Spy Printing-Office,
> October '98.* pp. (16). 8vo.   AAS. BA.

> A Reply to William Eaton this year.

34440   REPUBLICAN JOURNAL. [Motto.] VOL. II. No. 63. MONDAY, JANUARY 1, [—VOL.
III. No. 114. MONDAY, DECEMBER 31, 1798.]
> *Printed & published by Douglas & Nichols near the Court-House, in Danbury.*
> 1798. fol.   AAS.

> In October, the imprint was changed to: Danbury: Compiled by Stiles
> Nichols for Douglas & Nichols.

34441   RHEES, MORGAN JOHN   1760–1804
THE ALTAR OF PEACE, BEING THE SUBSTANCE OF A DISCOURSE DELIVERED IN THE
COUNCIL HOUSE, AT GREENVILLE, JULY 5TH, 1795, BEFORE THE OFFICERS OF THE
AMERICAN ARMY AND MAJOR GENERAL WAYNE, COMMANDER IN CHIEF, AND MIN-
ISTER PLENIPOTENTIARY FROM THE UNITED STATES TO TREAT WITH THE INDIAN
TRIBES, NORTH-WEST OF THE OHIO. BY MORGAN J. RHEES. TO WHICH IS PRE-
FIXED, AN ADDRESS OF THE MISSIONARY SOCIETY, WITH THEIR CONSTITUTION. "I
WILL GIVE THEE THE HEATHEN FOR AN INHERITANCE."
> *Philadelphia: Printed by Ephraim Conrad. Price 12½ cents. The profits
> arising from the sale to be applied to the funds of the Society.* 1798. pp. 15. 8vo.
>   AAS. JCB. MHS. NYPL.

34442   —— LETTERS ON LIBERTY AND SLAVERY: AN ANSWER TO A PAMPHLET, ENTITLED,
"NEGRO SLAVERY DEFENDED BY THE WORD OF GOD," BY PHILANTHROPOS. SEC-
OND EDITION.
> *New-York: Printed by R. Wilson.* 1798. pp. 24. 8vo.

34443   RHOADS, Asa

AN AMERICAN SPELLING-BOOK DESIGNED FOR THE USE OF OUR COMMON SCHOOLS; AND AS AN EASY INTRODUCTION TO THE ART OF SPELLING AND READING THE ENGLISH LANGUAGE WITH PROPRIETY. IN TWO PARTS. PART THE FIRST, CONTAINING EASY AND FAMILIAR WORDS, DIVIDED, ACCENTED AND METHODICALLY ARRANGED, AGREEABLY TO THEIR PROPER SOUNDS; WITH LESSONS OF READING INTERSPERSED. PART SECOND, TO CONTAIN WORDS MORE DIFFICULT AND IRREGULAR; ACCENTED, THEIR PROPER SOUNDS POINTED OUT AND THE VARIOUS SIGNIFICATIONS RANGED (IN GENERAL) IN ONE LINE; WITH INSTRUCTIVE AND ENTERTAINING READING LESSONS; AND THE MOST USEFUL PARTS OF GRAMMAR. COMPILED BY ASA RHOADS.

New-York: 1798.

68th New York District Copyright, issued to Daniel S. Dean and Joseph Talcott, as Proprietors, 14 November, 1798.

34444   RHODE ISLAND. STATE.

DECEMBER, 1797. AT THE GENERAL ASSEMBLY OF THE GOVERNOR AND COMPANY OF THE STATE OF RHODE-ISLAND, AND PROVIDENCE-PLANTATIONS, BEGUN AND HOLDEN, BY ADJOURNMENT, AT BRISTOL, WITHIN AND FOR THE STATE AFORESAID, ON THE SECOND MONDAY IN DECEMBER, IN THE YEAR OF OUR LORD ONE THOUSAND SEVEN HUNDRED AND NINETY-SEVEN, AND IN THE TWENTY-SECOND YEAR OF INDEPENDENCE. [Colophon:]

Warren (Rhode-Island): Printed by Nathaniel Phillips, Printer to the State. M,DCC,XCVIII. pp. 12. fol.   AAS. JCB. LOC. RIHS.

34445   —— JANUARY, 1798. AT THE GENERAL ASSEMBLY OF THE GOVERNOR AND COMPANY OF THE STATE OF RHODE-ISLAND AND PROVIDENCE-PLANTATIONS, BEGUN AND HOLDEN, BY ADJOURNMENT, AT PROVIDENCE, WITHIN AND FOR THE STATE AFORESAID, ON THE LAST MONDAY IN JANUARY, IN THE YEAR OF OUR LORD ONE THOUSAND SEVEN HUNDRED AND NINETY-EIGHT, AND IN THE TWENTY-SECOND YEAR OF INDEPENDENCE. [Colophon:]

Warren (Rhode-Island): Printed by Nathaniel Phillips, Printer to the State. M,DCC,XCVIII. pp. 21. fol.   AAS. JCB. LOC. RIHS.

34446   —— MAY, 1798. AT THE GENERAL ASSEMBLY OF THE GOVERNOR AND COMPANY OF THE STATE OF RHODE-ISLAND, AND PROVIDENCE-PLANTATIONS, BEGUN AND HOLDEN, AT NEWPORT, WITHIN AND FOR THE STATE AFORESAID, ON THE FIRST WEDNESDAY IN MAY, IN THE YEAR OF OUR LORD ONE THOUSAND SEVEN HUNDRED AND NINETY-EIGHT, AND IN THE TWENTY-SECOND YEAR OF INDEPENDENCE. [Colophon:]

Warren (Rhode-Island): Printed by Nathaniel Phillips, Printer to the State. M,DCC,XCVIII. pp. 31. fol.   AAS. JCB. LOC. RIHS.

34447   —— JUNE, 1798. AT THE GENERAL ASSEMBLY OF THE GOVERNOR AND COMPANY OF THE STATE OF RHODE-ISLAND AND PROVIDENCE-PLANTATIONS, BEGUN AND HOLDEN, BY ADJOURNMENT, AT NEWPORT, WITHIN AND FOR THE STATE AFORESAID, ON THE SECOND MONDAY IN JUNE, IN THE YEAR OF OUR LORD ONE THOUSAND SEVEN HUNDRED AND NINETY-EIGHT, AND IN THE TWENTY-SECOND YEAR OF INDEPENDENCE. [Colophon:]

Providence: Printed by Bennett Wheeler. [1798.] pp. 27. fol.
    AAS. JCB. HSP. LOC. RIHS.

34448   —— AN ACT FOR CALLING OUT THE MILITIA.

Newport: Printed by Henry Barber, 1798. Broadside.   RIHS.

RHODE ISLAND. STATE, continued.

34449 —— BY HIS EXCELLENCY ARTHUR FENNER, ESQ.; [Seal.] GOVERNOR, CAPTAIN-GEN-ERAL, AND COMMANDER IN CHIEF, OF THE STATE OF RHODE-ISLAND AND PROV-IDENCE PLANTATIONS. A PROCLAMATION. [Giving full force and effect, in thirty days to "The public laws of the State of Rhode-Island and Providence Plantations, as revised by a committee, and finally enacted by the honourable General Assembly, at their session in January, 1798."] GIVEN UNDER MY HAND, AND THE SEAL OF THE SAID STATE, THIS SIXTH DAY OF OCTOBER, IN THE YEAR OF OUR LORD ONE THOUSAND SEVEN HUNDRED AND NINETY-EIGHT, AND OF INDEPENDENCE THE TWENTY-THIRD. ARTHUR FENNER. BY HIS EXCELLENCY'S COMMAND, SAMUEL EDDY, SEC'RY. [Colophon:]
Providence: Printed by Carter and Wilkinson. [1798.] Broadside. fol.
AAS. JCB. RIHS.

34450 —— IN GENERAL ASSEMBLY. OCTOBER SESSION. AN ACT FOR GRANTING AND AP-PORTIONING A TAX OF TWENTY THOUSAND DOLLARS.
Newport: Printed by H. & O. Farnsworth, 1798. Broadside. RIHS.

34451 —— INSTRUCTIONS FOR PRINCIPAL ASSESSORS: TO   WE THE COMMISSIONERS FOR THE STATE OF RHODE-ISLAND, UNDER THE ACT OF CONGRESS . . . PROVIDENCE, THE [fifth] DAY OF [November] ONE THOUSAND SEVEN HUNDRED AND NINETY-EIGHT.
[Providence: Printed by Carter and Wilkinson, 1798.] Broadside. fol.

34452 —— INSTRUCTIONS FOR ASSISTANT ASSESSORS. [" For the valuation of lands and dwelling-houses and the enumeration of slaves within the United States."]
[Providence: Printed by Carter and Wilkinson. 5 November, 1798.] pp. (2), fol. AAS.

34453 —— THE PUBLIC LAWS OF THE STATE OF RHODE-ISLAND AND PROVIDENCE PLANTA-TIONS, AS REVISED BY A COMMITTEE, AND FINALLY ENACTED BY THE HONOURABLE GENERAL ASSEMBLY, AT THEIR SESSION IN JANUARY, 1798. TO WHICH ARE PRE-FIXED, THE CHARTER, DECLARATION OF INDEPENDENCE, ARTICLES OF CONFED-ERATION, CONSTITUTION OF THE UNITED STATES, AND PRESIDENT WASHINGTON'S ADDRESS OF SEPTEMBER, 1796. PUBLISHED BY AUTHORITY. IGNORANTIA LEGIS NEMINEM EXCUSAT. IGNORANCE OF THE LAW IS NO EXCUSE FOR ITS VIOLATION.
Printed at Providence, by Carter and Wilkinson, and sold at their Book-Store. 1798. pp. 652. 8vo. AAS. BU. HC. JCB. LOC. RIHS.

34454 —— PUBLIC LAWS OF THE STATE OF RHODE-ISLAND AND PROVIDENCE PLANTATIONS, PASSED SINCE THE SESSION OF THE GENERAL ASSEMBLY IN JANUARY, A. D. 1798.
Newport: Printed by H. & O. Farnsworth. [1798.] pp. 232. 8vo. AAS.
Under this general title has been assembled the Session Laws, some with imprints of other publishers, from May, 1798 – June 1813, continuously paged.

34455 —— A STATEMENT OF THE CLAIM OF THE RHODE-ISLAND BRIGADE, COMMANDED BY COLS. CRARY, TOPHAM, AND ELLIOT. FOR THE DEPRECIATION OF THEIR PAY DURING THE LATE WAR WITH GREAT-BRITAIN, AS SETTLED AND ADJUSTED BY THE LEGIS-LATURE OF THE STATE OF RHODE-ISLAND AT THEIR OCTOBER SESSIONS, 1785.
Boston: From J. Bumstead's Printing-Office, Union-Street. 1798. pp. 13. 8vo.
Imprint blotted out with ink. AAS. LOC.

34456 RHODE ISLAND COLLEGE, now BROWN UNIVERSITY.
CATALOGUS EORUM QUI IN COLLEGIO RHODIÆ INSULÆ QUOD EST PROVIDENTIÆ, AB ANNO MDCCLXIX AD ANNUM MDCCXCVIII, ALICUJUS GRADÛS LAUREÂ DONATI SUNT.
Providentiae: Typis Carter et Wilkinson. [1798.] pp. 22. 8vo.
AAS. BU. JCB. RIHS.

34457 RHODE ISLAND COLLEGE, continued.
—— COMMENCEMENT OF RHODE-ISLAND COLLEGE, SEPTEMBER 5, 1798. ORDER OF THE EXERCISE. . . .
[Providence: Printed by Bennett Wheeler, 1798.] Broadside. 4to.

34458 —— EXHIBITION, IN COLLEGE CHAPEL, 22 AUGUST, BY PART OF JUNIOR AND SOPHOMORE CLASSES.
[Providence: Printed by Bennett Wheeler, 1798.] Broadside. BU.

34459 —— EXHIBITION, 5 DECEMBER, SENIOR CLASS.
Providence: Printed by Bennett Wheeler. [1798.] Broadside. BU.

34460 —— ILLUSTRISSIMO JABEZ BOWEN, ARMIGERO, COLLEGII RHOD. INSULÆ QUOD PROVIDENTIÆ EST CANCELLARIO; REVERENDO JONATHANI MAXCY, S.T.P. PRÆSIDI, [Four lines]; HÆCCE PHILOSOPHEMATA JUVENES IN ARTIBUS INITIATI. [Eighteen names.] HUMILLIME DEDICANT. [Three columns.] [Colophon:]
Habita in solennibus Academicis Providentiæ, in Rep. Ins. Rhod. et Prov. Plant. die quinto Septembris, A. D. M,DCC,XCVIII. Rerumpublicarum fœderatarum Americæ summæ potestatis XXIII. [Providentiæ: Typis Bennett Wheeler.] Broadside. fol. BU.

34461 RHODES, JOHN　　　　　　　　　　　　1755-
THE SURPRISING ADVENTURES AND SUFFERINGS OF JOHN RHODES, A SEAMAN OF WORKINGTON. CONTAINING AN ACCOUNT OF HIS CAPTIVITY AND CRUEL TREATMENT DURING EIGHT YEARS WITH THE INDIANS, AND FIVE YEARS IN DIFFERENT PRISONS AMONG THE SPANIARDS IN SOUTH AMERICA. BY A GENTLEMAN PERFECTLY ACQUAINTED WITH THE UNFORTUNATE SUFFERER.
New-York: Printed for R. Cotton, by G. Forman, No. 64 Water-Street. - - 1798. pp. 250. 12mo. JCB. LOC. NYPL.

34462 RICHARD, OLD FATHER, pseudonym.
POOR RICHARD REVIVED: OR; BARBER & SOUTHWICK'S ALMANACK: FOR THE YEAR OF OUR LORD, 1799: BEING THE THIRD AFTER BISSEXTILE OR LEAP-YEAR — AND THE TWENTY THIRD OF AMERICAN INDEPENDENCE, UNTIL THE FOURTH OF JULY.— CONTAINING — ALL THE NECESSARY CALCULATIONS, BESIDES A VARIETY OF USEFUL AND ENTERTAINING MATTER. CALCULATED FOR THE MERIDIAN OF ALBANY; N. LAT. 42 DEG. 45 MIN. FROM THE ENGLISH OBSERVATORY, 73 DEG. AND 8 MIN. WEST. BY OLD FATHER RICHARD, MATHEMAT.
Albany: Printed and sold by Barber and Southwick, at their Book-Store, two doors north of the City-Hall, in Court-Street; and at their Printing-Office, Sign of Faust's Statue, lower end of State-Street. Sold also by the Post-Riders from their Office. ☞ *Generous allowances to retailers.* [1798.] pp. (40). 8vo. AAS.

Contains, Courts, and Government of the State of New-York. An Act to lay and collect a direct tax within the United States. An extract from the Act to provide for the valuation of lands, etc.

34463 RICHARDSON, SAMUEL　　　　　　　　1689–1761
CLARISSA: OR THE HISTORY OF A YOUNG LADY. COMPREHENDING THE MOST IMPORTANT CONCERNS OF PRIVATE LIFE. ABRIDGED FROM THE WORKS OF SAMUEL RICHARDSON, ESQ. AUTHOR OF PAMELA, AND SIR CHARLES GRANDISON.
Printed at Suffield, by H. & O. Farnsworth, for Oliver D. & I. Cooke, Book-Sellers Hartford. MDCCXCVIII. pp. 138, (1). 12mo. AAS. LOC. NYPL.

34464 —— — THE HISTORY OF MISS CLARISSA HARLOWE.
Philadelphia: 1798. 12mo.

34465   RICHARDSON, SAMUEL, continued.

—— THE HISTORY OF SIR CHARLES GRANDISON, ABRIDGED FROM THE WORKS OF SAMUEL RICHARDSON, ESQ. AUTHOR OF PAMELA AND CLARISSA. FROM THE TENTH LONDON EDITION. [Ornament.]

Suffield: Printed by Havila & Oliver Farnsworth, for Oliver D. & I. Cooke, Book-Sellers—Hartford. MDCCXCVIII. pp. 143. 12mo.   AAS. JCB. LOC.

34466   —— — BOSTON, APRIL 2, 1798. PROPOSALS, BY CALEB P. WAYNE, FOR PUBLISHING BY SUBSCRIPTION, THE HISTORY OF SIR CHARLES GRANDISON.

[Boston: Printed by Caleb P. Wayne. 1798.] Broadside.   MHS.

34467   RICHMOND, EDWARD   1767–1842

A SERMON, PREACHED OCTOBER 11TH, 1797, AT THE ORDINATION OF THE REV. LEMUEL WADSWORTH, TO THE PASTORAL CARE OF THE CHURCH AND CHRISTIAN SOCIETY IN RABY. BY EDWARD RICHMOND, A.M. PASTOR OF THE CHURCH IN STOUGHTON.

Samuel Preston, Printer, Amherst, New-Hampshire. 1798. pp. 40. 8vo.

                           AAS. BA. JCB. LOC. MHS. NYPL.

The Charge, by the Rev. Mr. Chaplin, of Groton. The Right hand of fellowship, by the Rev. Mr. Bullard, of Pepperell. The town of Raby, New Hampshire, is now known as Brookline.

34468   RIGHTS OF MAN:— BY JOHN WINTER. VOL. IV. NUMBER 207. WEDNESDAY, JANUARY 3, [— VOL. V. NUMBER 258. WEDNESDAY, DECEMBER 26, 1798.]

Frederick-Town, (State of Maryland): Printed by John Winter, at his Office in Patrick-Street, near Mr. Samuel Duvall's . . . 1798. fol.

34469   RIGHTS OF MAN, OR THE KENTUCKY MERCURY. VOL. I. NO. 32. WEDNESDAY, JANUARY 3, [— NO. 33. WEDNESDAY, JANUARY 10, 1798.]

Paris: Printed by Darius Moffett. 1798. fol.

The above is the last number located.

34470   RILEY, GEORGE

BEAUTIES OF THE CREATION: OR, A NEW MORAL SYSTEM OF NATURAL HISTORY; DISPLAYED IN THE MOST SINGULAR, CURIOUS AND BEAUTIFUL QUADRUPEDS, BIRDS, INSECTS, TREES, SHRUBS & FLOWERS. DESIGNED TO INSPIRE YOUTH WITH HUMANITY TOWARDS THE BRUTE CREATION, AND BRING THEM EARLY ACQUAINTED WITH THE WONDERFUL WORKS OF THE DIVINE CREATOR. BY GEORGE RILEY. [Three lines from] BLACKMORE ON THE CREATION. THIRD AMERICAN EDITION.

Worcester: Printed by Isaiah Thomas, jun. Sold by him at his Bookstore, opposite the Gaol. September—1798. pp. xii, ix, (3), (13)–274, (2), frontispiece. 24mo.   AAS. JCB. LOC. NYPL.

34471   RIPLEY, EZRA   1751–1841

A SERMON, DELIVERED AT YORK, OCTOBER 10, 1798, AT THE ORDINATION OF THE REV. ROSEWELL MESSINGER TO THE PASTORAL CHARGE OF THE FIRST CHURCH, AS COLLEAGUE PASTOR WITH THE REV. ISAAC LYMAN. BY EZRA RIPLEY, A.M. PASTOR OF THE CHURCH OF CHRIST IN CONCORD, MASS. [Quotation.]

Portsmouth, New-Hampshire: Printed by Charles Peirce at the Oracle-Press. 1798. pp. 24. 8vo.   AAS. BA. HC. JCB. LOC. MHS.

34472   RIPLEY, HEZEKIAH   1743–1831

A SERMON, DELIVERED AT THE INSTALLATION OF THE REV. WILLIAM R. RIPLEY, IN THE PASTORAL OFFICE OVER THE CHURCH IN LEBANON-GOSHEN, NOV. 14, 1798. BY HEZEKIAH RIPLEY, A.M. PASTOR OF THE CHURCH IN GREENSFARMS. PUBLISHED AT THE REQUEST OF THE SOCIETY IN LEBANON-GOSHEN.

Norwich: Printed by Thomas Hubbard. [1798.] pp. 30. 8vo.   JCB.

34473 RISING SUN. VOL. V. NO. 224. SATURDAY, JANUARY 6, [— VOL. V. NO. 240. SATURDAY, APRIL 28 ? 1798.]

    Kingston, (Ulster County): Printed by William Copp and Samuel Freer. 1798. fol.

    Succeeded in May by the *Ulster County Gazette.*

34474 THE RISING SUN. [Motto.] VOL. III. NO. 22. WHOLE NO. 126. SATURDAY, JANUARY 6, [— NO. 46. WHOLE NO. 150. SATURDAY, JUNE 23, 1798.]

    [Printed and published] By Cornelius Sturtevant, jun. & Co. Keene, (New-hampshire). 1798. fol.

    The firm of Sturtevant & Co. was dissolved in March; and from April 7th, for the next three months, the Sun was published by Elijah Cooper, and then discontinued.

34475 ROBERTS, WILLIAM   1767–1849

    TOO HIGH A PITCH MAY BE GIVEN TO THE MIND IN EARLY LIFE. STORY OF EUGENIO AND AMELIA: OR, THE VICISSITUDES OF LIFE. EXTRACTED FROM THAT CELEBRATED WORK THE "LOOKER ON." BY THE REVEREND WILLIAM ROBERTS, A. M. F. R. S. FELLOW OF CORPUS CHRISTINI COLLEGE. OXFORD. . . . FIRST EDITION.

    Worcester: Printed by Isaiah Thomas, jun. September—1798. pp. 156. 12mo.   AAS. JCB. NYPL.

34476 ROBERTSON, WILLIAM   1721–1793

    THE HISTORY OF AMERICA. BY WILLIAM ROBERTSON, PRINCIPAL OF THE UNIVERSITY AT EDINBURGH, HISTORIOGRAPHER TO HIS MAJESTY FOR SCOTLAND, AND MEMBER OF THE ROYAL ACADEMY AT MADRID. IN TWO VOLUMES. VOL. I. – [II.] NEW EDITION — CORRECTED.

    New-York: Printed for Samuel Campbell, by Robert Wilson. M.DCC.-XCVIII. 2 vols. pp. 512; (2). (5)–511, (32). 8vo.   AAS. JCB.

34477 ROBISON, JOHN   1739–1805

    PROOFS OF A CONSPIRACY AGAINST ALL THE RELIGIONS AND GOVERNMENTS OF EUROPE, CARRIED ON IN THE SECRET MEETINGS OF FREE MASONS, ILLUMINATI, AND READING SOCIETIES. COLLECTED FROM GOOD AUTHORITIES, BY JOHN ROBISON, A. M. PROFESSOR OF NATURAL PHILOSOPHY, AND SECRETARY TO THE ROYAL SOCIETY OF EDINBURGH. NAM TUA RES AGITUR PARIES CUM PROXIMUS ARDET. THE THIRD EDITION. TO WHICH IS ADDED A POSTSCRIPT.

    Philadelphia: Printed for T. Dobson, No. 41, South Second Street, and W. Cobbet [sic], No. 25, North Second Street. 1798. pp. 204, [197]–391 [sic 403.] 8vo.   AAS. BA. HC. LCP. LOC. NYPL.

34478 —— — PROOFS OF A CONSPIRACY AGAINST ALL THE RELIGIONS AND GOVERNMENTS OF EUROPE, CARRIED ON IN THE SECRET MEETINGS OF FREE MASONS, ILLUMINATI, AND READING SOCIETIES. COLLECTED FROM GOOD AUTHORITIES. BY JOHN ROBISON, A. M. PROFESSOR OF NATURAL PHILOSOPHY, AND SECRETARY TO THE ROYAL SOCIETY OF EDINBURGH. [One line of Latin.] THE FOURTH EDITION. TO WHICH IS ADDED, A POSTSCRIPT.

    New-York: Printed by George Forman, No. 64, for Cornelius Davis, bookseller, No. 94, Water-Street. 1798. pp. 399. 8vo.   AAS. BA. BM. HC. JCB. LCP. LOC. NYPL.

34479 ROBSON, JOHN C.

    A SCRIPTURAL VIEW OF THE RISE OF THE HEATHEN, JEWISH AND CHRISTIAN MONARCHIES IN THE WORLD; WITH AN ACCOUNT OF THE DISSOLUTION OF THE PRESENT EUROPEAN SYSTEM, ACCORDING TO THE PROPHECIES OF ISAIAH, DANIEL AND JOHN, IN THE REVELATION AND OTHERS. [Six lines of Scripture texts.]

    New-York: Printed and sold by J. Buel, No. 74, William Street. 1798.

    59th New York District Copyright, issued to John C. Robson, as Proprietor, 27 March, 1798.

34480   ROCHE, Regina Maria Dalton   1764–1845
The Children of the Abbey. A tale. By Regina Maria Roche.
Philadelphia: 1798. 4 vols. in two.

34481   —— Clermont. By mrs. Roche.
Philadelphia: 1798.

34482   ROGERS, Ransford
The Morris-Town ghosts delineated, and patriotic Revolutionary songs.
Morris-Town: Printed by E. Cooper & Co. 1797.   NJHS.

34483   ROLAND DE LA PLATIERE, Manon Jeanne Phlipon   1754–1793
An Appeal to impartial posterity: by madame Roland, wife of the minister
of the Interior: or, a collection of tracts written by her during her
confinement in the prisons of the Abbey, and St. Pelagie, in Paris. In four
parts. Translated from the French original, published for the benefit
of her only daughter, deprived of the fortune of her parents by seques-
tration. First American edition — corrected. . . .
*New-York: Printed by Robert Wilson, for A[rondt] Van Hook, Proprietor
of the Reading-room.* 1798. Four parts in 2 vols. pp. (202); (164); (202); (235).
8vo.   JCB. LOC. NYPL.

34484   ROMAN CATHOLIC CHURCH.
A Short abridgment of christian doctrine. Newly revised for the use of
the Catholic Church in the United States of America. To which is added,
a Short daily exercise. Fourteenth edition.
Baltimore: Printed by Michael Duffy. 1798. pp. 51. 18mo.

34485   ROOT, Jesse   1736–1822
Reports of cases adjudged in the Superior Court and Supreme Court of
Errors, from July A. D. 1789 to June A. D. 1793; with a variety of cases
anterior to that period. Prefaced with observations upon the government and laws of Connecticut. To which is subjoined, sundry law points
adjudged, and rules of practice adopted in the Superior Court. By Jesse
Root, a judge of the Superior Court. Vol. I.
Hartford: Printed by Hudson and Goodwin. 1798. pp. (2), (2), 584, (2),
(38). (8), (4). 8vo.   AAS. BA. BM. HC.
Contains, a four-page list of Subscribers' names. A second volume was
printed in Hartford, in 1802.

34486   ROSS, James   1744–1827
A Plain, short, comprehensive, practical Latin grammar, comprising all the
rules and observations necessary to an accurate knowledge of the Latin
classics, with the signs of quantity affixed to certain syllables to shew
their right pronunciation. By James Ross, a. m. teacher of the Latin and
Greek languages, and rector of the Franklin Academy in Chambersburg.
[Seven lines of quotations.]
Chambersburg: Printed for the Author, by Robert Harper, MDCCXCVIII.
pp. viii, [158], (1). 12mo.   AAS. JCB.
213th Pennsylvania District Copyright, issued to James Ross, as Author,
19 June, 1798,

34487   ROWE, Elizabeth Singer   1674–1737
Devout exercises of the heart, in meditation, soliloquy, prayer, and praise.
By the late pious and ingenious mrs. Rowe. Revised and published, at her
request, by I. Watts, d.d.
*Printed at Northampton, by Andrew Wright, for Daniel Wright and Com-
pany.* MDCCXCVIII. pp. 158. 16mo.   FL. JCB.

34488   ROWE, ELIZABETH SINGER, continued.

—— — DEVOUT EXERCISES OF THE HEART, IN MEDITATION AND SOLILOQUY, PRAYER AND PRAISE. BY THE LATE PIOUS AND INGENIOUS MRS. ELIZABETH ROWE. ABRIDGED FOR THE USE OF THE METHODIST SOCIETY.

Philadelphia: Printed by Henry Tuckniss: Sold by John Dickins, No. 41, Market Street. 1798. [Price one-fourth of a dollar.] pp. 214, (6), (4). 32mo.

Contains, a four-page list of books for the use of the Methodist Societies.   AAS.

34489   ROWSON, SUSANNA HASWELL   1761–1824

THE LITTLE SAILOR BOY. A BALLAD. SUNG AT THE THEATRES AND OTHER PUBLIC PLACES IN PHILADELPHIA, BALTIMORE, NEW YORK, &c. BY MESSRS. J. DARLEY WILLIAMSON, MISS BROADHURST, MR. HODGKINSON AND MR. OLDMIXON. WRITTEN BY MRS. ROWSON. COMPOSED BY B. CARR. PRICE 25 CENTS.

Printed and sold at the Author's Musical Repository, Philadelphia. J. Carr's, Baltimore & J. Hewitt's, New-York. Entered according to law. [1798.] pp. 2. 4to.

                     AAS. BU. HC. HSP. JCB. LOC. NYPL.

201st Pennsylvania District Copyright, issued to Benjamin Carr, as Author and Proprietor, 22 January, 1798.

34490   —— REUBEN AND RACHEL; OR, TALES OF OLD TIMES. A NOVEL. BY MRS. ROWSON, AUTHOR OF CHARLOTTE, TRIALS OF THE HEART, FILLE DE CHAMBRE, &c. &c. [Thirteen lines of verse.] PUBLISHED ACCORDING TO ACT OF CONGRESS.

Boston: Printed by Manning & Loring, for David West, at Book-Store, No. 56, Cornhill, sold by him and by the Author, in Winter-Street; also by Ebenezer S. Thomas, Charleston, South-Carolina, and by Solomon Cotton & Co. Baltimore. 1798. 2 vols. in one. pp. iv, 364. 12mo.   AAS. BA. BU. HC. LOC. NYPL. WL. YC.

140th Massachusetts District Copyright, issued to David West, as Proprietor, 23 April, 1798.

34491   RUDDIMAN, THOMAS   1674–1757

THE RUDIMENTS OF THE LATIN TONGUE; OR, A PLAIN AND EASY INTRODUCTION TO LATIN GRAMMAR: WHEREIN THE PRINCIPLES OF THE LANGUAGE ARE METHODICALLY DIGESTED BOTH IN ENGLISH AND LATIN. WITH USEFUL NOTES AND OBSERVATIONS, EXPLAINING THE TERMS OF GRAMMAR, AND FURTHER IMPROVING ITS RULES. BY THOMAS RUDDIMAN, M.A. THE TWENTY-SECOND GENUINE EDITION. CAREFULLY CORRECTED AND IMPROVED.

Philadelphia: Printed for Robert Campbell & Co. By John Bioren. MDCCXCVIII. pp. ii, 130. nar. 12mo.   JCB. LOC.

34492   RULHIÈRE, CLAUDE CARLOMAN DE   1734–1791

A HISTORY, OR ANECDOTES OF THE REVOLUTION IN RUSSIA, IN THE YEAR 1762. TRANSLATED FROM THE FRENCH OF M. DE RULHIERE.

Boston: Printed by Manning & Loring, for J. Nancrede, No. 49, Marlbro'-street. 1798. pp. (195), (3), portrait of Catharine II. 24mo.   AAS. BM. JCB.

34493   RURAL FELICITY, OR HISTORY OF TOMMY AND SALLY. PRICE FOUR CENTS.

Boston: Printed and sold by John W. Folsom, No. 30, Union-Street. 1798. 32mo.

34494   THE RURAL [cut] MAGAZINE. [Motto.] VOLUME I. NUMBER 1. SATURDAY, FEBRUARY 17, [— NUMBER 46. SATURDAY, DECEMBER 29, 1798.]

Newark—Printed by John H. Williams, for the Proprietors. 1798. 4to.

                     JCB. LOC. NYHS.

Discontinued at the end of the first volume in February, 1799, for "the want of sufficient subscription, and literary assistance, two essentials to the support of all similar publications." Its motto was: Prodesse et delectare. And join both profit and delight in one.

34495   RUSH, BENJAMIN   1745–1813
ESSAYS, LITERARY, MORAL & PHILOSOPHICAL. BY BENJAMIN RUSH, M. D. AND PROFES-
SOR OF THE INSTITUTES OF MEDICINE AND CLINICAL PRACTICE IN THE UNIVERSITY
OF PENNSYLVANIA.

 *Philadelphia: Printed by Thomas & Samuel F. Bradford, No. 8, South Front
Street.* 1798. pp. (2), (2), (2), (2), 378. 8vo.

        AAS. BA. BM. HC. LOC. NL. NYHS. NYPL. SGO.

 198th Pennsylvania District Copyright, issued to Thomas and Samuel
F. Bradford, as Proprietors, 12 January, 1798.

34496   —— MEDICAL INQUIRIES AND OBSERVATIONS: CONTAINING AN ACCOUNT OF THE YEL-
LOW FEVER, AS IT APPEARED IN PHILADELPHIA IN 1797, AND OBSERVATIONS UPON
THE NATURE AND CURE OF THE GOUT AND HYDROPHOBIA. BY BENJAMIN RUSH, M.D.
PROFESSOR OF MEDICINE IN THE UNIVERSITY OF PENNSYLVANIA. VOLUME V.

 *Philadelphia: Printed by Budd and Bartram, for Thomas Dobson, at the
Stone House, No. 41, South Second Street.*—1798.—pp. xii, 236. 8vo.

 Forming Volume v. of his Works.   AAS. LOC. NYPL. SGO.

34497   —— A SYLLABUS OF A COURSE OF LECTURES ON THE INSTITUTES AND PRACTICE OF
MEDICINE, BY BENJAMIN RUSH, M. D. PROFESSOR OF THE INSTITUTE OF MEDICINE
AND OF CLINICAL PRACTICE IN THE UNIVERSITY OF PENNSYLVANIA.

 *Philadelphia: Printed by Thomas & Samuel F. Bradford, No. 8, South
Front-Street.* 1798. pp. 15. 12mo.   NYHS. SGO.

34498   RUSH, JACOB   1746–1820
A CHARGE DELIVERED BY THE HON. JUDGE RUSH TO THE GRAND JURY OF LUZERNE
COUNTY, PENNSYLVANIA, 30TH JUNE, 1798.

 Philadelphia: Printed by Andrew Brown? 1798. 12mo.

 Reprinted in Glasgow in 1798.

34499   RUSSEL, or RUSSELL, ROBERT
SEVEN SERMONS ON DIFFERENT IMPORTANT SUBJECTS; VIZ. I. OF THE UNPARDONABLE
SIN AGAINST THE HOLY GHOST; OR THE SIN UNTO DEATH. II. THE SAINT'S DUTY
AND EXERCISE; IN TWO PARTS. BEING AN EXHORTATION TO AND DIRECTIONS FOR
PRAYER. III. THE ACCEPTED TIME, AND DAY OF SALVATION. IV. THE END OF TIME,
AND BEGINNING OF ETERNITY. V. JOSHUA'S RESOLUTION TO SERVE THE LORD. VI.
THE WAY TO HEAVEN MADE PLAIN. VII. THE FUTURE STATE OF MAN; OR, A TREA-
TISE OF THE RESURRECTION. BY ROBERT RUSSEL, AT WARDHURST, IN SUSSEX.

 New-Haven: Printed by George Bunce. 1798. pp. 144. 12mo. AAS.

34500   RUSSELL, JOHN MILLER   1768–1840
A POEM, ON THE FOURTH OF JULY, 1798. BEING THE ANNIVERSARY OF THE INDEPEND-
ENCE OF THE UNITED STATES OF AMERICA. TO WHICH IS ADDED, A SONG, TO THE
TUNE OF "GOD SAVE THE KING." BY J. M. RUSSELL, A. M.

 Boston: Printed by Manning & Loring. 1798. pp. 16. 8vo. AAS. BA. BU.

34501   RUSSELL, JOSEPH   1775–1861
A SERMON PREACHED AT PRINCETON, (MASSACHUSETTS) APRIL 8TH, 1798. AND OC-
CASIONED BY THE DEATH OF MADAM REBECCA GILL, CONSORT OF HIS HONOR MOSES
GILL, ESQ. LIEUTENANT-GOVERNOR OF THE COMMONWEALTH OF MASSACHUSETTS.
WHO DIED MARCH 9TH, 1798. ÆTAT 70. BY JOSEPH RUSSELL, A. M. PASTOR OF
THE CHURCH IN PRINCETON.

 Boston: Printed by Rhoades & Laughton, Court-Street. 1798. pp. [26.] 8vo.
        AAS. JCB. LOC. MHS. NYPL.

34502   RUSSEL'S ECHO: OR, THE NORTH STAR. VOL. I. No. 1. THURSDAY, FEBRUARY 22, [— No. 40. FRIDAY, DECEMBER 28, 1798.]

         Published by Elijah Russel, Fryeburg. District of Muine, Massachusetts. 1798. fol.   HC.

         Established, as a weekly, and published, somewhat irregularly, by Elijah Russel, or Russell, to the issue for January 11, 1799, when it was suspended for want of paper, and never revived. With the issue for November 28, 1798, after a lapse in publication of two months, the title was shortened to *Russel's Echo.*

34503   RUSSELL'S GAZETTE. COMMERCIAL AND POLITICAL. VOL. IV. No. 27. THURSDAY, JUNE 7, [— VOL. V. No. 33. MONDAY, DECEMBER 31, 1798.]

         Published on Mondays and Thursdays, by John Russell, at his Office, in Quaker-Lane, Boston. 1798. fol.   AAS. BA. MHS.

         In continuation of *The Boston Price-Current and Marine Intelligencer.* With the issue for June 7th, the paper was enlarged to the folio size of the other Boston newspapers. With the issue for December 17th, the title becomes *J. Russell's Gazette. Commercial and political.*

34504   THE RUTLAND HERALD: A REGISTER OF THE TIMES. [Motto.] VOL. IV. No. 1. MONDAY, JANUARY 1, [— No. 53. MONDAY, DECEMBER 31, 1798.]

         Printed at Rutland, (Vermont) by Josiah Fay, for S. Williams & Co. a few rods south of the State House. 1798. fol.   AAS. VtSL.

         In September, the sub-title was dropped from the heading, and John Walker, jun. took the place of Josiah Fay, as Printer.

34505   S., H.

     THE HISTORY OF THE DAVENPORT FAMILY: IN WHICH IS DISPLAYED A STRIKING CONTRAST BETWEEN HAUGHTY INDOLENCE AND HEALTHFUL ACTIVITY, IN THE CHARACTERS OF THE YOUNG DAVENPORTS, AND THEIR COUSINS, SOPHIA AND AMELIA EASY. INTERSPERSED WITH MORAL REFLECTIONS. BY H. S. TWO VOLUMES IN ONE. EMBELLISHED WITH [eleven] ENGRAVINGS,

         Boston: Printed and sold by Spotswood and Etheridge. 1798. pp. 144, frontispiece. 24mo.   AAS. LOC.

34506   S., R.

     JACHIN AND BOAZ; OR, AN AUTHENTIC KEY TO THE DOOR OF FREE-MASONRY, BOTH ANCIENT AND MODERN. CALCULATED NOT ONLY FOR THE INSTRUCTION OF EVERY NEW MADE MASON; BUT ALSO FOR THE INFORMATION OF ALL WHO INTEND TO BECOME BRETHREN. CONTAINING, I. A CIRCUMSTANTIAL ACCOUNT OF ALL THE PROCEEDINGS IN MAKING A MASON, WITH THE SEVERAL OBLIGATIONS OF AN ENTERED APPRENTICE, FELLOW-CRAFT, AND MASTER; THE PRAYERS, AND ALSO THE SIGN, GRIP, AND PASS-WORD OF EACH DEGREE, WITH THE CEREMONY OF THE MOP AND PAIL. II. THE MANNER OF OPENING A LODGE AND SETTING THE CRAFT TO WORK. III. THE ENTERED APPRENTICE, FELLOW-CRAFT, AND MASTER'S LECTURES, VERBATIM, AS DELIVERED IN ALL LODGES; WITH THE SONG AT THE CONCLUSION OF EACH PART. IV. THE ORIGIN OF MASONRY; DESCRIPTION OF SOLOMON'S TEMPLE; HISTORY OF THE MURDER OF THE GRAND MASTER HIRAM BY THE THREE FELLOW-CRAFTS; THEIR DISCOVERY AND PUNISHMENT; THE BURIAL OF HIRAM BY KING SOLOMON'S ORDER; WITH THE FIVE POINTS OF FELLOWSHIP, &C. V. THE CEREMONY OF THE INSTALMENT OF THE MASTERS OF DIFFERENT LODGES ON ST. JOHN'S DAY. — DESCRIPTION OF THE REGALIA, &C. VI. CEREMONIES USED AT THE FUNERAL OF A MASON. VII. A SAFE AND EASY METHOD PROPOSED, BY WHICH A MAN MAY OBTAIN ADMITTANCE INTO ANY LODGE, WITHOUT PASSING THROUGH THE FORM REQUIRED, AND THEREBY SAVE A GUINEA OR TWO IN HIS POCKET. VIII. ANTHEMS, ODES, SONGS, TOASTS, &C. ILLUSTRATED WITH A BEAUTIFUL FRONTISPIECE OF THE REGALIA, JEWELS, AND

AUCTION
VALUES

S., R., continued.

EMBLEMATICAL ORNAMENTS BELONGING TO MASONRY. AND AN ACCURATE PLAN OF
THE DRAWING ON THE FLOOR OF A LODGE, INTERSPERSED WITH A VARIETY OF NOTES
AND REMARKS, NECESSARY TO EXPLAIN AND RENDER THE WHOLE CLEAR TO THE
MEANEST CAPACITY. BY A GENTLEMAN BELONGING TO THE JERUSALEM LODGE; A
FREQUENT VISITOR AT THE QUEEN'S ARMS, ST. PAUL'S CHURCH-YARD; THE HORN,
IN FLEET-STREET; CROWN AND ANCHOR, STRAND; AND THE SALUTATION, NEW-
GATE-STREET. TRY ME — PROVE ME. A NEW EDITION, GREATLY ENLARGED AND
IMPROVED. TO WHICH ARE ADDED, A SELECT COLLECTION OF SONGS, AND A LIST OF
TOASTS AND SENTIMENTS, PROPER FOR THE SOCIETY OF FREE MASONS.

> *Boston : Printed by J. Bumstead, for E. Larkin.* 1798. pp. 64, frontispiece.
> 8vo.
> NYPL.

34507   SAGE, SYLVESTER   1765–1841
A SERMON, DELIVERED AT THE INSTALLATION OF REV. JESSE TOWNSEND, A. M. TO THE
PASTORAL CARE OF CHRIST'S CHURCH IN DURHAM, STATE OF NEW-YORK, JUNE 20,
1798. BY SYLVESTER SAGE, A. M. PASTOR OF CHRIST'S CHURCH, IN WESTMINSTER,
STATE OF VERMONT.

> *Catskill: Printed by M. Croswell.* [1798.] pp. 24. 8vo.   NYPL.

The Charge, by Rev. Beriah Hotchkin, of Newry.

34508   SAINT PIERRE, JACQUES HENRI BERNARDIN DE   1737–1814
STUDIES OF NATURE. BY JAMES HENRY BERNARDIN DE ST. PIERRE. MISERIS SUC-
CURRERE DISCO. TRANSLATED BY HENRY HUNTER, D. D. MINISTER OF THE SCOTS
CHURCH, LONDON WALL. FIRST AMERICAN EDITION. IN THREE VOLUMES. VOL. II.

> *Worcester: Printed [by Thomas, Son & Thomas] for J. Nancrede, Marlbor-*
> *ough Street, Boston.* 1798. pp. 496. 8vo.   AAS. BM. HC. NYPL.

34509   SALEM. MASSACHUSETTS.
RULES AND REGULATIONS TO BE OBSERVED BY THE COMPANIES BELONGING TO THE
SEVERAL FIRE ENGINES IN THE TOWN OF SALEM: AGREEABLY TO AN ACT OF THE
GENERAL COURT OF THIS COMMONWEALTH, PASSED ON THE SEVENTH OF FEBRU-
ARY, 1786.

> [*Salem: Printed by Thomas C. Cushing, May 7, 1798.*] Broadside.   EI.

34510   THE SALEM GAZETTE. VOL. XII. NUMB. 669. TUESDAY, JANUARY 2, [— NUMB. 772.
FRIDAY, DECEMBER 29, 1798.]

> *Published on Tuesdays and Fridays, by Thomas C. Cushing, Essex-Street, be-*
> *tween Washington and Market-Streets, Salem, Massachusetts.* 1798. fol.
> AAS. EI. HC. LOC.

34511   —— TO THE PATRONS OF THE SALEM GAZETTE, THE CARRIER PRESENTS THE COM-
PLIMENTS OF THE SEASON AND THE FOLLOWING ADDRESS. O THOU, IN AIRY GARRET
PERCH'D WHERE BAILIFF'S PRYING EYE N'ER SEARCH'D. . . . BY WILLIAM BIG-
LOW, A. M.

> [*Salem: Printed by Thomas C. Cushing, January 1, 1798.*] Broadside.   EI.

34512   SANDERS, DANIEL CLARKE   1768–1850
A SERMON, ON OCCASION OF THE DEATH OF MR. MARTIN HARMON, A. B. WHO DIED IN
THE CITY OF VERGENNES, JULY 25, 1798. ÆT. 24. PUBLISHED BY DESIRE OF THE
HEARERS. BY DANIEL CLARKE SANDERS, A. M. MINISTER OF THE CONGREGATION
IN VERGENNES.

> *Vergennes: Printed by G. and R. Waite.* 1798. pp. 22. 8vo.   NYPL.

34513   SANDERS, Daniel Clarke, continued.

—— A Sermon, preached before his excellency Isaac Tichenor, esq. governor; his honor Paul Brigham, esq., lieutenant governor; the honorable Council and House of Representatives of the State of Vermont, October 11, 1798. In the city of Vergennes, on occasion of general election. By Daniel Clarke Sanders, a. m. minister of the congregation in Vergennes. Printed by order of the legislative assembly.

     Vergennes: Printed by G. and R. Waite. 1798. pp. 22. 8vo.   aas. ba. bm. loc.

34514   SANGER, Zedekiah   1748–1820

A Sermon, preached Feb. 28, 1798, at the ordination of the rev. Samuel Watson, to the pastoral care of the church and united Congregational society in Barrington. By Zedekiah Sanger, a. m,

     Warren, (Rhode-Island): Printed by Nathaniel Phillips. M,DCC,XCVIII. pp. 30. 8vo.   aas. hc. jcb. rihs.

34515   THE SARATOGA Register: or, Farmer's Journal. Vol. I. No. 1. Wednesday, June 13, [— No. 29. Wednesday, December 26, 1798.]

     Ballston Spa: Published by Increase & William Child. 1798. fol.

Established, as a weekly, by Increase, and William Child. The firm was dissolved by the retirement of Increase Child in April, 1800. It probably was succeeded by the *Republican Telescope* in March, 1801.

34516   SCHAFFER, Francis C.

A Pocket companion for the German flute and violin, containing a selection of airs, songs, duets, and trios, from the works of Haydn, Pleyel, Devienne, Hoofmaster [sic] Doctor Arnold, Shield, Hook, Dibden, Linley, Carter, etc. together with correct and easy instructions for the flute. By F. C. Schaffer, professor of music, teacher of the flute, clarinet, violin, etc.

     Boston: 1798.

34517   SCHENECTADY. New York.

Charter of the city of Schenectady, enacted by the people of the State of New York in Senate and Assembly convened at Albany the 26th of March, 1798.

     Albany: Printed by C. R. & G. Webster. [1798.] pp. 34, (2). 12mo.

34518   SCOTT, Job   1751–1793

Journal of the life, travels and gospel labours of that faithful servant and minister of Christ, Job Scott. Fourth edition.

     New-York: Printed and sold by Isaac Collins, No. 189, Pearl-street. 1798. pp. xii, 360. 12mo.   loc.

34519   SCOTT, Joseph

The New and universal gazetteer; or, modern geographical dictionary.

     Philadelphia: Printed by Francis and Robert Bailey. 1798.

First published in numbers. To be comprised in thirty-two numbers. "July 3, 1798. Just published No. 1 of Scott's New Universal Gazetteer (embellished with a handsome map of Africa)."

34520 SCOTT, JOSEPH WARREN 1778–1871
AN ORATION, DELIVERED ON THE TWENTY-SECOND ANNIVERSARY OF AMERICAN IN-
DEPENDENCE, JULY 4, 1798, IN THE PRESBYTERIAN CHURCH AT NEW-BRUNSWICK.
BY JOSEPH WARREN SCOTT, A. B. PUBLISHED BY REQUEST.
New Brunswick: Printed by A. Blauvelt.—1798. pp. (16). 8vo. AAS.

34521 SCOTT, WILLIAM
LESSONS IN ELOCUTION: OR A SELECTION OF PIECES IN PROSE AND VERSE, FOR THE
IMPROVEMENT OF YOUTH IN READING AND SPEAKING. BY WILLIAM SCOTT. THE
SEVENTH AMERICAN, FROM THE FIFTH BRITISH EDITION. TO WHICH ARE PREFIXED,
ELEMENTS OF GESTURE . . . [By John Walker], AND RULES FOR EXPRESSING,
WITH PROPRIETY, THE VARIOUS PASSIONS AND EMOTIONS OF THE MIND. [By James
Burgh.
Philadelphia: Printed by William Young. 1798. pp. 436, 4 plates. 12mo.
AAS. NYPL.

34522 THE SCRIPTURE WARNING AND SIGNS OF THE LAST TIMES: TOUCHED UPON IN A
SHORT DISCOURSE, FROM EZEKIEL, 7TH CHAP. 12TH VERSE. "THE TIME IS COME,
THE DAY DRAWETH NEAR, LET NOT THE BUYER REJOICE, NOR THE SELLER MOURN,
FOR WRATH IS UPON ALL THE MULTITUDE THEREOF." BY A PLAIN SINGULAR MAN,
WHO PROFESSES TO BELIEVE THE PROPHECIES AND DOCTRINES OF THE BIBLE.
Portsmouth: Printed by Charles Peirce. 1798.

34523 SEABURY, SAMUEL 1729–1796
DISCOURSES ON SEVERAL IMPORTANT SUBJECTS. BY THE LATE RIGHT REV. SAMUEL
SEABURY, D. D. BISHOP OF THE PROTESTANT EPISCOPAL CHURCH IN THE STATES
OF CONNECTICUT AND RHODE-ISLAND. PUBLISHED FROM MANUSCRIPTS PREPARED
BY THE AUTHOR FOR THE PRESS.
New-York: Printed and sold by T. & J. Swords, No. 99 Pearl-Street. 1798.
pp. vii, 279. 8vo. AAS. BA. BPL. JCB. NYPL. YC.

The first discourse, in six parts, entitled, Observations on the history of
Pharaoh, occupies over one hundred pages. Proposals for printing this
volume by subscription were made in November, 1794. A second edition
was published in Hudson, in 1815.

34524 SEIXAS, GERSHOM MENDEZ 1745–1816
A DISCOURSE, DELIVERED IN THE SYNAGOGUE IN NEW-YORK, ON THE NINTH OF MAY,
1798, OBSERVED AS A DAY OF HUMILIATION, &C. &C. CONFORMABLY TO A RECOM-
MENDATION OF THE PRESIDENT OF THE UNITED STATES OF AMERICA. BY REV. G.
SEIXAS. [Two lines from] PSALM 133.
New-York: Printed by William A. Davis & Co. for Naphtali Judah, 1798.
pp. 32. 8vo. AAS. CLA. LOC, NYHS.

34525 SELECT STORIES, OR MISCELLANEOUS EPITOME OF ENTERTAINMENT, SELECTED FROM
THE NEWEST PUBLICATIONS OF MERIT. [Two lines from] CREECH.
*New York: Printed by John Harrisson, and sold at his Book Store, No, 3 Peck
Slip.* 1798. pp. (2), (2), 252, frontispiece. 12mo. AAS.

Contains, The horrors of a monastery. — The heiress of Devon. — The
generous lady. Translated from the French. — Jacquot. — The Cornish
curate. — The history of Pauline. — The deserted infant.— Drusilla, or
the fate of Harold. — Youthful imprudence. By Miss St. Leger. —
History of Maria Feodorovna. — Albert and Emma.

34526 SENSIBILITY. A DRAMA.
Boston: 1798. 24mo.

34527 A SERIES OF LETTERS ON COURTSHIP AND MARRIAGE. TO WHICH ARE ADDED, WITH-ERSPOON'S LETTERS ON MARRIAGE. — MRS. PIOZZI'S LETTER TO A GENTLEMAN NEWLY MARRIED. — SWIFT'S LETTER TO A NEWLY MARRIED LADY, &C. &C. *Springfield: Printed by F. Stebbins. For C. Davis, Bookseller, New-York.* [1798.] pp. (2), 195. 8vo.   LOC.

Contains.—Reflections on courtship and marriage, by Benjamin Frank-lin.—Letters on marriage. Ascribed to the Reverend John Witherspoon. — A letter to a very young lady on her marriage. By Dean Swift. — Letter to a young gentleman on his marriage. By Mrs. Piozzi.—Letter from a young gentleman to his sister, on her removing from the country to live in the city. From the Guardian, No. 113. — Letter from Dr. Franklin, to John Alleyne, esq. on early marriage.—Marriage; a vision. By Dr. Cotton.—An epistle to a lady. By Mr. Nugent.

34528 SEVER, THOMAS, JUNIOR
AN ODE, ON THE SUDDEN DEATH OF MR. DANIEL HOLT, LATE OF TOWNSEND, WHO WAS INSTANT KILLED BY THE UNEXPECTED FALL OF A TREE, AUGUST 31ST, 1798. ADDRESSED TO THE PUBLIC IN GENERAL, AND HIS FRIENDS IN PARTICULAR. BY THOMAS SEVER, JUN. [Thirty four-line verses.]
[Leominster? Printed by Charles & John Prentiss, 1798.] Broadside. BU. MHS.

34529 SEWALL, DANIEL   1755–1842
AN ASTRONOMICAL DIARY, OR ALMANAC, FOR THE YEAR OF CHRISTIAN ÆRA, 1799; BE-ING THIRD AFTER LEAP YEAR. CALCULATED FOR THE MERIDIAN OF PORTSMOUTH, NEW-HAMPSHIRE, LAT. 43 DEG. 5 MIN. NORTH. AND DESIGNED CHIEFLY FOR THE STATE OF NEW-HAMPSHIRE, AND DISTRICT OF MAINE. CONTAINING EVERY THING NECESSARY FOR AN ALMANAC, WITH A VARIETY OF USEFUL AND ENTERTAINING MATTER. BY DANIEL SEWALL.
Portsmouth, New-Hampshire: Printed by Charles Peirce, No. 5, Daniel-street; sold by him wholesale and retail; also, by the Author at his Office in York, and by most of the shopkeepers in town and country. [1798.] pp. (24). 12mo. AAS. NHHS.

Contains, Astronomy. A poem.

34530 —— — BICKERSTAFF'S ASTRONOMICAL DIARY, OR, ALMANACK FOR THE YEAR OF OUR LORD, 1799: BEING THIRD AFTER LEAP-YEAR. CALCULATED FOR THE MERIDIAN OF PORTSMOUTH, NEW-HAMPSHIRE, LAT. 43 DEG. 5 MIN. NORTH, BUT WILL SERVE FOR ANY OF THE NEIGHBOURING STATES. CONTAINING EVERY THING NECESSARY FOR AN ALMANACK, WITH A VARIETY OF ENTERTAINING AND USEFUL MATTERS. [Six lines of verse.]
Portsmouth, New-Hampshire: Printed by Charles Peirce, No. 5, Daniel-Street, sold by him wholesale and retail; and by most of the shopkeepers in town and coun-try. [1798.] pp. (24). 12mo.

The same as Daniel Sewall's Almanac, with a change of title-page only.

34531 —— — WEATHERWISE'S ASTRONOMICAL DIARY. OR, ALMANACK, FOR THE YEAR OF OUR LORD, 1799: BEING THIRD AFTER LEAP-YEAR. CALCULATED FOR THE MERIDIAN OF PORTSMOUTH, NEW-HAMPSHIRE, LAT. 43 DEG. 5 MIN. NORTH, BUT WILL SERVE FOR ANY OF THE NEIGHBOURING STATES. CONTAINING EVERY THING NECESSARY FOR AN ALMANACK, WITH A VARIETY OF ENTERTAINING AND USEFUL MATTERS. [Six lines of verse.]
Portsmouth, New-Hampshire: Printed by Charles Peirce, No. 5, Daniel-Street, sold by him wholesale and retail; and by most of the shopkeepers in town and coun-try. pp. (24). 12mo.

The same as Daniel Sewall's Almanac, with a change of title-page only.

34532   SEWALL, Jonathan Mitchell.   1748–1808
A Versification of President Washington's excellent Farewell-Address, to the citizens of the United States. By a Gentleman of Portsmouth, N. H. Published according to Act of Congress.

> *Portsmouth, New-Hampshire: Printed and sold by Charles Peirce, at the Columbian Bookstore, No. 5 Daniel-Street. 1798.* pp. (54.) 4to.

Reprinted in Tarrytown, in 1925.   AAS. BA. BU. HC. JCB. LOC. NYPL.

34533   SEWARD, Anna   1747–1809
Monody on major André. By miss Seward. Fourth American edition.

> *Boston: Printed for and sold by W. Spotswood, and C. P. Wayne. 1798.* pp. 22.
> 12mo.   AAS. BU. HC. JCB. LCP. LOC. NYPL.

Also included with "Amelia" and Florian's "Galatea," this year.

34534   SHAFTSBURY. Vermont. Baptist Association.
Minutes of the Shaftsbury Association, at their annual convention, held in Stephentown, 1798.

> *[Without place, or printer. 1798.]*

34535   SHARP, Joshua
Poor Robin's Almanac, for the year 1799. Being the third after bissextile, or leap-year. Containing, (besides the astronomical calculations, by Joshua Sharp), The Stamp Act, Hail Columbia, &c. [U. S. arms.]

> *Philadelphia: Printed and sold by John M'Culloch, No. 1, North Third-Street.*
> [1798.] pp. (23.) 8vo.   AAS.

Contains, Courts of Law, United States, Pennsylvania, New-Jersey, Delaware, Maryland, Virginia.

34536   SHAW, Josiah Crocker   –1847
An Oration, delivered July 4th, 1798, at the request of the inhabitants of the town of Little Compton; in celebration of the anniversary of American independence. By Josiah C. Shaw, m. a. [One line of Latin from] Virgil.

> *Newport: Printed by H. & O. Farnsworth. M,DCC,XCVIII.* pp. [22.] 8vo.
>   AAS. RIHS.

34537   SHELDON, William
Cursory remarks on the laws concerning usury. And on some late proceedings, in cases of usury. By W. Sheldon, of Norwich, Connecticut. [Two lines from] Job xxi : 3.

> *Norwich: Printed and sold by John Trumbull. May, 1798.* pp.–63.– 8vo.   AAS.

34538   SHEPARD, Samuel   1739–1815
The Principle of universal salvation examined and tried by the law and testimony, and found to be a direct contradiction to the doctrine of Christ and his inspired witnesses. In an epistle to a friend. By Samuel Shepard, preacher of the Gospel.

> *Printed at Exeter, by Henry Ranlet, for the Author. M,DCC,XCVIII.* pp. 36.
> 12mo.   JCB. NYPL.

34539   SHIELD, William   1748–1829
Johnny and Mary. A Scots song.

> *New York. Printed & sold at J. Hewitt's Musical Repository, No. 131 William Street. Sold also by B. Carr, Philadelphia & J. Carr, Baltimore.* [1798.]
> Broadside. 4to.   LOC.

SHIELD, WILLIAM, continued.

34540   —— THE MORNING IS UP. A FAVORITE HUNTING SONG. BY WILLIAM SHIELD.
New York: Published by J. Hewitt, No. 131 *William St.* 1798.

34541   —— WHAT ARE THE BOASTED JOYS OF LOVE. CAVATINA, BY WILLIAM SHIELD.
Philadelphia: Published at Carr's Musical Repository. 1798.

34542   SHOEMAKER, ABRAHAM
THE NEW-JERSEY AND NEW-YORK ALMANAC FOR THE YEAR OF OUR LORD 1799.
BEING THE THIRD AFTER LEAP-YEAR AND THE TWENTY-FOURTH OF AMERICAN
INDEPENDENCE AFTER THE FOURTH OF JULY. CONTAINING . . . CALCULATED
FOR THE LATITUDE AND MERIDIAN OF NEW-JERSEY. BY ABRAHAM SHOEMAKER.
    Newark: Printed by John H. Williams, for Pennington and Dodge. [1798.]
pp. (36). 12mo.   HEH.

34543   —— THE NEW-JERSEY AND PENNSYLVANIA ALMANAC, FOR THE YEAR OF OUR LORD,
1799. BEING THE THIRD AFTER BISSEXTILE, OR LEAP-YEAR, AND THE TWENTY-
FOURTH OF AMERICAN INDEPENDENCE, AFTER THE FOURTH OF JULY. [Sixteen
lines.] CALCULATED FOR THE LATITUDE AND MERIDIAN OF PHILADELPHIA. BY
ABRAHAM SHOEMAKER.
    Trenton: Printed and sold, wholesale and retail, by Matthias Day. [1798.]
pp. (36). 12mo.   AAS. LOC. NJSL. NYHS.

34544   —— POULSON'S TOWN AND COUNTRY ALMANAC, FOR THE YEAR OF OUR LORD, 1799;
BEING THE THIRD AFTER LEAP - YEAR. THE NAMES AND CHARACTERS OF THE
TWELVE CONSTELLATIONS, THE TIME OF THE SUN'S ENTRANCE INTO EACH OF THEM,
AND THE MANNER IN WHICH THEY ARE SAID TO GOVERN THE HUMAN BODY. [Cut.
Three lines.]
    —*Philadelphia:—Printed and sold by Zachariah Poulson, junior, No.* 106,
*Chesnut-street, between Third and Fourth-streets, nearly opposite to the Bank of
North America.* [1798.] pp. (48). 12mo.   AAS. LOC. MHS. NYPL.

    Contains, Contemplations on the commencement of the new year. On
the importance of real Christians to a nation. Of Sir William Jones.
On the reunion of friends in a future state of existence. Of man. De-
scriptions of Aurora Borealis, the Water-spout, the Ignis Fatuus, of
Mount Ætna. Singularities of John Howard. Advice to farmers. Anecdotes. Poems. Tables. Courts.

34545   —— — THE TOWN AND COUNTRY ALMANAC, FOR THE YEAR OF OUR LORD 1799.
    *Philadelphia: Printed by Zachariah Poulson, jun. for and sold by Isaac
Pearson, No.* 139 *Market-Street.* [1798.] pp. 44. 12mo.

34546   —— THE UNITED STATES ALMANAC, FOR THE YEAR OF OUR LORD 1799: BEING THE
SECOND [*sic*] AFTER LEAP-YEAR, AND THE XXIIID OF AMERICAN INDEPENDENCE,'TILL
4TH JULY: CONTAINING EVERY THING THAT IS USEFUL OR NECESSARY IN AN AL-
MANAC. ALSO, A VARIETY OF ENTERTAINING MATTER IN PROSE AND VERSE. BY
ABRAHAM SHOEMAKER.
    Elizabeth-Town: Printed by Shepard Kollock, for Naphtali Judah, No. 47,
Water-Street, near Coenties Slip, New-York. [1798.] pp. (36). 12mo. AAS. NJHS.

34547   —— — THE UNITED STATES ALMANAC, FOR THE YEAR OF OUR LORD 1799: BEING
THE SECOND [*sic*] AFTER LEAP-YEAR, AND THE XXIIID OF AMERICAN INDEPENDENCE,
'TILL 4TH JULY: CONTAINING EVERY THING THAT IS USEFUL OR NECESSARY IN AN
ALMANAC. ALSO, A VARIETY OF ENTERTAINING MATTER IN PROSE AND VERSE. BY
ABRAHAM SHOEMAKER.
    Elizabeth-Town: Printed by Shepard Kollock, for David Dunham. [1798.]
pp. (36). 12mo.   LOC.

34548 SHURTLEFF, JAMES
A CONCISE REVIEW OF THE SPIRIT WHICH SEEMED TO GOVERN IN THE TIME OF THE
LATE AMERICAN WAR, COMPARED WITH THE SPIRIT WHICH NOW PREVAILS; WITH
THE SPEECH OF THE GODDESS OF FREEDOM, WHO IS REPRESENTED AS MAKING HER
APPEARANCE UPON THE ALARMING OCCASION. [Five lines from] SOLOMON. ECC. V.
VIII.
Augusta: Printed by Peter Edes. 1798. 12mo.   AAS.

34549 SIMMONS, AMELIA
AMERICAN COOKERY, OR THE ART OF DRESSING VIANDS, FISH, POULTRY, AND VEGE-
TABLES, AND THE BEST MODES OF MAKING PASTES, PUFFS, PIES, TARTS, PUDDINGS,
CUSTARDS AND PRESERVES, AND ALL KINDS OF CAKES, FROM THE IMPERIAL PLUMB
TO PLAIN CAKE. ADAPTED TO THIS COUNTRY, AND ALL GRADES OF LIFE. BY AMELIA
SIMMONS, AN AMERICAN ORPHAN. PUBLISHED ACCORDING TO ACT OF CONGRESS.
Hartford: Printed [by Hudson & Goodwin] for Simeon Butler, Northampton.
1798. pp. 48. 8vo.   AAS. FL.

"Just republished, and for sale, by Simeon Butler, at Northampton,
October 31, 1798. (Price 33 cents)."

34550 —— — AMERICAN COOKERY: OR, THE ART OF DRESSING VIANDS, FISH, POULTRY, AND
VEGETABLES, AND THE BEST MODES OF MAKING PASTES, PUFFS, PIES, TARTS, PUD-
DINGS, CUSTARDS AND PRESERVES, AND ALL KINDS OF CAKES, FROM THE IMPERIAL
PLUMB TO PLAIN CAKE. ADAPTED TO THIS COUNTRY, AND ALL GRADES OF LIFE. BY
AMELIA SIMMONS, AN AMERICAN ORPHAN. THE SECOND EDITION.
New-York: Printed by Thomas Greenleaf, No. 54, Wall-Street. 1798.

"This day, May 1, 1798, published. The second edition of American
cookery: or, the art of dressing, etc.," as above.

34551 A SKETCH OF THE HISTORY OF THE WAR IN EUROPE, FROM ITS COMMENCEMENT TO
THE TREATY OF PEACE BETWEEN FRANCE AND AUSTRIA. BY A SOCIETY OF LIT-
ERARY MEN IN ENGLAND. TO WHICH IS ADDED, MEMOIRS OF GEN. BUONAPARTE,
BY PAULTIER, MEMBER OF THE COUNCIL OF ANCIENTS. [Seven lines from] YOUNG'S
NIGHT THOUGHTS.
New-York: Printed by T. Kirk, No. 112, Chatham-Street. 1798. pp. 260.
12mo.   AAS. LOC.

34552 A SMILE FROM THE YOUTH THAT I LOVE. WRITTEN BY THE AUTHOR OF THE MAR-
VELLOUS PLEASANT LOVE STORY, AND SET TO MUSIC BY THOMAS WRIGHT.
Philadelphia: Printed & sold by G. Willig, No. 185 Market Street. [1798.]
pp. (2).   LOC.

34553 SMITH, ELIHU HUBBARD   1771–1798
ALCUIN; A DIALOGUE.
New-York: Printed by T. & J. Swords, No. 99 Pearl-Street. [March] 1798.
pp. 77. 16mo.   LOC. NYHS. NYPL. YC.

61st New York District Copyright, issued to Elihu Hubbard Smith, as
Proprietor, 1 May, 1798. Attributed, also, to Charles Brockden Brown,
with some probability that it was a joint production.

34554 —— A DISCOURSE, DELIVERED APRIL 11, 1798, AT THE REQUEST OF AND BEFORE
THE NEW-YORK SOCIETY FOR PROMOTING THE MANUMISSION OF SLAVES, AND PRO-
TESTING SUCH OF THEM AS HAVE BEEN OR MAY BE LIBERATED. BY E. H. SMITH, A
MEMBER OF THE SOCIETY.
New-York: Printed by T. & J. Swords, No. 99 Pearl-Street. 1798. pp. 30.
8vo.   AAS. LOC. NYHS. NYPL. RIHS. YC.

34555   SMITH, EUNICE
SOME MOTIVES TO ENGAGE THOSE WHO HAVE PROFESSED THE NAME OF THE LORD
JESUS, TO DEPART FROM ALL INIQUITY, AND STUDY A CLOSE WALK WITH GOD. TO
WHICH ARE AFFIXED, A NUMBER OF SONGS, PRESENTED TO THOSE WHO LOVE THE
LORD. BY EUNICE SMITH.
Printed at Greenfield, (Mass.) for the Proprietor. 1798. pp. 24. 12mo.   NYPL.

34556   SMITH, JOHN COTTON   1765–1845
AN ORATION, PRONOUNCED AT SHARON, ON THE ANNIVERSARY OF AMERICAN INDE-
PENDENCE, 4TH OF JULY, 1798. BY JOHN C. SMITH. PUBLISHED AT THE REQUEST
OF THE COMMITTEE. [U. S. arms.]
Printed at Litchfield by T. Collier. [1798.] pp. 23. 8vo.   AAS. BM. NYPL. YC.

34557   SMITH, PRESERVED   1759–1843
A MASONICK DISCOURSE; DELIVERED AT GREENFIELD, MASSACHUSETTS. BEFORE THE
OFFICERS AND BRETHREN OF THE REPUBLICAN LODGE, OF FREE AND ACCEPTED
MASONS, IN THAT TOWN; JOINED BY THE OFFICERS AND BRETHREN OF HARMONY
LODGE, FROM NORTHFIELD; ON THE FESTIVAL OF ST. JOHN THE BAPTIST; JUNE,
26TH, A. L. 5798. BY THE REV. BROTHER PRESERVED SMITH. . . . PUBLISHED
BY THE UNITED REQUEST OF THE BRETHREN.
Printed at Greenfield, by Francis Barker. 1798. pp. 11. 4to.   AAS.

34558   SMITH, SAMUEL HARRISON   1772–1845
REMARKS ON EDUCATION: ILLUSTRATING THE CLOSE CONNECTION BETWEEN VIRTUE
AND WISDOM. TO WHICH IS ANNEXED, A SYSTEM OF LIBERAL EDUCATION. WHICH,
HAVING RECEIVED THE PREMIUM AWARDED BY THE AMERICAN PHILOSOPHICAL
SOCIETY, DECEMBER 15TH, 1797, IS NOW PUBLISHED BY THEIR ORDER. BY SAMUEL
HARRISON SMITH, A. M. MEMBER OF THE AM. PHIL. SOCIETY.
Philadelphia: Printed for John Ormrod. M,DCC,XCVIII. pp. 92. 8vo.
Copyright secured according to law.   AAS. JCB. LOC. NYPL.

34559   SMITH, THOMAS PETERS
Half-title: ANNUAL ORATION DELIVERED BEFORE THE CHEMICAL SOCIETY OF PHILA-
DELPHIA, APRIL 11TH, 1798.
Title: A SKETCH OF THE REVOLUTIONS IN CHEMISTRY. BY THOMAS P. SMITH.
Philadelphia: Printed by Samuel H. Smith, No. 118, *Chesnut Street.* M,DCC,-
XCVIII. pp. 40. 8vo.   AAS. BA. BM. HSP. JCB. LOC. NYHS. NYPL. SGO.

34560   SMITH, VENTURE   1729 ? – 1805
A NARRATIVE OF THE LIFE AND ADVENTURES OF VENTURE, A NATIVE OF AFRICA; BUT
RESIDENT ABOVE SIXTY YEARS IN THE UNITED STATES OF AMERICA. RELATED BY
HIMSELF. [AND ATTESTED BY RESPECTABLE WITNESSES. VENTURE IS A NEGRO
REMARKABLE FOR SIZE, STRENGTH, INDUSTRY, FIDELITY, AND FRUGALITY, AND WELL
KNOWN IN THE STATE OF RHODE-ISLAND, ON LONG ISLAND, AND IN STONINGTON,
EAST HADDAM, AND SEVERAL OTHER PARTS OF THIS STATE. DESCENDED FROM A
ROYAL RACE, BENEVOLENT AND BRAVE; ON AFRIC'S SAVAGE PLAINS A PRINCE, IN
THIS FREE LAND A SLAVE.]
New London: Printed by C. Holt, at the Bee Office. 1798. pp. 32. 16mo.

The bracketed part of the title is as advertised. The Narrative is said to
have been written by Elisha Niles, a schoolmaster, of Chatham. Venture
was so named by his first master, who bought him as a venture; and he
assumed the name of his last owner, from whom he purchased his freedom. Reprinted, by a descendant of Venture, in 1835; and in a reprint
of the latter, in Middletown, Connecticut, in 1897.

34561   SMITH, WILLIAM   1754–1821
A DISCOURSE, DELIVERED ON THE 18TH OF OCTOBER, 1797. [BEING THE FESTIVAL OF ST. LUKE.] IN TRINITY CHURCH, IN NEW-HAVEN, BEFORE THE ECCLESIASTICAL CONVENTION, OF THE STATE OF CONNECTICUT; ASSEMBLED THERE TO WITNESS THE CONSECRATING OF THE RIGHT REV. ABRAHAM JARVIS, D.D. TO THE EPISCOPAL CHAIR OF SAID STATE; AND TO RECOGNIZE HIM AS THEIR ECCLESIASTICAL SUPERIOR. BY THE REV. WILLIAM SMITH, D.D. RECTOR OF ST. PAUL'S CHURCH, NORWALK.

     Newfield: Printed by Lazarus Beach, for the Convention. [1798.] pp. [20.] 8vo.   BA. NYPL. UTS. YC.

34562   —— DOCTOR SMITH'S ANSWER TO MR. BLATCHFORD'S LETTER. [Seven lines of quotations.]

     Printed at Newfield, by Lazarus Beach. 1798. pp. [144.] 8vo.
     AAS. BPL. HEH. NYPL. UTS. YC.

34563   SMOLLETT, TOBIAS GEORGE   1721–1771
THE HISTORY AND ADVENTURES OF PEREGRINE PICKLE, WITH THE MANY DROLL TRICKS THAT PEREGRINE PLAYED HIS MOTHER AND OTHERS; ALSO OF HIS TWO COMPANIONS, HATCHWAY AND PIPES. A NEW AMERICAN EDITION.

     Leominster, Massachusetts, Printed by Charles & John Prentiss, for Robert B. & Aaron Thomas, Sterling. June, 1798. pp. 104. 12mo.   AAS.

     Contains, eight pages of Selections.

34564   SMOLLETT, TOBIAS GEORGE, and others.
THE HISTORY OF ENGLAND, FROM THE REVOLUTION, TO THE END OF THE AMERICAN WAR, AND PEACE OF VERSAILLES IN 1783. IN SIX VOLUMES. DESIGNED AS A CONTINUATION OF MR. HUME'S HISTORY. BY A SOCIETY OF GENTLEMEN. VOL. V. A NEW EDITION, WITH CORRECTIONS AND IMPROVEMENTS.

     Philadelphia: Printed for Robert Campbell & Co. by Richard Folwell. M.DCC.XCVIII. pp. 511, portrait of Franklin. 8vo.   JCB. NYPL.

34565   —— —— THE HISTORY OF ENGLAND, FROM THE REVOLUTION, TO THE END OF THE AMERICAN WAR, AND PEACE OF VERSAILLES IN 1783. IN SIX VOLUMES. DESIGNED AS A CONTINUATION OF MR. HUME'S HISTORY. BY A SOCIETY OF GENTLEMEN. VOL. VI. A NEW EDITION, WITH CORRECTIONS AND IMPROVEMENTS.

     Philadelphia: Printed for Robert Campbell & Co. by John Biorsn. M.DCC.-XCVIII. pp. (2), 452, 59, (6), (1), portrait. 8vo.   AAS. JCB. LCF. NYPL.

     Contains a six page list of Subscribers' names.

34566   SNOW, WILLIAM
THE FALL OF MAN, AND RECOVERY BY CHRIST. BY WILLIAM SNOW. [Between heavy lines.]

     West-Springfield: Printed for the Author. 1798. pp. 12. 12mo.   NYHS.

34567   SNOWDEN, NATHANIEL R.
A FREE MASON SERMON PREACHED AT HARRISBURGH BY THE REV. MR. NATHANIEL R. SNOWDEN, BEFORE THE TWO LODGES, HARRISBURGH AND CARLISLE.

     Carlisle: Printed by George Kline. [February 28, 1798.]

34568   SNYDER, G. W.
THE AGE OF REASON UNREASONABLE; OR, THE FOLLY OF REJECTING REVEALED RELIGION. IN A SERIES OF LETTERS TO A FRIEND. BY G. W. SNYDER, A.M.

     Philadelphia: Published by William Cobbett, opposite Christ Church, May, 1798. pp. 213. 8vo.   JCB. LOC.

     214th Pennsylvania District Copyright, issued to William Cobbett, as Proprietor, 25 June, 1798.

34569   SOME DOUBTS RESPECTING THE DEATH, RESURRECTION, AND ASCENSION OF JESUS CHRIST. FROM THE AUTHOR'S MANUSCRIPT. TO WHICH ARE ADDED, REASONS FOR SCEPTICISM IN REVEALED RELIGION, BY JOHN HOLLIS: THE HISTORY OF THE "MAN AFTER GOD'S OWN HEART!" AND DIANA OF THE EPHESIANS.

New-York: Printed for John Fellows. 1797. pp. 6, 42. 12mo.   LOC.

34570   SOME MISCELLANEOUS OBSERVATIONS ON MASONRY. BY A BROTHER.

Boston: Printed and sold at Ede's Office, Kilby-Street—1798.—pp. [15,] 8vo.   AAS.

34571   A SONG BOOK. CONTAINING UPWARDS OF FORTY OF THE MOST MODERN AND ELEGANT SONGS NOW IN VOGUE.

Amherst, Newhampshire: Printed by Samuel Preston. 1798.

34572   SORLIE, SHOLTO
A TREATISE ON THE NEW SWORD EXERCISE, FOR CAVALRY. BY SHOLTO SORLIE, OF THE SEVENTH (OR QUEEN'S OWN) REGIMENT OF LIGHT DRAGOONS. "WITHOUT DISCIPLINE, SOLDIERS ARE BUT AN ARMED MOB." MARSHAL SAXE.

Philadelphia: Re-published by William Cobbett. 1798. pp. 24. 8vo.   HC.

34573   SOUTH CAROLINA. STATE.
ACTS AND RESOLUTIONS OF THE GENERAL ASSEMBLY, OF THE STATE OF SOUTH-CAROLINA. PASSED IN DECEMBER, MDCCXCIV.

Charleston: Printed by Young & Faust, Printers to the State, Franklin's Head, No. 43, Broad-Street. 1795. pp. 80, (3). fol.   BM. HC. NYBA.

34574   —— — ACTS AND RESOLUTIONS OF THE GENERAL ASSEMBLY, OF THE STATE OF SOUTH-CAROLINA. PASSED IN DECEMBER, MDCCXCIV.

Columbia: Printed by Young & Faust, Printers to the State, corner of Richardson and Plain Streets. 1795. pp. 80, (3). fol.   LOC. MSL.

34575   —— ACTS AND RESOLUTIONS OF THE GENERAL ASSEMBLY, OF THE STATE OF SOUTH-CAROLINA, FROM DECEMBER, 1794 [1795] TO DECEMBER, 1797, INCLUSIVE.

Printed in Charleston. [Colophon:] *Printed by Daniel Faust & Co. Printers to the State.* [1798.] pp. 155; 172, (10). fol.   HEH. MSL.

The original sheets of the Acts of 1795, 1796 and 1797, with a new title-page, and index. "Directions to binders, &c. Cancel the title and indexes for 1795, 1796, and 1797, take out the Resolutions and put them together, according to their folios, and then prefix the title, with this index, to the beginning of the laws."

34576   —— ACTS AND RESOLUTIONS OF THE GENERAL ASSEMBLY, OF THE STATE OF SOUTH-CAROLINA. PASSED IN DECEMBER, 1797. [Arms.]

Charleston: Printed by W. P. Young, for Daniel Faust and Company, Printers to the State, Columbia. M.DCC.XCVIII. pp. (2), (103)–155, (2); (133)–172, (2), (1). fol.   LOC.

34577   SOUTH CAROLINA SOCIETY FOR PROMOTING AGRICULTURE.
ADDRESS AND RULES OF THE SOUTH-CAROLINA SOCIETY FOR PROMOTING AND IMPROVING AGRICULTURE, AND OTHER RURAL CONCERNS.

Charleston: Printed by Freneau & Paine. 1798. pp. 8. 8vo.   LOC.

34578   THE SOUTH-CAROLINA & GEORGIA ALMANAC, FOR THE YEAR OF OUR LORD 1799: BEING THE THIRD AFTER BISSEXTILE, OR LEAP-YEAR, AND ('TILL THE 4TH OF JULY) THE TWENTY-THIRD OF AMERICAN INDEPENDENCE. [Fourteen lines.]

Charleston: Printed by Freneau & Paine, No. 47, Bay. [1798.] pp. (48). 12mo.   LOC. NYHS.

34579   SOUTH-CAROLINA [cut] State-Gazette, and Timothy's Daily Advertiser. Vol. lvii. No. 5714. Monday, January 1, [— Vol. lvii. No. 6026. Monday, December 31, 1798.]
> *Charleston: Printed by Benjamin Franklin Timothy.* 1798. fol.

34580   THE SOUTH-CAROLINA State Gazette, and General Advertiser. Friday, January 5, [— Friday, December 28, 1798.]
> *Columbia, South-Carolina. Published by Young & Faust.* 1798. fol.

Before April 27th, the imprint was changed to Daniel Faust & Company.

34581   SOUTH-CAROLINA Weekly Museum; and complete magazine of entertainment and intelligence. [Vignette cut of] Geo. Washington, esq. Vol. ii. No. 52. Saturday, January 6, [— Vol. iii. No. 26. Whole no. 78. Saturday, July 7, 1798.]
> *Charleston: (South-Carolina). Printed by Thomas B. Bowen, No. 32, Church-Street, near the City Theatre.* 1798. pp. 30, — ; 826, vi. 4to.   NYHS.

No further evidence of publication is known.

34582   SOUTHERN Centinel, and Gazette of the State. Vol. v. Numb. 239. Thursday, January 4, [— Numb. 293. Thursday, December 27, 1798.]
> *Augusta: Printed by Alexander M'Millan, Printer to the State.* 1798. fol.

34583   SOUTHEY, Robert   1774–1843
Joan of Arc, an epic poem, by Robert Southey. [One line of Greek.]
> *Boston: Printed by Manning & Loring, for J. Nancrede, No. 49, Marlbro'-Street.* 1798. pp. 254. 12mo.   AAS.

At the foot of page 254 is an announcement that the publisher proposes to publish a volume of Southey's Poems, just received. Page 69 is misnumbered 66.

34584   —— — Joan of Arc, an epic poem, by Robert Southey. [One line of Greek.]
> *Boston: Printed by Manning & Loring, for J. Nancrede, No. 49, Marlbro'-Street.* 1798. pp. 264. 12mo.   LOC.

This variety contains on pages 255-264, a Catalogue of books, published or for sale by Joseph Nancrede.

34585   —— — Joan of Arc, an epic poem, by Robert Southey. [One line of Greek.]
> *Boston: Printed by Manning & Loring, for J. Nancrede, No. 49, Marlbro'-Street.* 1798. pp. 270. 12mo.   AAS. BA. JCB. LCP. MHS.

In this variety, pages 253-270, are misnumbered 153-170; and the space at the foot of page 254 is blank; with a list of subscribers on pages 255-258; a review of Southey's Poems, on pages 258-268; and a Catalogue of books for sale by J. Nancrede, on pages 264-270.

34586   —— — Joan of Arc, an epic poem, by Robert Southey. [One line of Greek.]
> *Boston: Printed by Manning & Loring, for J. Nancrede, No. 49, Marlbro'-Street.* 1798. pp. 270. 12mo.   HEH.

In this variety, pages 255-270, are misnumbered 155-170—253-254 being correctly numbered, and the space at the foot of page 254 is blank, but the proposal to publish Southey's Poems is on page 258. The list of Subscribers, reviews of Poems, and Catalogue of books, are as given in the various previous issues.

AUCTION
VALUES

34587   SPARHAWK, THOMAS STEARNS   1769–1807
AN ORATION, DELIVERED AT BUCKSTON, IN THE COUNTY OF HANCOCK, BEFORE CAPT. CURTIS'S, AND CAPT. HANCOCK'S COMPANIES OF MILITIA, AND A NUMBER OF OTHER CITIZENS, JULY 4TH, A. D. 1798. BEING THE TWENTY-SECOND ANNIVERSARY OF AMERICAN INDEPENDENCE. BY THOMAS S. SPARHAWK, A.M.

     Boston: Printed by Manning & Loring. 1798. pp. 20. 8vo.   AAS. YC.

34588   THE SPECTATOR. VOL. I. NUMBER 27. WEDNESDAY, JANUARY 3, [— VOL. II. NUMBER 132. SATURDAY, DECEMBER 29, 1798.]

     New-York, No. 40, Pine-Street: Published (Wednesdays and Saturdays) by George F. Hopkins, Printers of the Laws of the United States for the district of New-York. . . . 1798. fol.   AAS. BA. BPL. LOC. MHS. NYHS. NYPL. WHS. YC.

34589   SPOONER'S VERMONT JOURNAL. VOLUME XV. NUMBER 754. WEDNESDAY, JANUARY 3, [— VOLUME XVI. NUMBER 805. TUESDAY, DECEMBER 25, 1798.]

     [Windsor:] Printed and published by Alden Spooner, on the west side of the Main Street. 1798. fol.   AAS.

34590   SPRING, SAMUEL   1746–1819
A THANKSGIVING SERMON, PREACHED NOVEMBER 29, 1798. BY THE REV SAMUEL SPRING, A.M. PASTOR OF THE NORTH CONGREGATIONAL SOCIETY IN NEWBURYPORT. PUBLISHED BY DESIRE.

     Newburyport: Printed by Angier March, for the Subscribers. M.DCC.-XCVIII. pp. 26. 8vo.   AAS. BA. BM. CLA. JCB. LOC. MHS. NYHS. NYPL. YC.

34591   SPRINGER'S WEEKLY ORACLE. VOL. II. NO. 64. SATURDAY, JANUARY 6, [—VOL. III. NO. 115. MONDAY, DECEMBER 31, 1798.]

     New-London: Printed and published by James Springer, at his Printing-Office, Beach-Street. 1798. fol.

In continuation of his *Weekly Oracle.* On June 9th, the Printing-Office was removed "to the dwelling-house and store lately occupied by Dr. Pelouze, opposite the market," and the day of publication changed from Saturday to Monday, beginning June 30th.

34592   SQUIBB, ROBERT
THE GARDENER'S CALENDER IMPROVED.

     Augusta: Printed by John E. Smith. 1798.

Proposals for printing a new edition of Squibb's Gardener's Calender improved, to be put to press as early as possible, were made May 3, 1798.

34593   STAFFORD, CORNELIUS WILLIAM
THE PHILADELPHIA DIRECTORY, FOR 1798: CONTAINING THE NAMES, OCCUPATIONS, AND PLACES OF ABODE OF THE CITIZENS, ARRANGED IN ALPHABETICAL ORDER: ALSO A REGISTER OF THE EXECUTIVE, LEGISLATIVE, AND JUDICIAL MAGISTRATES OF THE UNITED STATES — THE CONSTITUTION OF THE UNITED STATES — OFFICERS OF THE COMMONWEALTH OF PENNSYLVANIA — AND THE MAGISTRATES OF THE CITY: WITH AN ACCURATE TABLE OF THE DUTIES ON GOODS, WARES, AND MERCHANDIZE; TOGETHER WITH A GENERAL ABSTRACT FROM THE REVENUE LAWS, RELATIVE TO THE DUTY OF MASTERS OF VESSELS — OF THE OWNERS OR CONSIGNEES OF GOODS — OF OFFICERS OF THE CUSTOMS — OF PAYMENT OF DUTIES, &C. — AND THE FORM OF ENTRY AT THE CUSTOM-HOUSE ON THE IMPORTATION OF GOODS: TO ALL WHICH ARE ADDED, AN ACCOUNT OF THE POST-OFFICE ESTABLISHMENT—THE BANKS—TABLES OF MONIES — SOME REMARKS ON THE YELLOW FEVER, &C. — WITH AN ALPHABETICAL LIST OF THE STREETS, LANES AND ALLEYS. BY CORNELIUS WILLIAM STAFFORD.

     Printed for the Editor, by William W. Woodward, No. 17, Chesnut Street. 1798. pp. [160]; [77], (2). 8vo.   AAS. HC. LCP. LOC. YC.

34594   STAFFORD, JOHN NATHAN, JUNIOR
     AN ALMANACK, FOR THE YEAR 1799. BEING THE THIRD AFTER LEAP-YEAR. BY
     JOHN NATHAN STAFFORD, JUN. [Six lines of verse. U. S. arms.]
       Printed at Litchfield, by T. Collier, and sold by the thousand, gross, dozen or
     single. [1798.] pp. [24.] 12mo.   AAS. LHS. NYPL.

34595   STANHOPE, PHILIP DORMER, 4th earl of CHESTERFIELD   1694–1773
     Half-title: PRINCIPLES OF POLITENESS. BY THE LATE LORD CHESTERFIELD. TO-
     GETHER WITH A FATHER'S LEGACY TO HIS DAUGHTERS. BY THE LATE DR. GREGORY.
     Title: PRINCIPLES OF POLITENESS AND OF KNOWING THE WORLD: BY THE LATE
     LORD CHESTERFIELD. WITH ADDITIONS, BY THE REV. DR. JOHN TRUSLER. CON-
     TAINING EVERY INSTRUCTION NECESSARY TO COMPLETE THE GENTLEMAN AND MAN
     OF FASHION, TO TEACH HIM A KNOWLEDGE OF LIFE, AND MAKE HIM WELL RECEIVED
     IN ALL COMPANIES. FOR THE IMPROVEMENT OF YOUTH: YET NOT BENEATH THE
     ATTENTION OF ANY. SECOND WORCESTER EDITION.
       Printed at Worcester: by Isaiah Thomas, jun. for Ephraim Goodale, Book-
     binder, Mendon. August—1798. pp. (2), 198. 12mo.   AAS. BA. HC.
       Second heading: A FATHER'S LEGACY TO HIS DAUGHTERS. BY THE LATE DR.
     GREGORY. pp. (129) – 198.

34596   THE STARRY CALCULATOR; BEING AN ALMANAC FOR THE YEAR OF OUR LORD, 1799.
     ☞ INSTRUCTIVE AND ENTERTAINING. SUN, MOON, AND STARS, I SCAN FROM POLE
     TO POLE, OBSERVE THEIR MOTIONS; TELL HOW SEASONS ROLL.
       Chambersburg, Printed by Robert Harper. [1798.] pp. (38). 12mo.   AAS.

34597   THE STATE GAZETTE & NEW-JERSEY ADVERTISER. INDEPENDENCE 22D YEAR.
     FEDERAL GOVERNMENT 9TH YEAR. NO. 18 OF VOL. VI. WHOLE NO. 278. TUESDAY,
     JANUARY 2, [— NO. 17 OF VOL. VII. WHOLE NO. 329. TUESDAY, DECEMBER 25,
     1798.]
       Printed by Matthias Day, Trenton. 1798. fol.   AAS.
      An "Extra" for October 3d, is devoted to an Address of the Mayor of
     Trenton, and Answer by Charles C. Pinckney. In November, "Printer to
     the State" was added to the imprint.

34598   STATE GAZETTE OF NORTH-CAROLINA. VOL. XIII. NUMB. 624. THURSDAY, JANUARY
     4, [— VOL. XIII. NUMBER 674. WEDNESDAY EVENING, DECEMBER 26, 1798.]
       Edenton: Printed by James Wills. 1798. fol.

34599   STAUGHTON, WILLIAM   1770–1829
     MISSIONARY-ENCOURAGEMENT: A DISCOURSE, DELIVERED ON WEDNESDAY EVENING,
     THE 16TH OF MAY, 1798, BEFORE THE PHILADELPHIA MISSIONARY SOCIETY AND
     THE CONGREGATION OF THE BAPTIST MEETING HOUSE, PHILADELPHIA. BY THE REV.
     WILLIAM STAUGHTON, PRINCIPAL OF BORDENTON ACADEMY. [Six lines of verse.]
       Philadelphia: Printed by Stephen C. Ustick, 1798. pp. 44. 8vo. AAS. JCB.

34600   STEARNS, CHARLES   1753–1826
     DRAMATIC DIALOGUES FOR THE USE OF SCHOOLS. BY CHARLES STEARNS, A. M. PASTOR
     OF THE CHURCH AND PRECEPTOR OF THE LIBERAL SCHOOL, IN LINCOLN. . . .
     PUBLISHED ACCORDING TO ACT OF CONGRESS.
       Leominster, Massachusetts, Printed by John Prentiss, & Co. for the Author.
     1798. pp. 540. 12mo.   AAS. BM. BU. HC. HEH. LCP. LOC. YC.
      134th Massachusetts District Copyright, issued to Charles Stearns, as
     Author, 11 November, 1797.

STEARNS, Charles, continued.

34601 —— Principles of religion and morality. In three parts. i. Of the evidences of religion. ii. Principles of religion. iii. Principles of morality, with four lessons on the cardinal virtues. The whole in short lessons, in the form of dialogues; adapted to schools, and private instruction in families. By Charles Stearns, a.m. pastor of the church and preceptor of the liberal school in Lincoln. Published according to Act of Congress.

Leominster, Massachusetts, Printed by Charles & John Prentiss, for the Author. 1798. pp. 79. 16mo.　　　　　　　　　AAS.

153d Massachusetts District Copyright, issued to Charles Stearns, as Author, 17 October, 1798.

34602 **STEARNS**, Samuel　　　　　　　　　　　　　1747–1819

Sir, Your being a member of the hon. the General Assembly of this State and our taking into our serious consideration, the great and important object of promoting the increase of medical knowledge in this country, must be our apology for troubling you with this letter. [Three columns. Proposing that the General Assembly of Rhode-Island, authorize a Medical Lottery, of thirty thousand dollars, for printing, and giving, gratis, to every physician, surgeon, apothecary, and others, in the State, a copy of Dr. Stearns's American Dispensatory, and the Columbian Practice of physic and system of surgery, in two large volumes in folio.] That a Petition upon the subject, will be presented to the Assembly; and as you are a member of the same; we trust you will not be backward in encouraging a scheme, which tends to promote your own felicity, as well as the health and happiness of mankind in general. We wish your health and prosperity; and have the honor to be, sir, your most obedient humble servants. [Space for signatures.]

Providence: Printed by Carter and Wilkinson? 1798.] Broadside. fol.
　　　　　　　　　　　　　　　　　AAS. JCB. RIHS.

34603 **STEPHENS**, Joseph

The Temple rent in twain and reared up in three days. . . . By Joseph Stephens.

Trenton. Printed by Matthias Day. 1797. pp. 34, (1). 8vo.

34604 **STEWART'S** Kentucky Herald. Vol. iii. No. 151. Tuesday, January 2, [—Vol. iv. No. 201. Tuesday, December 25, 1798.]

Lexington: Printed by James H. Stewart, . . . 1798. fol.

34605 **STONE**, Eliab　　　　　　　　　　　　　　1737–1822

A Sermon, preached in Cohasset, Jan. 10, 1798, at the ordination of the rev. mr. Jacob Flint. By Eliab Stone. a.m. pastor of a church in Reading. [Ornament.]

Boston: Printed by Thomas Adams, Court-Street. 1798. pp. [23.] 8vo.

The Charge, given by the Rev. Gad Hitchcock, D. D.　　　AAS. BA. JCB. LOC.

34606 **STONE**, John Hurford　　　　　　　　　　　1763–1818

Copies of original letters recently written by persons in Paris to dr. [Joseph] Priestley, in America. Taken on board of a neutral vessel. [Five lines of verse from] Pope. [Edited by William Cobbett.]

Philadelphia. Printed. from the second London edition, by James Humphreys, and sold by him, opposite the Bank of the United States in Third-street. pp. (21), (3). 8vo.　　　　　　　　　　AAS. JCB. LOC. NYHS.

The first Letter signed J. H. Stone. The writer of the second is not given.

34607   STONINGTON. Connecticut. Baptist Association.
Minutes of the Stonington Association. 1798.
     [*New London?* 1798.]

34608   STORACE, Stephen   1763–1796
The Willow. Song by Storace.
     New York: Published by J. Hewitt, No. 131 *William Street.* 1798.

34609   STORY, Isaac   1749–1816
A Sermon, preached August the 15th, 1798, at Hamilton, at the ordination
of the rev. Daniel Story, to the pastoral care of the church in Marietta,
and its vicinity, in the Territory of the United States, north-west of the
River Ohio. By his brother, Isaac Story, pastor of the second Congregational church in Marblehead.
     Printed by Thomas C. Cushing, Essex-Street, Salem. 1798. pp. [43.] 8vo.
                               AAS. BA. EI. JCB. LOC. NYES. NYPL. PU.

The Charge, by the Rev. Doctor Cutler, of Hamilton. The Right hand
of fellowship, by the Rev. Benjamin Wadsworth, of Danvers. Pages 34-
36, are principally devoted to the Antiquities of Marietta.

34610   STRONG, Cyprian   1743–1811
The Christian system the only source of true peace. A sermon, preached at
the installation of the rev. Elijah Gridley, to the pastoral office, in the
church, in Granby, Massachusetts. May 31, 1797. By Cyprian Strong, a.m.
pastor of the first church in Chatham. . . .
     Hartford: Printed by Hudson & Goodwin. M,DCC,XCVIII. pp.26. 8vo. JCB.

34611   STRONG, Jonathan   1761–1814
A Sermon, delivered at the ordination of the rev. Levi White, to the pas-
toral care of the church in Sandersfield [*sic* Sandisfield]; June 28th, 1798.
By Jonathan Strong, a.m. pastor of the church in Randolph. [Printers mark.]
     Hartford: Printed by Hudson & Goodwin. 1798. pp. 31. 8vo.
                                  AAS. BM. JCB. LOC. UTS.

34612   STRONG, Nathan   1748–1816
Political instruction from the prophecies of God's word—a sermon, preached
on the State thanksgiving, Nov. 29, 1798. By Nathan Strong, pastor of
the north Presbyterian church in Hartford, Connecticut. Published
according to Act of Congress, and by desire of the hearers.
     Hartford: Printed by Hudson and Goodwin. 1798. pp. 30. 8vo.
                  AAS. BA. BM. CHS. CLA. LOC. NYHS. NYPL. YC.

34613   —— A Sermon, preached at the installation of the rev. David Huntington,
a. m. to the pastoral charge of the second Congregational church in Middletown, on the 8th day of November, A. D. 1797, By Nathan Strong,
pastor of the north Presbyterian church in Hartford.
     Middletown: Printed by Tertius Dunning. 1798. pp. 24. 8vo.   AAS.

34614   —— A Sermon, preached on the State fast, April 6th, 1798. Published at
the request of the hearers. By Nathan Strong, pastor of the north
Presbyterian church in Hartford. [Printers mark.]
     Hartford: Printed by Hudson & Goodwin. 1798. pp. 20. 8vo.
                 AAS. CHS. CLA. JCB. LOC. MHS. NYPL. UTS. YC.

34615　STRONG, Nathan, continued.
—— Sermons, on various subjects, doctrinal, experimental and practical. By Nathan Strong, pastor of the north Presbyterian church in Hartford, Connecticut. Vol. I.

Hartford: Printed by Hudson & Goodwin. 1798. [Published and sold by Oliver D. & I. Cooke, Book-Sellers and Stationers, Hartford: According to Act of Congress.] pp. 396. 8vo.　　　　AAS. BA. BM. LOC. NYPL. UTS. YC.

The second volume was published in 1800.

34616　STRONG, Nehemiah　　　　　　　　　　　　1729–1807
An Astronomical diary, calendar, or Almanack, for the year of our Lord, 1799: and from the creation of the world, 5748, and till July 4th, the 23d of American independence. Being the third after bissextile or leap-year, containing, all things necessary for such a composition. Calculated for the meridian and horizon of Hartford, lat. 41 deg. 56 min. north; longit. 72 deg. 56 min. west. But may serve indifferently for all the towns in Connecticut. and adjacent States. By Nehemiah Strong, late professor of mathematicks, and natural philosophy of Yale College.

Hartford: Printed by Elisha Babcock. [For sale by gross, dozen or single by Henry Devier, ten rods north of the Court-House.] [1798.] pp. (24). 12mo.
　　　　　　　　　　　　　　　　　　　AAS. CHS. LOC. YC.

34617　—— Sheet Almanac for the year 1799.
Hartford: Printed by Elisha Babcock, 1798. Broadside.

"To which is added, Duties on stamped vellum, parchment and paper,—times of holding court, &c."

34618　—— An Astronomical diary, calendar, or Almanack, for the year of our Lord 1799. And from the creation of the world 5748. And till July 4th the 23d of American independence. Being the third after bissextile or leap-year. Containing all things necessary to such a composition. Calculated for the meridian and horizon of New-Haven, lat. 41 degrees 19 minutes north. And longt. 73 degrees 14 minutes west of the Royal Observatory or Flamsted-House in Greenwich, according to latest observations; but may, without any sensible error, serve indifferently for all the towns in Connecticut, and adjacent States. By H. Stafford. [Eight lines of verse.]

New-Haven: Printed & sold by T. & S. Green. [1798.] pp. [24.] 12mo.
　　　　　　　　　　　　　　　　　　AAS. CHS. LOC. NYPL.

Contains, Reflections on life. A poem.

34619　STUART, James
A Dissertation on the salutary effects of mercury, in malignant fevers. [An inaugural thesis submitted to the examination of the rev. John Ewing, s.t.p. provost: the trustees and medical faculty of the University of Pennsylvania, for the degree of doctor of medicine, on the 22d day of May, 1798.] By James Stuart, a native of Virginia, and resident member of the Academy of Medicine of Philadelphia. [Four lines of Latin quotations.]

Philadelphia: Printed by Thomas & Samuel F. Bradford. No. 8, South Front Street. 1798. pp. (2), (2), (2), (2), (4), (37). 8vo.　AAS. BM. JCB. LOC. RIMS. SGO.

Reprinted in Caldwell's Medical theses. Vol 2. 1806.

34620　SULLIVAN, James　　　　　　　　　　　　1744–1808
An Impartial review of the causes and principles of the French Revolution. By an American.

Boston: Printed by Benjamin Edes, Kilby-Street. 1798. pp. (101, (1). 8vo.
　　　　　　　　　　　　AAS. BA. BM. LOC. MHS. NYHS. NYPL.

34621 THE [cut] SUN. Dover Gazette, and County Advertiser. [Motto.] Number 18 of vol. 3. Whole number 122. Wednesday, January 3, [— Number 17 of vol. 4. Whole no. 178. Wednesday, December 26, 1798.]

Published on Wednesdays — By Samuel Bragg, jun. at his Printing-Office, Dover. . . . 1798. fol. AAS.

34622 THE SUNBURY and Northumberland Gazette. Vol. vi. No. 28. Saturday, January 6, [— Vol. vii. No. 27. Saturday, December 29, 1798.]

Northumberland — Printed by George Schurler. 1798. fol.

34623 SWEET amusement, for leisure hours: being an entertaining and instructive collection of stories. Every pretty moral tale Shall o'er the infant mind prevail. First Exeter edition. [Ornament.]

Printed and sold by H. Ranlet, Exeter. where a number [of] pretty books for Children are constantly for sale. 1797. pp. 64. 32mo.

34624 SWIFT, Samuel   1782–1875
An Oration, occasioned by the death of mr. John Merrill, late member of the freshman class in Dartmouth University. By Samuel Swift, member of the same class.

Haverhill: Printed by Angier March. 1798.

34625 SWIFT, Seth   1749–1807
The Work of the Gospel ministry of extensive and interesting influence, illustrated, in a sermon, preached at West-Rupert, at the ordination of the rev. John B. Preston, February 5th, 1798. By the rev. Seth Swift, a.m. pastor of the church at Williamstown. Published at the request of a number of the hearers. [Three lines of Scripture text.]

Bennington: Printed by Anthony Haswell. M,DCC,XCVIII. pp. [29.] 8vo.
BU. CHS. JCB. NYHS. NYPL.

34626 THE TABLET; and Weekly Advertiser. Vol. i. No. 11. Wednesday, January 3, [— No. 36. Wednesday, June 27, 1798.]

New-York: Published by Tiebout & Burling. 1798. fol.

In April, Thomas Burling withdrew; and publication was continued under the shortened title of *Tablet*, by John Tiebout, up to July, 1798, as above, when, apparently, it was discontinued.

34627 TAPPAN, David   1752–1803
A Discourse, delivered to the religious society in Brattle-street, Boston, and to the christian congregation in Charlestown, on April 5, 1798. Being the day of the annual fast in the Commonwealth of Massachusetts. By David Tappan. d.d. Hollis professor of divinity in Harvard College. Published by desire of the hearers, to whom it is respectfully inscribed. [Ornament.]

Printed by Samuel Hall, No. 53, Cornhill, Boston. 1798. pp. [31.] 8vo.
AAS. BA. BM. HC. JCB. LOC. MHS. NYHS. UTS. YC.

34628 —— — A Discourse, delivered to the religious society in Brattle-street, Boston, and to the christian congregation in Charlestown, on April 5, 1798. Being the day of the annual fast in the Commonwealth of Massachusetts. By David Tappan, d.d. Hollis professor of divinity in Harvard College. Second edition.

Printed by Samuel Hall, No. 53 Cornhill, Boston. 1798. pp. 31. 8vo.
AAS. JCB. NYPL.

34629   TAPPAN, DAVID, continued.
—— A DISCOURSE DELIVERED IN THE CHAPEL OF HARVARD COLLEGE, JUNE 19, 1798. OCCASIONED BY THE APPROACHING DEPARTURE OF THE SENIOR CLASS FROM THE UNIVERSITY. BY DAVID TAPPAN, D. D. HOLLIS PROFESSOR OF DIVINITY IN SAID COLLEGE.
Boston: Printed by Manning and Loring. 1798. pp. [28.] 8vo.
AAS. BA. HC. JCB. LOC. MHS. NYHS. NYPL. UTS.

34630   TATTLE, TOM, pseudonym.
FATHER ABRAHAM'S ALMANAC, FOR THE YEAR OF OUR LORD, 1799; BEING THE THIRD AFTER LEAP-YEAR, AND THE 24TH OF AMERICAN INDEPENDENCE, AFTER THE 4TH OF JULY. CONTAINING, (BESIDES THE ASTRONOMICAL CALCULATIONS, BY TOM TATTLE,). [Fourteen lines.] CALCULATED FOR THE MERIDIAN OF PHILADELPHIA, BUT MAY, WITHOUT SENSIBLE VARIATION, SERVE FOR ANY OF THE MIDDLE STATES.
Philadelphia: Printed and sold by Peter Stewart, No. 34, South Second-Street. [1798.] pp. (40). 12mo.   AAS. LOC.

> Contains, An instance of Turkish justice. Glorious magnanimity of a peasant. The way to make money plenty in every man's pocket, by Dr. Benjamin Franklin. The internal state of America. A sermon lately preached to a numerous congregation at Hackney, England. A comparative view of the utility of different branches of education. Tables of interest. Courts of law,—the United States. Thoughts on duelling. Roads.

34631   —— THE PENNSYLVANIA, NEW-JERSEY, DELAWARE, MARYLAND AND VIRGINIA ALMANAC, FOR THE YEAR OF OUR LORD, 1799; BEING THE THIRD AFTER LEAP-YEAR, AND THE 24TH OF AMERICAN INDEPENDENCE, AFTER THE 4TH OF JULY. CONTAINING, (BESIDES THE ASTRONOMICAL CALCULATIONS, BY TOM TATTLE,) [Sixteen lines.]
Philadelphia: Printed and sold by Peter Stewart, No. 34, South Second-Street. [1798.] pp. (40). 12mo.   AAS. HSP.

34632   TAYLOR, JOHN   1762–1840
A SERMON, DELIVERED ON THE DAY OF PUBLIC THANKSGIVING, AT DEERFIELD;— NOV. 29, '98. BY JOHN TAYLOR, A. M. PASTOR OF THE CHURCH IN DEERFIELD.
Printed at Greenfield, by Francis Barker. [1798.] pp. [19.] 4to.
AAS. CHS. CLA. JCB. MHS. YC.

34633   TAYLOR, RAYNOR   1747–1825
RUSTIC FESTIVITY. A NEW SONG COMPOSED BY R. TAYLOR.
Philadelphia: Republished by B. Carr, at his Repository, Marketstreet. [1798.]

34634   —— SUMMER, A PASTORALE SONG BY RAYNOR TAYLOR.
Philadelphia: Published by B. Carr, at his Repository, Market Street. 1798.

34635   TELEGRAPHE AND DAILY ADVERTISER. NUM. 831. MONDAY, JANUARY 1, [— NUM. 1143. MONDAY, DECEMBER 31, 1798.]
Baltimore—Printed by T. E. Clayland and T. Dobbin, No. 36, Market-Street, opposite the Vendue Store. 1798. fol.

> Beginning January 1, 1799, publication was continued in the name of Thomas Dobbin.

34636   TELL ME FAIREST, TELL ME TRUE. SONG.
New-York: Published by George Gilbert, at his Music Store, 177 Broadway, Apollo's Head. 1798.

34637 TENNESSEE. STATE.
A PROCLAMATION, BY HIS EXCELLENCY JOHN SEVIER, GOVERNOR, IN AND OVER THE
STATE OF TENNESSEE. BY VIRTUE OF THE POWER AND AUTHORITY IN ME VESTED
BY THE CONSTITUTION, TO CONVENE THE GENERAL ASSEMBLY ON EXTRAORDINARY
OCCASIONS I DO REQUIRE THE SENATORS AND REPRESENTATIVES OF THE RESPEC-
TIVE COUNTIES OF THE STATE OF TENNESSEE, TO CONVENE IN GENERAL ASSEMBLY,
AT KNOXVILLE, ON MONDAY THE THIRD OF DECEMBER NEXT. GIVEN UNDER MY
HAND AND SEAL AT KNOXVILLE, THIS 15TH DAY OF OCTOBER 1798. JOHN SEVIER.
BY THE GOVERNOR, WILLIAM MACLIN, SEC'Y.

Knoxville: Printed by George Roulstone. 1798. Broadside.

34638 THACHER, PETER   1715–1785
SELECT DISCOURSES ON PRACTICAL SUBJECTS. BY THE REV. PETER THACHER, A. M.
LATE PASTOR OF THE CHURCH AT ATTLEBOROUGH. [Ornament.]

*Leominster, Massachusetts, Printed by John Prentiss & Co. for Thomas
Thacher — Princeton.* 1798. pp. 114. 8vo.   AAS.

34639 THACHER, PETER   1752–1802
BRIEF ACCOUNT OF THE SOCIETY FOR PROPAGATING THE GOSPEL AMONG THE INDIANS
AND OTHERS IN NORTH-AMERICA. [With a list of the officers and members of the
Society. Signed, Peter Thacher, sec'y. Boston, January, 1798.]

[Printed by S. Hall, in Cornhill, Boston. 1798.] pp. (7). 4to. BM. LOC. MHS.

34640 —— TO THE MEMBERS OF THE SOCIETY FOR PROPOGATING THE GOSPEL AMONG THE
INDIANS, AND OTHERS IN NORTH AMERICA.

[Printed by S. Hall, in Cornhill, Boston, 1798.]   LOC.

34641 —— A SERMON PREACHED TO THE SOCIETY IN BRATTLE-STREET, BOSTON, MARCH 25,
1798, ON THE DEATH OF MADAM REBECCA GILL, CONSORT OF HIS HONOR MOSES
GILL, L.T.-GOV. OF THE COMMONWEALTH OF MASSACHUSETTS, WHO DIED MARCH 19.
1798. BY PETER THACHER, D. D.

Boston: Printed by Rhoades & Laughton, 1798. pp. 23. 8vo.
AAS. BA. JCB. LOC. MHS. NYPL.

34642 —— A SERMON, DELIVERED AT THE FIRST CHURCH IN BOSTON, APRIL 6, 1798, AT THE
INTERMENT OF THE REVEREND JOHN CLARKE, D. D., WHO EXPIRED SUDDENLY, APRIL
2, 1798. Æ 43. BY PETER THACHER, PASTOR OF THE CHURCH IN BRATTLE-STREET.

Boston: Printed by Samuel Hall. 1798. pp. 27. 8vo.
AAS. BA. BM. HC. JCB. LOC. MHS. NYHS. NYPL.

Contains, Remarks on Dr. Clarke, delivered by the Rev. Joseph Willard
at the first church, the Lord's day after the funeral; and an Account of
him published in the Columbian Centinel the day after the interment.
By Jeremy Belknap, D. D.

34643 THACKARA, JAMES
THE YOUNG LADIES' & GENTLEMEN'S COMPLETE DRAWING-BOOK. CONTAINING AN
EXTENSIVE COLLECTION OF EXAMPLES ON A VARIETY OF SUBJECTS (FOR THE IM-
PROVEMENT OF YOUTH) IN THE PLEASING, ELEGANT AND USEFUL ART OF DRAWING.
BEAUTIFULLY ENGRAVED ON A GREAT NUMBER OF COPPER PLATES: TO WHICH ARE
ANNEXED, INTRODUCTORY RULES FOR THE USE OF LEARNERS, WITH AN ACCOUNT
OF INSTRUMENTS AND MATERIALS USED IN DRAWING.

Philadelphia: Printed for the Author, No. 72, Spruce-Street. 1798.

34644   THARP, PETER
A NEW AND COMPLETE SYSTEM OF FEDERAL ARITHMETIC; IN THREE PARTS. WITH AN APPENDIX, CONTAINING BOARD AND TIMBER MEASURE. DESIGNED FOR THE USE OF SCHOOLS. BY PETER THARP, MATH.
     Newburgh: Printed by D. Denniston for the Author.—1798. pp. (138), (2). 16mo.   AAS.

     77th New York District Copyright, issued to Peter Tharp, as Author, 8 April, 1799.

34645   THATCHER, THOMAS   1756–1812
A SERMON, PREACHED IN THE EPISCOPAL CHURCH IN DEDHAM, DECEMBER 25, 1797; BEING THE FESTIVAL OF CHRISTMAS. BY THOMAS THATCHER, A. M. MINISTER OF A CONGREGATIONAL CHURCH IN DEDHAM. [Two lines of Latin from] TACITUS.
     Dedham: Printed by Mann and Adams. 1798. pp. (30). 8vo.
                            AAS. BA. JCB. LOC.

34646   THAYER, JOHN   1755–1818
A DISCOURSE, DELIVERED, AT THE ROMAN CATHOLIC CHURCH IN BOSTON, ON THE 9TH. OF MAY, 1798, A DAY RECOMMENDED BY THE PRESIDENT, FOR HUMILIATION AND PRAYER THROUGHOUT THE UNITED STATES. BY THE REVEREND JOHN THAYER, CATHOLIC MISSIONER. PRINTED AT THE PRESSING SOLICITATION OF THOSE WHO HEARD IT. [Ornament.]
     Printed by Samuel Hall, No. 53, Cornhill, Boston. 1798. pp. 31. 8vo.
              AAS. BA. CHS. HC. JCB. LOC. MHS. YC.

34647   —— — A DISCOURSE, DELIVERED, AT THE ROMAN CATHOLIC CHURCH IN BOSTON, ON THE 9TH OF MAY, 1798, A DAY RECOMMENDED BY THE PRESIDENT, FOR HUMILIATION AND PRAYER THROUGHOUT THE UNITED STATES. BY THE REVEREND JOHN THAYER, CATHOLIC MISSIONER. PRINTED AT THE PRESSING SOLICITATION OF THOSE WHO HEARD IT. THE SECOND EDITION.
     Printed by Samuel Hall, Boston. 1798. pp. 31. 8vo.   AAS. JCB. NYPL.

     142d Massachusetts District Copyright, issued to John Thayer, as Author, 22 May, 1798.

34648   THAYER, NATHANIEL   1769–1840
A SERMON, DELIVERED BEFORE THE ANCIENT AND HONORABLE ARTILLERY COMPANY, IN BOSTON, JUNE 4, 1798; BEING THE ANNIVERSARY OF THEIR ELECTION OF OFFICERS. BY NATHANIEL THAYER, MINISTER OF THE CHURCH IN LANCASTER. [Vignette.]
     Boston: Printed by Manning & Loring. 1798. pp. [20.] 8vo.
                        AAS. BA. LOC. MHS.

34649   THE THEOLOGICAL MAGAZINE, OR SYNOPSIS OF MODERN RELIGIOUS SENTIMENT. ON A NEW PLAN. [Seven lines of quotations.] VOL. III. [No. 1. OCTOBER, NOVEMBER, AND DECEMBER, 1797— No. 5. SEPTEMBER, OCTOBER, AND NOVEMBER, 1798.]
     New-York: Printed by T. and J. Swords, for Cornelius Davis. 1798. pp. 408. 8vo.   AAS. BA. JCB. LOC. MHS. NYHS. NYPL. YC.

34650   THERE IS A SNAKE IN THE GRASS ! ! ! CITIZENS OF KENTUCKY, BE UPON YOUR GUARD, IF APPLICATIONS SHOULD BE MADE TO YOU TO SIGN ADDRESSES [in favor of the "late impolitic and unconstitutional measures of our government." Dated, Lexington, August 15, 1798.]
     [*Lexington: Printed by John Bradford.* 1798.] Broadside. 4to.

34651 THESPIAN ORACLE, OR MONTHLY MIRROR. CONSISTING OF ORIGINAL PIECES AND
SELECTIONS FROM PERFORMANCES OF MERIT, RELATING CHIEFLY TO THE MOST
ADMIRED DRAMATIC COMPOSITIONS, AND INTERSPERSED WITH THEATRICAL ANEC-
DOTES. VOLUME FIRST. [NO. 1. JANUARY, 1798.]
*Philadelphia: Printed for T. B. Freeman, No. 39, South Front Street, oppo-
site the Post-Office . . . 1798. pp. 36, portrait. 8vo.*   HC. HSP.

All that was published. 205th Pennsylvania District Copyright, issued
to T. B. Freeman, as Proprietor, 5 April, 1798.

34652 ISAIAH THOMAS'S MASSACHUSETTS, CONNECTICUT, RHODEISLAND, NEWHAMPSHIRE
& VERMONT ALMANACK, WITH AN EPHEMERIS, FOR THE YEAR OF OUR LORD 1799.
BEING THE THIRD AFTER BISSEXTILE, OR LEAP YEAR, AND TWENTY-THIRD OF THE
INDEPENDENCE OF UNITED COLUMBIA. FROM CREATION, ACCORDING TO THE SCRIPT-
URES, 5761. [Six lines. Cut. Four lines of verse.]
*Printed at Worcester, Massachusetts, by Isaiah Thomas. Sold by him, and by
I. Thomas, jun. in Worcester; by Thomas & Andrews, S. Hall, D. West, E. Lar-
kin, J. Boyle, W. Spotswood, and at the Boston Bookstore, in Boston; by Thomas
and Thomas, Walpole; by T. C. Cushing and J. Dabney, Salem; by Thomas, An-
drews and Penniman, Albany; and by all the Booksellers, in Town and country.
Price 7¼ dols. per gross—75 cents doz.—10 cents single. [1798.] pp. (48). 12mo.*
   AAS. LOC. NYPL. YC.

34653 THOMAS'S MASSACHUSETTS SPY: OR THE WORCESTER GAZETTE. [Mottos.] VOL. XXVI.
NO. 1290. WEDNESDAY, JANUARY 3, [— VOL. XXVII. NO. 1342. WEDNESDAY,
DECEMBER 26, 1798.]
*Printed at Worcester, (Massachusetts) by Leonard Worcester, at his Office, near
the South Meeting House, for Isaiah Thomas. . . . 1798. fol.*   AAS.

34654 THOMAS, ROBERT BAILEY   1766–1846
NO. VII. THE FARMER'S ALMANACK, CALCULATED ON A NEW AND IMPROVED PLAN,
FOR THE YEAR OF OUR LORD, 1799. BEING THE THIRD AFTER BISSEXTILE, OR LEAP-
YEAR, AND TWENTY-THIRD OF THE INDEPENDENCE OF AMERICA. [Six lines.] BY
ROBERT B. THOMAS. [Cut. Four lines of verse.]
*Boston: Printed by Manning & Loring, for John West, Proprietor of the copy-
right, and for sale at his Book-Store, No. 75, Cornhill, and by the other Booksellers
in Boston. Sold also by the Booksellers in Salem, Newburyport, &c. by the Author
at Sterling, and at various other places. [Price 7¼ dollars per gross, 75 cents per
dozen, and 10 cents single.] [1798.] pp. (48). 12mo.*   AAS. LOC. MHS.

34655 THOMAS, WILLIAM
HODGE'S NORTH-CAROLINA ALMANACK, FOR THE YEAR OF OUR LORD 1799; BEING
THE THIRD AFTER BISSEXTILE, OR LEAP YEAR, AND THE 23D – 24TH OF AMERICAN
INDEPENDENCE. CALCULATED FOR THE STATE OF NORTH-CAROLINA, BEING PRE-
CISELY ADAPTED TO THE MERIDIAN AND LATITUDE OF THE CITY OF RALEIGH; BUT
WILL SERVE WITHOUT SENSIBLE ERROR FOR ANY OF THE STATES ADJACENT. . . .
Halifax: Printed by Abraham Hodge. [1798.]

34656 THOMPSON, SIR BENJAMIN, COUNT OF RUMFORD   1753–1814
ESSAYS, POLITICAL, ECONOMICAL, AND PHILOSOPHICAL. BY BENJAMIN, COUNT OF RUM-
FORD, KNIGHT OF THE WHITE EAGLE, AND ST. STANISLAUS; CHAMBERLAIN, PRIVY
COUNSELLOR OF STATE, AND LIEUTENANT-GENERAL IN THE SERVICE OF HIS MOST
SERENE HIGHNESS THE ELECTOR PALATINE, REIGNING DUKE OF BAVARIA; COLONEL
OF HIS REGIMENT OF ARTILLERY, AND COMMANDER IN CHIEF OF THE GENERAL STAFF
OF HIS ARMY; F. R. S. ACAD. R. HIBER. BEROL. ELEC. BOICŒ. PALAT. ET AMER. SOC.
THE FIRST AMERICAN, FROM THE THIRD LONDON EDITION. VOL. I.
Boston: Printed by Manning & Loring, for David West. Sold at his Book-

THOMPSON, Sir BENJAMIN, continued.

store, No. 56, Cornhill; by Ebenezer S. Thomas, Charleston, S. Carolina, and by Solomon Cotton & Co. Baltimore. March, 1798. pp. xxiv, 464, portrait, and 6 plates in text. 8vo.   AAS. BA. BM. JCB. NL. NYPL.

First published in parts: No. 1. of volume II, in press, May 16, 1798. A second volume was published in Boston, in 1799, and a third volume in 1804.

34657 THOMPSON, or THOMSON, JOHN   1777–1799
       THE LETTERS OF CURTIUS. ADDRESSED TO GENERAL [John] MARSHALL. [Ornament.]
       Richmond: Printed by Samuel Pleasants, jun. December, 1798. pp. 40. 8vo.
                                                                AAS.
       Note from the Virginia Argus, April, 1799: "John Thompson, author of Curtius' Letters, which originally appeared in the Virginia Argus, died March 25, 1799, aged 23 years." Reprinted in Richmond in 1804.

34658 THOMPSON, OTIS   1776–1859
       AN ORATION, URGING THE NECESSITY OF RELIGION, AS THE ONLY PERMANENT BASIS OF CIVIL GOVERNMENT. PRONOUNCED IN THE BAPTIST MEETING-HOUSE IN PROVIDENCE, AT THE COMMENCEMENT OF RHODE-ISLAND COLLEGE, SEPTEMBER 5, A. D. 1798. BY OTIS THOMPSON, A. B. PUBLISHED AT THE REQUEST OF THE STUDENTS. [Four lines of Latin quotations.]
       Providence: Printed by Carter and Wilkinson. 1798. pp. (8). 8vo.
                                                                AAS. JCB. LOC. RIHS.

34659 —— A POEM, DELIVERED IN THE CHAPEL OF RHODE-ISLAND COLLEGE, AT THE PUBLIC EXHIBITION OF THE SENIOR CLASS, DECEMBER 27, 1797. BY OTIS THOMPSON. PUBLISHED AT THE REQUEST OF THE STUDENTS.
       [Providence:] Printed by B. Wheeler. [1798] pp. (8). 4to.   AAS. RIHS.

34660 THREE NEW MARCHES. [Buonaparte's March: The Pyrenees. Buonaparte's March: The Mantuane. Prussian March.]
       Philadelphia: Printed and sold by G. Willig, No. 185 Market Street. [1798.]
                                                                LCP.

34661 THRUM, TAM. pseudonym.
       LOOK BEFORE YE LOUP; OR, A HEALIN' SA' FOR THE CRACKIT CROWNS OF COUNTRY POLITICIANS. TAM THRUM, AN AULD WEAVER. . . .
       Philadelphia: Printed by Thomas Dobson, at the Stone House, No. 41, South Second Street. M.DCC.XCVIII. pp. 36. 16mo.   BU. LOC.

34662 THUMB, THOMAS, pseudonym.
       A BAG OF NUTS. SECOND WORCESTER EDITION.
       Worcester, Massachusetts: Printed by I. Thomas, jun. September, 1798. pp. 95, frontispiece. 32mo.   AAS.

34663 TIELKE, JOHANN GOTTLIEB   1731-1787
       INSTRUCTIONS FOR OFFICERS WHO WISH TO BECOME FIELD ENGINEERS: OR, WHO ARE DESIROUS OF BECOMING USEFUL IN THE FIELD. ILLUSTRATED BY EXAMPLES FROM THE LAST WAR, AND PROVIDED WITH THE NECESSARY PLANS. BY J. G. TIELKE, MAJOR OF THE SAXON ARTILLERY. TRANSLATED FROM THE GERMAN, BY CHARLES SMITH, CAPTAIN IN THE SECOND REGIMENT OF NEW-YORK MILITIA.
       New-York: Published by Charles Smith. 1798.
       Proposals to publish the above were made by Charles Smith this year.

34664 THE TIME Piece. Vol. ii. No. 47. Monday, January 1, [— Vol. iii. No. 150. Thursday, August 30, 1798.]

[New-York: | Published on Mondays, Wednesdays & Fridays, by P. Freneau & M. L. Davis, No. 26 Moore Street, near Whitehall. 1798. fol.

BA. LOC. NYHS. NYPL.

Beginning with the issue for March 21st, Philip Freneau's name was dropped from the imprint, and publication continued by M. L. Davis & Co., at the same printing-office, until June 18th, when it was published "at No 25, Maiden-Lane, by Robert Saunders, for the Proprietors"— John Daly Burk, and James Smith,— to July 11th. Saunders' name being omitted after that date, and the name of no other publisher is given before publication ceased, apparently, with the issue for 30 August, 1798: the days of publication from August 14th, being changed to Tuesdays, Thursdays, and Saturdays. On June 20th, announcement was made that "The Editor in addition to the Time piece, (which is intended to appear daily) contemplates the publication of a continental paper to be entitled *"The Friend of the People."*

34665 THE TIMES. [and] Alexandria [cut] Advertiser. [Motto.] Vol. i. No. 229. Monday, January 1, [— Vol. ii. No. 541. Monday, December 31, 1798.]

Printed daily, by Thomas and Westcott, Royal-Street, between the Post-Office and Coffee-House, Alexandria. 1798. fol. AAS. LOC.

34666 TINDAL, Matthew 1653–1733

Christianity as old as the creation: or the Gospel, a republication of the religion of nature. By Matthew Tindal, l. l. d. [Twelve lines of quotations.]

Newburgh: Printed and sold by David Denniston.— M,DCC,XCVIII. pp. 372. 8vo. AAS. BA. NYPL.

34667 A TIT-BIT for the public, or memoirs of an antiquated shaver, &c.

Baltimore: Printed by T. E. Clayland and T. Dobbin, 1798.

34668 TO the committee who fitted out William Kittletas, of New-York, to distribute scurrilous hand-bills, and propogate malicious falsehoods against Mr. Jay, in the western district. You did well to furnish your emissary with a number of circular addresses of your own and the committee of New-York. . . . An Elector of Herkimer.

[New-York? 1798.] pp. (2). fol. NYPL.

34669 TO the electors of Dutchess County. At a meeting of a number of the electors of the county of Dutchess, in Poughkeepsie, 29th March, 1798, . . . Resolved, that Robert R. Livingston be nominated for Governor, and Stephen Van Rensselaer for lieutenant governor . . . [With Address. Signed by Abraham Schenck, and others. Four columns. Colophon:]

Poughkeepsie: Printed by Powers and Southwick. [1798.] Broadside. 4to.

34670 TO the free and independent voters of the city and County of Baltimore. Fellow-citizens, The opposers of General Smith, finding that they are not able to rally to the standard of opposition, any number like a majority of the free, virtuous and independent American citizens, have descended to disgrace their country, and insult their countrymen, by enlisting to their services a band of British seamen, belonging to a privateer of that nation, now laying in our port—[With affidavits to the opposition of J. John O'Donnell to the mechanics voting for General Smith.]

[Baltimore: Printed by William Pechin, 1798.] Broadside.

34671   TO THE FREEMEN OF THE STATE OF RHODE-ISLAND, &C. TO THE END THAT THE MINDS OF THE PEOPLE MAY NO LONGER BE HELD IN SUSPENSE, WHETHER OR NOT MR. JOHN BROWN WILL ACCEPT THE APPOINTMENT, AND PERFORM THE DUTIES, OF A REPRE-SENTATIVE IN CONGRESS, IN CASE HE SHOULD BE ELECTED, IT IS THOUGHT PROPER TO PUBLISH HIS ANSWER TO AN APPLICATION ON THIS SUBJECT. [Accepting the nomination. Fourteen lines.] AN ELECTOR. PROVIDENCE, AUG. 20, 1798.

       [Providence, Printed by Carter and Wilkinson. 1798.] Broadside. fol.

                                                     LOC. RIHS.

34672   TO THE FRIENDS OF ISRAEL ISRAEL. YOU HAVE AGREED TO SUPPORT THIS MAN AT THE ELECTION, THIS DAY, FOR A SENATOR. [Advocating the re-election of Benjamin R. Morgan, instead.] ONE OF THE PEOPLE. FEBRUARY 22, 1798.

       [Philadelphia: 1798.] Broadside. 4to.   HSP.

34673   —— AN DIE FREUNDE DES ISRAEL ISRAEL. IHR SIND EINIG WORDEN, DIESSEN MANN FÜR EINEN SENATOR. . . . EINER VON DEM VOLK. DEN 22STEN FEBRUAR, 1798.

       [Philadelphia: 1798.] Broadside. 4to.   HSP.

34674   TO THE PUBLIC. A FEW DAYS AGO I WAS AT MY NEIGHBORS AND WHILE THERE HE RE-CEIVED A VISIT FROM AN OLD FRIEND OF HIS, WHO BELONGS TO THE SENATE OF THIS STATE. AMONG OTHER TOPICS, OUR CONVERSATION TURNED ON THE ELECTION . . . [refuting charges against the administration of Governor John Jay. Signed,] A FARMER. COLUMBIA. APRIL 17, 1798.

       Hudson: Printed by A. Stoddard. 1798. Broadside. fol.   NYPL.

34675   TRACY, URIAH   1755–1807
       REFLECTIONS ON MONROE'S VIEW, OF THE CONDUCT OF THE EXECUTIVE, AS PUBLISHED IN THE GAZETTE OF THE UNITED STATES, UNDER THE SIGNATURE OF SCIPIO. IN WHICH THE COMMERCIAL WARFARE OF FRANCE IS TRACED TO THE FRENCH FACTION IN THIS COUNTRY, AS ITS SOURCE, AND THE MOTIVES OF OPPOSITION, &C.

       [Philadelphia: Printed by John Fenno. 1798.] pp. (88). 8vo.

                                 BA. CLS. HSP. JCB. LOC. NYPL.

34676   —— — SCIPIO'S REFLECTIONS ON MONROE'S VIEW OF THE CONDUCT OF THE EX-ECUTIVE, ON THE FOREIGN AFFAIRS OF THE UNITED STATES, CONNECTED WITH A MISSION TO THE FRENCH REPUBLIC IN THE YEARS, 1794, '95, '96.

       Boston: Printed by Caleb P. Wayne, publisher of the Boston "Federal Gazette and daily advertiser," No. 17, *Kilby-Street,* 3 *doors from State-Street.*—1798. pp. (2), (2), 140. 8vo.   AAS. BA. HSP. JCB LOC. MHS. NYHS. NYPL. YC.

       There is considerable variation in the two editions. The Philadelphia edition has appended five pages of matter not contained in the Boston edition.

34677   THE TRAGICAL HISTORY OF THE CHILDREN IN THE WOOD. CONTAINING A TRUE AC-COUNT OF THEIR UNHAPPY FATE. WITH THE HISTORY OF THEIR PARENTS, AND THEIR UNNATURAL UNCLE. INTERSPERSED WITH INSTRUCTIVE MORALS. EMBELLISHED WITH CUTS.

       Boston: Printed and sold by S. Hall, No. 53, *Cornhill.* [1798.] pp. 91. 32mo.

       Contains, The Children in the wood. A favorite ballad. pp. 79–91.   LOC.

34678   TRENCK, FRIEDRICH, freiherr VON DER   1726–1794
       THE LIFE AND ADVENTURES OF BARON FREDERICK TRENCK. CONTAINING HIS CRUEL AND EXCESSIVE SUFFERINGS DURING TEN YEARS IMPRISONMENT AT THE FORTRESS OF MAGDEBURG, BY COMMAND OF THE LATE KING OF PRUSSIA.

       Philadelphia: 1798. 12mo.

34679   TRENTON. NEW JERSEY. LIBRARY COMPANY.
LAWS AND REGULATIONS OF THE TRENTON LIBRARY COMPANY.
Trenton: Printed by Matthias Day. 1798.

34680   TRIPLETT, THOMAS
AN INAUGURAL DISSERTATION ON APOPLEXY. BY THOMAS TRIPLETT, OF ALEXANDRIA,
HONORARY MEMBER OF THE PHILADELPHIA MEDICAL SOCIETY. [Two lines from]
HALLIFAX.
Philadelphia: Printed by Way & Groff, No. 27, Arch-Street. 1798. pp. (32).
8vo.   AAS. JCB. LOC. SGO.

34681   THE TRUE AMERICAN. VOL. I. No. 1. TUESDAY, NOVEMBER 27, [— No. 5. TUES-
DAY, DECEMBER 25, 1798.]
Leesburg, (Virginia). Published by Patrick M'Intyre. 1798. fol.
Established, as a weekly, by Patrick M'Intyre, and continued by him to
December 30, 1800—the last, and only number located.

34682   THE TRUE AMERICAN AND COMMERCIAL [cut] ADVERTISER. No. 1. MONDAY MORN-
ING, JULY 2, [No. 152. MONDAY. DECEMBER 31, 1798.]
*[Philadelphia: Published] By Samuel F. Bradford, No. 8, South Front-
Street.* 1798. fol.   AAS. HSP. LCP.
Established, as a daily, by Samuel F. Bradford, in continuation of *The
Merchants' Daily Advertiser,* and continued by him to July 1801, when
he disposed of his interests to his father, Thomas Bradford, who continued publication to December, 1813. With the issue for December 6,
1818, his interests were purchased by James Elliot, and Thomas T. Stiles,
who, under the firm name of Elliot & Stiles, published it, with a new
serial numbering, as the *True American and Commercial Advertiser.* In
July, 1815. Elliot withdrew, and Stiles continued publication, shortening
the title to *The True American,* to June, 1816, when Charles Miner was
admitted to partnership as Stiles & Miner, up to early in 1817, when
Miner retired, and shortly after Stiles disposed of his interests to Thomas
Smith, and Ebenezer Cummins. The firm of Smith & Cummins continued publication into March, 1818, when it was united with the
"United States' Gazette," to form a new paper called *The Union.* The
motto, on the cut, reads, "United we stand, Divided we fall." Owing
to the epidemic of yellow fever, the paper was suspended in September,
and printed on a half sheet in October, 1798.
In July, 1798, Samuel F. Bradford purchased "The Philadelphia Minerva," and continued its publication weekly, as a literary supplement to
"The True American," as *The Dessert to the True American* from July 14,
1798, to August 19, 1799, gratis to subscribers, and two dollars per
annum to others.

34683   TUDOR, WILLIAM   1750–1819
A DISCOURSE, DELIVERED AT THE REQUEST OF THE MASSACHUSETTS CHARITABLE
FIRE SOCIETY, JUNE 1, 1798.
Boston: Printed by Samuel Etheridge, No. 22, Marlborough-Street. 1798.
pp. 21, (1), (2). 8vo.   AAS. BA. BM. HC. JCB. LOC. MHS. NYPL.
The last two pages contain: Adams and Liberty, the Boston patriotic
song—Composed by Thomas Paine, A. M. First sung at the anniversary
of the Massachusetts Charitable Fire Society, by Doctor Fay ; Tune "To
Anacreon in Heaven."

34684   TWELVE CENTS WORTH OF WIT; OR, LITTLE STORIES FOR LITTLE FOLKS OF ALL DE-
NOMINATIONS. [Two lines from] POPE.
*Philadelphia: Printed for David Hogan, in George-street, 3d door below
South-street.* 1798.

34685   TYLER, JOHN   1742–1823
UNIVERSAL DAMNATION, AND SALVATION, CLEARLY PROVED BY THE SCRIPTURES OF THE OLD AND NEW TESTAMENT. SPECIALLY RECOMMENDED TO THE PERUSAL OF THOSE WHO BELIEVE IN THE SALVATION OF ALL MANKIND. [Twelve lines of Scripture texts.]

Boston: Printed and sold by B. Edes, jun.—1798.—pp.(2),[79.] 8vo. AAS, JCB.

Reprinted in Shirley, Massachusetts, in 1802; Salem, 1805; and Boston, 1826; Also, with the title of "The Law and the Gospel clearly demonstrated in six sermons," in Norwich, in 1815.

34686   ULSTER COUNTY GAZETTE. VOL. I. NUMBER 1. SATURDAY, MAY 5, [— NUMBER 35. SATURDAY, DECEMBER 29, 1798.]

Published at Kingston, (Ulster County,) by Samuel Freer and Son. 1798. fol.

Established, in continuation of the *Rising Sun*, by Samuel Freer, and his son, Samuel S. Freer. For a short time, in 1798, it was called, *Ulster and Delaware Gazette*, and was published by Samuel Freer alone. Early in the following year it reverted to its first title and both publishers, and this arrangement continued, apparently, (for only scattering numbers are known), into the year 1803, when the title was shortened to *Ulster Gazette*, published by Samuel S. Freer, alone. About the year 1816, Anthony Freer was admitted to partnership under the firm name of S. S. & A. Freer, and this arrangement continued until after the year 1820.

34687   UNITED STATES OF AMERICA.
ACTS PASSED AT THE FIRST SESSION OF THE FIFTH CONGRESS OF THE UNITED STATES, BEGUN AND HELD AT THE CITY OF PHILADELPHIA, IN THE STATE OF PENNSYLVANIA, ON MONDAY, THE FIFTEENTH OF MAY, [— 10 JULY] ONE THOUSAND SEVEN HUNDRED AND NINETY-SEVEN. [Ornament.]

Richmond: Printed by Augustine Davis, Printer to the Commonwealth. M,-DCC,XCVIII. pp. [18], (1). fol.   NYPL. VSL.

34688   —— ACTS PASSED AT THE SECOND SESSION OF THE FIFTH CONGRESS OF THE UNITED STATES OF AMERICA, BEGUN AND HELD AT THE CITY OF PHILADELPHIA, IN THE STATE OF PENNSYLVANIA, ON MONDAY, THE THIRTEENTH OF NOVEMBER IN THE YEAR M,DCC,XCVII. AND OF THE INDEPENDENCE OF THE UNITED STATES, THE TWENTY-SECOND. [— 16 JULY, 1798.]

Philadelphia: Printed by Richard Folwell, No. 33, Carter's-Alley. [1798.] pp. (2), [51]–[240.], vii, (1). 8vo.   AAS LOC. MHS.

34689   —— ACTS PASSED AT THE SECOND SESSION OF THE FIFTH CONGRESS OF THE UNITED STATES: BEGUN AND HELD AT THE CITY OF PHILADELPHIA, IN THE STATE OF PENNSYLVANIA, ON MONDAY, THE THIRTEENTH OF NOVEMBER, ONE THOUSAND SEVEN HUNDRED AND NINETY-SEVEN. [— 16 JULY, 1798.] [Ornament.]

Richmond: Printed by Augustine Davis, Printer for the Commonwealth. M,-DCC,XCVIII. pp, [84], [iv.] fol.   NYPL. VSL.

34690   —— AN ACT CONCERNING ALIENS. APPROVED, JUNE 22D, 1798.

[Philadelphia: 1798.] Broadside. fol.

34691   —— AMENDMENTS OF THE SENATE, TO THE BILL, INTITULED "AN ACT FOR THE ESTABLISHING AND ORGANIZING A BATTALION OF INFANTRY, TO BE CALLED THE MARINE CORPS." [PRINTED BY ORDER OF THE HOUSE OF REPRESENTATIVES.]

[Philadelphia: Printed by William Ross, 1798.] pp. (4). 8vo.   AAS.

UNITED STATES, continued.

34692 —— AN ACT FOR THE GOVERNMENT AND REGULATION OF SEAMEN IN THE MERCHANTS' SERVICE. [With shipping] ARTICLES OF AGREEMENT, BETWEEN THE MASTER AND MARINERS OF THE . . . [Colophon:]
Baltimore: Printed and sold by W. Pechin, No. 15, Baltimore-street. [1798.] pp. (2). fol. LOC.

34693 —— AMENDMENTS TO THE BILL, INTITULED "AN ACT FOR THE MORE EFFECTUAL COLLECTION OF CERTAIN INTERNAL REVENUES OF THE UNITED STATES." [PUBLISHED BY ORDER OF THE HOUSE OF REPRESENTATIVES.]
[Philadelphia: Printed by William Ross, 1798.] pp. (4). 8vo. AAS.

34694 —— AMENDMENT, IN COMMITTEE OF THE WHOLE HOUSE, TO THE BILL IN ADDITION TO THE ACT FOR THE RELIEF OF AMERICAN SEAMEN. 15 FEBRUARY, 1798.
[Philadelphia: 1798.] 8vo. BA.

34695 —— *Caption:* TO CAPTAIN [JAMES DEVEREUX] COMMANDER OF THE PRIVATE ARMED [SHIP] CALLED THE [FRANKLIN]. INSTRUCTIONS FOR THE PRIVATE ARMED VESSELS OF THE UNITED STATES. . . .
AN ACT FURTHER TO PROTECT THE COMMERCE OF THE UNITED STATES. . . . ENACTED INTO A LAW, JULY 9, 1798. BY COMMAND OF THE PRESIDENT OF THE UNITED STATES OF AMERICA. [Signed, Timothy Pickering.] SECRETARY OF STATE.
[Philadelphia: 1798.] pp. (8). 8vo. AAS.

34696 —— AMENDMENTS TO THE BILL, INTITULED, "AN ACT MAKING APPROPRIATIONS FOR THE MILITARY ESTABLISHMENT FOR THE YEAR ONE THOUSAND SEVEN HUNDRED AND NINETY-EIGHT; AND FOR OTHER PURPOSES." 6TH JUNE, 1798, COMMITTED TO A COMMITTEE OF THE WHOLE HOUSE, TO-MORROW. [PUBLISHED BY ORDER OF THE HOUSE OF REPRESENTATIVES.]
[Philadelphia: Printed by William Ross, 1798.] pp. 4. 8vo. AAS.

34697 —— AN ACT MORE EFFECTUALLY TO PROTECT THE COMMERCE AND COASTS OF THE UNITED STATES. . . . [Authorizing commanders of armed vessels to capture any French vessel found on the coasts of the United States.] JOHN ADAMS.
[Philadelphia: 1798.] Broadside. fol.

34698 —— AMENDMENTS OF THE SENATE TO THE BILL, INTITULED "AN ACT TO AUTHORIZE THE DEFENCE OF THE MERCHANT VESSELS OF THE UNITED STATES AGAINST FRENCH DEPREDATIONS." 20TH JUNE, 1798, COMMITTED TO A COMMITTEE OF THE WHOLE HOUSE, TO-MORROW. [PUBLISHED BY ORDER OF THE HOUSE OF REPRESENTATIVES.]
[Philadelphia: Printed by William Ross, 1798.] pp. 4. 8vo. AAS. BA.

34699 —— AN ACT TO CONTINUE . . . AN ACT PROHIBITING . . . EXPORTATION OF ARMS. . . . APPROVED, APRIL 7, 1798.
[Philadelphia: 1798.] Broadside. 8vo.

34700 —— AN ACT SUPPLEMENTARY TO, AND TO AMEND THE ACT, INTITULED, "AN ACT TO ESTABLISH AN UNIFORM RULE OF NATURALIZATION; AND TO REPEAL THE ACT HERETOFORE PASSED ON THAT SUBJECT. APPROVED JUNE 18, 1798.
[Philadelphia: 1798.] pp. (2) fol. JCB.

34701 —— FEDERAL SYSTEM OF DIRECT TAXATION, ENACTED BY CONGRESS, JULY 9, 1798; TO WHICH IS ADDED AN ACT LEVYING A TAX OF TWO MILLIONS OF DOLLARS.
Hudson: Printed and sold by Ashbel Stoddard. [1798.] pp. 66. 18mo. NYPL.

34702 —— AMENDMENTS OF THE SENATE, TO THE BILL, INTITULED, "AN ACT TO LAY AND COLLECT A DIRECT TAX WITHIN THE UNITED STATES." [PRINTED BY ORDER OF THE HOUSE OF REPRESENTATIVES.]
[Philadelphia: Printed by William Ross, 1798.] pp. (4). 8vo. AAS.

UNITED STATES, continued.

34703 —— Amendments of the Senate, to the bill, intituled, "An Act to make a further appropriation for the additional naval armament. [Printed by order of the House of Representatives.]
[Philadelphia: Printed by William Ross, 1798.] pp. (4). 8vo.   AAS.

34704 —— *Caption-title:* An Act to provide for the valuation of lands and dwelling-houses, and the enumeration of slaves within the United States.
[Boston: 1798.] pp. 22, (1), 26–35, 2 folded tables. 8vo.   NYPL.

Second title: State of Massachusetts. At a general meeting of the commissioners for the State of Massachusetts, appointed in pursuance of the Act of the United States (as above) to carry the same Act into effect in said State. . . . pp. 25–35.

34705 —— Extract from the Act, entitled, "An Act to provide for the valuation of land and dwelling-houses, and the enumeration of slaves within the United States.
[Philadelphia? 1798.] pp. 15. 8vo.

34706 —— Extract from the Instructions to the assessors appointed under the Act, entitled, "An Act to provide for the valuation of lands and dwelling-houses, and the enumeration of slaves, within the United States." [Twenty-two lines.]
[Philadelphia: 1798.] Broadside. 4to.   HSP.

34707 —— *Caption title:* Laws of the United States. An Act to provide for the valuation of lands and dwelling-houses, and the enumeration of slaves within the United States.
Trenton, Printed by Matthias Day. 1798. pp. 22. 8vo.   LOC.

34708 —— Abstract of An Act to provide for the valuation of lands and dwelling-houses, and the enumeration of slaves within the United States. To which are added, instructions and regulations for the principal and assistant assessors, made in pursuance of said Act: and the instructions of the Secretary of the Treasury of the United States. Published by order of the Board of Commissioners.
Vergennes: Printed by G. and R. Waite. 1798. pp. 35. 8vo.   HEH. LOC.

34709 —— — The Commissioners of the United States, under the Act of the Congress of the United States, passed on the ninth day of July 1798, entitled "An Act to provide for the valuation of lands and dwelling-houses, and the enumeration of slaves within the United States." To all to whom these presents shall come; send Greeting. . . . [Form of warrant for assistant assessors in the State of Vermont. Signed, Royall Tyler, clerk to the commissioners.]
Vergennes: Printed by G. and R. Waite, [1798.] obl. fol.

34710 —— An Act to suspend . . . intercourse . . . with France. Approved, June 13th, 1798.
[Philadelphia: 1798.] pp. 4. fol.

34711 —— The Alien and Sedition laws, and Virginia and Kentucky Resolutions. Published by order of the Legislature of Massachusetts. [Colophon:]
[Boston:] Printed by Young & Minns, Printers to the State. [1798.] pp. (2). fol.   AAS.

UNITED STATES, continued.

34712 —— — A Bill to establish an uniform system of bankruptcy throughout the United States. 8th February, 1798. Read the first and second time, and committed to a committee of the whole House, on Monday next. [Published by order of the House of Representatives.]

[Philadelphia: Printed by Joseph Gales. 1798.] pp. 32. 8vo. LOC. NYHS.

34713 —— A Bill to establish an uniform system of bankruptcy throughout the United States. 14th December, 1798. Read the first and second time, and committed to a committee of the whole House on Monday next. [Published by order of the House of Representatives.]

[Philadelphia: Printed by Joseph Gales, 1798.] pp. 32. 8vo. AAS.

34714 —— — Amendments proposed by Mr. Otis. To the tenth section of the bill to establish an uniform system of bankruptcy throughout the United States, . . .

[Philadelphia:] J. Gales, Printer. [1798.] pp. 2. 8vo. AAS.

34715 —— A Bill to provide for organizing, arming and disciplining the militia of the United States. Reported in pursuance of the following Resolution; [Eleven lines.] January 1st, 1798. Committed to a committee of the whole House, on Monday next.

Philadelphia: Printed by Joseph Gales, No. 116, North Second Street. [1798.] pp. (18). 8vo. AAS. BA.

34716 —— Extracts from the internal revenue laws, of the United States, printed for the use of the officers of the revenue, within the district of New-York.

New-York: Printed by Louis Jones. [1798.] pp. (2), 88. 8vo. NYPL.

34717 —— — Extracts from the revenue laws of the United States: comprehending such parts of the excise laws, — laws laying duties on licenses for selling wines, &c.—on riding carriages,—on property sold at auction, —and on stamps; as appears best calculated for the information of such as have not an opportunity of perusing the laws of the general government.

Lexington, Printed by J. Bradford, 1798. pp. 26. 8vo. LOC.

34718 —— [No. 1.] In Senate of the United States, July 9th 1798. The Committee to whom was referred a bill, entitled, "An Act for the relief of John Vaughan," with instruction to make a particular report, Report thereon, . . .

[Philadelphia: 1798.] pp. (6). 8vo. AAS.

34719 —— Journal of the House of Representatives of the United States, at the second session of the Fifth Congress, and of the Independence of the United States the twenty-second. [13 November, 1797—16 February, 1798.]

Philadelphia: Printed by William Ross, near Congress Hall. 1797. [1798.] pp. 683, lii. 8vo. AAS. BA. JCB.

34720 —— Journal of the Senate of the United States of America. Being the second session of the Fifth Congress, begun and held at the city of Philadelphia, November 13th, 1797 [— 16 July, 1798.] and in the twenty-second year of the sovereignty of the said United States.

Philadelphia: Printed by John Fenno, Printer to the Senate of the United States. 1798. pp. 501. 8vo. AAS. BA. MHS.

UNITED STATES, continued.

34721   —— Mr. Dwight Foster's Motion, June 6, 1798. [That the Treaty with France was no longer obligatory.]

     [Philadelphia: Printed by J. Gales? 1798. Broadside. 8vo.   AAS. BA.

34722   —— Mr. Harper's Motion. [To raise, arm and equip an army of ten thousand men.] 5th June, 1798, ordered to lie on the table. [Published by order of the House of Representatives.]

     [Philadelphia: Printed by William Ross, 1798.] pp. (4). 8vo.   AAS. BA.

34723   —— Mr. Harper's Motion, 3d July, 1798. [For a provisional army of ten thousand men, etc.]

     [Philadelphia:] J. Gales, Printer. [1798.] Broadside. 8vo.   AAS.

34724   —— Mr. Harper's Motion, 6th July, 1798. Referred to the committee of the whole House on the bill sent from the Senate intituled "An Act in addition to the Act intituled "An Act for the punishment of certain crimes against the United States."

     [Philadelphia: 1798.] pp. (3). 8vo.   AAS.

34725   —— Mr. Harper's Motion. [On State indebtedness to the government.] 12th December, 1798. Committed to a committee of the whole House to-morrow. Published by order of the House of Representatives.

     Philadelphia: Printed by J. Gales, No. 23, South Third-Street. [1798.] pp. 4. 8vo.   AAS. BA.

34726   —— Mr. Sitgreave's Motion, 22d May, 1798. [Regarding French cruziers.]

     [Philadelphia:] Printed by J. Gales. [1798.] Broadside. 8vo.   AAS.

34727   —— Report of the committee of claims, on a Motion relative to the amendments in the Acts respecting invalid pensioners; 26 March, 1798.

     [Philadelphia: 1798.] pp. 10. 8vo.   BA.

34728   —— Report of the committee of claims on a Resolution of the House on the expediency of extending the provisions of the "Act in addition to the Act for making farther and more effectual provision for the protection of the frontiers of the United States." To the widows and orphan children of the officers of the army of the United States, who were killed in an action with the Indians in the Territory northwest of the Ohio, 4th of November, 1791.

     [Philadelphia: 1798.] pp. 2. 8vo.   BA.

34729   —— Report of the committee of claims, on the Memorial of William Alexander. 4 January, 1798.

     [Philadelphia: 1798.] 8vo.   BA.

34730   —— Report of the committee of claims, on the Memorials of Joseph Ball. [Bills of credit.] 26 February, 1798.

     [Philadelphia: 1798.] 8vo.   BA.

34731   —— Report of the committee of claims, on the Memorials and Petitions of George P. Frost, Charles Jackson, and others. 19 March, 1798.

     [Philadelphia: 1798.] 8vo.   BA.

UNITED STATES, continued.

34732 —— REPORT OF THE COMMITTEE OF CLAIMS, TO WHOM WAS REFERRED THE MEMORIAL OF ALEXANDER MACOMB, AND WILLIAM EDGAR, PRESENTED THE THIRTEENTH OF MAY, 1796. 30TH JANUARY, 1798. COMMITTED TO A COMMITTEE OF THE WHOLE HOUSE, TO-MORROW. PUBLISHED BY ORDER OF THE HOUSE OF REPRESENTATIVES.

[Philadelphia:] Printed by W. Ross. [1798.] pp. (2), (1), 314–316, (2). 8vo. BA.

34733 —— REPORT OF THE COMMITTEE OF CLAIMS, ON THE MEMORIAL OF J. PERRY. 22 MARCH, 1798.

[Philadelphia: 1798.] 8vo. BA.

34734 —— REPORT OF THE COMMITTEE OF CLAIMS, ON THE PETITION OF S. ALEXANDER, WIDOW OF THE LATE MAJOR GENERAL EARL OF STIRLING. 2 JANUARY, 1798.

[Philadelphia: 1798.] 8vo. BA.

34735 —— REPORT OF THE COMMITTEE OF CLAIMS, TO WHOM WAS REFERRED, ON THE TWENTY-FIRST ULTIMO, THE PETITION OF JOHN CARR, PRESENTED THE 21ST OF FEBRUARY, 1794.

[Philadelphia: 1798.] 8vo. BA.

34736 —— — REPORT OF THE COMMITTEE OF CLAIMS, TO WHOM WAS REFERRED, ON THE TWENTY-FIRST ULTIMO, THE PETITION OF JOHN CARR, PRESENTED THE 21ST OF FEBRUARY, 1794, AND THE REPORT OF A COMMITTEE THEREON. 17TH JANUARY, 1798. COMMITTED TO A COMMITTEE OF THE WHOLE HOUSE, TOMORROW. [PUBLISHED BY ORDER OF THE HOUSE OF REPRESENTATIVES.]

[Philadelphia: Printed by William Ross. 1798.] pp. (2), 277–278. 8vo. JCB.

34737 —— REPORT OF THE COMMITTEE OF CLAIMS, ON THE PETITION OF L. CLARK. 18 JANUARY, 1798.

[Philadelphia: 1798.] 8vo. BA.

34738 —— REPORT OF THE COMMITTEE OF CLAIMS, ON THE PETITION OF T. ELLIOT. 2 APRIL, 1798.

[Philadelphia: 1798.] 8vo. BA.

34739 —— REPORT OF THE COMMITTEE OF CLAIMS, ON THE PETITION OF J. FRANK. 8 JANUARY, 1798.

[Philadelphia: 1798.] 8vo. BA.

34740 —— REPORT OF THE COMMITTEE OF CLAIMS, TO WHOM WAS REFERRED, ON THE 30TH OF MARCH LAST, THE PETITION OF JONATHAN HASKELL. 16TH APRIL, 1798, COMMITTED TO A COMMITTEE OF THE WHOLE HOUSE, TO-MORROW. 24TH DECEMBER, 1798, COMMITTED TO A COMMITTEE OF THE WHOLE HOUSE, ON THURSDAY NEXT. [PUBLISHED BY ORDER OF THE HOUSE OF REPRESENTATIVES.]

[Philadelphia: Printed by William Ross, 1798.] pp. 4. 8vo. AAS. BA.

34741 —— REPORT OF THE COMMITTEE OF CLAIMS, TO WHOM WAS RECOMMITTED, ON THE 5TH OF DECEMBER LAST, THE PETITION OF HENRY HILL, AND THE SEVERAL REPORTS THEREON, WITH INSTRUCTION "TO REPORT A STATEMENT OF THE FACTS RELATIVE TO THE DEMANDS AGAINST WHICH THE UNITED STATES HAVE INDEMNIFIED GENERAL GREENE, AS SURETY FOR JOHN BANKS." 14TH FEBRUARY, 1798. COMMITTED TO A COMMITTEE OF THE WHOLE HOUSE, ON MONDAY NEXT. [PUBLISHED BY ORDER OF THE HOUSE OF REPRESENTATIVES.]

[Philadelphia: Printed by William Ross. 1798.] pp. (2), 381–394. 8vo. BA. JCB.

UNITED STATES, continued.

34742 —— REPORT OF THE COMMITTEE OF CLAIMS, ON THE PETITION OF THOMAS LEWIS. 15TH FEBRUARY, 1798, ORDERED TO LIE ON THE TABLE. 25TH APRIL, 1798, COMMITTED TO A COMMITTEE OF THE WHOLE HOUSE, ON MONDAY NEXT. [PUBLISHED BY ORDER OF THE HOUSE OF REPRESENTATIVES.]

[Philadelphia: Printed by William Ross, 1798.] pp. (4). 8vo.   AAS. BA.

34743 —— REPORT OF THE COMMITTEE OF CLAIMS, ON THE PETITIONS OF J. NELSON AND S. RUSSELL. 23 JANUARY, 1798.

[Philadelphia: 1798.] 8vo.   BA.

34744 —— REPORT OF THE COMMITTEE OF CLAIMS, ON THE PETITION OF THE CORPORATION OF RHODE ISLAND COLLEGE. 12 DECEMBER, 1798.

[Philadelphia: 1798.] 8vo.   BA.

34745 —— REPORT OF THE COMMITTEE OF CLAIMS, ON THE PETITION OF COMFORT SANDS. 20 DECEMBER, 1798.

[Philadelphia: 1798.] 8vo.   BA.

34746 —— REPORT OF THE COMMITTEE OF CLAIMS, ON THE PETITION OF JOHN VAUGHAN; 19 MAY, 1798.

[Philadelphia: 1798.] 8vo.   BA.

34747 —— REPORT OF THE COMMITTEE OF CLAIMS, TO WHOM WAS REFERRED, ON THE 25TH ULTIMO, THE PETITION OF JOHN BAPTISTE VERDIER. COMMITTED TO A COMMITTEE OF THE WHOLE HOUSE, ON MONDAY NEXT. [PUBLISHED BY ORDER OF THE HOUSE OF REPRESENTATIVES.]

[Philadelphia: Printed by William Ross. 1798.] pp. 21. 8vo.   JCB.

34748 —— REPORT OF THE COMMITTEE OF CLAIMS, ON THE PETITION OF B. WELLS. 2 MAY, 1798.

[Philadelphia: 1798.] 8vo.   BA.

34749 —— REPORT OF THE COMMITTEE OF CLAIMS, ON THE PETITION OF ANNA WELSH. 7TH FEBRUARY, 1797, COMMITTED TO A COMMITTEE OF THE WHOLE HOUSE, ON MONDAY NEXT. 5TH DECEMBER, 1797, COMMITTED TO A COMMITTEE OF THE WHOLE HOUSE, ON MONDAY NEXT. [PUBLISHED BY ORDER OF THE HOUSE OF REPRESENTATIVES.]

[Philadelphia: Printed by William Ross. 1798.] pp. (2), [65]–68. 8vo.   AAS.

34750 —— REPORT OF THE COMMITTEE OF COMMERCE AND MANUFACTURES, ON THE PETITION OF P. AUPOIX. 2 JANUARY, 1798.

[Philadelphia: 1798.] 8vo.   BA.

34751 —— REPORT OF THE COMMITTEE OF COMMERCE AND MANUFACTURES, ON THE PETITION OF W. BELL. 4 JANUARY, 1798.

[Philadelphia: 1798.] 8vo.   BA.

34752 —— .REPORT OF THE COMMITTEE OF COMMERCE AND MANUFACTURES, ON THE PETITION OF G. AND H. COLHOUN; 18 APRIL, 1798.

[Philadelphia: 1798.] 8vo.   BA.

34753 —— REPORT OF THE COMMITTEE OF COMMERCE AND MANUFACTURES, ON THE PETITION OF O. COOK, A. WOOD, JR., AND R. HOOPER. 29 DECEMBER, 1797.

[Philadelphia: 1798.] 8vo.   BA.

34754 —— REPORT OF THE COMMITTEE OF COMMERCE AND MANUFACTURES, ON THE PETITION OF R. CUTTER. 10 JANUARY, 1798.

[Philadelphia: 1798.] 8vo.   BA.

UNITED STATES, continued.

34755 —— Report of the Committee of Commerce and Manufactures, on the Petition of P. J. Flamend in behalf of Louis Le Guen; . . . 8 December, 1798.
[*Philadelphia:* 1798.] 8vo. BA.

34756 —— Report of the Committee of Commerce and Manufactures, on the Petition of J. Heron and others. 9 February, 1798.
[*Philadelphia:* 1798.] 8vo. BA.

34757 —— Report of the Committee of Privileges, to whom was referred, on the thirtieth ultimo, a motion relative to the "expulsion from this House, of Matthew Lyon, for a violent attack, and gross indecency committed upon the person of Roger Griswold, a member from Connecticut, in the presence of the House, while sitting." 2nd February, 1798.
[*Philadelphia:* 1798.] pp. (4). 8vo. BA.

34758 —— Report of the Committee of Privileges. Testimony, by members of the House of Representatives, before a committee of the whole House, relative to a Report of the Committee of Privileges on the conduct of Matthew Lyon. [12 February, 1798.]
[*Philadelphia:* 1798.] 8vo. BA.

34759 —— Report of the Committee of Privileges, to whom was referred, on the sixteenth instant, a motion for the expulsion of Roger Griswold and Matthew Lyon, members of this House, for riotous and disorderly behaviour, committed in the House. 20th February, 1798, ordered to lie on the table. [Published by order of the House of Representatives.]
[*Philadelphia: Printed by William Ross.* 1798.] pp. 24. 8vo. AAS. BA.

34760 —— The Testimony given before a committee of the whole of the House of Representatives of the United States, in relation to a Report of their committee of Privileges, 5th, 6th and 8th of February, 1798.
[*Philadelphia: Printed by Joseph Gales.* 1798.] pp. (30). 8vo. AAS.
The relations of witnesses to the Lyon-Griswold affair in the House of Representatives.

34761 —— Report of the Committee of Revisal and Unfinished Business, on bills, reports, and other matters of business depending and undetermined upon, at the last session. 11th December, 1798, ordered to lie on the table. [Published by order of the House of Representatives.]
[*Philadelphia: Printed by William Ross,* 1798.] pp. 10. 8vo. AAS.

34762 —— Further Report of the Committee of Revisal & Unfinished Business, on such Laws of the United States, as are near expiring. 27th December, 1798, ordered to lie on the table. [Published by order of the House of Representatives.]
[*Philadelphia: Printed by William Ross,* 1798.] pp. 4. 8vo. AAS.

34763 —— Report of the Committee of Revisal and Unfinished Business, on the Memorial of W. Simmons; 7 May, 1798.
[*Philadelphia:* 1798.] 8vo. BA.

34764 —— Report of the Committee of Revisal and Unfinished Business, to whom was referred the Message of the President with representation of the Secretary of War on the subject of clerks in his office. 31 January, 1798.
[*Philadelphia:* 1798.] 8vo. BA.

UNITED STATES, continued.

34765   —— [Ornament.] REPORT OF THE COMMITTEE OF WAYS AND MEANS, INSTRUCTED ON THE SIXTH ULTIMO, TO ENQUIRE WHETHER ANY AND WHAT ADDITIONAL REVENUES, WILL BE WANTED FOR THE PUBLIC SERVICE. 1ST MAY, 1798. RECOMMITTED TO THE COMMITTEE OF WAYS AND MEANS. 2D MAY, 1798. COMMITTED TO A COMMITTEE OF THE WHOLE HOUSE ON FRIDAY NEXT. [PUBLISHED BY ORDER OF THE HOUSE OF REPRESENTATIVES.] [Ornament.]

    [Philadelphia: 1798.] pp. (18). fol.   AAS. BA. JCB.

34766   —— FURTHER REPORT OF THE COMMITTEE OF WAYS AND MEANS, INSTRUCTED ON THE FIFTH OF DECEMBER LAST, TO ENQUIRE WHAT ALTERATIONS MAY BE NECESSARY, IN THE ACT, ENTITLED AN ACT LAYING DUTIES ON STAMPED VELLUM, PARCHMENT AND PAPER. 14TH FEBRUARY, 1798. COMMITTED TO A COMMITTEE OF THE WHOLE HOUSE, ON MONDAY NEXT. PUBLISHED BY ORDER OF THE HOUSE OF REPRESENTATIVES.

    [Philadelphia:] Printed by W. Ross. [1798?] pp. (2), 395–403. 8vo.

                                      BA. JCB.

34767   —— REPORT ON ALTERATIONS IN ACTS IMPOSING DUTIES ON SPIRITS DISTILLED WITHIN THE UNITED STATES. 14 FEBRUARY, 1798.

    [Philadelphia: 1798.] 8vo.   BA.

34768   —— REPORT OF THE COMMITTEE TO WHOM WAS REFERRED A REPORT OF THE DIRECTOR OF THE MINT. 8 DECEMBER, 1797.

    [Philadelphia: 1798.] 8vo.   BA.

34769   —— REPORT IN PART, OF THE COMMITTEE TO WHOM WAS REFERRED, ON THE 29TH OF NOVEMBER LAST, SO MUCH OF THE PRESIDENT'S SPEECH, AS RELATES TO THE PROTECTION OF COMMERCE, AND THE DEFENCE OF THE COUNTRY. 8TH MARCH, 1798, REFERRED TO THE COMMITTEE OF THE WHOLE HOUSE, ON THE STATE OF THE UNION. [PUBLISHED BY ORDER OF THE HOUSE OF REPRESENTATIVES.]

    [Philadelphia: Printed by William Ross, 1798?] pp. (2), 441–445. 8vo. JCB.

34770   —— REPORT OF THE COMMITTEE TO WHOM WAS REFERRED, ON THE 29TH OF NOVEMBER LAST, SO MUCH OF THE PRESIDENT'S SPEECH AS RELATES TO THE PROTECTION OF COMMERCE AND THE DEFENCE OF THE COUNTRY. 9TH APRIL, 1798, COMMITTED TO A COMMITTEE OF THE WHOLE HOUSE, ON THE STATE OF THE UNION. [PUBLISHED BY ORDER OF THE HOUSE OF REPRESENTATIVES.]

    [Philadelphia: Printed by William Ross, 1798.] pp. (4). 8vo.   AAS. BA.

34771   —— REPORT OF THE COMMITTEE TO WHOM WAS REFERRED, ON THE 29TH OF NOVEMBER LAST, SO MUCH OF THE PRESIDENT'S SPEECH AS RELATES TO THE PROTECTION OF COMMERCE, AND THE DEFENCE OF THE COUNTRY. 22D MAY, 1798, COMMITTED TO A COMMITTEE OF THE WHOLE HOUSE, TO-MORROW. [PUBLISHED BY ORDER OF THE HOUSE OF REPRESENTATIVES.]

    [Philadelphia: Printed by William Ross, 1798.] pp. (4). 8vo.   AAS. BA.

34772   —— REPORT FROM THE COMMITTEE TO WHOM WAS REFERRED, ON THE 29TH OF NOVEMBER LAST, SO MUCH OF THE PRESIDENT'S SPEECH AS RELATES TO THE REIMBURSEMENT OF CERTAIN ADVANCES MADE BY THE CONSULS OF THE UNITED STATES IN FOREIGN COUNTRIES. 14TH FEBRUARY, 1798. COMMITTED TO A COMMITTEE OF THE WHOLE HOUSE ON FRIDAY NEXT. PRINTED BY ORDER OF THE HOUSE OF REPRESENTATIVES.

    Philadelphia: Printed by Joseph Gales, No. 126, North Second Street. [1798.] pp. (2), (369)–(376). 8vo.   AAS. BA.

UNITED STATES, continued.

34773 —— REPORT FROM THE COMMITTEE TO WHOM WAS REFERRED, ON THE TWENTY-THIRD OF JANUARY LAST, THE MESSAGE FROM THE PRESIDENT OF THE UNITED STATES, RELATIVE TO THE EXECUTION OF THE ACT FOR RELIEF OF PERSONS IMPRISONED FOR DEBT. 26TH FEBRUARY, 1798. COMMITTED TO A COMMITTEE OF THE WHOLE HOUSE TO-MORROW. PRINTED BY ORDER OF THE HOUSE OF REPRESENTATIVES.

Philadelphia: Printed by Joseph Gales, No. 126, North Second Street. [1798.] pp. (3). 8vo.   AAS. BA.

34774 —— REPORT OF THE COMMITTEE TO WHOM WAS REFERRED THE ACT FOR THE RELIEF OF PERSONS IMPRISONED FOR DEBT, AND AN ACT MITIGATING OR REMITTING THE FORFEITURES, PENALTIES, ETC. ALSO THE PETITION OF JAMES GREENLEAF. 25 APRIL, 1798.

[Philadelphia: 1798.] 8vo.   BA.

34775 —— REPORT OF THE COMMITTEE TO WHOM WAS REFERRED A MOTION OF THE 6TH INSTANT, RELATIVE TO THE BALANCES DUE TO THE UNITED STATES. 7TH JULY, 1798. COMMITTED TO A COMMITTEE OF THE WHOLE HOUSE ON MONDAY NEXT. PRINTED BY ORDER OF THE HOUSE OF REPRESENTATIVES.

Philadelphia: Printed by Joseph Gales, No. 23, South Third Street. [1798.] pp. (3). 8vo.   AAS.

34776 —— REPORT OF THE COMMITTEE APPOINTED ON THE TENTH INSTANT, TO PREPARE AN ADDRESS TO THE PRESIDENT OF THE UNITED STATES. 12TH DECEMBER, 1798, COMMITTED TO A COMMITTEE OF THE WHOLE HOUSE, TO-MORROW. [PUBLISHED BY ORDER OF THE HOUSE OF REPRESENTATIVES.]

[Philadelphia: Printed by William Ross, 1798.] pp. 6. 8vo.   AAS. BA.

34777 —— REPORT OF THE COMMITTEE, ALTERATIONS IN THE ACTS ESTABLISHING THE EXECUTIVE DEPARTMENTS. 5 JULY, 1798.

[Philadelphia: 1798.] pp. 10. 8vo.   BA.

34778 —— REPORT OF COMMITTEE ON AMENDMENTS TO THE BILL FOR THE RELIEF OF THE REFUGEES FROM THE BRITISH PROVINCES. 27 FEBRUARY, 1798.

[Philadelphia: 1798.] 8vo.   BA.

34779 —— REPORT OF THE COMMITTEE ON THE LETTERS OF R. PUTNAM. 13 JUNE, 1798.

[Philadelphia: 1798.] 8vo.   BA.

34780 —— REPORT OF THE COMMITTEE TO WHOM WAS REFERRED THE ACT PROVIDING FOR THE SALE OF THE LANDS NORTH-WEST OF THE OHIO. 13 JUNE, 1798.

[Philadelphia: 1798.] 8vo.   BA.

34781 —— REPORT OF THE COMMITTEE TO WHOM WAS REFERRED THE MEMORIAL AND PETITION OF MARGARET LAPSLEY. AGREED TO BY THE SENATE—MARCH 19TH, 1798. PUBLISHED BY ORDER OF THE SENATE OF THE UNITED STATES.

[Philadelphia:] Printed by Way & Groff, No. 27, Arch-Street. [1798.] pp. (4). 8vo.   AAS. BA.

34782 —— REPORT OF THE COMMITTEE ON A MESSAGE FROM THE PRESIDENT, INCLOSING A MEMORIAL FROM THE COMMISSIONERS OF THE CITY OF WASHINGTON. 8 MARCH, 1798.

[Philadelphia: 1798.] 8vo.   BA.

34783 —— REPORT OF THE COMMITTEE TO WHOM WAS REFERRED THE MOTION OF THE SEVENTEENTH JANUARY LAST, RESPECTING THE TERRITORY OF THE UNITED STATES SOUTHWARD AND WESTWARD OF THE STATE OF GEORGIA. PUBLISHED BY ORDER OF THE SENATE OF THE UNITED STATES.

[Philadelphia:] Printed by W. Ross. [1798.] pp. 6. 8vo.   AAS. BA. DeRGL. YC.

UNITED STATES, continued.

34784 —— REPORT OF THE COMMITTEE TO WHOM WAS REFERRED, ON THE 30TH OF NOVEMBER LAST, A REPRESENTATION AND REMONSTRANCE OF THE LEGISLATURE OF THE STATE OF GEORGIA. 3D MAY, 1788, COMMITTED TO A COMMITTEE OF THE WHOLE HOUSE, ON THURSDAY NEXT. 24TH DECEMBER, 1798, COMMITTED TO A COMMITTEE OF THE WHOLE HOUSE, ON MONDAY NEXT. [PUBLISHED BY ORDER OF THE HOUSE OF REPRESENTATIVES.

[Philadelphia: Printed by William Ross, 1798.] pp. 4. 8vo.

AAS. BA. DeRGL. JCB.

34785 —— REPORT OF THE COMMITTEE OF THE HOUSE OF REPRESENTATIVES OF THE UNITED STATES, APPOINTED TO PREPARE AND REPORT ARTICLES OF IMPEACHMENT AGAINST WILLIAM BLOUNT, A SENATOR OF THE UNITED STATES, IMPEACHED OF HIGH CRIMES AND MISDEMEANORS, MADE IN PURSUANCE OF A RESOLUTION OF THE HOUSE OF REPRESENTATIVES, AUTHORIZING THE SAID COMMITTEE TO SIT DURING THE RECESS OF CONGRESS, AND INSTRUCTING THEM "TO ENQUIRE, AND, BY ALL LAWFUL MEANS, TO DISCOVER THE WHOLE NATURE AND EXTENT OF THE OFFENCE WHEREOF THE SAID WILLIAM BLOUNT STANDS IMPEACHED, AND WHO ARE THE PARTIES AND ASSOCIATES THEREIN." PRINTED BY ORDER OF THE HOUSE OF REPRESENTATIVES.

[Philadelphia:] Printed by John Fenno. [1798.] pp. (2), (vi.), (16), (clx). 8vo.

AAS. BA. CLS. HSP. JCB. LOC. NYHS.

34786 —— — DEPOSITION OF GEN. ELIJAH CLARK[E], OF THE STATE OF GEORGIA, RESPECTING A LETTER FROM HIM TO DON DIEGO MORPHY, CONSUL OF HIS CATHOLIC MAJESTY, AT CHARLESTON, SOUTH-CAROLINA, CONTAINING THE ANSWERS OF THE SAID DEPONENT, TO CERTAIN INTERROGATORIES FRAMED BY THE COMMITTEE APPOINTED ON THE 2D OF FEBRUARY LAST. "TO TAKE ALL SUCH STEPS AS MAY BE NECESSARY FOR OBTAINING THE TESTIMONY OF THE SAID ELIJAH CLARK[E], OR ANY OTHER PERSON OR PERSONS, ON THE SUBJECT MATTER OF SAID LETTER." TAKEN BEFORE CERTAIN COMMISSIONERS EMPOWERED BY THE SAID COMMITTEE, FOR THE PURPOSE OF TAKING THE SAID DEPOSITION. 27TH APRIL, 1798, ORDERED TO LIE ON THE TABLE.

[Philadelphia: Printed by William Ross, 1798.] pp. 8. 8vo.

Relating to the impeachment of William Blount.   AAS. BA. LOC. MHS.

34787 —— — FURTHER REPORT FROM THE COMMITTEE OF IMPEACHMENT AGAINST WILLIAM BLOUNT. [DEPOSITION OF A. HOLDEN, JR.] 30 DECEMBER, 1797.

[Philadelphia: 1798.] 8vo.   BA.

34788 —— — LETTERS OF CHEV. D'YRUJO, AND J. P. RIPLEY, TO THE CHAIRMAN OF THE COMMITTEE OF IMPEACHMENT AGAINST WILLIAM BLOUNT. 19 JANUARY, 1798.

[Philadelphia: 1798.] 8vo.   BA.

34789 —— — REPORT, IN PART, OF THE COMMITTEE, APPOINTED ON THE 18TH INSTANT, TO CONSIDER WHAT RULES ARE NECESSARY TO BE ADOPTED BY THE SENATE, IN THE TRIAL OF WILLIAM BLOUNT. 20TH DECEMBER, 1798. PRINTED BY ORDER OF THE SENATE OF THE UNITED STATES.

Philadelphia: Printed by Way & Groff, No. 48, North Third-Street. [1798.] pp. (4). 8vo.   AAS. BA.

34790 —— — FURTHER REPORT OF THE MANAGERS APPOINTED TO CONDUCT THE IMPEACHMENT AGAINST WILLIAM BLOUNT 20TH DECEMBER, 1798, ORDERED TO LIE ON THE TABLE. [PUBLISHED BY ORDER OF THE HOUSE OF REPRESENTATIVES.]

[Philadelphia: Printed by William Ross, 1798.] pp. 4. 8vo.   AAS. LOC.

UNITED STATES, continued.

34791 —— — MESSAGE FROM THE SENATE, COMMUNICATING A COPY OF THE PLEA, FILED BY THE COUNSEL IN BEHALF OF WILLIAM BLOUNT. 26TH DECEMBER, 1798. REFERRED TO THE MANAGERS APPOINTED TO CONDUCT THE IMPEACHMENT AGAINST WILLIAM BLOUNT, WITH INSTRUCTIONS TO PROCEED THEREON, AS THEY SHALL DEEM ADVISABLE. [PUBLISHED BY ORDER OF THE HOUSE OF REPRESENTATIVES.]
[Philadelphia: Printed by William Ross, 1798.] pp. 4. 8vo.   AAS. BA.

34792 —— — FURTHER REPORT OF THE COMMITTEE, APPOINTED ON THE EIGHTH JULY LAST, TO PREPARE AND REPORT ARTICLES OF IMPEACHMENT AGAINST WILLIAM BLOUNT, A SENATOR OF THE UNITED STATES. IMPEACHED BY THE HOUSE OF REPRESENTATIVES, OF HIGH CRIMES AND MISDEMEANORS. 25TH JANUARY, 1798. [COMMITTED TO A COMMITTEE OF THE WHOLE HOUSE, ON MONDAY NEXT.]
[Philadelphia:] Printed by John Fenno. [1798.]. pp. (11). 8vo.
AAS. BA. LOC.

34793 —— — FURTHER REPORT FROM THE COMMITTEE APPOINTED ON THE EIGHTH OF JULY LAST, TO PREPARE AND REPORT ARTICLES OF IMPEACHMENT AGAINST WILLIAM BLOUNT, A SENATOR OF THE UNITED STATES, IMPEACHED BY THE HOUSE OF REPRESENTATIVES, OF HIGH CRIMES AND MISDEMEANORS.
[Philadelphia: 1798.] pp. iv, 4. 8vo.   AAS. LOC.

34794 —— THE CONSTITUTION OF THE UNITED STATES OF AMERICA, AS AGREED UPON BY THEIR DELEGATES IN CONVENTION, SEPTEMBER 17TH, 1787: TOGETHER WITH THE ARTICLES OF AMENDMENT, AS ADOPTED BY THE CONGRESS OF THE SAID STATES, IN THE YEAR 1789.
Bennington: Printed by Anthony Haswell. 1798. pp. 23. 12mo.   JCB.

34795 —— — CONSTITUTION OF THE UNITED STATES OF AMERICA, AND OF THE STATE OF NEW-JERSEY. TO WHICH IS ANNEXED, THE DECLARATION OF INDEPENDENCE, AS AGREED UPON BY THE REPRESENTATIVES OF THE UNITED STATES OF AMERICA, CONGRESS ASSEMBLED, JULY 4, 1776. AND A COMPENDIUM OF THE DECLARATION OF RIGHTS, SELECTED FROM SOME OF THE STATE CONSTITUTIONS.
Newark, N.J.: Printed by Pennington and Dodge. 1798. pp. 40. 8vo. NJHS.

34796 —— — THE CONSTITUTION OF THE UNITED STATES OF AMERICA, WITH ALL THE AMENDMENTS.
Newport: Printed by H. and O. Farnsworth. 1798. pp. 22. 18mo.

34797 —— [Arms.] BY THE PRESIDENT OF THE UNITED STATES OF AMERICA. A PROCLAMATION. AS THE SAFETY AND PROSPERITY OF NATIONS ULTIMATELY AND ESSENTIALLY DEPEND ON THE PROTECTION AND THE BLESSING OF ALMIGHTY GOD; . . . I DO HEREBY RECOMMEND, THAT WEDNESDAY THE NINTH DAY OF MAY NEXT, BE OBSERVED THROUGHOUT THE UNITED STATES, AS A DAY OF SOLEMN HUMILIATION, FASTING AND PRAYER; . . . GIVEN UNDER MY HAND AND THE SEAL OF THE UNITED STATES OF AMERICA, AT PHILADELPHIA, THIS TWENTY-THIRD DAY OF MARCH, IN THE YEAR OF OUR LORD ONE THOUSAND SEVEN HUNDRED AND NINETY-EIGHT, AND OF THE INDEPENDENCE OF THE UNITED STATES THE TWENTY-SECOND. JOHN ADAMS. BY THE PRESIDENT, TIMOTHY PICKERING, SECRETARY OF STATE.
[Philadelphia: 1798.] Broadside. fol.   AAS. HSP. MHS. NYPL.

34798 —— MESSAGE OF THE PRESIDENT OF THE UNITED STATES RELATIVE TO THE AFFAIR OF WILLIAM BLOUNT: AND THE REPORT OF A COMMITTEE OF CONGRESS CONTAINING THE EVIDENCE RELATIVE THERETO. PROCEEDINGS ON IMPEACHMENT.
[Philadelphia:] July 5, 1797. pp. 182. 8vo.

UNITED STATES, continued.

34799 —— MESSAGE FROM THE PRESIDENT OF THE UNITED STATES, ACCOMPANYING A RE-
PORT FROM THE SECRETARY OF STATE, AND COPIES OF ACTS OF THE LEGISLATURES
OF THE STATES OF CONNECTICUT, MARYLAND AND VIRGINIA, RATIFYING THE AMEND-
MENT PROPOSED BY CONGRESS, CONCERNING THE SUABILITY OF STATES, IN PURSU-
ANCE OF A RESOLUTION OF THE TWO HOUSES OF THE SECOND OF MARCH LAST. 1ST
JANUARY, 1798. ORDERED TO LIE ON THE TABLE. 17TH OF JANUARY, 1798.
REFERRED TO MR. BALDWIN, MR. HINDMAN, MR. SITGREAVES. [PUBLISHED BY
ORDER OF THE HOUSE OF REPRESENTATIVES.]

[Philadelphia: Printed by William Ross. 1798.] pp. 12. 8vo.   AAS. BA.

34800 —— MESSAGE FROM THE PRESIDENT OF THE UNITED STATES, ACCOMPANYING A REP-
RESENTATION FROM THE JUDGE OF THE DISTRICT OF PENNSYLVANIA, AND A RE-
PORT OF THE ATTORNEY-GENERAL, RELATIVE TO CERTAIN INCONVENIENCES AND
DISAGREEABLE CONSEQUENCES WHICH HAVE OCCURRED IN THE EXECUTION OF THE
ACT PASSED THE TWENTY-EIGHTH OF MAY, 1796, INTITULED "AN ACT FOR THE
RELIEF OF PERSONS IMPRISONED FOR DEBT." JANUARY 18TH, 1798. COMMITTED
TO THE COMMITTEE OF THE WHOLE HOUSE, TO WHOM IS COMMITTED THE REPORT
OF THE COMMITTEE OF COMMERCE AND MANUFACTURES ON THE PETITION OF WIL-
LIAM BELL. PRINTED BY ORDER OF THE HOUSE OF REPRESENTATIVES.

Philadelphia: Printed by Joseph Gales, No. 126, North Second Street. [1798.]
pp. 8. 8vo.   AAS. BA.

34801 —— MESSAGE FROM THE PRESIDENT OF THE UNITED STATES, ACCOMPANYING A RE-
PORT TO HIM FROM THE SECRETARY OF STATE, AND SUNDRY DOCUMENTS, RELATIVE
TO THE AFFAIRS OF THE UNITED STATES ON THE MISSISSIPPI; THE INTERCOURSE
WITH THE INDIAN NATIONS, AND THE INEXECUTION OF THE TREATY BETWEEN THE
UNITED STATES AND SPAIN. 23D JANUARY, 1798. ORDERED TO LIE ON THE TABLE.
PUBLISHED BY ORDER OF THE HOUSE OF REPRESENTATIVES.

[Philadelphia: Printed by William Ross. 1798.] pp. 91. 8vo.   AAS. BA. JCB.

34802 —— MESSAGE FROM THE PRESIDENT OF THE UNITED STATES, ACCOMPANYING COPIES
OF TWO ACTS OF THE PARLIAMENT OF GREAT-BRITAIN, PASSED ON THE 4TH AND
19TH OF JULY, 1797, RELATIVE TO THE CARRYING INTO EXECUTION THE TREATY
OF AMITY, COMMERCE AND NAVIGATION, CONCLUDED BETWEEN HIS MAJESTY AND
THE UNITED STATES OF AMERICA; AND REGULATING THE TRADE TO BE CARRIED
ON WITH THE BRITISH POSSESSIONS IN INDIA, BY THE SHIPS OF NATIONS IN AMITY
WITH HIS MAJESTY. 2D FEBRUARY, 1798. REFERRED TO THE COMMITTEE OF
COMMERCE AND MANUFACTURES. PUBLISHED BY ORDER OF THE HOUSE OF REPRE-
SENTATIVES.

[Philadelphia: Printed by William Ross. 1798.] pp. 29. 8vo.   AAS. BA.

34803 —— MESSAGE FROM THE PRESIDENT OF THE UNITED STATES, INCLOSING A LETTER
TO HIM FROM THE GOVERNOR OF SOUTH-CAROLINA, ACCOMPANYING A NUMBER OF
DEPOSITIONS OF WITNESSES TO SEVERAL CAPTURES AND OUTRAGES COMMITTED WITHIN
AND NEAR THE LIMITS OF THE UNITED STATES, BY A FRENCH PRIVATEER, CALLED
THE VERTITUDE, OR FORTITUDE; AND ALSO COPIES OF CERTAIN OTHER DEPOSITIONS
RELATIVE TO THE SAME SUBJECT, TRANSMITTED BY THE COLLECTOR OF THE DISTRICT
OF CHARLESTON. FEBRUARY 5TH, 1798. REFERRED TO THE COMMITTEE TO WHOM
WAS COMMITTED, ON THE 29TH OF NOVEMBER LAST, SO MUCH OF THE PRESIDENT'S
SPEECH AS RELATED TO THE PROTECTION OF COMMERCE AND THE DEFENCE OF THE
COUNTRY. PRINTED BY ORDER OF THE HOUSE OF REPRESENTATIVES.

Philadelphia: Printed by Joseph Gales, No. 126, North Second Street. [1798.]
pp. (22). 8vo.   AAS. BA.

UNITED STATES, continued.

34804 —— MESSAGE FROM THE PRESIDENT OF THE UNITED STATES, TRANSMITTING AN OFFI-CIAL STATEMENT OF THE EXPENDITURE, TO THE END OF THE YEAR ONE THOUSAND SEVEN HUNDRED AND NINETY-SEVEN, FROM THE SUMS HERETOFORE GRANTED TO DEFRAY THE CONTINGENT CHARGES OF THE GOVERNMENT. 12TH FEBRUARY, 1798. RECEIVED 13TH FEBRUARY, 1798. READ, AND ORDERED TO LIE ON THE TABLE. PRINTED BY ORDER OF THE HOUSE OF REPRESENTATIVES.

Philadelphia: Printed by Joseph Gales, No. 126, North Second Street. [1798.] pp. (7). 8vo   AAS. BA.

34805 —— MESSAGE FROM THE PRESIDENT OF THE UNITED STATES, ACCOMPANYING A RE-PORT MADE TO HIM BY THE SECRETARY OF STATE, EXHIBITING A STATEMENT OF THE LOSSES RECOVERED BY THE CITIZENS OF THE UNITED STATES UNDER THE TREATY MADE WITH GREAT BRITAIN. "SPECIFYING THOSE CASES WHICH HAVE BEEN ACTU-ALLY DECIDED IN THE COURT OF APPEALS;" MADE IN PURSUANCE OF A RESOLUTION OF THE FIRST INSTANT. 19TH FEBRUARY, 1798. ORDERED TO LIE ON THE TABLE. [PUBLISHED BY ORDER OF THE HOUSE OF REPRESENTATIVES.]

[Philadelphia: Printed by William Ross, 1798.] pp. 11, table. 8vo.   AAS. JCB.

34806 —— MESSAGE FROM THE PRESIDENT OF THE UNITED STATES, ACCOMPANYING A REPORT TO HIM FROM THE SECRETARY OF STATE, ALSO, AN ACCOUNT OF THE EX-PENDITURES FOR THE PROSECUTION OF THE CLAIMS OF CERTAIN CITIZENS OF THE UNITED STATES, FOR PROPERTY CAPTURED BY THE BELLIGERENT POWERS, AND OF THE REIMBURSEMENTS ARISING FROM THE DEDUCTIONS OF COSTS IN THE CASES MEN-TIONED IN THE SAID ACCOUNT OF THE 18TH OF AUGUST, 1797.—IN PURSUANCE OF AN ACT PASSED THE 3D OF MARCH, 1797. 20TH FEBRUARY, 1798. ORDERED TO LIE ON THE TABLE. [Ornament.] PUBLISHED BY ORDER OF THE HOUSE OF REP-RESENTATIVES.

[Philadelphia:] Printed by W. Ross. [1798.] pp. (8). fol.   AAS.

34807 —— MESSAGE FROM THE PRESIDENT OF THE UNITED STATES, INCLOSING A MEMORIAL OF THE COMMISSIONERS APPOINTED UNDER THE "ACT FOR ESTABLISHING THE TEM-PORARY AND PERMANENT SEAT OF THE GOVERNMENT OF THE UNITED STATES," REPRESENTING THE SITUATION AND CIRCUMSTANCES OF THE CITY OF WASHINGTON. 23D FEBRUARY, 1798. REFERRED TO MR. CRAIK, MR. SITGREAVES. MR. BRENT, MR. STANFORD, MR. VARNUM, MR. ALLEN, AND MR. SUMTER. PRINTED BY ORDER OF THE HOUSE OF REPRESENTATIVES.

Philadelphia: Printed by Joseph Gales, No. 126, *North Second Street.* [1798.] pp. 14. 8vo.   AAS. BA. LOC.

34808 —— MESSAGE FROM THE PRESIDENT OF THE UNITED STATES. [Relations with Tunis.] 23 FEBRUARY, 1798.

[Philadelphia: 1798.] 8vo.

34809 —— THE MESSAGE OF THE PRESIDENT OF THE UNITED STATES, OF 5TH MARCH, 1798; WITH A LETTER FROM OUR ENVOYS EXTRAORDINARY AT PARIS, WITH OTHER DOCU-MENTS. PRINTED BY ORDER OF THE SENATE OF THE UNITED STATES.

Philadelphia: Printed by Way & Groff, No. 27, *Arch-Street.* [1798.] pp. (8). 8vo.   AAS.

34810 —— MESSAGE CONCERNING THE DISPATCHES FROM THE ENVOYS EXTRAORDINARY OF THE UNITED STATES TO THE FRENCH REPUBLIC. MARCH 19, 1798.

[Philadelphia: 1798.] 8vo.   BA.

34811 —— —— POSTSCRIPT TO THE MERCURY. TUESDAY, MARCH 27. OFFICIAL AND IM-PORTANT. [Message of John Adams to Congress. March 19, 1798.]

[Boston: Printed by Young and Minns. 1798.] Broadside.

UNITED STATES, continued.

34812 —— MESSAGE OF THE PRESIDENT OF THE UNITED STATES TO BOTH HOUSES OF CONGRESS. APRIL 3D, 1798.

[Philadelphia: Printed by John Fenno. 1798.] pp. [71.] 8vo.

AAS. BA. JCB. LOC.

Consists of the famous "X Y Z" correspondence. Reprinted in London, also, this year.

34813 —— —— IN SENATE OF THE UNITED STATES. APRIL 5TH, 1798. ORDERED, THAT FIVE HUNDRED COPIES OF THE MESSAGE OF THE PRESIDENT OF THE UNITED STATES, OF THE THIRD INSTANT, TOGETHER WITH THE DISPATCHES FROM THE ENVOYS OF THE FRENCH REPUBLIC, ACCOMPANYING THE SAME, BE PUBLISHED FOR THE USE OF THE SENATE.

[Philadelphia: 1798.] pp. 71. 8vo.

34814 —— —— MESSAGE OF THE PRESIDENT OF THE UNITED STATES, TO BOTH HOUSES OF CONGRESS, APRIL 3D, 1798. [Ornament.]

Philadelphia: Printed by T. Dobson and J. Ormrod. 1798. pp. (60). 8vo.

AAS. LOC.

34815 —— —— AMERICA AND FRANCE. THE INTIRE MESSAGE OF THE PRESIDENT OF THE UNITED STATES, TO BOTH HOUSES OF CONGRESS: COVERING THE FULL POWERS TO, AND DISPATCHES FROM, THE ENVOYS EXTRAORDINARY OF THE UNITED STATES, TO THE FRENCH REPUBLIC. PUBLISHED BY ORDER OF CONGRESS.

Boston, Massachusetts, Published for universal information by B. Russell, State-Street. [1798.] pp. 71. 8vo.   AAS. HSP. JCB. LOC. MHS.

34816 —— —— DOCUMENTS AND DISPATCHES WHICH ACCOMPANIED THE MESSAGE OF THE PRESIDENT OF THE UNITED STATES TO BOTH HOUSES OF CONGRESS, APRIL 3, 1798. WITH THE INSTRUCTIONS TO THE ENVOYS EXTRAORDINARY OF THE UNITED STATES TO THE FRENCH REPUBLIC.

Carlisle: Printed by George Kline, for A. Loudon. [May 1, 1798.]

34817 —— —— IMPORTANT DOCUMENTS AND DISPATCHES, WHICH ACCOMPANIED THE MESSAGE OF THE PRESIDENT OF THE UNITED STATES, TO BOTH HOUSES OF CONGRESS, APRIL 3, 1798.

Charleston: Printed by W. P. Young, No. 43, Broad-Street. April 26, 1798. pp. (51). 8vo.   CLS.

34818 —— —— BERICHT DES PRÄSIDENTEN DER VER. STAATEN AN DIE BEIDEN HÄUSER DES CONGRESSES AM 3. APRIL 1798.

Philadelphia: Gedruckt bey H. Schweitzer. 1798.

34819 —— MESSAGE OF THE PRESIDENT OF THE UNITED STATES, TO BOTH HOUSES OF CONGRESS. MAY 4TH, 1798.

[Philadelphia: 1798.] pp. (72). 8vo.   AAS. BA. JCB. LCP. LOC.

34820 —— —— MEMORIAL FROM THE ENVOYS AT PARIS TO THE FRENCH REPUBLIC, COMMUNICATED BY THE PRESIDENT TO CONGRESS, MAY 4TH, 1798.

Carlisle: Printed by George Kline. [July 4, 1798]

34821 —— MESSAGE OF THE PRESIDENT OF THE UNITED STATES TO BOTH HOUSES OF CONGRESS. JUNE 5TH, 1798.

[Philadelphia: 1798.] pp. (15). 8vo.   BA. LOC.

UNITED STATES, continued.

34822 —— — MESSAGE FROM THE PRESIDENT OF THE UNITED STATES, ACCOMPANYING THE COMMUNICATIONS FROM THE ENVOYS EXTRAORDINARY TO THE FRENCH REPUBLIC, RECEIVED SINCE THE FOURTH OF MAY LAST. 5TH JUNE, 1798.—ORDERED TO LIE ON THE TABLE. PRINTED BY ORDER OF THE HOUSE OF REPRESENTATIVES OF THE UNITED STATES.

Philadelphia: Printed by Way & Groff, No. 27, Arch-Street. [1798.] pp. (17). 8vo. AAS. BA. JCB.

34823 —— — MESSAGE FROM THE PRESIDENT OF THE UNITED STATES, TO BOTH HOUSES OF CONGRESS, ACCOMPANYING COMMUNICATION NO. 8, FROM THE ENVOYS EXTRAORDINARY TO THE FRENCH REPUBLIC; JUNE 18TH, 1798.

[Philadelphia: 1798.] pp. 64. 8vo. BA. JCB.

34824 —— — MESSAGE FROM THE PRESIDENT OF THE UNITED STATES, ACCOMPANYING A COMMUNICATION, NO. 8, FROM THE ENVOYS EXTRAORDINARY TO THE FRENCH REPUBLIC. RECEIVED AT THE OFFICE OF THE SECRETARY OF STATE ON THURSDAY THE 14TH INSTANT. 18TH JUNE, 1798. ORDERED TO LIE ON THE TABLE. PRINTED BY ORDER OF THE HOUSE OF REPRESENTATIVES.

Philadelphia: Printed by Joseph Gales, No. 23, South Third Street. [1798.] pp. (72). 8vo. AAS. JCB. UTS.

34825 ——— MESSAGE OF THE PRESIDENT OF THE UNITED STATES, TO BOTH HOUSES OF CONGRESS. JUNE 21ST, 1798.

[Philadelphia: 1798.] pp. (8). 8vo. AAS. BA. JCB.

34826 —— MESSAGE FROM THE PRESIDENT OF THE UNITED STATES, INCLCING [*sic*] A LETTER, AND SUNDRY DOCUMENTS, FROM THE GOVERNOR OF THE STATE OF PENNSYLVANIA, RESPECTING THE ARRIVAL IN THE PORTS OF THE UNITED STATES, OF SUNDRY FRENCH INHABITANTS OF THE WEST-INDIES. 27TH JUNE, 1798. COMMITTED TO THE COMMITTEE ON SO MUCH OF THE PRESIDENT'S SPEECH, AS RELATES TO THE PROTECTION OF COMMERCE AND DEFENCE OF THE COUNTRY. PRINTED BY ORDER OF THE HOUSE OF REPRESENTATIVES.

Philadelphia: Printed by Joseph Gales, No. 23, South Third Street. [1798.] pp. (8). 8vo. AAS. BA.

34827 —— MESSAGE OF THE PRESIDENT OF THE UNITED STATES. TRANSMITTING A LETTER FROM GENERAL WASHINGTON, ACCEPTING HIS APPOINTMENT AS LIEUTENANT-GENERAL AND COMMANDER IN CHIEF OF THE ARMY. JOHN ADAMS. UNITED STATES. JULY 17TH, 1798.

[Philadelphia: Printed by John Fenno. 1798.] pp. (2). 8vo.

34828 —— — THE LETTER FROM GENERAL WASHINGTON TO THE PRESIDENT OF THE UNITED STATES, COMMUNICATING THE ACCEPTANCE OF HIS LATE APPOINTMENT.

Philadelphia: Printed by John Fenno. 1798. 8vo.

"Printed in octavo form on fine paper."

34829 —— — GENERAL WASHINGTON'S LETTER, DECLARING HIS ACCEPTANCE OF THE COMMAND OF THE ARMIES OF THE UNITED STATES. IN SENATE, JULY 18, 1798. GENTLEMEN OF THE SENATE. BELIEVING THAT THE LETTER RECEIVED THIS MORNING FROM GENERAL WASHINGTON, WILL GIVE HIGH SATISFACTION TO THE SENATE, I TRANSMIT THEM A COPY OF IT, AND CONGRATULATE THEM AND THE PUBLIC ON THIS GREAT EVENT, THE GENERAL'S ACCEPTANCE OF HIS APPOINTMENT, AS LIEUTENANT-GENERAL AND COMMANDER IN CHIEF OF THE ARMY. JOHN ADAMS. UNITED STATES, JULY 17TH, 1798. [Followed by Washington's Letter, dated, Mount Vernon, 13th July, 1798, in double columns.]

[Philadelphia: (Published for general information.) 1798.] Broadside. fol. AAS. EI. JCB.

UNITED STATES, continued.

34830 —— — [Arms.] Washington's Letter, declaring his acceptance of the command of the armies of the United States. July 13, 1798.

   [Boston: John Russell, print.] [1798.] Broadside.   EI.

Printed on silk.

34831 —— Speech of the President of the United States to both Houses of Congress. Delivered the eighth of December, 1798. 8th December, 1798. Committed to a committee of the whole House on Monday next. Published by order of the House of Representatives.

   Philadelphia: Printed by J. Gales, No. 23, South Third-Street. [1798.] pp. 8. 8vo.   AAS. BA. JCB.

34832 —— — Speech of the President of the United States, to both Houses of Congress, December 8th, 1798. [Two columns.] John Adams.

   [Philadelphia: 1798.] Broadside. fol.   AAS.

34833 —— — President's Speech. Providence, Saturday evening, December 15, 1798. After a considerable number of this day's Gazette had been circulated, we received, from a honourable member of the Senate, a copy of the President's interesting communication to Congress, at the opening of the present session, and hasten to present it to the public. [Three columns.] John Adams.

   [Providence:] *[Printed by Carter and Wilkinson.]* [1798.] Broadside. fol.   RIHS.

34834 —— — Newburyport Herald-Office, December 17, 1798. Having procured an extra paper published yesterday morning at Boston, containing the President's Speech to both Houses of Congress, we hasten to lay it before our patrons at an early hour. [Colophon:]

   [A. March's Printing-Office, State-Street.] 1798. Broadside. fol.   NYHS.

34835 —— — The President's Speech, to both Houses of Congress. ☞ We felicitate our patrons in being able to gratify their most ardent wishes, by an early perusal of the President's Speech. It was received at a late hour last evening, and repose has been a stranger to our eye-lids, from that moment to the present. Oracle-Office, (No. 5, Daniel-street,) December 18, 4 o'clock a.m. [Four columns.] John Adams. United States, December 8, 1798. [Colophon:]

   Printed by Charles Peirce, Portsmouth, N. H. [1798.] Broadside. fol.   AAS.

34836 —— President's Answer to the inhabitants of Providence. . . . Your noble declaration of your readiness, with your lives and fortunes, to support the dignity and independence of the United States, will receive the applause of your country. . . . John Adams.

   [Providence:] *Printed by Carter and Wilkinson.* [1798.] Broadside. 4to.

34837 —— Instructions to Charles Cotesworth Pinckney, John Marshall and Elbridge Gerry, envoys extraordinary and ministers plenipotentiary to the French Republic, referred to in the Message of the President of the United States of the third [April] instant.

   Philadelphia: Printed by Way & Groff, No. 27, Arch-Street. 1798. pp. [20.] 8vo.   AAS. BA. HSP. JCB. LOC. MHS.

Signed, Timothy Pickering, Secretary of State. Five hundred copies printed for the use of the Senate.

UNITED STATES, continued.

34838 —— —— INSTRUCTIONS TO THE ENVOYS EXTRAORDINARY AND MINISTERS PLENIPO-
TENTIARY FROM THE UNITED STATES OF AMERICA, TO THE FRENCH REPUBLIC,
THEIR LETTERS OF CREDENCE AND FULL POWERS, AND THE DISPATCHES RECEIVED
FROM THEM RELATIVE TO THEIR MISSION. PUBLISHED BY THE SECRETARY OF
STATE, IN CONFORMITY WITH THE RESOLUTION OF CONGRESS, OF THE 22D JUNE,
1798. [Printer's mark.]

> *Philadelphia: Printed by W. Ross, in Locust-Street, near the corner of South
> Ninth-Street.* [1798.] pp. (131). 8vo.   AAS. BA. BU. HSP. JCB. LOC. NYHS.

34839 —— —— VERHALTUNGSBEFEHLE AN CHARLES COTESWORTH PINCKNEY, JOHN MAR-
SCHALL UND ELDRIDGE GERRY, AUSSERORDENTLICHE ABGESANDTE UND BEVOLL-
MÄCHTIGTE MINISTER AN DIE FRANZÖSISCHE REPUBLIK. AUS DEM ENGLISCHEN
ÜBERSETZT.

> *Philadelphia: Gedruckt bey H. Schweitzer.* 1798. pp. 54. 8vo.   APS.

34840 —— —— A LETTER FROM MR. PICKERING, SECRETARY OF STATE, TO MR. PINCKNEY, MIN-
ISTER PLENIPOTENTIARY AT PARIS, IN ANSWER TO THE COMPLAINTS COMMUNICATED
BY MR. ADET, MINISTER OF THE FRENCH REPUBLIC, AGAINST THE UNITED STATES
OF AMERICA.

> *Richmond: Printed and sold by T. Nicolson.* [1798.] pp. 93. 12mo.   BA.

> One thousand copies were printed at private expense, to counteract the
> Virginia Resolutions of 1798.

34841 —— —— LETTER FROM THE SECRETARY OF STATE, ACCOMPANYING A REPORT AND AB-
STRACT OF ALL THE RETURNS OF REGISTERED AMERICAN SEAMEN, AND OF THE
PROTESTS AND RETURNS RESPECTING IMPRESSED SEAMEN, SINCE THE 17TH OF FEB-
RUARY, 1797, THE DATE OF HIS LAST REPORT, WHICH HAVE BEEN TRANSMITTED TO
HIM, BY THE COLLECTORS OF THE DIFFERENT PORTS, AGREEABLY TO THE DIRECTIONS
OF THE "ACT FOR THE RELIEF AND PROTECTION OF AMERICAN SEAMEN;" AND ALSO,
COPIES OR ABSTRACTS OF SUCH COMMUNICATIONS FROM THE AGENTS EMPLOYED BY
VIRTUE OF THE SAME ACT, IN FOREIGN PORTS, AS HAVE BEEN RECEIVED:— WITH
SUNDRY COMMUNICATIONS FROM THE MINISTER PLENIPOTENTIARY OF THE UNITED
STATES, AT LONDON, ON THE SAME SUBJECT: IN PURSUANCE OF A RESOLUTION OF
THIS HOUSE, OF THE 29TH OF NOVEMBER LAST. 1ST MARCH, 1798. REFERRED TO
THE COMMITTEE OF COMMERCE AND MANUFACTURES. PUBLISHED BY ORDER OF THE
HOUSE OF REPRESENTATIVES OF THE UNITED STATES.

> *Philadelphia: Printed by Way & Groff, No. 27, Arch-Street.* [1798.] pp.
> (55). fol.   AAS. BA. JCB.

34842 —— —— PASSPORT AND ROLL OF EQUIPAGE, AGREEABLY TO THE 25TH AND 27TH ARTICLES
OF THE TREATY BETWEEN FRANCE AND THE UNITED STATES, MADE THE 6TH OF
FEBRUARY, 1798.

> *[Philadelphia? May 2, 1798.]* Broadside.

34843 —— —— PASSPORT & ROLL D'EQUIPAGE, AGREEABLE TO THE TREATY BETWEEN
FRANCE AND AMERICA.

> *Newburyport: Printed and sold by Angier March.* 1797.

34844 —— —— PASSPORT AND ROLL OF EQUIPAGE, AGREEABLE TO THE 25TH AND 27TH
ARTICLES OF THE TREATY BETWEEN FRANCE AND THE UNITED STATES, MADE THE
6TH OF FEBRUARY, 1798.

> *Portland: Printed by John Rand.* 1798.

34845 —— —— ROLE D'EQUIPAGE, LAID DOWN AGREEABLY TO THE DECREE OF THE EXEC-
UTIVE DIRECTORY OF FRANCE.

> *Wilmington: Printed by W. C. Smyth.* 1798.

UNITED STATES, continued.

34846 —— — Passport and Roll of Equipage. agreeable to the 25th and 27th articles of the Treaty between France and the United States, made the 6th of February, 1798.

Wiscasset: Printed by Hoskins & Scott. 1798.

34847 —— An Account of the receipts and expenditures of the United States, for the year 1797. Stated in pursuance of the standing order of the House of Representatives of the United States, passed on the thirtieth day of December, one thousand seven hundred and ninety-one. Published by order of the House of Representatives.

Philadelphia: Printed by John Ward Fenno, No. 119, Chesnut Street. [1798.] pp. (88), 4 folded tables. fol.   AAS. JCB. LOC. MHS.

34848 —— Accounts of the treasurer of the United States, of payments and receipts of public monies, commencing the first of January. and ending the thirty-first of December, 1797. Also, his account of receipts and expenditures for the War Department, from the first of January, to the thirty-first of December, 1797. [Published by order of the House of Representatives.]

[Philadelphia: Printed by William Ross, 1798.] pp. 143. 8vo.   AAS. BA.

34849 —— Articles of agreement made on the fourth day of September, one thousand seven hundred and ninety-eight, between Oliver Wolcott, Secretary of the Treasury of the United States, of the one part, and And. Welton, of Waterbury in the State of Connecticut of the other part. [Contract for one thousand muskets of the Charleville-model, complete with stocks of black walnut, or maple, ramrods and bayonets tempered. locks hardened, and barrels proved, for $13.47 each, delivery in eighteen months. Signed by both contracting parties, and witnessed by James Hillhouse, and Richard Law. With seal.]

[Philadelphia: 1798.] pp. (2). fol.

34850 —— Circular to the collector of customs [modifying former instructions.] March 21, 1798.

[Philadelphia: 1798.] Broadside. 4to.

34851 —— [Form of customs] Return of seamen . . . of monies . . . Register of white persons . . . [and certification.]

[Boston: 1798.] pp. (4). fol.   LOC.

34852 —— Letter and report of the Secretary of the Treasury, accompanied with sundry statements relative to the military and naval establishments [1791–1796] and to the fortification of the ports and harbours of the United States, in pursuance of three Resolutions of the House of Representatives, of the 3d of March,1797. . . .

[Philadelphia:] Printed by W. Ross. [1798.] pp. 56. 8vo.   LOC.

34853 —— Letter from the Secretary of the Treasury, accompanying his Report, made in pursuance of a Resolution of the House of Representatives of the 14th of December last. January 8, 1798. Referred to a committee of the whole House on the Report of the committee of claims, on the expediency or inexpediency of designating certain claims to be excepted from the operation of the Acts of limitation. Printed by order of the House of Representatives.

Philadelphia: Printed by Joseph Gales, No. 126, North Second Street. [1798.] pp. (8). 8vo.   AAS. BA. JCB.

UNITED STATES, continued.

34854 —— LETTER FROM THE SECRETARY OF THE TREASURY, TRANSMITTING STATEMENTS OF GOODS, WARES AND MERCHANDIZE, IMPORTED INTO THE UNITED STATES, FOR TWO YEARS; ONE COMMENCING ON THE FIRST OF OCTOBER, 1794,—AND THE OTHER ON THE FIRST DAY OF OCTOBER, 1795. IN PURSUANCE OF A RESOLUTION OF THE THIRD OF MARCH, 1797. [Ornament.] 8TH JANUARY, 1798. ORDERED TO LIE ON THE TABLE. [Ornament.] PUBLISHED BY ORDER OF THE HOUSE OF REPRESENTATIVES.

[Philadelphia:] Printed by W. Ross. [1798.] pp. (4), 2 folded tables. fol.
AAS. BA. JCB.

34855 —— LETTER FROM THE SECRETARY OF THE TREASURY, ACCOMPANYING HIS REPORT RESPECTING THE EXECUTION OF THE THIRD SECTION OF THE ACT REGULATING FOREIGN COINS, AND FOR OTHER PURPOSES; IN PURSUANCE OF A RESOLUTION OF THE HOUSE, OF THE FIFTH INSTANT. 11TH JANUARY, 1798. REFERRED TO THE COMMITTEE OF THE WHOLE HOUSE, TO WHOM WAS COMMITTED, ON THE 8TH ULTIMO, THE REPORT OF THE COMMITTEE, ON A LETTER FROM THE SECRETARY OF STATE, INCLOSING A REPORT OF THE DIRECTOR OF THE MINT. PUBLISHED BY ORDER OF THE HOUSE OF REPRESENTATIVES.

[Philadelphia:] Printed by W. Ross. [1798.] pp. 6. 8vo.   AAS. BA.

34856 —— LETTER AND REPORT OF THE SECRETARY OF THE TREASURY, ACCOMPANYING A PLAN FOR REGULATING THE COLLECTION OF DUTIES ON IMPORTS AND TONNAGE, PREPARED IN PURSUANCE OF A RESOLUTION OF THIS HOUSE, OF THE SECOND OF FEBRUARY LAST. 25TH JANUARY, 1798, REFERRED TO THE COMMITTEE OF COMMERCE AND MANUFACTURES. [PUBLISHED BY ORDER OF THE HOUSE OF REPRESENTATIVES.]

[Philadelphia: Printed by William Ross. 1798.] pp. 158. 8vo.
AAS. BA. UTS. YC.

34857 —— LETTER FROM THE SECRETARY OF THE TREASURY, ACCOMPANYING HIS REPORT ON THE PETITIONS ON SUNDRY INHABITANTS OF THE TOWN OF NEWPORT, IN THE STATE OF RHODE-ISLAND,—OF THE CORPORATION OF THE MARINE SOCIETY OF THE CITY OF NEW-YORK—OF THE CORPORATION OF THE CHAMBER OF COMMERCE OF THE CITY OF NEW-YORK, OF THE PRESIDENT AND DIRECTORS OF THE UNITED INSURANCE COMPANY, AND OF THE PRESIDENT AND DIRECTORS OF THE NEW-YORK INSURANCE COMPANY. 6TH FEBRUARY. 1798, REFERRED TO THE COMMITTEE OF COMMERCE AND MANUFACTURES, WITH INSTRUCTIONS TO REPORT THEREON, BY BILL, OR OTHERWISE. [PUBLISHED BY ORDER OF THE HOUSE OF REPRESENTATIVES.]

[Philadelphia: Printed by William Ross. 1798.] pp. 4. 8vo. AAS. BA. JCB.

34858 —— LETTER FROM THE SECRETARY OF THE TREASURY, ACCOMPANYING A REPORT OF THE LATE COMMISSIONER OF THE REVENUE, AND SUNDRY STATEMENTS, IN RELATION TO THE INTERNAL REVENUES OF THE UNITED STATES, PURSUANT TO A RESOLUTION OF THIS HOUSE, OF THE SIXTH OF JANUARY, 1797. 23D FEBRUARY, 1798. ORDERED TO LIE ON THE TABLE. [PUBLISHED BY ORDER OF THE HOUSE OF REPRESENTATIVES.]

[Philadelphia:] Printed by J. H. Oswald. [1798.] pp. (2), 12, 24 tables. fol.
BA. JCB.

34859 —— LETTER FROM THE SECRETARY OF THE TREASURY, TRANSMITTING A STATEMENT OF GOODS, WARES AND MERCHANDIZE, EXPORTED FROM THE UNITED STATES, DURING ONE YEAR, PRIOR TO THE FIRST DAY OF OCTOBER, 1797. 6TH MARCH, 1798. ORDERED TO LIE ON THE TABLE. [PUBLISHED BY ORDER OF THE HOUSE OF REPRESENTATIVES.]

[Philadelphia:] Printed by John H. Oswald. [1798.] pp. (4), table. fol.
BA. JCB.

UNITED STATES, continued.

34860 —— LETTER FROM THE SECRETARY OF THE TREASURY, ACCOMPANYING A LETTER TO HIM FROM THE COMPTROLLER OF THE TREASURY; AS ALSO, AN ABSTRACT OF THE EMOLUMENTS AND EXPENDITURES OF THE OFFICERS OF THE CUSTOMS, PURSUANT TO AN ACT OF CONGRESS, PASSED THE 14TH FEBRUARY, 1795. 20TH MARCH, 1798. REFERRED TO THE COMMITTEE OF COMMERCE AND MANUFACTURES. PUBLISHED BY ORDER OF THE HOUSE OF REPRESENTATIVES.

[Philadelphia:] Printed by W. Ross. [1798.] pp. (8), 2 folded tables. fol.
AAS. BA.

34861 —— LETTER FROM THE SECRETARY OF THE TREASURY, ACCOMPANYING A REPORT AND ESTIMATE OF AN APPROPRIATION OF MONIES FOR THE COMPENSATION OF THE CLERKS IN THE OFFICES OF THE COMMISSIONER OF LOANS, AND AN ALLOWANCE TO CERTAIN LOAN-OFFICERS, IN LIEU OF CLERK HIRE, AND TO DEFRAY THE AUTHORIZED EXPENSES OF THE SEVERAL LOAN-OFFICES, FOR THE YEAR 1798. 28TH MAY, 1798, ORDERED TO LIE ON THE TABLE. [PUBLISHED BY ORDER OF THE HOUSE OF REPRESENTATIVES.]

[Philadelphia: Printed by William Ross, 1798.] pp. (4). 8vo.   AAS.

34862 —— LETTER FROM THE SECRETARY OF THE TREASURY, ACCOMPANYING A REPORT AND SATEMENT [*sic*] OF THE SUMS NECESSARY TO BE APPROPRIATED ON ACCOUNT OF THE COMPENSATION OF THE SECRETARY OF THE NAVY, HIS CLERKS AND MESSENGER, FOR THE PRESENT YEAR, AND FOR OTHER PURPOSES. 11TH JULY, 1798. REFERRED TO THE COMMITTEE OF WAYS AND MEANS, WITH INSTRUCTION TO REPORT BY BILL OR OTHERWISE. PRINTED BY ORDER OF THE HOUSE OF REPRESENTATIVES.

Philadelphia: Printed by Joseph Gales, No. 23, South Third Street. [1798.] pp. (7). 8vo.   AAS.

34863 —— LETTER FROM THE SECRETARY OF THE TREASURY, ACCOMPANYING A STATEMENT EXHIBITING THE AMOUNT OF DRAWBACKS PAID UPON THE DUTIABLE ARTICLES EXPORTED FROM THE UNITED STATES DURING THE YEAR 1794–1795– AND 1796, COMPARED WITH THE DUTIES ON SIMILAR ARTICLES, DURING THE SAME PERIOD; IN PURSUANCE OF A RESOLUTION OF THE HOUSE OF REPRESENTATIVES, OF THE 3D OF MARCH, 1797. 9TH FEBRUARY, 1798. ORDERED TO LIE ON THE TABLE. PUBLISHED BY ORDER OF THE HOUSE OF REPRESENTATIVES.

[Philadelphia:] Printed by W. Ross. [1798.] pp. (2), folded table. fol.
AAS. BA. JCB.

34864 —— LETTER FROM THE SECRETARY OF THE TREASURY, ACCOMPANYING A STATEMENT OF THE SEVERAL EXISTING CONTRACTS, MADE FOR THE SUBSISTANCE OF THE ARMY, IN PURSUANCE OF A RESOLUTION OF THIS HOUSE OF THE 28TH INSTANT. 30TH MARCH, 1798. — ORDERED TO LIE ON THE TABLE. PUBLISHED BY ORDER OF THE HOUSE OF REPRESENTATIVES OF THE UNITED STATES.

Philadelphia: Printed by Way & Groff, No. 27, Arch-Street. [1798.] pp. (6). 8vo.   AAS.

34865 —— LETTER FROM THE SECRETARY OF THE TREASURY, ACCOMPANYING TWO STATEMENTS, MARKED A & B, EXHIBITING THE TONNAGE OF SHIPPING BELONGING TO THE SEVERAL DISTRICTS OF THE UNITED STATES AT THE CLOSE OF THE YEAR 1796; ALSO, A COMPARATIVE VIEW OF THE TONNAGE OF ALL VESSELS WHICH PAID DUTIES IN THE PORTS OF THE UNITED STATES, IN EACH YEAR, FROM 1790 TO 1796, INCLUSIVE: DISTINGUISHING, GENERALLY THE EMPLOYMENTS OF THE VESSELS OF THE UNITED STATES, AND THE TONNAGE OF VESSELS BELONGING TO DIFFERENT NATIONS. IN PURSUANCE OF A RESOLUTION OF THIS HOUSE OF THE 4TH INSTANT. 6TH APRIL, 1798—ORDERED TO LIE ON THE TABLE. [Ornament.] PUBLISHED BY ORDER OF THE HOUSE OF REPRESENTATIVES OF THE UNITED STATES. [Ornament.]

Philadelphia: Printed by Way & Groff, No. 27, Arch-Street. [1798.] pp. (8). fol.   AAS. BA.

34866 UNITED STATES, continued.
—— LETTER FROM THE SECRETARY OF THE TREASURY, ACCOMPANYING HIS REPORT ON THE MEMORIAL OF SUNDRY MERCHANTS AND TRADERS OF THE CITY OF PHILADELPHIA. 13TH APRIL, 1798. COMMITTED TO A COMMITTEE OF THE WHOLE HOUSE, ON MONDAY NEXT. [PUBLISHED BY ORDER OF THE HOUSE OF REPRESENTATIVES.]
[Philadelphia: Printed by William Ross. 1798.] pp. 8. 8vo. AAS. BA. HSP.

34867 —— LETTER FROM THE SECRETARY OF THE TREASURY, INCLOSING HIS REPORT ON THE PETITION OF JONATHAN JACKSON, AND THE MEMORIAL OF ABEL WHITNEY, PRESENTED THE 28TH OF NOVEMBER, AND 11TH OF DECEMBER LAST. 18TH APRIL, 1798. ORDERED TO LIE ON THE TABLE. PRINTED BY ORDER OF THE HOUSE OF REPRESENTATIVES.
Philadelphia: Printed by Joseph Gales, No. 23, South Third Street. [1798.] pp. (16). 8vo. AAS. BA. JCB.

34868 —— LETTER FROM THE SECRETARY OF THE TREASURY, TO THE CHAIRMAN OF THE COMMITTEE OF WAYS & MEANS, EXHIBITING A CALCULATION OF THE QUOTAS OF THE RESPECTIVE STATES, IN A TAX OF TWO MILLIONS OF DOLLARS, PROPORTIONED TO THE NUMBER OF FREE WHITE PERSONS, AND THREE-FIFTHS OF THE NUMBER OF SLAVES, AS ASCERTAINED BY THE CENSUS. 25TH MAY, 1798, REFERRED TO THE COMMITTEE OF THE WHOLE HOUSE, TO WHOM IS COMMITTED THE BILL TO PROVIDE THE ASSESSMENT AND COLLECTION OF DIRECT TAXES. [PUBLISHED BY ORDER OF THE HOUSE OF REPRESENTATIVES.]
[Philadelphia: Printed by William Ross, 1798.] pp. 8. 8vo. AAS. BA.

34869 —— LETTER FROM THE SECRETARY OF THE TREASURY, TRANSMITTING A COPY OF A LETTER FROM THE COMMISSIONERS APPOINTED UNDER THE "ACT ESTABLISHING THE TEMPORARY AND PERMANENT SEAT OF THE GOVERNMENT OF THE UNITED STATES," WITH SUNDRY DOCUMENTS MARKED A, B, C, AND D, EXHIBITING A VIEW OF ALL THE RECEIPTS AND EXPENDITURES OF ALL MONIES ENTRUSTED TO THEM, AND ALSO OF THE PROGRESS AND STATE OF THE BUSINESS, AND OF THE FUNDS UNDER THEIR ADMINISTRATION, FROM THE 18TH OF NOVEMBER, 1797, TO THE 18TH OF MAY, 1798. 29TH MAY, 1798, ORDERED TO LIE ON THE TABLE. [PUBLISHED BY ORDER OF THE HOUSE OF REPRESENTATIVES.]
[Philadelphia: Printed by William Ross, 1798.] pp. 40. 8vo. AAS. BA. JCB.

34870 —— LETTER FROM THE SECRETARY OF THE TREASURY, ACCOMPANYING THE COPY OF A LETTER FROM THE COMMISSIONERS OF THE CITY OF WASHINGTON, IN THE DISTRICT OF COLUMBIA, AND SUNDRY STATEMENTS MARKED A. B. C. D. AND E., EXHIBITING A VIEW OF THE RECEIPTS AND EXPENDITURES OF ALL MONIES ENTRUSTED TO THEM; ALSO, OF THE PROGRESS AND STATE OF THE BUSINESS AND OF THE FUNDS UNDER THEIR ADMINISTRATION, FROM THE 18TH OF MAY, 1790, TO THE 18TH OF NOVEMBER FOLLOWING. [Ornament.] 11TH DECEMBER, 1798. ORDERED TO LIE ON THE TABLE. [Ornament.]
Philadelphia: Printed by John Ward Fenno, No. 119, Chesnut-Street. 1798. pp. (8). fol. AAS. BA. JCB.

34871 —— LETTER FROM THE SECRETARY OF THE TREASURY, ACCOMPANYING SUNDRY STATEMENTS, EXHIBITING THE AMOUNT OF DUTIES UPON DOMESTIC DISTILLED SPIRITS AND STILLS, FOR THE YEAR ENDING THE 30TH OF JUNE, 1797; ALSO, THE AMOUNT OF DUTIES UPON SALES AT AUCTION, REFINED SUGAR, CARRIAGES, AND LICENSES TO RETAILERS, FOR THE YEAR ENDING THE 30TH OF SEPTEMBER, 1797; TOGETHER WITH AN EXPLANATORY LETTER THEREON, FROM THE COMMISSIONER OF THE REVENUE. 13TH DECEMBER, 1798.—ORDERED TO LIE ON THE TABLE. PUBLISHED BY ORDER OF THE HOUSE OF REPRESENTATIVES OF THE UNITED STATES.
Philadelphia: Printed by Way & Groff, No. 48, North Third-Street. [1798.] pp. 12. fol. AAS.

UNITED STATES, continued.

34872 —— LETTER FROM THE SECRETARY OF THE TREASURY, INCLOSING A REPORT AND ESTIMATES OF THE SUMS NECESSARY TO BE APPROPRIATED FOR THE SERVICE OF THE YEAR 1799: ALSO, A STATEMENT OF THE RECEIPTS AND EXPENDITURES AT THE TREASURY OF THE UNITED STATES, FOR ONE YEAR PRECEDING THE 1ST OF OCTOBER, 1798. 24TH DECEMBER, 1798. REFERRED TO THE COMMITTEE OF WAYS AND MEANS. PUBLISHED BY ORDER OF THE HOUSE OF REPRESENTATIVES OF THE UNITED STATES.

Philadelphia: Printed by Way & Groff, No. 48, North Third-Street. [1798.] pp. (110). 8vo.   AAS. BA.

34873 —— REPORT OF THE SECRETARY OF THE TREASURY, MADE IN PURSUANCE OF A RESOLUTION OF THE HOUSE, OF THE 22D INSTANT, RELATIVE TO THE CLAIM OF GENERAL KOSCIUSKO, AGAINST THE UNITED STATES. HOUSE OF REPRESENTATIVES, DEC. 28, 1797. COMMITTED TO A COMMITTEE OF THE WHOLE HOUSE ON MONDAY NEXT.

Philadelphia: Printed by Joseph Gales, No. 126, North Second Street. [1798.] pp. (8). 8vo.   AAS. BA. JCB.

34874 —— ABSTRACT OF THE STAMP LAW. TREASURY DEPARTMENT, MARCH 1, 1798. PUBLIC NOTICE IS HEREBY GIVEN, [Two columns.] THOMAS DOBSON, AT THE STONE HOUSE, NO. 41, SOUTH SECOND STREET, PHILADELPHIA, HAS FOR SALE AN ASSORTMENT OF THE ABOVE STAMPS, ALSO A LARGE AND VERY GENERAL ASSORTMENT OF STATIONERY. [Three columns.]

[Philadelphia: Printed by Thomas Dobson, 1798.] Broadside. fol.   HSP.

34875 —— — AN AUTHENTIC COPY OF THE AMERICAN STAMP ACT.

New-London: Printed by Charles Holt. 1798. Broadside. fol.

34876 —— — THE SEVERAL ACTS RELATIVE TO THE STAMP DUTIES PASSED AT THE LATE AND PRESENT SESSION OF CONGRESS, AND WHICH BECAME PAYABLE FROM AND AFTER THE FIRST DAY OF JULY, 1798. TO WHICH IS ADDED, A TABLE OF THE SEVERAL DUTIES, BY WHICH THEY MAY BE SEEN AT ONE VIEW.

Frankfort: Printed by Hunter and Beaumont. 1798.

"Printed on fine paper, and adapted for a pocket-book."

34877 —— — STAMP DUTIES. ANY CERTIFICATE OF NATURALIZATION, . . . BONDS, NOTES, &C. . . . [Colophon:]

Printed by Barber & Southwick, and sold at their Book-store, in Court-Street, two doors north of the City-Hall, Albany.— Price 6d. single — 4s. a dozen. [1798.] Broadside. fol.   MHS. NYPL.

34878 —— — STAMP DUTIES.

Lexington: Printed by John Bradford. 1798.

"Printed on thick paper, and calculated to be fitted into a pocket-book."

34879 —— — A TABLE OR LIST OF THE DIFFERENT RATES OF STAMP DUTIES UPON STAMPED PAPER.

Newburyport: Printed by Angier March, 1798. Broadside. fol.

34880 —— — A TABLE OR LIST OF THE DIFFERENT RATES OF STAMP DUTIES UPON STAMPED PAPER, AGREEABLY TO AN ACT OF CONGRESS.

Salem: Printed by Thomas C. Cushing. 1798.

34881

UNITED STATES, continued.

—— REPORT OF THE COMMISSIONERS OF THE SINKING FUND INCLOSING A REPORT TO THEM, FROM THE SECRETARY OF THE TREASURY, AND SUNDRY OFFICIAL STATEMENTS OF THE ACCOUNTING OFFICERS OF THE TREASURY DEPARTMENT, RELATIVE TO THE MEASURES WHICH HAVE BEEN AUTHORIZED BY THE SAID COMMISSIONERS FOR PURCHASING THE PUBLIC DEBT, SUBSEQUENT TO THEIR REPORT OF THE 4TH OF DECEMBER, 1797. 17TH DECEMBER, 1798. ORDERED TO LIE ON THE TABLE. PUBLISHED BY ORDER OF THE HOUSE OF REPRESENTATIVES OF THE UNITED STATES.

Philadelphia: Printed by Way & Groff, No. 49, North Third-Street. [1798.] pp. (11). 8vo.   AAS. BA. JCB.

34882

—— TERMS, CONDITIONS, AND CIRCUMSTANCES TOUCHING LANDS FOR SALE IN THE UNITED STATES OF AMERICA.

[Philadelphia? 1798.] Broadside. fol.   BM.

34883

—— TO ALL WHOM IT MAY CONCERN. I DO HEREBY CERTIFY, THAT JOHN VAUGHAN . . . DID . . . LODGE IN THE MINT OF THE UNITED STATES, FOR COINAGE, BULLION WHICH CONTAINED 230,888, OF STANDARD SILVER . . .

[Philadelphia: July 11, 1798.] pp. (2). 8vo.   AAS.

34884

—— TREASURY DEPARTMENT, TRENTON, SEPTEMBER 8, 1798. [A Circular letter transmitting forms to be observed "in the execution of the Act to provide for the valuation of lands, and dwelling-houses, and the enumeration of slaves." Signed by Oliver Wolcott.]

[Trenton: Printed by Matthias Day ? 1798.] pp. (2) fol.

34885

—— TREASURY OF THE UNITED STATES, DECEMBER 20, 1798. SIR, MY SPECIE AND WAR DEPARTMENT ACCOUNTS ENDING 30TH OF JUNE, AND WAR AND NAVY DEPARTMENTS ENDING THE 30TH OF SEPTEMBER, HAVING PASSED THE OFFICES, PERMIT ME THROUGH YOU TO LAY THEM BEFORE YOUR HONOURABLE HOUSE, AND TO ASSURE YOU, THAT, I AM, WITH PERFECT RESPECT, YOUR MOST HUMBLE SERVANT, SAMUEL MEREDITH, TREASURER OF THE UNITED STATES. THE HONOURABLE JONATHAN DAYTON.

[Philadelphia: 1798.] pp. 83. 8vo.   AAS.

34886

—— LETTER FROM THE SECRETARY AT WAR, ACCOMPANYING HIS REPORT RELATIVE TO THE RUNNING OF A LINE OF EXPERIMENT FROM CLINCH RIVER TO CHILHOWEE MOUNTAIN, BY ORDER OF THE GOVERNOR OF THE TERRITORY OF THE UNITED STATES SOUTH OF THE OHIO, IN PURSUANCE OF A RESOLUTION OF THE HOUSE OF REPRESENTATIVES OF THE 28TH ULTIMO. JANUARY 5TH, 1798. COMMITTED TO THE COMMITTEE OF THE WHOLE HOUSE ON THE REPORT OF THE COMMITTEE TO WHOM WAS REFERRED THE REMONSTRANCE AND PETITION OF THE LEGISLATURE OF THE STATE OF TENNESSEE. PRINTED BY ORDER OF THE HOUSE OF REPRESENTATIVES.

Philadelphia: Printed by Joseph Gales, No. 126, North Second Street. [1798.] pp. (18). 8vo.   AAS. BA.

34887

—— LETTER FROM THE SECRETARY OF WAR, INCLOSING HIS REPORT ON THE PETITION OF STEPHEN CANTRILL, REFERRED TO HIM ON THE 27TH OF NOVEMBER, 1797. 5TH APRIL, 1798. COMMITTED TO A COMMITTEE OF THE WHOLE HOUSE ON MONDAY NEXT. PRINTED BY ORDER OF THE HOUSE OF REPRESENTATIVES.

Philadelphia: Printed by Joseph Gales, No. 126, North Second Street. [1798.] pp. (24). 8vo.   AAS. BA. JCB.

UNITED STATES, continued.

34888 —— LETTER FROM THE SECRETARY AT WAR, TO THE CHAIRMAN OF THE COMMITTEE, ON SO MUCH OF THE PRESIDENT'S SPEECH AS RELATES TO THE PROTECTION OF COMMERCE, AND THE DEFENCE OF THE COUNTRY, INCLOSING SUNDRY PAPERS, RELATIVE TO THE PROVISIONAL MEASURES WHICH, IN THE OPINION OF THE SAID SECRETARY, SHOULD BE IMMEDIATELY TAKEN TO PROTECT THE COMMERCE, AND SECURE AND DEFEND THE TERRITORY AND SOVEREIGNTY OF THE UNITED STATES. 11TH APRIL, 1798, COMMITTED TO THE COMMITTEE OF THE WHOLE HOUSE, ON THE STATE OF THE UNION. [PUBLISHED BY ORDER OF THE HOUSE OF REPRESENTATIVES.]

[Philadelphia: Printed by William Ross, 1798.] pp. 16. 8vo.   AAS. BA. JCB.

34889 —— LETTER FROM THE SECRETARY OF WAR, INCLOSING A STATEMENT OF THE NUMBER OF CANNON PURCHASED FOR THE USE OF THE FRIGATES, THE REVENUE CUTTERS AND FORTIFICATIONS, SINCE JANUARY, 1794; WITH THE SIZES OF THE CANNON, AND WHAT PORTION OF THEM HAVE BEEN CAST IN THE UNITED STATES, AND AT WHAT FOUNDRIES THEY WERE CAST; WITH A STATEMENT OF THE PRICES FOR EACH SIZE. IN PURSUANCE OF A RESOLUTION OF THIS HOUSE, OF THE 28TH OF MARCH, 1798. 12TH APRIL, 1798.— ORDERED TO LIE ON THE TABLE. PUBLISHED BY ORDER OF THE HOUSE OF REPRESENTATIVES OF THE UNITED STATES.

Philadelphia: Printed by Way & Groff, No. 27, *Arch-Street.* [1798.] pp. (7). 8vo.   AAS. BA. JCB.

34890 —— LETTER FROM THE SECRETARY OF WAR, INCLOSING A REPORT AND SUNDRY STATEMENTS, MARKED A TO I INCLUSIVE; IN PURSUANCE OF TWO RESOLUTIONS OF THE HOUSE OF REPRESENTATIVES, OF THE 28TH OF MARCH LAST. 16TH APRIL, 1798. COMMITTED THE COMMITTEE OF THE WHOLE HOUSE, TO WHOM IS COMMITTED THE BILL MAKING APPROPRIATIONS FOR THE MILITARY ESTABLISHMENT, FOR THE YEAR 1798; AND FOR OTHER PURPOSES. PUBLISHED BY ORDER OF THE HOUSE OF REPRESENTATIVES OF THE UNITED STATES.

Philadelphia: Printed by Way & Groff, No. 27, *Arch-Street.* [1798.] pp. (32). fol.   AAS. JCB.

34891 —— LETTER FROM THE SECRETARY AT WAR, ACCOMPANYING A REPORT AND SUNDRY STATEMENTS, SUPPLEMENTARY TO HIS REPORT RECEIVED THE 16TH INSTANT, IN PURSUANCE OF TWO RESOLUTIONS OF THIS HOUSE OF THE 28TH OF MARCH LAST. 23D APRIL, 1798. REFERRED TO THE COMMITTEE OF THE WHOLE HOUSE, TO WHOM IS COMMITTED THE BILL MAKING APPROPRIATIONS FOR THE MILITARY ESTABLISHMENT FOR THE YEAR ONE THOUSAND SEVEN HUNDRED AND NINETY-EIGHT, AND FOR OTHER PURPOSES. PRINTED BY ORDER OF THE HOUSE OF REPRESENTATIVES.

Philadelphia: Printed by Joseph Gales, No. 23, *South Third Street.* [1798.] pp. (15). 8vo.   AAS. BA.

34892 —— LETTER FROM THE SECRETARY AT WAR, TO THE CHAIRMAN OF THE COMMITTEE, APPOINTED ON THE 15TH OF JANUARY LAST, TO ENQUIRE INTO THE EXPENDITURES OF THE MONIES HERETOFORE APPROPRIATED FOR A NAVAL ARMAMENT; AND ALSO, INTO THE CAUSES OF THE DELAY IN COMPLETING THE SAME: ACCOMPANYING SUNDRY STATEMENTS, MADE IN PURSUANCE OF THE RESOLUTIONS OF THE 15TH OF JANUARY, AND THE 16TH OF MARCH LAST. 1ST MAY, 1798, ORDERED TO LIE ON THE TABLE. PUBLISHED BY ORDER OF THE HOUSE OF REPRESENTATIVES.

[Philadelphia:] Printed by W. Ross, in Locust-Street, near the corner of 9th —South. [1798.] pp. 54, folded table. fol.   BA. JCB.

34893 —— MARINE RULES AND REGULATIONS.

[Philadelphia:] Printed by John Fenno. M.DCC.XCVIII. pp. (56), (6), folded quarter bill. 8vo.   LOC.

Contains an autograph order for execution of the above, signed by James McHenry, Secy. of War.

34894   UNITED STATES, continued.
   —— Military rules and regulations. Respecting the recruiting service. [Signed, James M'Henry, Secretary of War.]
    [Philadelphia: 1798.] 8vo.   BA.

34895   —— Steuben's Manual exercise.
    Frankfort: Printed by Hunter and Beaumont. 1798.
   "Neatly printed on writing paper and calculated for a pocket-book."

34896   —— — Steuben's Manual exercise.
    Hartford: Printed and sold by John Babcock. 1798.

34897   —— Steuben's Military Regulations, with eight plates. As ordered both by Congress, and by our late Legislature. To which is added, Cavalry instructions, and Manual.
    New-York: Printed by Thomas Greenleaf. 1798.

34898   —— — Regulations for the order and discipline of the troops of the United States. By baron de Steuben, late major general and inspector general in the American army. Part I. The tenth edition. To which is added, the Manual exercise, and Evolutions of the cavalry: as practised in the late American army.
    New-York: Printed by Hugh Gaine, at the Bible, Pearl-street. 1798. pp. (4), 73, 15, 4, 8 folded plates. 12mo.   NYHS.

34899   —— — Regulations for the order and discipline of the troops of the United States. Part I.
    Philadelphia: Printed by Charles Cist, No.104, North Second-Street. M,DCC,-XCVIII. pp. (4), [151], (8), folded plate. 12mo.   VSL.

34900   —— — Regulations for the order and discipline of the troops of the United States. Part I.
    Philadelphia: Printed by Charles Cist, No.104, North Second-Street. M,DCC,-XCVIII. pp. (2), (2), [151], (8), 8 plates. 12mo.
   Together with: An Act for the regulation of the militia of the Commonwealth of Pennsylvania.
    [Philadelphia: Printed by Charles Cist, 1798.] pp. 60+

34901   —— — Regulations for the order and discipline of the troops of the United States.
    White-Hall: Printed for William Young, Bookseller and Stationer, No. 52, South Second-Street, Philadelphia. M,DCC,XCVIII. pp. [73], (1), (4), 10 folded plates. 12mo.   AAS. SGO.

34902   —— Rules and regulations respecting the recruiting service.
    [Philadelphia: 1798.] pp. 14, (4), 1 folded sheet. 8vo.   BA.

34903   —— Letter from the assistant postmaster-general, accompanying a Specification of the various post offices, and of the compensations which have been allowed to the deputy post-masters, from the first of April, to the thirtieth of September, 1797, inclusive, In pursuance of the 5th section of an Act entitled, "An Act in addition to the Act, entitled, An Act to establish the post office and post roads within the United States." 26th March, 1798. Referred to the committee appointed, on the 6th December last, to inquire whether any, and if any, what alterations are necessary in the law establishing the post office and post roads within the United States.
    Philadelphia: Printed by Way & Groff, No. 27, Arch-Street. [1798.] pp. (24). 8vo.   AAS. BA. MHS.

UNITED STATES, continued.

34904 —— The Post-Office law, with instructions, forms and tables of distances, published for the regulation of the post-offices. 1798.

Philadelphia: Printed by Charles Cist. [1798.] pp. 99, (8). + 8vo.   LOC.

34905 —— Return of the whole number of persons within the several districts of the United States, according to "An Act providing for the enumeration of the inhabitants of the United States," passed March the first, one thousand seven hundred and ninety. Printed by order of the House of Representatives.

Philadelphia: Printed by Joseph Gales, No. 23, South Third Street, [1798.] pp. [56.] 8vo.   AAS. JCB. LOC. MHS. RIHS.

34906 —— Commissioners on the Sixth Article of the Treaty with Great Britain of 1794. The Claim and Answer, in the case of William Cunningham & Co. against the United States; under the sixth article of the Treaty of amity, commerce and navigation, between His Britannic Majesty and the United States of America.

Philadelphia: Printed by John Fenno. M,DCC,XCVIII. pp. (12), (6), (72), (xx). 4to.   AAS. BA. BM. LOC. MHS. NYPL.

Second title: The Reply of William Cunningham & Co. to the Answer of the United States to their Claim and Memorial.

Philadelphia: Printed by James Humphreys. 1798. pp. [36.] 4to.

     AAS. BA. JCB. LOC. NYPL.

Third title: Observations on the part of the United States, by their agent, to the Reply of Daniel Dulany. Under the sixth article of the Treaty of amity, commerce and navigation, between His Britannic Majesty and the United States of America. [Signed, John Read, jun.]

[Philadelphia: Printed by John Fenno. 1798.] pp. (17); (16). 4to.

     AAS. BA. LOC. NYPL.

34907 —— Sundry resolutions of the Board of Commissioners for carrying into effect the sixth article of the Treaty of amity, commerce, and navigation, concluded between His Britannic Majesty and the United States of America. Published for the information of the claimants under the said article by the general agent for claimants. [By William Moore Smith, general agent for British creditors.]

Philadelphia: Printed by James Humphreys, 1798. pp. 18. 8vo.   HSP. NYPL.

Second title: A Candid examination of the objections to the Treaty of amity, commerce, and navigation, between the United States and Great Britain, as stated in the report of the committee, appointed by the citizens of the United States, in Charleston, South-Carolina. By a Citizen of South-Carolina [William Loughton Smith.]

[Philadelphia: Printed by James Humphreys. 1798.]

34908 UNITED STATES. Circuit Court. Rhode-Island District.

Declaration. Rhode-Island District &c. Circuit Court of the United States, June term, 1798. Nathaniel Russel of Charleston in the State of South Carolina, . . . Complains of John Innis Clark of Providence . . . surviving partner of the – – firm of Clarke and Nightingale, . . .

[Providence: 1798.] pp. (8). 8vo.   JCB. RIHS.

34909 [U. S. arms.] UNITED STATES Chronicle. [R. I. arms.] Vol. xv. Numb. 729. Thursday, January 4, [— Numb. 780. Thursday, December 27, 1798.]

Published by B. Wheeler, at his Office in Westminster Street, a few rods westward of the Great Bridge, Providence. 1798. fol.   AAS. HC. LOC. RIHS.

34910 THE UNIVERSAL GAZETTE. VOL. I, No. 8. THURSDAY, JANUARY 4, [— No. 59. THURSDAY, DECEMBER 27, 1798.]
Philadelphia: Printed by Samuel Harrison Smith. 1798. fol. AAS. BA. LOC.

34911 DER UNPARTHEYISCHE READINGER ADLER. No. 54. DIENSTAG, JANUAR 2, [— No. 105. DIENSTAG, DEZEMBER 25, 1798.]
Herausgegeben von Jacob Schneider und Comp. in der Deutsch- und Englischen Buchdruckerey in Reading, in der Pennstrasse. 1798. fol. AAS.

34912 UPTON, WILLIAM
TO THE MAID I LOVE BEST. SONG. WRITTEN BY MR. UPTON.
New-York: Published by G. Gilfert at his Musical Magazine, No. 177 Broadway. 1798.

34913 VALUABLE SECRETS CONCERNING ARTS AND TRADES: OR, APPROVED DIRECTIONS, FROM THE BEST ARTISTS, FOR THE VARIOUS METHODS OF ENGRAVING ON BRASS, COPPER OR STEEL. OF THE COMPOSITION OF METAL AND VARNISHES. OF MASTICKS AND CEMENTS, SEALING WAX, &C. OF COLOURS AND PAINTING FOR CARRIAGE-PAINTERS. OF PAINTING ON PAPER. OF COMPOSITION FOR LIMNERS. OF TRANSPARENT COLOURS. HOW TO DYE SKINS OR GLOVES. TO COLOUR OR VARNISH COPPER-PLATE PRINTS. OF PAINTING ON GLASS. OF COLOURS OF ALL SORTS FOR OIL, WATER AND CRAYONS. OF THE ART OF GILDING. OF THE ART OF DYEING WOODS, BONES, &C. OF THE ART OF MOULDING. OF THE ART OF MAKING WINES. OF THE VARIOUS COMPOSITIONS OF VINEGARS. OF LIQUORS AND ESSENTIAL OILS. OF THE CONFECTIONARY ART. OF TAKING OUT ALL SORTS OF SPOTS AND STAINS, &C. &C. WITH AN APPENDIX, CONTAINING VALUABLE SELECTIONS, IN ADDITION TO, AND NEVER BEFORE PUBLISHED IN THIS WORK. THE THIRD AMERICAN EDITION.
Boston: From J. Bumstead's Printing Office, Union-Street. 1798. LOC.

34914 VAN HORNE, DAVID 1746–1801
INSTRUCTIONS FOR THE CAVALRY, OF THE STATE OF NEW-YORK. BY AN OFFICER OF THE MILITIA. PUBLISHED BY PERMISSION OF HIS EXCELLENCY THE COMMANDER IN CHIEF.
Albany: Printed by Charles R. & George Webster, at their Bookstore, in the White House, corner of State and Pearl-Streets. 1798. pp. 70. 12mo. NYPL.

34915 VAN HORNE, FREDERICK
A SERMON, DELIVERED BY THE REVEREND MR. VAN HORNE, OF ULSTER COUNTY, BEFORE THE BRETHREN OF SOLOMON'S LODGE AT POUGHKEEPSIE, THE 24TH OF JUNE. 1798. [Ornament.]
[Poughkeepsie:] Printed at the request of the Lodge, by Power and Southwick. [1798.] pp. 10. 4to. NYHS.

34916 DER VERBESSERTE HOCH DEUTSCHE AMERICANISCHE LAND UND STAATS CALENDER AUF DAS JAHR . . . 1799. DAS FÜNFZEHNTE MAL HERAUSGEGEBEN.
Friedrich-Stadt, Maryland: Gedruckt bey Matthias Bärtgis. [1798.]

34917 DER VEREINIGTEN STAATEN CALENDER AUF DAS JAHR JESU CHRISTI 1799.
Philadelphia: Gedruckt bey J. R. Kämmerer. [1798.]

34918 THE VERGENNES GAZETTE AND VERMONT AND NEW-YORK ADVERTISER. VOL. I. No. 1. THURSDAY, AUGUST 30, [— No. 16. THURSDAY, DECEMBER 27, 1798.]
Vergennes, State of Vermont: Printed and published every Thursday morning, by G. & R. Waite, at their Printing-Office adjoining the Court house: . . . 1798. fol. AAS. DC.

Established, as a weekly, by George, and Robert Waite. In November, the Waites suddenly departed, and after a suspension of two weeks, on November 29, 1798, Samuel Chipman, junior, resumed publication and continued it into August, 1800. On August 21, 1800, William Fessenden was admitted to partnership and this arrangement continued up to October 27, 1801, when the printing-office was destroyed by fire.

34919   VERMONT. State.

AN ACT ESTABLISHING FEES. PASSED BY THE LEGISLATURE OF THE STATE OF VERMONT, AT THEIR SESSION HOLDEN AT VERGENNES, OCTOBER, 1798. PUBLISHED BY AUTHORITY.

Vergennes. Printed by G. & R. Waite. 1798. pp. 15. 8vo.

34920   —— ACTS AND LAWS, PASSED BY THE LEGISLATURE OF THE STATE OF VERMONT, AT THEIR SESSION AT WINDSOR, OCTOBER, ONE THOUSAND SEVEN HUNDRED AND NINETY-SEVEN. PUBLISHED BY AUTHORITY.

Printed at Rutland, by Josiah Fay, for the Hon. Legislature. M,DCC,XCVIII. pp. 110. 8vo.

34921   —— BY HIS EXCELLENCY, ISAAC TICHENOR, ESQUIRE, GOVERNOUR OF THE STATE OF VERMONT. A PROCLAMATION, FOR A DAY OF PUBLIC HUMILIATION, FASTING AND PRAYER. . . . APPOINT WEDNESDAY, THE EIGHTEENTH DAY OF APRIL NEXT, . . . GIVEN UNDER MY HAND AT BENNINGTON, THE SIXTEENTH DAY OF MARCH, ANNO DOMINI, 1798, BEING THE 22D YEAR OF THE INDEPENDENCE OF THE UNITED STATES. ISAAC TICHENOR. BY HIS EXCELLENCY'S COMMAND, TRUMAN SQUIER, SECRETARY. GOD SAVE THE PEOPLE!

[Bennington: Printed by Anthony Haswell. 1798.] Broadside.

34922   —— BY ISAAC TICHENOR GOVERNOR OF THE STATE OF VERMONT. A PROCLAMATION. . . . APPOINT THE FIRST THURSDAY OF DECEMBER NEXT, BEING THE SIXTH DAY OF SAID MONTH, TO BE OBSERVED AS A DAY OF PUBLIC THANKSGIVING AND PRAISE THROUGHOUT THIS STATE; . . . GIVEN AT THE COUNCIL CHAMBER IN THE CITY OF VERGENNES, THIS 29TH DAY OF OCTOBER, A. D. 1798, AND IN THE 23D YEAR OF THE INDEPENDENCE OF THE UNITED STATES OF AMERICA. ISAAC TICHENOR. BY HIS EXCELLENCY'S COMMAND, R. WHITNEY, SECRETARY. GOD SAVE THE PEOPLE!

[Vergennes: Printed by G. and R. Waite. 1798.] Broadside.

34923   —— A JOURNAL OF THE PROCEEDINGS OF THE GENERAL ASSEMBLY OF THE STATE OF VERMONT, BEGUN AND HELD AT WINDSOR, OCTOBER THE TWELFTH, ONE THOUSAND, SEVEN HUNDRED AND NINETY SEVEN. PUBLISHED BY ORDER OF THE GENERAL ASSEMBLY.

Bennington: Printed by A. Haswell, for S. Williams. 1798. pp. 287. 8vo. VSL.

The Journal of the February, 1797, Session was never printed.

34924   —— JOURNAL OF THE GENERAL ASSEMBLY OF THE STATE OF VERMONT, BEGUN AND HELD AT THE CITY OF VERGENNES, OCTOBER XITH, M,DCC,XCVIII. [— 8 NOVEMBER, 1798.] [Ornament.]

Bennington: Printed by Anthony Haswell. [1798.] pp. [299.] 8vo. AAS.

34925   —— LAWS OF THE STATE OF VERMONT; REVISED AND PASSED BY THE LEGISLATURE, IN THE YEAR OF OUR LORD, ONE THOUSAND SEVEN HUNDRED AND NINETY-SEVEN. TOGETHER WITH THE DECLARATION OF INDEPENDENCE, THE CONSTITUTION OF THE UNITED STATES, WITH ITS AMENDMENTS, AND THE CONSTITUTION OF THE STATE OF VERMONT: WITH AN APPENDIX, CONTAINING THE SEVERAL LAWS, WHICH HAVE HERETOFORE BEEN PASSED BY THE LEGISLATURE, REGULATING PROPRIETORS' MEETINGS, GRANTING GENERAL LAND TAXES, EXCLUSIVE PRIVILEGES TO COMPANIES FOR LOCKS, TOLL BRIDGES, TURNPIKE ROADS, &C. AND THE TITLES OF ALL THE ACTS WHICH HAVE BEEN REPEALED, OR BECOME OBSOLETE. PUBLISHED BY AUTHORITY.

State of Vermont. Printed at Rutland, by Jonas Fay. M,DCC,XCVIII. pp. 621; 205, (2). 8vo. AAS. BA.

34926   VERMONT GAZETTE. [Motto.] VOL. I. NUMBER 18. TUESDAY, JANUARY 2, [—VOL. II. NUMBER 17. THURSDAY, DECEMBER 27. 1798.]

Printed and Published at Bennington, by Anthony Haswell. 1798. fol. AAS.

34927   VESPER; OR, THE EVENING COURIER. VOL. I. NO. 1. TUESDAY, JULY 31, [— NO. 32. FRIDAY, NOVEMBER 16, 1798.]

Charleston: Printed by Bonnetheau & Evans. 1798. fol.   HC.

Established, as a semi-weekly, by Gabriel M. Bonnetheau and John J. Evans, and continued by them to November 16, 1798—the last number located.

34928   A VIEW OF THE ADMINISTRATION OF THE FEDERAL GOVERNMENT. CONTAINING AN ADDRESS DELIVERED AT A PUBLIC MEETING OF THE CITIZENS OF MASON AND THE ADJACENT COUNTIES. BY A CITIZEN OF KENTUCKY.

Washington (K). Printed by Hunter and Beaumont. 1798.

34929   THE VIGIL: NO. I. TUESDAY, FEBRUARY 27, [— NO. VI. TUESDAY, APRIL 3, 1798.] [Three lines of Latin from] HOR. [Printer's mark.]

Charleston: Printed by W. P. Young, No. 43, Broad-Street 1798. pp. 48. 8vo.   CLS.

"A periodical paper upon the plan of the Spectator, Guardian, &c." Edited by Richard Beresford. Apparently all that was published.

34930   THE VILLAGE HARMONY, OR YOUTH'S ASSISTANT TO SACRED MUSICK. CONTAINING A CONCISE INTRODUCTION TO THE GROUNDS OF MUSICK, WITH SUCH A COLLECTION OF THE MOST APPROVED PSALM TUNES, ANTHEMS, AND OTHER PIECES, IN THREE, AND FOUR PARTS, AS ARE MOST SUITABLE FOR DIVINE WORSHIP. DESIGNED FOR THE USE OF SCHOOLS AND SINGING SOCIETIES. THE FOURTH EDITION, CORRECTED AND IMPROVED.

Printed at Exeter, by H. Ranlet, and sold at his Book-Store. 1798. pp. 203. obl. 8vo.

34931   VILLAGE MESSENGER. VOL. III. NO. 101. SATURDAY, JANUARY 6, [— VOL. III. NO. 157. SATURDAY, DECEMBER 29, 1798.]

[Printed and published] By Samuel Preston, Amherst. Newhampshire. 1798. fol.   AAS.

The title enclosed in an oval ornamental border. The Printing-Office was "a few rods west of the Meeting-House."

34932   THE VILLAGE RECRUIT. SONG.

New York: Published by George Gilbert, at his Music-Store, 177 Broadway, Apollo's Head. 1798.

34933   VINING, EBENEZER

A FUNERAL SERMON; DELIVERED AT THE INTERMENT OF MRS. MARY PIERCE, LATE WIFE OF MR. JONATHAN PIERCE, OF CHESTERFIELD, WHO DEPARTED THIS LIFE AUGUST 2D, 1798. BY THE REV. EBENEZER VINING, PASTOR OF THE BAPTIST CHURCH IN CHESTERFIELD. . . .

Conway: Printed by Theodore & A. H. Leonard. 1798. pp. 11. 12mo.

BA. JCB. NYPL.

34934   VIRGINIA. STATE.

ACTS PASSED AT A GENERAL ASSEMBLY OF THE COMMONWEALTH OF VIRGINIA: BEGUN, AND HELD AT THE CAPITOL, IN THE CITY OF RICHMOND, ON MONDAY, THE FOURTH DAY OF DECEMBER, ONE THOUSAND SEVEN HUNDRED AND NINETY-SEVEN. [— 25 JANUARY, 1798.] [Ornament.]

Richmond: Printed by Augustine Davis, Printer for the Public. M.DCC.- XCVIII pp. [51.] fol.   HSP. LOC. NYPL., VSL.

VIRGINIA. STATE, continued.

34935 —— DEBATES IN THE HOUSE OF DELEGATES OF VIRGINIA, UPON CERTAIN RESOLU-
TIONS BEFORE THE HOUSE, UPON THE IMPORTANT SUBJECT OF THE ACTS OF CONGRESS
PASSED AT THEIR LAST SESSION, COMMONLY CALLED, THE ALIEN AND SEDITION LAWS.
[By Theodosius Hansford.]

Richmond: Printed by Thos. Nicolson. M,DCC,CXVIII. [*sic*] [1798.] pp.
(189), (2). 8vo.   JCB. LOC. NYPL.

11th Virginia District Copyright, issued to Theodosius Hansford, as
Author, 2 January, 1799. Reprinted in Richmond, in 1829.

34936 —— JOURNAL OF THE HOUSE OF DELEGATES OF THE COMMONWEALTH OF VIRGINIA,
BEGUN AND HELD AT THE CAPITOL, IN THE CITY OF RICHMOND, ON MONDAY, THE
FOURTH DAY OF DECEMBER, ONE THOUSAND SEVEN HUNDRED AND NINETY-SEVEN.
[— 19 JANUARY, 1798.] [Ornament.]

Richmond: Printed by Augustine Davis, Printer to the Commonwealth. M,-
DCC,XCVII. [1798.] pp. 115. fol.   BU. JCB. NYPL. VSL.

34937 —— JOURNAL OF THE SENATE OF THE COMMONWEALTH OF VIRGINIA, BEGUN AND
HELD AT THE CAPITOL, IN THE CITY OF RICHMOND, ON MONDAY, THE FOURTH DAY
OF DECEMBER, ONE THOUSAND SEVEN HUNDRED AND NINETY-SEVEN. [— 25 JAN-
UARY, 1798.]

Richmond: Printed by Thomas Nicolson. 1798.

No copy in print, or in manuscript, is known to be extant.

34938 —— (CIRCULAR) IN COUNCIL, 8TH OF JANUARY, 1798. GENTLEMEN, MY OFFICIAL DUTY
CALLS UPON ME TO REQUEST YOUR PARTICULAR ATTENTION TO THE LAWS RELATIVE
TO THE APPOINTMENT AND DUTIES OF SHERIFFS. [Thirteen lines. Signed, James
Wood.]

[Richmond: Printed by Augustine Davis. 1798.] Broadside. 4to.   LOC.

34939 —— INSTRUCTIONS FROM THE GENERAL ASSEMBLY OF VIRGINIA, TO STEPHENS THOMP-
SON MASON, AND WILSON CARY NICHOLAS, SENATORS FROM THE STATE OF VIRGINIA,
IN THE CONGRESS OF THE UNITED STATES. [Two pages.] 1. TO PROCURE A RE-
DUCTION OF THE ARMY, . . . 2. TO PREVENT ANY AUGMENTATION OF THE NAVY,
. . . 3. TO OPPOSE . . . THE PRINCIPLE LATELY ADVANCED, "THAT THE COMMON
LAW OF ENGLAND IS IN FORCE UNDER THE GOVERNMENT OF THE UNITED STATES.
4. TO PROCURE A REPEAL OF THE ACTS OF CONGRESS COMMONLY CALLED THE ALIEN
AND SEDITION LAWS.

[Richmond: Printed by Augustine Davis. 1798.] pp. (2). fol.   AAS.

34940 —— LIST OF PENSIONERS CONTINUED BY THE HONORABLE THE EXECUTIVE, FOR THE
YEAR 1797, TO BE PAID OUT OF THE REVENUE FOR THAT YEAR. [Forty-two pensioners, and allowances.] AUDITOR'S-OFFICE, FEBRUARY 1, 1798.

[Richmond: Printed by Augustine Davis. 1798.] Broadside. fol.   LOC.

34941 —— VIRGINIA, IN THE HOUSE OF DELEGATES, TUESDAY, DECEMBER THE 13TH, 1798.
[Resolutions recommending that the people instruct their representatives in the
next session of the General Assembly, upon the propriety of calling a convention
for revising the Constitution of the Commonwealth.]

[Richmond: Printed by Jones and Dixon. 1798.] Broadside. fol.   LOC.

34942

VIRGINIA. STATE, continued.
—— VIRGINIA TO WIT. IN THE HOUSE OF DELEGATES, FRIDAY, DECEMBER 21ST, 1798. RESOLVED, THAT THE GENERAL ASSEMBLY OF VIRGINIA DOTH UNEQUIVOCALLY EXPRESS A FIRM RESOLUTION TO MAINTAIN AND DEFEND THE CONSTITUTION OF THE UNITED STATES, AND THE CONSTITUTION OF THIS STATE, AGAINST EVERY AGGRESSION, EITHER FOREIGN OR DOMESTIC, AND THAT THEY WILL SUPPORT THE GOVERNMENT OF THE UNITED STATES IN ALL MEASURES WARRANTED BY THE FORMER. [Protesting against the Alien and Sedition acts as unconstitutional.] ATTEST JOHN STEWART, C. H. D. 1798, DECEMBER THE 24TH. AGREED TO BY THE SENATE, H. BROOKE, C. S.

[Richmond: Printed by Augustine Davis. 1798.] pp. (2). 4to.   LOC.

34943

THE VIRGINIA ALMANAC, FOR THE YEAR OF OUR LORD 1799, BEING THE THIRD AFTER BISSEXTILE OR LEAP YEAR, THE TWENTY THIRD OF AMERICAN INDEPENDENCE, AND THE ELEVENTH YEAR OF OUR FEDERAL GOVERNMENT. WHICH MAY THE GOVERNOR OF THE WORLD PROSPER. CONTAINING THE MOTIONS OF THE SUN AND MOON; THE TRUE PLACES AND ASPECTS OF THE PLANETS; THE RISING AND SETTING OF THE SUN AND MOON; ALSO, THE LUNATIONS, CONJUNCTIONS, ECLIPSES, JUDGMENT OF THE WEATHER, REMARKABLE DAYS, LENGTH OF DAYS AND NIGHTS, TIMES COURTS ARE HELD IN VIRGINIA, MARYLAND AND PENNSYLVANIA, ROADS, &C. LIKEWISE, A VARIETY OF ESSAYS IN PROSE & VERSE. THE WHOLE CALCULATED FOR GENERAL UTILITY AND ENTERTAINMENT. BY THE NORTH MOUNTAIN PHILOSOPHER.

Winchester: Printed and sold by Richard Bowen, opposite the Episcopal Church, in Loudoun Street. [1798.] pp. (36). 12mo.   AAS.

34944

THE VIRGINIA ARGUS. [Motto.] VOL. V. No. 75. WHOLE NO. 490. TUESDAY, JANUARY 2, [— VOL. VI. No. 72. WHOLE NO. 593. FRIDAY, DECEMBER 28, 1798.]

Richmond: Printed (on Tuesdays and Fridays) by Samuel Pleasants, jun. near the Vendue Office of M. Vandewall. 1798. fol.

The motto reads: A free press maintains the sovereignty of the people.

34945

THE VIRGINIA GAZETTE, AND GENERAL ADVERTISER. VOL. XII. NUMB. 600. WEDNESDAY, JANUARY 3, [— NUMB. 654. TUESDAY, DECEMBER 25, 1798.]

Richmond: Printed by Aug. Davis. 1798. fol.

An extra number was issued October 2d. containing the Remonstrance of the citizens of Albemarle County against the "Alien and Sedition laws."

34946

VIRGINIA GAZETTE, AND PETERSBURG INTELLIGENCER. NUMBER 860. TUESDAY, JANUARY 2, [— NUMBER 963. FRIDAY, DECEMBER 28, 1798.]

[Petersburg:] Published every Tuesday and Friday by William Prentis. 1798. fol.

34947

VIRGINIA GAZETTE, AND STAUNTON WEEKLY ADVERTISER. VOL. II. No. 44. FRIDAY, JANUARY 5, [— No. 52. FRIDAY, MARCH 2, 1798.]

Staunton: Printed by John Wise. 1798. fol.

Beginning March 14th. with continuous numbering, Wise changed the title to *The Phenix.*

34948

THE VIRGINIA HERALD. VOL. X. NUMB. 691. TUESDAY, JANUARY 2, [— VOL. XI. NUMB. 792. FRIDAY, DECEMBER 28, 1798.]

Fredericksburg (Va.) Published on Tuesdays and Fridays by T. Green. 1798. fol.

34949   VOLNEY, Constantin François Chassebœuf Boisgivais, comte DE   1757–1820
Travels through Syria and Egypt, in the years 1783, 1784 and 1785. Containing the present natural and political state of those countries, their productions, arts, manufactures, and commerce; with observations on the manners, customs, and government of the Turks and Arabs. By C-F. Volney. Translated from the French.

    New-York: Printed by Thomas Greenleaf, No. 54, Wall Street. 1798. 2 vols. 8vo.   BM.

    "Printed on good paper, fair type, in 8 numbers, each to contain 72 pages octavo. 1 shilling per number stitched in blue paper. With a list of subscribers, and a portrait of the Author, by an American artist."

34950   VOSE, Solomon
A Masonic charge: delivered at Greenfield, Massachusetts. Before the officers and brethren of the Republican Lodge, of Free and Accepted Masons, in that town; joined by the officers and brethren of Harmony Lodge, from Northfield; on the festival of St. John the Baptist: June 26th, A.L. 5798. By the rt. worshipful brother Solomon Vose. Published by the united request of the brethren.

    Printed at Greenfield, by Francis Barker. 1798. pp. 11. 4to.   AAS.

34951   WALLACE, Jonathan
Carlisle, October, 1798. Fellow-citizens, The present sheriff's time being about to expire, and a respectable number of you having encouraged me to offer myself a candidate for the sheriff's office, at the ensuing general election: [Fifty-five lines.] Jonathan Wallace.

    [Carlisle: Printed by George Kline, 1798.] Broadside. fol.   HSP.

34952   WALSH, Thomas   1730–1759
The Whole armour of God. A sermon on Eph. chap. VI. verse II. By the late Thomas Walsh, preacher of the Gospel.

    New-York: Printed by T. Kirk. 1798. pp. 36. 12mo.   NYPL.

34953   WALTER, William   1737–1800
A Discourse delivered before the Humane Society of the Commonwealth of Massachusetts, at the semi annual meeting twelfth of June, 1798. By William Walter, D.D. rector of Christ church in Boston. [Printers mark.]

    Boston: Printed by John & Thomas Fleet, at the Bible and Heart, Cornhill. MDCCXCVIII. pp. 48. 4to.   AAS. BA. BM. HC. JCB. MHS. NYHS. NYPL. SGO.

34954   WARD, Edward   1667–1731
Female policy detected: or the arts of a designing woman laid open. By E. W. author of the London Spy, and a Trip to Jamaica.

    New-York: 1798. 12mo.

34955   WAREHAM. Massachusetts. Social Library.
Catalogue of books, belonging to Wareham Social Library, 1798. To be returned the first Tuesday of April, July, October, & January. [180 volumes.]

    Printed at Newbedford, by J. Spooner, for the Proprietors.— 1798. pp. 7. 16mo.   AAS.

34956   WARREN. Rhode Island. Warren Association.
Minutes of the Warren Association, held at the Baptist meeting-house in Barnstable, September 11 and 12, 1798.

    Boston: Printed by Manning and Loring. M,DCC,XCVIII. pp. 8. 8vo.
                                         AAS. BM. JCB. NYPL.

34957   WARWICK. New York. Baptist Association.
MINUTES OF THE WARWICK BAPTIST ASSOCIATION, HELD AT WARWICK. MAY 29TH,
1798. [Colophon:]
     Goshen: Printed by John G. Hurtin. [1798.] 4to.

34958   WASHINGTON, Bushrod   1762–1829
REPORTS OF CASES ARGUED AND DETERMINED IN THE COURT OF APPEALS OF VIRGINIA.
By BUSHROD WASHINGTON. VOL. I. [1790–1794.]
     Richmond: Printed by Thomas Nicolson. MDCCXCVIII. pp. viii, 392, 16,
(1). 8vo.   AAS. BM. HC. JCB. NYPL. VSL.

     13th Virginia District Copyright, issued to Bushrod Washington, as
Author. 29 June, 1798. Reprinted in Philadelphia, in 1823.

34959   WASHINGTON AND INDEPENDENCE. A NEW PATRIOTIC SONG.
     *Boston: Published by P. A. von Hagen, jun. and Co's Musical Magazine, No.
62, Newbury-Street.* 1798.

34960   THE WASHINGTON GAZETTE. NUMBER 25 OF VOL. II. FROM SATURDAY, DECEMBER
30, TO SATURDAY, JANUARY 6, [— NUMBER 35. SATURDAY, MARCH 17–24, 1798.]
     *City of Washington: Published by Benjamin More, every Saturday, price two
and a half dollars per ann. at the house next west of the Hotel, where subscriptions
will be thankfully received. Handbills, &c. printed at the shortest notice.* 1798. fol.
                                                   AAS. HC. LOC.

     Discontinued in March, at the above date. The issue for March 17–24,
editorially states: "I shall not be able to continue the publication of the
Washington Gazette, except some friend should lend a helping hand.
HOPE has led me into a thicket of difficulties — and appears to be
departing from me."

34961   WATSON, Richard   1737–1816
AN ADDRESS TO THE PEOPLE OF GREAT BRITAIN. BY R. WATSON, LORD BISHOP OF
LANDAFF. FIRST NEW-YORK EDITION.
     New-York: Printed by J. Buel, for C. Davis, No. 94, Water Street. 1798.
pp. [24.] 12mo.   AAS. JCB. LOC.

34962   —— — AN ADDRESS TO THE PEOPLE OF GREAT BRITAIN. BY R. WATSON, LORD
BISHOP OF LANDAFF.
     Philadelphia: Published by William Cobbett, opposite Christ Church. April,
1798. pp. [40.] 8vo.   AAS. BA. BM. BU. JCB. LCP. LOC.

34963   WATTS, Isaac   1674–1748
A CATECHISM FOR CHILDREN. BY ISAAC WATTS, D. D. [Five lines from] MOSES.
     Windham: Printed by John Byrne. 1798. pp. 46, portrait. 48mo.   AAS.

34964   —— A COMPREHENSIVE ABRIDGMENT OF DR. WATTS'S LYRIC POEMS AND MISCELLA-
NEOUS THOUGHTS. TOGETHER WITH THE HYMNS SUBJOINED TO HIS FOURTY-FOUR
SERMONS, AND A FEW PIECES FROM POPE, ADDISON, ROWE &c. . . . BY SOLOMON
HOWE. IN TWO PARTS.
     *Northampton, Massachusetts: Printed for the Editor. Sold by him in Green-
wich.* 1798. pp. 48; 16. 8vo.   BA. BM. NYPL.

     Second title: SUBLIMITY AND DEVOTION UNITED, IN A NUMBER OF HYMNS COM-
POSED BY DR. ISAAC WATTS—NOT IN PRINT WITH HIS OTHER HYMNS. TO WHICH IS
PREFIXED, HIS POEM, ENTITLED, FEW HAPPY MATCHES: AND SOME ELEGANT PIECES
FROM OTHER AUTHORS, DESIGNED FOR THE ENTERTAINMENT OF ALL CLASSES. . . . .
[Edited by Solomon Howe.]
     [Northampton:] Printed for, and sold by S. Howe, of Greenwich. [1798.]
pp. 16.

WATTS, ISAAC, continued.

34965 —— DIVINE SONGS, ATTEMPTED IN EASY LANGUAGE, FOR THE USE OF CHILDREN. BY ISAAC WATTS, D. D. "OUT OF THE MOUTHS OF BABES AND SUCKLINGS THOU HAST PERFECTED PRAISE." MAT. XXI. 16.

> *Boston: Printed by B. Edes, jun.*—1798. pp. 47, cut. 48mo.   AAS.
>
> Contains, a slight specimen of Moral songs. pp. 45–47.

34966 —— HORÆ LYRICÆ. POEMS, CHIEFLY OF THE LYRIC KIND. IN THREE BOOKS. BOOK I. SACRED TO DEVOTION AND PIETY. BOOK II. TO VIRTUE, HONOR AND FRIENDSHIP. BOOK III. TO THE MEMORY OF THE DEAD. BY ISAAC WATTS, D.D. [Three lines of Latin from] HOR. OD. I. IMITAT.

> *Printed at Windham, (Connecticut) by John Byrne.* M,DCC,XCVIII. pp. 208. 12mo.   AAS. NYPL.

34967 **THE WAVES** WERE HUSH'D, THE SKY SERENE. SONG.

> *New-York: Published by G. Gilfert at his Musical Magazine, No. 177 Broadway.* 1798.

34968 **WEATHERWISE, J.**, pseudonym.

THE FARMER'S ALMANACK, FOR THE YEAR OF OUR LORD, 1799. BEING THE THIRD AFTER BISSEXTILE, OR LEAP YEAR, AND TWENTY-THIRD OF AMERICAN INDEPENDENCE. CALCULATED FOR THE MERIDIAN OF NORWICH—BUT WILL SERVE FOR THE STATE OF CONNECTICUT, RHODE ISLAND, NEW HAMPSHIRE, MASSACHUSETTS, NEW YORK AND VERMONT. [Nine lines.] BY J. WEATHERWISE, ASTRONOMER.

> *Printed and sold by J. Trumbull, Norwich, and by S. Trumbull, Printer, Stonington Port.* [1798.] pp. (24). 12mo.   AAS. CHS. LOC. WL.

34969 **WEATHERWISE'S** MASSACHUSETTS, CONNECTICUT, RHODE-ISLAND, NEW-HAMPSHIRE AND VERMONT ALMANACK, FOR THE YEAR 1799. BEING THE THIRD AFTER BISSEXTILE, OR LEAP-YEAR, AND TWENTY THIRD OF THE INDEPENDENCE OF THE UNITED STATES OF AMERICA. FITTED TO THE LATITUDE AND LONGITUDE OF THE TOWN OF BOSTON, BUT WILL SERVE WITHOUT ESSENTIAL VARIATION FOR THE ADJACENT STATES. TOGETHER WITH MATTER, BOTH USEFUL AND ENTERTAINING. [Cut.]

> *Medford: Printed by Nathaniel Coverly. Price 3 dollars and 75 cents per groce, 42 cents per dozen, and 6 cents single.* [1798.] pp. (24). 12mo.   AAS.

34970 **WEATHERWISE'S** MASSACHUSETTS, CONNECTICUT, RHODEISLAND, NEWHAMPSHIRE AND VERMONT ALMANACK, FOR THE YEAR OF OUR LORD 1799. BEING THE THIRD AFTER BISSEXTILE, OR LEAP YEAR, AND TWENTY THIRD OF THE INDEPENDENCE OF THE UNITED STATES OF AMERICA. FITTED TO THE LATITUDE AND LONGITUDE OF THE TOWN OF BOSTON, BUT WILL SERVE WITHOUT ESSENTIAL VARIATION FOR THE ADJACENT STATES. TOGETHER WITH MATTERS, BOTH USEFUL AND ENTERTAINING. [Cut.]

> *Printed by Nathaniel & John Coverly, sold by them at their Book store in Salem. Price 3 dollars and 75 cents per groce, 42 cents per dozen, and 6 cents single.* [1798.] pp. (24). 12mo.   AAS. LOC.
>
> The American Antiquarian Society has another variety with a different wood cut on the title page. There is no difference, except the title pages, between this and The Farmer's Almanack, and Bickerstaff's, printed by the same printers this year.

34971 **WEBB, CONRADE**

UNION CONSIDERED AS THE ONLY SAFETY OF THE UNITED STATES. AN ORATION, TOGETHER WITH THE VALEDICTORY ADDRESSES, PRONOUNCED IN THE BAPTIST MEETING-HOUSE IN PROVIDENCE, AT THE COMMENCEMENT OF RHODE-ISLAND COLLEGE, SEPTEMBER 5, A. D. 1798. BY CONRADE WEBB, A. B. PUBLISHED BY REQUEST.

> *Providence: Printed by Bennett Wheeler.* M,DCC,XCVIII. pp. (19). 8vo.
>
>   AAS. BU. NYPL.

34972 WEBB, Elizabeth
EINIGE GLAUBENS-BEKENNTNISSE UND GÖTTLICHE ERFAHRUNGS-PROBEN IN EINEM SENDSCHREIBEN VON ELISABETHA WEBB AN ANTON WILHELM BÖHM, CAPELLAN ZUM PRINZEN GEORG VON DÄNEMARK IM JAHR 1712. AUS DER ENGLISCHEN SPRACHE ÜBERSETZT VON J. M. JORCK. ZWEYTE AUSGABE.

    Philadelphia: Gedruckt bey Carl Cist, in der Zweyten Strasse. 1798. pp. iv, 48. 12mo.   AAS. JCB.

34973 ——— — A LETTER FROM ELIZABETH WEBB, TO ANTHONY WILLIAM BOEHM, WITH HIS ANSWER. THE THIRD EDITION.

    Philadelphia: Printed by Henry Tuckniss. 1798.   LOC.

34974 WEBB, William
AN INAUGURAL DISSERTATION ON THE COLIC, SUBMITTED TO THE EXAMINATION OF THE REV. JOHN EWING, S. S. T. P. PROVOST, THE TRUSTEES AND MEDICAL PROFESSORS, OF THE UNIVERSITY OF PENNSYLVANIA. ON THE TWENTY-SECOND DAY OF MAY, 1798, FOR THE DEGREE OF DOCTOR OF MEDICINE. BY WILLIAM WEBB, OF VIRGINIA. MEMBER OF THE PHILADELPHIA MEDICAL SOCIETY. [Two lines from] DARWIN.

    Philadelphia: Printed by John Ormrod, No. 41, Chesnut-Street. 1798. pp. (17) [*sic* 27.] 8vo.   AAS. LCP. LOC. SGO.

34975 WEBSTER, Noah, JUNIOR   1758–1843
THE AMERICAN SELECTION OF LESSONS IN READING AND SPEAKING. CALCULATED TO IMPROVE THE MINDS AND REFINE THE TASTE OF YOUTH, TO WHICH ARE PREFIXED RULES IN ELOCUTION, AND DIRECTIONS FOR EXPRESSING THE PRINCIPAL PASSIONS OF THE MIND. BEING THE THIRD PART OF A GRAMMATICAL INSTITUTE OF THE ENGLISH LANGUAGE. BY NOAH WEBSTER, JUN. AUTHOR OF 'DISSERTATIONS ON THE ENGLISH LANGUAGE,' 'COLLECTION OF ESSAYS AND FUGITIVE WRITINGS,' 'THE PROMPTER,' &c. THE THIRTEENTH EDITION.

    Hartford: Printed by Hudson & Goodwin. [With the privilege of copy right.] [1798.] pp. 240. 12mo.   JCB. LOC. NYPL. RIHS. YC.

34976 ——— THE AMERICAN SPELLING BOOK: CONTAINING AN EASY STANDARD OF PRONUNCIATION. BEING THE FIRST PART OF A GRAMMATICAL INSTITUTE OF THE ENGLISH LANGUAGE. TO WHICH IS ADDED, AN APPENDIX CONTAINING A MORAL CATECHISM, AND A FEDERAL CATECHISM. BY NOAH WEBSTER, JUN. ESQUIRE. AUTHOR OF "DISSERTATIONS ON THE ENGLISH LANGUAGE," "COLLECTION OF ESSAYS AND FUGITIVE WRITINGS," &c. THOMAS & ANDREWS' SEVENTEENTH EDITION. WITH MANY CORRECTIONS AND IMPROVEMENTS BY THE AUTHOR.

    Printed at Boston, by Isaiah Thomas and Ebenezer T. Andrews, Faust's Statue, No. 45, Newbury Street. Sold wholesale and retail, at their Bookstore; by said Thomas at his Bookstore in Worcester; and by Thomas, Andrews & Penniman, in Albany; and by Thomas, Andrews & Butler, in Baltimore. - - 1798. pp. 156, (2), portrait. 12mo.   LOC.

34977 ——— THE AMERICAN SPELLING BOOK: CONTAINING AN EASY STANDARD OF PRONUNCIATION. BEING THE FIRST PART OF A GRAMMATICAL INSTITUTE OF THE ENGLISH LANGUAGE. TO WHICH IS ADDED, AN APPENDIX CONTAINING A MORAL CATECHISM, AND A FEDERAL CATECHISM. BY NOAH WEBSTER, JUN. ESQUIRE. AUTHOR OF "DISSERTATIONS ON THE ENGLISH LANGUAGE," "COLLECTION OF ESSAYS AND FUGITIVE WRITINGS", &c. THOMAS & ANDREWS' EIGHTEENTH EDITION. WITH MANY CORRECTIONS AND IMPROVEMENTS BY THE AUTHOR.

    Printed at Boston by Isaiah Thomas and Ebenezer T. Andrews, Faust's Statue, No. 45, Newbury Street. Sold, wholesale and retail, at their Bookstore; by said Thomas in Worcester; by Thomas, Andrews & Penniman, in Albany: and by Thomas, Andrews & Butler, in Baltimore. - - 1798. pp. 156, (2), portrait. 12mo.

WEBSTER, Noah, junior, continued.

34978   —— —— The American spelling book: containing an easy standard of pronunciation. Being the first part of a Grammatical institute of the English language. To which is added, an Appendix containing a Moral catechism, and a Federal catechism. By Noah Webster, jun. esquire. Author of "Dissertations on the English language," "Collection of essays and fugitive writings," &c. Thomas & Andrews' nineteenth edition. With many corrections and improvements by the Author.
    Printed at Boston, by Isaiah Thomas and Ebenezer T. Andrews, Faust's Statue, No. 45, Newbury Street. Sold, wholesale and retail, at their Bookstore; by said Thomas in Worcester; by Thomas, Andrews & Penniman, in Albany; and by Thomas, Andrews & Butler, in Baltimore. – – 1798. pp. 156, (2), portrait. 12mo.

34979   —— —— The American spelling book: containing an easy standard of pronunciation. Being the first part of a Grammatical institute of the English language. In three parts. By Noah Webster, junr. esquire The twentieth Connecticut edition.
    Hartford: Printed by Hudson & Goodwin. [*With the privilege of copy right.*] [1798.] pp. 165, (1). 12mo.

34980   —— A Grammatical institute of the English language; comprising an easy, concise and systematic method of education. Designed for the use of English schools in America. In three parts. Part second. Containing a plain and comprehensive grammar. Grounded on the true principles and idioms of the language. By Noah Webster, jun. Author of "Dissertations on the English language," Collection of essays and fugitive writings" &c.
    New-York: Printed by Robert Wilson, for Evert Duyckinck, & Co. Booksellers and Stationers. 1798. pp. 119, (1). 12mo.   AAS. LOC. MHS. NYPL.

34981   —— A Letter to the governors, instructors and trustees of the universities, and other seminaries of learning, in the United States, on the errors of English grammar. By Noah Webster, jun.
    New-York: Printed by George F. Hopkins, for the Author. 1798. pp. 36. 8vo.   AAS. BM. CHS. HC. JCB. LOC. NYHS. NYPL. UTS. WL. YC.

34982   —— The Little reader's assistant: containing, 1st. A number of stories, mostly taken from the History of America, and adorned with cuts. 2d. Rudiments of English grammar. 3d. A Federal catechism, being a short and easy explanation of the Constitution of the United States. 4th. General principles of government and commerce. 5th. The Farmer's catechism, containing plain rules of husbandry, All adapted to the capacities of children. By Noah Webster. jun.
    Hartford: Printed and sold by Elisha Babcock. 1798.

34983   —— —— The Little reader's assistant: containing, 1st. A number of stories, mostly taken from the History of America, and adorned with cuts. 2d. Rudiments of English grammar. 3d. A Federal catechism, being a short and easy explanation of the Constitution of the United States. 4th. General principles of government and commerce. 5th. The Farmer's catechism, containing plain rules of husbandry. All adapted to the capacities of children. By Noah Webster, jun. The fourth edition.
    Printed at Northampton (Mass.) By William Butler. 1798. pp. 138. 16mo.   LOC. NYPL.

34984   —— An Oration pronounced before the citizens of New-Haven on the anniversary of the independence of the United States, July 4th, 1798; and published at their request. By Noah Webster, jun.
    New-Haven: Printed by T. & S. Green. [1798.] pp. 16. 8vo.
    AAS. BA. BM. CHS. HC. JCB. LOC. MHS. NYHS. WL. YC.

34985   WEBSTER, NOAH, JUNIOR, continued.

—— To THE CLERGYMEN OR OTHER WELL-INFORMED GENTLEMEN IN THE SEVERAL TOWNS IN CONNECTICUT. [Proposition to compile statistics of Connecticut. Dated, New Haven, May 7, 1798.]

[New-Haven: Printed by T. & S. Green. 1798.] Broadside. fol.

34986   WEED, ENOS, JUNIOR

THE AMERICAN ORTHOGRAPHER, IN THREE BOOKS. BOOK I. THE BIBLIOGRAPHICAL-SPELLING-BOOK. BOOK II. THE GEOGRAPHICAL-SPELLING-BOOK. BɔK III. PART I. ɯVMERRIKAN-STANDARD ɟOR PRONUNSIVSHON. PART II. ɯVMERRIKANZ JEO-GRAFFIKAL STANDARD. PART III. ɯVMERRIKANZ-DIKSONVRIAN STANDARD. [Three lines from] II. TIM. III. 15. BY ENOS WEED, JUN. PHYSICIAN AND SURGEON IN DIFFICULT CASES.

Danbury: Printed by Douglas & Nichols, for the Author. [Copy-right secured to the Author.] [1798.] pp. 60. 8vo.   JCB.

Connecticut District Copyright, issued to Enos Weed, junior, of Stanford, as Author, 8 February, 1798. Advertised as: The American orthographer. Book I. Containing the sum of the Scriptural proper names, both of the Old and New Testaments, compiled in tables according to their accent and number of syllables, with essays, extracts, First and Scriptural Catechisms.

34987   —— — THE AMERICAN ORTHOGRAPHER. BOOK II. THE GEOGRAPHICAL SPELLING-BOOK. [Eight lines of Scripture texts.] BY ENOS WEED, JUN. PHYSICIAN AND SURGEON IN DIFFICULT CASES.

Danbury: Printed by Douglas & Nichols, for the Author. 1798. pp. 36. 8vo.

Advertised as: The American orthographer. Book II. The Geographical   AAS. spelling-book. Or poor man's gazetteer. By Enos Weed, jun. Containing, Geographical definitions, names of places with their difference of longitude from Philadelphia, and difference of latitude from the Equator, rules for finding the difference of latitude and longitude, names of places alphabetically arranged in tables, with their latitude and longitude, a compendious system of Federal arithmetic, &c. &c.

34988   —— — THE AMERICAN ORTHOGRAPHER. BɔK III. ɯ KOMMON MANZ ɟIZZIKKAL INMUKT-TER IN TU BOKS. BOK I. EVRI MAN HIZ EEN ɟIZI ◌ SHAN. ɯ KOMMON MANZ ɟIZZIKAL INMUKT-TER IN TU BOKS. BOK I. EVRI MAN HIZ EEN ɟIZI ◌ SHAN. BOK II. EVRI WOMMON HER OON ɟIZI ◌ SHAN. BY ENOS WEED, JUN. V4 OR OV ɯ VMERRIKAN. OR4OGGRVɅER & ɟIZI ◌ SHAN & SURJEN IN DIFFIKULT KVSEZ.

Danbury: Printed by Douglas & Nichols, for the Author. 1798.

A weed in the garden of American Literature.

34989   THE WEEKLY ADVERTISER, OF READING, IN THE COUNTY OF BERKS. No. 88. SATURDAY, JANUARY 6, [— No. 139. SATURDAY, DECEMBER 29, 1798.]

This paper is published every Saturday by Gottlob Jungmann and Company in the Printing-Office of Reading, at the rate of one dollar per annum, one half dollar to be paid at subscribing and half a dollar at the expiration of every six months. 1798. 4to.

34990   WEEKLY COMPANION: AND THE COMMERCIAL CENTINEL. VOL. I. No. 20. SATURDAY, SEPTEMBER 15, [— No. 35. SATURDAY, DECEMBER 29, 1798.]

Newport, Rhode-Island: Printed by H. & O. Farnsworth. 1798. fol.   AAS.

In continuation of The Companion; and Commercial Centinel.

34991 THE WEEKLY MAGAZINE OF ORIGINAL ESSAYS, FUGITIVE PIECES, AND INTERESTING
INTELLIGENCE. VOL. I. FEBRUARY 3—APRIL 28 [1798.] WITH AN APPENDIX OF
STATE PAPERS.

*Philadelphia: Printed and published by James Watters & Co. and sold at the
Printing Office, Lœtitia Court; at James Watters, Willing's Alley; by Mr. Alexander Somerville, New-York; Mr. George Hill, Baltimore; and the principal Booksellers in this City.* 1798. pp. (2), xii, (1), 464, 2 plates. 8vo.
      AAS. HC. HSP. LCP. LOC. NYHS. NYPL. NYSL. WHS. YC.

APPENDIX TO VOLUME I OF THE WEEKLY MAGAZINE, CONTAINING THE MESSAGE OF
THE PRESIDENT OF THE UNITED STATES, TO BOTH HOUSES OF CONGRESS. DELIV-
ERED APRIL THIRD, 1798. AND THE INSTRUCTIONS AND DISPATCHES TO WHICH IT
REFERS. pp. (2), (419)–464.

34992 —— THE WEEKLY MAGAZINE OF ORIGINAL ESSAYS, FUGITIVE PIECES, AND INTEREST-
ING INTELLIGENCE. VOL. II. MAY 5 — JULY 28, [1798.] WITH AN APPENDIX OF
STATE PAPERS.

*Philadelphia: Printed for James Watters, by H. Maxwell; and sold by the
Proprietor, Willing's Alley; Mr. Alexander Somerville, New-York; Mr. George
Hill, Baltimore; and the principal Booksellers in this City.* 1798. pp. (2), 506,
plate. 8vo.   AAS. LOC. NYHS.

34993 —— THE WEEKLY MAGAZINE OF ORIGINAL ESSAYS, FUGITIVE PIECES, AND INTEREST-
ING INTELLIGENCE. VOL. III. [AUGUST 4 – 25, 1798.]

Philadelphia: Printed for James Watters, by H. Maxwell. [1798.] pp. 128.
8vo.   LOC. NYHS.

The death of James Watters, by yellow fever, in the epidemic then raging
in Philadelphia, discontinued the publication of the Weekly Magazine
until February, 9, 1799, when it was resumed by Ezekiel Forman.
Charles Brockden Brown contributed to the first volume, a series of
papers entitled: "The Man at home"; which were followed, in the second volume, by his "Arthur Mervyn."

34994 WEEKLY MONITOR. VOL. 14. No. 648. WEDNESDAY, JANUARY 3. [— VOL. 14. No.
655. WEDNESDAY, FEBRUARY 21, 1798.]

Litchfield, (Connecticut): Printed by Thomas Collier. 1798. fol.

Continued as *The Monitor.*

34995 THE WEEKLY MUSEUM. VOL. X. NUMBER 504. SATURDAY, JANUARY 6, [— VOL.
XI, NUMBER 555. SATURDAY, DECEMBER 29, 1798.]

*New-York: Printed and published by John Harrisson, at his Printing-Office,
(Yorick's Head) No. 3, Peck-Slip.* 1798. 4to.   LOC. NYHS. NYPL. WHS.

With the issue for June 23d, the title was changed to *Weekly Museum.*

34996 WEEMS, MASON LOCKE   1759–1825
THE LOVER'S ALMANAC, No. 1. CONTAINING BESIDES WHAT IS COMMON IN THE BEST
VIRGINIA ALMANAC, A NEW AND CHARMING DISSERTATION ON LOVE, COURTSHIP AND
MATRIMONY—WITH A FINE FLOURISH ON TRUE BEAUTY, DISCLOSING IN THE PLEAS-
ANTEST MANNER IMAGINABLE, THOSE TWO GREAT SECRETS, 1ST. HOW A HOMELY
GIRL MAY BECOME HANDSOME, AND A HANDSOME ONE AN ANGEL; AND 2DLY. HOW A
SINGLE MAY BECOME MARRIED AND THE MARRIED HAPPY. BEING A PRETTY PRES-
ENT TO A WIFE, OR DAUGHTER, A SISTER OR SWEETHEART. GOD PROSPER LONG
OUR NOBLE STATE, IN PLENTY LOVE AND PEACE, AND GRANT HENCEFORTH, THAT
BACH'LORS OLD, 'MONGST PRETTY MAIDS MAY CEASE.

Alexandria: Printed for M. L. Weems, by Thomas and Westcott. 1798.

34997   WELD, Ezra   1736–1816
A FUNERAL ADDRESS, AT THE INTERMENT OF ATHERTON THAYER, ESQ. DELIVERED AT BRAINTREE, JULY 4, 1798. AND NOW PRINTED AT THE REQUEST OF THE MOURNERS. BY EZRA WELD, A. M. PASTOR OF THE CHURCH IN BRAINTREE.

Printed by S. Hall, No. 53, Cornhill, Boston. 1798. pp. [14], (2). 8vo.   BA.

34998   WELLS, John   1770–1823
AN ORATION, DELIVERED ON THE FOURTH OF JULY, 1798, AT ST. PAUL'S CHURCH, BEFORE THE YOUNG MEN OF THE CITY OF NEW-YORK, ASSEMBLED TO COMMEMORATE THEIR NATIONAL INDEPENDENCE. BY JOHN WELLS, ESQ.

New-York: Printed by M'Lean & Lang. 1798. pp. 22. 8vo.
AAS. BA. BM. JCB. LOC. NYHS. NYPL.

34999   WELLS, William   1744–1827
A SERMON, DELIVERED AT PUTNEY, VERMONT, ON THE SIXTEENTH DAY OF NOVEMBER, 1797; AT THE FUNERAL OF THE REV. JOSIAH GOODHUE. BY THE REV. WILLIAM WELLS, LATE OF BLOOMSGROVE, ENGLAND, NOW OFFICIATING PASTOR OF THE CHURCH OF CHRIST IN BRATTLEBORO', VERMONT.

From the Press of C. Sturtevant, jun. & Co. Putney, Vermont. [1798.] pp. (12). 12mo.   JCB. UTS.

35000   —— A SERMON, PREACHED AT BRATTLEBOROUGH. VERMONT, JULY 3, A D. 1797. BY THE REV. WILLIAM WELLS, OFFICIATING PASTOR OF CHRIST'S CHURCH . 'HAT PLACE; AT THE INTERMENT OF MESS. PARDON TAYLOR, A   )WARD   .ER, WHO THE DAY BEFORE WERE DROWNED IN CONNECTICUT RIVER. . . . Pi   HED AND PUBLISHED AT THE REQUEST OF THE MOURNING RELATIVES.

Brattleborough: From the Press of Ben. Smead. M,DCC,XCVIII. pp. 20. 8vo.   JCB.

35001   WEST, Benjamin   1730–1813
BICKERSTAFF'S MASSACHUSETTS, CONNECTICUT, RHODE-ISLAND, NEWHAMPSHIRE AND VERMONT ALMANACK, FOR THE YEAR OF OUR LORD 1799. BEING THE THIRD AFTER BISSEXTILE, OR LEAP-YEAR, AND TWENTY-THIRD OF THE INDEPENDENCE OF THE UNITED STATES OF AMERICA. FITTED TO THE LATITUDE AND LONGITUDE OF THE TOWN OF BOSTON, BUT WILL SERVE WITHOUT ESSENTIAL VARIATION FOR THE ADJACENT STATES. TOGETHER WITH MATTER, BOTH USEFUL AND ENTERTAINING. [Cut.]

Printed by Nathaniel & John Coverly. Sold by them, at their Book-Store in Salem—Price 3 dollars and 75 cents per groce, 12 cents per dozen and 6 cents single. [1798.] pp. (24). 12mo.   AAS. NYPL.

This, and the publishers' Weatherwise Almanac for 1799, except for the title-page, are the same.

35002   —— THE NEW-ENGLAND ALMANACK, OR LADY'S AND GENTLEMAN'S DIARY, FOR THE YEAR OF OUR LORD CHRIST 1799: BEING THE THIRD AFTER BISSEXTILE, OR LEAP-YEAR, AND THE TWENTY-THIRD OF AMERICAN INDEPENDENCE, WHICH COMMENCED JULY 4, 1776. [Sixteen lines.] BY ISAAC BICKERSTAFF, ESQ; PHILOM.

Printed at Providence, (R. I.) by Carter and Wilkinson. and sold, wholesale and retail, at their Book and Stationary Store, opposite the Market. | Great allowance made to those who purchase quantities.] [1798.] pp. (24). 12mo.
AAS. HSP. JCB. LOC. NYPL. RIHS.

35003

WEST, BENJAMIN, continued.

—— THE TOWN AND COUNTRY ALMANACK, FOR THE YEAR OF OUR LORD 1799. BEING THE THIRD AFTER BISSEXTILE, OR LEAP YEAR, AND THE TWENTY-THIRD OF THE INDEPENDENCE OF AMERICA. FITTED TO THE TOWN OF NORWICH, BUT WILL SERVE FOR ANY OF THE NEW-ENGLAND STATES. CONTAINING ALL THE ASTRONOMICAL CALCULATIONS THAT IS NECESSARY FOR AN ALMANACK, TOGETHER WITH MANY OTHER MATTERS THAT IS CURIOUS, ENTERTAINING AND USEFUL. BY ISAAC BICKERSTAFF, ASTRONOMER.

 Norwich, (Connecticut), Printed by John Trumbull. and sold in large or small quantities at his Printing-Office, and Book-Shop, a few rods west from the Court House. [1798.] pp. (24). 12mo.

35004

—— WHEELER'S NORTH-AMERICAN CALENDAR, OR AN ALMANACK, FOR THE YEAR OF OUR LORD 1799: BEING THE 3D AFTER BISSEXTILE, OR LEAP YEAR, AND THE TWENTY-THIRD OF AMERICAN INDEPENDENCE. [U. S. arms.]

 Printed at Providence, and sold by B. Wheeler, at his Book-Store, No. 1, Westminster Street. [1798] pp. (24). 12mo.   AAS. RIHS.

35005

WEST, JOHN

THE BOSTON DIRECTORY, CONTAINING THE NAMES OF THE INHABITANTS, THEIR OCCUPATIONS, PLACES OF BUSINESS, AND DWELLING-HOUSES. ALSO, A LIST OF THE CIVIL GOVERNMENT OF MASSACHUSETTS, AND OF THE TOWN OFFICERS, PUBLIC OFFICES, BANKS, &C. LIKEWISE, A TABLE OF DUTIES ON STAMPED PAPER, VELLUM, &C. (CONFORMABLY TO THE STAMP ACT, PASSED JULY 6, '97,) AND A LIST OF ALL THE STAGES THAT RUN FROM BOSTON, WITH THE PLACES AT WHICH THEY PUT UP, &C. TO WHICH IS PREFIXED, A GENERAL DESCRIPTION OF BOSTON. ORNAMENTED WITH A PLAN OF THE TOWN, FROM ACTUAL SURVEY.

 Boston: Printed by Rhoades and Laughton. for John West, No. 75, Cornhill. 1798. pp. 148, plan. 12mo.   AAS.

Title of plan: A PLAN OF BOSTON, FROM ACTUAL SURVEY; BY OSGOOD CARLETON. 1796.

 Published by John West, No. 75, Cornhill, Boston. 8.1 x 14.1

This is the third Boston Directory.

35006

WEST, STEPHEN   1735–1819

A DISSERTATION ON INFANT-BAPTISM: IN REPLY TO THE REV. CYPRIAN STRONG'S SECOND INQUIRY ON THAT SUBJECT. BY STEPHEN WEST. D.D. PASTOR OF THE CHURCH IN STOCKBRIDGE. [Ornament.]

 Hartford: Printed by Hudson & Goodwin. 1798. pp. 106. 8vo.
       AAS. BM. CHS. LOC. NYPL. UTS. YC.

35007

THE WESTERN ALMANAC, FOR THE YEAR OF OUR LORD, 1797. BEING THE FIRST AFTER LEAP-YEAR, AND THE 22D OF AMERICAN INDEPENDENCE AFTER THE 4TH OF JULY. ADAPTED TO THE LATITUDE OF PENNSYLVANIA AND THE ADJOINING STATES. CONTAINING BESIDES THE USUAL CONTENTS OF AN ALMANAC, A VARIETY OF PIECES IN PROSE AND VERSE, USEFUL TABLES, REMEDIES, ETC.

 Carlisle: Printed for Archibald Loudon by George Kline. [October 17, 1796.]

Contains: Speech of Miss Polly Baker, before a court of judicature in Connecticut, wherein she was prosecuted the fifth time for having bastard children. The character of a bachelor. The character of a married man. Drunkenness — the honest fellow — the tippler — the drunken woman. Aphorisms. Anecdotes. Poetry: The Connecticut Sabbath—American independence — Advice to the married — To the ladies — The distinction. Remarkable events. Postal rates. A useful hint for the needy. Deacon Marvin's publishment. Tables, of courts, roads, exchange, interest, depreciation. Hints to horsemen from the Gentlemen's pocket farrier.

35008 THE WESTERN ALMANAC, FOR THE YEAR OF OUR LORD 1798. BEING THE SECOND AFTER LEAP-YEAR, AND THE 23D OF AMERICAN INDEPENDENCE AFTER THE 4TH OF JULY. ADAPTED TO THE LATITUDE OF PENNSYLVANIA AND THE ADJOINING STATES. CONTAINING, BESIDES THE USUAL CONTENTS OF AN ALMANAC, A VARIETY OF PIECES IN PROSE AND VERSE, USEFUL TABLES, REMEDIES, ETC. ETC. ETC.

Carlisle: Printed for Archibald Loudon by George Kline. [1797.] pp. (36). 12mo.

AAS.

35009 WESTERN ALMANAC, FOR THE YEAR OF OUR LORD, 1799. BEING THE THIRD AFTER LEAP-YEAR, AND THE 24TH OF AMERICAN INDEPENDENCE AFTER THE 4TH OF JULY. ADAPTED TO THE LATITUDE OF PENNSYLVANIA AND THE ADJOINING STATES. CONTAINING, BESIDES THE USUAL CONTENTS OF AN ALMANAC, A VARIETY OF PIECES IN PROSE AND VERSE, USEFUL TABLES, REMEDIES, ETC. ETC. ETC.

Carlisle: Printed by George Kline. [*October 24, 1798.*]

35010 WESTERN CENTINEL. VOL. V. No. 1. WEDNESDAY, JANUARY 4, [— No. 52. WEDNESDAY, DECEMBER 26, 1798.]

Whitestown, New-York: Printed by Lewis & Webb. 1798. fol.

35011 WESTERN INLAND LOCK NAVIGATION COMPANY. AT A MEETING OF A BOARD OF DIRECTORS OF THE WESTERN INLAND LOCK NAVIGATION COMPANY, HELD THE 12TH DAY OF FEBRUARY, 1798. RESOLVED, THAT THE ORDER PASSED BY THIS BOARD ON THE 18TH DAY OF AUGUST LAST, DIRECTING THE RATE OF TOLL TO BE RECEIVED FOR PASSING THE CANAL AT FORT SCHUYLER (FORMERLY STANWIX) AND IN THE RIVER AND CREEK IN THE NEIGHBOURHOOD THEREOF, BE REPEALED, AND THAT THE FOLLOWING RATES OF TOLL BE ESTABLISHED IN LIEU THEREOF, . . . BY ORDER OF THE BOARD, GERARD WALTON, VICE-PRES. NEW-YORK, FEBRUARY 12, 1798.

[*Albany: Printed by Charles R. and George Webster.* 1798.] Broadside. NYPL.

35012 —— REPORT OF THE DIRECTORS OF THE WESTERN INLAND LOCK-NAVIGATION COMPANY TO THE LEGISLATURE, 16TH FEBRUARY, 1798.

Albany: Printed by Charles R. and George Webster, corner of State and Pearl-streets. [1798.] pp. 32. 8vo. HC. HEH. NYHS. NYPL.

35013 THE WESTERN [cut] STAR. No. 7 OF VOL. IX. WHOLE NO. 423. MONDAY, JANUARY 1, [— No. 6 OF VOL. X. WHOLE NO. 474. TUESDAY, DECEMBER 25, 1798.]

Printed at Stockbridge, (Mass.) by Rosseter & Willard. 1798. fol. AAS.

With the issue for August 7th, Heman Willard withdrew, and publication was made in the name of Benjamin Rosseter.

35014 THE WESTERN TELEGRAPHE, AND WASHINGTON ADVERTISER. FREE, BUT NOT LICENTIOUS. VOL. III. No. 125. TUESDAY, JANUARY 2, [— VOL. IV. No. 176. TUESDAY, DECEMBER 25, 1798.]

Washington (Pennsylvania): Printed by John Colerick.—Subscriptions and advertisements taken in at Washington, by the Editor; Morgan-Town by Hugh M'Neely; in Union-Town, by Samuel King; Brownsville, by Jacob Bowman; in Frederick-Town, by Isaac Jenkinson; in Greensburgh, by Charles Ferry; in Waynesburgh, by Wm. Hunter; in West-Liberty, by Wm. M'Kinley and Wm. Skinner; in Charlestown (Mouth of Buffaloe) by John Connel and Richard Speer, [Bezaleel Wells]; in West Baltimore, by Philip Ducombe; in George Town, by Samuel Lyons; in Middletown, by Samuel Urie; in Canonsburgh, by Andrew Munroe and William Clark; Pittsburgh, by Jeremiah Barker; M'Kee's Port, by Samuel Bailey; in Williams Port, Samuel Black; and in Marietta, by Joseph Lincoln. 1798. fol.

35015   WETHERILL, Samuel

An Apology for the religious society called Free Quakers, in the city of Philadelphia, shewing that all churches who excommunicate act inconsistently with the Gospel of Jesus.

Philadelphia: [1798.] pp. 37. 8vo.

35016   WETMORE, Robert Griffith   1774–1803

Address to the Episcopal congregations in Schenectady and Duanesborough, July, 1798.

Catskill: Printed by Mackay Croswell. [1798.] pp. 31. 8vo.

35017   WETMORE, Robert William

To the honourable General Assembly of the State of Connecticut, to be holden at Hartford, in said State, on the second Thursday of May next. The Petition of Robert William Wetmore, and Victory Wetmore, of Stratford, in the County of Fairfield, late partners in trade with Prosper Wetmore, late of the city, County and State of New-York, deceased . . . Humbly sheweth, That . . . they now owe about forty thousand dollars . . . and pray that your honors would pass an Act of insolvency. . . . [Four columns.]

[New-Haven: Printed by T. & S. Green. April, 1798.] Broadside. fol.   aas.

35018   WHARTON, Charles Henry   1748–1833

Caption title: An Elegy to the memory of mrs. Mary Wharton, who died at Philadelphia, on the second day of June, 1798. By her husband. [Signed, C. H. W. Colophon:]

[Philadelphia:] Printed by John Ormrod. [1798.] pp. 7. 8vo.   nypl.

35019   WHITESTOWN Gazette. Vol. ii. No. 83. Tuesday, January 2, [— Vol. iii. No. 117. Tuesday, August 28, 1798.]

Published by William M'Lean — Whitestown (Herkimer County), opposite the Meeting-House. 1798. fol.

In September, M'Lean removed his Press to Utica, and resumed publication there, without change of numbering, as the:

35020   WHITESTOWN Gazette. And Cato's Patrol. Vol. iii. No. 118. Monday, September 3, [— Vol. iii. No. 135. Monday, December 31, 1798.]

Utica: Published by William M'Lean. 1798. fol.

In continuation of the *Whitestown Gazette.*

35021   WHITING, Thurston   1752–1829

A Discourse delivered in the meeting house in Pownalborough, March 1, 1798. Occasioned by the death of David Silvester, esq. right worshipful master of the ancient and honorable fraternity of Free and Accepted Masons of Lincoln Lodge; and who was on that day interred with masonic honors. By the rev. brother Thurston Whiting.

Wiscasset: Printed by Henry Hoskins & John W. Scott. 1798. pp. 27. 8vo.   jcb.

35022   —— An Oration, delivered in the Baptist meeting house in Thomaston, July 4th, 1798. At the request of the Friendly Society, and in commemoration of American independence. By the rev. Thurston Whiting,

Hallowell: Printed by Howard S. Robinson. [1798.] pp. 21. 12mo.   ba. jcb.

35023   WHITMAN, BENJAMIN
AN ORATION, DELIVERED IN TAUNTON, (MASSACHUSETTS) BEFORE KING DAVID'S
LODGE OF FREE AND ACCEPTED MASONS, SEPTEMBER 13TH, 5798. BY BROTHER
BENJAMIN WHITMAN, MASTER OF OLD COLONY LODGE. PRINTED AT THE REQUEST
OF THE BRETHREN.

Newbedford, (Massachusetts) Printed by John Spooner. — 1798. — pp. [18.]
8vo.   AAS. LOC.

Contains, A Masonic Ode—[Composed and set to music, by Mr. Jezaniah
Sumner.]

35024   WHITMAN, KILBORN   –1835
AN ORATION, PRONOUNCED AT BRIDGEWATER, OCTOBER 4, 1798, AT THE REQUEST OF
THE COLUMBIAN SOCIETY. BY KILBORN WHITMAN. PUBLISHED BY THE DESIRE
OF THE HEARERS. [Two lines from] PRESIDENT ADAMS'S REPLY TO AN ADDRESS.

Boston: Printed by Samuel Etheridge, No. 22, Marlborough-Street. 1798.
pp. 39. 8vo.   AAS. HSP. JCB. MHS. NYHS.

35025   WHITTEMORE, JOSEPH
JOSEPH WHITTEMORE, PRESENTS THE FOLLOWING ADDRESS TO HIS FRIENDS AND
CUSTOMERS, WISHING THEM MOST SINCERELY, A HAPPY NEW YEAR. BOSTON, JANU-
ARY 1, 1798.

[Boston: 1798.] Broadside.   HSP.

35026   WILBERFORCE, WILLIAM   1759–1833
A PRACTICAL VIEW OF THE PREVAILING RELIGIOUS SYSTEM OF PROFESSED CHRISTIANS,
IN THE HIGHER AND MIDDLE CLASSES, CONTRASTED WITH REAL CHRISTIANITY. BY
WILLIAM WILBERFORCE, ESQ. MEMBER OF PARLIAMENT FOR THE COUNTY OF YORK.
[Five lines from] MILTON. FIRST AMERICAN EDITION.

Philadelphia: Printed by John Ormrod, No. 41, Chesnut-Street. 1798. pp.
343, (9), (4). 8vo.   AAS. JCB. NYPL. WiPL.

Contains a List of Subscribers.

35027   WILDER, JOHN   1759–1836
Half-title: MR. WILDER'S SERMON, ON THE FEDERAL FAST.
Title: A DISCOURSE, DELIVERED MAY 9, 1798, ON THE IMPORTANCE OF SPECIAL
HUMILIATION. BY JOHN WILDER, A. M. PASTOR OF THE FIRST CHURCH IN ATTLE-
BOROUGH. [Ornament.]

Printed at Wrentham, Massachusetts, by Nathaniel and Benjamin Heaton.
M,DCC,XCVIII. pp. (27). 8vo.   AAS. BM. CLA. JCB. NYHS. NYPL.

35028   THE WILKESBARRE GAZETTE, AND LUZERNE ADVERTISER. VOL. I. NO. 6 TUES-
DAY, JANUARY 2, [— VOL. II. NO. 5. TUESDAY, DECEMBER 25, 1798.]

Wilkesbarre: Printed by Josiah Wright. 1798. fol.   NYHS.

In February, "The" was dropped from the title; and, in December,
Josiah Wright withdrew, the paper was published for the Proprietor,
Thomas Wright.

35029   WILKINSON, EDWARD   1727–1809
WISDOM A POEM [Seven lines.] BY A QUAKER, (OR FRIEND) OF R. ISLAND. THE
SECOND LITCHFIELD EDITION.

[Printed at Litchfield, by T. Collier.] 1798. pp. 24. 24mo.   CHS.

35030   WILLIAMS, HELEN MARIA   1762–1827
A RESIDENCE IN FRANCE, DURING THE YEARS 1792, 1793, 1794, AND 1795; DESCRIBED IN A SERIES OF LETTERS FROM AN ENGLISH LADY: WITH GENERAL AND INCIDENTAL REMARKS ON THE FRENCH CHARACTER AND MANNERS. PREPARED FOR THE PRESS BY JOHN GIFFORD, ESQ. . . . FIRST AMERICAN EDITION.

> *Elizabeth-Town: Printed by Shepard Kollock, for Cornelius Davis, No. 94 Water Street, New-York.* 1798. pp. 517. 8vo.   HEH.

35031   WILLIAMS, SAMUEL   1743–1817
THE VERMONT ALMANAC AND REGISTER, FOR THE YEAR OF OUR LORD, 1799. FITTED TO THE LATITUDE AND LONGITUDE OF RUTLAND.

> *Printed at Rutland, (Vermont), by John Walker, jun. for S. Williams.* [1798.] pp. 42. 12mo.   BM. LOC.

Contains, Hail Columbia, four verses.

35032   WILLIAMS, W.
FIRST PRINCIPLES OF GEOGRAPHY, SELECTED FROM APPROVED AUTHORS.

> *Charleston: Printed by T. B. Bowen, No. 32, Church-street, near the City Theatre,* 1798. pp. (2), 11, 3 plates, table. 4to.   LOC.

35033   WILLIAMSON, CHARLES   1757–1808
DESCRIPTION OF THE GENESEE COUNTRY, ITS RAPIDLY PROGRESSIVE POPULATION AND IMPROVEMENTS: IN A SERIES OF LETTERS FROM A GENTLEMAN TO HIS FRIEND.

> *Albany: Printed by Loring Andrews & Co.* 1798. pp. –37,– 2 maps, plate, 4to.   AAS. JCB. LOC. NYHS. NYPL.

35034   WILLISON, JOHN   1680–1750
THE MOTHER'S CATECHISM, CONTAINING SHORT AND EASY QUESTIONS. DESIGNED AS AN INTRODUCTION TO UNDERSTAND THE ASSEMBLY'S SHORTER CATECHISM.

> *Trenton: Printed and sold by Matthias Day.* 1798.

35035   WILLOCK, JOHN
THE VOYAGES AND ADVENTURES OF JOHN WILLOCK, MARINER. INTERSPERSED WITH REMARKS ON DIFFERENT COUNTRIES IN EUROPE, AFRICA, AND AMERICA; WITH THE CUSTOMS AND MANNERS OF THE INHABITANTS; AND A NUMBER OF ORIGINAL ANECDOTES.

> *Philadelphia: Printed for George Gibson, by Hogan & M'Elroy, No. 222, South Third-street.* 1798. pp. (2), [ix],–xi, [13]–283, 8, frontispiece. 12mo.

Contains, an eight-page list of Subscribers' names.   AAS. BA. BM. JCB. LOC. NYPL.

35036   WILMINGTON MERCURY. PRINTED OCCASIONALLY AND DELIVERED GRATIS—TO THE PATRONS OF THE DELAWARE GAZETTE.— BY SMYTH. SUNDAY EVENING, SEPT. 23, 1798.

> [*Wilmington: Printed by W. C. Smyth.* 1798.] Broadside. 4to.   NYPL.

Bulletin of the Board of Health, giving list of deaths, from yellow fever, during the past twenty-four hours, hospital report, and list of donations.

35037   WILSON, JAMES   1751–1799
THE UTILITY OF THE SCRIPTURES OF THE OLD TESTAMENT: A DISCOURSE DELIVERED AT THE OPENING OF A SESSION OF THE PRESBYTERY OF BALTIMORE, HELD IN ALEXANDRIA, SEPTEMBER 27, 1797. BY JAMES WILSON, A. M. ONE OF THE MEMBERS OF SAID PRESBYTERY. COPY-RIGHT SECURED.

> *Alexandria: Printed for the Author by Thomas and Westcott, Royal-Street, between the Coffee-House and Post-Office.* M,DCC,XCVIII. pp. (61). 8vo.

10th Virginia District Copyright.   AAS. LOC. NYPL.

35038   WILSON, James   1760–1839
APOSTOLIC CHURCH GOVERNMENT DISPLAYED; AND THE GOVERNMENT AND SYSTEM OF
THE METHODIST EPISCOPAL CHURCH INVESTIGATED. TO WHICH IS ADDED, AN AP-
PENDIX, CONTAINING A CONCISE DISSERTATION ON THE NATURE AND DURATION OF
APOSTOLIC PERSONAL AUTHORITY AND OFFICE. BY JAMES WILSON, PASTOR OF THE
BENEFICENT CONGREGATIONAL CHURCH IN PROVIDENCE. [One line from] I THESS.
v. 21.

    Printed at Providence: by Bennett Wheeler, and sold at his Book-store, No. 1,
Westminster-street, 1798. pp. xii, (4), 234, (1). 12mo.

    "Copyright secured according to Law."   AAS. BU. JCB. NYHS. NYPL. RIHS.

35039   WILSON, Samuel
THE KENTUCKY ENGLISH GRAMMAR.
    Lexington: Printed by John Bradford, 1798.

35040   WINCHESTER [scroll with] THE CENTINEL. GAZETTE. [Motto.] VOL. XI. NUMBER
521 ? WEDNESDAY, APRIL 4 ? [— VOL. XI. NUMBER 561. WEDNESDAY, DECEM-
BER 26, 1798.]

    *Winchester (Virginia) Printed and published (every Wednesday) by Richard
Bowen, opposite the Episcopal Church, in Loudoun-Street.* 1798. fol.

    In continuation of *Bowen's Virginia Gazette: and the Winchester Centinel.*

35041   WINDHAM HERALD. VOL. VIII. NUMB. 372. THURSDAY, APRIL 19, [— NUMB. 408.
THURSDAY, DECEMBER 27, 1798.]

    Windham: Printed by John Byrne, in the lower-room of the Court-House.
1798. fol.   AAS. CHS. NYHS.

    In continuation of *The Phenix: or Windham Herald.*

35042   WINSTON, Isaac
AN INAUGURAL DISSERTATION ON THE POLYGALA SENECA, COMMONLY CALLED SENECA
SNAKE-ROOT; SUBMITTED TO THE EXAMINATION OF REV. JOHN EWING, S. S. T. P.
PROVOST; THE TRUSTEES & MEDICAL FACULTY, OF THE UNIVERSITY OF PENNSYLVA-
NIA, ON THE 22D DAY OF MAY, 1798, FOR THE DEGREE OF DOCTOR OF MEDICINE.
BY ISAAC WINSTON, OF VIRGINIA . . .

    Philadelphia: Printed by Way & Groff, No, 27, *Arch-Street.* 1798. pp. 29.
8vo.   LOC. SGO.

35043   WISCASSET ARGUS. VOL. I. NO. 3. SATURDAY, JANUARY 6, [— NO. 4. SATURDAY,
JANUARY 13, 1798.]

    Wiscasset, District of Maine. Published by Laughton & Rhoades. 1798. fol.

    Publication was discontinued early in this year.

35044   THE WISCASSET TELEGRAPH. [Motto.] VOL. II. NO. 8. FRIDAY, JANUARY 5, [—
VOL. II. NO. 52 ?. TUESDAY, NOVEMBER 27 ? 1798.]

    *Wiscasset: | District of Maine] Printed by Henry Hoskins & John W. Scott,
at their Office, corner of Main & Water Streets.* 1798. fol.

    Discontinued on, or before, the end of the second volume, in November,
as above.

35045   WISDOM IN MINIATURE; OR THE YOUNG GENTLEMAN AND LADY'S MAGAZINE. BEING A
COLLECTION OF SENTENCES, DIVINE AND MORAL. TRAIN UP A CHILD IN THE WAY
HE SHOULD GO, AND WHEN HE IS OLD HE WILL NOT DEPART FROM IT.
    Hartford: Printed by J. Babcock. 1798. 32mo.

AUCTION VALUES

35046   WITS or WITSIUS, HERMANN   1636–1708
THE OECONOMY OF THE COVENANT BETWEEN GOD AND MAN. COMPREHENDING A COMPLETE BODY OF DIVINITY. BY HERMANN WITSIUS, D. D. LATE PROFESSOR OF DIVINITY IN THE UNIVERSITIES OF FRANEQUER, UTRECHT AND LEYDEN; AND ALSO REGENT OF THE DIVINITY-COLLEGE OF THE STATES OF HOLLAND AND WEST FRIESLAND. TO WHICH IS PREFIXED, THE LIFE OF THE AUTHOR. A NEW TRANSLATION FROM THE ORIGINAL LATIN. IN THREE VOLUMES. VOLUME I [— III.]

New-York: Printed by George Forman, No. 64, Water-Street, for Lee & Stokes, No. 25, Maiden Lane. 1798. 3 vols. pp. 460, (4); iv, 448; iv, 455. 8vo.

AAS. LOC. NYPL.

Although dated 1798, publication of the second and third volumes was not made until 1799.

35047   THE WONDERS OF THE INVISIBLE WORLD DISPLAYED. BEING AN AUTHENTIC AND PARTICULAR HISTORY OF SALEM WITCHCRAFT, WITH THE SUFFERINGS, TORTURES, AND CRUEL EXECUTIONS, OF THE UNFORTUNATE VICTIMS TO SUPERSTITION.

New-London: Printed and sold by Charles Holt. 1798.

35048   WOOD, JOHN
CAPT. JOHN WOOD'S LOTTERY, ASSIGNED TO COL. MATHEW [*sic*] LYON. THE HONORABLE THE GENERAL ASSEMBLY OF THE STATE OF VERMONT, HAVING, BY THEIR ACT, PASSED THE 9TH OF MARCH, 1797, GIVEN LIBERTY TO JOHN WOOD TO RAISE BY LOTTERY THE SUM OF FIVE HUNDRED DOLLARS, TO REIMBURSE HIM FOR SERVICES RENDERED THE PUBLIC BEFORE THE EXISTANCE OF SAID STATE; THE MANAGERS, THEREFORE, HAVING GIVEN THE AMPLE AND NECESSARY BONDS, WITH SECURITY FOR THE PAYMENT OF THE PRIZES, AND THE REGULAR MANAGEMENT OF THE LOTTERY, PRESENT THE FOLLOWING SCHEME TO THE PUBLIC. [Three columns.] ELIAS BUELL, MANAGER.

[*Rutland: Printed by John Walker, jun. November 28, 1798.*] Broadside. fol.   AAS.

35049   WOODBRIDGE, WILLIAM   1755–1836
A SERMON ON THE CARE OF THE SOUL, DELIVERED TO THE SOCIETY IN NORTH-KILLINGWORTH. AND PUBLISHED AT THEIR REQUEST. BY WILLIAM WOODBRIDGE, A. M. [Five lines of quotations.]

Middletown: Printed by Tertius Dunning. 1798. pp. (40). 8vo.

AAS. BA. BU. CHS. JCB. NYPL. UTS YC.

35050   WOODWARD, ISRAEL BEARD   1767–1810
AMERICAN LIBERTY AND INDEPENDENCE. [Ornament.] A DISCOURSE, DELIVERED AT WATERTOWN, ON THE FOURTH OF JULY, 1798. BY THE REV. ISRAEL B. WOODWARD, A. M. [Printer's mark.]

Printed at Litchfield by T. Collier. [1798.] pp. 26. 8vo.   CHS. HEH.

35051   WOODWARD, WILLIAM HENRY   1774–1813
AN ORATION, DELIVERED AT HANOVER, NEWHAMPSHIRE, AT THE REQUEST OF THE BRETHREN OF FRANKLIN LODGE—NO. 6; AT THE CELEBRATION OF THE FESTIVAL OF ST. JOHN THE BAPTIST; AND PUBLISHED BY THEIR DESIRE, IN THE YEAR OF MASONRY, 5798. BY WILLIAM WOODWARD, ESQ. SECRETARY OF SAID LODGE. . . .

Printed at Hanover, Newhampshire; by Benjamin True. [1798.] pp. 15. 8vo.

JCB.

35052 WOODWORTH, John   1768–1858
THE SPUNKIAD: OR HEROISM IMPROVED. A CONGRESSIONAL DISPLAY OF SPIT AND
CUDGEL. A POEM, IN FOUR CANTOES. BY AN AMERICAN YOUTH.
Newburgh: Printed and sold by D. Denniston. M,DCC,XCVIII. pp. 23. 12mo.
AAS. BU. HC. HSP. LOC. NYPL.

Copyright secured. A satire on the Matthew Lyon — Roger Griswold
affair. For full account see Historical Magazine. January, 1864.

35053 WORCESTER, Noah   1758–1837
THE NATURAL TEACHER: OR, THE BEST SPELLING BOOK FOR LITTLE CHILDREN. THE
SECOND EDITION, WITH ADDITIONS. BY NOAH WORCESTER, A. M. PUBLISHED AC-
CORDING TO ACT OF CONGRESS.
Concord: Printed by George Hough, for the Author, 1798. pp. 59. 24mo.
NYPL.

35054 WORCESTER, Thomas
AN ORATION DELIVERED AT SALISBURY, ON THE ANNIVERSARY OF AMERICAN INDE-
PENDENCE, JULY 4TH, 1798. BY THOMAS WORCESTER.
Printed by Geo. Hough, at Concord. 1798.
BM.

35055 —— THE SOLEMNITY OF MARRIAGE ILLUSTRATED: A DISCOURSE, OCCASIONED BY THE
RE-MARRIAGE OF THE REV. NOAH WORCESTER, DELIVERED AT THORNTON, MAY 31,
1798. BY THOMAS WORCESTER, V. D. M. PASTOR OF THE CONGREGATIONAL CHURCH
IN SALISBURY.
Printed by Geo. Hough, at Concord. M.DCC.XCVIII. pp. (26). 8vo.
AAS. JCB. LOC.

35056 WORCESTER. MASSACHUSETTS. FIRE SOCIETY.
ARTICLES: CONTAINING THE RULES AND REGULATIONS OF THE WORCESTER FIRE
SOCIETY. INSTITUTED JANUARY 21ST, MDCCXCIII. REVISED AND CORRECTED,
JANUARY, 1798.
Worcester: From the Press of Isaiah Thomas, jun. April—1798. pp. 12.
12mo.
AAS.

35057 WORKMAN, Benjamin
FATHER TAMMANY'S ALMANAC, FOR THE YEAR 1799.
Philadelphia: Printed and sold by John M'Culloch. [1798.] 12mo.
BM.

35058 YALE COLLEGE.
CATALOGUE OF THE MEMBERS OF YALE-COLLEGE, IN NEW-HAVEN, 1797.
[New-Haven: Printed by Thomas & Samuel Green, 1797.] Broadside.
YC.

35059 —— CATALOGUE OF THE MEMBERS OF YALE-COLLEGE, IN NEW-HAVEN. NOVEMBER,
1798.
[New-Haven: Printed by Thomas & Samuel Green, 1798.] Broadside.
YC.

35060 —— SCHEME OF THE EXHIBITIONS AT THE PUBLIC COMMENCEMENT AT YALE-COL-
LEGE, 1796.
[New-Haven: Printed by Thomas & Samuel Green, 1796.] Broadside.
YC.

35061 —— SCHEME OF THE EXHIBITIONS AT THE PUBLIC COMMENCEMENT AT YALE-COL-
LEGE, 1797.
[New-Haven: Printed by Thomas & Samuel Green, 1797.] Broadside.
YC.

35062 —— SCHEME OF THE EXHIBITIONS AT THE PUBLIC COMMENCEMENT AT YALE-COL-
LEGE, SEPTEMBER 12TH, 1798.
[New-Haven: Printed by Thomas & Samuel Green, 1798.] Broadside.
YC.

35063   YANKEE DOODLE. A NEW FEDERAL SONG. COLUMBIANS ALL, THE PRESENT HOUR, AS BROTHERS SHOULD UNITE US — UNION AT HOME'S THE ONLY WAY, TO MAKE EACH NATION RIGHT US. YANKEE DOODLE, GUARD YOUR COAST, YANKEE DOODLE DANDY — FEAR NOT THEN NOR THREAT NOR BOAST, YANKEE DOODLE DANDY. [Five four-line verses, with chorus change with each verse — the last one reading:] THEN YANKEE DOODLE, BE DIVINE, YANKEE DOODLE DANDY — BENEATH THE FIG-TREE AND THE VINE, SING YANKEE DOODLE DANDY.

> As sung in Portland, Maine, Alexandria, Edenton, North Carolina, May, 1798.

35064   —— NEW YANKEE DOODLE. TOUGH TIMES. AN ODE FOR THE 4TH OF JULY, 1798. THERE'S ICHABOD HAS COME TO TOWN, FROM PHILADELPHIA CITY, HE STROLL'D THE STREETS ALL UP AND DOWN, AND BROUGHT NICE TALES TO FIT YE. YANKEE DOODLE, DOODLE DOO, YANKEE DOODLE, DANDY, WHEN TIMES RUN TOUGH, THE HEART THAT'S TRUE IS SWEET AS 'LASSES [sugar] CANDY. [Twenty verses, with chorus.]

> As sung at the Theatre in New York, and at meetings of the Society of the Cincinnati in Philadelphia, and Salem, Massachusetts.

35065   YARROW, THOMAS
AN ORATION DELIVERED AT MOUNT PLEASANT, NEW-YORK, JULY 4, 1798. BEING THE 22D ANNIVERSARY OF AMERICAN INDEPENDENCE. BY THOMAS YARROW.
> *Mount Pleasant, New-York: Printed by William Durell.* 1798. pp. 16. 8vo.

35066   YEATMAN, CHARLETON
THE MARINER'S GUIDE, OR PLAIN INSTRUCTIONS TO THEM HOW TO TREAT EVERY DISEASE WHICH THEY ARE LIABLE TO WITH THEIR GENERAL SYMPTOMS; TO KNOW ONE DISORDER FROM ANOTHER, TO ACCOMPANY MEDICINE CHESTS, PUT UP AGREEABLY TO AN ACT OF CONGRESS. BY CHARLETON YEATMAN, M.D. . . .
> *Philadelphia: Printed by John Bioren, No. 75, Dock-Street.* 1798.   LOC.

35067   YOUNG, EDWARD   1684–1765
THE COMPLAINT: OR, NIGHT-THOUGHTS ON LIFE, DEATH, AND IMMORTALITY. TO WHICH IS PREFIXED, THE LIFE OF THE AUTHOR. [One line of Latin from] VIRG.
> *Philadelphia: Printed by W. W. Woodward, No. 17, Chesnut-Street, for Cornelius W. Stafford.* 1798. pp. x, 266, frontispiece. 12mo.   AAS. JCB. LOC. NYPL.

35068   YOUNG, JOHN
ESSAYS ON THE FOLLOWING INTERESTING SUBJECTS: I. GOVERNMENT. II. REVOLUTIONS. III. THE BRITISH CONSTITUTION. IV. KINGLY GOVERNMENT. V. PARLIAMENTARY REPRESENTATION . . . VI. LIBERTY AND EQUALITY. VII. TAXATION. AND VIII. THE PRESENT WAR AND THE STAGNATION OF CREDIT CONNECTED WITH IT. BY JOHN YOUNG, D.D. MINISTER OF HAWICK, SCOTLAND. FIFTH EDITION.
> *Glasgow, printed: London, re-printed and Philadelphia: Re-printed by Jas. Humphreys.* 1798. pp. 148, (2). 12mo.   BA. LOC. NYPL.

35069   YOUNG, WILLIAM P.
PALLADIUM OF KNOWLEDGE: OR, THE CAROLINA AND GEORGIA ALMANAC, FOR THE YEAR OF OUR LORD, 1799, AND 23–24 OF AMERICAN INDEPENDENCE.
> *Charleston: Printed by W. P. Young, No. 43 Broad-Street.* [1798.]

1799

35070 ABBOT, ABIEL   1770–1828
A DISCOURSE DELIVERED AT NORTH-COVENTRY, JULY 4TH, 1799, BEING THE TWENTY-THIRD ANNIVERSARY OF AMERICAN INDEPENDENCE. BY ABIEL ABBOT.
Hartford: Printed by Hudson and Goodwin. 1799. pp. 16. 8vo.   JCB.

35071 —— TRAITS OF RESEMBLANCE IN THE PEOPLE OF THE UNITED STATES OF AMERICA TO ANCIENT ISRAEL. IN A SERMON DELIVERED AT HAVERHILL, ON THE TWENTY-EIGHTH OF NOVEMBER, 1799, THE DAY OF ANNIVERSARY THANKSGIVING. BY ABIEL ABBOT, PASTOR OF THE FIRST CHURCH IN HAVERHILL. [Vignette.]
Haverhill: From the Press of Moore & Stebbins. Published for the Subscribers.—Dec. 1799. pp. 25. 8vo.   AAS. BA. BM. CLA. UTS.

35072 AN ACCOUNT OF THE LIFE AND DEATH OF THE LATE PIOUS MRS. JONES OF MECK-LENBURG.
Richmond: Printed by Samuel Pleasants, jun. 1799.

"To be had at Mr. John Allen's store in Richmond, the lower side of the Bridge. And at Mr. Nathaniel Quarles' in Manchester."

35073 ADAM, ALEXANDER   1741–1809
THE RUDIMENTS OF LATIN AND ENGLISH GRAMMAR; DESIGNED TO FACILITATE THE STUDY OF BOTH LANGUAGES, BY CONNECTING THEM TOGETHER. BY ALEXANDER ADAM, LL. D. RECTOR OF THE HIGH SCHOOL OF EDINBURGH. [Five lines of Latin from] QUINCTILLIAN I. 4, 5. FIRST AMERICAN FROM THE FIFTH ENGLISH EDITION, WITH IMPROVEMENTS. RECOMMENDED BY THE UNIVERSITY AT CAMBRIDGE (MASS-ACHUSETTS) TO BE USED BY THOSE WHO ARE INTENDED FOR THAT SEMINARY.
Boston: Printed by Manning & Loring, for S. Hall, W. Spotswood, J. White, Thomas & Andrews, D. West, E. Larkin, W. P. & L. Blake, and J. West. December, 1799. pp. xi, (3), 302. 12mo.   AAS. JCB. NYPL.

35074 ADAMS, DANIEL   1773–1864
AN INAUGURAL DISSERTATION ON THE PRINCIPLE OF ANIMATION; READ AND DEFENDED AT A PUBLIC EXAMINATION. BEFORE THE HON. JOHN WHEELOCK, LL. D. PRESIDENT, AND THE GOVERNORS OF DARTMOUTH COLLEGE, FOR THE DEGREE OF BATCHELOR IN MEDICINE, JULY 18, 1799. BY DANIEL ADAMS, A.B.
Hanover, New-Hampshire: Printed by Moses Davis. 1799. pp. 27. 8vo.
   AAS. JCB. NYPL.

35075   ADAMS, HANNAH   1755–1832
A SUMMARY HISTORY OF NEW-ENGLAND, FROM THE FIRST SETTLEMENT AT PLYMOUTH,
TO THE ACCEPTANCE OF THE FEDERAL CONSTITUTION. COMPREHENDING A GENERAL
SKETCH OF THE AMERICAN WAR. BY HANNAH ADAMS. [Ten lines from] DWIGHT'S
GREENFIELD HILL, p. 13–15. PUBLISHED ACCORDING TO ACT OF CONGRESS.
     Dedham: Printed for the Author, by H. Mann and J. H. Adams. M.DCC.-
XC.IX. pp. 513, (3). 8vo.   AAS. BA. BM. BU. HC. JCB. LOC. MHS. NL. NYPL.
     With a list of Subscribers' names. 158th Massachusetts District Copy-
right, issued to Hannah Adams, as Author, 17 December, 1798.

35076   ADAMS, MOSES   –1819
A SERMON, DELIVERED AT THE ORDINATION OF THE REV. THOMAS NOYES, TO THE
PASTORAL CARE OF THE SECOND CHURCH IN NEEDHAM, JULY 10, 1799. BY MOSES
ADAMS, A.M. PASTOR OF THE CHURCH IN ACTON. TO WHICH ARE ADDED, THE
CHARGE, BY THE REV. MR. BRIDGE, OF EAST-SUDBURY, AND THE RIGHT HAND OF
FELLOWSHIP, BY THE REV. MR. PALMER, OF NEEDHAM.
     Printed at the Minerva Press, by Herman Mann. 1799. pp. 27. 8vo.
                                  AAS. BA. JCB. LOC.

35077   ADDISON, ALEXANDER   1759–1807
ON THE ALIEN ACT. A CHARGE TO THE GRAND JURIES OF THE COUNTY COURTS OF
THE FIFTH CIRCUIT OF THE STATE OF PENNSYLVANIA, AT DECEMBER SESSIONS,
1798; BY ALEX. ADDISON, PRESIDENT OF THOSE COURTS. PUBLISHED AT THE RE-
QUEST OF THE GRAND JURIES OF THE COUNTIES OF ALLEGHENY, WESTMORELAND,
SOMERSET, AND GREENE.
     Washington, [Pennsylvania]: Printed by John Colerick, 1799. pp. (2), (21).
12mo.   AAS. BA. LOC. NYPL. RIHS.

35078   —— — A CHARGE TO THE GRAND JURIES OF THE COUNTY COURTS OF THE FIFTH CIR-
CUIT OF THE STATE OF PENNSYLVANIA. BY ALEXANDER ADDISON, PRESIDENT OF
THOSE COURTS.
     Vergennes: Printed [by Samuel Chipman, jun.] for Samuel Chipman. 1799.
pp, (32). 12mo.   AAS.

35079   AN ADDRESS FROM A MINISTER IN VIRGINIA, TO HIS PEOPLE IN A SPECIAL MEETING
•   ON WEEK DAY, MARCH, 1798. OCCASIONED BY THEIR OPPOSITION TO THE MEASURES
ADOPTED BY THE FEDERAL GOVERNMENT: WITH AN APPENDIX CONTAINING A NOBLE
CONFESSION AND SINCERE CONVERSION OF A JACOBIN TO FEDERALISM. [Ornament.]
     Printed at Hanover, New-Hampshire. By Benjamin True. M.DCC.XCIX.
pp. 23. 8vo.   AAS. NYHS. NYPL.
     Second heading: AN APPENDIX, CONTAINING THE CONFESSION OF A JACOBIN; MADE
IN PUBLIC MEETING. pp. [17] – 23.

35080   AN ADDRESS TO THE FARMERS OF PENNSYLVANIA.
     [Without place or Printer. 1799.] pp. 16. 8vo.

35081   AN ADDRESS TO THE FREEMEN OF PENNSYLVANIA, FROM THE COMMITTEE OF COR-
RESPONDENCE FOR THE CITY OF PHILADELPHIA, APPOINTED, BY THE FRIENDS OF
JAMES ROSS, TO CORRESPOND WITH THEIR FELLOW CITIZENS ON THE SUBJECT OF
THE ELECTION OF A GOVERNOR.
     Germantown: Printed by Zachariah Poulson, junior. 1799. pp. 24. 8vo.
                                      LOC. NYPL.

35082   —— EINE ADDRESSE AN DIE FREYEN LEUTE VON PENNSYLVANIEN, VON DER CORRES-
PONDENZ-COMMITTEE DIE FÜR DIE STADT PHILADELPHIA VON DEN FREUNDEN DES
JAMES ROSS BESTIMMT WURDE, MIT IHREN MITBÜRGERN UEBER DEN GEGENSTAND
DER GOUVERNÖRS-WAHL ZU CORRESPONDIREN.
     Philadelphia: Gedruckt bey Carl Cist. 1799. pp. 24. 8vo.   LOC.

35083 ADGATE, ANDREW   —1793
RUDIMENTS OF MUSIC. BY ANDREW ADGATE, P.U.A. THE SIXTH EDITION.

Philadelphia: Printed for, and sold by Mathew Carey, No. 118, *Market-Street.*
Jan. 14*th,* 1799. [Entered according to Act of Congress.] pp. 102. obl. 24mo. JCB.

Second title: PHILADELPHIA HARMONY, OR, A COLLECTION OF PSALM TUNES, HYMNS,
AND ANTHEMS. SELECTED BY ANDREW ADGATE. PART II. pp. 77–102.

35084 THE ADVERTISEMENT FOR A HUSBAND. A NOVEL: IN A SERIES OF LETTERS BE-
TWEEN BELINDA BLACKET, LOUISA LENOX, AND OTHERS. TWO VOLUMES IN ONE.
[Printer's mark.]

Worcester: Printed by Isaiah Thomas, jun. and sold by him at his Printing-
Office. September— 1799. pp. 203, (1). 12mo.   AAS. HEH.

35085 ÆSOPUS   619–564 B.C.
FABULÆ ÆSOPI SELECTÆ; OR, SELECT FABLES OF ÆSOP; WITH AN ENGLISH
TRANSLATION, MORE LITERAL THAN ANY YET EXTANT, DESIGNED FOR THE READIER
INSTRUCTION OF BEGINNERS IN THE LATIN TONGUE. BY H. CLARKE, TEACHER OF
THE LATIN LANGUAGE. FIRST EXETER EDITION, PRINTED FROM THE LONDON TENTH
EDITION, CORRECTED.

New-Hampshire: Printed by H. Ranlet, Exeter, for Thomas and Andrews, E.
Larkin and J. West, Boston. M,DCC,XCIX. pp. 132. 12mo.

                                              AAS. BM. JCB. LOC. NYPL.
With the Latin text, and the English translation, in adjoining columns.

35086 THE AFFECTING HISTORY OF THE CHILDREN IN THE WOOD. . . . FIRST NEWPORT
EDITION.

Newport: Printed by H. & O. Farnsworth. 1799. pp. 32, illustrated. 32mo.

35087 AIKIN, JOHN   1747–1822
EVENINGS AT HOME, OR THE JUVENILE BUDGET OPENED, CONSISTING OF A VARIETY OF
MISCELLANEOUS PIECES FOR THE INSTRUCTION AND AMUSEMENT OF YOUNG PERSONS.

Printed in London: Re-printed at Salem, for Thomas C. Cushing and sold at
the Bible and Heart. 1799. pp. 156. 12mo.   EI.

35088 THE ALBANY CENTINEL. NO. 53 OF VOL. II. TUESDAY, JANUARY 1, [— NO. 53 OF
VOL. III. TUESDAY, DECEMBER 31, 1799.]

Published every Tuesday and Friday, by Loring Andrews, Printer to the State
at the Printing-Office in Court-Street, a few rods south of the City Hall; . . .
1799. fol.

35089 —— THE NEWS-BOY'S ADDRESS, TO THE PATRONS OF THE ALBANY CENTINEL, JANU-
ARY 1, 1799. [Twelve verses.]

[*Albany: Printed by Loring Andrews,* 1799.] Broadside. nar. fol.

35090 THE ALBANY GAZETTE. VOL. XV. NUMB. 1264. FRIDAY, JANUARY 4, [—VOL. XVI.
NUMB. 1367. MONDAY, DECEMBER 30, 1799.]

Printed every Monday and Friday [Thursday] by Charles R. and George
Webster, at their Bookstore in the White House, corner of State and Pearl-Streets.
1799. fol.

35091 THE ALBANY [N. Y. arms] REGISTER. VOL. XI. NUMBER 730. MONDAY, JANU-
ARY 7, [—VOL. XII. NUMBER 833. TUESDAY, DECEMBER 31, 1799.]

Published every Monday and Friday by Barber & Southwick.——Subscriptions,
advertisements, &c. for the Register, will be received at their Printing-Office, Sign
of Faust's Statue, State-Street, or at their Book-Store, two doors north of the City-
Hall, in Court-Street. 1799. fol.   NYPL.

Beginning in September publication was made on Tuesdays and Fridays.

35092　ALEXANDER, Caleb　　　　　　　　　　　　　　1755–1828
A Grammatical system of the English language: comprehending a plain and
familiar scheme, of teaching young gentlemen and ladies the art of
speaking and writing correctly their native tongue. By Caleb Alexander, a. m. Scientiarum janitrix grammatica. The fifth edition, corrected
by the Author.

*Printed at Boston, by I. Thomas and E. T. Andrews. [Proprietors of the
work.] Sold, wholesale and retail, by them at Faust's Statue, No. 45, Newbury-
Street; by said Thomas, in Worcester; by Thomas, Andrews & Butler, in Baltimore; and by Thomas, Andrews & Penniman, in Albany. Nov. 1799. pp. 95.*
12mo.　　　　　　　　　　　　　　　　　　　AAS. JCB. NYPL. YC.

35093　—— The Young ladies' and gentlemen's spelling book: on a new and improved
plan; containing a criterion of rightly spelling and pronouncing the
English language: interspersed with many easy lessons, in reading, entertaining fables and collections of moral sentences. Intended for the use
of common schools. By Caleb Alexander, a. m. Published according to Act
of Congress.

*Printed at Worcester, by I. Thomas, jun. for I. Thomas & Son. Sold whole-
sale and retail by them; also, by Thomas and Andrews, and other Booksellers in Boston.—* 1799. pp. 144. 12mo.　　　　　　　　AAS. LOC. NYPL.

Frontispiece headed: First Worcester edition. 174th Massachusetts District Copyright, issued to Isaiah Thomas, as Proprietor, 23 November,
1799.

35094　ALLEN, Paul, junior　　　　　　　　　　　　　1775–1826
An Oration, delivered at the Beneficent Congregational meeting-house, at
the election of the officers of the Independent Companies of the town
of Providence; on the twenty-ninth day of April, 1799. By Paul Allen,
jun. esq. Published at the request of the Independent Company of Cadets.

*Providence: Printed by John Carter, jun. at the New Printing-Office, west
side of the great Bridge.* 1799. pp. 14. 8vo.　　　AAS. JCB. LOC. RIHS.

35095　ALLEN, Thomas　　　　　　　　　　　　　　1743–1810
Benefits of affliction. A funeral sermon, occasioned by the death of Mrs.
Elizabeth White consort of mr. William White; who departed this life
in London, on Friday the 2d. day of Feb. 1798, and delivered at Pittsfield,
the place of her nativity. April 22d. in commemoration of that event the
next Lords day after the receipt of the melancholy tidings. By Thomas
Allen, a. m. pastor of the church in Pittsfield. To which are added two
letters from a respectable gentleman, in London, relating to her sickness and death. [One line from] Eccl. vii. 14. The second edition.

Pittsfield: Printed by Holly & Smith. 1799. pp. [27,] portrait. 8vo.
　　　　　　　　　　　　　　　　　　　　AAS. BA. BM. JCB. MHS.

35096　ALLYN, John　　　　　　　　　　　　　　　1767–1833
A Sermon, delivered on the 29th of November, 1798, the day of public
thanksgiving in the State of Massachusetts. By John Allyn, minister of
the church in Duxborough.

Printed by Samuel Hall, No. 53, Cornhill, Boston. 1799. pp. [21.] 8vo.
　　　　　　　　　　　　　　　　　　　　AAS. HC. MHS.

35097　AN ALMANACK for the year 1800.
Frankfort: Printed by Hunter and Beaumont. [1799.]

35098 AMBROSE AND ELEANOR, OR THE ADVENTURES OF TWO CHILDREN DESERTED ON AN
UNINHABITED ISLAND. (TRANSLATED FROM THE FRENCH.) [By Lucy Peacock.]—
"PROVIDENCE IS THEIR PILOT,"—TO WHICH IS ADDED AUGUSTE AND MADELAINE,
A REAL HISTORY, BY MISS HELEN MARIA WILLIAMS.
*— Baltimore:— Printed for Thomas, Andrews and Butler, No. 184, Market
Street. By Warner and Hanna, Harrison Street. 1799. pp. 215. 12mo.* AAS.

35099 —— AMBROSE AND ELEANOR; OR, THE ADVENTURES OF TWO CHILDREN ON AN
UNINHABITED ISLAND. [TRANSLATED FROM THE FRENCH.] [By Lucy Peacock.]
☞ PROVIDENCE IS THEIR PILOT. TO WHICH IS ADDED, AUGUSTE AND MADELAINE,
— A REAL HISTORY. BY MISS HELEN MARIA WILLIAMS.
Philadelphia: Printed by William W. Woodward. 1799. plate. 12mo.

35100 AMERICAN AND DAILY ADVERTISER. VOL. I. No. 1. TUESDAY, MAY 14, [— No. 199.
TUESDAY, DECEMBER 31, 1799.]
Baltimore: Published by Alex. Martin. 1799. fol.

Established, as a daily, by Alexander Martin, and founded on the subscription list of *The Baltimore Intelligencer.* With the issue for May 17,
1802, Martin disposed of his interests to Thomas Burling. With the
issue for August 17, 1802, Burling disposed of his interests to William
Pechin, the former proprietor of the "Intelligencer." With the issue for
January 1, 1803, Leonard Frailey was admitted to partnership, as Pechin
& Frailey, and the title was changed to *American, and commercial daily
advertiser.* With the issue for August 10, 1805, Frailey withdrew, and
William Pechin continued publication alone to July, 1810, when George
Dobbin, and Thomas Murphy were admitted to partnership, as W.
Pechin & G. Dobbin & Murphy, and the title was slightly changed to
American & commercial daily advertiser. George Dobbin died December
3, 1811, but his name was retained in the interest of his widow. With
the issue for July 4, 1815, William Bose was admitted to partnership,
as Pechin, Dobbin, Murphy & Bose. With the issue for July 1, 1817,
Pechin withdrew, leaving the firm name, Dobbin, Murphy & Bose, who
continued publication beyond the period of this work. A tri-weekly
paper for the country was also issued from 1800 to 1821, with slight
changes of title.

35101 THE AMERICAN EAGLE. VOL. I. No. 1. FRIDAY, MAY 10, [— No. 34. THURSDAY,
DECEMBER 26, 1799.]
Easton, Pennsylvania. Published by Samuel Longcope. 1799. fol.

Established, as a weekly, by Samuel Longcope, and continued by him
into November, 1805, when it was discontinued.

35102 AMERICAN [cut] FARMER, AND DUTCHESS COUNTY ADVERTISER. VOL. I. No. 31.
THURSDAY, JANUARY 3, [— VOL. II. No. 31. (WHOLE NO. 83.) TUESDAY, DECEM-
BER 31, 1799.]
*Poughkeepsie, (State of New York) Printed by John Woods, by whom printing
in all its branches is executed on moderate terms. 1799. fol.* NJHS.

35103 AMERICAN INDEPENDENCE, IN VINDICATION OF THE PRESIDENT'S NOMINATION OF A
NEW EMBASSY TO FRANCE. AS PUBLISHED IN THE COMMERCIAL GAZETTE, NOVEM-
BER 21ST, 1799. [Cut of Eagle.]
*Boston: Printed by John Russell, at his office, Quaker Lane. [1799.] pp. (2),
16. 16mo.* AAS. BA. BM. NYPL.

35104 AMERICAN [U. S. arms] MERCURY. VOL. XV. No. 757. THURSDAY, JANUARY 3, [—
VOL. XVI. No. 808. THURSDAY, DECEMBER 26, 1799.]
Published by Elisha Babcock — Hartford. 1799. fol. AAS. CHS. YC.

35105   THE AMERICAN Museum: or, annual register of fugitive pieces, ancient and modern. For the year 1798. [Vol. xiii.] [One line of Latin.]

Printed for Mathew Carey, Philadelphia. By W. & R. Dickson, Lancaster, June 20, M,DCC,XCIX. pp. 416, 5. 8vo.   AAS. BA. LOC. NYHS.

35106   AMERICAN PHILOSOPHICAL SOCIETY.
Transactions of the American Philosophical Society, held at Philadelphia, for promoting useful knowledge. Volume iv.

Philadelphia: Printed and sold by Thomas Dobson, at the Stone-House, No. 41, South Second Street. 1799. pp. xliv, 281, 288–450, (1), 451–534, errata, 14 plates. 8vo.   JCB.

35107   THE AMERICAN Primer. Improved. Or, an easy and pleasant guide to the art of reading. Adorned with cuts. To which is added, The Assembly of Divines' Catechism.

Medford: Printed by N. Coverly [junior] for Charles Cambridge, of Amherst. 1798. pp. (64). 32mo.   PPL.

35108   THE AMERICAN songster; or federal museum of melody and wit. In four parts, containing a collection of much admired songs; selected from the writings of various English and American authors.

Baltimore: Printed and sold by Warner & Hanna, No. 2 North Gay Street, 1799. pp. 245, (7). 16mo.   BU.

35109   AMERICAN Telegraphe. By Lazarus Beach, Newfield, Connecticut. [Motto.] Vol. iv. No. 40. Whole no. 196. Wednesday, January 2, [— Vol. v. No. 39. Whole no. 247. Thursday, December 26, 1799.]

Newfield near Fairfield: Printed and published by Lazarus Beach, Printer, Bookseller and Stationer, opposite Mr. Hinman's Inn. 1799. fol.

35110   AMERICANISCHER Stadt und Land Kalender auf das 1800ste Jahr Christi, welches ein Gemeines Jahr ist von 365 Tagen.

Philadelphia: Gedruckt und zu haben bey Carl Cist, in der Zweyten Strasse, No. 104, nah am Eck der Rehs-Strasse. [1799.] pp. (44). 4to.   AAS. LOC.

Title enclosed in a fanciful border illustrating articles of commerce and agriculture.

35111   ANDERSON, John E.
The Contract for the purchase of western territory, made with the Legislature of Georgia in the year 1795; considered with a reference to the subsequent attempt of the State, to impair its obligation. By John E. Anderson & William J. Hobby, esq'rs. (Published at the instance of the purchasers.)

Augusta: Printed by Randolph & Bunce, 1799. pp. 93, (2). 4to.
     BA. DERGL. JCB. LOC. NYPL.

In some copies of this work the sections, pages 17–24, 74–90, relating to the Yazoo land companies, have been cancelled. The New York Public Library has both forms.

35112   ANDROS, Thomas   1759–1845
An Oration, delivered at Dighton, (Massachusetts), July 4th, 1799. In commemoration of the independence of the United States of America. By Thomas Andros.

Newbedford (Massachusetts): Printed by John Spooner. 1799. pp. 15. 8vo.
     AAS. NYPL.

35113   THE ANNUAL REGISTER, AND VIRGINIAN REPOSITORY FOR THE YEAR 1800.
> *From the Blandford Press. Sold by Ross and Douglas, Petersburg, and by all
> the Booksellers in Virginia.* [1799.] pp. xii, 204. 12mo.   LOC.

35114   THE ANNUAL VISITOR; OR ALMANAC, FOR THE YEAR OF OUR LORD, 1800; CALCULATED
FOR THE MERIDIAN OF BALTIMORE, BUT WITHOUT ANY CONSIDERABLE VARIATION,
WILL SUIT THE STATES OF MARYLAND, PENNSYLVANIA, VIRGINIA, KENTUCKY, OR
TENNESSEE. CONTAINING, BESIDES *every* THING NECESSARY IN AN ALMANAC, A
variety OF PIECES, IN PROSE & VERSE — USEFUL & ENTERTAINING.
> *Baltimore: Printed for Thomas, Andrews & Butler, No.* 184 —*by W. Pechin,
> No.* 15, *Market-st.* [1799.] pp. (36), interleaved. 12mo.   AAS.

> Contains, Post Office establishment. Courts of law. Post towns. Trux-
> ton's victory. Love's ingenuity: or cupid's cunning. Approved method
> of making wine from American grape. Anecdotes, etc.

35115   ARGUS. GREENLEAF'S NEW [cut] DAILY ADVERTISER. [Motto.] NUMBER 1091.
TUESDAY, JANUARY 1, [— NUMBER 1397. TUESDAY, DECEMBER 31, 1799.]
> *New-York— Printed and published (every morning) by Ann Greenleaf, No.* 54,
> *Wall-Street — six doors from the Tontine Coffee-House.* 1799. fol.   LOC. NYHS.

35116   ARISTOTLE, pseudonym.
THE EXPERIENCED MIDWIFE: ABSOLUTELY NECESSARY FOR SURGEONS, MIDWIVES,
NURSES, AND CHILDBEARING WOMEN. A NEW EDITION.
> *Philadelphia: Printed for the Booksellers.* 1799. pp. 100. 12mo. AAS. SGO.

35117   ARNAUD, FRANÇOIS THOMAS MARIE DE BACULARD D'   · 1718–1805
FANNY, OR THE HAPPY REPENTANCE. TRANSLATED FROM THE FRENCH. FIFTH EDI-
TION.
> *Hartford: Printed by J. Babcock.* 1799. pp. 68, (1). 12mo.   AAS.

35118   ASH, JOHN   1724–1779
GRAMMATICAL INSTITUTES; OR, AN EASY INTRODUCTION TO DR. LOWTH'S ENGLISH
GRAMMAR: DESIGNED FOR THE USE OF SCHOOLS, AND TO LEAD YOUNG GENTLEMEN
AND LADIES INTO THE KNOWLEDGE OF THE FIRST PRINCIPLES OF THE ENGLISH
LANGUAGE. BY JOHN ASH, L. L. D. WITH AN APPENDIX, CONTAINING I. THE DE-
CLENSION OF IRREGULAR AND DEFECTIVE VERBS. TO WHICH ARE ADDED, SELECT
LESSONS, TO INSTIL JUST SENTIMENTS OF VIRTUE INTO YOUTH. A NEW EDITION,
REVISED AND CORRECTED.
> *New-York: Printed by M. L. & W. A. Davis, for T. S. Arden.* 1799. pp.
> 142. 18mo.   NYPL.

35119   ASSOCIATE REFORMED CHURCH IN NORTH AMERICA.
THE CONSTITUTION AND STANDARDS OF THE ASSOCIATE-REFORMED CHURCH IN NORTH-
AMERICA.
> *New-York: Printed by T. & J. Swords, No.* 99 *Pearl-street.* 1799. pp. 612,
> (1); (1), (1). 8vo.   AAS. BM. HSP. JCB. NYPL.

> *Second title:* THE CONFESSION OF FAITH, AGREED UPON BY THE ASSEMBLY OF DI-
> VINES AT WESTMINSTER, WITH THE ASSISTANCE OF COMMISSIONERS FROM THE
> CHURCH OF SCOTLAND, AS RECEIVED BY THE ASSOCIATE-REFORMED CHURCH IN
> NORTH-AMERICA. WITH THE PROOFS FROM THE SCRIPTURE.
> > *New-York: Printed by T. & J. Swords, No.* 99 *Pearl-street.* 1799. pp. (9)–174.

> *Third title:* THE LARGER CATECHISM, AGREED UPON BY THE ASSEMBLY OF DIVINES
> AT WESTMINSTER, WITH THE ASSISTANCE OF COMMISSIONERS FROM THE CHURCH
> OF SCOTLAND, AS RECEIVED BY THE ASSOCIATE-REFORMED CHURCH IN NORTH-
> AMERICA. WITH THE PROOFS FROM THE SCRIPTURE.
> > *New-York: Printed by T. & J. Swords, No.* 99 *Pearl-street.* 1799. pp. (175)–418.

ASSOCIATE REFORMED CHURCH, continued.

Fourth title: THE SHORTER CATECHISM, AGREED UPON BY THE ASSEMBLY OF DIVINES AT WESTMINSTER, WITH THE ASSISTANCE OF COMMISSIONERS FROM THE CHURCH OF SCOTLAND, AS RECEIVED BY THE ASSOCIATE-REFORMED CHURCH IN NORTH-AMERICA. WITH THE PROOFS FROM THE SCRIPTURE.

    New-York: Printed by T. & J. Swords, No. 99 Pearl-street. 1799. pp. (419)–469.

Fifth title: THE GOVERNMENT, DISCIPLINE, AND WORSHIP, OF THE ASSOCIATE-REFORMED CHURCH IN NORTH-AMERICA.

    New-York: Printed by T. & J. Swords, No. 99 Pearl-street. 1799. pp. (471)–(586).

Sixth title: THE SUM OF SAVING KNOWLEDGE; OR A BRIEF SUM OF CHRISTIAN DOCTRINE, CONTAINED IN THE HOLY SCRIPTURES, AND HELD FORTH IN THE FOREGOING CONFESSION OF FAITH AND CATECHISMS; TOGETHER WITH THE PRACTICAL USE THEREOF. JOHN VI. 37. [Two lines.]

    New-York: Printed by T. & J. Swords, No. 99 Pearl-street. 1799. pp. (587)–612, (1), (1), (1).

35120   —— EXTRACTS FROM THE MINUTES OF THE ACTS AND PROCEEDINGS OF THE ASSOCIATE REFORMED SYNOD. MET AT PHILADELPHIA MAY   1799, AND CONTINUED BY ADJOURNMENTS. PUBLISHED BY ORDER OF SYNOD.

    New-York: Printed by T. & J. Swords. 1799. 8vo.

35121   ATHERTON, CHARLES HUMPHREY   1773–1853
AN ORATION DELIVERED AT CONCORD, NEW-HAMPSHIRE, AT THE INSTALLATION OF THE BLAZING-STAR LODGE. MAY 6, A. L. 5799. BY CHARLES H. ATHERTON.

    Samuel Preston, Printer, Amherst. June —— 1799. pp. 16. 8vo.

                               AAS. BA. BM. JCB. LOC.

35122   AUGUSTA. DISTRICT OF MAINE. FIRE CLUB.
Caption title: ARTICLES AND REGULATIONS OF THE AUGUSTA FIRE CLUB. A NUMBER OF THE INHABITANTS OF THE TOWN OF AUGUSTA HAVING ASSOCIATED TO PROCURE A FIRE ENGINE, AND IT HAVING BEEN PROPOSED BY THEM TO FORM A FIRE CLUB—IT IS HEREBY AGREED, . . . [Names of twenty-five associates.]

    [Augusta: Printed by Peter Edes. 19th March, 1799.] pp. 8. 16mo.   JCB.

35123   AUGUSTA [cut] HERALD. VOL. I. NUMBER 1. WEDNESDAY, JULY 17, [— NUMBER 24. WEDNESDAY, DECEMBER 25, 1799.]

    [Augusta, Georgia.] Printed by George F. Randolph & William J. Bunce, in Washington-Street. 1799. fol.

    Established, as a weekly, by George F. Randolph and William J. Bunce. With the issue for August 20, 1800, Randolph withdrew, and publication was continued by William J. Bunce. In July ? 1804, William J. Hobby was admitted to partnership, as Hobby and Bunce. In January, 1817, publication was made by William J. Bunce, alone, and this arrangement continued beyond the period of this work.

35124   AURORA [cut] GENERAL ADVERTISER. SURGO UT PROSIM. NUM. 2442. TUESDAY, JANUARY 1, [— NUM. 2735. TUESDAY, DECEMBER 31, 1799.]

    Published (daily) for the heirs of Benj. Franklin Bache, at No. 112 Market Street, between Third and Fourth Streets, Philadelphia. 1799. fol.

                AAS. BM. HC. HSP. LCP. MdHS. NYPL. PSL. YC.

    Because of the yellow fever in Philadelphia, the Aurora was published at Bristol, from August 30th, to October 19th, 1799.

35125   AUSTIN, David   1759–1831
THE DANCE OF HERODIAS, THROUGH THE STREETS OF HARTFORD, ON ELECTION DAY, TO THE TUNE OF THE STARS OF HEAVEN, IN THE DRAGON'S TAIL; OR, A GENTLE TRIP AT THE HEELS OF THE STRUMPET OF BABYLON, PLAYING TRICKS IN THE ATTIRE OF THE DAUGHTERS OF ZION.

[East-Windsor: Printed by Luther Pratt.] For the Author, 1799. 12mo.

35126   —— *Caption:* THE FIRST VIBRATION OF THE JUBILEE TRUMP! NUMBER I–IX.

[Elizabeth-Town: Printed by Shepard Kollock, Nov. 22, 1799.] [pp. 16.]
8vo.   AAS.

Signed, David Austin, jun. Elizabeth-Town, 11th month.

35127   —— MASONRY IN ITS GLORY; OR, SOLOMON'S TEMPLE ILLUMINATED: DISCERNED THROUGH THE FLASHES OF PROPHETIC LIGHT . . . BY DAVID AUSTIN. JUNR. CITIZEN OF THE WORLD.

East-Windsor, (Connecticut.) Printed by Luther Pratt. 1799. pp. 86. 12mo.
                                           CHS.

35128   —— THE MILLENIAL DOOR THROWN OPEN, OR, THE MYSTERIES OF THE LATTER DAY GLORY UNFOLDED, IN A DISCOURSE DELIVERED AT EAST-WINDSOR, STATE OF CONNECTICUT. JULY FOURTH, 1799, THE TWENTY-THIRD YEAR OF THE DECLARATION OF INDEPENDENCE OF THE UNITED STATES. BY DAVID AUSTIN, JUNR. CITIZEN OF THE WORLD.

East-Windsor: Printed by Luther Pratt. 1799. pp. 48. 12mo.   CHS. SGO.

35129   THE AUTHOR WISHING IT MAY BE IMPROVED AND ENLARGED, BY SOME ABLER PEN, NOW CASTS IN HER MITE, TO THE MEMÓRY OF THAT WORTHY PERSON [George Washington] WHOSE LOSS WE SEVERELY FEEL. MY FATHER CRIES THE UNITED STATES, PRAY LEAVE US NOT OUR GUIDE AND LIGHT: . . .

[Without place or printer. 1799.] Broadside.

35130   AVERY, David   1746–1818
A SERMON, ON THE DUTY OF CHRISTIAN PITY, PREACHED AT THE INTERMENT OF MR. WALTER MOOR, STUDENT OF PHILLIPS ACADEMY, ANDOVER, MASSACHUSETTS; WHO DIED AT UNION, IN CONNECTICUT, JUNE 20TH, 1798, IN THE 22D YEAR OF HIS AGE. BY DAVID AVERY, MINISTER OF THE WORD OF GOD. [Printer's mark.]

Charlestown: Printed by Samuel Etheridge. 1799. pp. [47.] 8vo.
                               AAS. BM. HC. JCB. YC.
Second heading: LINES IN MEMORY OF MR. WALTER MOOR, BY A STUDENT OF PHILLIPS ANDOVER ACADEMY. [Fourteen four-line verses.] pp. 45–47.

35131   AWFUL DEATH OF AN IMPIOUS YOUTH: A FRAGMENT. [Double line.]

Philadelphia: Printed by H. Maxwell; for A. Dickins, Bookseller, No. 41, Market Street. 1799. pp. [12.] 8vo.   AAS.

35132   BACHE'S PHILADELPHIA AURORA. WEDNESDAY, JANUARY 2D, AND THURSDAY, JANUARY 3, [— MONDAY, DECEMBER 30, AND TUESDAY, DECEMBER 31, 1799.]

Published (tri-weekly) for the heirs of Benj. Franklin Bache, at No. 112 *Market Street.* 1799. fol.

Owing to the yellow fever epidemic in Philadelphia, publication was made at Bristol, from August 30th, to October 21, 1799.

35133   BACKUS, CHARLES   1749–1803
THE HIGH IMPORTANCE OF LOVE TO JESUS CHRIST IN THE MINISTERS OF THE GOSPEL.
A SERMON, DELIVERED AT THE ORDINATION OF THE REVEREND JOHN HUBBARD
CHURCH, TO THE PASTORAL CHARGE OF THE CHURCH IN PELHAM, NEW-HAMPSHIRE.
OCTOBER 31, 1798. BY CHARLES BACKUS, A. M. PASTOR OF A CHURCH IN SOMERS,
CONNECTICUT.
        Amherst, New-Hampshire, From the Press of Samuel Preston, Jan. – 1799.
pp. 38. 8vo.   AAS. CLA. JCB. LOC. NYPL.
        The Charge, by the Rev. Solomon Aiken of Dracutt. The Right hand
        of fellowship, by the Rev. Jabez Pond Fisher, of Nottingham West.

35134   ——   THE LIVING WARNED TO BE PREPARED FOR DEATH. A SERMON, OCCASIONED BY
THE DEATH OF SIX YOUNG PERSONS, WHO WERE DROWNED IN A POND IN WILBRAHAM,
MASSACHUSETTS, APRIL 29, 1799: AND DELIVERED MAY 2, WHEN THE FUNERAL OF
FIVE OF THEM WAS ATTENDED. BY CHARLES BACKUS, A. M. PASTOR OF A CHURCH IN
SOMERS, CONNECTICUT. TO WHICH IS SUBJOINED, TWO DISCOURSES, DELIVERED IN
WILBRAHAM MAY 12, '99, ON THE SAME OCCASION. BY REV. MR. WITTER, PASTOR
OF THE NORTH CHURCH IN WILBRAHAM. TOGETHER WITH AN APPENDIX, GIVING
SOME ACCOUNT OF THE PARTICULARS OF THE MELANCHOLY EVENT.
        Printed at Springfield. [*By Timothy Ashley.*] M,DCC,XCIX. pp. (16); (11);
(12). 8vo.   AAS. CLA.
        Second title: RESIGNATION TO THE AFFLICTIVE DISPENSATIONS OF DIVINE PROVI-
DENCE, RECOMMENDED IN A DISCOURSE, DELIVERED IN WILBRAHAM, MAY 12, 1799.
OCCASIONED BY THE DEATH OF SIX PERSONS WHO WERE DROWNED IN THAT PLACE,
APRIL 29, 1799. BY EZRA WITTER, PASTOR OF THE NORTH CHURCH IN THAT TOWN.
PUBLISHED BY DESIRE. [Three lines of Scripture texts.]
        Springfield: Printed by T. Ashley. M,DCC,XCIX. pp. (11).
        Third title: GRATITUDE AND OBEDIENCE TO THE PRESERVER OF MEN, FROM A
SIGNAL DELIVERANCE; AND WARNING FROM THE AWFUL AND UNTIMELY FATE OF
OTHERS; RECOMMENDED AND ENFORCED IN A DISCOURSE, DELIVERED IN WILBRA-
HAM, MAY 12, 1799. OCCASIONED BY THE DEATH OF SIX YOUNG PERSONS WHO WERE
DROWNED IN THAT PLACE, APRIL 29, 1799. BY EZRA WITTER, PASTOR OF THE NORTH
CHURCH IN THAT TOWN. PUBLISHED BY DESIRE. [Five lines of Scripture texts.]
        Springfield: Printed by T. Ashley. 1799. pp. (12).

        Pages 10-12 contain; An Appendix, giving some account of the particu-
        lars of the melancholy event which gave rise to the preceding Discourses.

35135   ——   A SERMON, PREACHED AT ENFIELD, FEBRUARY 16, 1799; AT THE FUNERAL OF
MRS. AGNES PRUDDEN, CONSORT OF THE REV. NEHEMIAH PRUDDEN. BY CHARLES
BACKUS, A. M. PASTOR OF A CHURCH IN SOMERS. [Printers mark.]
        Hartford: Printed by Hudson & Goodwin. 1799. pp. 27. 8vo.
                                        CHS. JCB. NYPL. UTS. YC.

35136   BACON, ASA   1771–1857
AN ORATION DELIVERED AT CANTERBURY, JUNE 27, 1799, BEFORE MORIAH LODGE,
ON THE CELEBRATION OF THE FESTIVAL OF ST. JOHN THE BAPTIST. BY ASA BACON.
        Printed by George Hough at Concord. 1799.

35137   BACON, EZEKIEL   1776–1870
AN ORATION DELIVERED AT WILLIAMSTOWN, ON THE 4TH OF JULY, 1799. BEING THE
ANNIVERSARY OF AMERICAN INDEPENDENCE. BY EZEKIEL BACON, ESQUIRE. [Five
lines from] THOMSON.
        Bennington: Printed by Anthony Haswell. [1799.] pp. 32. 8vo.
                                        BA. CHS. JCB. LOC. NYHS. NYPL.
        A copy of this anti-federal oration was publicly burnt by the students
        of Williams College.

35138   BAILEY, Francis   1735–1815
Bailey's Pocket Almanac, for the year of our Lord, MDCCC; and of the
independence of the United States, the twenty fourth. Fourth * after
bissextile, or leap-year. * Because the length of a solar year is about 11
minutes less than 365 days, 6 hours, in 25 leap-years, or a century, there
is an excess of 18 hours, or three quarters of a day; therefore the leap-
year is dropped in every centurial year not divisible by 400 without a
remainder. [U. S. arms.]
    Philadelphia: Printed by Francis & Robert Bailey, at Yorick's Head, No. 116,
High-Street. [1799.] pp. (32) interleaved. 32mo.   AAS. LOC.

35139   BALDWIN, Thomas   1753–1825
A Brief account of the late revivals of religion in a number of towns in
the New-England States. Extracted chiefly from letters written by
several gentlemen of unquestionable veracity.
    Boston: Printed and sold by Manning & Loring. May, 1799. pp. [8]. 8vo.
                                            AAS. HC. JCB. NYHS. NYPL.

35140   —— — A Brief account of the late revivals of religion in a number of
towns in the New-England States, and also in Nova-Scotia. Extracted
chiefly from letters written by several gentlemen of unquestionable
veracity. To which is added, a very interesting letter from a minister
in London to his friend in Massachusetts.
    Boston: Printed by Manning & Loring. Sept. 1799. pp. [24.] 12mo.
                                            AAS. JCB. LOC. NYPL.

35141   —— — A Brief account of the late revivals of religion in a number of
towns in the New England States. Extracted chiefly from letters written by several gentlemen of unquestionable veracity.
    Newburyport: Printed and sold by Parker & Robinson. May 22, 1799. pp.
(15). 8vo.   AAS.

35142   —— — A Brief account of the late revivals of religion in a number of
towns in the New-England States, and also in Nova-Scotia. Extracted
chiefly from letters written by several gentlemen of unquestionable
veracity. To which is added, a very interesting letter, from a minister
in London to his friend in Massachusetts.
    Worcester: Printed by Mower & Greenleaf. Dec. 1799. pp. [36.] 12mo.   AAS.

35143   —— Brief vindication of the particular communion of the Baptist churches;
being a reply to the remarks of the rev. Noah Worcester, a. b. in his
"Friendly letter" to the Author. By Thomas Baldwin. Third edition.
    Suffield: Printed by E. Gray. M,DCC,XCIX. pp. 112. 12mo.

35144   —— A Sermon, delivered at Boston, on Tuesday, April 2, 1799; at a quarterly meeting of several churches for special prayer. By Thomas Baldwin,
a. m. pastor of the second Baptist church in Boston. Published by desire
of many who heard it.
    Boston: Printed by Manning & Loring. 1799. pp. [24.] 8vo.
                                    AAS. BA. BM. HC. JCB. LOC. NYPL. YC.

35145   —— A Sermon, delivered at Boston, July 11, 1799, at the ordination of the
rev. William Collier. (Ordained at large.) By Thomas Baldwin, a. m.
pastor of the second Baptist church in Boston.
    Boston: Printed by Manning & Loring. 1799. pp. [27.] 8vo. AAS. JCB. LOC.

35146　BALLOU, Hosea　　　　　　　　　　　　　　1771–1852
A Literary correspondence, between Joel Foster, a. m. minister of the Congregational Society in New-Salem, and Hosea Ballou, an itinerant preacher of the sect called Universalists. In which, the question concerning future punishment, and the reasons, for and against it, are considered. [Seven lines from] Sherlock.

Printed at Northampton, (Massachusetts) by William Butler. M,DCC,XCIX. pp. [68.] 8vo.　　　　　　　　　　　　AAS. BA. BM. JCB.

35147　BALTIMORE. Maryland. Marine Insurance Office.
Whereas it is contemplated to establish an office or society for insurance, in the city of Baltimore, under the name and style of the Marine Insurance Office, we the subscribers, do hereby severally associate and bind ourselves . . . [Thirty-six names.]

[Baltimore: 1799.] Broadside. fol.

35148　BALTIMORE. Maryland. Society of St. George.
Rules and Constitution of the Society of St. George, in Maryland; established in the city of Baltimore, for the purpose of relieving their brethren in distress: as revised by a committee appointed for that purpose, and approved and adopted at a special meeting, April 2, 1799.

Baltimore: Printed by John Hayes, No. 8, Baltimore-Street. 1799. pp. 15. 8vo.　　　　　　　　　　　　　　　　　　NYPL.

35149　THE BALTIMORE Intelligencer. Vol. iii. No. 130. Wednesday, January 2, [— No. 185 ? Friday, May 10 ? 1799.]

Baltimore: Published by William Pechin. 1799. 4to.

In May, the Intelligencer was absorbed into the *American and daily advertiser*, which continued its subscription list.

35150　THE BALTIMORE repository, for the year 1800: containing, An Almanac; Government of the U. S. List of Congress; Department of State, Treasury, War, Navy, and Judiciary, with an account of what is important in each; Federal Courts of law: Army and Navy of the U. S. Mint establishment; Post-Office establishment, and list of post-towns, &c. Times of receiving and closing the mails at Philadelphia and Baltimore; Abstract of the Revenue law, list of duties, tonnage, drawbacks, &c. Abstract of the Stamp Act, with a list of stamp duties; Duties payable on domestic articles; An Act to value property, and an Act to lay a direct tax, &c. Officers of the Revenue; Ministers, consuls, &c. to and from the United States; Alien and Sedition laws; Appropriations by Congress for 1799; An account of the corporation of the city of Baltimore; Banks and insurance companies, &c. in ditto; Government of the State of Maryland, with a list of the General Assembly; Militia law of do. abridged; Several useful tables, and a great variety of other interesting matter.

Baltimore: Printed and sold by Bonsal and Niles, No. 173, Market-Street. [1799.] pp. [160.] 24mo.　　　　　　　　MdHS.

Title enclosed in ornamental border. Unpaged. Almanac interleaved. Bound as a pocket-book.

35151　BANKER, Robert
Keatinge' Maryland Almanack for 1800. The astronomical calculations by Robert Banker: to which is added, extracts from the Ordinances of the city of Baltimore, together with the names of the officers of government. Entertaining stories, &c. &c. [State seal.]

Baltimore: Printed by and for George Keatinge. [1799.] pp. (36). 12mo. JCB.

35152   BARLOW, Joel   1754–1812
HASTY PUDDING: A POEM. IN THREE CANTOS. WRITTEN AT CHAMBERY, IN SAVOY, JANUARY, 1793. OMNE TULIT PUNCTUM QUI MISCUIT UTILI DULCI. HE MAKES A GOOD BREAKFAST WHO MIXES PUDDING WITH MOLASSES.

     Salem: Printed by Joshua Cushing, 1799. pp. 21. 12mo.

                                     AAS. BA. BU. EI. HC. LOC.

35153   BARRUEL, Augustin de, l'abbé   1741–1820
MEMOIRS, ILLUSTRATING THE HISTORY OF JACOBINISM. A TRANSLATION FROM THE FRENCH OF THE ABBE BARRUEL. [By Robert Clifford.] PART I.—VOL. I. THE ANTICHRISTIAN CONSPIRACY. [Printers mark.]

     Hartford: Printed by Hudson & Goodwin for Cornelius Davis, No. 94, Water-Street, New-York. 1799. pp. xviii, 226. 8vo.   AAS. HC. LOC. NYPL.

35154   —— — MEMOIRS, ILLUSTRATING THE HISTORY OF JACOBINISM. A TRANSLATION FROM THE FRENCH OF THE ABBE BARRUEL. PART II. — VOL. II. THE ANTIMONARCHICAL CONSPIRACY. [Printers mark.]

     Hartford: Printed by Hudson & Goodwin for Cornelius Davis, No. 94, Water-Street, New-York. 1799. pp. viii, v, 264. 8vo.   AAS. HC. LOC. NYPL.

35155   —— — MEMOIRS, ILLUSTRATING THE HISTORY OF JACOBINISM. A TRANSLATION FROM THE FRENCH OF THE ABBE BARRUEL. PART III.—VOL. III. THE ANTISOCIAL CONSPIRACY. [U. S. arms.]

     New-York: Printed by Isaac Collins, for Cornelius Davis, No. 94, Water-Street. 1799. pp. xii, 256. 8vo.   AAS HC. LOC. NYPL.

35156   —— — MEMOIRS, ILLUSTRATING THE HISTORY OF JACOBINISM, WRITTEN IN FRENCH BY THE ABBÉ BARRUEL, AND TRANSLATED INTO ENGLISH BY THE HON. ROBERT CLIFFORD, F. R. S. & A. S. [Two lines from] WEISHAUPT'S DISCOURSE FOR THE MYSTERIES. PART IV.—VOL. IV. ANTISOCIAL CONSPIRACY; HISTORICAL PART. FIRST AMERICAN EDITION, FROM THE SECOND LONDON EDITION.

     Elizabeth-Town: Printed by Shepard Kollock for Cornelius Davis, No. 94, Water-Street, New-York. 1799. pp. 16, (2), (17)–400. 8vo.   AAS. HC. LOC. NYPL.

35157   BARTGIS'S FEDERAL [U. S. arms] GAZETTE, OR THE FREDERICK COUNTY WEEKLY ADVERTISER. VOL. VI. WHOLE NO. 347. WEDNESDAY, JANUARY 2, [— VOL. VII. No. 23. WHOLE NO. 398. WEDNESDAY, DECEMBER 25, 1799.]

     Printed every Wednesday, by Matthias Bartgis, at his English & German Printing-Office, at the corner of Market & Patrick-Streets, Frederick-Town; . . . 1799. fol.

                                             MdHS.

35158   BARTLETT, Joseph   1763–1827
PHYSIOGNOMY, A POEM, DELIVERED AT THE REQUEST OF THE SOCIETY OF P B K, IN THE CHAPEL OF HARVARD UNIVERSITY, ON THE DAY OF THEIR ANNIVERSARY, JULY 18TH, 1799. BY JOSEPH BARTLETT. [Three lines of quotations.]

     Boston: Printed by John Russell, 1799. pp. 16. 4to.

                             AAS. BA. BM. BU. HC. LOC. NYPL.

AUCTION
VALUES

35159   BARTON, Benjamin Smith   1766–1815
Fragments of the natural history of Pennsylvania. By Benjamin Smith Barton, m.d. correspondent-member of the Society of Antiquaries of Scotland; member of the American Philosophical Society; fellow of the American Academy of Arts and Sciences of Boston; corresponding member of the Massachusetts Historical Society; member of the Physical Society of Jena; one of the foreign members of the Linnæan Society of London; and professor of materia medica, natural history and botany, in the University of Pennsylvania. Part first. [Two lines of Latin quotations.]

     Philadelphia: Printed, for the Author, by Way & Groff, No. 48, North Third-Street. 1799. pp. (xviii), (24). fol.   BM. JCB. LOC. NYHS. NYPL.

     All that was published. 234th Pennsylvania District Copyright, issued to Benjamin Smith Barton, as Author, 27 May, 1799. Reprinted in London in 1883.

35160   BARZONI, Vittorio   1764–1829
The Romans in Greece. An ancient tale, descriptive of modern events. Translated from the Italian. Copy-right secured according to Act of Congress.

     Boston: Printed by Manning & Loring, for J. Nancrede, No. 49, Marlbro'-Street. 1799. pp. [80], (4). 12mo.   AAS. LOC.

     172d Massachusetts District Copyright, issued to Joseph Nancrede, as Proprietor, 7 October, 1799.

35161   BAYLEY, Richard   1745–1801
Letters from the Health-Office, submitted to the Common Council, of the city of New-York. By Richard Bayley. [Between heavy lines.]

     [New-York:] Printed by John Furman, No. 102, Pearl-Street, third door below the corner of Old-Slip. [1799.] pp. 100. 8vo.   LOC. NYHS. SGO.

35162   THE [cut] BEE. Volume II. Number 73. Wednesday, January 2, [— Vol. III. Number 123. Wednesday, December 25, 1799.]

     New-London: Printed and published by Charles Holt. 1799. fol.   LOC.

35163   BEEDÉ, Thomas   –1848
An Oration, delivered at Roxbury, July 4, 1799, in commemoration of American independence. By Thomas Beede.

     Boston: Printed by Ebenezer Rhoades. 1799. pp. 15. 8vo.   AAS. BA. HC. MHS.

35164   BEERS, Andrew   1749–1824
Beers' Almanac for the year of our Lord, 1800: being the completion of the eighteenth century, and twenty-fourth year of American independence, 'till 4th of July. Calculated for the meridian of Hartford, latitude 41 degrees, 56 min. north—longitude 72 degrees, 50 min. west, and will serve for any of the adjacent States, without any essential difference. [Six lines.] By Andrew Beers, philom.

     Hartford: Printed by Hudson & Goodwin. [1799.] pp. [36.] 12mo.
                                     AAS. CHS. LOC. NYPL.

     Contains, Courts. Concise Calendar for young farmers and gardeners. Collection round a tea table. Singular method of duelling. The difference between a lover and a husband. Friar Philip's geese. Humphrey Gubbin's courtship. Anecdotes. Interest.

BEERS, ANDREW, continued.

35165 —— CROSWELL'S DIARY: OR, THE CATSKILL ALMANACK, FOR THE YEAR OF OUR LORD 1800: NO BISSEXTILE OR LEAP YEAR, IT BEING THE COMPLETION OF THE 18TH CENTURY, AND OF AMERICAN INDEPENDENCE (WHICH WAS DECLARED THE 4TH OF JULY, 1776) PART OF THE 24TH AND 25TH YEARS: CALCULATED FOR LATITUDE 42 DEGREES NORTH, AND FOR A MERIDIAN 3 DEGREES EAST OF GEORGETOWN, THE INTENDED PERMANENT RESIDENCE OF CONGRESS. CONTAINING, BESIDES WHAT IS USUAL AND NECESSARY IN COMPOSITIONS OF THIS NATURE, MANY THINGS, NEW, USEFUL AND ENTERTAINING. BY ANDREW BEERS, PHILOM.

Catskill: Printed and sold by Mackay Croswell. ☞ *Great allowance to those who purchase quantities.* [1799.] pp. (36). 12mo. AAS.

Contains, Courts. Interest. Anecdote of Dean Swift. The humours of a wet Sunday. Humorous story of a robbery. The Sexton of Cluni. A Norman tale. Extract from "Letters on Egypt." The Un-Natural son. Anecdotes. Jewish economy. Points of honor. Humour.

35166 —— EQUAL TO HUTCHINS. AN ALMANACK AND EPHEMERIS FOR THE YEAR OF OUR LORD, 1800.

State of New-York: Kingston (Ulster County) Printed and sold by Samuel Freer and Son. Wholesale and retail. [1799.] pp. (36). 12mo.

35167 —— THE FARMERS ALMANAC, FOR THE YEAR OF OUR LORD CHRIST, 1800, AND FROM THE CREATION, 5749. NO BISSEXTILE, OR LEAP YEAR, IT BEING THE COMPLETION OF THE 18TH CENTURY. THE 24TH YEAR OF AMERICAN INDEPENDENCE, TILL THE 4TH OF JULY. CALCULATED FOR THE MERIDIAN OF DANBURY, IN THE STATE OF CONNECTICUT, LATITUDE 41° 50" N. LONG. 78° 57" W. BUT MAY SERVE FOR THE ADJACENT STATES. CONTAINING, A GREAT VARIETY OF USEFUL AND ENTERTAINING MATTER. BY ANDREW BEERS, PHILOM.

Danbury: Printed & sold by the gross, dozen or single, by Douglas & Nichols. [1799.] pp. [36.] 12mo. AAS. CHS.

Contains, A Discourse, supposed to be delivered at midnight; the preacher standing in the door of a gambling room, in which were seated a number at play.

35168 —— THE FARMERS' ALMANAC FOR THE YEAR OF OUR LORD, 1800. CALCULATED FOR THE MERIDIAN OF NEWFIELD.

Newfield: Printed and sold by Lazarus Beach. [1799.]

35169 —— FRANKLIN'S LEGACY: OR, THE NEW-YORK AND VERMONT ALMANACK, FOR THE YEAR OF OUR LORD, 1800; BEING THE 24TH YEAR OF AMERICAN INDEPENDENCE, UNTIL JULY 4TH. . . . BY ANDREW BEERS, PHILOM.

Troy: Printed by R. Moffitt & Co. and sold by them, at their Office, opposite Messrs. G. & B. Tibbitt's Store, by the wholesale, gross, dozen or single. [1799.] LOC.

35170 —— GLORIA GREENLEAF'S NEW-YORK, CONNECTICUT & NEW-JERSEY ALMANACK, OR DIARY, FOR THE YEAR OF OUR LORD, 1800; [Eighteen lines, with cut.]

Brooklyn: Printed and for sale by T. Kirk. Mundi. [1799.] pp. (36). 12mo. AAS. LIHS.

35171 —— —— GLORIA GREENLEAF'S NEW-YORK, CONNECTICUT, & NEW-JERSEY ALMANACK, OR DIARY, FOR THE YEAR OF OUR LORD, 1800; BEING THE FOURTH AFTER BISSEXTILE, OR LEAP YEAR, THE TWENTY-FOURTH OF THE INDEPENDENCE OF THE U. STATES OF AMERICA, AND FROM CREATION (PER BIBLE) 5804. FITTED FOR THE MERIDIAN AND HORIZON OF NEW-YORK, BUT WILL SERVE WITHOUT ESSENTIAL

BEERS, ANDREW, continued.
VARIATION, FOR CONNECTICUT AND NEW-JERSEY. CONTAINING USUAL ASTRONOMICAL
CALCULATIONS, AND A GREATER VARIETY OF OTHER MATTER THAN IS COMMON IN
AN ALMANACK — ALL OF WHICH IS USEFUL — CURIOUS — AND ENTERTAINING. TO
WHICH IS ADDED, WITH DIRECTIONS, THE NEW FRENCH CALENDAR. [Cut. Five lines
of verse from] MILTON.

Brooklyn: Printed by T. Kirk, for Benjamin Gomez. Mundi. [1799.] pp.
[36.] 12mo.   NYPL.

Contains, An Act for supplying the city of New-York with pure and
wholesome water, and incorporating the Manhattan Company. Passed
2d April, 1799.

35172   ——   HUTCHINS IMPROVED: BEING AN ALMANAC, FOR THE YEAR OF OUR LORD 1800;
NO BISSEXTILE OR LEAP-YEAR; IT BEING THE COMPLETION OF THE 18TH CENTURY.
OF THE INDEPENDENCE OF THE UNITED-STATES THE 24TH YEAR. CONTAINING THE
MOTIONS OF THE SUN AND MOON; THE TRUE PLACES AND ASPECTS OF THE PLANETS;
THE RISING AND SETTING OF THE SUN; THE RISING, SETTING AND SOUTHING OF THE
MOON; THE LUNATIONS, CONJUNCTIONS, ECLIPSES; RISING AND SETTING OF THE PLAN-
ETS; LENGTH OF DAYS AND NIGHTS; JUDGMENT OF THE WEATHER; FESTIVALS, AND
OTHER REMARKABLE DAYS; DAYS FOR HOLDING COURTS IN NEW-YORK AND NEW-
JERSEY; A COLLECTION OF USEFUL TABLES, AND A GREATER VARIETY OF OTHER
MATTER THAN IS USUALLY FOUND IN AN ALMANAC; ALL OF WHICH WILL BE FOUND
USEFUL AND ENTERTAINING. BY ANDREW BEERS, PHILOM.

State of New-York: Poughkeepsie, printed by John Woods. [1799.] pp. (36).
12mo.   AAS.

Tide table. The Devil. A man-fish. A remarkable fact. Valuable receipts. Duties on Spirits, and Carriages. Government of the United
States. New-York courts. Coins of the United States. Interest. Remarkable occurrences. Roads.

35173   ——   STODDARD'S DIARY: OR, THE COLUMBIA ALMANAC, FOR THE YEAR OF OUR LORD
1800: NO BISSEXTILE OR LEAP YEAR, IT BEING THE COMPLETION OF THE 18TH
CENTURY, AND OF AMERICAN INDEPENDENCE (WHICH WAS DECLARED THE 4TH OF
JULY, 1776) PART OF THE 24TH AND 25TH YEARS. CALCULATED FOR LATITUDE 42
DEGREES NORTH, AND FOR A MERIDIAN 3 DEGREES EAST OF GEORGETOWN, THE
INTENDED RESIDENCE OF CONGRESS. CONTAINING, BESIDES WHAT IS USUAL AND
NECESSARY IN COMPOSITIONS OF THIS NATURE, MANY THINGS, NEW, USEFUL AND
ENTERTAINING. BY ANDREW BEERS, PHILOM.

Hudson: Printed and sold by Ashbel Stoddard. ☞ *Great allowance to those
who purchase quantities.* [1799.] pp. (34). 12mo.   AAS.

With slight variation this is the same as Croswell's Diary, by Andrew
Beers.

35174   ——   WEBSTER'S CALENDAR: OR THE ALBANY ALMANACK, FOR THE YEAR OF OUR LORD,
1800: NO BISSEXTILE OR LEAP YEAR — IT BEING THE COMPLETION OF THE 18TH
CENTURY. OF AMERICAN INDEPENDENCE (WHICH WAS DECLARED THE 4TH OF JULY,
1776) PART OF THE 24TH & 25TH YEARS. CALCULATED FOR THE MERIDIAN OF
ALBANY — NORTH LATITUDE 42 DEGREES 45 MINUTES — FROM THE ENGLISH
OBSERVATORY, 73 DEGREES AND 8 MINUTES WEST. BY ANDREW BEERS, PHILOM.
CONTAINING, AS USUAL, A GREAT VARIETY OF NEW, USEFUL AND ENTERTAINING
PIECES.

*Albany:— Printed by Charles R. and George Webster, corner of State and
Pearl-streets.* ☞ *Great allowance to those who buy by wholesale.* [1799.] pp.
(37). 12mo.   NYPL.

35175 BELAIR, ALEXANDRE PIERRE JULIENNE DE   1747–1819
THE ELEMENTS OF FORTIFICATION. TRANSLATED FROM THE FRENCH.

[Philadelphia:] Printed for the War Office. By John Ward Fenno. 1799.
pp. (42), 6 folded copper plates, by Thackara. 8vo.   AAS.

35176 BELL, WILLIAM   1731–1816
A PRACTICAL INQUIRY INTO THE AUTHORITY, NATURE, AND DESIGN OF THE LORD'S
SUPPER; AS THEY ARE EXPLAINED IN THE NEW TESTAMENT ITSELF. BY WILLIAM
BELL, D.D. PREBENDARY OF ST. PETER'S, WESTMINSTER.

*Printed at London. New-London: Re-printed by Charles Holt for James
Springer.* 1799. pp. 36. 12mo.   AAS. JCB.

35177 BELLINGER, JOHN SKOTTOWE
AN INAUGURAL DISSERTATION ON CHRONIC PNEUMONY, OR PULMONARY CONSUMPTION:
SUBMITTED TO THE EXAMINATION OF THE REV. JOHN EWING, S.T.P. PROVOST; THE
TRUSTEES & MEDICAL FACULTY, OF THE UNIVERSITY OF PENNSYLVANIA, ON THE
SIXTH DAY OF JUNE, 1799, FOR THE DEGREE OF DOCTOR OF MEDICINE. BY JOHN
SKOTTOWE BELLINGER, OF CHARLESTON, SOUTH CAROLINA, MEMBER OF THE PHIL-
ADELPHIA MEDICAL AND CHEMICAL SOCIETIES.

Philadelphia: Printed by Way & Groff, No. 48, North Third-Street. 1799.
pp. 78. 8vo.   AAS. JCB. LOC. SGO.

35178 BENEZET, ANTHONY   1713–1784
A SHORT ACCOUNT OF THE PEOPLE CALLED QUAKERS: THEIR RISE, RELIGIOUS PRIN-
CIPLES, AND SETTLEMENT IN AMERICA. MOSTLY COLLECTED FROM DIFFERENT
AUTHORS, FOR THE INFORMATION OF ALL SERIOUS INQUIRERS, PARTICULARLY FOR-
EIGNERS. BY ANTHONY BENEZET.

New-Bedford: Printed by Abraham Shearman, jun. 1799. pp. [28.] 8vo.
                     AAS. BM. HC.

35179 BENJAMIN, JONATHAN
HARMONIA CŒLESTIS: A COLLECTION OF CHURCH MUSIC, IN TWO, THREE, AND FOUR
PARTS. WITH WORDS ADAPTED TO EACH, COMPREHENDING NOT ONLY THE METRES
IN COMMON USE, BUT THE PARTICULAR METRES, IN THE HARTFORD COLLECTION OF
HYMNS; THE TUNES CORRECTLY FIGURED FOR THE ORGAN AND HARPSICHORD.—
WITH AN INTTODUCTION [*sic*] TO MUSIC. CHIEFLY COLLECTED FROM THE GREATEST
MASTERS IN EUROPE, AND NEVER BEFORE PRINTED IN AMERICA. BY JONATHAN
BENJAMIN.

*Northampton: Printed, typographically, by Andrew Wright, for Oliver D. &
I. Cooke, Booksellers, Hartford.— Sept.* 1799. Published according to Act of
Congress. pp. 79, (1). obl. 16mo.   AAS. JCB. LOC. MHS. UTS.

"All of the Hymns may be found in the *Hartford Collection,* now publishing by the Rev. Messrs. Strong, Flint & Stewart, for the benefit of
the Missionary Society."

35180 BENTLEY, WILLIAM   1758–1819
AN ADDRESS, DELIVERED IN THE ESSEX LODGE, UPON THE FESTIVAL OF ST. JOHN
THE EVANGELIST, AT THE INDUCTION OF THE OFFICERS, BY BROTHER JOSEPH
HILLER, PAST MASTER, AND BROTHER BENJAMIN HODGES, MASTER ELECT, DECEM-
BER 27, 1798. BY WILLIAM BENTLEY, MEMBER OF ESSEX LODGE. [Five lines of
quotations.]

Printed at Salem, by Joshua Cushing. 1799. pp. [31.] 8vo.
                     AAS. BA. BM. EI. HC. JCB. LOC. MHS.

35181　　BENTLEY, William, continued.
—— Extracts from professor [John] Robison's "Proofs of a conspiracy," &c.
with brief reflections on the charges he has exhibited, the evidence he
has produced, and the merit of his performance. [Signed, Cornelius. Massachusetts, Dec. 1798.]

> *Boston: Printed by Manning & Loring.* 1799. pp. (30). 8vo.
> AAS. BM. HC. LCP. LOC. NYPL. UTS.

> "The name of the writer (a retired clergyman) is left with the Printers,
> who will communicate the same to any person who may wish to be in-
> formed of it."

35182　　BERESFORD, Richard　　　　　　　　　　　　　　　1755–1803
Half-title: A Dissertation on the uses of the learned languages.

> *Title:* A Dissertation on the uses of the learned languages. Delivered
> on the 19th of June, 1799, before the Charleston Library Society; and
> published by the said Society. By Richard Beresford.

> *Charleston: Printed by W. P. Young,* 43, *Broad-Street.* [1799.] pp. (2), 17.
> 8vo.
> CLS.

35183　　BERINGTON, Simon　　　　　　　　　　　　　　　　1680–1755
The Adventures of sig. Gaudentio di Lucca. Being the substance of his
examination before the fathers of the Inquisition at Bologna, in Italy:
giving an account of an unknown country, in the midst of the deserts of
Africa, the origin and antiquity of the people, their religion, customs,
and laws. Copied from the original manuscript in St. Mark's Library at
Venice. With critical notes of the learned signor Rhedi. To which is
prefixed: a letter of the secretary of the Inquisition, shewing the reasons of signor Gaudentio's being apprehended, and the manner of it.
Translated from the Italian [by E. T., gent.]

> *Philadelphia: Re-printed by William Conover.* 1799. pp. 320. 12mo.

Erroneously attributed to Bishop Berkeley.　　AAS. JCB. LOC. NYPL.

35184　　THE BERKELEY Intelligencer. Vol. i. No. 1. Wednesday, April 3, [— No.
39. Wednesday, December 25, 1799.]

> *Martinsburg, Virginia. Printed by John Alburtis.* 1799. fol.

> Established, as a weekly, by John Alburtis, and continued by him into
> the year 1810, when, without change in numbering, or ownership, it was
> succeeded by the *Martinsburgh Gazette.* In April, 1802, and continuing
> for a number of years, the title was changed to, *The Berkeley and Jef-
> ferson County Intelligencer and Northern Neck Advertiser.*

35185　　BERKSHIRE Gazette. [Motto.] Vol. i. No. 51. Wednesday, January 2, [—
Vol. ii, No. 44. Wednesday, December 25, 1799.]

> *Published by Holly & Smith, Pittsfield, Massachusetts.* 1799. fol.

> With the issue for March 6th, Nathaniel Holly withdrew, and publica-
> tion was made in the name of Chester Smith.

35186　　BERN or BERNE. Switzerland. Œconomische Gesellschaft.
Essays on the spirit of legislation, in the encouragement of agriculture,
population, manufactures, and commerce. — Containing—observations on
the political systems at present pursued in various countries of Europe,
for the advancement of those essential interests. Interspersed with
various remarks on the practice of agriculture. Societies of agriculture.
Rewards. Bounties. The police. Luxury. Industry. Machines. Exporta-

BERN or BERNE. SWITZERLAND, continued.
TION. TAXES. INOCULATION. MARRIAGE. NATURALIZATION, &C. TRANSLATED
FROM THE ORIGINAL FRENCH, WHICH GAINED THE PREMIUMS OFFERED BY THE
ŒCONOMICAL SOCIETY OF BERNE, IN SWITZERLAND, FOR THE BEST COMPOSITIONS
ON THIS SUBJECT.

Newark: Printed by Pennington & Dodge, for William Reid, Patterson [sic.]
pp. 479. 8vo.   AAS. LOC.

35187   BERRIMAN, JACOB M.
[Cut of snake.] THE FOLLOWING IS COPIED FROM THE JOURNAL KEPT BY MR. JACOB
M. BERRIMAN, DURING HIS TOUR TO THE WESTWARD OF FORT RECOVERY. [Two
column account of the killing of a monstrous snake, 36 feet 2 inches in length,
and 3 feet 1 inch, in diameter.] AS MANY PERSONS, PERHAPS, WILL DOUBT THE
TRUTH OF THE ABOVE ACCOUNT, THEY MAY SATISFY THEMSELVES BY CALLING AT MR.
PECK'S MUSEUM IN PHILADELPHIA, WHERE THE SKIN WAS PRESENTED. [Colophon:]

Suffield: Printed by Edward Gray. [1799.] Broadside. fol.   AAS.

35188   BIBLIA.
THE HOLY BIBLE, CONTAINING THE OLD AND NEW TESTAMENTS: TRANSLATED OUT
OF THE ORIGINAL TONGUES: AND WITH THE FORMER TRANSLATIONS DILIGENTLY
COMPARED AND REVISED. WITH MARGINAL REFERENCES.

*Philadelphia: Printed for Thomas Dobson, at the Stone House, No. 41, South
Second-Street,* 1799. [unpaged.] fol.   AAS. HSP.

Second title: THE NEW TESTAMENT OF OUR LORD AND SAVIOUR JESUS CHRIST,
TRANSLATED OUT OF THE ORIGINAL GREEK: AND WITH THE FORMER TRANSLATIONS
DILIGENTLY COMPARED AND REVISED: WITH MARGINAL REFERENCES.

*Philadelphia: Printed for Thomas Dobson, at the Stone House, No. 41, South
Second-Street,* 1799. [unpaged.]

35189   —— THE HOLY BIBLE, CONTAINING THE OLD AND NEW TESTAMENTS: TRANSLATED
OUT OF THE ORIGINAL TONGUES, AND WITH THE FORMER TRANSLATIONS DILIGENTLY
COMPARED AND REVISED. BY THE SPECIAL COMMAND OF KING JAMES I. OF ENGLAND.
[One line of Hebrew text from Genesis II. 17, enclosed in ornamental border.]

*United States of Columbia. Printed at Worcester, Massachusetts. By Isaiah
Thomas. Sold by him in Worcester, by wholesale, bound or in sheets. Sold also by
said Thomas and Andrews, in Boston, and by the Booksellers in the United States
of Columbia.* 1799. pp. (2), 674; (2), 288. [unpaged.] 12mo.   AAS. LOC. NYPL.

Second title: THE NEW TESTAMENT OF OUR LORD AND SAVIOUR JESUS CHRIST.
TRANSLATED OUT OF THE ORIGINAL GREEK, AND WITH THE FORMER TRANSLATION
DILIGENTLY COMPARED AND REVISED, BY THE SPECIAL COMMAND OF HIS MAJESTY
KING JAMES I. OF ENGLAND. [Two lines of Greek text, in an ornamental border.]

*United States of Columbia. Printed at Worcester, Massachusetts, by Isaiah
Thomas. Sold by him in worcester, by wholesale, bound or in sheets. Sold also by
said Thomas and Andrews, in Boston, and by the Booksellers in the United States
of Columbia.* 1799. pp. (2), (288). [unpaged.]

Thomas's standard duodecimo edition, with new title-pages only. The
error in Acts vi. 3, *ye* for *we*, is continued.

35190   —— THE BIBLE. THE NINTH EDITION.
New England, Printed for the Purchaser. [1799.]

35191   BIBLIA. OLD TESTAMENT. PSALMS.

PSALMS, CAREFULLY SUITED TO THE CHRISTIAN WORSHIP IN THE UNITED STATES OF AMERICA: BEING DR. WATTS' IMITATION OF THE PSALMS OF DAVID, AS IMPROVED BY MR. BARLOW. [Ornament.] ALLOWED BY THE REVEREND SYNOD OF NEW-YORK AND PHILADELPHIA, TO BE SUNG IN CONGREGATIONS AND FAMILIES. [Ornament.]

Philadelphia: Printed [by William Young] for Robert Campbell, No. 30, Chesnut-Street. M,DCC,XCIX. pp. 292, (10). 24mo.   AAS. BM.

Title within ornamental border.

35192   —— THE PSALMS OF DAVID, IMITATED IN THE LANGUAGE OF THE NEW TESTAMENT, AND APPLIED TO THE CHRISTIAN STATE AND WORSHIP. BY ISAAC WATTS, D.D. [Six lines of Scripture texts.]

Boston: Printed by Joseph Bumstead. Sold by him at No. 20, Union-Street, and by the principal Booksellers in Boston. 1799. pp. 595. 12mo.   NYPL.

Second title: HYMNS AND SPIRITUAL SONGS. IN THREE BOOKS. I. COLLECTED FROM THE SCRIPTURES. II. COMPOSED ON DIVINE SUBJECTS. III. PREPARED FOR THE LORD'S SUPPER. BY ISAAC WATTS, D.D. [Six lines of quotations.]

Boston: Printed by Joseph Bumstead. Sold by him at No. 20, Union-Street, and by the principal Booksellers in Boston. 1795. pp. (2), (319)–595.

There is no difference in this and the edition published by Bumstead in Boston in 1796, except the reversal of a 6 to make a 9, on the first title-page.

35193   —— THE PSALMS OF DAVID, IMITATED IN THE LANGUAGE OF THE NEW TESTAMENT, AND APPLIED TO THE CHRISTIAN STATE AND WORSHIP. BY ISAAC WATTS, D.D. CORRECTED, AND ACCOMMODATED TO THE USE OF THE CHURCH OF CHRIST IN AMERICA. [Six lines of Scripture texts.]

Brookfield: Printed by E. Merriam & Co. Sold by them in Brookfield, by G. Merriam, Worcester; by West & Greenleaf, E. & S. Larkin, Thomas & Andrews, J. West, J. White, W. P. & L. Blake, C. Bingham, Boston; by B. B. Macanulty, Salem; Thomas & Thomas, Walpole, N. H. [1799.] pp. (2), (9),(3)–288; 245, (9). 24mo.   NYPL.

Second title: HYMNS AND SPIRITUAL SONGS, IN THREE BOOKS: I. COLLECTED FROM THE SCRIPTURES. II. COMPOSED ON DIVINE SUBJECTS. III. PREPARED FOR THE LORD'S SUPPER. BY ISAAC WATTS, D.D. CORRECTED, AND ACCOMMODATED TO THE USE OF THE CHURCH OF CHRIST IN AMERICA. [Six lines of quotations.]

Brookfield: Printed by E. Merriam & Co. Sold by them in Brookfield, by G. Merriam, Worcester; by West & Greenleaf, E. & S. Larkin, Thomas & Andrews, J. West, J. White, W. P. & L. Blake, C. Bingham, Boston; by B. B. Macanulty, Salem; Thomas & Thomas, Walpole, N. H. [1799.] pp. 245, (9).

35194   —— — THE PSALMS OF DAVID, IMITATED IN THE LANGUAGE OF THE NEW TESTAMENT, AND APPLIED TO THE CHRISTIAN STATE AND WORSHIP. BY ISAAC WATTS, D.D. CORRECTED, AND ACCOMMODATED TO THE USE OF THE CHURCH OF CHRIST IN AMERICA. [Six lines of Scripture texts.]

Brookfield: Printed by E. Merriam & Co. Sold by them in Brookfield, by G. Merriam, Worcester; by West & Greenleaf, E. & S. Larkin, Thomas & Andrews, J. West, J. White, W. P. & L. Blake, C. Bingham, Boston; by B. B. Macanulty, Salem; Thomas & Thomas, Walpole, N. H. [1799.] pp. (2), (9), (3)–288; 245, (9). 24mo.   NYPL.

Second title: HYMNS AND SPIRITUAL SONGS, IN THREE BOOKS. I. COLLECTED FROM THE SCRIPTURES. II. COMPOSED ON DIVINE SUBJECTS. III. PREPARED FOR THE LORD'S SUPPER. BY ISAAC WATTS, D.D. CORRECTED, AND ACCOMMODATED TO THE USE OF THE CHURCH OF CHRIST IN AMERICA. [Six lines of quotations.]

Brookfield: Printed by E. Merriam & Co. Sold by them in Brookfield, by G. Merriam, Worcester, the Booksellers in Boston, Thomas & Thomas, Walpole, and S. Butler, Northampton. [1799.] pp. 245, (9).

35195　BIBLIA. Psalms, continued.
—— The Psalms of David, imitated in the language of the New Testament, and applied to the christian state and worship. By I. Watts, d. d.
　　Hartford: Printed by Hudson & Goodwin? 1799.

35196　—— The Psalms of David, imitated in the language of the New-Testament, and applied to the christian state and worship. Together with Hymns, and spiritual songs, in three books. I. Collected from the Scriptures. II. Composed on divine subjects. III. Prepared for the Lord's Supper. With indexes and tables complete. By Isaac Watts, d. d. [Six lines of quotations.]
　　Printed at Northampton, by William Butler. MDCCXCIX. pp. 233. sm. 4to.　　　　　　　　　　　AAS. BM. FL. JCB. IÓC. NYPL.
　　Title within ornamental border. Text in two columns.

35197　BIBLIA. New Testament.
The New Testament of our Lord and Saviour Jesus Christ, newly translated out of the original Greek; and with the former translations diligently compared and revised.
　　Philadelphia: Printed by Charles Cist, No. 104, North Second Street, near Race Street. M.DCC.XCIX. [unpaged.] 12mo.　　　　　NYPL.
　　An error in I. Timothy IV. 16, *thy* for *the* doctrine has been noted.

35198　—— — The New Testament of our Lord and Saviour Jesus Christ: translated out of the original Greek; and with the former translations diligently compared and revised. (Appointed to be read in churches and families.)
　　Philadelphia: Printed [by Charles Cist] for Isaac Pearson, No. 109, Market-Street. M,DCC,XCIX. [unpaged.] 12mo.　　　AAS.
　　Has the same error in I. Timothy, IV. 16.

35199　—— The New Testament of our Lord and Saviour Jesus Christ, translated out of the original Greek: and with the former translations diligently compared and revised by his majesty's special command. Appointed to be read in churches.
　　New-Haven: 1799.
　　This unidentified edition is referred to in the following advertisement: "To Printers. For sale. The whole of the New Testament, standing in forms, corrected & ready for press. Apply to Prescott & Sherman. New-Haven. January 1, 1799."

35200　BIBLIA. New Testament. Gospels.
The Four Gospels, translated from the Greek. With preliminary dissertations, and notes critical and explanatory. By George Campbell, d.d., f.r.s. Edinburgh; principal of Marischal College; Aberdeen. [One line of Greek.]
　　Philadelphia: Printed by A. Bartram. 1799. pp. viii, xvi, 488; 196, (16). 4to.　　　　　　　　　　　　　AAS.
　　Apparently Dobson's 1796 edition, with a new title-page.

35201　—— Die Geschichte von der Marterwoche, Auferstebung und Himmelfahrt unsers Herrn und Heilandes Jesu Christi. Uebersetzt in die Aruwackische Sprache, und erklärend umschrieben.
　　Philadelphia: Gedruckt bey Carl Cist, 1799. pp. 213. 8vo.　　NYPL.
　　Indian title: Wadaijahun Wuussada – goanti Wappussida – goanti baddia Jesus Christus Amonaigaddunnua, heikann akkarraddi giddunnia baddia, waijàlukkùduwa ùssondàgan, laggünnegunnua hitti ulluggu wara ku, wu-

BIBLIA. New Testament, continued.

WUSSÀ – WA LAGGUJUNNUA BADDIA AIJÙMUNIRU UKKUNNA MUNTU ADIAꞚ, DUHU GARDA: BIBITI GUNNU EVANGELISTINU, NARI HIDDIA MUTTU MATTHÆUS, MARCUS, LUCAS, JOHANNES, MUTTI AÏBUSSIA GUBA WAMUM ABBULLIDIN, NADDIKIN ULLUKKUDI RÈN, JESUS UMATTINNI HINNA GUBA JE.

Philadelphia mün 1799. Assabbaduhügan duhu gàrda hiddia muttu wijuakkkunna: Ein Tausend Sieben Hundert und Neun und Neunzig wijua tabbugoaua, Wadaijahün Wappussida goanti Jesus Christus elontin apuddi giddin benna guba dannuhu hidda.

A Translation of the History of the Passion, Resurrection and Ascension of the Saviour, into the language of the Arawaks, in Guiana, by the Rev. Johannes Jacob Gottlob Fischer, missionary.

35202   BIBLIA. New Testament. Matthew.
SPIEGEL FÜR ALLE MENSCHEN ODER NUTZANWENDUNGEN ÜBER DAS EVANGELIUM ST. MATTHÄI.

Philadelphia: Gedruckt bey Henrich Schweitzer. 1799. pp. 70. 8vo.

35203   BICKNELL, Alexander   –1796
THE ENGLISH HERMIT; OR, THE ADVENTURES OF PHILIP QUARLL. WHO WAS DISCOVERED BY MR. DORRINGTON, A BRISTOL MERCHANT, UPON AN UNINHABITED ISLAND: —WHERE HE HAD LIVED ABOVE FIFTY YEARS, WITHOUT ANY HUMAN ASSISTANCE, STILL CONTINUES TO RESIDE, AND WILL NOT COME AWAY. ADORNED WITH [twelve] CUTS. [Double line.]

Hartford [in vignette.] *Printed by John Babcock.* 1799. pp. [95,] (1). 24mo.
AAS.

Contains, Eight Riddles, in verse.

35204   BIGLOW, William   1773–1874
EDUCATION: A POEM, SPOKEN AT CAMBRIDGE, AT THE REQUEST OF THE PHI BETA KAPPA, JULY 18TH, 1799. BY WILLIAM BIGLOW. [Two lines from] SOLOMON.

Printed at Salem, by Joshua Cushing.— 1799. pp. [17.] 8vo.
AAS. BA. EI. HC. JCB. LOC. UTS.

35205   BINGHAM, Caleb   1757–1817
THE AMERICAN PRECEPTOR; BEING A NEW SELECTION OF LESSONS FOR READING AND SPEAKING. DESIGNED FOR THE USE OF SCHOOLS. BY CALEB BINGHAM, A.M. AUTHOR OF THE COLUMBIAN ORATOR, CHILD'S COMPANION, &C. "TRAIN UP A CHILD IN THE WAY HE SHOULD GO." THE SIXTH EDITION. PUBLISHED ACCORDING TO ACT OF CONGRESS.

Boston: Printed by Manning and Loring, for the Author; and sold at his Book-Store, No. 44, Cornhill, sold also by the Booksellers in general. 1799. pp. 228. 12mo.

35206   —— — THE AMERICAN PRECEPTOR; BEING A NEW SELECTION OF LESSONS FOR READING AND SPEAKING. DESIGNED FOR THE USE OF SCHOOLS. BY CALEB BINGHAM, A.M. AUTHOR OF THE COLUMBIAN ORATOR, CHILD'S COMPANION, &C. "TRAIN UP A CHILD IN THE WAY HE SHOULD GO." THE SEVENTH EDITION. PUBLISHED ACCORDING TO ACT OF CONGRESS.

Boston: Printed by Manning and Loring, for the Author; and sold at his Book-Store, No. 44, Cornhill, sold also by the Booksellers in general. 1799. pp. 228. 12mo.
AAS. JCB.

35207 BINGHAM, CALEB, continued.
—— —— THE AMERICAN PRECEPTOR; BEING A NEW SELECTION OF LESSONS FOR READING AND SPEAKING. DESIGNED FOR THE USE OF SCHOOLS. BY CALEB BINGHAM, A.M. AUTHOR OF THE YOUNG LADY'S ACCIDENCE, AND CHILD'S COMPANION. "TRAIN UP A CHILD IN THE WAY HE SHOULD GO.—" FIRST WALPOLE EDITION. PUBLISHED ACCORDING TO ACT OF CONGRESS.

Printed at Walpole, Newhampshire, by David Carlisle, for Thomas and Thomas, and sold wholesale and retail at the Walpole Bookstore. 1799. pp. 228. 12mo. AAS.

35208 —— THE COLUMBIAN ORATOR: CONTAINING A VARIETY OF ORIGINAL AND SELECTED PIECES; TOGETHER WITH RULES; CALCULATED TO IMPROVE YOUTH AND OTHERS IN THE ORNAMENTAL AND USEFUL ART OF ELOQUENCE. BY CALEB BINGHAM, A.M. AUTHOR OF THE AMERICAN PRECEPTOR, YOUNG LADY'S ACCIDENCE, &C. [Three lines from] ROLLIN. PUBLISHED ACCORDING TO ACT OF CONGRESS. SECOND EDITION.

Boston: Printed by Manning & Loring, for the Author, and sold at his Bookstore, No. 44, Cornhill, and by the Booksellers in general. May, 1799. pp. 300. 12mo. AAS. BM. JCB. LOC. NYPL.

Designed as a Second part of his "American Preceptor."

35209 —— THE YOUNG LADY'S ACCIDENCE: OR, A SHORT AND EASY INTRODUCTION TO ENGLISH GRAMMAR. DESIGNED, PRINCIPALLY, FOR THE USE OF YOUNG LEARNERS, MORE ESPECIALLY THOSE OF THE FAIR SEX, THOUGH PROPER FOR EITHER. BY CALEB BINGHAM, A.M. AUTHOR OF THE CHILD'S COMPANION, AMERICAN PRECEPTOR, AND COLUMBIAN ORATOR. [Two lines of verse.] THE ELEVENTH EDITION. PUBLISHED ACCORDING TO ACT OF CONGRESS.

Boston: Printed by Manning & Loring, for David West. 1799. pp. 60, 12mo. AAS. NYYL.

35210 BIRCH, THOMAS LEDLIE   –1808
A LETTER FROM AN IRISH EMIGRANT, TO HIS FRIEND IN THE UNITED STATES. GIVING AN ACCOUNT OF THE RISE AND PROGRESS OF THE COMMOTIONS IN IRELAND, OF THE UNITED IRISHMEN, AND ORANGE SOCIETIES, AND OF SEVERAL BATTLES AND MILITARY EXECUTIONS.

Philadelphia: Printed [at the Aurora Office] and sold at the Book-sellers. 1799. pp. (2), [56.] 8vo. LOC. NYHS.

35211 BLACKSTONE, Sir WILLIAM   1723–1780
COMMENTARIES ON THE LAWS OF ENGLAND. IN FOUR BOOKS. BY SIR WILLIAM BLACKSTONE, KNT. ONE OF THE LATE JUSTICES OF HIS BRITANNIC MAJESTY'S COURT OF COMMON PLEAS. IN FOUR VOLUMES. SECOND AMERICAN EDITION, CAREFULLY REPRINTED FROM THE LAST LONDON EDITION. CONTAINING THE LAST CORRECTIONS OF THE AUTHOR. THE ADDITIONS BY RICHARD BURN, LL.D. AND CONTINUED TO THE PRESENT TIME, BY JOHN WILLIAMS, ESQ. VOL. I. – BOOK I. [—VOL. IV.—BOOK IV.]

Printed at Boston, by I. Thomas and E. T. Andrews. Sold by them at Faust's Statue, No. 45, Newbury-Street; by I. Thomas, Worcester; by Thomas, Andrews and Penniman, Albany; by Thomas, Andrews, and Butler, Baltimore; and by E. S. Thomas, Charleston, S. C. 1799. 4 vols. pp. 8, 512, portrait; vi, 520, xviii; vi, 455, xxviii; vi, 442, vii, (52). 12mo. AAS.

The imprints of the third and fourth volumes vary from the first two as: "Boston: From J. Bumstead's Printing-Office, Union-Street. Sold to Mess. Thomas and Andrews, and for sale at their Bookstore, No. 45, Newbury-Street, Boston;" with no further alteration in paper, type, or format.

AUCTION VALUES

35212   BLAIR, Samuel   1741–1818
A Funeral discourse, delivered in the third Presbyterian church in the city of Philadelphia, on the 17th day of November, on occasion of the death of the Rev. Dr. John B. Smith, late pastor of said church, who departed this life, on the 22d of August, 1799. By the Rev. Dr. Samuel Blair. 14th chap. Rev. 13th verse. [One line.] Published at the desire of the congregation.
     Philadelphia: Printed by W. W. Woodward, No. 17, Chesnut Street. 1799. pp. (2), 38. 8vo.   AAS. BA. JCB. LOC. PU.

35213   BLAUVELT, Abraham
The American Almanac for the year of our Lord, 1800.
     New-Brunswick, N. J. Printed by Abraham Blauvelt. [1799.] pp. (36). 12mo.
                                                      LOC.

35214   —— The New-Jersey Pocket Almanac for the year 1800.
     New-Brunswick: Printed by Abraham Blauvelt. [1799.]

35215   —— A Sheet Almanac for the year 1800.
     New-Brunswick: Printed by Abraham Blauvelt, 1799. Broadside. fol.

35216   BORDLEY, John Beale   1727–1804
Essays and notes on husbandry and rural affairs. By J. B. Bordley. Still let me country culture scan: My farm's my home: "My brother, man: "And God is every where."
     Philadelphia: Printed by Budd and Bartram, for Thomas Dobson, at the Stone House, No. 41, South Second Street. 1799. [Copy-right secured according to law.] pp. viii, 591, 7, 4 plates, (8), errata. 8vo.   AAS. BM. NYPL.

35217   —— Hemp. [Signed, B. January, 1799.]
     [Philadelphia: Printed by Charles Cist, 1799.] pp. 7. 8vo.   LOC.

35218   BOSTON. Massachusetts.
Notification. The freeholders and other inhabitants of the town of Boston, . . . are hereby notified to meet at Faneuil-Hall, on Wednesday, the 25th day of September. . . . [Appended:] Abstract of the Will of the late Thomas Boylston, esq. Published by order of the selectmen for the information of the inhabitants.
     [Boston: September 19, 1799.] Broadside. nar. fol.   AAS.

35219   —— Schedule of the expenses of the town of Boston, from May 1, 1798, to May 1, 1799. Published conformably to the vote of the town, May 14, 1799.
     [Boston: 1799.] Broadside. fol.   HC. LOC. MHS.

35220   BOSTON. Massachusetts. Board of Health.
Board of Health, To their constituents. . . . Paul Revere, president.
     [Boston: March 30, 1799.] Broadside.   MHS.

35221   BOSTON. Massachusetts. Marine Insurance Company.
An Act, to incorporate the Boston Marine Insurance Company. [Cut of ship.]
     Printed by John Russell, at his Office, Quaker-Lane, Boston. [1799.] pp. 13. 8vo.   LOC. NYPL.

35222   BOSTON. Massachusetts. West Boston Society.
A Collection of Psalms and Hymns, for publick worship.
     Boston: Printed by Manning and Loring. 1799. pp. 254, (10). 12mo.
                                             AAS. BA. HC. LOC.
     The Psalms, selected principally from Tate and Brady. For the "Church in Tremont Street, Boston."

35223 BOSTWICK, NUEL
THE FIRST BOOK OF CHRONICLES. THE POLITICAL WAR IN BALLSTON. BY NUEL
BOSTWICK.
[Ballston Spa: Printed by Increase & William Child.] 1799. pp. 4. 8vo.
LOC. NYPL.

35224 BOWDOINHAM. MAINE. BAPTIST ASSOCIATION.
MINUTES OF THE BOWDOINHAM ASSOCIATION, HELD AT THE BAPTIST MEETING-HOUSE
IN LIVERMORE, AUGUST 28 AND 29, 1799.
Portland: Printed by B. Titcomb. 1799. pp. (12). 8vo.   AAS.

35225 BOWEN, DANIEL
THE COLUMBIAN MUSEUM, AT THE HEAD OF THE MALL, BOSTON. 100 [115] ELEGANT
PAINTINGS. . . .
[Boston: Printed by D. Bowen, at his Museum Office. 1799.] Broadside. MHS.

35226 —— — MUSEUM, HEAD OF THE MALL, BOSTON, IS OPENED EVERY DAY, AND TUESDAY,
THURSDAY AND FRIDAY EVENINGS. WITH MUSIC ON A LARGE CONCERT ORGAN. CON-
TAINING THE FOLLOWING WAX FIGURES . . . PAINTINGS, [123], CURIOSITIES, . . .
[Boston: Printed by D. Bowen, at his Museum Office. 1799.] Broadside. MHS.

35227 —— — [Cuts.] COLUMBIAN MUSEUM, NEAR THE MALL, BOSTON. THE COLUMBIAN
MUSEUM CONTAINS A VERY EXTENSIVE COLLECTION OF ARTIFICIAL AND NATURAL
CURIOSITIES. . . .
[Boston:] Printed at D. Bowen's Ornamental Printing Office, under the Colum-
bian Museum, where hand-bills, shop-bills, cards, blanks, &c. is done with neatness,
on reasonable terms. [1799.] Broadside. fol.   MHS.

35228 BRADLEY, CALEB   1751–1861
MR. BRADLEY'S THANKSGIVING SERMON, DELIVERED AT BETHEL, (MAINE), NOVEM-
BER 29, 1798.
Fryeburgh, District of Maine. Printed by Elijah Russell. 1798.

35229 BRADLEY, WILLIAM CZAR   1782–1867
WILLIAM C. BRADLEY'S ORATION TO THE CITIZENS OF WESTMINSTER, ON THE FOURTH
OF JULY, 1799, BEING THE ANNIVERSARY OF AMERICAN INDEPENDENCE. [Three
lines of Latin from] M. T. CICERO.
Walpole: Printed by David Carlisle, for Thomas and Thomas. 1799. pp. 16.
4to.   AAS. JCB.

35230 BRAILSFORD, EDWARD
AN EXPERIMENTAL DISSERTATION ON THE CHEMICAL AND MEDICAL PROPERTIES OF THE
NICOTIANA TABACUM OF LINNAEUS, COMMONLY KNOWN BY THE NAME OF TOBACCO.
BY EDWARD BRAILSFORD, OF CHARLESTON, SOUTH-CAROLINA, MEMBER OF THE
MEDICAL AND CHEMICAL SOCIETIES OF PHILADELPHIA.
Philadelphia: Printed by John Ormrod, No. 41, Chesnut Street. 1799. pp.
77. 8vo.   LOC.

35231 —— — AN EXPERIMENTAL DISSERTATION ON THE CHEMICAL AND MEDICAL PROPER-
TIES OF THE NICOTIANA TABACUM OF LINNÆUS, COMMONLY KNOWN BY THE NAME OF
TOBACCO. BY EDWARD BRAILSFORD, OF CHARLESTON, SOUTH-CAROLINA, MEMBER
OF THE MEDICAL AND CHEMICAL SOCIETIES OF PHILADELPHIA.
Philadelphia: Printed by John Ormrod, No. 41, Chesnut Street. 1799. pp.
78, folded colored plate. 8vo.   BM. LOC. NYPL. SGO.

35232   BREVITT, JOSEPH
THE HISTORY OF ANATOMY, FROM HIPPOCRATES, WHO LIVED FOUR HUNDRED YEARS
BEFORE CHRIST. TOGETHER WITH THE DISCOVERIES AND IMPROVEMENTS OF SUC-
CEEDING ANATOMISTS, IN THE REGULAR SUCCESSION OF TIMES IN WHICH THEY LIVED
AND FLOURISHED TO THE PRESENT PERIOD. BY J. BREVITT, M.D. & F.S.C.
> *Baltimore: Printed by Samuel Sower, in Fayette-Street.* M,DCC,XCXIX.
> pp. 29. 12mo.   AAS.

35233   BRIGGS, ISAAC   1775–1862
SERMON DELIVERED AT YORK, THE SABBATH AFTER HIS ORDINATION. BY REV. ISAAC
BRIGGS.
> *Portsmouth: Printed by Charles Peirce,* 1799.

35234   BRIGGS, ISAAC
THE GEORGIA AND SOUTH-CAROLINA ALMANAC, FOR THE YEAR OF OUR LORD 1800.
> *Augusta: Printed and sold by John E. Smith.* [1799.]

Contains, a Gardener's calender, by Robert Squibb.

35235   —— THE MARYLAND & VIRGINIA ALMANAC, FOR THE YEAR OF OUR LORD, 1800; BEING
ONE OF THE CENTENNIAL YEARS, AND THEREFORE NOT A LEAP YEAR; CONTAINING
BESIDES THE ASTRONOMICAL CALCULATIONS, &C. TABLE OF INTEREST AT SIX PER
CENT, TABLE OF THE WEIGHT AND VALUE OF COINS, TIMES OF HOLDING FEDERAL
COURTS AND STATE COURTS IN MARYLAND, LIST OF THE PRINCIPAL EXECUTIVE OF-
FICERS OF THE GOVERNMENT OF THE UNITED STATES, WITH THEIR RESPECTIVE
SALARIES. LIST OF THE MEMBERS OF CONGRESS. RATES OF POSTAGE OF LETTERS.
ALSO, A VARIETY OF INSTRUCTIVE & ENTERTAINING MATTER, IN PROSE AND VERSE.
> *George-Town: Printed and sold by Green, English & Co.* [1799.]

35236   —— PALLADIUM OF KNOWLEDGE: OR, THE CAROLINA AND GEORGIA ALMANAC, FOR
THE YEAR OF OUR LORD 1800, AND 24-25 OF AMERICAN INDEPENDENCE. [Sixteen
lines.] THE ASTRONOMICAL PART BY ISAAC BRIGGS.
> *Charleston: Printed and sold by W. P. Young, No. 43, Broad-Street: Sold
> also by Bailey, Waller & Bailey, No. 104, Broad-Street, and at Thomas C. Cox's
> Printing-Office, No. 137, Tradd-Street* [1799.] pp. (36), 25–36. 12mo.
>   CLS. JCB. LOC.

35237   —— THE VIRGINIA ALMANAC, FOR THE YEAR OF OUR LORD, 1800.
> *Richmond: Printed and sold by Merewether Jones.* [1799.]

35238   —— THE VIRGINIA ALMANAC OR EPHEMERIS, FOR THE YEAR OF OUR LORD 1800.
. . . THE ASTRONOMICAL PART, BY ISAAC BRIGGS.
> *Richmond: Printed and sold by Samuel Pleasants, jun.* [1799.]

35239   —— THE VIRGINIA AND NORTH-CAROLINA ALMANACK AND ANNUAL REGISTER FOR THE
YEAR 1800. . . . THE ASTRONOMICAL PART BY ISAAC BRIGGS; THE EDITORIAL
PART BY AMERICANUS URBAN.
> *Blandford: Printed and sold by G. Douglas.* [1799.] pp. xii, 94.   BM. LOC.

35240   —— THE VIRGINIA AND N. CAROLINA ALMANACK, FOR THE YEAR OF OUR LORD, 1800.
> *Norfolk: Printed and sold by Willetts & O'Cortnor.* [1799.]

35241   BROADGRIN, BILLY, pseudonym.
THE MERRY FELLOW'S POCKET COMPANION CONTAINING A LARGE NUMBER OF WITTY
ANECDOTES, BON MOTS, AND CURIOUS STORIES. [Cut.] BY BILLY BROADGRIN. YOU
THAT IN PLEASANT TALES DELIGHT, TO PASS THE TEDIOUS TIME AWAY, SOME COLD
AND STORMY WINTER'S NIGHT, PERUSE THIS SMALL BOOK, I PRAY; 'TWILL MAKE A
PRIEST OR DEACON LAUGH HIS FILL; AND CURE THE SPLEEN BEYOND THE DOCTOR'S
SKILL.
> *Boston— Printed by Tom Hazard— Price 9d.* [1798.] pp. 24. 8vo.   LOC.

35242   THE BROTHER'S GIFT; OR THE NAUGHTY GIRL REFORMED. PUBLISHED FOR THE ADVANTAGE OF THE RISING GENERATION.

      Printed at Worcester, Massachusetts, by Isaiah Thomas, jun. Sold wholesale and retail by him. 1799.

35243   BROWN, CHARLES BROCKDEN   1771–1810
      ARTHUR MERVYN; OR, MEMOIRS OF THE YEAR 1793. BY THE AUTHOR OF WIELAND; AND ORMOND, OR THE SECRET WITNESS. COPY-RIGHT SECURED. [VOL. I.]

      Philadelphia: Printed and published by H. Maxwell, No. 3, Lætitia Court— and sold by Messrs. T. Dobson, R. Campbell, H. and P. Rice, A. Dickins, and the principal Booksellers in the neighbouring States. 1799. pp. (2), 224. 12mo.
                                        AAS. BA. HC. JCB. LOC. NYPL.

      224th Pennsylvania District Copyright, issued to Charles B. Brown, as Author, 25 February, 1799.

      A graphic portrayal of the epidemic of yellow fever in Philadelphia, in 1793. The second volume was printed in New York, in 1800. Publication was first begun in the second volume of "The Weekly Magazine."

35244   —— EDGAR HUNTLY; OR, MEMOIRS OF A SLEEP-WALKER. BY THE AUTHOR OF ARTHUR MERVYN, WIELAND,—-ORMOND, &c. VOL. I. [— III.]

      Philadelphia: Printed by H. Maxwell, No. 3 Letitia Court, and sold by Thomas Dobson, Asbury Dickins, and the principal booksellers. 1799. 3 vols. pp. 250; 252; 193; 48. 12mo.   AAS. JCB. LOC. NYPL.

      "Copy-right secured."

35245   —— ORMOND; OR THE SECRET WITNESS. BY THE AUTHOR OF WIELAND; OR THE TRANSFORMATION.

      New-York: Printed by G. Forman, for H. Caritat. 1799.—pp. 338. 12mo.
      75th New York District Copyright, issued to Hocquet Caritat, as Proprietor, 16 January, 1799.   AAS.

35246   —— — ORMOND OU LE TÉMOIN SECRET. PAR L'AUTEUR DE WIELAND.

      New-York: Imprimés pour le compte de H. Caritat, libraire, dans Broad-Way, No. 153. 1799. 12mo. Prix une gourde relié.

      The French version is probably the work of John Davis, who boasted equal facility in adapting both languages to each other.

35247   —— WIELAND, OU LA TRANSFORMATION, CONTE AMÉRICAIN. PAR UN AMÉRICAIN.

      New-York: Imprimés pour le compte de H. Caritat, libraire, dans Broad-Way, No. 153. 1799. 12mo. Une gourde relié.

      The French version is probably the work of John Davis.

35248   BROWN, CLARK   1772–1817
      THE CHARACTER OF OUR LORD AND SAVIOUR JESUS CHRIST, ILLUSTRATED IN TWO DISCOURSES: IN WHICH IS SHOWN IN WHAT MANNER ALL THOSE DESCRIPTIVE AND SUBLIME REPRESENTATIONS OF HIM, IN THE SACRED VOLUME, ARE TO BE CONSIDERED, IN CONSISTENCY WITH THE ABSOLUTE UNITY OF THE DEITY; AND WITH HIS BEING THE MIGHTY SAVIOUR, THE LOGOS OF THE MOST DISTINGUISHED REPRESENTATIONS AND COMMUNICATIONS FROM THE FATHER ALMIGHTY AND WITH HIS DEPENDENCE UPON HIM FOR ALL HIS POWER AND AUTHORITY. BY CLARK BROWN, A. M. MINISTER OF THE GOSPEL CONGREGATIONAL CHURCH AND SOCIETY IN BRIMFIELD, MASSACHUSETTS. [Three lines from] CHRIST.

      Stonington-Port, (Connecticut). Printed by Samuel Trumbull. 1799. pp. 63, (1). 8vo.   AAS. BA. JCB. LOC. MHS.

35249 BROWN, CLARK, continued.
—— CHRISTIAN CHARITY, THE PERFECTION OF EVERY MORAL SYSTEM, ILLUSTRATED IN A SERMON, DELIVERED AT NORTHFIELD, MASSACHUSETTS, BEFORE THE OFFICERS AND BRETHREN OF THE HARMONY LODGE OF FREE AND ACCEPTED MASONS IN THAT TOWN, JOINED BY THE REPUBLICAN LODGE, FROM GREENFIELD: ON THE FESTIVAL OF ST. JOHN, THE BAPTIST, JUNE 24TH, 1799.—A. L. 5799. BY CLARK BROWN, A. M. MINISTER OF THE CHRISTIAN CONGREGATIONAL CHURCH AND SOCIETY IN BRIMFIELD.
Printed at Greenfield, Massachusetts by Thomas Dickman.— 1799. pp. 31. 8vo.
AAS. NYHS.

35250 BROWN, GEORGE
PROVIDENCE, APRIL 13, SIR, GEORGE BROWN IS A CANDIDATE . . .
[Providence: Printed by John Carter, jun. 1799.] Broadside.   RIHS.

35251 BROWN, WILLIAM   1764–1803
AN ORATION, SPOKEN AT HARTFORD, IN THE STATE OF CONNECTICUT, ON THE ANNIVERSARY OF AMERICAN INDEPENDENCE, JULY 4TH, A. D. 1799. BY WILLIAM BROWN. [Ornament.]
Hartford: Printed by Hudson and Goodwin. 1799. pp. 23. 8vo.
AAS. BM. HC. JCB. NYHS. NYPL. UTS. YC.

35252 BUCHAN, WILLIAM   1729–1805
DOMESTIC MEDICINE: OR, A TREATISE ON THE PREVENTION AND CURE OF DISEASES, BY REGIMEN AND SIMPLE MEDICINES: WITH AN APPENDIX, CONTAINING A DISPENSATORY FOR THE USE OF PRIVATE PRACTITIONERS. BY WIILLIAM BUCHAN, M.D. FELLOW OF THE ROYAL COLLEGE OF PHYSICIANS, EDINBURGH. ADAPTED TO THE CLIMATE AND DISEASES OF AMERICA, BY ISAAC CATHRALL.
Philadelphia: Printed by Richard Folwell. 1799. pp. 512. 8vo.   AAS.
Copy-right secured according to law.

35253 BUCKMINSTER, JOSEPH   1751–1812
A SERMON [ON THE DUTY OF MINISTERS], PREACHED AT CONCORD, BEFORE THE ECCLESIASTICAL CONVENTION OF NEW-HAMPSHIRE, JUNE 5, 1799. BY JOSEPH BUCKMINSTER, A. M. PASTOR OF THE FIRST CHURCH IN PORTSMOUTH. [One line from] ISAIAH. PUBLISHED BY REQUEST OF THE CONVENTION.
Concord: Printed by George Hough. July — 1799. pp. [31.] 8vo.
AAS. CHS. JCB. LOC. NYHS. NYPL.

35254 BURGES, TRISTAM   1770–1853
THE ART OF EXCELLING, AN ORATION: DELIVERED IN THE BENEVOLENT CONGREGATIONAL MEETING-HOUSE AT PROVIDENCE, BEFORE THE SOCIETY OF THE FEDERAL ADELPHI ON THEIR ANNIVERSARY, SEPTEMBER 5, A. D. 1799. BY TRISTAM BURGES, A. M.
Providence: Printed by John Carter, jun. at the New Printing-Office, Market-Street. 1799. pp. 22. 8vo.   AAS. BA. JCB. NYPL. RIHS.

35255 —— WAR, NECESSARY, JUST AND BENEFICIAL: AN ORATION, PRONOUNCED ON COMMENCEMENT AT RHODE-ISLAND COLLEGE, SEPTEMBER 4TH, A. D. 1799. BY TRISTAM BURGES, A CANDIDATE FOR THE SECOND DEGREE.
Providence: Printed by B. Wheeler. 1799. pp. 8. 8vo.   AAS. JCB. RIHS.

35256 BURK, JOHN DALY   1775–1808
HISTORY OF THE LATE WAR IN IRELAND, WITH AN ACCOUNT OF THE UNITED IRISH ASSOCIATION FROM THE FIRST MEETING AT BELFAST, TO THE LANDING OF THE FRENCH AT KILALA. BY JOHN BURK. WITH AN APPENDIX, CONTAINING A WELL-AUTHENTICATED SERIES OF BRITISH CRUELTIES, VARIOUS DETACHED PAPERS, ADDRESSES, NOTES, &C. &C. &C. [Fourteen lines of quotations.]
Philadelphia: Printed by Francis and Robert Bailey, at Yorick's Head, No. 116, High street. 1799. pp. 140, (1), 40. 8vo.   AAS. JCB. LOC. MHS. NYPL.

35257   BURNAP, JACOB   1748–1821
A SERMON DELIVERED AT MERRIMAC, ON THE DAY OF THE NATIONAL FAST, APRIL 25, 1799. BY JACOB BURNAP, A. M. PASTOR OF THE CHURCH IN MERRIMAC. [Three lines from] REV. II. 20.
From Preston's Printing-Office, Amherst, July, 1799. pp. 15. 8vo. AAS. HC.

35258   BURNET, GEORGE WHITEFIELD   –1800
AN ORATION, DELIVERED TO THE MASONIC SOCIETY IN CINCINNATI, ON THE ANNIVERSARY OF ST. JOHN, THE EVANGELIST. BY GEORGE W. BURNET, ESQUIRE. DECEMBER 27TH, A. L. 5798.
Printed by Joseph Carpenter, Cincinnati. 1799. pp. 15. 8vo. LOC.

35259   BURNET, JAMES   1779–1806
AN ORATION, DELIVERED ON THE FOURTH OF JULY, 1799. AT THE MEETING-HOUSE, IN WESTON: IN COMMEMORATION OF THE INDEPENDENCE OF AMERICA. BY JAMES BURNET, A. B.
Newfield: Printed by Lazarus Beach. [1799.] pp. 22, (1). 8vo. AAS.

35260   BURROUGHS, JOSIAH
THE ASSISTANT, OR A TREATISE ON THE CURRENCY OF THE UNITED STATES. CONTAINING ARITHMETICAL RULES TO OBTAIN THE PRICES OF ALL KINDS OF COMMODITIES IN AN EASY AND SHORT WAY IN THE FEDERAL CURRENCY. ALSO A METHOD OF REDUCING THE CURRENCIES OF A NUMBER OF STATES TO THE FEDERAL, AND THE FEDERAL TO THOSE OF THE STATES. TOGETHER WITH AN EASY METHOD OF CASTING INTEREST; WITH MANY USEFUL TABLES.
Newburyport: Printed and sold by Angier March, 1799.
164th Massachusetts District Copyright, issued to Josiah Burroughs, as Author, 8 March, 1799.

35261   BURTON, JOHN   1746–1806
LECTURES ON FEMALE EDUCATION AND MANNERS. BY J. BURTON. THE FIFTH AMERICAN EDITION.
Elizabeth-Town: Printed by S. Kollock for Cornelius Davis, No. 94, Water-Street, New-York. 1799. pp. 280, (4). 12mo. AAS. BA. JCB. LOC.

35262   CALDWELL, CHARLES   1772–1853
AN EULOGIUM TO THE MEMORY OF DR. SAMUEL COOPER, DELIVERED, BY APPOINTMENT, BEFORE THE PHILADELPHIA MEDICAL SOCIETY, ON THE FOURTH DAY OF MARCH, 1799. BY CHARLES CALDWELL, A. M. M. D. A MEMBER OF THE SOCIETY.
Philadelphia: Printed by Henry Tuckniss, for Mathew Carey, No. 118, Market-Street. 1799. pp. (48). 8vo. AAS. JCB. LOC. SGO.

35263   —— A SEMI-ANNUAL ORATION, ON THE ORIGIN OF PESTILENTIAL DISEASES, DELIVERED BEFORE THE ACADEMY OF MEDICINE OF PHILADELPHIA, ON THE 17TH DAY OF DECEMBER, 1798. BY CHARLES CALDWELL, A. M. M. D. SENIOR VICE-PRESIDENT OF THE ACADEMY.
Philadelphia: Printed by Thomas and Samuel F. Bradford, No. 8, South Front-Street. 1799. pp. 59. 8vo. AAS. BM. JCB. LOC. NYPL. SGO.
The copy in the British Museum is printed on blue tinted paper.

35264   CAMP, SAMUEL   1744–1813
THANKSGIVING AND PRAISE DUE TO GOD, FOR HIS WISDOM, POWER AND GOODNESS, DISPLAYED IN THE LATE AND PRESENT DISPENSATIONS OF HIS PROVIDENCE. A DISCOURSE DELIVERED AT RIDGBURY, ON THE DAY OF PUBLIC THANKSGIVING: NOVEMBER 29, 1798. BY SAMUEL CAMP, A. M. PASTOR OF THE CHURCH IN RIDGBURY. PUBLISHED BY DESIRE.
Printed in Danbury, by Douglas & Nichols. M,DCC,XCIX. pp. [23.] 8vo.
AAS. CHS. CLA. LOC. NYPL.

35265   CAMPBELL, Donald   1751–1804
A Narrative of the extraordinary adventures, and sufferings by shipwreck
& imprisonment, of Donald Campbell, esq. of Barbreck: with the singular
humours of his Tartar guide, Hassan Artaz; comprising the occurrences
of four years and five days, in an overland journey to India. In a series
of letters to his son. [Three lines from] Young. Second American edition.

*New-York: Printed by John Tiebout, No. 358, Pearl-Street, for Thomas B.
Jansen. 1799. pp. 417, frontispiece. 12mo.*   AAS. NYPL.

The supposed route intended by Napoleon Buonaparte for his invasion
of India.

35266   CAMPBELL, Samuel
Something new, in eight letters to Joseph Meeker, Elizabeth-Town. Occa-
sioned by reading Miscellaneous essays, by Joseph Lyon, sen. of Lyon's
Farms. By Samuel Campbell, of Connecticut-Farms, New Jersey.

[Elizabeth-Town:] Printed [by Shepard Kollock] for the Author. [1799.]
pp. 60. 12mo.   BU. LOC.

35267   CAMPBELL, Samuel
Samuel Campbell's Sale Catalogue of books, for 1798 & 1799. Comprehending, above twenty thousand volumes, in arts, sciences, and miscellaneous
literature; forming a general assortment of the principal authors, ancient and modern. Among which will be found, many scarce and valuable
books: viz. divinity, physic, surgery, midwifery, philosophy, novels, architecture, voyages, travels, poetry, dramatic works, geography, miscellanies,
history, biography, arts, sciences, law, dictionaries and grammars for
English, Latin, Greek and French classes, &c. The books in general are
good editions and well bound, except otherwise expressed in the Catalogue; and will be sold for cash, at the most reasonable prices. Country
booksellers, merchants, traders and teachers, will particularly find it
their interest in applying for books or stationary, at Samuel Campbell's
Book & Stationary Store, No. 124, Pearl-Street, where Catalogues will
be delivered gratis, to gentlemen who please to call or send for them.
N. B. Orders from the country executed with the utmost care and attention; and a large discount made to those who purchase quantities.

[New-York: Printed for Samuel Campbell, 1799.] pp. (2), 53, (1). 8vo. AAS.

35268   CAREY, James
The Collected wisdom of ages, the most stupendous fabric of human inven-
tion, the English Constitution. A true copy from the original, in the
possession of William Pitt, & Co. By Timothy Telltruth. [Three lines from]
J. Adams.

*Philadelphia: Printed by James Carey, No. 7, South Front-Street. 1799.
[Copy right secured [sic.] pp. (47). 8vo.*   AAS. HSP. JCB. LOC. MHS. NYPL.

35269   —— A View of the New-England Illuminati: who are indefatigably engaged
in destroying the religion and government of the United States; under a
feigned regard for their safety—and under an impious abuse of true
religion.

*Philadelphia: Printed by James Carey, No. 16, Chesnut-Street. 1799. [Copy-
Right secured.] pp. (20). 8vo.*   AAS. BA. BM. JCB. LOC. NYPL.

238th Pennsylvania District Copyright, issued to James Carey, as Proprietor, 1 November, 1799.

35270   CAREY, James, continued.
—— — A View of the New-England Illuminati: who are indefatigably
engaged in destroying the religion and government of the United States;
under a feigned regard for their safety—and under an impious abuse of
true religion. The second edition.
*Philadelphia: Printed by James Carey, No. 16, Chesnut-street. 1799. [Copy-
right secured.]* pp. (20). 8vo.   AAS. HC. HSP. JCB. LOC. MHS.

35271   CAREY, Mathew   1760–1839
The Columbian reading book or historical preceptor: a collection of authentic histories, anecdotes, characters, &c. &c. Calculated to incite in young
minds a love of vertue from its intrinsic beauty and a hatred of vice from
its disgusting deformity.
Philadelphia: Printed for Mathew Carey. 1799.

240th Pennsylvania District Copyright, issued to Mathew Carey, as Author, 11 December, 1799.

35272   —— A Plumb pudding for the humane, chaste, valiant, enlightened Peter
Porcupine. By his obliged friend, Mathew Carey. [Five lines of quotations.
Vignette.]
*Philadelphia: Printed for the Author. [Copy right secured according to an
Act of Congress.]* [1799.] pp. (48). 8vo.   AAS. BA. BM. BU. JCB. LOC. NYHS. NYPL.

Preface dated January 16, 1799. 219th Pennsylvania District Copyright,
issued to Mathew Carey, as Author, 19 January, 1799.

35273   —— — A Plumb pudding for the humane, chaste, valiant, enlightened
Peter Porcupine. By his obliged friend, Mathew Carey. The second edition. [Five lines of quotations. Vignette.]
*Philadelphia: Printed for the Author. [Copy right secured according to Act
of Congress.]* [1799.] pp. (48), [8.] 8vo.   AAS. BM. CLS. JCB. LOC.

35274   —— *Caption title:* Philadelphia, Feb. 5, 1799. To the public. [An account of
his controversy with John Ward Fenno and William Cobbett.] Mathew Carey.
[Philadelphia: Printed for Mathew Carey. 1799.] pp. 8. 8vo.   AAS. LOC. NYPL.
Also appended to the second edition of his "Plumb pudding."

35275   —— The Porcupiniad. A hudibrastic poem. In four cantos. Addressed to
William Cobbett. By Mathew Carey. Canto I. [Six lines from] Porcupine's
Gazette.
Philadelphia: Printed for and sold by the Author. March 2, 1799. pp. 52,
frontispiece. 8vo.   AAS. BA. BU. JCB. LOC. NYPL.

225th Pennsylvania District Copyright, issued to Mathew Carey, as
Author, 1 March, 1799.

35276   —— — The Porcupiniad: a hudibrastic poem. In three cantos. Addressed
to William Cobbett. By Mathew Carey. Canto II. & III. [Six lines from]
Porcupine's Gazette.
Philadelphia: Printed for and sold by the Author. April 15, 1799. pp. 44,
frontispiece. 8vo.   AAS. BA. BU. JCB. LOC. MHS. NYPL.

35277   —— — The Porcupiniad: a hudibrastic poem. In three cantos. Addressed
to William Cobbett. By Mathew Carey. Canto I. Second edition improved.
[Six lines from] Porcupine's Gazette.
*Philadelphia: Printed for and sold by the Author. April 22, M,DCC,XCIX.
(Copy-right secured according to Act of Congress.)* pp. 35, frontispiece. 8vo.
                                                      AAS. BU.

35278   CARITAT, HOCQUET
CATALOGUE DES LIVRES FRANCAIS QUI SE TROUVENT CHEZ H. CARITAT, LIBRAIRE ET
BIBLIOTHÉCAIRE DANS BROAD-WAY, No. 157 A NEW-YORK. 1799.
[New-York: Imprimé par M. L. & W. A. Davis, 1799.] pp. [29.] 8vo.
AAS. NYPL.

35279   —— THE FEAST OF REASON AND THE FLOW OF SOUL. A NEW * EXPLANATORY CATA-
LOGUE OF H. CARITAT'S GENERAL & INCREASING CIRCULATING LIBRARY. INTENDED
ALSO TO ANSWER THE PURPOSE OF A SALE CATALOGUE, RESPECTING THOSE BOOKS
MARKED WITH A STAR (*) WHICH H. CARITAT HAS AN ASSORTMENT OF FOR SALE, IN
HIS BOOK-STORE, No. 153, BROAD-WAY. N.B. BY THE WORD * *explanatory*, IS TO
BE UNDERSTOOD, BOTH THE ARRANGEMENT OF THE BOOKS, THE INFORMATION OF
THEIR CHARACTERS, AND THE NAMES OF THEIR AUTHORS: THE TWO LAST ARE EITHER
TAKEN FROM THE REVIEWERS, OR FROM THE WORKS THEMSELVES; AND THE WHOLE
HAS BEEN DONE, IN ORDER TO PREPARE THE READER FOR AN EASY CHOICE OF HIS
BOOKS, AND A SUITABLE DISPOSITION TO RELISH AND BE PLEASED WITH THEM.
*** HOURS OF ATTENDANCE, FROM HALF AFTER EIGHT O'CLOCK IN THE MORNING
TILL ONE, AND FROM THREE O'CLOCK IN THE AFTERNOON TILL EIGHT IN THE EVEN-
ING.
New-York: Printed by M. L. & W. A. Davis. 1799. pp. 215, (1). 12mo.
AAS. NYPL.

82d New York District Copyright, issued to Hocquet Caritat, as Author,
30 August, 1799.

In the closing years of the eighteenth century, the book trade annals of
the United States were enriched by three Frenchmen who left an indel-
lible impression upon its high character: Joseph de Nancrede, at Boston; Moreau de St. Méry, at Philadelphia; and Hocquet Caritat, at New
York, elevated its standard by their scholarship and enterprising literary
industry, until the blundering diplomacy of Talleyrand disrupted our
peaceful relations with France, and ended their hopes of permanent
settlement amongst us.

In the above, the mantle of Librarian is worthily worn by this cultured
bookseller. No better selection of contemporary English and French
literature was to be found anywhere in the United States than what he
placed at the use and service of the citizens of New York in Caritat's
Circulating Library. For six dollars a year; three and a half for six
months; two a quarter year; or seventy-five cents monthly, from two to
six volumes might be drawn out; or for three cents a day, on leaving
the value of the book, the use of any volume was obtainable.

"I would place the bust of Caritat," says John Davis, "among those of
the Sosii of Horace and the Trypho of Quintillian. He was my only friend
at New York when the energies of my mind were depressed by the chilling
prospect of poverty. His talents were not meanly cultivated by letters:
he could tell a good book from a bad one, which few modern librarians
can do. But *place aux dames* was his maxim, and all the ladies of New
York declared that the library of Mr. Caritat was charming. Its shelves
could scarsely sustain the weight of 'Female frailty' the 'Posthumous
Daughter' and the 'Cavern of Woe'—(all imaginary titles): they required
the aid of the carpenter to support the burden of the 'Cottage-on-the
Moor' (by Elizabeth Helme), 'The House of Tyrnian' (by George Walker,
bookseller), and the 'Castles of Athlin and Dunbayne' (by Ann Radcliffe);
or they groaned under the multiplied editions of the 'Devil in love' (unknown), 'More Ghosts' (by Mrs. F. C. Patrick), and 'Rinaldo Rinaldini'
(from the German of Vulpius, by John Walker). Novels were called for
by the young and old; from the tender virgin of thirteen, whose little
heart went pit-a-pat at the approach of a beaux, to the experienced ma-
tron of three score, who could not read without spectacles."

35280 THE CAROLINA GAZETTE. VOL. II. No. 1. THURSDAY, JANUARY 3, [— No. 52.
THURSDAY, DECEMBER 26, 1799.]
Charleston: Published by Freneau and Paine. 1799. fol.   MdHS.

35281 CARPENTER, THOMAS
THE TRIALS OF JOHN FRIES AND OTHERS ON INDICTMENTS FOR TREASON: TOGETHER
WITH A BRIEF REPORT OF THE TRIALS OF SEVERAL OTHER PERSONS FOR INSUR-
RECTION, IN THE COUNTIES OF BUCKS, NORTHAMPTON AND MONTGOMERY, IN THE
CIRCUIT COURT OF THE UNITED STATES, BEFORE THE HON: JAMES IREDELL AND
RICHARD PETERS ESQUIRES, BEGUN AT THE CITY OF PHILADELPHIA, APRIL 10,
1799. TAKEN IN SHORT HAND BY THOMAS CARPENTER.
Philadelphia: 1799.
231st Pennsylvania District Copyright, issued to Thomas Carpenter, as
Proprietor, 7 May, 1799.

35282 —— — THE TRIAL OF JOHN FRIES ON AN INDICTMENT FOR TREASON; TOGETHER
WITH A BRIEF REPORT OF THE TRIALS OF SEVERAL OTHER PERSONS FOR INSUR-
RECTION, IN THE COUNTIES OF BUCKS, NORTHAMPTON AND MONTGOMERY, IN THE
CIRCUIT COURT OF THE UNITED STATES, BEFORE THE HON: JAMES IREDELL AND
RICHARD PETERS, ESQUIRES. BEGUN AT THE CITY OF PHILADELPHIA, APRIL 30.
1799. TAKEN IN SHORT HAND BY THOMAS CARPENTER.
Philadelphia: Printed and sold by William W. Woodward. 1799.
233d Pennsylvania District Copyright, issued to William W. Wood-
ward, as Proprietor, 20 May, 1799.

35283 CARR, BENJAMIN   1769–1831
THREE BALLADS, VIZ. THE NEW SOMEBODY. MARY WILL SMILE. AND POOR RICHARD.
COMPOSED BY B. CARR.
Philadelphia: 1799.
232d Pennsylvania District Copyright, issued to Benjamin Carr, as Au-
thor, 17 May, 1799.

35284 CARROLL, JOHN   1735–1815
A PASTORAL LETTER FROM THE RIGHT REV. DR. JOHN CARROLL . . . BISHOP OF
BALTIMORE, TO . . . THE CONGREGATION OF TRINITY CHURCH, PHILADELPHIA.
[Baltimore:] Printed by J. Hayes. [1799.] pp. 8. 4to.

35285 THE CASTINE JOURNAL, AND UNIVERSAL ADVERTISER. NO. I. OF VOL. I. WEDNES-
DAY, JANUARY 3 [*sic* 2.] [— NO. 52 OF VOL. I. FRIDAY, DECEMBER 27, 1799.]
*Castine [Mouth Penobscot River, District of Maine] Printed by David J.
Waters.* 1799. fol.
Established, as a weekly, by David J. Waters, and continued by him to
the issue for October 30, 1801, when it was discontinued for want of
support. With the issue for May 1, 1799, the title was changed to *The
Castine Journal and the Eastern Advertiser.* In April, 1802, David J.
Waters & Co. established, in continuation, and with consecutive num-
bering, *The Columbian Informer; and the Eastern Advertiser.*

35286 CATE, JAMES
DEVASTATION BY THE "KING OF TERROURS," IN THE FAMILY OF MR. JEREMIAH SAN-
BORN, &C. OF SANBORNTON, IN THE YEAR 1798, &C. BY JAMES CATE. [Six lines.
Cuts of three coffins. Forty-three four-line verses.] TO MR. JEREMIAH SANBORN.
FROM YOUR AFFECTIONATE FRIEND, JAMES CATE. FEBRUARY 12, 1799. [Colophon:]
[Exeter:] Printed by J[ohn] L[amson] for the Author. 1799. Broadside. fol.
Reprinted in New Haven, in an edition of two hundred and ten copies
in 1909.

35287   CATLIN, Jacob   1758–1826
THE GENTILES INHERITANCE OF THE BLESSING OF ABRAHAM, THROUGH JESUS CHRIST: A SERMON, RESPECTING INFANT BAPTISM. WITH AN APPENDIX, CONFUTING THE MODE OF BAPTISM BY IMMERSION. BY JACOB CATLIN, M. A. MINISTER OF THE GOSPEL IN NEW-MARLBOROUGH. WITH THE ADDITION OF EXTRACTS FROM THE MANUSCRIPTS OF AN ANONYMOUS WRITER ON THE INSTITUTION AND MODE OF CHRISTIAN BAPTISM.
       Canandaigua: Printed by Lucius Carey. 1799. pp. 44. 12mo.   BA. UTS.

35288   —— — THE GENTILES INHERITANCE OF THE BLESSING OF ABRAHAM, THROUGH JESUS CHRIST; ILLUSTRATED IN A SERMON, DELIVERED AT NEW-MARLBOROUGH, IN THE YEAR OF OUR LORD, 1798. BY JACOB CATLIN, A. M.
       Hartford: Printed by Hudson and Goodwin. 1799. pp. 36. 12mo.
                                      AAS. JCB. UTS. YC.

       Second title: A SERMON, DELIVERED AT THE FUNERAL OF THE REVEREND JOHN STEVENS, PASTOR OF THE SECOND CHURCH IN NEW-MARLBOROUGH, WHO DEPARTED THIS LIFE, JANUARY 6TH, 1799. pp. 27–36.

35289   THE CENTINEL [cut] OF FREEDOM. [Motto.] VOL. III. No. 14. TOTAL NUMB. 118. TUESDAY, JANUARY 1, [— VOL. IV. No. 14. TOTAL NUMB. 170. TUESDAY, DECEMBER 31, 1799.]
       Newark, (New-Jersey): Aaron Pennington & Daniel Dodge, Publishers. 1799. fol.
       On October 1st, the Centinel passed into the possession of Jabez Parkhurst, and Samuel Pennington, a brother of the former editor; and, in December, Parkhurst sold his interest to Stephen Gould. The motto, from Cowper, reads: "This folio of four pages, happy work! What is it but a map of busy life, Its fluctuations, and its vast concerns?"

35290   THE CENTINEL OF LIBERTY, AND GEORGE-TOWN AND WASHINGTON ADVERTISER. [Motto.] No. 63. VOL. III. TUESDAY, JANUARY 1, [— No. 63. VOL. IV. TUESDAY, DECEMBER 31, 1799.]
       From the Press of Green, English & Co. George-Town (Potomak) every Tuesday and Friday, at four dollars per annum. 1799. fol.

35291   CHALWILL, WILLIAM G.
A DISSERTATION ON THE SOURCES OF MALIGNANT BILIOUS OR YELLOW FEVER, AND MEANS OF PREVENTING IT; SUBMITTED TO THE EXAMINATION OF THE REV. JOHN EWING, S. T. P. PROVOST; THE TRUSTEES AND MEDICAL FACULTY, OF THE UNIVERSITY OF PENNSYLVANIA, ON THE SIXTH DAY OF JUNE, 1799, FOR THE DEGREE OF DOCTOR OF MEDICINE. BY WILLIAM G. CHALWILL, OF TORTOLA, MEMBER OF THE PHILADELPHIA MEDICAL AND CHEMICAL SOCIETIES.
       Philadelphia: Printed by Way & Groff, No. 48, North Third-Street. 1799. pp. 31. 8vo.   AAS. LCP. LOC. SGO.

35292   CHAMBERSBURG. PENNSYLVANIA. CARPENTERS.
A BILL OF RATES FOR CARPENTER AND HOUSE JOINER WORK SETTLED AND AGREED ON, BY THE SUBSCRIBERS, CHAMBERSBURG, APRIL 13, 1790. TO WHICH IS AFFIXED AN APPENDIX BY OTHER SUBSCRIBERS. CHAMBERSBURG, DECEMBER, 1799.
       Chambersburg: Printed by Robert Harper. 1799. pp. 14. 16mo.

35293   CHARLESTON. SOUTH CAROLINA. ARTILLERY.
RULES OF THE CHARLESTON ANCIENT BATTALION OF ARTILLERY. CONSIDERED AND APPROVED BY DANIEL STEPHENS, MAJOR COMMANDANT.
       Charleston: [1799.]

35294   CHARLESTON. SOUTH CAROLINA. BAPTIST ASSOCIATION.
MINUTES OF THE CHARLESTON BAPTIST ASSOCIATION, CONGAREE, 1799.
       Charleston: 1799. pp. 12. 12mo.

35295 CHAUDRON, SIMON   –1846
    Caption title: ODE SUR LA CONQUÊTE DE L'ITALIE. . . . PAR LE CITOYEN CHAUD-
    RON. 6 DÉCEM. 1796. ODE SUR L'ASSASSINAT DES DÉPUTÉS FRANÇAIS, À RASTADT.
    . . . 27 OCTOBRE, 1799.

      [*Philadelphia: Printed by John Ormrod ? 1799.*] pp. 7. 8vo.   NYPL.

35296 CHEAP REPOSITORY TRACTS.
    THE ENTERTAINING, MORAL, AND RELIGIOUS REPOSITORY; CONTAINING UPWARDS OF
    THREE SCORE SEPARATE PERFORMANCES, ALL OF WHICH ARE WRITTEN IN A SIMPLE,
    YET PLEASING STILE, AND ARE EMINENTLY CALCULATED FOR THE AMUSEMENT AND
    INSTRUCTION OF THE YOUTH OF BOTH SEXES. PUBLISHED BY A SOCIETY IN GREAT
    BRITAIN, INSTITUTED FOR THE BENEFICENT PURPOSE OF AIDING THE INTENTION
    OF HIS MAJESTY, AS EXPRESSED IN HIS ROYAL PROCLAMATION FOR THE SUPPRESSION
    OF VICE AND IMMORALITY. IN TWO VOLUMES. VOL. I.–[II.]

      Elizabeth-Town: Printed by Shepard Kollock for Cornelius Davis, No. 94,
    Water-Street, New-York. 1798. 2 vols. pp. —; 324. 12mo.   AAS.

35297 —— THE ENTERTAINING, MORAL, AND RELIGIOUS REPOSITORY; CONTAINING, UPWARDS
    OF THREE SCORE SEPARATE PERFORMANCES, ALL OF WHICH ARE WRITTEN IN A
    SIMPLE YET PLEASING STILE, AND ARE EMINENTLY CALCULATED FOR THE AMUSE-
    MENT AND INSTRUCTION OF THE YOUTH OF BOTH SEXES. PUBLISHED BY A SOCIETY
    IN GREAT BRITAIN, INSTITUTED FOR THE BENEFICENT PURPOSE OF AIDING THE
    INTENTION OF HIS MAJESTY, AS EXPRESSED IN HIS ROYAL PROCLAMATION FOR THE
    SUPPRESSION OF VICE AND IMMORALITY. [VOL. I.]

      New-York: Printed by George Forman, for Cornelius Davis, No. 94, Water-
    Street. 1799. pp. 396. 12mo.   AAS. LOC.

    Contents: THE SHEPHERD OF SALISBURY PLAIN. PART I.—THE SHEPHERD'S HYMN.
    —THE SHEPHERD OF SALISBURY PLAIN. [Signed Z–Hannah More.]—THE HISTORY
    OF TOM WHITE, THE POSTILION. PART I.—HYMN ON DIVINE PROVIDENCE.—THE
    WAY TO PLENTY: OR THE SECOND PART OF TOM WHITE. [Signed Z–Hannah More.]
    —THE LIFE OF WILLIAM BAKER. BY THE REV. MR. GILPIN.—FUNERAL SERMON.—
    ON HONEST LABOR. — THE TWO SOLDIERS. — A JEWISH TRADITION CONCERNING
    MOSES. — THE TWO SHOEMAKERS. PART I. — THE APPRENTICE TURNED MASTER;
    OR, THE SECOND PART OF THE TWO SHOEMAKERS. SHEWING HOW JAMES STOCK, FROM
    A PARISH APPRENTICE BECAME A CREDITABLE TRADESMAN.—THE HISTORY OF IDLE
    JACK BROWN. CONTAINING THE MERRY STORY OF THE MOUNTEBANK, WITH SOME
    ACCOUNT OF THE BAY MARE, SMILER. BEING THE THIRD PART OF THE TWO SHOE-
    MAKERS.—JACK BROWN IN PRISON; OR, THE PITCHER NEVER GOES SO OFTEN TO THE
    WELL, BUT IT IS BROKE AT LAST. BEING THE FOURTH PART OF THE HISTORY OF THE
    TWO SHOEMAKERS. [Signed Z–Hannah More.]— HISTORY OF THE PLAGUE IN LON-
    DON IN 1665. — THE LANCASHIRE COLLIER GIRL. A TRUE STORY. — THE HAPPY
    WATERMAN. — THE TWO WEALTHY FARMERS; OR THE HISTORY OF MR. BRAGWELL.
    PART I.—THE TWO WEALTHY FARMERS, &C. PART II.—THE TWO WEALTHY FARMERS;
    OR THE HISTORY OF MR. BRAGWELL. PART III.—THE TWO WEALTHY FARMERS; OR
    THE HISTORY OF MR. BRAGWELL. PART IV.—THE TWO WEALTHY FARMERS; WITH
    THE SAD ADVENTURES OF MISS BRAGWELL. PART V. [Signed Z–Hannah More.]—
    THE GOOD MOTHER'S LEGACY. [Signed S–Sarah More.]—SORROWFUL SAM; OR THE
    TWO BLACKSMITHS. — WONDERFUL ESCAPE FROM SHIPWRECK. — BABAY. A TRUE
    STORY OF A GOOD NEGRO WOMAN.—THE COMFORTS OF RELIGION.—A TRUE ACCOUNT
    OF A PIOUS NEGRO.—THE BEGGARLY BOY. A PARABLE.—THE WONDERFUL ADVAN-
    TAGES OF ADVENTURING IN THE LOTTERY.—DANIEL IN THE DEN OF LIONS.—NOAH'S
    FLOOD. — THE HARVEST HOME. — THE PARABLE OF THE LABORERS IN THE VINE-
    YARD. — THE TROUBLES OF LIFE; OR THE GUINEA AND THE SHILLING. — A TRUE
    EXAMPLE OF THE INTERPOSITION OF PROVIDENCE, IN THE DISCOVERY AND PUNISH-
    MENT OF MURDER. BY THAT FAMOUS MAGISTRATE, MR. JUSTICE FIELDING.

35298

CHEAP REPOSITORY TRACTS, continued.

—— THE ENTERTAINING, MORAL, AND RELIGIOUS REPOSITORY; CONTAINING, UPWARDS
OF THREE SCORE SEPARATE PERFORMANCES, ALL OF WHICH ARE WRITTEN IN A
SIMPLE YET PLEASING STILE, AND ARE EMINENTLY CALCULATED FOR THE AMUSE-
MENT AND INSTRUCTION OF THE YOUTH OF BOTH SEXES. PUBLISHED BY A SOCIETY
IN GREAT-BRITAIN, INSTITUTED FOR THE BENEFICENT PURPOSE OF AIDING THE IN-
TENTION OF HIS MAJESTY, AS EXPRESSED IN HIS ROYAL PROCLAMATION FOR THE
SUPPRESSION OF VICE AND IMMORALITY. [VOL. II.]

*Elizabeth-Town: Printed by Shepard Kollock, for Cornelius Davis, No. 94,
Water-Street, New-York. 1799. pp. (2), 324. 12mo.* AAS.

Contents: THE HISTORY OF CHARLES JONES, THE FOOTMAN. WRITTEN BY HIMSELF.
—— THE CHEAPSIDE APPRENTICE; OR, THE HISTORY OF MR. FRANCIS H * * * *.
FULLY SETTING FORTH THE DANGER OF PLAYING WITH EDGE TOOLS. SHEWING ALSO
HOW A GAY LIFE MAY PROVE A SHORT ONE, AND THAT A MERRY EVENING MAY PRO-
DUCE A SORROWFUL MORNING.—THE HYMN.—THE STORY OF POOR TRICKET, THE
GAMESTER. SHEWING HOW HE FIRST LOST HIS PLACE BY GAMING, AND THEN HAD
WELL NIGH BEEN THE DEATH OF HIS WIFE THROUGH THE SAME CAUSE, AND HOW
LASTLY, HIS GAMING WAS THE OCCASION OF HIS BEING TRANSPORTED AS A CONVICT
TO BOTANY BAY.—BETTY BROWN, THE ST. GILES'S ORANGE GIRL: WITH SOME AC-
COUNT OF MRS. SPONGE, THE MONEY LENDER.—BLACK GILES THE POACHER; WITH
SOME ACCOUNT OF A FAMILY WHO HAD RATHER LIVE BY THEIR WITS THAN THEIR
WORK. PART I.—BLACK GILES THE POACHER; WITH THE HISTORY OF WIDOW
BROWN'S APPLE TREE. PART II.—SOME NEW THOUGHTS FOR THE NEW-YEAR.
SHEWING HOW MR. THRIFTY, THE GREAT MERCER, SUCCEEDED IN HIS TRADE, BY
ALWAYS EXAMINING HIS BOOKS SOON AFTER CHRISTMAS, AND HOW MR. CARELESS,
BY NEGLECTING THIS RULE, LET ALL HIS AFFAIRS RUN TO RUIN BEFORE HE WAS
AWARE OF IT. AFTER WHICH SOME CHRISTIAN HELP IS OFFERED TO ALL THOSE
PERSONS, HIGH OR LOW, WHO HAVE A MIND TO EXAMINE INTO THE ACCOUNT OF THEIR
OWN LIVES DURING THE LAST YEAR.—A HYMN FOR THE NEW-YEAR.—A TRUE EX-
AMPLE OF THE INTERPOSITION OF PROVIDENCE, IN THE DISCOVERY AND PUNISHMENT
OF MURDER. BY THAT FAMOUS MAGISTRATE, MR. JUSTICE FIELDING.—THE TOUCH-
STONE; OR, THE WAY TO KNOW A TRUE CHRISTIAN. BEING A DESCRIPTION OF THE
CHARACTER OF OUR BLESSED SAVIOUR, WITH AN ENQUIRY WHETHER WE ARE LIKE
HIM. TO WHICH IS ADDED, AN APPEAL FIRST TO INFIDELS, AND THEN TO PERSONS
WHO CALL THEMSELVES BY THE NAME OF CHRISTIANS.—ONESIMUS; OR, THE
RUN-AWAY SERVANT CONVERTED. A TRUE STORY, SHEWING WHAT A WONDERFUL
IMPROVEMENT IN HIS CONDITION ONESIMUS EXPERIENCED AFTER HE BECAME A
CHRISTIAN. TO WHICH IS ADDED, AN AFFECTIONATE ADDRESS TO ALL THOSE UNHAPPY
PERSONS, BOTH MEN AND WOMEN, WHO, LIKE ONESIMUS, HAVE LEFT THEIR HOME,
AND HAVE GOT INTO A BAD WAY OF LIVING, AND WHO HAVE ALSO A MIND TO HEAR
HOW THEY MAY GET OUT.—LOOK AT HOME; OR, THE ACCUSERS ACCUSED. BEING
AN ACCOUNT OF THE MANNER IN WHICH OUR SAVIOUR PUT TO SILENCE THE SCRIBES
AND PHARISEES, WHEN THEY BROUGHT TO HIM THE WOMAN TAKEN IN ADULTERY.
—A HYMN.—THE GRAND ASSIZES; OR, GENERAL GAOL DELIVERY.—BEAR YE ONE
ANOTHER'S BURDENS; OR, THE VALLEY OF TEARS. A VISION.—THE STRAIT GATE
AND THE BROAD WAY, BEING THE SECOND PART OF THE VALLEY OF TEARS. [By
Hannah More.]—THE COTTAGE COOK; OR, MRS. JONES'S CHEAP DISHES; SHEWING
THE WAY TO DO MUCH GOOD WITH A LITTLE MONEY.—THE SUNDAY SCHOOL.—THE
HISTORY OF HESTER WILMOT; OR, THE NEW GOWN. PART II. BEING A CONTINUA-
TION OF THE SUNDAY SCHOOL.—ON THE SACRAMENT OF THE LORD'S SUPPER.—THE
HISTORY OF MR. FANTOM, THE NEW FASHIONED PHILOSOPHER AND HIS MAN WILLIAM.
—THE HUB-BUB; OR, THE HISTORY OF FARMER RUSSEL, THE HARD-HEARTED OVER-
SEER. [By Sarah More.]—TAWNY RACHEL, OR, THE FORTUNE TELLER; WITH SOME
ACCOUNT OF DREAMS, OMENS, AND CONJURERS. [By Hannah More.]—THE EXPLANA-
TION OF THE TEN COMMANDMENTS. PART I.—EXPLANATION OF THE NATURE OF
BAPTISM. DESIGNED ESPECIALLY FOR ALL THOSE PARENTS WHO ARE ABOUT TO
BRING A CHILD TO BE BAPTIZED.—THE SERVANT MAN TURNED SOLDIER; OR, THE

CHEAP REPOSITORY TRACTS, continued.
FAIR WEATHER CHRISTIAN. A PARABLE. — THE GENERAL RESURRECTION. PART I.
BEING A DESCRIPTION TAKEN FROM SCRIPTURE, OF SOME OF THE EVENTS WHICH
WILL COME TO PASS AT THE END OF THE WORLD. — AN HYMN ON THE SECOND COM-
ING OF CHRIST. — PRAYERS TO BE USED BY A CHILD OR YOUNG PERSON — BY A GROWN
PERSON — BY THE MASTER OR MISTRESS OF A SUNDAY SCHOOL — AND BY THE MASTER
OR MISTRESS OF A FAMILY.

35299   CHETWOOD, WILLIAM RUFUS   –1766
THE VOYAGES AND ADVENTURES OF CAPTAIN ROBERT BOYLE, IN SEVERAL PARTS OF
THE WORLD. INTERMIXED WITH THE STORY OF MISS VILLARS, AN ENGLISH LADY,
WITH WHOM HE MADE HIS SURPRISING ESCAPE FROM BARBARY. LIKEWISE IN-
CLUDING THE HISTORY OF AN ITALIAN CAPTIVE, AND THE LIFE OF DON PEDRO
AGUILIO, &C. FULL OF VARIOUS AND AMAZING TURNS OF FORTUNE.
*Walpole, Newhampshire: Printed by David Carlisle, for Thomas & Thomas,
and sold at the Walpole Bookstore.* 1799. pp. 244. 12mo.   AAS. NYPL.

35300   CHEVY CHACE.
THE HUNTING OF CHEVY-CHASE. A BALLAD.
Printed for every Purchaser. [1799.] pp. 8. 16mo.

35301   THE CHILD'S READING BOOK. DESIGNED TO INSTRUCT CHILDREN IN ONE ALPHABET
AND THE SPELLING AND READING OF WORDS OF ONE, TWO, THREE AND FOUR SYL-
LABLES. LESSONS OF READING, FROM THE SCRIPTURES, FABLES, AND OTHER AMUSING
PIECES. ARE ARRANGED IN A METHOD TO DIVERT THE MINDS, AND GAIN THE ATTEN-
TION OF CHILDREN. BY A FRIEND TO THE EDUCATION OF CHILDREN. [Three lines
from] SHERLOCK.
Windham: Printed and sold by John Byrne. 1799.

35302   CHISHOLM, COLIN   1755–1855
AN ESSAY ON THE MALIGNANT PESTILENTIAL FEVER INTRODUCED INTO THE WEST
INDIAN ISLANDS FROM BOULLAM, ON THE COAST OF GUINEA, AS IT APPEARED IN
1793 AND 1794. BY C. CHISHOLM, M.D. AND SURGEON TO HIS MAJESTY'S ORDNANCE
IN GRENADA. TO WHICH IS ANNEXED, A DESCRIPTION OF THE AMERICAN YELLOW
FEVER, WHICH PREVAILED AT CHARLESTON IN 1748. IN A LETTER FROM DR. JOHN
LINING.
*Philadelphia: Printed for Thomas Dobson, at the Stone House, No. 41, South
Second Street.* 1799. pp. xvi, [308.] 8vo.   AAS. BA. LOC. NYPL. SGO.

A second edition was printed, in two volumes, in London, in 1801.

35303   THE CHRISTIAN'S MONITOR; OR THEOLOGIAL MAGAZINE. [Motto.] No. 3. SATUR-
DAY, JANUARY 5, [— No. 14. — SATURDAY, JUNE 8, '99.]
By Rand & Burdick, Portland, Maine. [1799.] pp. (17)–112. 8vo.   AAS.

The above is the last number located.

35304   CHURCH, JAMES
A BRIEF DISSERTATION ON THE VENEREAL DISEASE, SEMINAL WEAKNESSES, GLEET, &C.
&C. INCLUDING THE HISTORY, CURE AND PREVENTION OF THOSE DISEASES, BY AN
APPROVED METHOD, BY WHICH PERSONS OF BOTH SEXES MAY CURE THEMSELVES
WITH EASE, CERTAINTY, SAFETY AND SECRECY, AT AN EASY EXPENSE. BY JAMES
CHURCH, M.D. FORMERLY PUPIL OF DR. DENNISON, LONDON HOSPITAL. [One line
from] SWIFT.
New-York: Printed by G. and R. Waite ? 1799.

83d New York District Copyright, issued to James Church, as Author,
18 November, 1799.

35305   CHURCH, James, continued.
—— The Efficacy of dr. Church's cough drops, demonstrated in the cure of
coughs, colds, asthmas, & consumptions, invented and prepared by James
Church, m. d. . . . Illustrated with many remarkable and authentic
facts. . . .

> *New-York: Printed for the Proprietor, by G. and R. Waite.* 1799. pp. 24.
> 8vo.   JCB. LOC.

35306   CHURCH, John Hubbard   1772-1840
The Ministry of reconciliation, and the duty of ministers and people considered: in two sermons, delivered at Pelham, New Hampshire, November
4, 1798. By John Hubbard Church. Being the Sabbath after his ordination
to the pastoral office in that place.

> *Amherst, Newhampshire: From the Press of Samuel Preston.* Feb. 1799. pp.
> 44. 8vo.   NYPL.

35307   CICERO; or, a discovery of a clan of conspirators against all religions and
governments in the whole world. Extracted from Robison, Mounier and
Barruel; and interspersed with hints in due season. By a Citizen of the
United States.

> *Baltimore: Printed by J. Hayes, No. 8, Baltimore-Street* 1799. pp. 61. 8vo.
>   LOC.

35308   CITY Gazette and [seal] Daily Advertiser. [Motto.] Vol. xviii. No. 3557.
Tuesday, January 1, [— Vol. xvii [sic]. No. 3863. Tuesday, December 31,
1799.]

> *Charleston: Published by Freneau & Paine, Printers to the City, No. 47, Bay.*
> 1799. fol.   CLS. LOC.

    In May, the Printers were appointed official printers to the State, also,—
the imprint reading: Charleston: — Published by Freneau & Paine,
Printers to the City, and to the State, No. 47, Bay, at 7 dollars per ann.
payable half yearly.

35309   CLARK, Jonas   1730–1805
A Sermon preached at the ordination of the rev. William Muzzy, to the
pastoral care of the church of Christ in Sullivan, (Newhampshire) February 7, 1798. By Jonas Clark, a. m. pastor of the church in Lexington.

> *Printed by John Prentiss – – Keene, (Newhampshire.)* November, 1799. pp.
> .24, 8vo.   BM. JCB. MHS.

35310   CLARKE, Abraham Lynson   1768–1810
The Secrets of masonry illustrated and explained; in a discourse, preached
at South-Kingstown, before the Grand Lodge of the State of Rhode-
Island; convened for the installation of Washington-Lodge, September 3d,
A. L. 5799. By Abraham Lynson Clarke, a. m. rector of St. John's church,
Providence.

> *Providence: Printed by brother Bennett Wheeler.* [1799.] pp. [15.] 8vo.
>   AAS. LOC. RIHS.

35311 CLARKE, JOHN   1687–1734
AN INTRODUCTION TO THE MAKING OF LATIN. COMPRISING, AFTER AN EASY, COMPEN-
DIOUS METHOD, THE SUBSTANCE OF THE LATIN SYNTAX. WITH PROPER ENGLISH
EXAMPLES, MOST OF THEM TRANSLATIONS FROM THE CLASSIC AUTHORS, IN ONE
COLUMN, AND THE LATIN WORDS IN ANOTHER. TO WHICH IS SUBJOINED, IN THE
SAME METHOD, A SUCCINCT ACCOUNT OF THE AFFAIRS OF ANTIENT GREECE AND
ROME, INTENDED AT ONCE TO BRING BOYS ACQUAINTED WITH HISTORY, AND THE
IDIOM OF THE LATIN TONGUE: WITH RULES FOR THE GENDER OF NOUNS. A NEW
EDITION, DILIGENTLY REVISED AND CAREFULLY CORRECTED. BY JOHN CLARKE,
LATE MASTER OF THE PUBLIC GRAMMAR-SCHOOL IN HULL.

> *London: Printed. New-York, Re-printed, by James Oram,* 1799. pp. xii,
> 276. 12mo.   BA.

35312 CLARKE, JOHN   1755–1798
SERMONS, BY THE LATE REVEREND JOHN CLARKE, D.D. MINISTER OF THE FIRST
CHURCH IN BOSTON, MASSACHUSETTS. COPY RIGHT SECURED ACCORDING TO ACT OF
CONGRESS. [Ornament.]

> *Boston: Printed by Samuel Hall, and sold at his Book-Store in Cornhill.*
> July, 1799. pp. 501, (3), portrait by Hill. 8vo.   AAS. BA. BM. JCB. MHS. NYPL.

> With a biographical sketch of the Author; and a list of the names of his
> predecessors at the First Church in Boston. 169th Massachusetts Dis-
> trict Copyright, issued to Esther Clarke, as Proprietor, 24 June, 1799.

35313 CLAYPOOLE'S AMERICAN DAILY ADVERTISER. NUMBER 6875. TUESDAY, JANUARY 1,
[— NUMBER 7188. TUESDAY, DECEMBER 31, 1799.]

> *Printed and sold by David C. Claypoole, No. 48, Market-Street, Philadelphia.*
> 1799. fol.   AAS. BM. HSP. LCP. LOC.

35314 CLÉRY, JEAN BAPTISTE CANT-HANET   1759–1809
A JOURNAL OF OCCURRENCES IN THE TOWER OF THE TEMPLE, DURING THE CONFINE-
MENT OF LOUIS XVI. KING OF FRANCE. [One line of Latin from] VIRG. BY M.
CLÉRY, THE KING'S VALET-DE-CHAMBRE. TRANSLATED FROM THE ORIGINAL MANU-
SCRIPT, BY R. C. DALLAS, ESQ.

> *Boston: Printed by Manning & Loring, for David West.* 1799. pp. 154.
> 12mo.   AAS. BU. HC. JCB. NYPL.

> An edition in French was also "Imprimé a la Nouvelle Imprimerie" in
> Quebec this year.

35315 COBB, WILLIAM, JUNIOR
THE COUNTRY TRADER'S ASSISTANT; OR YOUNG CLERK'S DIRECTORY IN THE ART OF
BOOK-KEEPING, ON A NEW AND APPROVED PLAN. TO WHICH IS ADDED, A RECORD OF
TRADE, A RECORD OF NOTES AND BILLS. ALSO, A FEW FORMS OF NOTES, ORDERS,
RECEIPTS, BILLS, &C. BY WILLIAM COBB, JUN.

> *Brookfield, Printed for the Author.* [*By E. Merriam & Co.*] 1799. pp. 46.
> sq. 16mo.   AAS.

> 173d Massachusetts District Copyright, issued to William Cobb, as Au-
> thor, 10 October, 1799.

35316 COBBETT, WILLIAM   1762–1835
BY WILLIAM COBBETT, OF THE CITY OF PHILADELPHIA. PROPOSALS FOR PUBLISHING
BY SUBSCRIPTION; A NEW, ENTIRE, AND NEAT EDITION OF PORCUPINE'S WORKS.
. . . SUBSCRIBERS NAMES.

> [*Philadelphia: Printed by William Cobbett, Feb. 5th,* 1799.] pp. 8. 8vo. JCB.

35317 COFFIN, PAUL   1737–1821
A SERMON, PREACHED BEFORE HIS HONOR MOSES GILL, ESQ. LIEUTENANT GOVERNOR, THE HONORABLE THE COUNCIL, SENATE AND HOUSE OF REPRESENTATIVES OF THE COMMONWEALTH OF MASSACHUSETTS, MAY 29, 1799, BEING THE DAY OF GENERAL ELECTION. BY REV. PAUL COFFIN, A.M. PASTOR OF THE CHURCH IN BUXTON.
  Boston: Printed by Young & Minns, State Printers. MDCCXCIX. pp. 31. 8vo.   AAS. BA. BM. HC. JCB. LOC. MHS. NYHS. NYPL.

35318 COGAN, THOMAS   1736–1818
LETTERS TO WILLIAM WILBERFORCE, ESQ. M.P. ON THE DOCTRINE OF HEREDITARY DEPRAVITY. BY A LAYMAN. [Two lines from] POPE.
  Boston: Printed by Manning & Loring, for J. Nancrede, No. 49, Marlbro'- Street. 1799. pp. 132. 12mo.   AAS. HC. JCB. MHS. NYPL.

  Contains, a seven-page list of Books published by J. Nancrede.

35319 COLE, JOHN   1774–1855
SACRED HARMONY, CONTAINING A VARIETY OF PLAIN AND SIMPLE AIRS, ADAPTED TO ALL THE METRES IN DR. WATTS' PSALMS, IMPROVED BY MR. BARLOW; AND A CHOICE COLLECTION OF THE MOST APPROVED HYMN TUNES, ADAPTED TO ALL THE METRES IN THE METHODIST POCKET HYMN BOOK, TOGETHER WITH A CONCISE INTRODUCTION TO THE ART OF SINGING. BY JOHN COLE.
  Baltimore: Printed for J. Carr, at his Music Store, Gay Street. 1799.

  Maryland District Copyright, issued to Joseph Carr, as Proprietor, 25 February, 1799.

35320 A COLLECTION OF CONTRA DANCES, OF LATE, APPROVED, AND FASHIONABLE FIGURES.
  Walpole: Printed at the Museum Press. And sold at the Walpole Bookstore. 1799. pp. 12. 12mo.   AAS.

35321 THE COLUMBIAN ALMANAC: OR, THE NORTH-AMERICAN CALENDAR, FOR THE YEAR OF OUR LORD 1800. BEING ONE OF THE CENTURIAL YEARS, NOT BISSEXTILE. [Cut of] ARMS OF THE UNITED STATES.
  Wilmington: Printed and sold by Peter Brynberg, in Market-street. [1799.] pp. (48). 12mo.   HSP. LOC.

35322 COLUMBIAN [U.S.A. in star] CENTINEL. VOL. XXX. NO. 35. WEDNESDAY, JANUARY 2, [— VOL. XXXII. NO. 34. SATURDAY, DECEMBER 28, 1799.]
  Printed and published on Wednesdays and Saturdays, by Benjamin Russell, Printer of the Laws of the Union, for the northern States— south side State Street, next to the Coffee-House, Boston, (Massachusetts). 1799. fol.
     AAS. BA. BM. EI. HC. LOC. MHS. NYHS.

  With the issue for October 5th, the title was altered to *Columbian Centinel & Massachusetts Federalist.* With the issue for November 13th, "&" was changed to "and."

35323 —— LIBERTY OF SPEECH, AND OF THE PRESS. A CHARGE TO THE GRAND JURIES OF THE COUNTY COURTS OF THE FIFTH CIRCUIT OF THE STATE OF PENNSYLVANIA. BY ALEXANDER ADDISON, PRESIDENT OF THOSE COURTS. [PRESENTED TO THE READERS OF THE COLUMBIAN CENTINEL AS A NEW-YEAR'S GIFT.]
  [Boston: Printed by Benjamin Russell, 1799.] pp. (2). fol.
     AAS. EI. HC. LOC. MHS. NYHS. NYPL.

35324 COLUMBIAN COURIER. VOL. I. NO. 5. SATURDAY, JANUARY 5, [— VOL. II. NO. 4. FRIDAY, DECEMBER 27, 1799.]
  New-Bedford, Massachusetts. Printed and published by Abraham Shearman, jun. 1799. fol.

35325   COLUMBIAN [U. S. arms.] GAZETTE. VOL. I. No. 1. SATURDAY, APRIL 6, [— No. 12. SATURDAY, JUNE 22, 1799.]

> *[New-York: Printed by Hurtin & M'Farlane, at the Literary Printing-Office, No. 29 Gold-Street.] For J. M. Williams, No. 24, Maiden-Lane. 1799. fol.*   BA.

> Established, as a weekly, by John Mason Williams, better known by his pseudonym of "Anthony Pasquin," and printed by Robert M. Hurtin, and Monteith M'Farlane. Publication was discontinued after twelve numbers had been published, as above.

35326   COLUMBIAN [Cut of eagle] MINERVA. VOL. III. No. 117. THURSDAY, JANUARY 3, [—VOLUME IV. NUMBER 168. THURSDAY, DECEMBER 26, 1799.]

> *Dedham, (Massachusetts): Published by Herman Mann, near the Court-House.* 1799. fol.   AAS.

> In continuation of *The Minerva*. In April, the cut was changed to a seated Minerva, with the motto, Lux Sapientiæ.

35327   THE COLUMBIAN MIRROR AND ALEXANDRIA GAZETTE. VOL. VII. No. 893. TUESDAY, JANUARY 1, [— VOL. VIII. No. 1048. TUESDAY, DECEMBER 31, 1799.]

> *Alexandria: Printed every Tuesday, Thursday, and Saturday, by Henry Gird, jun.* 1799. fol.

> In December, Gird withdrew, and was succeeded by Ellis Price.

35328   COLUMBIAN MUSEUM & SAVANNAH ADVERTISER. [Motto.] VOL. III. No. 88. WHOLE NUMBER 296. TUESDAY, JANUARY 1, [— VOL. IV. No. 88. WHOLE NUMBER 400. TUESDAY, DECEMBER 31, 1799.]

> *Savannah— Published on Tuesday and Friday, by Gurdon I. Seymour and Philip D. Woolhopter, on the Bay: at six dollars per annum, payable half yearly.* 1799. fol.   GHS.

35329   COLUMBIAN PATRIOTIC GAZETTE. VOL. I. No. 1. THURSDAY, AUGUST 8, [—No. 21. THURSDAY, DECEMBER 26, 1799.]

> *Rome, [New-York.] Published by Ebenezer Eaton & Thomas Walker.* 1799. fol.

> Established, as a weekly, by Ebenezer Eaton, and Thomas Walker. The word "Patriotic" is in smaller type, and may not have been intended to form part of the title. With the issue for August 4, 1800, the imprint reads: Printed by Thomas Walker, for Eaton & Walker; and, with the issue for August 3, 1801, Ebenezer Eaton withdrew from the firm. Thomas Walker continued publication to March, 1803, when he removed his Press to Utica, New York, and, with a new serial numbering, began publication there of the *Columbian Gazette*.

35330   THE COLUMBIAN PRIMER, ENLARGED AND IMPROVED: OR, AN EASY AND PLEASANT GUIDE TO THE ART OF READING. ADORN'D WITH CUTS. TO WHICH IS ADDED, THE ASSEMBLY OF DIVINES CATECHISM.

> *Boston: [P]rinted by Thomas Fleet.* MDCCXCIX. pp. (56). 24mo.   BPL.

35331   THE COLUMBIAN SONGSTER. BEING A LARGE COLLECTION OF FASHIONABLE SONGS, FOR GENTLEMEN & LADIES. IN A SERIES OF NUMBERS. [I–VII.]

> *Printed by Nathaniel Heaton, jun.* M,DCC,XCIX. *Wrentham, Mass.* pp. 36; 36; 36; 36; 36; 36; 30. 12mo.   BU. LOC.

35332   COMMERCIAL [cut of ship] ADVERTISER. VOL. II. NUMBER 391. TUESDAY, JANU-
ARY 1, [— VOL. III. NUMBER 703. TUESDAY, DECEMBER 31, 1799.]

> *[New-York:] Published (daily) at No. 40, Pine-Street, by Geo. F. Hopkins,
> Printer of the Laws of the United States for the District of New-York. 1799. fol.*
> BA. LOC. NYHS. NYPL.

With the issue for July 1st, Hopkins withdrew, and Noah Webster,
junior, formed a partnership with his nephew, Ebenezer Belden, as E.
Belden & Co.

35333   THE COMPANION: BEING A SELECTION OF THE BEAUTIES OF THE MOST CELEBRATED
AUTHORS, IN THE ENGLISH LANGUAGE. IN PROSE AND VERSE. [Two lines from]
AKENSIDE.

> *Printed by Nathaniel and Benjamin Heaton, for Joseph J. Todd, Providence,
> at the Sign of the Bible and Anchor,* M,DCC,XCIX. pp. 280. 16mo.
> AAS. BU. JCB. LOC. RIHS.

35334   CONDIE, THOMAS
A BIOGRAPHICAL SKETCH OF GEORGE WASHINGTON. WITH NOTES, AND A PARTICULAR
ACCOUNT OF HIS LATE ILLNESS, DEATH AND FUNERAL.

> *Philadelphia: Printed by Richard Folwell, for Thomas Condie, No. 20, Car-
> ter's Alley.* 1799. 8vo.

35335   —— HISTORY OF THE PESTILENCE, COMMONLY CALLED YELLOW FEVER, WHICH ALMOST
DESOLATED PHILADELPHIA, IN THE MONTHS OF AUGUST, SEPTEMBER & OCTOBER,
1798. BY THOMAS CONDIE & RICHARD FOLWELL.

> *Philadelphia: From the Press of R. Folwell.* [1799.] pp. 108, xxxii, (67).
> 8vo.   AAS. BA. JCB. LOC. NYHS. NYPL. 8GO.

With An alphabetical list of the names of the persons who died in Philadelphia, and the neighborhood, from the 1st of August to the 1st of
November, 1798. pp. (67). Also included in the Select pamphlets
collected and issued in a volume, by Mathew Carey, in 1799.

35336   —— — HISTORY OF THE PESTILENCE, COMMONLY CALLED THE YELLOW FEVER,
WHICH ALMOST DESOLATED PHILADELPHIA, IN THE MONTHS OF AUGUST, SEPTEMBER
& OCTOBER, 1798. BY THOMAS CONDIE & RICHARD FOLWELL.

> *Philadelphia: From the Press of R. Folwell.* [1799.] pp. 108, XXXII, (72).
> 8vo.   LOC. NYPL. 8GO.

An alphabetical list of the names of the 3521 persons who died in Philadelphia and the neighborhood, from the 1st of August, to the 1st of
November, 1798. pp. (72).

35337   CONDY, JEREMY   1709–1768
MERCY EXEMPLIFIED, IN THE CONDUCT OF A SAMARITAN; AND RECOMMENDED TO
UNIVERSAL IMITATION. A SERMON PREACHED AT BOSTON, IN THE PROVINCE OF THE
MASSACHUSETTS-BAY. BY JEREMY CONDY, A. M. AT CAMBRIDGE, IN THAT PROVINCE.

> *Boston: Re-printed and sold by Benjamin Edes, Kilby-Street,* — 1799. pp.
> [23.] 8vo.   LOC.

35338   CONGREGATIONAL CHURCH IN CONNECTICUT.
Caption title: AN ADDRESS TO THE YOUNG PEOPLE, IN THE WESTERN DISTRICT OF
FAIRFIELD COUNTY. WE THE MINISTERS OF THE GOSPEL IN THE WESTERN DISTRICT
OF THE COUNTY OF FAIRFIELD, MET IN CONSOCIATION . . . BY ORDER OF CON-
SOCIATION, AMZI LEWIS, MODERATOR. CANAAN. DEC. 11, 1799.

> *[Newfield: Printed by Lazarus Beach.* 1799.] pp. 4. 8vo.   NYPL.

35339   CONGREGATIONAL CHURCH in Massachusetts.
An Address, from the Convention of Congregational ministers in the Commonwealth of Massachusetts, to their christian brethren of the several Associations, and others not associated throughout this State. . . .
[*Boston: May 30, 1799.*] pp. 3. fol.   EI.

35340   —— Boston, April 15th, 1799. Rev. and dear brethren, Deeply impressed ourselves with the critical and very alarming state of our country, and of our holy religion . . .
[*Boston: 1799.*] pp. (2).   HC. MHS.

On the Harvard College Library Copy is noted: "The draft of your humble servt. J. Morse. The Address of Convention grew out of this. A delegation from the several Associations met agreeably to the above proposal and agreed to address their brethren. Great good has, it is believed, resulted from these measures."

35341   CONNECTICUT. State.
[Seal.] Acts and laws, made and passed in and by the General Court or Assembly of the State of Connecticut, in America, holden at Hartford, (in said State) on the second Thursday of May, Anno Domini 1799.
[*Hartford: Printed by Hudson and Goodwin. 1799.*] pp. 499–510. 8vo.
CHS. CSL. YC.

35342   —— — [Seal.] Acts and laws, made and passed in and by the General Court or Assembly of the State of Connecticut, in America, holden at New-Haven (in said State) on the second Thursday of October, Anno Domini 1799. [Colophon:]
Hartford: Printed by Hudson and Goodwin. [1799.] pp. 511–520. 8vo.
CHS. CSL. PLA.

35343   —— By his excellency Jonathan Trumbull, esquire, governor and commander in and over the State of Connecticut. A Proclamation . . . appoint Friday the 22d day of March next to be set apart and reserved as a day of solemn fasting, humilation and prayer . . . Given under my hand at Lebanon, in said State, this twenty-fifth day of February, in the year of our Lord, one thousand seven hundred and ninety nine, and of the independence of the United States, the twenty third. Jonathan Trumbull. By his excellencys command, Samuel Wyllys, secretary.
[*Hartford: Printed by Hudson and Goodwin?* 1799.] Broadside. fol.

35344   CONNECTICUT ACADEMY of Arts and Sciences.
Constitution of the Connecticut Academy of Arts and Sciences.
[*Hartford: Printed by Hudson & Goodwin?* 1799.] pp. (2). fol.

35345   CONNECTICUT LAND Company.
The Connecticut Gore title, stated and considered, showing the rights of the proprietors, to the lands lately purchased by them, from the State of Connecticut: lying west of the Delaware River. [Ornament.]
Hartford: Printed by Hudson & Goodwin. 1799. pp. 80. 8vo.
AAS. JCB. LOC. NYPL. UTS.

35346   THE CONNECTICUT Courant. Vol. xxxiv. Number 1772. Monday, January 7, [— Number 1823. Monday, December 30, 1799.]
Hartford: Printed by Hudson & Goodwin. 1799. fol.   AAS. CHS. YC.

35347   CONNECTICUT [arms] GAZETTE. VOL. XXXVI. No. 1834. WEDNESDAY, JANUARY 2, [— VOL. XXXVII. NO, 1885. WEDNESDAY, DECEMBER 25, 1799.]

      New-London: Printed and published by Samuel Green, at his Office adjoining the Bank. 1799. fol.   CHS. NYHS. WHS.

      With the issue for January 1, 1800, the title was changed to *Connecticut Gazette and the Commercial Intelligencer.*

35348   CONNECTICUT JOURNAL & WEEKLY ADVERTISER. VOL. XXXII. No. 1627. THURS-DAY, JANUARY 3, [— No. 1678. THURSDAY, DECEMBER 26, 1799.]

      Printed at New-Haven, by Thomas Green and Son, near the College. 1799. fol.   AAS. LOC. YC.

      For the first three months of this year the Journal bore the above heading, changing, on April 4th, to, *Connecticut* [arms] *Journal*, with the motto, Qui transuit.

35349   THE CONSTITUTIONAL DIARY AND PHILADELPHIA EVENING ADVERTISER. VOL. I. No. 1. MONDAY, DECEMBER 2, [— No. 26. TUESDAY, DECEMBER 31, 1799.]

      Philadelphia: Published by James Carey. 1799. fol.

      Established, as a daily, by James Carey, and continued by him to January 23, 1800—the last number located.

35350   THE CONSTITUTIONAL [cut] TELEGRAPHE. VOL. I. No. 1. WEDNESDAY. OCTO-BER 2, [— No. 26. SATURDAY, DECEMBER 28, 1799.]

      [Boston:] Published every Wednesday and Saturday, at Parker's Printing Office, south side, State Street, east corner Kilby Street, where subscriptions will be gratefully received. 1799. fol.   BA. LOC. MHS. YC.

      Established, as a semi-weekly, by Samuel S. Parker. With the issue for July 19, 1800, the paper was Published by Jonathan S. Copp, for the Proprietor, at Parker's Printing Office. At the end of the first volume, in September, 1800, Parker disposed of his interests to John S. Lillie, who kept a dry goods store, and whose ardent Jeffersonianism landed him in the Boston Gaol for three months, on a sentence for libel, in March, 1802. Lillie disposed of his interests, with the issue for April 10, 1802, to John Moseley Dunham, a practical printer, who continued publication to the issue for May 22, 1802, when he changed the title to *Republican Gazetteer.*

35351   CONVERSATION CARDS, OR LADIES' & GENTLEMEN'S LEISURE HOUR'S AMUSEMENT.

      Wilmington, (Del.) Printed by James Wilson, 1799.

35352   COOK, DAVID, JUNIOR

      COOK'S AMERICAN ARITHMETIC: BEING A SYSTEM OF DECIMAL ARITHMETIC COMPORT-ING WITH THE FEDERAL CURRENCY OF THE UNITED STATES OF AMERICA. TO WHICH IS ANNEXED, BY WAY OF SECOND PART, THE AMERICAN SURVEYOR: THE WHOLE ON AN ENTIRE NEW PLAN, TO WHICH IS ADDED A DRAFT OF INSTRUMENTS, ADAPTED TO CARRY THE ABOVE INTO EFFECT, &c. BY DAVID COOK, JUN.

      [Printed by Thomas Green & Son, New-Haven ? 1799.]

      Connecticut District Copyright, issued to David Cook, jun. as Author, 26 September, 1799.

35353   COOPER, EZEKIEL   1763–1847
A FUNERAL DISCOURSE, ON THE DEATH OF THAT EMINENT MAN THE LATE REVEREND
JOHN DICKINS. BY THE REVEREND EZEKIEL COOPER. [Nine lines from] PAUL
TO TIMOTHY.

Philadelphia: Printed by H. Maxwell, for Asbury Dickins, Bookseller, No.
41, Market Street. 1799. pp. 36. 12mo.   JCB.

221st Pennsylvania District Copyright, issued to Asbury Dickins, as
Proprietor, 31 January, 1799.

35354   COOPER, THOMAS   1759–1840
POLITICAL ESSAYS, ORIGINALLY INSERTED IN THE NORTHUMBERLAND GAZETTE, WITH
ADDITIONS. BY THOMAS COOPER, ESQ.

Northumberland: Printed by Andrew Kennedy. 1799. pp. (2), (64). 8vo.
AAS. JCB. LOC. NYHS. NYPL.

35355   COSGRAVE, J.
A GENUINE HISTORY OF THE LIVES AND ACTIONS OF THE MOST NOTORIOUS IRISH
HIGHWAYMEN, TORIES AND RAPPAREES, FROM REDMOND O'HANLON, THE FAMOUS
GENTLEMAN-ROBBER, TO CAHIER NA GAPPUL, THE GREAT HORSE-CATCHER, WHO
WAS EXECUTED AT MARYBOROUGH, IN AUGUST, 1735. TO WHICH IS ADDED, THE
GOLD-FINDER: OR, THE HISTORY OF MARCUS MAC ONEIL, WHO UNDER THE APPEAR-
ANCE OF A STUPID, IGNORANT COUNTRY FELLOW, (ON THE BOG OF ALLEN, BY THE
HELP OF HIS MAN ANDREW) PLAYED THE MOST NOTORIOUS CHEATS, AND REMARK-
ABLE TRICKS ON THE PEOPLE OF IRELAND, THAT EVER WAS KNOWN. ALSO, THE
REMARKABLE LIFE OF GILDER ROY, A MURDERER, RAVISHER, INCENDIARY AND
HIGHWAYMAN, WITH SEVERAL OTHERS, NOT IN ANY FORMER EDITIONS. THE EDI-
TION, WITH ADDITIONS. BY J. COSGRAVE.

Wilmington: Printed and sold by Bonsal & Niles. 1799. pp. 140. 24mo. AAS.

35356   COUNTRY PORCUPINE. VOL. II. No. 30. TUESDAY AND WEDNESDAY JANUARY 1 AND
2, [— VOL. III. No. 232. TUESDAY AND WEDNESDAY, AUGUST 28, AND 29, 1799.]
[Philadelphia: Printed and published by William Cobbett. 1799.] fol.

Discontinued with the above number.

35357   THE COURIER. VOL. III. NUMBER 6. WEDNESDAY, JANUARY 2, [— VOL. IV. NUM-
BER 5, WEDNESDAY, DECEMBER 25, 1799.]
Norwich (Chelsea Society). Printed by Thomas Hubbard. 1799. fol.   HC.

35358   THE COURIER, AND LONG ISLAND ADVERTISER. VOL. I. No. 1. WEDNESDAY, JUNE
26, [— No. 27. WEDNESDAY, DECEMBER 25, 1799.]
Brooklyn. Long Island: Printed by Thomas Kirk. 1799. fol.

Established, as a weekly, by Thomas Kirk, and continued by him to
October, 20, 1802.

35359   COURIER OF NEW HAMPSHIRE. No. 49. VOL. IX. WHOLE NO. 465. SATURDAY, JAN-
UARY 5, [— No. 48. VOL. X. WHOLE NO. 516. SATURDAY, DECEMBER 28, 1798.]
Devoted to news and national politicks: Published by George Hough, at Con-
cord. 1799. fol.

35360   COX, ZACHARIAH
AN ESTIMATE OF COMMERCIAL ADVANTAGES, BY WAY OF THE MISSISSIPPI AND MOBILE
RIVERS, TO THE WESTERN COUNTRY. PRINCIPLES OF A COMMERCIAL SYSTEM; AND
THE COMMENCEMENT AND PROGRESS OF A SETTLEMENT ON THE OHIO RIVER, TO
FACILITATE THE SAME, WITH A STATEMENT OF FACTS. BY ZACHARIAH COX.

Nashville: Printed by John M'Laughlin. 1799. pp. 70. 8vo.   LOC.

"From a pamphlet published by the Author at Knoxville in the year
1797, corrected from data, observation and experience."

AUCTION
VALUES

35361   COXE, TENCH   1755–1824
Caption title: AN AUTHENTIC VIEW OF THE PROGRESS OF THE STATE OF PENNSYL-
VANIA, SINCE THE ESTABLISHMENT OF THE INDEPENDENCE OF THE UNITED STATES
OF AMERICA. [Colophon:]

Printed by D. Humphreys, . . . Philadelphia, May, 1799. pp. 8. 8vo. NYPL.

35362   CRAWFORD, CHARLES
AN ESSAY UPON THE PROPAGATION OF THE GOSPEL. [Two lines from] MARK xvii, 15.
BY CHARLES CRAWFORD, ESQ.

Philadelphia: Printed by J. Gales, and sold by the Booksellers. 1799. pp. 60.
12mo.   AAS. LOC.

A second edition was printed in Philadelphia in 1801.

35363   CUMINGS, HENRY   1737–1823
A SERMON, PREACHED ON THE 9TH DAY OF OCTOBER, 1799, AT THE ORDINATION OF
THE REV. CALEB BRADLEY, TO THE PASTORAL CARE OF THE CHURCH AND PEOPLE
OF GOD, IN THE SECOND PARISH OF FALMOUTH. BY HENRY CUMMINGS [*sic*] A. M.
PASTOR OF THE CHURCH IN BILLERICA

Portland: Printed by E. A. Jenks. [1799.] pp. 36. 12mo.
                  AAS. BA. BM. JCB. LOC. MHS. NYHS. NYPL.

35364   CUMMINGS, ABRAHAM   1755–1827
THE PRESENT TIMES PERILOUS. A SERMON, PREACHED AT SULLIVAN, ON THE NATIONAL
FAST, APRIL 25, 1799. BY ABRAHAM CUMMINGS, A. M.

Printed for David J. Waters, Castine. [1799.] pp. [24.] 8vo.
                           AAS. JCB. LOC. NYHS.

35365   CURRIE, JAMES   1756–1806
AN ABRIDGEMENT OF THE SECOND EDITION OF A WORK WRITTEN BY DR. CURRIE OF
LIVERPOOL, IN ENGLAND, ON THE USE OF WATER, IN THE DISEASES OF THE HUMAN
FRAME: AND ON FEVER, OPIUM, STRONG DRINK, ABSTINENCE FROM FOOD, AND THE
PASSAGE THROUGH THE HUMAN SKIN; WITH OCCASIONAL REMARKS.

*Printed by Peter Edes of Augusta, in the District of Maine. Sold by Mr. Edes
of Augusta, and Mr. Bass of Hallowell, in Maine: and by the Booksellers of Boston,
New-York and Philadelphia.* [1799.] pp. viii, 53, (1). 16mo. AAS. BA. MEHS. SGO.

35366   CURTIS, SAMUEL
Cover title: CURTIS'S POCKET ALMANACK, FOR THE YEAR 1800: TO WHICH IS ADDED
A REGISTER OF NEW-HAMPSHIRE, CONTAINING A LIST OF THE OFFICERS, EXECUTIVE,
LEGISLATIVE AND JUDICIARY IN THE SERVICE OF THE UNITED STATES, WITH MANY
OTHER COMMUNICATIONS, IN THIS STATE, BOTH USEFUL AND INTERESTING. ☞ ER-
RORS POINTED OUT, OR INFORMATION ON THE SUBJECT, SUITABLE TO BE INSERTED
IN A REGISTER, WILL BE THANKFULLY RECEIVED, (BY THE POST-MASTER AT AM-
HERST) FOR THE NEXT REGISTER. ☞ INFORMATION WILL BE TOO LATE AFTER
THE 20TH AUGUST ANNUALLY. DRUGS AND MEDICINES. SHAVING-SOAP, AND A GOOD
ASSORTMENT OF THE BEST LIQUORS, CONSTANTLY KEPT AT THE POST-OFFICE, AM-
HERST. ALSO ☞ GOOD ATTENTION PAID TO GENTLEMEN'S HORSES,

Title: CURTIS'S POCKET ALMANACK FOR THE YEAR 1800: TO WHICH IS ADDED A
REGISTER OF NEW-HAMPSHIRE, CONTAINING, A LIST OF THE OFFICERS, EXECUTIVE,
LEGISLATIVE AND JUDICIARY IN THE SERVICE OF THE UNITED STATES, WITH MANY
OTHER COMMUNICATIONS, IN THIS STATE, BOTH USEFUL AND INTERESTING.

Exeter: Printed by H. Ranlet, for the Compiler. 1799. pp. (2), (106). 18mo.
                                   AAS. NHHS. NL. NYHS.
Reprinted in Chicago, for John Wentworth.

35367 CUTLER, MANASSEH   1742–1823
A SERMON, DELIVERED AT HAMILTON, ON THE DAY OF THE NATIONAL FAST, APRIL
25, 1799; APPOINTED BY THE PRESIDENT OF THE UNITED STATES OF AMERICA. BY
MANASSEH CUTLER, LL. I MINISTER OF THE CHURCH IN HAMILTON. PUBLISHED AT
THE REQUEST OF THE HEARERS.
> *Printed by Joshua Cushing, Salem* — 1799. pp. 32. 8vo.
>> BA. CLA. EI. JCB. LOC. NYHS. YC.

35368 DABOLL, NATHAN   1750–1818
THE NEW-ENGLAND ALMANAC, AND GENTLEMEN AND LADIES' DIARY, ENLARGED, FOR
THE YEAR OF OUR LORD CHRIST, 1800: BEING THE FOURTH AFTER BISSEXTILE OR
LEAP-YEAR, AND THE 24TH OF AMERICAN INDEPENDENCE. [Six lines.] BY NATHAN
DABOLL. [Six lines of verse.]
> *New-London: Printed and sold by Samuel Green.* [1799.] pp. (34). 12mo.
>> AAS. WL.

35369 —— SHEET ALMANAC FOR THE YEAR 1800.
> *New-London: Printed by Samuel Green,* 1799. Broadside.

35370 DAGGETT, DAVID   1764–1851
SUN-BEAMS MAY BE EXTRACTED FROM CUCUMBERS, BUT THE PROCESS IS TEDIOUS. AN
ORATION, PRONOUNCED ON THE FOURTH OF JULY, 1799, AT THE REQUEST OF THE
CITIZENS OF NEW-HAVEN. BY DAVID DAGGETT.
> *New-Haven: Printed by Thomas Green and Son.* [*Copy right secured.*]
> 1799. pp. 28. 8vo.   AAS. BM. CHS. JCB. NYPL. YC.

35371 —— — SUN-BEAMS MAY BE EXTRACTED FROM CUCUMBERS, BUT THE PROCESS IS
TEDIOUS. AN ORATION, PRONOUNCED ON THE FOURTH OF JULY, 1799. AT THE RE-
QUEST OF THE CITIZENS OF NEW-HAVEN. BY DAVID DAGGETT. THE SECOND
EDITION.
> *New-Haven: Printed by Thomas Green and Son.* [*August*] 1799. [*Copy
> right secured.*] pp. 28. 8vo.   AAS. BA. JCB. LOC. MHS. NYHS. NYPL. UTS.

Connecticut District Copyright, issued to Thomas Green, and Thomas
Green, junior, as Proprietors, 20 July, 1799.

35372 DAGGETT, HERMAN   1766–1832
A DISCOURSE, DELIVERED AT EAST-HAMPTON, (LONG-ISLAND,) LORD'S-DAY, JULY 22,
1798. OCCASIONED BY THE DEATH OF REV. SAMUEL BUELL, D. D. AND PASTOR OF
THE CHURCH THERE, WHO DEPARTED THIS LIFE, JULY 19, 1798. BY HERMAN
DAGGETT, A. M. AND PASTOR OF THE CHURCH IN WEST-HAMPTON.
> *New-London: Printed by Samuel Green.* 1799. pp. 23. 8vo.
>> AAS. JCB. LOC. MHS. NYPL.

35373 THE DAILY [cut of eagle] ADVERTISER. VOL. XV. No. 4337. TUESDAY, JANUARY
1, [— No. 4648. TUESDAY, DECEMBER 31, 1799.]
> *New-York: Printed by Charles Snowden, at his Office, No. 71, Pine-Street.*
> 1799. fol.   LOC. NYHS.

35374 DALLAS, ALEXANDER JAMES   1759–1817
REPORTS OF CASES, RULED AND ADJUDGED IN THE SEVERAL COURTS OF THE UNITED
STATES, AND OF PENNSYLVANIA, HELD AT THE SEAT OF THE FEDERAL GOVERNMENT.
BY A. J. DALLAS. VOL. III. [Three lines of Latin from] GROTIUS.
> *Philadelphia: Printed for the Reporter, by J. Ormrod.* 1799. pp. (2), (2),
> (3), 519, xiii. 8vo.   AAS. BM.

237th Pennsylvania District Copyright, issued to Alexander James
Dallas, as Author, 1 August, 1799.

AUCTION
VALUES

35375   DAMON'S SOLILOQUY. A NEW SONG. ADIEU YE STREAMS THAT GENTLY FLOWING, MURMUR THRO THE FLOW'RY MEAD, . . .

       [Boston:] Printed by Jonathan Nichols. 1799. Broadside.   BPL.

35376   DANA, DANIEL   1771–1859
      TWO SERMONS, DELIVERED APRIL 25, 1799: THE DAY RECOMMENDED BY THE PRESIDENT OF THE UNITED STATES FOR NATIONAL HUMILIATION, FASTING AND PRAYER. BY DANIEL DANA, A. M. PASTOR OF A CHURCH IN NEWBURYPORT. PUBLISHED BY DESIRE.

       Printed by Angier March, Newburyport, July, MDCCXCIX. pp. (56). 8vo.
                    AAS. BA. BM. CHS. CLA. HC. JCB. LOC. NYPL. UTS. YC.

35377   DANA, JAMES   1735–1812
      CHRISTIANITY THE WISDOM OF GOD. A SERMON, PREACHED OCTOBER 17, 1798, AT THE ORDINATION OF THE REV. DAN HUNTINGTON, TO THE PASTORAL CARE OF THE FIRST CHURCH AND SOCIETY IN LITCHFIELD, CONNECTICUT. BY JAMES DANA, D. D. PASTOR OF THE FIRST CONGREGATIONAL CHURCH IN NEW-HAVEN.

       Litchfield: Printed by Thomas Collier. 1799. pp. (30). 8vo.
                      AAS. BA. JCB. LOC. NYHS. NYPL. UTS.

      With a list of the former pastors at Litchfield.

35378   DANA, JOSEPH   1742–1827
      THE DUTY AND REWARD OF LOVING OUR COUNTRY, AND SEEKING IT'S PROSPERITY. A DISCOURSE DELIVERED IN TWO PARTS, AT THE NATIONAL FAST, APRIL 25TH, 1799. BY JOSEPH DANA, A. M. PASTOR OF THE SOUTH CHURCH IN IPSWICH.

       Boston: Printed by Manning & Loring. 1799. pp. 41. 8vo.
                 AAS. BA. BM. CLA. HC. JCB. LOC. MHS. NYHS. NYPL. YC.

35379   DANA, JOSEPH
      A NEW AMERICAN SELECTION OF LESSONS, IN READING AND SPEAKING. CONSISTING OF SACRED, MORAL, AND HISTORICAL EXTRACTS; HUMOROUS, ENTERTAINING AND DESCRIPTIVE PIECES; SELECT SENTENCES AND MAXIMS, POETRY, DIALOGUES, &C. TO WHICH ARE ADDED, ELEMENTS OF GESTURE. ILLUSTRATED WITH FOUR COPPERPLATE ENGRAVINGS. DESIGNED FOR THE USE OF SCHOOLS. BY JOSEPH DANA, A. B. PUBLISHED ACCORDING TO ACT OF CONGRESS. THIRD EDITION, CORRECTED AND IMPROVED.

       Printed at Exeter, by H. Ranlet, for Thomas and Andrews. Sold by them at their Book-Store, No. 45, Newbury-Street, Boston; by I. Thomas, Worcester; by Thomas, Andrews and Penniman, Albany; by Thomas, Andrews and Butler, Baltimore, &c. &c. Jan. 1799. pp. 300, 4 plates. 12mo.   AAS. LOC.

35380   DANE, NATHAN   1752–1835
      BEVERLY, JANUARY 19, 1799. CIRCULAR. SIR, AS THE FOLLOWING QUESTIONS HAVE (AMONG OTHERS OF LESS IMPORTANCE) BEEN STATED BY ASSESSORS IN THE DIFFERENT PARTS OF THE THIRD DIVISION — . . . . NATHAN DANE.

       [Salem: Printed by Thomas C. Cushing ? 1799.] Broadside.   MHS.

35381   DARTMOUTH UNIVERSITY.
      A CATALOGUE OF THE GRADUATES AT DARTMOUTH UNIVERSITY, AUGUST 28, 1799. [Two columns.] [Colophon:]

       From the Press of M. Davis, Concord. [1799.] Broadside. 4to.   AAS. DU.

35382   DARTMOUTH Gazette. [Motto.] Vol. i, Numb. 1. Tuesday, August 27, [— Numb. 19. Monday, December 30, 1799.]

Hanover, New-Hampshire: Printed on the College Plain, by Moses Davis. 1799. fol.

The motto reads: Here range the World, Explore the dense and rare And view all nature in your elbow chair.

Established, as a weekly, by Moses Davis, and continued by him to his death, 24 July, 1808. The issue for July 27th, bore his name, that for August 3d, had no publisher's name, and that for August 10th, was Printed for the Proprietor, by Colburn & Day. In November, 1808, Charles, and William S. Spear became the Publishers. And, with the issue for October 31, 1810, Henry Spear was admitted to partnership, as C. W. S. & H. Spear. In May ?, 1811, the firm was dissolved, Charles Spear continuing publication, changing the title in November, 1813, to *Dartmouth Gazette, and Grafton and Coo's Advertiser*, up to February 21, 1816, when the sub-title was dropped, into the year 1820.

35383   DAVIE, William Richardson   1756–1820
Instructions to be observed for the formation and movements of the cavalry. Published agreeably to a resolution of the Legislature of North-Carolina. By William Richardson Davie, esquire, governor, captain-general and commander in chief of the militia of the State of North-Carolina.

Halifax: Printed by Abraham Hodge. MDCCXCIX. pp. ix, 1, 1, 180, 3 folded plates. 8vo.   BA. NCU. NYPL.

35384   DAVIES, Benjamin
The American repository, and annual register, for 1799. Containing: a complete and correct list of the executive, legislative, and judiciary departments of government; of the ministers and consuls to and from the United States; lists of the custom-house officers at all the different ports; the times of receiving and closing the mails at Philadelphia; rates of postage; the distances on the main post roads, as well as on the cross-roads; a list of the chief governors in the United States, their salaries, and the expenses of the civil list in each State; an alphabetical table of import duties; an abstract of the law imposing duties, on stamped paper, &c. and an account of the duties payable on domestic articles; the civil government of Pennsylvania, its executive, legislative, judiciary, and land officers; the police officers of Philadelphia; the wardens of the port, and the board of health, the number of pleasure carriages, carts, drays, and public licensed houses; the times of holding the federal courts in the State of Pennsylvania; a table of fees payable in certain offices and courts of the United States; and a variety of other tables necessary to be known in every State of the Union. Embellished with a very handsome engraving.

Philadelphia: Printed for Benjamin Davies, No. 68, High-Street. 1799. BM.

35385   —— A Map of Philadelphia, taken from actual survey, and engraved in the neatest manner, on a plate twenty-six inches square. Exhibiting a correct view of all the streets, lanes, and alleys in the city. The Northern Liberties, and Southwark, and shewing the present extent of building in each.

Philadelphia: Published by Benjamin Davies, No. 68, High-Street. 1799. 26 x 26.

35386 DAVIS, JOHN 1761–1847
AN ADDRESS, DELIVERED BEFORE THE MEMBERS OF THE MASSACHUSETTS CHARITABLE FIRE SOCIETY, AT THEIR ANNUAL MEETING, IN BOSTON, MAY 31, 1799. SPERATE MISERI; CAVETE FELICES. [Printer's mark.]
Boston: Printed by John Russell. 1799. pp. 24. 8vo.
AAS. BA. BM. JCB. LOC. MHS. NYHS. NYPL.

35387 DAVIS, JOHN 1776–
Caption title: NUMBER I. POEMS, WRITTEN AT COOSAHATCHIE. IN SOUTH-CAROLINA. BY JOHN DAVIS. [Colophon:]
Printed by T. C. Cox, No. 137, *Tradd-Street, Charleston.* [1799.] pp. 12. 12mo.
CLS.

35388 DEARBORN, BENJAMIN 1755–1838
A DESCRIPTION OF THE VIBRATING STEELYARD, OR JUST BALANCE. INVENTED BY THE SUBSCRIBER, AND SECURED TO HIM BY PATENT. . . . TAUNTON, SEPT. 1799.
[*New-Bedford: Printed by John Spooner?* 1799.] Broadside. MHS.

35389 [THE DEATH OF BRAVE WOLF[e.] Sixteen four-line verses, in two columns.]
Norwich: Printed [by John Trumbull ?] 1799. Broadside. 4to. JCB.

35390 DECALOGUE, JEAN MARIE
THE LIFE OF JOHN MARY DECALOGUE, STUDENT IN THE UNIVERSITY OF PARIS. (TRANSLATED FROM THE FRENCH.)
Baltimore: Printed by Warner & Hanna. 1799. LOC.

35391 DECALVES, ALONSO, pseudonym.
NEW TRAVELS TO THE WESTWARD; OR, UNKNOWN PARTS OF AMERICA. BEING A TOUR OF ALMOST FOURTEEN MONTHS. CONTAINING AN ACCOUNT OF THE COUNTRY, UPWARDS OF TWO THOUSAND MILES WEST OF THE CHRISTIAN PARTS OF NORTH-AMERICA; WITH AN ACCOUNT OF WHITE INDIANS, THEIR MANNERS, HABITS, AND OTHER PARTICULARS. BY DON ALONSO DECALVES, CONFIRMED BY THREE OTHER PERSONS. THE FIFTH EDITION.
Hudson: Printed and sold by A. Stoddard. 1799. pp. 44. 16mo. HEH.

35392 DECAMBON, MARIA GEERTRUIDA VAN DE WERKEN
LETTERS AND CONVERSATIONS BETWEEN SEVERAL YOUNG LADIES, ON INTERESTING AND IMPROVING SUBJECTS. TRANSLATED FROM THE DUTCH OF MADAME DECAMBON, WITH ALTERATIONS AND IMPROVEMENTS. THIRD EDITION.
Richmond: Sold by W. Pritchard. 1799. pp. 318. 12mo. LOC.
Probably the Philadelphia 1797, edition on sale.

35393 DELANOE, S.
MISCELLANEOUS THOUGHTS ON THE DOCTRINE OF LIMITED ELECTION AND REPROBATION, AS IT STANDS CONTRASTED WITH SCRIPTURE AND REASON. BY A PRIVATE CITIZEN OF VERMONT. PART II.
Windsor: Printed by Alden Spooner for the Author. 1799.

35394 DELAWARE. STATE.
JOURNAL OF THE HOUSE OF REPRESENTATIVES OF THE STATE OF DELAWARE, AT A SESSION OF THE GENERAL ASSEMBLY, WHICH WAS BEGUN AND HELD AT DOVER, ON TUESDAY, THE FIRST DAY OF JANUARY, AND ENDED ON SATURDAY, THE SECOND DAY OF FEBRUARY, IN THE YEAR OF OUR LORD ONE THOUSAND SEVEN HUNDRED AND NINETY-NINE AND OF THE INDEPENDENCE OF THE UNITED STATES OF AMERICA THE TWENTY-THIRD. [— 2 FEBRUARY, 1799.]
New-Castle: Printed by Samuel and John Adams. 1799. fol. LOC.

35395 DELAWARE. STATE, continued.
—— JOURNAL OF THE SENATE OF THE STATE OF DELAWARE, AT A SESSION OF THE GENERAL ASSEMBLY, COMMENCED AND HOLDEN AT DOVER, ON TUESDAY, THE FIRST DAY OF JANUARY, IN THE YEAR OF OUR LORD ONE THOUSAND SEVEN HUNDRED AND NINETY-NINE. [— 2 FEBRUARY, 1799], PURSUANT TO THE DIRECTION OF THE FOURTH SECTION OF THE SECOND ARTICLE OF THE CONSTITUTION OF THE SAID STATE, AND IN THE TWENTY-THIRD YEAR OF THE INDEPENDENCE OF THE UNITED STATES. [Arms.]
New-Castle: Printed by S. and Jno. Adams, nearly opposite the Court-House. 1799. pp. 85. fol. AAS. LOC.

35396 —— THE LAWS OF THE STATE OF DELAWARE, FROM THE EARLIEST TIMES TO THE YEAR 1798; WITH AN APPENDIX, CONTAINING VARIOUS PUBLIC RECORDS, AND CERTAIN LEGISLATIVE ACTS, WHICH FROM THEIR CONNECTION IN SOME RESPECTS WITH THE EXISTING LAWS, REQUIRE TO BE PRESERVED. TO WHICH ARE PREFIXED, THE CONSTITUTION OF THE UNITED STATES, AND THE CONSTITUTION OF THE STATE OF DELAWARE.
[New-Castle: Printed by Samuel and John Adams, 1799.]

35397 THE DELAWARE AND EASTERN-SHORE ADVERTISER. No. 485. THURSDAY, JANUARY 3, [— No. 545. THURSDAY, AUGUST 1, 1799.]
Wilmington: Printed on Mondays and Thursdays, by Samuel & John Adams, corner of King and High-Streets, . . . 1799. fol.

The above is the last number located.

35398 THE DELAWARE GAZETTE. "THE NOBLEST MOTIVE IS THE PUBLIC GOOD." No. 895. WEDNESDAY, MARCH 14, [— No. 946. SATURDAY, SEPTEMBER 7, 1799.]
Printed by Bonsal & Niles for Vaughan & Coleman, Market-Street, Wilmington. 1799. fol. DHS.

September 7th, John Vaughan and Daniel Coleman, disposed of their interests to James Wilson, and publication was suspended at that date. On November 20th, Wilson established, in continuation, with a new serial numbering, the *Mirror of the Times, & General Advertiser.*

35399 DELAWARE AND SCHUYLKILL CANAL COMPANY.
ADDRESS OF THE COMMITTEE OF THE DELAWARE AND SCHUYLKILL CANAL COMPANY, TO THE COMMITTEES OF THE SENATE AND HOUSE OF REPRESENTATIVES, ON THE MEMORIAL OF SAID COMPANY.
Printed by John Ormrod, Philadelphia. [1799.] pp. 32,7. 8vo. HC. LOC. MHS.

Second caption title: REMARKS ON A SECOND PUBLICATION OF B. HENRY LATROBE, ENGINEER, SAID TO BE PRINTED BY ORDER OF THE COMMITTEE OF THE COUNCILS [of Philadelphia]: AND DISTRIBUTED AMONG THE MEMBERS OF THE LEGISLATURE. pp. 7.

35400 THE DEMOS IN COUNCIL: OR 'BIJAH IN PANDEMONIUM. BEING A SWEEP OF THE LYRE, IN CLOSE IMITATION OF MILTON. A POEM. [Four lines of verse.]
Boston: Printed by James Cutler, and for sale at the Bookstores.—April, 1799. pp. 16. 8vo. AAS. BA. BU. HC. LOC.

Reprinted in Tarrytown, in 1925.
Clef of characters: 'Bijah–Samuel Adams; Hones– —— Austin; Junius– —— Jarvis; Tummas–Thomas Edwards; Mozard–Dr. Linnehard? Niffey N– —— Noyes; Dr. V–Dr. Vinal; Dr. H– —— Hall; Gov. H– John Hancock?

35401   DEMOSTHENES, VERSUS CICERO; ALIAS, THE WOLF IN THE SHEEP'S COAT; OR, THE IMPOSTER [*sic*] DETECTED. BEING A SUITABLE REPLY TO THE ANTI-MASONIC, ANTI-ILLUMINATI, ANTI-REPUBLICAN REVERIES, IN A LATE PUBLICATION, UNDER THE INSIDIOUS SIGNATURE OF A CICERO. SUB OVIS PELLE ECCE LUPUM!

      Baltimore: Printed for the Author. [1799.] pp. [49.] 12mo.   HSP. LOC.

35402   THE DESSERT TO THE TRUE AMERICAN. VOL. I. NO. 26. SATURDAY, JANUARY 5, [— VOL. II. NO. 7. MONDAY, AUGUST 19, 1799.]

      [*Philadelphia: Published by*] *Samuel F. Bradford, Editor & Proprietor.* 1799. 4to.   AAS. HSP. LCP. WHS. YC.

      The above is the last number located.

35403   DER DEUTSCHE PORCUPEIN UND LANCÄSTER ANZEIGS-NACHRICHTEN. NUM. 53. MITTWOCH, JANUAR 2, [— NUM. 104. MITTWOCH, DEZEMBER 25, 1799.]

      Lancaster: Gedruckt bey Johann Albrecht und Comp. 1799. fol.   LOC.

      Discontinued at the above date. With the issue for January 1, 1800, without change in numbering, the title was changed to *Der Americanische Staatsbothe, und Lancäster anzeigs-Nachrichten.*

35404   DEVENS, RICHARD, JUNIOR   1749–1835

      THE WITNESS OF THE SPIRIT. A DISCOURSE, DELIVERED TO THE STUDENTS OF NEW JERSEY COLLEGE, MDCCLXXIII. BY RICHARD DEVENS, JUN. A.M. THEN TUTOR IN THE COLLEGE; AUTHOR OF A PARAPHRASE OF A PART OF THE BOOK OF JOB, AND OF A DISCOURSE, DELIVERED TO THE STUDENTS IN DIVINITY IN THE SAID COLLEGE.

      Charlestown: Printed by Samuel Etheridge. 1799. pp. [16.] 8vo.   BA.

35405   DEWEY, SHERMAN   1772–1813

      ACCOUNT OF A HAIL STORM, WHICH FELL ON PART OF THE TOWNS OF LEBANON, BOZRAH AND FRANKLIN, ON THE 15TH OF JULY, 1799; PERHAPS NEVER EQUALED BY ANY OTHER EVER KNOWN, NOT EVEN IN EGYPT. BY SHERMAN DEWEY. [COPY RIGHT SECURED.]

      Walpole, Newhampshire, Printed at the Press of Thomas & Thomas, by David Carlisle, for the Author. 1799. pp. (27). 8vo.   AAS. BA. JCB. NYPL.

      Vermont District Copyright, issued to Sherman Dewey, as Author, 4 October, 1799.

35406   DEWEY, SOLOMON

      A SHORT AND EASY METHOD OF SURVEYING; ADAPTED TO EVERY CAPACITY; DESIGNED CHIEFLY FOR SCHOOLS AND COMMON PRACTICE: TO WHICH IS ADDED THE SQUARE ROOT. BY SOLOMON DEWEY . . .

      Hartford. Printed by E. Babcock. 1799. pp. 24. 12mo.   LOC.

      Sold also by the Author, in Bolton.

35407   DIBDIN, CHARLES   1745–1814

      A COLLECTION OF SONGS, SELECTED FROM THE WORKS OF THE CELEBRATED MR. DIBDIN. TO WHICH ARE ADDED, THE NEWEST AND MOST FAVORITE AMERICAN PATRIOTIC SONGS. [Seven lines of quotation.]

      Philadelphia: Printed by J. Bioren for H. & P. Rice, and sold by J. Rice, Baltimore. 1799. pp. 328, x. 12mo.   AAS. LOC. NYPL.

35408   DICKSON, WILLIAM and ROBERT

      DICKSON'S BALLOON ALMANAC, FOR THE YEAR 1800. CONTAINING (BESIDES THE USUAL ASTRONOMICAL CALCULATIONS) A VARIETY OF ENTERTAINMENT, IN VERSE AND PROSE, . . .

      Lancaster: Printed by W. & R. Dickson. [1799.]

35409   DILWORTH, THOMAS   –1780
A NEW GUIDE TO THE ENGLISH TONGUE: IN FIVE PARTS. BY THOMAS DILWORTH.
Wilmington, Printed and sold by Peter Brynberg, 1799. pp. 142 incl. fron-
tispiece portrait. Illus. 12mo.   LOC.

35410   —— THE SCHOOLMASTER'S ASSISTANT: BEING A COMPENDIUM OF ARITHMETIC, BOTH
PRACTICAL AND THEORETICAL. IN FIVE PARTS. . . . TO WHICH IS PREFIXED, AN
ESSAY ON THE EDUCATION OF YOUTH: HUMBLY OFFERED TO THE CONSIDERATION
OF PARENTS, BY THOMAS DILWORTH . . .
*Philadelphia: Printed and sold by John Bioren, No. 83, Chesnut, four doors
below Third-street.* 1799. pp. xiv, (8), 194, folded plate. 12mo.   HEH.

35411   —— — THE SCHOOLMASTERS ASSISTANT: BEING A COMPENDIUM OF ARITHMETIC,
BOTH PRACTICAL AND THEORETICAL. IN FIVE PARTS. CONTAINING I. ARITHMETIC
IN WHOLE NUMBERS: WHEREIN ALL THE COMMON RULES, HAVING EACH OF THEM A
SUFFICIENT NUMBER OF QUESTIONS, WITH THEIR ANSWERS ARE METHODICALLY AND
BRIEFLY HANDLED. II. VULGAR FRACTIONS: WHEREIN SEVERAL THINGS, NOT COM-
MONLY MET WITH, ARE THERE DISTINCTLY TREATED OF, AND LAID DOWN IN THE MOST
PLAIN AND EASY MANNER. III. DECIMALS, IN WHICH, AMONG OTHER THINGS, ARE
CONSIDERED THE EXTRACTION OF ROOTS; INTEREST, BOTH SIMPLE AND COMPOUND;
ANNUITIES, REBATE, & EQUATION OF PAYMENTS. IV. A LARGE COLLECTION OF
QUESTIONS, WITH THEIR ANSWERS, SERVING TO EXERCISE THE FOREGOING RULES;
TOGETHER, WITH A FEW OTHERS, BOTH PLEASANT AND DIVERTING. V. DUODEC-
IMALS, COMMONLY CALLED CROSS MULTIPLICATION; WHEREIN THAT SORT OF ARITH-
METIC IS THOROUGHLY CONSIDERED, AND RENDERED VERY PLAIN AND EASY;
TOGETHER WITH THE METHOD OF PROVING ALL THE FOREGOING OPERATIONS AT
ONCE, BY DIVISION OF SEVERAL DENOMINATIONS, WITHOUT REDUCING THEM TO THE
LOWEST TERM MENTIONED. THE WHOLE BEING DELIVERED IN THE MOST FAMILIAR
WAY OF QUESTION AND ANSWER, IS RECOMMENDED BY SEVERAL EMINENT MATHE-
MATICIANS, ACCOMPTANTS AND SCHOOLMASTERS, AS NECESSARY TO BE USED IN
SCHOOLS BY ALL TEACHERS, WHO WOULD HAVE THEIR SCHOLARS THOROUGHLY UN-
DERSTAND, AND MAKE A QUICK PROGRESS IN ARITHMETIC. BY THOMAS DILWORTH,
AUTHOR OF THE NEW GUIDE TO THE ENGLISH TONGUE; YOUNG BOOKKEEPER'S
ASSISTANT; &C. AND SCHOOLMASTER IN WAPPING.
*Wilmington: Printed and sold by Bonsal and Niles. Also sold at their Book-
store, No. 173, Market-street, Baltimore.* [1799.] pp. (2), (2), 192, folded table,
portrait. 12mo.   AAS. JCB.

35412   DIVINE BREATHINGS: OR, A PIOUS SOUL THIRSTING AFTER CHRIST: IN A HUNDRED
PATHETICAL MEDITATIONS. FIRST AMERICAN EDITION. PSALM LXXIII. 25. [TWO
lines.]
*Printed at Leominster, (Mass.) by Charles Prentiss, for Robert B. Thomas,
Sterling.* 1799. pp. 167, (6). 24mo.   AAS. JCB.

35413   DOBSON, THOMAS
LETTERS ON THE EXISTENCE AND CHARACTER OF THE DEITY, AND ON THE MORAL
STATE OF MAN.
*Philadelphia: Printed for Thomas Dobson, at the Stone House, No. 41, South
Second Street.* 1799. pp. (144). 16mo.   AAS. JCB.
229th Pennsylvania District Copyright, issued to Thomas Dobson, as
Author, 23 April, 1799. A second part was published by Thomas Dob-
son, in Philadelphia, in 1802.

35414   DODDRIDGE, PHILIP   1702–1751
PLAIN AND SERIOUS ADDRESS TO THE MASTER OF A FAMILY, ON THE IMPORTANT SUB-
JECT OF FAMILY-RELIGION. BY PHILIP DODDRIDGE, D.D. REPRINTED FOR THE USE
OF THE TRUSTEES OF THE MISSIONARY SOCIETY. [Ornament.]
Hartford: Printed by John Babcock. 1799. pp. 24. 8vo.   AAS.

DODDRIDGE, PHILIP, continued.

35415 —— THE PRINCIPLES OF THE CHRISTIAN RELIGION: DIVIDED INTO LESSONS AND
ADAPTED TO THE CAPACITIES OF CHILDREN. [Vignette.]
> *Printed at Worcester, by Isaiah Thomas, jun. sold wholesale and retail at his
Store.* 1799. pp. (32), 6 cuts. 32mo.   AAS.

35416 —— — THE PRINCIPLES OF THE CHRISTIAN RELIGION, EXPRESSED IN PLAIN AND
EASY VERSE, AND DIVIDED INTO SHORT LESSONS, FOR THE USE OF CHILDREN AND
YOUTH. COMPOSED AT NORTHAMPTON, (IN ENGLAND;) AND FIRST PUBLISHED A.D.
1743. BY PHILIP DODDRIDGE, D.D.
> *Worcester: Printed by Mower & Greenleaf.* 1799. pp. 24. 12mo.   AAS.

35417 —— A SERMON, [ON THE ONE THING NEEDFUL], PREACHED AT MAIDWELL, IN NORTH-
AMPTONSHIRE, JUNE 22, 1735. BY PHILLIP [*sic*] DODDRIDGE, D.D. [Four lines of
Scripture texts.]
> *Dedham: Printed by Herman Mann, for the Rev. Mr. Haven.* M,DCC,-
LXXXXIX. pp. (23). 8vo.   AAS. JCB.

> Reprinted evidently for presentation to the members of his congrega-
tion by their friend and pastor, Jason Haven,

35418 DOGGETT, SIMEON, JUNIOR   1765–1852
AN ORATION, DELIVERED AT TAUNTON, ON THE 4TH OF JULY, 1799. BY SIMEON DOG-
GETT, JUN. A.M. PRECEPTOR OF BRISTOL ACADEMY. . . .
> *Newbedford (Massachusetts): Printed by John Spooner.* 1799. pp. 20. 8vo.
> BA. JCB. MHS. NYPL.

35419 DOUGLAS, GEORGE
PRINTING-OFFICE, PETERSBURGH. G. DOUGLAS HAVING OPENED A PRINTING-OFFICE,
FURNISHED WITH A COMPLETE SET OF TYPES AND THE NECESSARY MATERIALS, IS
READY TO UNDERTAKE ANY KIND OF PRINTING WORK WITH WHICH MERCHANTS OR
OTHERS, EITHER IN TOWN OR COUNTRY, MAY BE PLEASED TO EMPLOY HIM, AND
WHICH HE WILL EXECUTE WITH EXPEDITION IN THE NEATEST MANNER, AND ON THE
MOST REASONABLE TERMS – – – – SEPT. 1, 1799. N.B. ORDERS LEFT AT THE
STORE OF ROSS & DOUGLAS, AT THE HEAD OF BOLLINGBROOK-STREET, WILL BE
PUNCTUALLY ATTENDED TO. [On the verso is the advertisement of Ross & Doug-
las, Petersburgh. Two columns.]
> *[Petersburgh: Printed by G. Douglas, 1799.]* pp. (2). fol.   LOC.

> In ms. "Sold to Lady Skipwith, 1 set Sillery on education 10/6; Tri-
umph of temper 6/ ; National spelling-book 3/ ; Universal spelling-book
(lately published in Philadelphia) 1/10.

35420 DOVER. VIRGINIA. BAPTIST ASSOCIATION.
MINUTES OF THE BAPTIST DOVER ASSOCIATION, HELD AT HICKORY-NECK MEETING-
HOUSE, JAMES CITY COUNTY, VIRGINIA, OCTOBER 12TH, 1799.
> *Richmond: Printed by Samuel Pleasants jun.* [1799.] pp. [11.] 8vo. AAS.

35421 DOW, HENDRICUS or HENDRICK   1761–1814
A POEM IN TWO LETTERS. ARGUMENT. A CANDIDATE FOR THE MINISTRY OF THE
GOSPEL IS HIGHLY CENSURED BY A PHYSICIAN, FOR SOME LITTLE FAMILIARITIES
TAKEN WITH A YOUNG MAIDEN, WHOM HE ACCIDENTLY MET WITH IN HIS RAMBLES
INTO THE FIELDS, IN THE SEASON FOR STRAWBERRIES. — THE REVEREND DIVINE
MAKES A SPIRITED REPLY, AND SEEMS TO JUSTIFY HIMSELF.
> *Printed at Brattleborough [by Benjamin Smead.]* 1799. pp. 11. 12mo. HEH.

35422 —— — A POEM. CONTAINING TWO LETTERS BETWEEN A MINISTER AND A PHYSICIAN.
> *New-Haven: Printed for the Flying Stationers.* 1799. pp. 11. 12mo. HEH.

35423 DREW, SAMUEL   1765–1833
REMARKS ON THE FIRST PART OF THOMAS PAINE'S AGE OF REASON. BY SAMUEL DREW.
Brooklyn: Printed by Thomas Kirk. 1799.

A second edition was printed in New York in 1831.

35424 DUANE, WILLIAM   1760–1835
A REPORT OF THE EXTRAORDINARY TRANSACTIONS WHICH TOOK PLACE AT PHILA-
DELPHIA, IN FEBRUARY 1799. IN CONSEQUENCE OF A MEMORIAL FROM CERTAIN
NATIVES OF IRELAND TO CONGRESS, PRAYING A REPEAL OF THE ALIEN BILL;—CON-
TAINING—AN ACCOUNT OF THE PROCEEDINGS WHICH PRODUCED THE MEMORIAL—
THE ASSAULT ON THE COMMITTEE AT ST. MARY'S CHURCH.—AND THE PROCEEDINGS
AT THE MAYOR'S OFFICE, UPON THE ARREST OF THE MEMORIALISTS. A COPY OF THE
MEMORIAL. AND, THE TRIAL, WITH THE NAMES OF THE JURY, THE EVIDENCE AT
LARGE, THE SPEECHES OF COUNSEL ON BOTH SIDES, AND THE CHARGE TO THE JURY.
BY WILLIAM DUANE.
Philadelphia: Printed at the Office of the Aurora. 1799. pp. (4), [47], (6).
8vo.   HSP. LOC.

35425 DUBOIS-FONTANELLE, JEAN GASPARD   1737–1812
THE SHIPWRECK AND ADVENTURES OF MONSIEUR PIERRE VIAUD. A NATIVE OF
BORDEAUX AND CAPTAIN OF A SHIP. TRANSLATED FROM THE FRENCH, BY MRS.
GRIFFITH. FIRST AMERICAN EDITION. . . .
Dover, N. H. Printed and sold by Samuel Bragg, jr. 1799. pp. viii, 203.
18mo.   BA. BM. JCB. LOC. NYPL.

35426 DUKE OF YORK'S MARCH.
Printed and sold. Philadelphia by G. Willig. Market Street No. 185. [1799.]

35427 DU PRÉ, LEWIS
OBSERVATIONS ON THE CULTURE OF COTTON. BY LEWIS DU PRE.
Georgetown: [S. C.] Printed by Elliott & Burd. 1799.

35428 DWIGHT, NATHANIEL   1770–1831
A SHORT BUT COMPREHENSIVE SYSTEM OF THE GEOGRAPHY OF THE WORLD: BY WAY
OF QUESTION AND ANSWER. PRINCIPALLY DESIGNED FOR CHILDREN, AND COMMON
SCHOOLS. BY NATHANIEL DWIGHT. THE SECOND ALBANY EDITION. FROM THE
SECOND HARTFORD EDITION, ENLARGED AND IMPROVED. [Four lines of quotations.]
*Albany: Printed by Charles R. & George Webster. [With privilege of copy
-right.] Sold at their Bookstore, in the White-House, corner of State and Pearl
streets*—MDCCXCIX. pp. 187, (4). 12mo.   AAS.

35429 THE EAGLE. VOLUME VI. NUMBER 24. TUESDAY, JANUARY 1, [—VOLUME VI. NUM-
BER 45. SATURDAY, JUNE 1, 1799.]
*Hanover, Newhampshire, Printed at the northwest corner of College Square, in
the Academy, by Benjamin True.* 1799. fol.   AAS.

The above is the last number located.

35430 THE EAGLE, OR, CARLISLE HERALD. VOL. I. NO. 1. WEDNESDAY, OCTOBER 2, [—
NO. 13. WEDNESDAY, DECEMBER 25, 1799.]
Carlisle: Published by John P. Thompson. 1799. fol.

Established, as a weekly, by John P. Thompson, deputy-postmaster, and
continued by him to June, 1802, when he removed to Frederick Town,
Maryland. And succeeded in June, 1802, by the *Carlisle Herald*, which
was continued under various owners down to the year 1921, bringing it
within the small group of centennial newspapers.

35431   EAST INDIA COMPANY OF NORTH AMERICA.
CONSTITUTIONAL ARTICLES OF THE ASSOCIATION OF THE EAST INDIA COMPANY OF NORTH-AMERICA.
> *Philadelphia: Printed by John Ward Fenno.* 1799. pp. (14). 8vo.
>> AAS. LOC. NYPL.

35432   EASTERN HERALD [cut] AND GAZETTE OF MAINE. THE PEOPLE AND THE GOVERNMENT. [Motto.] VOL. XIV. MONDAY, JANUARY 7, [—VOL. XV. MONDAY, DECEMBER 30, 1799.]
> *Published by Baker & George, Fish Street, Portland. [District of Maine.] [Massachusetts.]* 1799. fol.

> The motto, from Shakespeare, reads: Who is so vile as not to love his country? If any, speak, for him shall we offend.

35433   EATON, PETER   1765–1848
A SERMON, PREACHED AT BOXFORD, NOVEMBER 28, 1799. THE DAY OF ANNIVERSARY THANKSGIVING IN THE COMMONWEALTH OF MASSACHUSETTS. BY PETER EATON, A. M. MINISTER OF A CHURCH IN SAID TOWN. [Ornament.]
> *Haverhill. From the Press of Moore & Stebbins. Published for the Subscribers.—Dec.* 1799. pp. 24. 8vo.   AAS. BM. JCB. LOC. NYHS.

35434   EDDY, SAMUEL   1769–1839
ADDRESS OF SAMUEL EDDY TO THE GENERAL ASSEMBLY, JUNE SESSION, A. D. 1799. [Presenting an Act to establish free schools.]
> *Newport: Printed by Oliver Farnsworth,* 1799. pp. 12. 12mo.

35435   EDMOND, DAVID   1778–1824
AN ORATION, DELIVERED AT RIDGFIELD, ON THE FOURTH OF JULY, 1799, BEFORE A LARGE CONCOURSE OF PEOPLE, ASSEMBLED TO COMMEMORATE THEIR INDEPENDENCE. BY DAVID EDMOND.
> *Danbury: Printed by Douglas & Nichols.* 1799. pp. 15. 8vo.   LOC. NYYL.

35436   EDSON, JESSE   1773–1805
A DISCOURSE, DELIVERED TO THE YOUNG PEOPLE OF HALIFAX, OCTOBER 17TH, 1799, AND MADE PUBLIC AT THEIR REQUEST. BY JESSE EDSON, A. M. PASTOR OF THE CONGREGATIONAL CHURCH IN HALIFAX. . . .
> *Printed at Greenfield, Massachusetts, by Thomas Dickman.* [1799.] pp. 23. 8vo.   AAS. JCB.

35437   EDWARDS, JONATHAN   1703–1758
Half-title: TWO DISCOURSES, PREACHED BY THE LATE PRESIDENT EDWARDS. REPRINTED FOR THE USE OF THE TRUSTEES OF THE MISSIONARY SOCIETY.
Title: THE JUSTICE OF GOD IN THE DAMNATION OF SINNERS. A DISCOURSE DELIVERED AT NORTHAMPTON, AT THE TIME OF THE REVIVAL OF RELIGION THERE, IN THE YEAR 1734.
Second title: A DISCOURSE ON TRUE GRACE DISTINGUISHED FROM THE EXPERIENCE OF DEVILS. BY JONATHAN EDWARDS, A. M. PASTOR OF THE CHURCH OF CHRIST IN NORTHAMPTON, AND AFTERWARDS PRESIDENT OF PRINCETON COLLEGE.
> *Hartford: Printed by John Babcock.* 1799. pp. 132. 12mo.   NYPL.

35438   EDWARDS, JONATHAN   1745–1801
A FAREWELL SERMON, TO THE PEOPLE OF COLEBROOK, DELIVERED JULY 14TH, 1799. BY JONATHAN EDWARDS, D. D. RESIDENT [*sic*] OF UNION COLLEGE. PRINTED AT THE REQUEST OF THE HEARERS. [Ornament.]
> *Suffield: Printed by Edward Gray,* M,DCC,XCIX. pp. (15). 8vo.
>> JCB. LOC. PU. UTS.

35439 ELMINA; OR, THE FLOWER THAT NEVER FADES. A TALE FOR YOUNG PEOPLE. ORNA-
MENTED WITH ELEGANT CUTS.
Hartford: Printed by John Babcock. 1799. pp.48, cuts in text. 24mo. AAS. JCB.

35440 ELY, JOHN   1763–1827
A SERMON, DELIVERED IN THE FIRST PRESBYTERIAN CHURCH IN DANBURY, NOVEM-
BER 25, 1798: IT BEING THE DAY APPOINTED ON WHICH THE ADDRESS FROM THE
GENERAL ASSEMBLY OF CONNECTICUT WAS TO BE READ UNTO THE PEOPLE ASSEMBLED
FOR PUBLIC WORSHIP THROUGH THE STATE: AND ALSO IN THE SECOND PRESBYTE-
RIAN CHURCH IN DANBURY, DECEMBER 9, 1798. BY JOHN ELY, A.M. PASTOR OF
THE SECOND PRESBYTERIAN CHURCH IN DANBURY. . . .
Danbury: Printed by Douglas & Nichols. 1799. pp. 14. 8vo. CHS. NYPL. UTS.

35441 ELY, JOHN
THE CHILD'S INSTRUCTOR: CONSISTING OF EASY LESSONS FOR CHILDREN; ON SUBJECTS
WHICH ARE FAMILIAR TO THEM IN LANGUAGE ADAPTED TO THEIR CAPACITIES. BY A
TEACHER OF LITTLE CHILDREN IN PHILADELPHIA. SECOND CONNECTICUT EDITION.
Newfield: Printed by Lazarus Beach. 1799. pp. 108. 12mo.

35442 ELY, ZEBULON   1759–1824
EVANGELICAL CONSOLATION. A SERMON, DELIVERED AT THE FUNERAL OF MRS. BE-
THIAH HUNTINGTON, THE AMIABLE CONSORT OF CAPTAIN WILLIAM HUNTINGTON.
WHO DEPARTED THIS LIFE, JULY 12, 1799.— IN THE 61ST YEAR OF HER AGE. BY
ZEBULON ELY, PASTOR OF THE FIRST CHURCH IN LEBANON. [Three lines from]
REV. XIV. 13.
Printed in Norwich, by John Trumbull. M,DCC,XCIX. pp. [16.] 8vo.
AAS. CHS. NYPL.

35443 EMERSON, WILLIAM   1769–1811
PIETY AND ARMS. A SERMON, PREACHED AT THE REQUEST OF THE ANCIENT AND
HONOURABLE ARTILLERY COMPANY, IN BOSTON. JUNE 3, 1799; THE ANNIVERSARY
OF THEIR ELECTION OF OFFICERS. BY WILLIAM EMERSON.
Boston: Printed by Manning & Loring. 1799. pp. [23.] 8vo.
BA. HC. LOC. NYHS. RIHS.

35444 EMMONS, NATHANAEL   1745–1840
A DISCOURSE, DELIVERED ON THE NATINOAL [*sic*] FAST, APRIL 25, 1799. BY NA-
THANAEL EMMONS, D.D. PASTOR OF THE CHURCH IN FRANKLIN.
Printed at Wrentham, Massachusetts, by Nathaniel and Benjamin Heaton.
M,DCC,XCIX. pp. 31. 8vo.   AAS. BA. CHS. CLA. HC. JCB. NYPL. UTS. YC.

35445 —— A DISCOURSE, DELIVERED MAY 9, 1798. BEING THE DAY OF FASTING AND PRAYER
THROUGHOUT THE UNITED STATES. BY NATHANAEL EMMONS, A.M. PASTOR OF THE
CHURCH IN FRANKLIN. SECOND EDITION.
Newburyport: Re-printed by Angier March. [1799.] pp. 24. 8vo.
BA. BM. HC. NYPL.

35446 ENFIELD, WILLIAM   1741–1797
THE SPEAKER; OR, MISCELLANEOUS PIECES, SELECTED FROM VARIOUS AUTHORS. AND
DISPOSED UNDER PROPER HEADS, WITH A VIEW TO FACILITATE THE IMPROVEMENT
OF YOUTH IN READING AND SPEAKING. TO WHICH IS PREFIXED, AN ESSAY ON ELO-
CUTION. BY WILLIAM ENFIELD, L.L.D. LECTURER ON THE BELLES LETTRES IN THE
ACADEMY AT WARRINGTON. FROM THE SIXTH EUROPEAN EDITION [Three lines of
Latin from] OVID.
*Philadelphia: Printed by William Wallis Woodward, No. 17, Chesnut near
Front Street. Franklin's Head.* 1799. pp. (20), 17–503, frontispiece. 8vo.
AAS. JCB. LCP. NYPL.
Contains, a List of Subscribers' names. The frontispiece, engraved by
H. W. Weston, is headed: Woodward's first American edition 1799.

35448   EPITOME [cut] OF THE TIMES. [Motto.] No. 82. VOL. I. THURSDAY, JANUARY 3,
[—VOL. II. No. 80. WHOLE NO. 185. MONDAY, DECEMBER 30, 1799.]

> *Norfolk: Printed every Monday and Thursday, by Augustus C. Jordan, oppo-
site the Post-Office; . . . 1799. fol.*

A weekly edition for the country, without title heading, was also published.

35449   ERDMANN, CARL
DAS GELBE FIEBER IN PHILADELPHIA IM JAHRE 1798. NEBST EINER LISTE DER
TODTEN, VOM 1 AUGUST BIS ZUM 31 OCTOBER 1798.

> *Philadelphia: Gedruckt bey J. R. Kammerer u. Comp. 1799.* pp. (2), 85. 8vo.
HC. SGO.

35450   EIN ERNSTLICHER RUF AN DIE DEUTSCHEN IN PENNSYLVANIEN. VON EINEM IHRER
LANDSLEUTE, DEM DIE EHRE DES DEUTSCHEN NAMENS THEUER UND WERTH IST.
[Signed, Ein Pennsylvanischer Deutscher.]

> *Lancaster: Gedruckt bey Johann Albrecht und Comp. in der Prinz-Strasse.*
[1799.] pp. 15. 8vo.   AAS. LOC. NYPL.

A federalist pamphlet, advocating James Ross for Governor.

35451   ERRA PATER, pseudonym.
THE BOOK OF KNOWLEDGE, TREATING OF THE WISDOM OF THE ANCIENTS. IN FOUR
PARTS. I. SHEWING THE VARIOUS AND WONDERFUL OPERATION OF THE SIGNS AND
PLANETS, AND OTHER CELESTIAL CONSTELLATIONS, ON THE BODIES OF MEN, &C. II.
PROGNOSTICATIONS FOREVER NECESSARY TO KEEP THE BODY IN HEALTH; WITH
SEVERAL CHOICE RECEIPTS IN PHYSIC AND SURGERY. III. AN ABSTRACT [*sic*] OF THE
ART OF PHYSIOGNOMY AND PALMISTRY; TOGETHER WITH THE SIGNIFICATION OF
MOLES, AND THE INTERPRETATION OF DREAMS, &C. IV. THE FARMER'S CALENDAR,
CONTAINING, 1. PERPETUAL PROGNOSTICATIONS FOR WEATHER. 2. THE WHOLE
MYSTERY OF HUSBANDRY. 3. THE COMPLEAT EXPERIENCED FARRIER AND COW-
LEECH, &C. WRITTEN BY ERRA PATER. A JEW DOCTOR IN ASTRONOMY & PHYSIC,
BORN IN BETHANY, NEAR MOUNT OLIVE, IN JUDEA. MADE ENGLISH BY W. LILLY,
STUDENT IN PHYSIC AND ASTROLOGY. TO WHICH IS ADDED, THE TRUE FORM OF ALL
SORTS OF BILLS, BONDS, COUNTER BONDS, INDENTURES, LETTERS OF ATTORNEY AND
LICENCE, DEEDS OF GIFT, BILLS OF EXCHANGE, &C.

> *Suffield: Printed by Edward Gray.* M,DCC,XCIX. pp. 117, frontispiece,
and cuts in text. 12mo.   HC. JCB. NYPL.

35452   [ESSAYS RELATING TO YELLOW FEVER. FIRST PUBLISHED IN THE NEW JERSEY GA-
ZETTE. SIGNED, A PHILADELPHIAN.]

> *Philadelphia:* 1799. pp. v, 7–42. 8vo.   SGO.

35453   EVANGELICAL REFORMED CHURCH IN THE UNITED STATES OF AMERICA.
DAS NEUE UND VERBESSERTE GESANGBUCH, WORINNEN DIE PSALMEN DAVIDS, SAMT
EINER SAMMLUNG ALTER UND NEUER GEISTREICHER LIEDER, SOWOHL FÜR PRIVAT
UND HAUSANDACHTEN, ALS AUCH FÜR DEN ÖFFENTLICHEN GOTTESDIENST ENTHAL-
TEN SIND. NEBST EINEM ANHANG DES HEYDELBERGISCHEN CATECHISMUS, WIE
AUCH ERBAULICHER GEBÄTER. NACH EINEM SYNODAL SCHLUSS ZUSAMMENGETRA-
GEN UND EINGERICHTET VOR DIE EVANGELISCH-REFORMIRTEN GEMEINEN IN DEN
VEREINIGTEN STAATEN VON AMERICA. ZWEITE AUFLAGE.

> *Germantaun: Gedruckt bey Michael Billmeyer, 1799.* pp. (2), (4), 148; (2),
(6), 585, (9), 26. 8vo.   AAS. JCB. LCP. LOC. NYPL.

EVANGELICAL REFORMED CHURCH, continued.

Second title: SAMMLUNG ALTER UND NEUER GEISTREICHER LIEDER, ZUR ÖFFENT-LICHEN UND BESONDERN ERBAUUNG DER EVANGELISCH-REFORMIRTEN GEMEINEN IN DEN VEREINIGTEN STAATEN VON AMERICA. AUF VERORDNUNG DES SYNODS BESAGTER GEMEINEN ZUSAMMENGETRAGEN VON EINIGEN DAZU ERWÄHLTEN GLIEDERN DESSELBEN. ZWEYTE AUFLAGE.

Germantaun: Gedruckt bey Michael Billmeyer, 1799. pp. (2), (6), 585, (9).

Heading: CATECHISMUS, ODER KURZER UNTERRICHT CHRISTLICHER LEHRE, WIE DERSELBE IN KIRCHEN UND SCHULEN DER EVANGELISCH-REFORMIRTEN GEMEINDEN GELEHRET WIRD. pp. 26.

35454   EVERETT, DAVID   1770–1813

COMMON SENSE IN DISHABILLE: OR, THE FARMER'S MONITOR. CONTAINING A VARIETY OF FAMILIAR ESSAYS ON SUBJECTS MORAL & ECONOMICAL. TO WHICH IS ADDED, A PERPETUAL CALENDAR, OR ECONOMICAL ALMANACK. BY DAVID EVERETT, A. M. [Six lines of verse.] PUBLISHED ACCORDING TO ACT OF CONGRESS.

Printed at Worcester, Massachusetts: by Isaiah Thomas, jun. for Isaiah Thomas. Sold at the Worcester Bookstore. March, 1799. pp. 120. 12mo.

AAS. BM. BU. JCB. LOC.

Second title: PERPETUAL CALENDAR; OR, ECONOMICAL ALMANACK. CALCULATED FOR THE MERIDIAN OF THE RURAL OBSERVATORY, IN THE SHOP OF MESSRS. COLON AND SPONDEE; BUT WILL ANSWER, WITHOUT ESSENTIAL VARIATION, FOR ANY SHOP, KITCHEN, OR PARLOR IN THE NEWENGLAND STATES, WHILE THERE SHALL BE ICE IN DECEMBER, OR FLOWERS IN MAY. CONTAINING "LESSONS OF COMMON SENSE AND FAMILY LECTURES, ON HOUSEHOLD AND BARNHOLD ECONOMY." ADAPTED TO EACH MONTH IN THE YEAR. [Seven lines of verse from] THOMSON. pp. (2), (95)–120.

Originally published in the Farmer's Weekly Museum.
155th Massachusetts District Copyright, issued to Isaiah Thomas, as Proprietor, 4 March, 1799.

35455   THE EXAMINER. [Motto.] VOL. I. NUM. 10. TUESDAY, JANUARY 1, [— VOL. II. NUM. 12. SATURDAY, DECEMBER 28, 1799.]

Richmond: Printed on Tuesdays and Fridays, by Meriwether Jones & John Dixon. 1799. fol.

With the issue for May 31st, Dixon withdrew, and publication was continued by Meriwether Jones, Printer to the Commonwealth.

35456   EXETER FEDERAL MISCELLANY. VOL. I. No. 7. WEDNESDAY, JANUARY 16, [— No. 43. TUESDAY, SEPTEMBER 24, 1799.]

Exeter (New-Hampshire) Printed and published by Henry Ranlet. 1799. fol.

In continuation of *Ranlet's Federal Miscellany.* With the issue for October 1st the title was altered to *Political Banquet, and farmer's feast.*

35457   THE FAIRING; OR, A GOLDEN TOY FOR CHILDREN OF ALL SIZES AND DENOMINATIONS. IN WHICH THEY MAY SEE ALL THE FUN OF THE FAIR, AND AT HOME BE AS HAPPY AS IF THEY WERE THERE.

Printed at Worcester, Massachusetts, by Isaiah Thomas, jun. 1799.

35458   A FAMILY BOOK FOR CHILDREN. CONTAINING, PART 1. THE NEW TESTAMENT OF OUR LORD AND SAVIOUR, JESUS CHRIST. TO WHICH IS ADDED, A NUMBER OF HYMNS, AND PLAIN RULES, FOR THE BEHAVIOR OF CHILDREN, AT THE MEETING-HOUSE; AT HOME; AT THE TABLE; AT THE SCHOOL; WHEN ABROAD; AND WHEN AMONG OTHER CHILDREN: WITH AN ADMONITION TO THEM. PART 2. DR. WATTS'S DIVINE AND MORAL SONGS, WITH A NUMBER OF HYMNS, BY OTHER AUTHORS; THE SHORTER CATECHISM; DR. WATTS'S CATECHISM FOR LITTLE CHILDREN, AND HIS SECOND CATECHISM FOR YOUTH; MORNING AND EVENING PRAYERS, &C.

Hartford: Printed by John Babcock, 1799. pp. 120, cuts in text. 24mo. JCB.

35459 FARLEY, Amos
    Farley & Goss' Almanac, or Vermont Calendar, for the year of our Lord
    1800: being the fourth after bissextile, or leap year, and the twenty-
    fourth of Columbian independence. [Seven lines.]

     *Peacham: Printed by Farley & Goss, and for sale at their Printing Office; at
    the different stores in this town; and various other places. Price 50 cents per dozen,
    —6 cts. single.* [1799.] pp. (24). 12mo.   LOC.

35460 THE FARMERS Almanac, for the year of our Lord, 1800; being one of the
    centurial years, not bissextile. Containing, besides the astronomical
    calculations, judgment of the weather; length of days; festivals and
    other remarkable days; tables of interest, &c. times of holding the fed-
    eral courts and the courts of Pennsylvania, together with a large and
    correct list of roads, &c. interspersed with a variety of instructing and
    entertaining matter, in prose and verse. The astronomical parts calcu-
    lated to the meridian of Greensburg; but may without sensible variation,
    serve for Pennsylvania, or any of the middle States.

     *Greensburgh, (Westmoreland, Pennsylvania): Printed by Snowden & M'Cor-
    kle; where storekeepers and others may be supplied. Price, single, 6d.—per dozen,
    3s. 9d.* [1799.] pp. (36). 12mo.   AAS. LOC.

35461 THE FARMER'S Weekly Museum: Newhampshire and Vermont Journal. [Mot-
    to.] Vol. vi. No. 301. Monday, January 7, [— No. 312. Monday, March 25,
    1799.]

     Printed at Walpole, Newhampshire, by David Carlisle, for Thomas & Thomas,
    . . . 1799. fol.   AAS. LOC.

    The issue for March 25th, completed the sixth year of publication; and
    on April 1st, appeared, in a new dress of type and other improvements,
    the *Farmers' Museum, or Lay preacher's gazette.*—the sub-title honoring
    the Sermons of the editor, Joseph Dennie, which had been one of the
    prominent features under his editorship. The old motto, from Bunyan,
    was also discarded with the old and worn-out types, and the following
    from Goldsmith adopted: Hither, each week, the peasant shall repair,
    To sweet oblivion of his daily care; Again the farmer's news—the bar-
    ber's tale, Again the woodman's ballad shall prevail.

35462 FARMERS' Museum, or [cut] Lay Preacher's Gazette. [Four lines of verse from]
    Goldsmith. Vol. vii. No. 313. Monday, April 1, [— Vol. vii. No. 352. Mon-
    day, December 30, 1799.]

     Printed at Walpole Newhampshire, by David Carlisle, for Thomas & Thomas.
    . . . *The price of the Museum, printed on common paper, is one dollar and fifty
    cents per annum, and on the superfine, two dollars and fifty cents.* . . . 1799. fol.
                 AAS.

35463 THE FARMERS' [cut] Register. Vol. i. No. xxxviii. Wednesday, January 2,
    [— Vol. i. No. lii. Wednesday, April 10, 1799.]

     *Chambersburg: (Penn.) Printed and published every Wednesday, by Snowden
    & M'Corkle, in Market-Street, near the Bridge.* 1799. pp. 153–211, (1). fol. HSP.

    The issue for April 10th, has an Index to the first volume. In May,
    Snowden & M'Corkle removed their Press to Greensburg, Pennsylvania,
    and continued publication of The Farmer's Register there, with a new
    serial numbering, as follows:

AUCTION
VALUES

35464 THE FARMERS [cut] REGISTER. VOL. I. No. 1. FRIDAY, MAY 24, [— No. XXXII.
SATURDAY, DECEMBER 28, 1799.]

*Greensburg, (Penn.) Printed and published every Friday by Snowden &
M'Corkle.* 1799. pp. 124. fol.   HSP.

Paged. In September publication was changed to Saturdays. Established by John M. Snowden and William M'Corkle in continuation of
a weekly newspaper, with the same title, they had been publishing at
Chambersburg. In May, 1803, M'Corkle withdrew, and publication was
continued in the name of John M. Snowden into January, 1808, when
it was discontinued and, apparently, succeeded by the *Greensburg & In-
diana Register.*

35465 FARRAR, STEPHEN   1738–1809
A SERMON DELIVERED AT TOWNSEND (MS.) NOVEMBER 15TH, AT THE INTERMENT OF
THE REVEREND SAMUEL DIX, A.M. WHO DIED NOVEMBER 12TH, 1797; IN THE SIXTY-
SECOND YEAR OF HIS AGE, AND THIRTY-SEVENTH OF HIS MINISTRY. BY STEPHEN
FARRAR, A.M. PASTOR OF THE CHURCH IN NEW-IPSWICH, N.H. PUBLISHED AT THE
REQUEST OF THE CHURCH AND PEOPLE IN TOWNSEND, TO WHOM IT IS RESPECTFULLY
DEDICATED.

Amherst, N.H.—Printed by Samuel Preston, 1799. pp. 15. 8vo.   BM. JCB.

35466 THE FATHER'S GIFT; OR THE WAY TO BE WISE AND HAPPY.

Printed at Worcester, Massachusetts, by Isaiah Thomas, jun. 1799.

35467 A FAVORITE SONG TRANSLATED FROM THE IRISH.

*New-York: Printed & sold at J. Hewitt's Musical Repository, No. 23 Maiden
Lane.* [1799.] Broadside. 4to.   HSP.

35468 FAYETTE COUNTY. KENTUCKY.
RESOLUTIONS ON ADOPTING PROPER PERSONS TO REPRESENT THAT COUNTY IN CON-
VENTION. . . . JOHN M'DOWELL. JANUARY 28, 1799.

[Lexington: Printed by John Bradford, 1799.] Broadside. fol.

35469 THE FAYETTE GAZETTE, AND UNION ADVERTISER. VOL. I. No. 52. FRIDAY, JANU-
ARY 4, [— VOL. II. No. 51. FRIDAY, DECEMBER 27, 1799.]

Uniontown: Printed by Stewart and Mowry, near the Court-House. 1799. fol.

35470 FEDERAL GALAXY. [Motto.] VOL. III. No. 105. TUESDAY, JANUARY 1, [— No. 156.
SATURDAY, DECEMBER 28, 1799.]

*Published for Windham County, by Benjamin Smead, in Brattleborough, Ver-
mont.* 1799. fol.   AAS.

In August, a cut of the moon in its first quarter, and sixteen stars, with
a flying eagle was added to the heading.

35471 FEDERAL GAZETTE AND BALTIMORE DAILY ADVERTISER. VOL. VIII? No. 1611. TUES-
DAY, JANUARY 1, [— No. 1907. TUESDAY, DECEMBER 31, 1799.]

*[Baltimore:] Printed and sold by Yundt and Brown, South Gay Street, No.
12.* 1799. fol.

35472 FEDERAL OBSERVER. NUMB. 7. THURSDAY, JANUARY 3, [— NUMB. 58. THURSDAY,
DECEMBER 26, 1799.]

Portsmouth: Printed and published by Treadwell & Hart. 1799. fol.   BA.

With the issue for August 1st, Samuel G. Hart withdrew. Publication
being continued by William Treadwell.

35473   THE FEDERAL Spy. Vol. vii. No. 1. Tuesday, January 1, [— Vol. viii. No. 1. Tuesday, December 31, 1799.]

> *Published by Francis Stebbins—Springfield—Massachusetts.* 1799. fol.

In November ? Stebbins disposed of his interests to Timothy Ashley.

35474   THE FEDERALIST; or [cut of eagle] New-Jersey Gazette. "Adams and Liberty." Vol. i. No. 27. Monday evening, January 7, [— Vol. ii. No. 78. Monday evening, December 30, 1799.]

> *Printed at Trenton, under the direction of G. Craft, Printer to the State, and Printer of the Laws of the United States for the District of New-Jersey, at his Office in the Main-Street, between the Indian Queen and City Hotel:* . . . 1799. fol.

35475   FELBINGER, Jeremias   1616–1690
Christliches Hand-Büchlein, darin gehandelt wird i. Von des Menschen Erschaffung, seinem Abfall, und Wieder-Aufrichtung. ii. Von Aufnehmung der unmündigen Kinder, in die sichtbare Gemeine des Herrn. iii. Von der heil. Taufe. iv. Von der Kirchenzucht. v. Von dem heil. Fusswaschen. vi. Von dem heil. Abendmahl. vii. Von dem Verbot des Eidschwörens. Allen Wahrheit-liebenden zum heilsamen Nutz und Gebrauch, sowohl zu Hause als auch auf Reisen und in Gesellschaften sich ossen nützlich zu ordnen. Von Jeremias Felbinger. Rechten und Ordnungen des Hauses Gottes, in Frag und Antwort. Grundforschende Fragen, welche den neuen Täufern im Mitgensteinischen zu beantworten vorgelegt wurden, nebst beygefügten Antworten auf dieselben. Von Alexander Mack. Dritte Auflage.

> *Baltimore: Gedruckt bey Samuel Saur,* 1799. pp. (2), (2), 129; 99, (1); 41. 12mo.   AAS. LOC.

> *Second title:* Kurze und einfältige Vorstellung der äussern, aber doch heiligen Rechten u. Ordnungen des Hauses Gottes, wie es der wahre Haus-Vater Jesus Christus befohlen, und in seinem Testament schriftlich hinterlassen. Vorgestellt in einem Gespräch unter Vater und Sohn, durch Frag und Antwort, von Alexander Mack, einem Mitberufenen zu dem grossen Abendmahl. Dritte Auflage.

> *Baltimore: Gedruckt bey Samuel Saur,* 1799. pp. 99, (1).

> *Third title:* Eberhard Ludwig Grubers Grundforschende Fragen, welche den neuen Täufern im Mitgensteinischen, insonderheit zu beantworten, vorgelegt waren, nebst beygefügten kurzen und einfältigen Antworten auf dieselben, vormals schriftlich herausgegeben von einem Aufrichtigen Mitglied der Gemeine zu Mitgenstein, und nun auf vieles Verlangen zum öffentlichen Druck befördert. Dritte Auflage.

> *Baltimore: Gedruckt bey Samuel Saur,* 1799. pp. 41.

Aufrichtigen Mitglied, is Alexander Mack. Another edition was printed in Lancaster, Pennsylvania, in 1822.

35476   FÉNELON, François de Salignac de La Mothe, archevêque de Cambray
Some advice to governesses and teachers. Written by the Author of the Evidence of the existence of God. Supposed to be translated by Bishop Barclay.

> *New-York: Printed by Isaac Collins, No. 189, Pearl-Street.* 1799. pp. 12. 12mo.   BA. HC.

35477 FENNING, DANIEL
THE READY RECKONER OR, TRADER'S USEFUL ASSISTANT, IN BUYING AND SELLING ALL
SORTS OF COMMODITIES. EITHER WHOLESALE OR RETAIL. SHEWING AT ONE VIEW,
THE AMOUNT OR VALUE OF ANY NUMBER OR QUANTITY OF GOODS OR MERCHANDISE,
FROM A FARTHING TO 20s. EITHER BY THE HUNDRED, HALF HUNDRED OR QUARTER,
POUND OR OUNCE, ELL OR YARD, &C. &C. IN SO PLAIN AND EASY A MANNER, THAT A
PERSON, QUITE UNACQUAINTED WITH ARITHMETICK, MAY HEREBY ASCERTAIN THE
VALUE OF ANY NUMBER OF HUNDREDS, POUNDS, OUNCES, ELLS OR YARDS, &C. AT ANY
PRICE WHATEVER.—TO THE MOST READY IN FIGURES IT WILL BE EQUALLY USEFUL,
BY CASTING UP WHAT IS HERE CORRECTLY DONE TO THEIR HAND. TO WHICH IS
ADDED SUNDRY USEFUL TABLES. BY DANIEL FENNING. THE TWELFTH EDITION.

Wilmington: Printed and sold by Peter Brynberg. 1799. pp. 189, (3).
12mo.
WiPL.

35478 —— THE UNIVERSAL SPELLING BOOK IMPROVED: BEING A NEW AND EASY GUIDE TO
THE ENGLISH LANGUAGE. CONTAINING I. TABLES OF USEFUL WORDS FROM ONE TO
EIGHT SYLLABLES DIVERSIFIED WITH A GREAT VARIETY OF RELIGIOUS AND MORAL
PRECEPTS AND ACCOMPANIED BY A NUMBER OF INSTRUCTIVE FABLES AND STORIES.
A LARGE COLLECTION OF WORDS NEARLY ALIKE IN SOUND BUT DIFFERENT IN SPEL-
LING AND SIGNIFICATION. REMARKS ON THE VARIOUS PRONUNCIATIONS OF THE VOW-
ELS AND CONSONANTS, AND A NEW CATALOGUE OF THE MOST USEFUL CONTRACTIONS.
II. AN EASY AND COMPREHENSIVE GUIDE TO ENGLISH GRAMMAR ADAPTED TO YOUNG
CAPACITIES IN A FAMILIAR DIALOGUE BETWEEN MASTER AND SCHOLAR WHEREBY
THE LEARNER MAY VERY SOON BECOME ACQUAINTED WITH THE FIRST PRINCIPLES
OF HIS NATIVE LANGUAGE. III. TABLES OF THE PRINCIPAL PARTS OF SPEECH, VIZ.
SUBSTANTIVES, ADJECTIVES, AND VERBS OF TWO, THREE AND FOUR SYLLABLES
RANGED ALPHABETICALLY UNDER THEIR RESPECTIVE HEADS AND EXPLAINED FROM
THE BEST AUTHORITY IN THE EASIEST AND MOST COMPREHENSIVE TERMS. IV. A
VARIETY OF SELECT ALPHABETICAL SENTENCES CALCULATED FOR WRITING PIECES,
MORAL POEMS AND PRECEPTS, CONCISE FORMS OF GRACES AND PRAYERS, WITH OTHER
USEFUL AND INSTRUCTIVE ARTICLES, VERY NECESSARY FOR THE INFORMATION OF
THE YOUNG SCHOLAR, AND A COPIOUS CHRONOLOGICAL TABLE OF THE MOST REMARK-
ABLE EVENTS FROM THE CREATION OF THE WORLD TO THE PRESENT PERIOD, &C.
&C. &C. BY DANIEL FENNING, LATE SCHOOLMASTER AT BURIES IN SUFFOLK, AUTHOR
OF THE ROYAL ENGLISH DICTIONARY, PRACTICAL ARITHMETIC, THE YOUNG MAN'S
BOOK OF KNOWLEDGE &C. [Two lines of verse.] THE FIRST AMERICAN EDITION,
WITH CONSIDERABLE ADDITIONS AND IMPROVEMENTS.

Philadelphia: 1799.

227th Pennsylvania District Copyright, issued to George Douglas, as
Proprietor, 19 March, 1799.

35479 FESSENDEN, THOMAS GREEN   1771–1807
A POEM, IN TWO CANTOS; IN WHICH IS PORTRAYED FRENCH POLITICS, INGRAFTED IN
HOPKINTONIAN SUPERSTITION; AS DISPLAYED BY CERTAIN PURITANS OF THE TRIBE
OF ROBINSONITES. BY THE RT. HON. SIMON SPUNKEY, ESQ. PUBLISHED ACCORDING
TO ACT OF CONGRESS.

Brattleboro', Vermont: Printed by Benjamin Smead. 1799.

"This work was calculated and designed for the Western District of
Vermont, but will answer, without any sensible variation, for France,
Kentucky, Pennsylvania, &c." Price 6 cents.

35480 FEVER; AN ELEGIAC POEM. DEDICATED TO THE CITIZENS OF PHILADELPHIA, BY A
CITIZEN.

Philadelphia: Printed for the Author, by John Ormrod, 1799. pp. 24.
12mo.
LOC.

35481   FIELDING, Henry   1707–1754
THE REMARKABLE HISTORY OF TOM JONES, A FOUNDLING.

      Printed and sold by N. and J. Coverly, Faust's Statue, Essex Street, Salem.
1799. pp. 29. 16mo.   EI.

35482   —— — THE REMARKABLE HISTORY OF TOM JONES, A FOUNDLING. THE FOURTH
WORCESTER EDITION.

      *Printed at Worcester, Massachusetts, by Isaiah Thomas, jun. Sold wholesale
and retail by him,* 1799. pp. (28), (2), (1), 12 cuts. 32mo.   AAS.

35483   FISHER, Jacob   –1840
AN ORATION PRONOUNCED AT KENNEBUNK, ON THE FOURTH DAY OF JULY, 1799;
BEING THE ANNIVERSARY OF AMERICAN INDEPENDENCE. BY DR. JACOB FISHER.

      Portland: Printed by E. A. Jenks. 1799. pp. (2), 20. 8vo.   AAS. BA. JCB. NYHS.

35484   FISKE, Abel   1752–1802
A DISCOURSE, DELIVERED AT WILTON, NOVEMBER 15, 1798; BEING THE DAY OF THE
ANNIVERSARY THANKSGIVING THROUGHOUT THE STATE OF NEW HAMPSHIRE. BY
ABEL FISKE, A. M. PASTOR OF THE CHURCH IN SAID TOWN. TO WHICH TWO OTHER
DISCOURSES, SINCE DELIVERED, ARE ADDED. PUBLISHED BY DESIRE.

      Amherst, Newhampshire. From the Press of Samuel Preston. 1799. pp. 44.
8vo.   AAS. BM. HC. NHHS.

35485   FISKE, Samuel   · 1769–1834
AN ORATION PRONOUNCED AT CLAREMONT, ON THE ANNIVERSARY OF AMERICAN
INDEPENDENCE, JULY 4TH, 1799. BY SAMUEL FISKE, A. M. [Three line quotation.]

      Windsor: Printed by Alden Spooner. M.DCC.XCIX. pp. 15. 8vo.   AAS.

35486   FITCH, Ebenezer   1756–1833
USEFUL KNOWLEDGE AND RELIGION, RECOMMENDED TO THE PURSUIT AND IMPROVEMENT
OF THE YOUNG; IN A DISCOURSE, ADDRESSED TO THE CANDIDATES FOR THE BACCALAU-
REATE IN WILLIAMS COLLEGE, SEPTEMBER 1, 1799. BY THE REV. EBENEZER
FITCH, PRESIDENT OF WILLIAMS COLLEGE.

      Pittsfield: Printed by Chester Smith. [1799.] pp. (34). 12mo.
                                  AAS. JCB. LOC. NYHS. UTS. WC. YC.

      Reprinted in Durfee's Sketch of President Fitch.

35487   FLEET, John, and Thomas
FLEETS' REGISTER, AND POCKET ALMANACK FOR THE YEAR OF OUR LORD 1800. BEING
THE FOURTH YEAR SINCE THE LAST LEAP YEAR, AND THE TWENTY-FOURTH OF AMER-
ICAN INDEPENDENCE, WHICH BEGAN JULY 4TH, 1776. CALCULATED CHIEFLY FOR
THE USE OF THE COMMONWEALTH OF MASSACHUSETTS, BOSTON, THE METROPOLIS,
BEING IN LATITUDE 42 DEG. 23 MIN. NORTH, AND 70 DEG. 58, 53 WEST LONG. 348
MILES N. E. OF PHILADELPHIA.

      Boston: Printed and sold by J. & T. Fleet, at the Bible and Heart in Cornhill.
[1799.] pp. [20], (172). 24mo.   AAS. BA. JCB. LOC. MHS. NYPL.

      The New York Public Library has two impressions of this Register.
The earliest ends with the card of "William Harris is a Notary Public
in Boston." The second impression, has an additional name on page 141,
and ends: "The result of the valuation in Massachusetts, agreeably to
a law of the United States lately published, was not secured in season
for this publication." The number of pages in both impressions is the
same. This is the last issue of the series, printed by the original publishers. Continued, annually, as the Massachusetts Register, and United
States Calendar. Printed by Manning and Loring, and published by
John West.

35488   FOBES, Peres   1742–1812
HUMAN AND DIVINE AGENCY UNITED, IN THE SALVATION OF MEN: CONSIDERED, IN A
SERMON, PREACHED TO THE CONGREGATIONAL SOCIETY, IN BERKLEY, A. D. 1795.
BY PERES FOBES, LL. D. PASTOR OF THE CHURCH IN RAYNHAM . . .
Windsor: Re-printed by Alden Spooner. 1799. pp. 24 8vo.   NYPL.

35489   FOLWELL, RICHARD
TERMS OF RICHARD FOLWELL IN PHILADELPHIA, FOR SUBSCRIBING TO THE JOURNALS
OF CONGRESS, FROM THE COMMENCEMENT OF THE AMERICAN WAR, IN 1774, TO THE
PRESENT TIME: INCLUDING THE REPORTS OF HEADS OF DEPARTMENTS, OF COMMIT-
TEES, AND OTHER OFFICIAL AND PRIVATE PAPERS OF THAT BODY, WHICH MAY NOW
BE MADE PUBLIC. TERMS: [Six paragraphs.] PAYMENTS TO BE MADE ON DELIVERY
OF EACH VOLUME.
[Philadelphia: Printed by Richard Folwell. 1799.] pp. 14. 8vo.
Several sample pages were enclosed in a separate wrapper.

35490   FORBES, ELI   1726–1804
THE INOFFENSIVE MINISTRY DESCRIBED, IN A SERMON, DELIVERED BEFORE THE CON-
VENTION OF THE CLERGY OF MASSACHUSETTS, IN BOSTON, MAY 30, 1799. BY THE
REV. ELI FORBES, PASTOR OF THE FIRST CHURCH IN GLOUCESTER.
Charlestown: Printed by Samuel Etheridge. 1799. pp. [22.] 8vo.
AAS. BA. BM. HC. JCB. LOC. MHS. NYPL.

35491   FORSYTH, WILLIAM
PALIDA MORS, ÆQUA PULSAT PEDE, PAUPERUM TABERNAS, REGUMQUE TERRES. A
SERMON, PREACHED AT WINDSOR, OCTOBER 10, 1799, BEFORE HIS EXCELLENCY THE
GOVERNOR, THE LIEUTENANT-GOVERNOR AND COUNCIL, AND THE HOUSE OF REPRE-
SENTATIVES, OF THE STATE OF VERMONT. BY WILLIAM FORSYTH, A. M.
Windsor: Printed for S. Williams, Printer to the State. M,DCC,XCIX. pp.
(2), (19). 8vo.   AAS. BM.

35492   FOSTER, JOEL   1755–1812
A LITERARY CORRESPONDENCE, BETWEEN JOEL FOSTER, A. M. MINISTER OF THE
CONGREGATIONAL SOCIETY IN NEW-SALEM, AND HOSEA BALLOU, AN ITINERANT
PREACHER OF THE SECT CALLED UNIVERSALISTS. IN WHICH, THE QUESTION CON-
CERNING FUTURE PUNISHMENT, AND THE REASONS, FOR AND AGAINST IT, ARE CONSID-
ERED. [Seven lines from] SHERLOCK.
Printed at Northampton, (Massachusetts) by William Butler. M,DCC,XCIX.
pp. (68). 8vo.   AAS. BA. BM. JCB.

35493   FOSTER, JOHN   1763–1829
A SERMON, PREACHED BEFORE THE ROXBURY CHARITABLE SOCIETY, AT THEIR ANNI-
VERSARY MEETING, SEPTEMBER 16, 1799. BY JOHN FOSTER, PASTOR OF THE THIRD
CHURCH IN CAMBRIDGE. PUBLISHED AT THE DESIRE OF THE SOCIETY.
Boston: Printed by Samuel Hall. 1799. pp. 22. 8vo. AAS. BA. JCB. MHS. NYPL.

35494   FOUSHEE, JOHN H.
AN INAUGURAL ESSAY ON THE STRICTURES IN THE URETHRA; SUBMITTED TO THE
EXAMINATION OF THE REV. JOHN EWING, S. T. P. PROVOST, THE TRUSTEES AND MED-
ICAL PROFESSORS OF THE UNIVERSITY OF PENNSYLVANIA, ON THE SIXTH DAY OF
JUNE, 1799, FOR THE DEGREE OF DOCTOR OF MEDICINE. BY JOHN H. FOUSHEE, OF
VIRGINIA, MEMBER OF THE PHILADELPHIA MEDICAL AND CHEMICAL SOCIETIES.
[Two lines of Latin from] HOR.
Philadelphia: Printed by John Ormrod, No. 41, Chesnut-Street. 1799. pp.
(39), (1), plate. 8vo.   LOC. NYPL. SGO. VSL.

35495 FOWLER, ABRAHAM   1745–1815
A FAREWELL SERMON, DELIVERED AT SALEM, IN WATERBURY, APRIL 17, 1799, BY
THE REV. ABRAHAM FOWLER; LATE PASTOR OF THE CHURCH IN THAT SOCIETY.
[With his dismission.]
> *Printed by George Bunce—-New-Haven.* M,DCC,XCIX. pp. 23, (2), errata. 8vo.
AAS.

35496 FRANCE. DIRECTORY.
COPIES OF ORIGINAL LETTERS FROM THE ARMY OF GENERAL BONAPARTE IN EGYPT,
INTERCEPTED BY THE FLEET UNDER THE COMMAND OF ADMIRAL LORD NELSON.
TRANSLATED FROM THE FRENCH. PART FIRST.
> *Philadelphia: Printed and sold by Way and Groff, No. 48, North Third-
Street.* 1799. pp. xxv, 133. 8vo.   AAS. BA.

35497 FRANKLIN, BENJAMIN   1706–1790
THE LIFE OF DOCTOR BENJAMIN FRANKLIN. WRITTEN BY HIMSELF. FOURTH [*sic*]
AMERICAN EDITION.
> *Wilmington: Printed and sold by Peter Brynberg.* 1799. pp. 178. (1). 12mo.
> LOC.
Extended to 1730; and with the Continuation by Dr. Henry Steuber.

35498 —— THE WORKS OF THE LATE DR. BENJAMIN FRANKLIN; CONSISTING OF HIS LIFE
WRITTEN BY HIMSELF: TOGETHER WITH ESSAYS, HUMOROUS, MORAL, AND LITERARY;
CHIEFLY IN THE MANNER OF THE SPECTATOR.
> *New-York: Printed and sold by John Tiebout, No. 358, Pearl-Street.* 1799.
2 vols. in one. pp. 184; 104, portrait. 16mo.   NYPL.

The Press forms of this edition are identical with Johnson and Manchester's edition, printed in 1797. Although paged for two volumes,
there was no title-page to the second part.

35499 THE FRANKLIN REPOSITORY. VOL. III. NO. 38. TOTAL NO. 142. THURSDAY, JANU-
ARY 3, [— THURSDAY, APRIL, 1799.]
> *Chambersburg: Published by Robert Harper.* 1799. fol.

From the scattering numbers known, it would appear that, owing to the
opposition of The Franklin Minerva, established by his brother, George
Kenton Harper, in February, publication was suspended in April; and,
in December, after transferring his proprietary rights in the Repository
to his brother, Robert Harper removed to Gettysburg, and there established, in 1800, *The Adams Centinel.*

35500 THE FRANKLIN MINERVA. VOL. I. NO. 1. WEDNESDAY, FEBRUARY 2, [—
WEDNESDAY, DECEMBER, 1799.]
> *Chambersburg: Published by George Kenton Harper.* 1799. fol.

Established, as a bi-weekly, by George Kenton Harper, with James
Magee as printer. Later in the year, his brother, Robert Harper, transferred to him his proprietary rights in *The Franklin Repository*, which
suspended publication in April, and the name of that paper was assumed,
and continued by him as publisher for thirty-nine years.

35501 FRASER, DONALD
PARTY-SPIRIT EXPOSED, OR REMARKS ON THE TIMES: TO WHICH IS ADDED SOME IM-
PORTANT HINTS TO THE LADIES. BY A GENTLEMAN OF NEW-YORK. [Between double
lines.] LET *Feds* AND *Demos*, FORM ONE FRIENDLY BAND, AND DRIVE FELL DISCORD
FROM OUR HAPPY LAND: *Columbia* UNITED, SHALL TO GLORY ARISE, "THE QUEEN
OF THE WORLD AND THE CHILD OF THE SKIES. LET THE CRIMES OF THE EAST NE'ER
ENCRIMSON *her* NAME, BE FREEDOM, AND SCIENCE AND VIRTUE HER FAME." [Or-
nament.]
> *New-York: Printed by Thomas Kirk.* 1799. pp. 16. 8vo.   NYHS. NYHS.

35503 FREE AND ACCEPTED MASONS. GRAND LODGE OF CONNECTICUT.
CONSTITUTION AND BYE-LAWS . . . ADOPTED BY THE GRAND LODGE OF CONNEC-
TICUT.
Hartford: Printed by M. Babcock. 1799. pp. 20. 12mo. BM.

35504 FREE AND ACCEPTED MASONS. GRAND ROYAL ARCH CHAPTER.
CONSTITUTION OF THE GENERAL GRAND ROYAL ARCH CHAPTER, OF THE NORTHERN
STATES OF AMERICA. [Ornament. Double line.]
Printed for Thomas S. Webb, Albany, 1799. pp. (19). 8vo. AAS. NYHS.

35505 —— REGULATIONS OF THE GRAND ROYAL ARCH CHAPTER OF THE STATE OF NEW-
YORK. [Double line.]
Albany. 5799. [1799.] pp. 8. 8vo. NYHS.

35506 FREE AND ACCEPTED MASONS. GRAND LODGE OF PENNSYLVANIA.
RULES AND REGULATIONS FOR THE GOVERNMENT OF THE GRAND LODGE OF PENNSYL-
VANIA.
Philadelphia: 1799. pp. 10. 8vo.

35507 FREE AND ACCEPTED MASONS. GRAND ROYAL ARCH CHAPTER.
RULES AND REGULATIONS FOR THE GOVERNMENT OF THE GRAND ROYAL ARCH CHAP-
TER.
Philadelphia: 1799. pp. 8. 8vo.

35508 FREE AND ACCEPTED MASONS. GRAND LODGE OF NEW-HAMPSHIRE.
REGULATIONS OF THE GRAND LODGE OF NEW-HAMPSHIRE. [Vignette.]
Portsmouth: New-Hampshire. Printed by J. Melcher, 5799 [1799.] pp. 7.
8vo. LOC.

35509 FREE AND ACCEPTED MASONS. GRAND LODGE OF RHODE ISLAND.
THE MASONIC BURIAL-OFFICE OF THE GRAND LODGE OF THE STATE OF RHODE ISLAND.
"DUST THOU ART, AND UNTO DUST THOU SHALT RETURN."
[Providence:] Printed by brother John Carter, 5799. [1799.] pp. [8.] 4to.
AAS. RIHS.
Five hundred copies were printed. The copy in the American Anti-
quarian Society has manuscript corrections throughout by Reverend
Brother Smith—the Author.

35510 FREE AND ACCEPTED MASONS. GRAND LODGE OF VIRGINIA.
EXTRACTS FROM THE RECORDS OF THE GRAND LODGE OF VIRGINIA.
*Richmond: Printed by Meriwether Jones & John Dixon, Printers to the Com-
monwealth. A. L.* 5799 [1799.] pp. 11. 8vo. NYPL.

On the back of the title-page it is stated that in the Resolution of Dec.
12, 1798, the grand secretary was directed to publish in a pamphlet all
the recent Resolutions. A list of all the expulsions, and a list of the
Lodges under the jurisdiction of the Grand Lodge.

35511 —— PROCEEDINGS OF A GRAND ANNUAL COMMUNICATION OF THE GRAND LODGE OF
VIRGINIA: BEGUN AND HELD IN THE MASONS' HALL IN THE CITY OF RICHMOND ON
MONDAY, THE NINTH DAY OF DECEMBER, A. L. 5799—A. D. 1799. [Ornament.]
Richmond: Printed by John Dixon, Printer to the Grand Lodge of Virginia.
[1799.] pp. [32.] 8vo. AAS.

35512   FREEMAN, JONATHAN   1765–1822
A SERMON DELIVERED AT NEW-WINDSOR AND BETHLEHEM, AUGUST 30, 1798. BEING THE DAY APPOINTED BY THE GENERAL ASSEMBLY OF THE PRESBYTERIAN CHURCH, IN THE UNITED STATES OF AMERICA: TO BE OBSERVED AS A DAY OF SOLEMN HUMILIATION, FASTING AND PRAYER, IN ALL THE CHURCHES UNDER THEIR CARE. BY JONATHAN FREEMAN.

New-Windsor: Printed by Jacob Schultz. MDCCXCIX. pp. [52.] 8vo.
AAS. NYPL.

Contains, a Hymn, by John Newton, of eight four-line verses, at end.

35513   FREEMAN, SAMUEL   1743–1831
THE TOWN OFFICER; OR THE POWER AND DUTY OF SELECTMEN, TOWN CLERKS, TOWN TREASURERS, OVERSEERS OF THE POOR, ASSESSORS, CONSTABLES, COLLECTORS OF TAXES, SURVEYORS OF HIGHWAYS, SURVEYORS OF LUMBER, FENCE VIEWERS, CLERKS OF THE MARKET, MEASURERS OF WOOD, AND OTHER TOWN OFFICERS. AS CONTAINED IN THE LAWS OF THE COMMONWEALTH OF MASSACHUSETTS. WITH A VARIETY OF FORMS, FOR THE USE OF SUCH OFFICERS. TO WHICH ARE ADDED, THE POWER AND DUTY OF TOWNS, PARISHES AND PLANTATIONS, AND A PLAIN AND REGULAR METHOD TO KEEP ACCOUNTS OF THE EXPENDITURES OF MONIES VOTED BY A TOWN; UPON AN INSPECTION OF WHICH, THE STATE OF ITS FINANCES MAY AT ANY TIME BE KNOWN. THE FOURTH EDITION, MUCH IMPROVED, AND GREATLY ENLARGED. BY SAMUEL FREEMAN, ESQ. AUTHOR OF THE MASSACHUSETTS JUSTICE, PROBATE AUXILIARY, AND AMERICAN CLERK'S MAGAZINE. PUBLISHED ACCORDING TO ACT OF CONGRESS.

Printed at Boston, by I. Thomas and E. T. Andrews, proprietors of the work, Faust's Statue, No. 45, Newbury Street. Feb. 1799. pp. 287, (1). 12mo. AAS. LOC.

35514   FREEMAN'S JOURNAL. [Motto.] VOL. III. NUMBER 29. SATURDAY, JANUARY 5, [— VOL. IV. NUMBER 19. TUESDAY, OCTOBER 1, 1799.]
Cincinnati: Printed by Edmund Freeman. 1799. fol.

Publication is said to have been continued into the year 1800—but the above is the last number located.

35515   FRENCH, JONATHAN   1740–1809
A SERMON, DELIVERED ON THE ANNIVERSARY THANKSGIVING, NOVEMBER 29, 1798. WITH SOME ADDITIONS IN THE HISTORICAL PART. BY JONATHAN FRENCH, A. M. PASTOR OF THE SOUTH CHURCH IN ANDOVER. PUBLISHED BY REQUEST.

Andover: Printed by Ames and Parker. 1799. pp. [31.] 8vo.
AAS. BA. CLA. HC. JCB. LOC. MHS. NYPL. YC.

35516   FRENEAU, PHILIP   1752–1832
LETTERS ON VARIOUS INTERESTING AND IMPORTANT SUBJECTS; MANY OF WHICH HAVE APPEARED IN THE AURORA. CORRECTED AND MUCH ENLARGED. BY ROBERT SLENDER, O.S.M. [Two lines from] POPE'S ESSAY.

Philadelphia: Printed for the Author. From the Press of D. Hogan—and sold at his store, No. 222, South Third-Street, and at the Office of the Aurora. December 30, 1799. pp. (142), (1). 8vo.   AAS. BM. CLS. HSP. LOC. NYHS. NYPL.

The initials O. S. M. stand for: One of the Swinish Multitude. 243d Pennsylvania District Copyright, issued to David Hogan, as Proprietor, 28 December, 1799.

35517   A FRIENDLY LETTER FROM A MINISTER OF CHRIST TO A BROTHER MINISTER, UNDER PECULIAR TRIALS, AND DESPONDING IN HIS ADVANCED AGE, . . .
Suffield: Printed by Edward Gray. 1799. pp. 12. 12mo.

35518   FRIENDS. SOCIETY OF
A COLLECTION OF RELIGIOUS TRACTS, FROM DIFFERENT AUTHORS. REPUBLISHED FOR
INFORMATION AND SERIOUS PERUSAL OF ALL SOBER ENQUIRERS.

Baltimore: Printed by William Pechin, No. 15, Market-Street. 1799. pp.
116. 8vo.   LOC.

> Contains: A concise view of the christian religion, as professed by the
> people called Quakers. By Robert Barclay.—A short account of the peo-
> ple called Quakers; their rise, religious principles & settlement in Amer-
> ica. By Anthony Benezet.—Further considerations on war (By the same
> author).—A few serious queries & observations. Addressed to the high
> perfessors [*sic*] of religion in this day, by one who was long in the pro-
> fession, but knew not the power; till it pleased the Lord, by the ministry
> and writings of the people called Quakers, to direct him to where alone
> the power is to be known, within. By John Spalding.—A few reasons
> for leaving the national established mode of worship, addressed prin-
> cipally to those who attend at the place called St. Giles's church, Read-
> ing.—Two letters written by Samuel Crisp, about the year 1702, to some
> of his acquaintance, upon his change from a chaplain of the Church of
> England, to join the people called Quakers.—Extracts from the writings
> of divers eminent authors of different religious denominations; and at
> various periods of time, representing the evils and pernicious effects of
> stage plays, and other vain amusements. By Lindley Murray. With
> some additions.

35519   —— AN EPISTLE FROM THE THREE MONTHLY-MEETINGS OF FRIENDS OF PHILADELPHIA,
TO THE MEMBERS OF OUR RELIGIOUS SOCIETY, IN THE CITY AND NEIGHBOURHOOD.
[Signed in behalf and by appointment of the said meetings held at Philadelphia
in the 2nd month, 1799, by James Pemberton, and seven others.]

Philadelphia: Printed by Benjamin & Jacob Johnson, No. 147, High-Street.
1799. pp. 8. 8vo.   AAS. JCB. LOC.

35520   —— THE EPISTLE FROM THE YEARLY MEETING, HELD IN LONDON, BY ADJOURNMENTS,
FROM THE 22D TO THE 31ST OF THE FIFTH MONTH, 1799, INCLUSIVE; TO THE QUAR-
TERLY AND MONTHLY MEETINGS OF FRIENDS IN GREAT-BRITAIN, AND IRELAND.

[Philadelphia: 1799.] pp. [3.] fol.   AAS. JCB.

35521   —— FROM OUR YEARLY MEETING HELD IN LONDON, BY ADJOURNMENTS, FROM THE 22D
OF THE FIFTH MONTH, TO THE 31ST OF THE SAME INCLUSIVE, 1799, TO THE ENSU-
ING YEARLY MEETING OF FRIENDS IN PHILADELPHIA.

[Philadelphia: 1799.] pp. [2.] fol.   AAS. JCB.

35522   —— TO OUR FELLOW CITIZENS OF THE UNITED STATES OF NORTH AMERICA AND
OTHERS TO WHOM IT MAY CONCERN. [On the evils of slavery.] SIGNED ON BEHALF
AND BY DIRECTION OF A MEETING REPRESENTING THE RELIGIOUS SOCIETY CALLED
QUAKERS IN PENNSYLVANIA, NEW JERSEY, &C. HELD IN PHILADELPHIA THE 15TH
OF THE 11TH MONTH, 1799. JOHN DRINKER, CLERK.

[Philadelphia: 1799.] pp. [3.] 8vo.   LOC.

35523   FRISBIE, LEVI   1748–1806
THE NATURE AND EFFECTS OF THE WORKS OF DARKNESS DETECTED AND DISPLAYED,
IN TWO DISCOURSES, DELIVERED AT THE FIRST PARISH IN IPSWICH, APRIL 4, 1799,
ON THE ANNIVERSARY FAST DAY THROUGHOUT THE STATE OF MASSACHUSETTS, BY
LEVI FRISBIE, A. M. PASTOR OF THE FIRST CHURCH IN IPSWICH. PUBLISHED AT THE
REQUEST OF MANY OF THE HEARERS. [Ornament.]

Printed by Angier March, Newburyport, MDCCXCIX. pp. (53). 8vo.

Page 53 is misprinted 42.   AAS. BA. CHS. CLA. JCB.

35524　FROM THEE ELIZA I MUST GO. SONG.
　　New-York: Published by J. and M. Paff. [1799.] pp. (2). 4to.　　LOC.

35525　FROTHINGHAM'S LONG-ISLAND HERALD. [Motto.] VOL. VII. NUMB. 320. MON-
DAY, JANUARY 7, [— DECEMBER ? 1799.]
　　Sag-Harbor: Printed by David Frothingham. 1799. fol.

　　The above is the last number located, and how much longer publication
was continued is not known. In 1802, Selleck Osborn bought the plant,
and changed the name to Suffolk County Herald; and, in 1804, transferred
the paper to Alden Spooner, who changed the name to Suffolk Gazette,
which he edited and published to 1811, when publication ceased.

35526　FULLER, SYLVESTER
NEW OHIO LANDS, AND TITLE INDISPUTABLE. THE SUBSCRIBER HAVING LATELY PUR-
CHASED A TRACT OF 21,401 ACRES OF LAND, LYING ON THE WATERS OF ELK RIVER,
ONE OF THE SOURCES OF THE GREAT KANHAWAY AND OHIO RIVER, IN THE COUNTY
OF RANDOLPH, STATE OF VIRGINIA. [Two columns.] SYLVESTER FULLER.
　　Providence, [Printed by John Carter, junior.] May 11, 1799. Broadside. fol.
　　　　　　　　　　　　　　　　　　　　　　AAS. JCB. RIHS.

35527　FULLING, THOMAS
THE ASTRONOMICAL REPOSITORY; OR, THE FAMILY CALENDAR, FOR THE YEAR OF OUR
LORD, 1800. CALCULATED FOR THE TOWN OF BOSTON; BUT WILL SERVE FOR ALL
THE NEIGHBOURING STATES. CONTAINING EVERY THING NECESSARY FOR AN ALMA-
NACK, AND MORE REMARKABLE EVENTS THAN IN ANY OTHER. BY THOMAS FULLING,
A.M. [Six lines of verse.]
　　Boston: Printed and sold by Benjamin Edes, in Kilby-Street. [1799.] pp.
(24). 12mo.　　　　　　　　　　　　　　　　　　AAS. LOC.

35528　—— THE ASTRONOMICAL REPOSITORY; OR THE FAMILY CALENDAR, FOR THE YEAR OF
OUR LORD 1800. CALCULATED FOR THE TOWN OF BOSTON; BUT WILL SERVE FOR
ALL THE NEIGHBOURING STATES. CONTAINING EVERY THING NECESSARY FOR AN
ALMANACK, AND MORE REMARKABLE EVENTS THAN IN ANY OTHER. BY ISAAC
BICKERSTAFF. [Six lines of verse.]
　　Boston: Printed and sold by Benjamin Edes, in Kilby-Street. [1799.] pp.
(24). 12mo.　　　　　　　　　　　　　　　　　　AAS.

　　With slight changes only, this is the same as Edes' Thomas Fulling Almanac for this year.

35529　—— THE ASTRONOMICAL REPOSITORY; OR THE FAMILY CALENDAR, FOR THE YEAR OF
OUR LORD 1800. CALCULATED FOR THE TOWN OF BOSTON; BUT WILL SERVE FOR
ALL THE NEIGHBOURING STATES. CONTAINING EVERY THING NECESSARY FOR AN
ALMANACK, AND MORE REMARKABLE EVENTS THAN IN ANY OTHER. BY ABRAHAM
WEATHERWISE. [Six lines of verse.]
　　Boston: Printed and sold by Benjamin Edes, in Kilby-Street. [1799.] pp.
(24). 12mo.　　　　　　　　　　　　　　　　　　AAS.

　　With change of authorship, only, there is no difference in Edes' Fulling,
Bickerstaff, or Weatherwise Almanacs for this year.

35530　GALLATIN, ABRAHAM ALBERT ALPHONSE　　　　　　　1761–1849
THE SPEECH OF ALBERT GALLATIN ON THE ALIEN AND SEDITION LAWS.
　　Philadelphia: 1799. 8vo.

35531　—— THE SUBSTANCE OF TWO SPEECHES OF MR. GALLATIN, ON THE BILL FOR
AUGMENTING THE NAVY ESTABLISHMENT OF THE UNITED STATES, IN THE HOUSE OF
REPRESENTATIVES, ON THE 7TH AND 11TH OF FEBRUARY, 1799.
　　Philadelphia: Printed by Joseph Gales. 1799. pp. 28. 8vo.
　　　　　　　　　AAS. BA. BM. HSP. JCB. LOC. NYHS. NYPL.

35532   THE GAMUT, OR SCALE OF MUSIC, ADAPTED FOR THE USE OF BEGINNERS IN PSALMODY.
     Lansingburgh: Printed by Gardiner Tracy. 1799.

35533   GAZETTE FRANCAISE. No. 437. MERCREDI, 2 JANVIER, [— No. 555. VENDREDI,
     4 OCTOBRE, 1799.]
         Imprime par Claude Parisot a New-York, Pearl-Street, No. 51. 1799. 4to.   HC.
     The above is the last number located.

35534   GAZETTE OF THE UNITED STATES, AND PHILADELPHIA DAILY ADVERTISER. VOL. XV.
     NUMBER 1962. TUESDAY, JANUARY 1, [— VOL. XVI. NUMBER 2269. TUESDAY,
     DECEMBER 31, 1799.]
         [*Philadelphia: Published] By John Ward Fenno, No.* 119, *Chesnut-Street.*
     1799. fol.   AAS. BA. HSP. LCP. LOC. MdHS.

35535   THE GENIUS OF LIBERTY. VOL. I. No. 33. THURSDAY, JANUARY 3, [— VOL. II.
     No. 84. THURSDAY, DECEMBER 26, 1799.]
         *Morris-Town: Printed and published by Jacob Mann, nearly opposite the
     Academy.* 1799. fol.

35536   THE GENIUS OF LIBERTY; AND FREDRICKSBURG & FALMOUTH ADVERTISER. VOL. II.
     No. 64. FRIDAY, JANUARY 4, [—VOL. III. No. 114. FRIDAY, DECEMBER 27, 1799.]
         Fredericksburg, (Va.) Printed by Mercer & Carter. 1799. fol.

     Sometime this year George Carter withdrew, and publication was for a
     time in the name of Robert Mercer. Owing to his illness the issue for
     November 22d, was skipped, and probably about this time — Field was
     admitted to partnership, as Mercer & Field.

35537   GENLIS, STÉPANIE FÉLICITÉ DUCREST DE SAINT-AUBIN, comtesse de   1746–1830
     ALPHONSO AND DALINDA: OR, THE MAGIC OF ART AND NATURE. A MORAL TALE.
     WRITTEN IN FRENCH BY MADAME LA COMTESSE DE GENLIS, TRANSLATED INTO
     ENGLISH BY THOMAS HOLCROFT. A NEW EDITION.
         Printed at Fairhaven by Judah P. Spooner? 1799. pp. 216. 12mo.   LOC. WRHS.

35538   GEORGE, DANIEL
     THE FARMERS' ALMANACK, FOR THE YEAR OF OUR LORD 1800: BEING THE FOURTH
     YEAR AFTER BISSEXTILE, OR LEAP YEAR: AND THE TWENTY FOURTH OF AMERICAN
     INDEPENDENCE. ADAPTED TO THE DISTRICT OF MAINE. CALCULATED FOR THE
     MERIDIAN OF PORTLAND. LAT. 43 DEG. 43 MIN. NORTH. [Four lines of verse.]
         Printed at Portland, by Baker & George. [1799.] pp. (36). 12mo.   AAS.

     Contains, Stamp duties. Interest. Court calendar. Probate. Postage,
     and Mails. Plaster of Paris as a manure, by John M. Blake. Roads.

35539   THE GEORGETOWN GAZETTE. [Motto.] VOL. II. No. 53. WEDNESDAY, JANUARY 2,
     [— No. 104. WEDNESDAY, DECEMBER 25, 1799.]
         *Georgetown, (S. C.) Printed every Wednesday, by Elliott & Burd, at five dol-
     lars per ann. payable half yearly.* 1799. fol.

     Owing to the "emoluments arising therefrom fall so far short of the
     support of two editors." Robert Elliott withdrew from the firm at the
     end of this year.

35540   GEORGIA. STATE.
     ACTS OF THE GENERAL ASSEMBLY OF THE STATE OF GEORGIA: PASSED AT LOUIS-
     VILLE, IN JANUARY AND FEBRUARY, 1799.
         *Louisville: Printed by Elisha H. Waldo, for Alexander M'Millan, Printer to
     the State.* 1799. pp. [150.] 8vo.   DeRGL. LOC.

35541   GEORGIA. STATE, continued.
——— THE CONSTITUTION OF THE STATE OF GEORGIA. AS REVISED, AMENDED AND
COMPILED BY THE CONVENTION OF THE STATE, AT LOUISVILLE, ON THE THIRTIETH
DAY OF MAY, MDCCXCVIII. [Ornament.]
        Augusta: Printed by John Erdman Smith. MDCCXCIX. pp. 36. 8vo. DERGL.

35542   GEORGIA. THE AUGUSTA CHRONICLE AND GAZETTE OF THE STATE. [Motto.] VOL.
XIII. No. 639. SATURDAY, JANUARY 5, [— VOL. XIV, No. 690. SATURDAY, DE-
CEMBER 28, 1799.]
        Augusta: Printed by John E. Smith, Printer to the State. 1799. fol. GHS.

35543   GEORGIA GAZETTE. (No. 793.) THURSDAY, JANUARY 3, [— No. 844. THURSDAY,
DECEMBER 26, 1799.]
        Savannah: Printed by N. Johnston and Co. 1799. fol.   GHS.
        With the issue for November 14th, a cut of an eagle was added to the
        heading.

35544   DIE GERMANTAUNER ZEITUNG. NUM. 443. DIENSTAG, DEN 2 JANUAR, [— NUM.
494. DIENSTAG, DEN 25 DECEMBER, 1799.]
        *Diese Zeitung wird wochentlich Dienstag Nachmittags herausgegeben von Michael
        Billmeyer, Buchdrucker, zu Germantaun,* . . . 1799. 4to.

35545   GETCHELL, DENNIS   1760–1791
A TESTIMONY CONCERNING ACCEPTABLE WORSHIP TO ALMIGHTY GOD. BY DENNIS
GETCHELL, LATE OF VASSALBOROUGH, IN NEW-ENGLAND.
        New-Bedford: Printed by Abraham Shearman, jun. for Stephen Buffington.
        1799. pp. [12.] 12mo.   LOC. NYPL.
        Contains, "Some account of Dennis Getchell aforesaid, as certified by a
        person who was well acquainted with him in years past."

35546   GIFFORD, WILLIAM   1756–1826
THE BAVIAD, AND MÆVIAD, BY WILLIAM GIFFORD, ESQUIRE. [Five lines of Latin.]
TO WHICH IS PREFIXED, A POETICAL EPISTLE TO THE AUTHOR, BY AN AMERICAN
GENTLEMAN. [William Cliffton.] A NEW EDITION REVISED.
        London—Printed—Philadelphia: Re-printed for William Cobbett. M.DCC.-
        XCIX. pp. [xx], (2), [145.] 12mo.   AAS. BU. JCB. LOC. NYPL.
        Printed on thick paper.

35547   GILL, SARAH PRINCE
DEVOTIONAL PAPERS, WROTE BY THE LATE MRS. SARAH GILL, OF BOSTON; THE SAME
AS CONTAINED IN THE APPENDIX TO THE SERMON ON HER DEATH, BY THE REV. MR.
HUNT. TOGETHER WITH HER TOUCHING LETTER, AS FROM THE DEAD. ALL PUB-
LISHED FOR THE BENEFIT OF THE LIVING.
        Windham: Re-printed by John Byrne. 1799. pp. 23. 12mo.   AAS. BA.

35548   GILLET, or GILLETT, ELIPHALET   1768–1848
A DISCOURSE, DELIVERED AT HALLOWELL, APRIL 25TH, 1799. BEING THE DAY AP-
POINTED BY THE CHIEF MAGISTRATE OF THE UNITED STATES FOR A NATIONAL FAST.
BY ELIPHALET GILLET, A. M. PASTOR OF THE CHURCH IN HALLOWELL.
        Augusta, (District of Maine.) Printed by Peter Edes. 1799. pp. 32. 8vo.
                                                BA. HEH. JCB. MHS. NYHS.

35549   ——— — A DISCOURSE, DELIVERED AT HALLOWELL, APRIL 25TH, 1799, BEING THE DAY
APPOINTED BY THE CHIEF MAGISTRATE OF THE UNITED STATES, FOR A NATIONAL FAST.
BY ELIPHALET GILLETT, A. M. PASTOR OF THE CHURCH OF CHRIST IN HALLOWELL.
        *Hallowell—Printed: New-York—Re-printed for, and sold by Cornelius Davis,
        No. 94, Water-Street.* 1799. pp. (2), 22. 8vo.
                AAS. BA. CHS. CLA. JCB. LOC. MeHS. MHS. NYHS. NYPL. UTS. YC.

35550   GILMANTON RURAL MUSEUM. VOL. I. NO. 1. MONDAY, OCTOBER 28, [— NO. 10. MONDAY, DECEMBER 30, 1799.]

> *Gilmanton, New-Hampshire. Printed and published by Elijah Russell.* 1799. fol.

Established, as a weekly, by Elijah Russell, and continued by him into 1800.

35551   THE GIRL WITH A CAST IN HER EYE.

> *New-York Printed & sold by J. Hewitt, No. 23 Maiden Lane. Price 12½ cents.*
> [1799.] Broadside. 4to.   LOC.

35552   GISBORNE, THOMAS   1758–1846
AN ENQUIRY INTO THE DUTIES OF THE FEMALE SEX. BY THOMAS GISBORNE, M.A.

> *London, Printed. Philadelphia, Re-printed, and sold by James Humphreys, South Third Street, opposite the Bank of the United States.* 1799. pp. iv, (2), 312. 12mo.   AAS.

35553   THE GLEBE HOUSE, A TALE. BY A LADY OF DISTINCTION. FIRST AMERICAN EDITION. [Cut.]

> *Salem, New-Jersey: From the Press of Black & North.* 1799. pp. 120. 12mo.
>   LOC. NYPL.

35554   GODDARD, JOSIAH
A NEW AND BEAUTIFUL COLLECTION OF SELECT HYMNS AND SPIRITUAL SONGS: SELECTED FROM ALL AUTHORS THAT ARE ENTERTAINING, SPIRITUAL AND DIVINE. FOR THE USE OF CHURCHES, RELIGIOUS SOCIETIES, AND CHRISTIAN CONFERENCES; AND IN PARTICULAR FOR THE COMFORT AND EDIFICATION OF PRIVATE CHRISTIANS, FOR WHICH IT IS MOSTLY DESIGNED. BY JOSIAH GODDARD. . . .

> [*Walpole, N. H. Printed at the Press of Thomas & Thomas, by David Carlisle, for the Author.* 1799 ?] pp. 396, (10). 16mo.

166th Massachusetts District Copyright, issued to Josiah Goddard, as Author, 25 March, 1799.

35555   GODWIN, MARY WOLLSTONECRAFT   1759–1797
MARIA: OR, THE WRONGS OF WOMAN. A POSTHUMOUS FRAGMENT. BY MARY WOLLSTONECRAFT GODWIN. AUTHOR OF A VINDICATION OF THE RIGHTS OF WOMAN. [Edited by William Godwin.]

> *Philadelphia: Printed by James Carey, No. 16, Chesnut-Street.* 1799. pp. 232. 12mo.   AAS. LOC.

35556   GODWIN, WILLIAM   1756–1836
MEMOIRS OF MARY WOLLSTONECRAFT GODWIN, AUTHOR OF "A VINDICATION OF THE RIGHTS OF WOMAN."

> *Philadelphia: Printed by James Carey, No. 16, Chesnut-Street.* 1799. pp. (158). 12mo.   AAS. BA. JCB. LOC. NYPL.

35557   GOLDSMITH, OLIVER   1728–1774
THE DESERTED VILLAGE. BY DR. GOLDSMITH.

> *Litchfield: Printed by Thomas Collier.* 1799.

35558   THE GOSHEN REPOSITORY. [Motto.] VOL. X. NO. 518. TUESDAY, JANUARY 1, [— VOL. XI. NO. 570. TUESDAY, DECEMBER 31, 1799.]

> *Published every Tuesday, by John G. & William Hurtin, in Goshen, (Orange County)* . . . 1799. fol.

Discontinued. In January, 1800, John G. Hurtin established, in continuation, the *Orange Patrol.*

35559 GRAEFF, JOHANN GEORG
LISBIA. A NEW CANZONET. COMPOSED BY J. C. GRAEFF.
New York: Printed & sold at J. Hewitt's Musical Repository, No. 23 Maiden Lane. Pr. 25 cents. [1799.] pp. (2). 4to. LOC.

35560 GRAHAM, WILLIAM 1745–1799
THE SCRIPTURAL DOCTRINE OF WATER BAPTISM. SHEWING I. THE SCRIPTURAL SUBJECTS OF THAT ORDINANCE. II. THE SCRIPTURAL MODE OF ITS ADMINISTRATION. AND, LASTLY, ANSWERING SOME QUESTIONS FOR THE SATISFACTION OF SERIOUS ENQUIRERS. BY THE REV. WILLIAM GRAHAM, A. M.
Richmond, Virginia: Printed by W. A. Rind, near the Market. 1799. pp. 41. 8vo. AAS. LOC. NYPL.
Prepared for publication, at the request of the Synod of Virginia.

35561 GRANT, THOMAS –1818
AN ORATION DELIVERED AT FLEMINGTON, JULY 4TH, 1799. BY THOMAS GRANT.
Trenton: Printed by G. Craft. 1799. pp. 16. 8vo.

35562 GRAY, THOMAS 1716–1771
AN ELEGY WRITTEN IN A COUNTRY CHURCH YARD. BY MR. GRAY. THE CURFEW TOLLS THE KNELL OF PARTING DAY, THE LOWING HERD WINDS SLOWLY O'ER THE LEA, THE PLOUGHMAN HOMEWARD PLODS HIS WEARY WAY, AND LEAVES THE WORLD TO DARKNESS AND TO ME.
Re-printed at T. Collier's Office, Litchfield. 1799. pp. 8. 16mo. CHS.

35563 GREEN, ASHBEL 1762–1848
A PASTORAL LETTER, FROM A MINISTER IN THE COUNTRY, TO THOSE OF HIS FLOCK WHO REMAINED IN THE CITY OF PHILADELPHIA DURING THE PESTILENCE OF 1798.
Philadelphia: Printed by John Ormrod, No. 41, Chesnut-Street. 1799. pp. 12. 12mo. JCB. NYPL. SGO.

35564 GREEN, JACOB 1722–1796
A VISION OF HELL, AND A DISCOVERY OF THE CONSULTATIONS AND SERVICES THERE. BY THEODORUS VAN SHERMAIN.
Portsmouth, N. H.: Printed and sold by Charles Peirce. 1799.

35565 THE GREEN MOUNTAIN PATRIOT. [Motto.] VOL. I. No. 46. FRIDAY, JANUARY 4, [— VOL. II. No. 97. THURSDAY, DECEMBER 26, 1799.]
Printed at Peacham, Vermont, by Farley & Goss, . . . 1799. fol. AAS.
In February, the day of publication was changed to Thursday.

35566 GREEN, SAMUEL
GREEN'S ALMANACK AND REGISTER FOR THE STATE OF CONNECTICUT; FOR THE YEAR OF OUR LORD, 1800; BEING THE TWENTY-FOURTH OF THE INDEPENDENCE OF THE UNITED STATES.
New-London: Printed and sold by Samuel Green. [1799.] pp. 156. 24mo. AAS. CHS. HC. JCB. LOC. YC.

35567 GREENFIELD GAZETTE. A REGISTER OF GENUINE FEDERALISM. No. 51 OF VOL. VII. WHOLE NO. 363. MONDAY, JANUARY 7, [— No. 50 OF VOL. VIII. WHOLE NO. 414. SATURDAY, DECEMBER 28, 1799.]
Printed at Greenfield, (Massachusetts) by Francis Barker. 1799. fol. AAS.
With the issue for June 17th, Barker disposed of his interests to Thomas Dickman, its former proprietor.

35568 | GREENLEAF'S NEW YORK JOURNAL & PATRIOTIC REGISTER. [Motto.] VOL. LII. NUMB. 88. TOTAL NUMB. 3339. WEDNESDAY, JANUARY 2, [— VOL. LIII. NUMB. . TOTAL NUMB 4342. SATURDAY, DECEMBER 28, 1799.]
New-York — Printed and published (on Wednesdays and Saturdays) by Ann Greenleaf, at her Printing-Office, No. 54, Wall-Street. . . . 1799. fol. NYHS. YC.

35569 | GRETTON, JOHN
JAVOTTE; OR. THE MAID OF THE ALPS. WRITTEN BY JOHN GRETTON. COMPOSED BY JOSEPH WILLSON, ORGANIST OF TRINITY CHURCH.
New York: Published by J. and M. Paff. [1799.] pp. (4). 4to.

35570 | GRIFFITH, WILLIAM   1766–1826
EUMENES: BEING A COLLECTION OF PAPERS, WRITTEN FOR THE PURPOSE OF EXHIBITING SOME OF THE MORE PROMINENT ERRORS AND OMISSIONS OF THE CONSTITUTION OF NEW-JERSEY, AS ESTABLISHED ON THE SECOND DAY OF JULY, ONE THOUSAND SEVEN HUNDRED AND SEVENTY-SIX; AND TO PROVE THE NECESSITY OF CALLING A CONVENTION, FOR REVISION AND AMENDMENT.
Trenton: Printed by G. Craft. 1799. pp. 149, (2), (2), (1). 8vo.
HSP. JCB. LOC. MHS. NYHS. NYPL.
Issued in fifty-two numbers, some of which "have been published in Mr. Day's [State] Gazette."

35571 | GROUT, JONATHAN, JUNIOR
THE YOUNG CHILD'S ACCIDENCE: BEING A SMALL SPELLING BOOK FOR LITTLE CHILDREN: CONTAINING A SELECTION OF WORDS IN MODERN USE, ARRANGED IN SUCH A MANNER AS WILL NATURALLY LEAD THE YOUNG PUPIL, STEP BY-STEP, TO A RIGHT PRONUNCIATION. DESIGNED FOR A CHEAP BOOK FOR LITTLE CHILDREN. BY JONATHAN GROUT, JUN. COPPY [*sic*] RIGHT SECURED.
Printed at Worcester, (Massa.) By Daniel Greenleaf. 1799. pp. 48. 24mo. AAS.
168th Massachusetts District Copyright, issued to Jonathan Grout, junior, as Author, 18 June, 1799.

35572 | GUARDIAN; OR, NEW-BRUNSWICK ADVERTISER. NUMB. 10 OF VOL. VII. WHOLE NUM. 322. TUESDAY, JANUARY 1, [— NUM. 10 OF VOL. VIII. WHOLE NUM. 374. TUESDAY, DECEMBER 31, 1799.]
New-Brunswick, New-Jersey; Printed by Abraham Blauvelt, in Albany-Street. 1799. fol.

35573 | THE GUARDIAN OF FREEDOM. [Motto.] No. 34 OF VOL. I. THURSDAY, JANUARY 3, [— No. 20 OF VOL. III. TOTAL NO. 71. THURSDAY, SEPTEMBER 19, 1799 ?]
Frankfort, (Kentucky): Printed by John Bradford & Son, at the Capitol. 1799. fol.
In May, the Printing-Office was changed to, "on Main Street." Apparently about the above date John Bradford withdrew, and his son James M. Bradford continued publication, with a new serial numbering, as follows:

35574 | THE GUARDIAN OF FREEDOM. THIS FOLIO OF FOUR PAGES, HAPPY WORK! WHAT IS IT BUT A MAP OF BUSY LIFE, ITS FLUCTUATIONS, AND ITS VAST CONCERNS?—COWPER. No. 1 OF VOL. I. WEDNESDAY, SEPTEMBER 25, [— No. 14. WEDNESDAY, DECEMBER 25, 1799.]
Frankfort (Kentucky): Printed by James M. Bradford, at the corner of Montgomery and St. Clair Streets. 1799. fol.
James M. Bradford continued publication to January 25, 1804, when he sold it to Thomas Anderson, whom he had chosen to succeed him. Anderson disposed of the establishment without making any use of it, to Elijah Conway Berry, who continued its publication into the year 1805 —and perhaps later.

35575   THE GUARDIAN OF LIBERTY AND HUNTINGDON CHRONICLE. VOL. I. No. 1. THURS-DAY, NOVEMBER 28, [— No. 5. THURSDAY, DECEMBER 26, 1799.]

     Huntingdon, Pennsylvania. Published by John R. Parrington. 1799. fol.

     Established, as a weekly, by John R. Parrington, and continued by him to August 14, 1800 — the last, and only number located.

35576   A GUIDE TO THE HEALTH OF CHILDREN.

     Hartford: Printed by John Babcock. 1799.

35577   GUIREY, WILLIAM

     THE HISTORY OF EPISCOPACY, IN FOUR PARTS, 1ST. FROM ITS RISE AND PROGRESS IN THE CHURCH OF ROME. 2D. A SHORT ACCOUNT OF ITS PROCEEDINGS IN THE CHURCH OF ENGLAND. 3D. THE RISE AND PROGRESS OF THE METHODISTS IN EUROPE. 4TH. THE RISE AND PROGRESS OF EPISCOPACY AMONG THE METHODISTS IN AMERICA. BY WILLIAM GUIREY, MINISTER OF THE GOSPEL. [Ten lines from] THO. TAYLOR.

     [Raleigh: Printed by Joseph Gales. 1799.] pp. x, 381, (3).   DERGL.

     There is a woodcut on page 260, of the "Baltimore Methodistical Bull." "Principally intended for the information of the inhabitants of the back-woods in Georgia."

35578   GURNEY, THOMAS   1705–1770

     GURNEY'S EASY AND COMPENDIOUS SYSTEM OF SHORT HAND; ADAPTED TO THE ARTS AND SCIENCES, AND TO THE LEARNED PROFESSIONS. IMPROVED BY THOMAS SERGEANT. SECOND AMERICAN EDITION. [Four lines of verse.]

     Printed for Mathew Carey, Philadelphia, by W. & R. Dickson, Lancaster, June 17, 1799. pp. 38, 12 plates, portrait. 12mo.   AAS. JCB. NYPL.

35579   HALE, ENOCH   1753–1837

     A SPELLING BOOK; OR THE FIRST PART OF A GRAMMAR OF THE ENGLISH LANGUAGE, AS WRITTEN AND SPOKEN IN THE UNITED STATES. BY ENOCH HALE, A.M. THE FIRST EDITION. . . . PUBLISHED ACCORDING TO ACT OF CONGRESS.

     Northampton: Printed by William Butler. M,DCC,XC,IX. pp. 120. 12mo.

     160th Massachusetts District Copyright, issued to Enoch Hale, as   HC. NYPL. Author, 31 December, 1798.

35580   HALL, DAVID   1683–1756

     A COMPASSIONATE CALL, AND HAND REACHED FORTH IN TENDER GOSPEL LOVE, TO ALL SUCH PERSONS, AS HAVING ONCE MADE PROFESSION OF THE BLESSED TRUTH, YET BY SOME MIS-CONDUCT OR OTHER, HAVE UNHAPPILY FORFEITED THEIR UNITY WITH THE SOCIETY OF FRIENDS; IN WHAT CAPACITY, POST OR STATION SOEVER IN THE CHURCH THEY MAY HAVE BEEN; OR IN WHAT CIRCUMSTANCE OF LIFE SOEVER THEY NOW STAND, IN THEIR PRESENT DISUNITED SITUATION. BY DAVID HALL.

     Philadelphia: Printed by Benjamin & Jacob Johnson. 1799. pp. 12. 12mo.

35581   HAMILTON, ALEXANDER, and others.

     THE FEDERALIST: A COLLECTION OF ESSAYS, WRITTEN IN FAVOUR OF THE NEW CONSTITUTION, AS AGREED UPON BY THE FEDERAL CONVENTION, SEPTEMBER 17, 1787. IN TWO VOLUMES. VOL. I. [— II.]

     New-York: Printed and sold by John Tiebout, . . . 1799. 2 vols. pp. vi, 227; vi, 384. 12mo.   JCB. LOC. NYPL. NL.

     This is the first edition of "The Federalist," with new title-pages only.

35582 HAMILTON, JOSEPH
OCCASIONAL REFLECTIONS ON THE OPERATIONS OF THE SMALL-POX OR, THE TRAVELLER'S POCKET DOCTOR. BY JOSEPH HAMILTON, PHYSICIAN.

New-York: 1799.

80th New York District Copyright, issued to Joseph Hamilton, as Author, 21 May, 1799.

35583 HAMPSHIRE COUNTY. MASSACHUSETTS. NORTHERN ASSOCIATION.
SERMONS, ON VARIOUS IMPORTANT DOCTRINES AND DUTIES OF THE CHRISTIAN RELIGION; SELECTED FROM THE MANUSCRIPTS OF SEVERAL MINISTERS, MEMBERS OF THE NORTHERN ASSOCIATION, IN THE COUNTY OF HAMPSHIRE.

Northampton: (Massachusetts) Printed by William Butler. 1799. pp. 448, (1). 8vo. AAS. BM. LOC. NYPL.

Contains, I. & II. The Christian religion of divine authority. By Mr. Strong, of Williamsburgh.—III. The true God known only from divine revelation. By Mr. Forward, of Belcherstown.—IV. A view of the divine perfections. By Mr. Emerson, of Conway.—V. A view of God, as creator and governor of the world. By Mr. Newton, of Greenfield.—VI. The essential divinity of Jesus Christ. By Mr. Hale, of Westhampton.—VII. The personality and divinity of the Spirit. By the same.—VIII. The glory of Christ, as mediator. By the same.—IX. On regeneration. By Mr. Emerson.—X. A belief of the peculiar doctrines of christianity essential to our acceptance with God. By Mr. Lyman, of Hatfield.—XI. The true christian character delineated. By Mr. Williston, of Easthampton.—XII. On living under the eye of God. By Mr. Emerson.—XIII. The advantages of pious society. By Mr. Williams, of Northampton.—XIV. Family government and filial duty. By Mr. Lyman.—XV. Symptoms of the decline, and importance of the revival of family religion. By Mr. Hayes, of South-Hadley.—XVI. The use and importance of christian institutions. By Mr. Strong, of Williamsburg.—XVII. Persuasives to an attendance on the Lord's Supper. By Mr. Taylor, of Deerfield.—XVIII & XIX. Infants of believers members of the church of Christ. By Mr. Hopkins, of Hadley.—XX. Upon the discipline of Christ's church. By Mr. Lyman.—XXI. Dissuasives from excessive and sinful diversions. By Mr. Taylor.—XXII. Habitual growth in grace essential to the christian character. By Mr. Forward.—XXIII. On what constitutes a criminal conformity to the world. By Mr. Judd, of Southampton.—XXIV. Religion frequently corrupted by human speculation. By Mr. Forward.—XXV. Reasons offered for frequent meditations on death and judgment. By Mr. Wells, of Whateley.—XXVI. The final and total disappointment of the wicked. By Mr. Williams, of Northampton.—XXVII. The happy and glorious state of the righteous. By the same.

35584 HAMPSHIRE GAZETTE. VOL. XIII., NUMB. 644. WEDNESDAY, JANUARY 2, [—VOL. XIV. NUMB. 695. WEDNESDAY, DECEMBER 25, 1799.]

Printed at Northampton, (Massachusetts,) by William Butler. 1799. fol.

35585 HANWAY, JONAS 1712–1786
TRAVELS OF JONAS HANWAY, ESQ. THROUGH RUSSIA INTO PERSIA, AND AFTERWADS [*sic*] THROUGH RUSSIA, GERMANY, & HOLLAND, [Ornament.]

Philadelphia: Printed and sold by Joseph & James Cruikshank, No. 87, High-Street. [1799.] pp. 111. 16mo. AAS.

35586   HARDIE, James   1758–1826
AN ACCOUNT OF THE MALIGNANT FEVER, LATELY PREVALENT IN THE CITY OF NEW YORK, CONTAINING I. A NARRATIVE OF ITS RISE. PROGRESS AND DECLINE WITH THE OPINIONS OF SOME MEDICAL GENTLEMEN WITH RESPECT TO ITS ORIGIN, &c. II. THE MANNER IN WHICH THE POOR WERE RELIEVED DURING THE AWFUL CALAMITY. III. A LIST OF THE DONATIONS, WHICH HAVE BEEN PRESENTED TO THE HEALTH COMMITTEE FOR THE RELIEF OF THE SICK AND INDIGENT. IV. A LIST OF THE NAMES OF THE DEAD, ARRANGED IN ALPHABETICAL ORDER, WITH THEIR PROFESSIONS OR OCCUPATIONS, AND AS FAR AS WAS PRACTICABLE TO OBTAIN INFORMATION, THE NAMES OF THE COUNTRIES OF WHICH THEY WERE NATIVES. V. A COMPARATIVE VIEW OF THE FEVER OF THE YEAR 1798, WITH THAT OF THE YEAR 1795. BY JAMES HARDIE, A. M. . . .

       New-York: Printed by Hurtin and M'Farlane at the Literary Printing-Office, and sold by the Author. . . . 1799. pp. 139, (9). 8vo.

                                 AAS. BM. HC. JCB. LOC. NYHS. NYPL. SGO.

     74th New York District Copyright, issued to James Hardie, as Author, 28 December, 1798.

35587   HARPER, Robert Goodloe   1765–1825
THE CASE OF THE GEORGIA SALES ON THE MISSISSIPPI CONSIDERED : WITH A REFERENCE TO LAW AUTHORITIES AND PUBLIC ACTS ; WITH AN APPENDIX, CONTAINING CERTAIN EXTRACTS, RECORDS, AND OFFICIAL PAPERS.

       Philadelphia: Printed by Richard Folwell, No. 33, Carter's-Alley. 1799. pp. 91. 4to.   DERGL. JCB. LOC. NYPL. YC.

     Page 57 omitted; 65 repeated: Signed on page 44, Rob. G. Harper.

35588   —— — THE CASE OF THE GEORGIA SALES ON THE MISSISSIPPI CONSIDERED : WITH A REFERENCE TO LAW AUTHORITIES AND PUBLIC ACTS : WITH AN APPENDIX, CONTAINING CERTAIN EXTRACTS, RECORDS, AND OFFICIAL PAPERS.

       Philadelphia: Printed [by Richard Folwell] for Benjamin Davies. 1799. pp. (4), 109. 8vo.   HC.

35589   —— MR. HARPER'S SPEECH ON THE NAVY: IN OPPOSITION TO THE MOTION OF MR. GALLATIN, FOR STRIKING OUT OF THE BILL FOR AUGMENTING THE NAVY, THAT PART WHICH PROVIDES FOR BUILDING SIX SEVENTY-FOURS. DELIVERED IN A COMMITTEE OF THE WHOLE HOUSE, FEBRUARY 8, 1799. TO WHICH IS ANNEXED A SPEECH OF THE SAME GENTLEMAN, IN THE COMMITTEE OF THE WHOLE, APRIL 18, 1798, ON THE PROPRIETY AND NECESSITY OF GRANTING CONVOY — THE IMPORTANCE OF A NAVY — THE CONNECTION BETWEEN AGRICULTURE AND COMMERCE — AND THE POLICY OF DEFENDING ONE, IN ORDER TO ENCOURAGE THE OTHER. MADE IN OPPOSITION TO A MOTION OF MR. NICHOLAS, AND RE-PUBLISHED FROM THE "AMERICAN DAILY ADVERTISER." OF APRIL 25, 1798.

       Philadelphia: Printed by Joseph Gales. 1799. pp. 24. 8vo.   AAS. BA.

35590   HARRIS, Thaddeus Mason   1768–1842
A DISCOURSE, ADDRESSED TO THE RELIGIOUS SOCIETY OF YOUNG MEN IN DORCHESTER, ON THE TERMINATION OF ONE HUNDRED YEARS FROM THE TIME OF ITS ESTABLISHMENT. BY THE REV. THADDEUS MASON HARRIS. [Two lines from] ST. JOHN.

       Charlestown (Massachusetts): Printed by Samuel Etheridge, next door to the Warren-Tavern. 1799. pp. 24. 8vo.   AAS. BM. HC. JCB. NYHS. NYPL.

35591   —— A SERMON, PREACHED AT WRENTHAM, OCT. 10TH, 1798. BEFORE THE GRAND LODGE OF FREE AND ACCEPTED MASONS FOR THE COMMONWEALTH OF MASSACHUSETTS, ON OCCASION OF THE CONSECRATION OF MONTGOMERY LODGE (OF FRANKLIN). BY THE REV. BROTHER T. M. HARRIS, MINISTER OF DORCHESTER, AND CHAPLAIN OF THE GRAND LODGE.

       Printed at Wrentham, by Nathaniel Heaton, jun. M,DCC,XCIX. pp. (19). 8vo.   AAS.

35592   HARRIS, Thaddeus Mason, continued.
—— A Sermon, preached before the Free Masons, at Oxford, September
13th, A.L. 5798, by the reverend brother Thaddeus Mason Harris, a.m.
chaplain to the Grand Lodge of Massachusetts, on the day when the
Olive Branch Lodge was publickly consecrated, and its officers installed,
by the r.w. Isaiah Thomas, esq. grand master, pro tem. [Two lines of Latin
from] Virgil, Æn.
  Printed at Worcester, by Leonard Worcester. A. L. 5799 [1799.] pp. 20. 8vo.
                                                                      AAS. BM.

35593   HARRIS, Walter   1761–1843
A Discourse, delivered at Dunbarton, New-Hampshire, April 25, 1799: being
the day of a national fast. By Walter Harris, a.m. pastor of a church in
Dunbarton.
  Concord: Printed by Geo. Hough. 1799. pp. [32.] 8vo.   AAS. CLA. JCB. LOC.

35594   HARRIS, William   1765–1829
A Sermon delivered at Trinity church in Boston, before the annual Con-
vention of the Protestant Episcopal Church in Massachusetts, on Tuesday,
the 28th of May, 1799. By William Harris, rector of St. Michael's church,
Marblehead.
  Boston: Printed by John & Thomas Fleet, Cornhill, 1799. pp. (22). 4to.
                          AAS. BA. BM. JCB. LOC. MHS. NYHS. NYPL.

35595   HART, Joseph   1712–1768
Hymns, &c. composed on various subjects. By J. Hart. With the Author's
experience, the Supplement and Appendix. [Four lines from] Psalm xcviii. i.
The fifteenth edition.
  Elizabeth-Town: Printed and sold by S. Kollock. 1799. pp. (2), (2), xix, (2),
  (4), 231, (3). 18mo.   AAS. LOC.

35596   HARTFORD. Connecticut.
Having received a confirmation of the distressing intelligence of the death
of the great, the highly beloved Washington, the inhabitants of the
town of Hartford, desirous of testifying their reverence and affection
for the memory of "the man, first in war, first in peace, and first in the
heart of his countrymen," propose to attend divine service at the North
meeting-house, on Friday next. [A procession, at which each citizen will wear
black crape on his left arm, will move from the State House at two o'clock, and
the shops and stores shut Friday. Committee.]
  Hartford: [Printed by Hudson and Goodwin.] Dec. 24, 1799. Broadside,
  fol.   AAS.

35597   HARVARD UNIVERSITY.
Harvard University, in Cambridge, Commonwealth of Massachusetts. The
Order of the exercises of commencement, July 17th, m,dcc,xcix. [Colophon:]
  (Printed by J. & T. Fleet.) [1799.] Broadside. fol.   AAS. BA. HC. NYHS.

35598   —— Honoratissimo Mosi Gill armigero, vice gubernatori; consiliariis et
senatoribus Reipublicæ Massachusettensis; reverendisque ecclesiarum
in oppidis sex vicinis, Presbyteris, Universitatis Harvardianæ curatoribus;
reverendo Josepho Willard, s.t.d. ll.d. præsidi; [Four lines.] Theses hasce,
juvenes in artibus initiati, [Forty-four names.] Humillimè dedicant. . . .
Habita in comitiis Universitatis Cantabrigiæ, Massachusettensis, die Julii
XVII, anno salutis m,dcc,xcix. Rerumque Publicarum Fœderatarum Americæ
summæ potestatis xxiv. [Colophon:]
  Bostoniæ: Typis Manning & Loring. [1799.] Broadside. fol.
                                          AAS. CHS. EI. HC. MHS. YC.

35599   HASWELL, ANTHONY   1756–1816
AN ORATION, DELIVERED AT BENNINGTON, VERMONT, AUGUST 16TH, 1799. IN COM-
MEMORATION OF THE BATTLE OF BENNINGTON. PUBLISHED AT THE REQUEST OF THE
AUDIENCE. BY ANTHONY HASWELL. [Five lines of quotations.]

Bennington: Printed by Anthony Haswell, 1799. pp. (36). 8vo.   LOC.

Pages 26 to 36 consists of odes, songs, &c. performed on the occasion.

35600   —— HASWELL'S VERMONT AND NEW YORK ALMANACK, FOR THE YEAR OF OUR LORD
1800; BEING THE TWENTY FOURTH YEAR OF AMERICAN INDEPENDENCE, UNTIL JULY
4TH. CALCULATED FOR THE MERIDIAN OF BENNINGTON, LATITUDE 42 DEGREES AND
58 MINUTES NORTH. CONTAINING THE LUNATIONS, ECLIPSES, RISING AND SETTING
OF THE SUN AND MOON, JUDGMENT OF THE WEATHER, COURTS, &C. TOGETHER WITH
USEFUL TABLES AND A GREATER VARIETY OF INSTRUCTIVE AND ENTERTAINING
PIECES, THAN ARE TO BE FOUND IN MOST OTHER PRODUCTIONS OF THE KIND. BY A
LOVER OF SCIENCE. [Five lines.]

Bennington   Printed by Anthony Haswell. [1799.] pp. (24). 12mo.
AAS. NYPL. VtHS.

35601   —— PATRIOTIC EXULTATION ON [Matthew] LYON'S RELEASE FROM THE FEDERAL BAS-
TILE IN VERGENNES, STATE OF VERMONT. BENNINGTON, THIRD DAY OF RELEASE,
FEBRUARY 12, 1799. NO THANKS TO POWER.

[Bennington: Printed by Anthony Haswell, 1799.] Broadside.

35602   HASWELL, LYDIA BALDWIN   1759–1799
RECORD OF THE FAMILY OF ANTHONY HASWELL, BY LYDIA, HIS DECEASED CONSORT.
TOGETHER WITH SEVERAL ELEGIAC POEMS, THE TRIBUTE OF CONNUBIAL LOVE, TO
UNAFFECTED VIRTUE. [Three four-line verses.]

[Bennington:] Printed by her Sons, in June, 1799.

Reprinted by her bereaved widower in June, 1815.

35603   HAVEN, SAMUEL   1727–1806
AN ORATION, SPOKEN AT DEDHAM, ON THE FOURTH OF JULY, 1799, AT THE REQUEST
OF A NUMBER OF THE INHABITANTS OF THAT TOWN, AND ITS VICINITY, WHO ASSEM-
BLED TO COMMEMORATE AMERICAN INDEPENDENCE. BY SAMUEL HAVEN. [Cut of
flying eagle.]

Printed at the Minerva Press, in Dedham, by Herman Mann. 1799. pp. (24).
8vo.   AAS. JCB. LOC. NYPL.

35604   HAVERHILL FEDERAL GAZETTE. VOL. I. NO. 11. FRIDAY, JANUARY 4, [— VOL. II.
NO. 6. WEDNESDAY, NOVEMBER 27, 1799.]

Printed at Haverhill, (Massachusetts), by Seth H. Moore & Chester Stebbins.
1799. fol.   MHS.

Discontinued in November, as above.

35605   HAY, GEORGE   1765–1830
AN ESSAY ON THE LIBERTY OF THE PRESS; RESPECTFULLY INSCRIBED TO THE REPUB-
LICAN PRINTERS THROUGHOUT THE UNITED STATES. BY HORTENSIUS.

Philadelphia: Printed at the Aurora Office. 1799. pp. (2), [51.] 12mo.
AAS. HC. HSP. JCB. LOC. NYPL.

Dated, Virginia, January, 1799. Copy-right secured according to law.
Reprinted in Richmond in 1803.

35606   HAYDN, Franz Joseph   1732–1809
      A Favorite rondo in the Gipsy style, composed by Dr. Haydn. Price 50 cts.
          Philadelphia: Published and sold at G. Willig's Musical Magazine. [1799.]
      pp. 5. 4to.

35607   HAYWOOD, John   1762–1826
      Reports of cases adjudged in the Superior Courts of law and equity of the
      State of North-Carolina, from the year 1789, to the year 1798. By John
      Haywood, esquire, one of the judges of the Superior Courts of law and
      equity.
          Halifax: Printed by Abraham Hodge. M,DCC,XCIX. pp. (2), (2), 502, (18).
      8vo.   AAS. JCB. MSL. NYPL.

      A second volume was printed in Raleigh in 1806.

35608   HEATON, Benjamin   1775–1800
      The Columbian spelling book; being an easy introduction to spelling and
      reading. Containing, a selection of words in common use properly ar-
      ranged and divided in such a manner as to lead the learners to the right
      pronunciation: interspersed with a variety of easy lessons, entertaining
      fables, and moral sentences for the use of schools throughout the United
      States. By Benjamin Heaton, A.M.
          Wrentham: Printed by Nath'l. and Benj. Heaton. 1799.

      175th Massachusetts District Copyright, issued to Benjamin Heaton, as
      Author, 17 December, 1799.

35609   THE HEIDELBERG Catechism, or method of instruction, in the christian
      religion, as the same is taught in the Reformed churches and schools of
      Holland. To which is added a Compendium of the christian religion for
      those who intend to approach the Holy Supper of the Lord. Translated
      for the use of the Reformed Protestant churches in America. The sixth
      edition.
          Albany: Printed by Charles R. and George Webster ? 1799. pp. 60. 8vo.
                                            BM. NYHS.

35610   HELME, Elizabeth
      Instructive rambles in London, and the adjacent villages. Designed to amuse
      the mind, and improve the understanding of youth. By Elizabeth Helme.
      [Five lines of quotation.]
          *Philadelphia: Printed by Budd and Bartram, for Thomas Dobson, at the Stone
      House, No. 41, South Second Street.* 1799. pp. 308, frontispiece. 12mo. AAS. JCB.

35611   HENING, William Waller   1768–1828
      The New Virginia justice, comprising the office and authority of a justice
      of the peace, in the Commonwealth of Virginia. Together with a variety
      of useful precedents adapted to the laws now in force. To which is added,
      an appendix containing all the most approved forms of conveyancing, com-
      monly used in this country, such as deeds, of bargain and sale, of lease
      and release, of trust, mortgages, &c.—Also the duties of a justice of the
      peace, arising under the laws of the United States. By William Waller
      Hening, attorney at law.
          Richmond—Printed by Aug. Davis. MDCCXCIX. pp. (2), (2), (3), (4), 468,
      xxiv, 32, xv. 8vo.   AAS. LOC. VSL.

      Virginia District Copyright, issued to William Waller Hening, as Au-
      thor, 3 May, 1799.

35612   HENING, WILLIAM WALLER, continued.
—— —— THE NEW VIRGINIA JUSTICE, COMPRISING THE OFFICE AND AUTHORITY OF A JUSTICE OF THE PEACE, IN THE COMMONWEALTH OF VIRGINIA. TOGETHER WITH A VARIETY OF USEFUL PRECEDENTS ADOPTED [*sic*] TO THE LAWS NOW IN FORCE. TO WHICH IS ADDED, AN APPENDIX CONTAINING ALL THE MOST APPROVED FORMS OF CONVEYANCING, COMMONLY USED IN THIS COUNTRY, SUCH AS DEEDS, OF BARGAIN AND SALE, OF LEASE AND RELEASE, OF TRUST, MORTGAGES, &C.—— ALSO, THE DUTIES OF A JUSTICE OF THE PEACE, ARISING UNDER THE LAWS OF THE UNITED STATES. BY WILLIAM WALLER HENING, ATTORNEY AT LAW.

     Richmond: Printed by T. Nicolson. 1799. pp. (19), (8), (1), 456, (11), xxiv, 32. 8vo.   LOC.

     Contains a nineteen page list of Subscribers' names.

35613   HERALD AND EASTERN SHORE [cut] INTELLIGENCER. VOL. XTH. NO. 490. TUESDAY, NOVEMBER 5, [—— NO. 498. TUESDAY, DECEMBER 31, 1799.]

     Easton —— (Maryland:) Published every Tuesday morning, by James Cowan. 1799. fol.

     In continuation of *The Maryland Herald and Eastern Shore Intelligencer.*

35614   THE HERALD OF FREEDOM. VOL. XIV. NUMBER 677. WEDNESDAY, FEBRUARY 27, [—— VOL. XV. DECEMBER, 1799.]

     Edenton: Published by James Wills. 1799. fol.

     In continuation, without change in numbering, of the *State Gazette of North-Carolina*. And succeeded in May, 1800, by *The Encyclopedian Instructor, and Farmer's Gazette.*

35615   THE HERALD OF LIBERTY. [Motto.] VOL. I. NO. 34. MONDAY, JANUARY 7, [—— VOL. II. NO. 85. MONDAY, DECEMBER 30, 1799.]

     Washington, Pennsylvania. Printed by John Israel. 1799. fol.

35616   HERALD OF THE UNITED STATES. NO. 39 OF VOL. VII. WHOLE NO. 351. SATURDAY, JANUARY 5, [—— NO. 38 OF VOL. VIII. WHOLE NO. 405. SATURDAY, DECEMBER 28, 1799.]

     Warren:—— Published at the Post-Office, by Nathaniel Phillips, Printer to the State. 1799. pp. 1401–1609. fol.   AAS. HC. RIHS.

35617   HERTY, THOMAS
A DIGEST OF THE LAWS OF MARYLAND, BEING AN ABRIDGMENT, ALPHABETICALLY ARRANGED, OF ALL THE PUBLIC ACTS OF ASSEMBLY NOW IN FORCE, AND OF GENERAL USE, FROM THE FIRST SETTLEMENT OF THE STATE, TO THE END OF NOVEMBER SESSION, 1797, INCLUSIVE, WITH REFERENCES TO THE ACTS AT LARGE. BY THOMAS HERTY.

     Baltimore: Printed for the Editor, [by Warner & Hanna.] 1799. pp. (2), (1), 522; (2), 55. 8vo.   AAS. HC. LOC.

     Second title: AN APPENDIX, TO A DIGEST OF THE LAWS OF MARYLAND; BEING AN ABRIDGMENT, ALPHABETICALLY ARRANGED, OF THE PUBLIC ACTS OF ASSEMBLY. PASSED NOVEMBER SESSION, 1798.

     ——Baltimore:—Printed for Thomas Herty, by Warner & Hanna. 1799. pp. 55.

     A second volume, continued to the end of November session, 1803, was printed in Washington, in 1804.

35618   HEWITT, JAMES
HOW HAPPY WAS MY HUMBLE LOT. A FAVORITE BALLAD. SUNG BY MRS. OLDMIXON & MISS BROADHURST. COMPOSED BY J. HEWITT.

     *New York: Printed and sold by J. Hewitt No. 2*3 *Maiden Lane. Price 25 cents.* [1799.] pp. (2). 4to.   LOC.

35619   HINDMAN, WILLIAM   1743–1822
AN ADDRESS TO THE PEOPLE OF MARYLAND ON THE ORIGIN, PROGRESS AND PRESENT
STATE OF FRENCH AGGRESSION . . .
> *Philadelphia: Printed by J. Fenno, 1798. pp. 76. 8vo.*   LOC.

35620   A HINT TO FREE-MASONS. [Signed, Mason, Connecticut, June, 1799,]
> *Newfield: Printed and sold by Lazarus Beach. 1799. pp. 14. 8vo.*   AAS.

35621   THE HISTORY OF LITTLE GOODY TWO SHOES; OTHERWISE CALLED MRS. MARGERY
TWO SHOES — WITH THE MEANS BY WHICH SHE ACQUIRED HER LEARNING AND IN
CONSEQUENCE THEREOF HER ESTATE.
> *Printed at Worcester, Massachusetts, by Isaiah Thomas, jun. 1799.*

35622   THE HISTORY OF MISS KITTY PRIDE. TOGETHER WITH THE VIRTUE OF A ROD; OR
THE HISTORY OF A NAUGHTY BOY. "VICE WILL ALWAYS BE DETESTED, VIRTUE EVER
BE PROTECTED." FIRST WORCESTER EDITION.
> *Printed at Worcester, Massachusetts, by Isaiah Thomas, jun. Sold wholesale
> and retail by him*—1799. pp. 26, (2), (2), (1), 17 cuts. 32mo.   AAS.

35623   THE HISTORY OF TOMMY CARELESS: OR THE MISFORTUNES OF A WEEK. ADORNED
WITH CUTS. THIRD WORCESTER EDITION.
> *Printed at Worcester: Massachusetts, by Isaiah Thomas, jun. Sold wholesale
> and retail by him* – – – 1799. pp. 32. 32mo.

35624   HITCHCOCK, ENOS   1745–1803
A SERMON, DELIVERED AT WRENTHAM, AT THE ORDINATION OF THE REV. ELISHA
FISK, JUNE THE 12TH, 1799. BY ENOS HITCHCOCK.
> *Printed at Providence, by Bennett Wheeler. 1799. pp. (28). 8vo.*
>   AAS. HC. JCB. NYHS. NYPL. RIHS. UTS.
> The Charge, by the Rev. Roland Greene, of Mansfield, the Right hand
> of fellowship, by the Rev. Mr. Wilder, of Attleboro'.

35625   HOBBY, WILLIAM J.   –1841
AN ORATION, DELIVERED IN ST. PAUL'S CHURCH, AUGUSTA, ON THE FOURTH OF JULY,
ONE THOUSAND SEVEN HUNDRED AND NINETY-NINE, BEING THE TWENTY-THIRD
ANNIVERSARY OF AMERICAN INDEPENDENCE. BY WILLIAM J. HOBBY, ESQ.
> *Augusta: Printed by Randolph & Bunce. 1799. pp. 27. 8vo.*   JCB. LOC. NYPL.

35626   HOBSON, JOHN
PROSPECTUS OF A PLAN OF INSTRUCTION FOR THE YOUNG OF BOTH SEXES, INCLUDING
A COURSE OF LIBERAL EDUCATION FOR EACH. DEDICATED TO THE PARENTS OF
THOSE CHILDREN WHOSE TUITION THE AUTHOR HAS SUPERINTENDED DURING HIS
RESIDENCE IN PHILADELPHIA. BY JOHN HOBSON. "CHANGEZ L'EDUCATION D'UN
PEUPLE, VOUS CHANGEREZ SON CARACTÈRE ET SES MŒURS." BERNARDIN DE ST.
PIERRE. [Double line.]
> *Philadelphia: Printed for the Author. From the Press of D. Hogan. 1799.*
> pp. 22, (1). 8vo.   BA. NYHS.

35627   DER HOCH-DEUTSCHE AMERICANISCHE CALENDER, AUF DAS JAHR 1800. NACH
DER GNADENREICHEN GEBURT UNSERS HERRN UND HEYLANDES JESU CHRISTI.
. . . ZUM SECHZEHNTENMAL HERAUSGEGEBEN.
> *Germantaun: Gedruckt und zu finden bey Michael Billmeyer.* . . . [1799.]
> pp. 32. 4to.   LOC.

35628   HOLMES, ABIEL   1763–1837
        A SERMON PREACHED AT BRATTLE-STREET CHURCH IN BOSTON, AND AT CAMBRIDGE,
        APRIL 25, 1799, THE DAY APPOINTED BY THE PRESIDENT OF THE UNITED STATES
        FOR A NATIONAL FAST. BY ABIEL HOLMES, A.M. PASTOR OF THE FIRST CHURCH IN
        CAMBRIDGE.
              Boston: Printed for Young & Minns. 1799. pp. [31.] 8vo.
                     AAS. BA. BM. CHS. CLA. HC. JCB. LOC. MHS. UTS. YC.

35629   —— A SERMON, PREACHED AT CAMBRIDGE THE LORD'S DAY AFTER THE INTERMENT OF
        HIS EXCELLENCY, INCREASE SUMNER, ESQUIRE, GOVERNOR OF THE COMMONWEALTH
        OF MASSACHUSETTS, WHO DIED JUNE 7, 1799, ÆTAT. 53. BY ABIEL HOLMES.
              Boston: Printed by Manning & Loring. [1799.] pp. 24. 8vo.
                     AAS. BA. BM. CHS. HC. JCB. LOC. MHS. NYPL. UTS.

35630   —— A SERMON, PREACHED AT THE ORDINATION OF THE REV. JONATHAN WHITAKER.
        TO THE PASTORAL CARE OF THE CHURCH AND SOCIETY IN SHARON, MASSACHUSETTS,
        FEBRUARY 27, 1799. BY ABIEL HOLMES, A.M. PASTOR OF THE FRST CHURCH IN
        CAMBRIDGE. [Cut of eagle.]
              Dedham: Printed by Herman Mann. 1799. pp. 49. 8vo.
                     AAS. BA. BM. CHS. HC. JCB. LOC. MHS. NYHS. NYPL. YC.

        The Charge, by the Rev. Mr. Cushing, of Waltham. The Right hand of
        fellowship, by the Rev. Mr. Howard, of Canton.

35631   HONEST AND SOLID OBJECTIONS AGAINST ENTRUSTING JAMES ROSS, ESQ. WITH THE OF-
        FICE OF GOVERNOR OF PENNSYLVANIA. [Signed, An Independent elector.]
              [*Philadelphia:* 1799.] pp. 8. 8vo.   LOC.

35632   THE HONEYCOMB; — WITH CHOICEST SWEETS ENRICH'D, FROM VARIOUS GARDENS
        CULL'D WITH CARE. CALCULATED TO GRATIFY THE LOVERS OF ANECDOTE, BIOGRA-
        PHY, CRITICISM, HISTORY, MORALITY, POETRY, SENTIMENT, AND THE BELLE-LETTRES
        IN GENERAL. NO. 1. AUGUST 28, 1799.
              New-London: Printed by Charles Holt, 1799.

        Proposals were made in November, 1798, by Charles Holt, at New Lon-
        don, to issue The Honeycomb, as a weekly periodical of eight pages,
        with title-page, index, and frontispiece, at the end of the year, in con-
        nection with his newspaper, The Bee.

35633   HOOK, JAMES   1746–1827
        THE HOURS OF LOVE. A COLLECTION OF SONNETS, CONTAINING MORNING, NOON, EVE-
        NING & NIGHT, PROPERLY ADAPTED FOR THE VOICE, HARPSICHORD, VIOLIN, GERMAN
        FLUTE OR GUITAR. COMPOSED BY JAMES HOOK.
              Printed for Carr & Co. Musical Repositorys Philadelphia & Baltimore.
        [1799.] pp. 9. 4to.   LOC.

35634   HOPKINS, LEMUEL, and others.
        THE POLITICAL GREEN-HOUSE, FOR THE YEAR 1798. ADDRESSED TO THE READERS OF
        THE CONNECTICUT COURANT, JANUARY 1ST, 1799. PUBLISHED ACCORDING TO ACT
        OF CONGRESS. [Vignette.]
              Hartford: Printed by Hudson & Goodwin. [1799.] pp. 24. 8vo.
                     AAS. BU. JCB. LOC. MHS. NYHS. NYPL.

        "By Richard Alsop, Theodore Dwight, and Lemuel Hopkins" according
        to a ms. note by John Trumbull in his copy of *The Echo*, where the poem
        is reprinted, on pages 233-259.

35635   HOPKINS, SAMUEL   1721–1803
THE LIFE AND CHARACTER OF MISS SUSANNA ANTHONY, WHO DIED, IN NEWPORT, (R. I.) JUNE 23, MDCCXCI, IN THE SIXTY-FIFTH YEAR OF HER AGE. CONSISTING CHIEFLY IN EXTRACTS FROM HER WRITINGS, WITH SOME BRIEF OBSERVATIONS ON THEM. COMPILED BY SAMUEL HOPKINS, D.D. PASTOR OF THE FIRST CONGREGATIONAL CHURCH IN NEWPORT. [Printers mark.]

> *Printed at Worcester, Massachusetts. Hartford Re-printed by Hudson and Goodwin.* 1799. pp. 168. 12mo.   AAS. BA. BU. JCB. LOC.

From the Worcester edition of 1796.

35636   —— MEMOIRS OF THE LIFE OF MRS. SARAH OSBORN, WHO DIED AT NEWPORT, RHODE-ISLAND, ON THE SECOND DAY OF AUGUST, 1796, IN THE EIGHTY-THIRD YEAR OF HER AGE. BY SAMUEL HOPKINS, D.D. PASTOR OF THE FIRST CONGREGATIONAL CHURCH IN NEWPORT, R. I.

> *Printed at Worcester, Massachusetts, by Leonard Worcester.* 1799. pp. 380. 16mo.   AAS. BM. BU. JCB. LOC. NYPL.

35637   HOPKINSON, JOSEPH   1770–1842
BROTHER SOLDIERS ALL HAIL. A NEW PATRIOTIC SONG IN FAVOR OF WASHINGTON, ORNAMENTED WITH AN ELEGANT LIKENESS OF THE GENERAL. TO WHICH IS ADDED A TOAST. WRITTEN AND COMPOSED BY J. HOPKINSON, ESQ.

> *Philadelphia: Printed and published by Benjamin Carr.* 1799. *Price* 17 *cents.*

35638   —— THE NEW PRESIDENT'S MARCH.

> *New York: Printed and sold by J. Hewitt, 23 Maiden Lane.* [1799.] 4to.

35639   HORRID INDIAN CRUELTIES! AFFECTING HISTORY OF THE DREADFUL DISTRESSES OF FREDERIC MANHEIM'S FAMILY. TO WHICH ARE ADDED, AN ENCOUNTER BETWEEN A WHITE MAN AND TWO SAVAGES. REMARKABLE BRAVERY OF A WOMAN. SUFFERINGS OF JOHN CORBLY'S FAMILY.

> *Boston: Printed by James White.* 1799. pp. 12. 12mo.   LOC.

35640   THE HORRORS OF OAKENDALE ABBEY. A ROMANCE. [Ornament.]

> *— New-York — Printed and sold by John Harrisson, Yorick's Head, No. 3 Peck-Slip.* 1799. pp. 204. 12mo.   AAS. JCB. LOC.

35641   HOUGH, SIMON
THE SIGN OF THE PRESENT TIME: OR, A SHORT TREATISE SETTING FORTH WHAT PARTICULAR PROPHECIES ARE NOW FULFILLING, IN THE AUTHOR'S JUDGMENT. TOGETHER WITH A FEW SHORT DIALOGUES, &c. BY SIMON HOUGH.

> *Stockbridge: Printed and sold by H. Willard; by the Author, and by the several post-riders.* 1799.

35642   HOUGHTON, ASA
THE GENTLEMEN'S AND LADIES' DIARY, AND ALMANAC; WITH AN EPHEMERIS, FOR THE YEAR OF THE CREATION, ACCORDING TO SACRED WRIT 5762; AND OF THE CHRISTIAN ERA, 1800: BEING, ACCORDING TO THE STYLE ESTABLISHED, NOT BISSEXTILE, OR LEAP YEAR: THE TWENTY-FOURTH YEAR OF THE INDEPENDENCE OF THE UNITED STATES OF AMERICA. CONTAINING, BESIDES MORE THAN USUAL ASTRONOMICAL CALCULATIONS, AS GREAT A VARIETY OF INSTRUCTIVE, USEFUL AND ENTERTAINING MATTER AS ANY OTHER ALMANAC. FITTED FOR THE LATITUDE AND LONGITUDE OF BOSTON, (MASS.) BUT WILL SERVE FOR THE ADJOINING STATES, WITHOUT SENSIBLE VARIATION. BY ASA HOUGHTON, PHILOM. [Ten lines of verse.]

> *Keene (N. H.) — Printed by John Prentiss. Price* 7½ *dols. per gross—75 cents doz.—10 cents single.* [1799.] pp. (48). 12mo.   AAS. BM. MeHS. NYHS.

Dated, Bolton, (Mass.) August 15, 1799.

35643 HOWE, SOLOMON 1750–1835
WORSHIPPER'S ASSISTANT. CONTAINING THE RULES OF MUSIC, AND A VARIETY OF EASY
AND PLAIN PSALM TUNES: ADAPTED TO THE WEAKEST CAPACITIES, AND DESIGNED
FOR EXTENSIVE UTILITY, AS AN INTRODUCTION TO MORE CRITICAL AND CURIOUS
MUSIC. BY SOLOMON HOWE, A.M. [Twenty-four lines of verse.] COPY RIGHT
SECURED, ACCORDING TO ACT OF CONGRESS.

> *Printed, typographically, at Northampton, Massachusetts. By Andrew Wright:*
> *—for the Author. Sold by him in Greenwich; by D. Wright, in Northampton; by*
> *B. Larkin, in Boston; by G. Merriam, in Worcester; by E. Merriam & Co. in*
> *Brookfield; by C. Smith & Co. Pittsfield; by J. Mycall, in Newburyport; by J.*
> *Babcock, in Hartford; by B. Woodward, esq. at Dartmouth College; by C. Davis,*
> *in Newyork; by O. Penniman, in Albany; by J. Carter, in Providence; by M.*
> *Carey, in Philadelphia; by S. Butler, in Baltimore; and by J. Dwight, in Conajo-*
> *hary.*—1799. pp. 32. obl. 16mo. AAS. JCB. LOC. NYPL. UTS.

Preface dated, Greenwich, (Mass.) Feb. 14, 1799. 179th Massachusetts
District Copyright, issued to Solomon Howe, as Author, 25 January,
1800.

35644 HOWLAND, JOHN 1757–1854
A LECTURE, READ BEFORE THE PROVIDENCE ASSOCIATION OF MECHANICS AND MANU-
FACTURERS, AT THEIR QUARTERLY MEETING, JANUARY 14, A.D. 1799; PURSUANT
TO A REQUEST OF THE ASSOCIATION, AT A PREVIOUS MEETING. BY JOHN HOWLAND,
MEMBER OF THE ASSOCIATION.

> *Printed at Providence, by Bennett Wheeler*, 1799. pp. (14). 4to.

Reprinted in Stone's Sketch of the Association. AAS. JCB. MHS. RIHS.

35645 HUBBARD, JOHN 1759–1810
AN ORATION, PRONOUNCED AT WALPOLE, ON THE ANNIVERSARY OF AMERICAN INDE-
PENDENCE; JULY 4TH, 1799. BY JOHN HUBBARD, ESQ.

> *Walpole: Printed by David Carlisle, for Thomas & Thomas.* 1799. pp. 24.
> 4to. AAS. JCB.

35646 HUBBARD, WILLIAM 1621–1704
A NARRATIVE OF THE INDIAN WARS, IN NEW ENGLAND. FROM THE FIRST PLANTING
THEREOF, IN THE YEAR 1607 TO THE YEAR 1677. CONTAINING A RELATION OF THE
OCCASION, RISE, AND PROGRESS OF THE WAR WITH THE INDIANS, IN THE SOUTHERN,
WESTERN, EASTERN, AND NORTHERN PARTS OF SAID COUNTRY. BY WILLIAM HUB-
BARD, A.M., MINISTER AT IPSWICH.

Proposals for printing the above, in a volume of over 300 pages, were
issued by Moses Davis, Concord, New Hampshire, in 1799.

35647 HUDSON GAZETTE. VOL. XIV. NUMB. 718. TUESDAY, JANUARY 1, [—VOL. XV. NUMB.
770. TUESDAY, DECEMBER 31, 1799.]

> *[Hudson:] Printed by Ashbel Stoddard.* 1799. fol. AAS.

35648 HURD, ISAAC –1844
A DISCOURSE DELIVERED IN THE CHURCH IN BRATTLE STREET, IN BOSTON, TUESDAY,
JUNE 11TH, 1799, BEFORE THE HUMANE SOCIETY OF THE COMMONWEALTH OF
MASSACHUSETTS. BY ISAAC HURD, A.M. FELLOW OF THE MASSACHUSETTS MEDICAL
SOCIETY.

> *Boston: Printed by John & Thomas Fleet, Cornhill,* 1799. pp. (23). 4to.
> AAS. BA. HC. JCB. LOC. MHS. NYHS. NYPL. SGO.

35649   HUTCHINS, JOHN NATHAN

HUTCHINS IMPROVED: BEING AN ALMANACK AND EPHEMERIS OF THE MOTIONS OF THE SUN AND MOON; THE TRUE PLACES AND ASPECTS OF THE PLANETS: THE RISING AND SETTING OF THE SUN; AND THE RISING, SETTING, AND SOUTHING OF THE MOON, FOR THE YEAR OF OUR LORD 1800: AND 24TH YEAR OF AMERICAN INDEPENDENCE, 'TILL 4TH JULY. [Five lines.] BY JOHN NATHAN HUTCHINS, PHILOM.

New-York: Printed and sold by H. Gaine, at his Printing-Office, at the Bible, in Pearl-Street. Where may be had the New-York Pocket Almanack. [1799.] pp. (36). 12mo.   AAS. BA. LOC. NYHS. NYPL. YC.

Contains, An Act for the assessment and collection of taxes, in the State of New-York. Passed 1st of April, 1799. Rules for health. Rules to make a good store-keeper, shop-keeper, or tradesman. Hard times and no money! Courts. Roads.

35650   HYDE, ELIJAH, and others

AN IMPARTIAL RELATION OF THE HAIL-STORM ON THE FIFTEENTH OF JULY AND THE TORNADO ON THE SECOND OF AUGUST, 1799. WHICH APPEARED IN THE TOWNS OF BOZRAH, LEBANON AND FRANKLIN, IN THE STATE OF CONNECTICUT. TO WHICH IS ANNEXED AN ESTIMATE OF THE DAMAGES DONE BY THE STORM, MADE BY A COMMITTEE, FROM SAID TOWNS. THE WHOLE PUBLISHED UNDER THEIR DIRECTION FOR THE INFORMATION OF THE PUBLIC.

Norwich: Printed by John Trumbull, 1799. *Copy-right secured according to law.* pp. (30). 8vo.   AAS. JCB. LOC. NYPL. UTS.

"To the public." Signed and dated, Elijah Hyde: Nehemiah Waterman, Elisha Edgerton, select committee: Franklin. August 28, 1799.

35651   IMPARTIAL HERALD. VOL. I. NO. 25. TUESDAY, JANUARY 1, [— NO. 47. TUESDAY, JUNE 4, 1799.]

Suffield, Connecticut. Published by Edward Gray. 1799. fol.

Discontinued in June, as above.

35652   IMPARTIAL [cut] JOURNAL. "OPEN TO ALL PARTIES, BUT INFLUENCED BY NONE." VOL. II. NO. 1. TUESDAY, OCTOBER 8, [— NO. 13. TUESDAY, DECEMBER 31 ? 1799.]

Stonington, (Connecticut,) Published by Samuel Trumbull. 1799. fol.   HC.

In continuation of *Journal of the times.*

35653   IMPARTIAL THE KNOXVILLE GAZETTE OBSERVER. LIBERTY THE OBJECT, TRUTH THE GUIDE. VOL. I. NO. 1. WEDNESDAY, AUGUST 28, [— NO. 18. WEDNESDAY, DECEMBER 25, 1799.]

Knoxville, (State of Tennessee) Printed and published every Wednesday by Roulstone and Wilson. 1799. fol.

Formed by a consolidation of The Observer, published by George Wilson; and, the *Knoxville Gazette,* published by George Roulstone, the words, "The Knoxville Gazette," are within an arc of rays, in the centre, with the motto underneath. The last leaf of the Knoxville Gazette had been imposed in octavo pages, reprinting some document issued by the general government, and this was continued into the year 1801 — making on February 11th, 144 pages issued in that way, without title. On November 28, 1800, the copartnership of Roulstone and Wilson was dissolved, George Roulstone continuing publication under the title of *Knoxville Gazette,* only, until his death, in 1804. George Wilson removed to Jonesborough, and, in November, 1801, established there the *Washington Newspaper and Advertiser.*

AUCTION
VALUES

35654   THE INDEPENDENT [Mass. arms] CHRONICLE: AND THE UNIVERSAL ADVERTISER. VOL. XXXI. NUMBER 1856. FROM MONDAY, DECEMBER 31, 1798—TO THURSDAY, JANUARY 3, [— NUMBER 1959. FROM THURSDAY, DECEMBER 26 — MONDAY, DECEMBER 30, 1799.]

Boston—(Massachusetts)—Printed and published every Monday and Thursday, by Thomas Adams, at his Printing-Office, opposite the Court-House, Court-Street. 1799. fol.   AAS. LOC. MHS.

"Warned by great bodily indisposition." on May 2nd, Thomas Adams disposed and transferred all his rights, title and interest in the Independent Chronicle to James White, and on May 10th he died, in the 42nd year of his age. The new proprietor engaged Ebenezer Rhoades to publish the paper for him; and, beginning with the issue for May 13th, it was "Printed every Monday and Thursday, by Ebenezer Rhoades, (for the Proprietor)" at the same printing-office.

35655   —— [Arms.] THE CARRIER OF THE INDEPENDENT CHRONICLE, TO HIS GENEROUS CUSTOMERS, WISHES A HAPPY NEW-YEAR. . . .

[Boston: Printed by Thomas Adams. January 1, 1799.] Broadside.   HSP.

35656   THE INTELLIGENCER & WEEKLY ADVERTISER. NUMBER 1. WEDNESDAY, JULY 31, [— NUMBER 23, WEDNESDAY, DECEMBER 25, 1799.]

Published by William & Robert Dickson, at their Printingoffice and Bookstore, north Queenstreet. Lancaster. 1799. fol.   HSP. PSL.

Established, as a weekly, by William and Robert Dickson, and continued by them to the death of Robert Dickson on the 12th September, 1802, when it was continued by William Dickson alone to beyond the period of this work.

35657   AN INVESTIGATION OF THE DOCTRINE OF BARON SWEDENBORG, OR, OF THE CHURCH CALLED, NEW JERUSALEM, IN TWO LETTERS, ADDRESSED TO THE REV. MR. H——. BY AN INHABITANT OF BALTIMORE COUNTY. "TOKAL: THOU ART WEIGHED IN THE BALANCE, AND ART FOUND WANTING — DAN. 5, 27."

Baltimore: Printed by Samuel Sower. M,DCC,IC,IX. [*sic* 1799.] pp. 46. 8vo.
               MdHS.
"Errata" printed on inside of end cover. In the first paragraph of the first letter, the Author states: "as I am not an Englishman, you will, I hope, patiently indulge when I produce bad grammar in that language." Rev. John Hargrove, 1750 – 1839, was pastor of the New Jerusalem Church, in Baltimore, from 1799 – 1830.

35658   IVES, JOHN H.
TWENTY-FOUR FIGURES OF THE MOST FASHIONABLE COUNTRY DANCES: TOGETHER WITH EIGHT COTILLIONS, FOR THE YEAR EIGHTEEN HUNDRED. COMPOSED AND SELECTED BY JOHN H. IVES.

New-Haven: Printed by Read & Morse. 1799. pp. 14. 16mo.   HEH.

Connecticut District Copyright, issued to John H. Ives, as Author, 21 November, 1799.

35659   JACKY DANDY'S DELIGHT, OR THE HISTORY OF BIRDS AND BEASTS, IN VERSE AND PROSE. ADORNED WITH [10] CUTS.

Printed and sold by Nathaniel Coverly. 1799. *Great allowance made to those who purchase by the gross or dozen.* pp. 16. 32mo.   AAS.

35660   JACOB, ELIZABETH HEAD   1674–1739
AN EPISTLE IN TRUE LOVE. CONTAINING: A FAREWELL EXHORTATION TO FRIENDS' FAMILIES, &C. ELIZABETH JACOB. WRITTEN WORCESTER THE 5TH OF THE 9TH MONTH, 1712.

Printed by S. C. Ustick, Mount Holly. [1799.] pp. 12. 12mo.

35661   JAMIE [or Jemmy] AND NANCY, OR THE YARMOUTH TRAGEDY. LAYING OPEN HOW BY
THE CRUELTY OF PARENTS, TWO LOVERS WERE DESTROYED.
> *Providence: Printed by Abel Wheeler.* 1799. 8vo.

35662   JANEWAY, JAMES   1636–1674
A TOKEN FOR CHILDREN: BEING AN EXACT ACCOUNT OF THE CONVERSION, HOLY AND
EXEMPLARY LIVES, AND JOYFUL DEATHS OF SEVERAL YOUNG CHILDREN. IN TWO
PARTS. BY THE REV. JAMES JANEWAY. LUKE X. 14. [Three lines.]
> *Northampton: Printed for Simeon Butler.* 1799. pp. iv, viii, 114. 16mo.

Together with Divine songs, for children. By Isaac Watts, D. D. pp.   AAS.
97 – 114.

35663   JARVIS, PETER
PETER JARVIS, AT THE COMMENCEMENT OF A NEW-YEAR, SALUTES HIS FRIENDS WITH
WISHING THEM HEALTH, WEALTH, & HAPPINESS, HOPING FOR A REPITITION OF THEIR
FORMER FAVOURS. . . .
> [*Without place or Printer.* 1799.] Broadside.   HSP.

35664   JENCKES, EBENEZER   1773–1799
SACRED TO THE MEMORY OF MR. EBENEZER JENCKES, SON OF THE LATE JOHN
JENCKES, ESQ.; AND FREELOVE, HIS WIFE. HE DIED AT THE ISLAND OF ST. THOMAS
(WHERE COMMERCIAL PURSUITS HAD CALLED HIM) APRIL 26, 1799, IN THE 26TH
YEAR OF HIS AGE; AND HIS REMAINS WERE RESPECTFULLY INTERRED IN THE CHURCH-
YARD OF THAT ISLAND. HE LEFT A WIDOW AND TWO SONS, TO LAMENT THE EARLY
EXIT OF A FOND HUSBAND, AND AN AFFECTIONATE PARENT. [Cut of three hour
glasses.] "THIS MODEST STONE, WHAT FEW VAIN MARBLES CAN, MAY TRULY SAY,
WE MOURN AN HONEST MAN."
> [*Providence: Printed by John Carter, junior.* 1799.] Broadside. 4to.
>> AAS. RIHS.

35665   JENKS, BENJAMIN   1646–1724
PRAYERS AND OFFICES OF DEVOTION FOR FAMILIES, AND FOR PARTICULAR PERSONS,
UPON MOST OCCASIONS. BY BENJAMIN JENKS, LATE RECTOR OF HARLEY, IN SHROP-
SHIRE, AND CHAPLAIN TO THE RIGHT HONOURABLE THE EARL OF BRADFORD. [Four
lines of Scripture texts.] THE TWENTY-FOURTH EDITION.
> *London:—Printed. New-York: Re-printed, by Hugh Gaine, at the Bible, No.*
> 148 *Pearl-Street.* 1799. pp. xix, (5), 372. 12mo.   NYPL.

35666   —— PRAYERS AND OFFICES OF DEVOTION FOR FAMILIES, AND FOR PARTICULAR
PERSONS, UPON MOST OCCASIONS. CONTAINING NEARLY TWO HUNDRED FORMS OF
PRAYERS. BY BENJAMIN JENKS, LATE RECTOR OF HARLEY, IN SHROPSHIRE, AND
CHAPLAIN TO THE RIGHT HONOURABLE THE EARL OF BRADFORD.
> *Walpole: Printed by David Carlisle, for Thomas and Thomas.* 1799.

"The above is said to have had thirty editions in Europe."

35667   JENKS, STEPHEN   1772–1856
LAUS DEO. THE NEW-ENGLAND HARMONIST: CONTAINING CONCISE AND EASY RULES
OF MUSIC; TOGETHER WITH A NUMBER OF TUNES ADAPTED TO PUBLIC WORSHIP
FITTED TO ALL THE VARIOUS METRES, MOST OF WHICH WERE NEVER BEFORE PUB-
LISHED. BY STEPHEN JENKS.
> *Danbury: Printed by Douglas and Nichols.* [1799.] pp. [8], 9–24. obl. 16mo.

The sixteen pages of engraved music bear the Colophon: New-Haven Engraved by A. Doolittle. The Preface is dated, Ridgfield, 24 September,
1799. Connecticut District Copyright, issued to Stephen Jenks, as Author and Proprietor, 12 November, 1799.

35668   JENKS' Portland Gazette. Vol. ii. No. 55. Monday, April 29, [— Vol. ii. No. 90. Monday, December 30, 1799.]

> *Published by E. A. Jenks, Portland, District of Maine. Massachusetts. 1799. fol.*

> In continuation of the *Portland Gazette.*

35669   JESS, Zachariah

The American tutor's assistant, improved: or, a compendious system of decimal, practical arithmetic; comprising the usual methods of calculation, with the addition of federal money, and other decimals, dispersed through the several rules of that useful science. Adapted for the easy and regular instruction of youth in the United States. Compiled by Zachariah Jess, schoolmaster in Wilmington.

> *Wilmington: Printed and sold by Bonsal and Niles. Also sold at their Book-Store, No. 173, Market-Street, Baltimore.* 1799. pp. (2), (2), 204, errata. 12mo.
>   AAS. LOC.

> (No. 4.) Delaware District Copyright, issued to Bonsal and Niles, as Proprietors, 20 December, 1799.

35670   —— A Compendious system of practical surveying, and dividing of land: concisely defined, methodically arranged, and fully exemplified. The whole adapted for the easy and regular instruction of youth, in our American schools. Compiled by Zachariah Jess, schoolmaster in Wilmington. Copy right secured according to law.

> *Wilmington: Printed by Bonsal and Niles—for the Compiler—*1799.—pp. v, (1), 212; (1), 91; (1), 60. 8vo.   AAS. DHS. JCB. LCP. LOC. NYHS. NYPL.

> (No. 3.) Delaware District Copyright, issued to Zachariah Jess, as Author, 4 April, 1799.

> *Second title:* Tables of difference of latitude and departure: constructed to every quarter of a degree of the quadrant, and continued from one, to the distance of one hundred miles or chains. [Ornament.] [By John Robertson.]
> *Wilmington: Printed by Bonsal and Niles, for Zachariah Jess.* M,DCC,-XCIX. pp. (1), 91, (1), 60. 8vo.   AAS. DHS. JCB. LOC. NYPL.

> Bound with the preceding. With a Table of logarithms. pp. 59, (1).

35671   JOHNSON, Thomas

Remarks on some principles contained in the Presbyterian system, or Confession of faith: likewise, remarks on the necessity of supporting Gospel ministers, according to Gospel rules. By Thomas Johnson, of Pelham.

> *Northampton: Printed by William Butler.* 1799. pp. 48. 8vo.   AAS.

35672   THE JOHNSTOWN Gazette. Vol. iv. Numb. 182. Wednesday, January 2, [— Vol. v. Numb. 233. Wednesday, December 25, 1799.]

> *Johnstown, (State of New-York:) Printed by Holden & Smith.* 1799. fol.

35673   JONES, Archibald

An Oration, delivered at a public exhibition, in the West-Parish meeting-house of Brookfield. On the 27th, of February. Written by Archibald Jones.

> *Printed at Brookfield, Massachusetts, February,* 1799. pp. 11. 8vo.   AAS.

35674   JONES, DAVID   1736–1820
DECLARATION OF THE REVEREND MR. DAVID JONES. TO THE CITIZENS OF THE STATE
OF PENNSYLVANIA. THE FOLLOWING OBSERVATIONS ARE SUBMITTED BY THE SUB-
SCRIBER. [Charging that James Ross attorney having reprobated the doctrine of
original sin in court consequently must be an infidel.] DAVID JONES, LATE CHAP-
LAIN TO GENERAL WAYNE. SEPTEMBER 26, 1799.

       [*Washington, Pennsylvania. Printed by John Colerick.* 1799.] Broadside.
4to.   LOC.

35675   JOSEPHUS, FLAVIUS   37–95
[Ornament.] THE WHOLE GENUINE AND COMPLETE WORKS OF FLAVIOUS [*sic*] JOSE-
PHUS, THE LEARNED AND AUTHENTIC JEWISH HISTORIAN, AND CELEBRATED WARRIOR.
TO WHICH IS ADDED VARIOUS USEFUL INDEXES, PARTICULARLY OF THE COUNTRIES,
CITIES, TOWNS, VILLAGES, SEAS. RIVERS, MOUNTAINS, &C. WHICH ARE RELATED IN
THE HISTORY. ALSO A CONTINUATION OF THE HISTORY OF THE JEWS, FROM JOSE-
PHUS DOWN TO THE PRESENT TIME, INCLUDING A PERIOD OF MORE THAN SEVENTEEN
HUNDRED YEARS. [Ornament.] BY GEORGE HENRY MAYNARD, L. L. D. [Ornament.]
ILLUSTRATED WITH MARGINAL REFERENCES AND NOTES, HISTORICAL, BIOGRAPHICAL,
CLASSICAL, CRITICAL, GEOGRAPHICAL, AND EXPLANATORY. BY THE REV. EDWARD
KIMPTON, AUTHOR OF THE COMPLETE UNIVERSAL HISTORY OF THE HOLY BIBLE,
[line.] EMBELLISHED WITH UPWARDS OF THIRTY COPPER PLATE ENGRAVINGS, EXE-
CUTED BY AMERICAN ARTISTS. [line.]

       *New-York: Printed by W. Durell, for Bell & Smith, Booksellers & Stationers,
corner of Magazine and Chatham Streets.* 1799. [Ornament.] pp. 721, + 30
plates. fol.   NYHS.

35676   JOURNAL OF THE TIMES. VOL. I. No. 13. WEDNESDAY, JANUARY. 2, [— No. 52.
TUESDAY, OCTOBER 1, 1799.]

       Stonington Port, (Connecticut,) Printed by Samuel Trumbull. 1799. fol.

With the issue for October 8th, the name was changed to *Impartial*   CHS. HC.
Journal.

35677   KEACH, BENJAMIN
THE TRAVELS OF TRUE GODLINESS AND UNGODLINESS; ABRIDGED FROM THE WORKS
OF MR. BENJAMIN KEACH; SHEWING THE DIFFERENT SUCCESS THEY MET WITH, IN
THEIR VARIOUS JOURNEYINGS AMONGST THAT RACE OF FALLEN SPIRITS, WHO ARE
CLOTHED FOR A SEASON WITH FLESH AND BLOOD, AND COMMONLY CALLED MEN AND
WOMEN. [Ornament.]

       *Philadelphia: Printed by Henry Tuckniss, for Ezekiel Cooper, No. 47, North
Fourth-Street, near Race-Street.* MDCCXCIX. 2 vols. in one. pp. 297, (2).
12mo.   AAS.

Second title: THE PROGRESS OF SIN; OR, THE TRAVELS OF UNGODLINESS. ABRIDGED
FROM THE WORKS OF MR. BENJAMIN KEACH. [Ornament.]

       *Philadelphia: Printed by Henry Tuckniss, for Ezekiel Cooper, No. 47, North
Fourth-Street, near Race-Street.* MDCCXCIX. pp. (2), (2), 165–297, (2).

Contains, a two-page List of books published for Methodists.

35678   [U. S. arms.] KENNEBECK INTELLIGENCER. [Seal of District of Maine.] [Motto.]
VOL. IV. No. 159. SATURDAY, JANUARY 5, [— VOL. IV. No. 196. SATURDAY, DE-
CEMBER 28, 1799.]

       [*District of Maine.*] *Published by Peter Edes, near the Court-House, in
Augusta. [Hallowell.]* 1799. fol.   AAS.

With the issue for July 26th, the place of publication is again given as
Hallowell. And, with the issue for August 30th, the spelling of Kennebeck in the title is changed to Kennebec.

35679   KENTUCKY. STATE.
AN ACCOUNT OF RECEIPTS AND EXPENDITURES OF GOVERNMENT, NOVEMBER 11, 1798, .
TO NOVEMBER 7, 1799. . . . GEORGE MADISON.
[Lexington: Printed by John Bradford, 1799.] Broadside. fol.

35680   —— ACTS PASSED AT THE FIRST SESSION OF THE SEVENTH GENERAL ASSEMBLY, FOR
THE COMMONWEALTH OF KENTUCKY, BEGUN AND HELD IN THE CAPITOL, IN THE
TOWN OF FRANKFORT, ON MONDAY THE FIFTH DAY OF NOVEMBER, IN THE YEAR
OF OUR LORD, ONE THOUSAND, SEVEN HUNDRED, AND NINETY-EIGHT, AND OF THE
COMMONWEALTH THE SIXTH. PUBLISHED BY AUTHORITY.
Frankfort: Printed by Hunter & Beaumont, Printers to the Commonwealth.
1799. pp. (2), (4), (3)–[182.] 8vo.   LOC. MHS.

35681   —— THE CONSTITUTION, OR FORM OF GOVERNMENT FOR THE STATE OF KENTUCKY.
PUBLISHED BY ORDER OF THE CONVENTION. [As altered, revised and confirmed by
the late Convention.]
Frankfort: Printed by Hunter and Beaumont, Printers to the Commonwealth.
1799. pp. 30. 8vo.   JCB. LOC.

35682   —— — THE CONSTITUTION OF THE STATE OF KENTUCKY.
Lexington: Printed by John Bradford. 1799.

35683   —— LAWS OF KENTUCKY; COMPREHENDING THOSE OF A GENERAL NATURE NOW IN
FORCE, AND WHICH HAVE BEEN ACTED ON BY THE LEGISLATURE THEREOF. TO-
GETHER WITH A COPIOUS INDEX AND A LIST OF LOCAL OR PRIVATE ACTS, WITH THE
DATES OF THE SESSIONS AT WHICH THEY WERE PASSED. TO WHICH IS PREFIXED THE
CONSTITUTION OF THE UNITED STATES, WITH THE AMENDMENTS. THE ACT OF
SEPARATION FROM THE STATE OF VIRGINIA. AND THE CONSTITUTION OF KENTUCKY.
[Volume one.]
Lexington: Printed by John Bradford, Main-Street. 1799. pp. [lxxxvii,]
(3)–[514.] 8vo.   AAS. BM. JCB. LOC.

The last official printing of John Bradford as State Printer. The public
printing for the following years was done at Frankfort. The second volume was printed in Lexington, in 1807. A third volume in Frankfort,
in 1811. And a fourth volume in Frankfort, in 1814.

35684   THE KENTUCKY ALMANAC, FOR THE YEAR OF OUR LORD, 1800, BEING THE FOURTH
AFTER BISSEXTILE OR LEAP YEAR; THE TWENTY-FOURTH OF AMERICAN INDEPEND-
ENCE; THE TWELFTH OF FEDERAL GOVERNMENT — AND THE NINTH OF THIS COM-
MONWEALTH. CONTAINING, THE LUNATIONS, CONJUNCTIONS AND ECLIPSES; JUDGMENT
OF THE WEATHER, REMARKABLE DAYS, LENGTH OF DAYS AND NIGHTS, TIME COURTS
ARE HELD, &C. TOGETHER WITH USEFUL TABLES, AND A VARIETY OF ENTERTAINING
PIECES, IN PROSE AND VERSE: AND SOME EXPLANATORY REASONS WHY THE YEAR
1800 WILL NOT BE A LEAP-YEAR. CALCULATED FOR THE LATITUDE OF 37° NORTH,
AND A MERIDIAN OF 15′ WEST OF PHILADELPHIA: AND WILL SERVE, WITHOUT ANY
SENSIBLE VARIATION, FOR THE NORTH-WESTERN TERRITORY, ST. VINCENNES, STATE
OF TENNESSEE AND THE WESTERN PARTS OF VIRGINIA.
Lexington: Printed by John Bradford, Main Street. [1799.] pp. (36).
12mo.   AAS.

Contains, Some explanatory reasons why the year 1800 will not be a leap-
year. A thief discovered by a stratagem. Artful evasion. The sensible
fool. A whimsical account how the famous Dr. Swift, became dean of
Sit [*sic*] Patrick's, in Ireland. You can't untie the knot. Moll Thompson's mark. The widow. Officers of State government. Time courts are
held. Tables of interest.

35685 THE KENTUCKY GAZETTE. VOL. XII. No. 641. THURSDAY, JANUARY 3, [— VOL. XIII. No. 692. THURSDAY, DECEMBER 26, 1799.]
Lexington: Printed by John Bradford, (on Main Street)—Price fifteen shillings per annum. 1799. fol.

35686 KETOCKTON. VIRGINIA. BAPTIST ASSOCIATION.
MINUTES OF THE KETOCKTON BAPTIST ASSOCIATION. AUGUST 4, 1799.
[Alexandria: Printed by Ellis Price ? 1799.]

35687 KING, ROBERT J.
AN INAUGURAL ESSAY ON BLISTERS: SUBMITTED TO THE EXAMINATION OF THE REV. JOHN EWING, S.T.P. PROVOST; THE TRUSTEES & MEDICAL FACULTY, OF THE UNIVERSITY OF PENNSYLVANIA, ON THE SIXTH DAY OF JUNE, 1799, FOR THE DEGREE OF DOCTOR OF MEDICINE. BY ROBERT J. KING, OF MARYLAND, MEMBER OF THE PHILADELPHIA CHEMICAL SOCIETY.
Philadelphia: Printed by Way & Groff, No. 48, North Third-Street. 1799. pp. 37. 8vo.
AAS. LOC. NYPL. SGO.

35688 KLINE'S CARLISLE WEEKLY GAZETTE. VOL. XIV. No. 674. WEDNESDAY, JANUARY 2, [— VOL. XV. No. 726. WEDNESDAY, DECEMBER 25, 1799.]
Carlisle: (State of Pennsylvania) Printed by George Kline. 1799. fol.

35689 KNIGHT, JOHN   –1838
NARRATIVE OF A LATE EXPEDITION AGAINST THE INDIANS; WITH AN ACCOUNT OF THE BARBAROUS EXECUTION OF COL. CRAWFORD; AND THE WONDERFUL ESCAPE OF DR. KNIGHT & JOHN STOVER FROM CAPTIVITY IN 1782. TO WHICH IS ADDED, A NARRATIVE OF THE CAPTIVITY & ESCAPE OF MRS. FRANCES SCOTT, AN INHABITANT OF WASHINGTON COUNTY, VIRGINIA.
Andover: Printed by Ames & Parker. [1799.] pp. 40. 16mo.   LOC. NYPL.

35690 KNOX, SAMUEL   1756–1832
AN ESSAY ON THE BEST SYSTEM OF LIBERAL EDUCATION, ADAPTED TO THE GENIUS OF THE GOVERNMENT OF THE UNITED STATES. COMPREHENDING ALSO, AN UNIFORM, GENERAL PLAN FOR INSTITUTING AND CONDUCTING PUBLIC SCHOOLS, IN THIS COUNTRY, ON PRINCIPLES OF THE MOST EXTENSIVE UTILITY. TO WHICH IS PREFIXED, AN ADDRESS TO THE LEGISLATURE OF MARYLAND ON THAT SUBJECT. BY THE REV. SAMUEL KNOX, M.A. PRESIDENT OF THE FREDERICK ACADEMY.
Baltimore: Printed by Warner & Hanna, Harrison-Street. 1799. pp. 173, iv. 8vo.
AAS. BA. LOC. NYPL.

35691 KNOX, VICESIMUS   1752–1821
THE SPIRIT OF DESPOTISM. [Eight lines of quotations.]
London:—Printed in the year 1795. *Morris-Town: Printed by Jacob Mann.* M,DCC,XCIX. pp. (10), 319. 12mo.
AAS JCB. LOC. NYPL. UTS.

35692 KNOXVILLE GAZETTE. VOL. I. No. i. WEDNESDAY EVENING, JULY 3, [— No. viii. WEDNESDAY EVENING, AUGUST 21, 1799.]
Knoxville, (State of Tennessee) Printed and published every Wednesday, by George Roulstone. 1799. fol.

This Gazette is a revival of the first Knoxville Gazette, which suspended publication in 1797. The establishment of the Observer, by George Wilson, was, evidently, the exciting cause of the revival. The futility of publishing two newspapers in Knoxville, at this time, soon led their publishers to merge their publications into one, which appeared August 28th under the compromise title of *Impartial The Knoxville Gazette Observer*, published by Roulstone and Wilson.

AUCTION
VALUES

35693   KOTZEBUE, AUGUST FRIEDRICH FERDINAND VON   1761–1819
THE CONSTANT LOVER; OR, WILLIAM AND JEANETTE: A TALE. FROM THE GERMAN
OF AUGUSTUS VON KOTZEBUE, AUTHOR OF THE STRANGER, LOVERS' VOWS, SELF
IMMOLATION, VIRGIN OF THE SUN, &c. TO WHICH IS PREFIXED, AN ACCOUNT OF THE
LITERARY LIFE OF THE AUTHOR. TWO VOLUMES IN ONE.
> *Boston: Printed for Joseph Bumstead. Sold by him at No. 20, Union-Street;*
> *by Thomas & Andrews, Newbury-Street; by E. Larkin, and Wm. P. and L. Blake,*
> *Cornhill. 1799. pp. 295, (2). 12mo.*   AAS. LOC.

35694   —— — THE CONSTANT LOVER; OR, WILLIAM AND JEANETTE: A TALE. FROM THE
GERMAN OF AUGUSTUS VON KOTZEBUE; AUTHOR OF THE STRANGER.
> *New-York: Printed for Naphthali Judah. 1799.*

35695   —— COUNT BERGOWSKY; OR, THE CONSPIRACY OF KAMTSCHATKA. A TRAGI-COMEDY,
IN FIVE ACTS. TRANSLATED FROM THE GERMAN OF AUGUSTUS VON KOTZEBUE, BY
REV. W. READER, TEACHER OF THE GERMAN LANGUAGE, IN THE UNIVERSITY OF
CAMBRIDGE.
> *New-York: Printed for Naphthali Judah. 1799.*

35696   —— LOVERS' VÓWS. A PLAY, IN FIVE ACTS. FROM THE GERMAN OF KOTZEBUE. BY
MRS. INCHBALD.
> *Boston: Printed for John West, No. 75, Cornhill. June, 1799. pp. 56, (2).*
> *12mo.*   AAS. JCB.

The original title of this play was "The Natural son." The preface to
the London edition says the German title is, "The Child of Love."

35697   —— — LOVERS' VOWS. A PLAY, IN FIVE ACTS. PERFORMING AT THE THEATRE
ROYAL, COVENT-GARDEN. FROM THE GERMAN OF KOTZEBUE. BY MRS. INCHBALD.
> *London — Printed: New-York — Re-printed by Geo. Forman, for Napthali*
> *Judah, No. 47, Water-Street. 1799. pp. 86, (2). 8vo.*   AAS.

35698   —— PIZARRO; A TRAGEDY: IN FIVE ACTS, AS PERFORMED AT THE THEATRE ROYAL IN
DRURY LANE. TAKEN FROM THE GERMAN DRAMA OF KOTZEBUE; AND ADAPTED TO
THE ENGLISH STAGE, BY RICHARD BRINSLEY SHERIDAN. FIRST CHARLESTON EDI-
TION (FROM THE TWENTIETH LONDON EDITION).
> *Charleston: Printed and sold by T. C. Cox, 1799.*

35699   —— — PIZARRO; A TRAGEDY, IN FIVE ACTS; TAKEN FROM THE GERMAN DRAMA OF
KOTZEBUE; AND ADAPTED TO THE ENGLISH STAGE, BY RICHARD BRINSLEY SHERI-
DAN. [Printer's mark.]
> *Charlestown: Printed | by Samuel Etheridge] for William P. & Lemuel Blake,*
> *at the Boston Bookstore. [1799.] pp. (2), (2), 60. 12mo.*   AAS. NYPL.

35700   —— — PIZARRO; A TRAGIC PLAY, IN FIVE ACTS, AS PERFORMED AT THE THEATRE
ROYAL IN DRURY LANE. TAKEN FROM THE GERMAN DRAMA OF KOTZEBUE; AND
ADAPTED TO THE ENGLISH STAGE, BY RICHARD BRINSLEY SHERIDAN.
> *New-York: Printed for Napthali Judah. 1799. pp. 74, (2). 16mo.*   LOC.

35701   —— — *Half-title:* SELECT PLAYS. VOL. [Costume plate of] FALSTAFF.
Title: GENUINE EDITION. PIZARRO; A TRAGEDY, IN FIVE ACTS; AS PERFORMED AT
THE THEATRE ROYAL IN DRURY LANE: TAKEN FROM THE GERMAN DRAMA OF
KOTZEBUE; AND ADAPTED TO THE ENGLISH STAGE, BY RICHARD BRINSLEY SHERI-
DAN.
> *Philadelphia: Printed for H. & P. Rice, No. 16, South Second-Street. 1799.*
> *pp. (2), (2), (2), (2), 59, (2), plate. 12mo.*   AAS. LOC.

KOTZEBUE, AUGUST FREIDRICH FERDINAND VON, continued.

35702 —— SELF IMMOLATION, OR, THE SACRIFICE OF LOVE. A PLAY — IN THREE ACTS. BY AUGUSTUS VON KOTZEBUE. FAITHFULLY TRANSLATED FROM THE GERMAN, BY HENRY NEUMAN, ESQ.

> *Boston: Printed for W. P. and L. Blake, at the Boston Book-Store, Cornhill.* 1799. pp. 57, (3). 12mo. AAS. LOC.

> "Universally acknowledged to be the best play the German Shakespeare has ever produced."

35703 —— THE STRANGER: OR, MISANTHROPY AND REPENTANCE. A DRAMA, IN FIVE ACTS. CORRECTLY TRANSLATED FROM THE GERMAN OF AUGUSTUS VON KOTZEBUE, DIRECTOR OF THE IMPERIAL THEATRE AT VIENNA. BY GEORGE PAPENDICK. [Two lines from] SHAKSPEARE.

> *Boston: Printed by John Russell, at his Office, in Quaker Lane. [Price 25 cents.]* [1799.] pp. 76. 12mo. AAS. BU.

35704 —— — THE STRANGER: OR MISANTHROPY AND REPENTANCE. A DRAMA IN FIVE ACTS. CORRECTLY TRANSLATED FROM THE GERMAN OF AUGUSTUS VON KOTZEBUE, DIRECTOR OF THE IMPERIAL THEATRE AT VIENNA, BY GEORGE PAPENDICK. [Two lines from] SHAKESPEARE.

> *Salem: Printed [by Thomas E. Cushing] for Bernard B. Macanulty.* 1799. pp. 84. 12mo. AAS. EI. HEH.

35705 —— — THE STRANGER: A COMEDY. FREELY TRANSLATED FROM KOTZEBUE'S GERMAN COMEDY OF MISANTHROPY AND REPENTANCE. [By A. Schinck.]

> *New-York: Printed for Napthali Judah.* 1799. pp. vi, 56. 12mo. NYPL.

> "Address to the publick" signed and dated: A. S * * * * k. 26th March, 1798.

35706 DER LANCASTER CORRESPONDENT. FREY, STANDHAFT UND GEMÄSIGT. NUM. 1. SONNABEND, DEN 25 MAI, [— NUM 32. SONNABEND, DEN 28 DEZEMBER, 1799.]

> *Diese Zeitung wird alle Sonnabend Morgen herausgegeben von Christian Jacob Hütter in den neuen Buchdruckerey, in der Konigs'strasse, die 2te Thüre vom Markt, in Lancaster: wo auch alle Arten von Buchdruckerarbeit aufs geschwindeste verfertiget werden.* 1799. fol. HSP. J&ML.

> Established, as a weekly, by Christian Jacob Hütter, and continued by him to September, 1803, when he discontinued publication, as a losing venture, and removed his Press to Easton, Pennsylvania, and established there, in 1805, *Der Northampton Correspondent*, which has been continued to the present day.

35707 LANCASTER JOURNAL. [Motto.] VOL. V. No. 33, SATURDAY, JANUARY 5, [— VOL. VI. No. 32. SATURDAY, DECEMBER 28, 1799.]

> *Lancaster: Printed by William Hamilton, at the German and English Printing-Office, Franklin's-Head, King-Street, west of the Court-House, at the low price of two dollars per annum. . . .* 1799. fol. LOC.

> Beginning August 14th, the Journal was printed every Wednesday and Saturday. Wednesday issues are not numbered, but are called "Extra." Saturday issues are numbered consecutively without regard to them. The motto reads: "Not too rash,—yet not fearful:—Open to all parties, —but not influenced by any."

35708 DAS LANDMANNS WOCHENBLATT. NUM. 45. DIENSTAG, JANUAR 1, [— NUM. 52. DIENSTAG, FEBRUAR 19, 1799.]

> *Lancaster: Gedruckt bey William Hamilton und Conrad Wortmann.* 1799. fol.

> Discontinued at the end of its first year, and succeeded by *Der Lancaster Wochenblatt.*

35709   DER LANCASTER WOCHENBLATT. NUM. 1. DIENSTAG, FEBRUAR 26, [— NUM. 12 ? DIENSTAG, MAI 14 ? 1799.]

     Lancaster: Gedruckt bey William Hamilton ? 1799. fol.

     Established, as a weekly, in continuation of *Das Landmanns Wochenblatt*, by William Hamilton ? and publication continued into May, 1799, when it was succeeded by *Der Lancaster Correspondent*. No copies are known.

35710   LANGHORNE, JOHN   1735–1779

   SOLYMAN AND ALMENA. AN ORIENTAL TALE. BY DR. JOHN LANGHORNE. [Two lines of Latin from] VIRG.

     London: Printed, East-Windsor: (Connecticut) Re-printed, and sold wholesale & retail, by Luther Pratt. MDCCXCIX. pp. (168). 12mo.

                                     AAS. JCB. LOC. NYPL.

     Contains, Account of the Anabaptists in Germany. A. D. 1534. Rural felicity: or the history of Colin and Celia. To Solitude. Female excellence. And a six-page list of Subscribers names.

35711   LANSINGBURGH GAZETTE. VOL. I. No. 16. TUESDAY, JANUARY 1, [— VOL. II. No. 68. TUESDAY, DECEMBER 31, 1799.]

     [*Lansingburgh:*] *Printed every Tuesday, by Gardiner Tracy, at the Printing-Office, in King's Street. 1799. fol.*

35712   LATHROP, JOHN   1740–1816

   PATRIOTISM AND RELIGION. A SERMON, PREACHED ON THE 25TH OF APRIL, 1799, THE DAY RECOMMENDED BY THE PRESIDENT OF THE UNITED STATES, TO BE OBSERVED AS A NATIONAL FAST. BY JOHN LATHROP, D.D. MINISTER OF A CHURCH IN BOSTON. PUBLISHED BY DESIRE. [Ornament.]

     Boston: Printed by John Russell. 1799. pp. (2), 30. 8vo.

          AAS. BA. BM. CHS. CLA. HC. JCB. LOC. MHS. NYPL. UTS. YC.

35713   LATHROP, JOHN, JUNIOR   1772–1820

   THE NORFOLK ALBUM, IN PROSE AND POETRY: BY JOHN LATHROP JUN. A.M.

     Proposals for printing the above in a volume of 250 pages, duodecimo, were made by Herman Mann, Dedham, this year.

35714   LATROBE, BENJAMIN HENRY   1764–1820

   REMARKS ON THE ADDRESS OF THE COMMITTEE OF THE DELAWARE AND SCHUYLKILL CANAL COMPANY TO THE COMMITTEE OF THE SENATE AND HOUSE OF REPRESENTATIVES, AS FAR AS IT NOTICES THE "VIEW OF THE PRACTICABILITY AND MEANS OF SUPPLYING THE CITY OF PHILADELPHIA WITH WHOLESOME WATER:" . . .

     Philadelphia: Printed by Zachariah Poulson, junior. 1799. pp. 18. 8vo.

35715   —— VIEW OF THE PRACTICABILITY AND MEANS OF SUPPLYING THE CITY OF PHILADELPHIA WITH WHOLESOME WATER. IN A LETTER TO JOHN MILLER, ESQUIRE, FROM B. HENRY LATROBE, ENGINEER. DECEMBER 29TH, 1798. PRINTED BY ORDER OF THE CORPORATION OF PHILADELPHIA.

     Philadelphia: Printed by Zachariah Poulson, junior, No. 106, Chesnut-Street. 1799. pp. 20. 8vo.   JCB. LOC. NYPL.

35716   LAUGH AND BE FAT, OR, AN ANTIDOTE AGAINST MELANCHOLY. CONTAINING A GREAT VARIETY OF COMICAL INTRIGUES AND FINE STORIES: WITTY EPIGRAMS AND COMICAL WHIMS: EPITAPHS, HUMOUROUS JESTS, ETC. WRITTEN BY THE MOST INGENIOUS AUTHORS OF THE AGE.

     Salem: Printed [by Nathaniel Coverly, junior] at Faust's Head, Essex Street. 1799. pp. 82. 12mo.   EI.

35717   LAVATER, JOHANN CASPAR   1741–1801
REMONSTRANCE, ADDRESSED TO THE EXECUTIVE DIRECTORY OF THE FRENCH REPUB-
LIC, AGAINST THE INVASION OF SWITZERLAND. BY JOHN CASPAR LAVATER, RECTOR
AT ZURICH. FIRST NEW YORK EDITION.

> *London, Printed; New-York, Reprinted by John Tiebout.* 1799. pp. 22. 8vo.
> NYHS.

35718   LAVOISIER, ANTOINE LAURENT   1743–1794
ELEMENTS OF CHEMISTRY, IN A NEW SYSTEMATIC ORDER, CONTAINING ALL THE MOD-
ERN DISCOVERIES. ILLUSTRATED WITH THIRTEEN COPPERPLATES. BY M. LAVOISIER,
MEMBER OF THE ACADEMIES AND SOCIETIES OF PARIS, LONDON, ORLEANS, BOLOGNA,
BASEL, PHILADELPHIA, HARLAEM, MANCHESTER, &C. &C. TRANSLATED FROM THE
FRENCH BY ROBERT KERR, F.R.S. AND A.SS. EDIN. MEMBER OF THE ROYAL COL-
LEGE OF SURGEONS, AND OF THE ROYAL PHYSICAL SOCIETY OF EDINBURGH. FOURTH
EDITION, WITH NOTES, TABLES AND CONSIDERABLE ADDITIONS.

> *Philadelphia: Printed for Mathew Carey,* Decem. 12, MDCCXCIX. pp. xliii,
> 592, 13 plates, table. 8vo.   BU. JCB. LOC. SGO.

> A French translation was printed in Paris, in 1920.

35719   LAW, ANDREW   1748–1821
THE MUSICAL MAGAZINE. CONTAINING A NUMBER OF FAVORITE PIECES EUROPEAN
AND AMERICAN. BY ANDREW LAW. NUMBER FIFTH.
> *Philadelphia:* 1799.

> 220th Pennsylvania District Copyright, issued to Andrew Law, as Au-
> thor, 21 January, 1799.

35720   LEAMING, JEREMIAH   1717–1804
AN ESSAY ON CONVERSION. BY JEREMIAH LEAMING, LATE RECTOR OF CHRIST'S
CHURCH IN STRATFORD.
> *Hartford: Printed by Elisha Babcock.* 1799.

35721   LEAVITT, DUDLEY   1772–1851
AN ASTRONOMICAL DIARY, OR ALMANACK, FOR THE YEAR OF CHRISTIAN ÆRA, 1800.
THIS YEAR BEGINS A NEW CYCLE: AND ALTHOUGH THE YEAR 1796 WAS A LEAP-YEAR,
AND CONSEQUENTLY, ACCORDING TO THE COMMON COMPUTATION, IN RECKONING
EVERY FOURTH YEAR A LEAP-YEAR, THE PRESENT YEAR WOULD BE BISSEXTILE; YET
THE 29TH DAY MUST THIS YEAR BE STRUCK OUT OF THE MONTH OF FEBRUARY, IN
ORDER TO MAKE THE NEW STILE KEEP PACE WITH THE OLD: TO DO WHICH, THREE
DAYS ARE OMITTED IN EVERY 400 YEARS. CALCULATED FOR THE MERIDIAN OF GIL-
MANTOWN, N. H.—LAT. 43° 30' NORTH— LONG. 71° WEST FROM LONDON: DESIGNED
FOR THE STATE OF NEW-HAMPSHIRE, BUT WILL SERVE FOR THE ADJACENT STATES.
BY DUDLEY LEAVITT. [Five lines from] VIRGIL.

> *Printed at Concord, New-Hampshire. by Joshua Leavitt.* [1799.] pp. (32).
> 12mo.   AAS. NHHS.

> Contains, An account of the simoon, from Bruce. Circle of human life.
> Remarkable instances of the force of imagination. The causes of ice,
> thunder & lightning, the aurora borealis, ignus fatuus, and the rainbow.
> On the equation of time. Courts. Interest. Roads.

35722   LEE, HARRIET   1756–1851
CONSTANTIA DE VALMONT. A NOVEL. BY HARRIET LEE. [Two lines from] SHAKE-
SPEARE.
> *Philadelphia: Printed for Mathew Carey, No. 118, Market-Street.* July 24,
> 1799. pp. 101. 12mo.   AAS. JCB. LOC.

AUCTION VALUES

35723   LEE, HENRY   1756–1818
Caption title: PLAIN TRUTH: ADDRESSED TO THE PEOPLE OF VIRGINIA. WRITTEN IN FEBRUARY 1799 — BY A CITIZEN OF WESTMORELAND COUNTY, (VIRG.) . . .
[Richmond ? 1799.] pp. 56. 8vo.   BA. HEH.

Issued in ten parts, paged consecutively.

35724   LEE, SILAS   1760–1814
AN ORATION, DELIVERED AT WISCASSET, AT THE REQUEST OF THE INHABITANTS, ON THE FOURTH OF JULY, 1799. BY SILAS LEE. "BEWARE OF FOREIGN INFLUENCE, WHICH WILL INVOLVE YOU, IN SPITE OF YOURSELVES, IN WARS, AND RUIN." MALLET DU PAN.
Wiscasset: Printed by Henry Hoskins. 1799. pp. [25], (1). 8vo.   BA.

35725   LESSONS FOR YOUTH, SELECTED FOR THE USE OF YOUTH.
Philadelphia: Printed by Benjamin & Jacob Johnson, No. 147, *High Street.* 1799. pp. (178), (3). 12mo.   AAS. JCB.

35726   A LETTER FROM AN EMINENT MINISTER OF THE CHURCH OF SCOTLAND: WRITTEN TO A MINISTER OF HIS ACQUAINTANCE AT SOME DISTANCE, IN THE SAME KINGDOM: GIVING AN ACCOUNT OF HIS CONVERSION, AND WONDERFUL CHANGE IN HIS PREACHING, AFTER HE HAD BEEN EIGHT YEARS IN THE MINISTRY. [Four lines of Scripture texts.]
Leominster, Massachusetts, Printed by Charles & John Prentiss, for the Editor. 1799. pp. (24). 12mo.   AAS. JCB. NYPL.

35727   LEVANA GAZETTE: OR, ONONDAGA ADVERTISER. VOL. I. NUMB. 29. WEDNESDAY, JANUARY 2, [— 1799.]
Scipio, (Onondago County, S. N. Y.) Printed by R. Delano. 1799. fol.

Known only through a few scattering numbers, and discontinued probably sometime this year.

35728   LEWIS, ENOCH   1776–1856
PHILADELPHIA ALMANAC, FOR THE YEAR OF OUR LORD, 1800; BEING THE FOURTH AFTER LEAP-YEAR. CALCULATED FOR THE STATES OF PENNSYLVANIA, NEW-JERSEY, MARYLAND, AND DELAWARE. [Cut.] [BY ENOCH LEWIS.]
—: Philadelphia :— Printed and sold by B. & J. Johnson, No. 147, *High-Street.* [1799.] pp. (48). 12mo.   HSP. LOC.

35729   LEWIS, MATTHEW GREGORY   1775–1818
AMBROSIO; OR, THE MONK. A ROMANCE. BY M. G. LEWIS, ESQ. M. P. AUTHOR OF "CASTLE SPECTRE," &C. &C. THREE VOLUMES IN TWO. VOL. I. [— II.] THE SECOND AMERICAN, FROM THE FOURTH BRITISH EDITION. WITH CONSIDERABLE ADDITIONS AND ALTERATIONS. [Four lines of quotations.]
Printed at Boston, by Samuel Etheridge, for Thomas & Andrews. Sold by them, the other Booksellers, and S. Etheridge, in Boston; by I. Thomas, Worcester; by Thomas, Andrews & Penniman, Albany; by Thomas, Andrews & Butler, Baltimore; and by E. S. Thomas, Charleston, (S. C.) Jan. 1799. 2 vols. pp. 258. 12mo.   AAS.

35730   —— THE CASTLE SPECTRE: A DRAMA. IN FIVE ACTS. BY M. G. LEWIS, ESQ. M. P. AUTHOR OF "THE MONK." AS PERFORMED WITH UNBOUNDED APPLAUSE AT THE THEATRES IN BOSTON.
Salem: Printed [by Thomas E. Cushing] for Bernard B. Macanulty. 1799. pp. 92. 8vo.   AAS. BU. JCB. LOC.

35731   LEWIS, ZECHARIAH   1773–1840
An Oration, on the apparent, and the real political situation of the United
States, pronounced before the Connecticut Society of Cincinnati, assembled at New-Haven, for the celebration of American independence, July
the 4th, 1799. By Zechariah Lewis, a tutor of Yale-College.

New-Haven: Printed by Thomas Green and Son. 1799. pp. 27. 8vo.
AAS. BA. BM. CHS. HC. JCB. LOC. NYHS. NYPL. UTS. YC.

35732   LINDLY, EDWARD
The Foundling: or, the history of Lucius Stanhope.

Rutland: Printed by John Walker, jun. ? 1799. 18mo.

35733   LINING, JOHN   1708–1760
A Description of the American yellow fever, which prevailed at Charleston, in South Carolina, in the year 1748. By doctor John Lining, physician
at Charleston.

*Philadelphia: Printed for Thomas Dobson, at the Stone-House, No. 41, South
Second-Street.* 1799. pp. 30, (2). 8vo.   BA. BM. SGO.

35734   LITTLE, EZEKIEL   –1840
The Usher. Comprising arithmetic in whole numbers; federal money; decimal
and vulgar fractions; a description and use of Coggeshall's sliding rule;
some uses of Gunter's scale; superficial and solid measuring; geometrical
definitions and problems; surveying; the surveyor's pocket companion, or
trigonometry made easy; a table of sines; a table of tangents; miscellany,
tables of the weight and value of gold coins. Calculated and designed
for youth. By Ezekiel Little, a.m. Published agreeably to Act of Congress. "Whoever thinks a faultless piece to see, Thinks what ne'er was.
nor is, nor e'er shall be."

*Exeter: Printed by H. Ranlet, and sold at his Book-Store; Sold also by the
Booksellers in Boston, Newburyport, Portsmouth, and other places.* 1799. pp. 240.
12mo.   AAS. BM. JCB.

Contains six pages of Subscribers' names.

35735   LITTLE Robin Red Breast; a collection of pretty songs, for children, entirely new.

Printed at Worcester, Massachusetts, by Isaiah Thomas, jun. 1799.

35736   LIVERMORE, EDWARD ST. LOE   1762–1832
An Oration, in commemoration of the dissolution of the political union
between the United States of America and France. Delivered on the
seventeenth of July, 1799, at St. John's church, in Portsmouth, N. H. by
Edward St. Loe Livermore, esq. Olim Punica nunc Gallica fides. Published
at the request of the gentlemen present.

Portsmouth, New-Hampshire:—Printed at the Oracle Press, by Charles Peirce.
1799. pp. (28). 4to.   AAS. BA. BM. HC. JCB. LOC. NYHS. NYPL.

35737   THE LIVES of Martin Luther and John Calvin, the two great reformers.

*Philadelphia: Printed by Robert Johnson, for B. & J. Johnson, No. 147, High-
Street.* 1799. pp. 105. 18mo.   AAS. JCB.

35738   LIVINGSTON, John Henry   1746–1825
Two sermons, delivered before the New-York Missionary Society; the first on April 23d, in the Scots Presbyterian church, by the Rev. Dr. Livingston. The second on April 24th, in the North Dutch church, by the Rev. Dr. M'Knight. To which is added, a Charge given to the first missionary, by the Rev. Dr. Rodgers; together with the Instructions to missionaries, and the Report of the directors.

> *New-York: Printed by Isaac Collins, No. 189, Pearl-street.* 1799. pp. 104. 8vo.   AAS. HC. JCB. LOC. NYPL. rU. YC.

First heading: The Glory of the Redeemer. A sermon, preached before the New-York Missionary Society in the Scots Presbyterian church, 23d of April, 1799, by John H. Livingston, d.d. s.t.p. one of the ministers of the Reformed Dutch Church of the city of New-York. pp. (3)-48.

Second heading: Life to the dead. A sermon, preached before the New-York Missionary Society in the North Dutch church, on the 24th of April, 1799, by John M'Knight, d.d. one of the ministers of the United Presbyterian congregations in the city of New-York. pp. (49)-73.

Third heading: A Charge to the rev. mr. Joseph Bullen, first missionary to the Indians, from the New-York Missionary Society, for propagating the Gospel among the heathen, delivered by appointment of the Society, in the new Dutch church, March 21st, 1799, by John Rodgers, d.d. senior minister of the United Presbyterian churches in the city of New-York, and president of said Society. pp. (75)-84.

Fourth heading: Instructions from the directors of the New-York Missionary Society, to their missionaries among the Indians. pp. (85)-97.

Fifth heading: The Report of the directors. pp. 97-104.

35739   LOCKWOOD, William   1753–1828
A Sermon, delivered at the funeral of mrs. Jerusha Woodbridge, relict of the late rev. Ashbel Woodbridge, of Glastenbury, August 1st, 1799. By William Lockwood, a.m. pastor of the first church in Glastenbury.

> *Middletown:—Printed by Tertius Dunning.* 1799. pp. (23), (1). 8vo.   AAS. BA. HC. JCB. MHS. NYPL. YC.

Contains, on verso of last leaf, an Account of the family of the Rev. Ashbel Woodbridge of Glastenbury, collected from historical and family records.

35740   LONGWORTH, David
Longworth's American Almanack, New-York Register, and city Directory, for the twenty-fourth year of American independence. Price 5s. stitched —half-bound 6s.

> *New-York: Printed by John C. Totten and Co. No. 66 Nassau-Street.* 1799. pp. 402. 24mo.   AAS. NYHS. NYPL.

Second title: Astronomical calculations for the twenty-fourth year of American independence, commencing the fourth of July, A.D. 1799: being third after leap year. Containing the rising, setting, places, and eclipses of the sun and moon; the rising, setting, and southing of the most conspicuous planets and fixed stars; the equation of time; and time of high water at New-York, &c. Also, the increase, decrease, and length of the days with the festivals, &c. Calculated for the latitude and meridian of New-York. By Abraham Shoemaker.

> *From the Press of J. C. Totten & Co.* [1799.] pp. (45).

35741   LOUISIANA. PROVINCE.
DON JUAN VENTURA MORALES, CONTADOR PRINCIPAL DE EXERCITO Y REAL HACI-
ENDA DE LAS PROVINCIAS DE LA LUISIANA Y FLORIDA. [Regulations, in Spanish,
and French, by the Intendant.]
Nueva Orleans: 1799. 8vo.   LCP.

35742   LOUISVILLE GAZETTE AND REPUBLICAN TRUMPET. VOL. I. NO. 1. WEDNESDAY,
APRIL 10, [— NO. 38. WEDNESDAY, DECEMBER 25, 1799.]
Louisville, Georgia. Published by Ambrose Day and James Hely. 1799. fol.

Established, as a weekly, by Ambrose Day, and James Hely. Before
December, 1803, publication was made by Day & Hely for Abner Ham-
mond. Before January, 1805, by Ambrose Day for Abner Hammond.
Before October, 1806, by Ambrose Day, alone. In August, 1809, George
W. Wheeler was admitted to partnership, as Day & Wheeler, and the
title shortened to *Louisville Gazette.* Before May, 1810, publication was
made by Ambrose Day & Co., and before September, 1810, by Ambrose
Day, alone. Publication was finally discontinued before November, 1811.

35743   LOUVET DE COUVRAY, JEAN BAPTISTE   1760–1797
EMILIA DE VARMONT, OR, THE NECESSARY DIVORCE; AND MEMOIRS OF CURATE SEVIN.
A MORAL AND POLITICAL TALE. FOUNDED ON FACTS. TRANSLATED FROM THE
FRENCH OF M. LOUVET, BY MELATIAH NASH. THREE VOLUMES IN ONE. . . .
New-York: Printed by T. & J. Swords, No. 99 Pearl-Street. 1799. 3 vols.
in one. 12mo.   HEH.

35744   —— LOVE AND PATRIOTISM! OR, THE EXTRAORDINARY ADVENTURES OF M. DUPOR-
TAIL, LATE MAJOR-GENERAL IN THE ARMIES OF THE UNITED STATES. INTERSPERSED
WITH MANY SURPRISING INCIDENTS IN THE LIFE OF THE LATE COUNT PULAUSKI.
[Printer's mark.]
*Boston: Printed by Samuel Etheridge, sold by him, and the principal Book-
sellers in town and country.—1799.—pp. 59.* 12mo.   AAS. BA. DERGI.. JCB.

35745   LOVE'S PILGRIMAGE: A STORY FOUNDED ON FACTS. COMPILED FROM THE JOURNAL OF
A DECEASED FRIEND. [Four lines from] SHAKESPEARE.
Philadelphia: Printed and sold by John Bioren, No. 83, Chesnut-Street.
1799. pp. [vi], 274. 12mo.   AAS.

35746   LOW, NATHANAEL   1740–1808
[Low's.] AN ASTRONOMICAL DIARY: OR ALMANACK, FOR THE YEAR OF CHRISTIAN
ÆRA 1800. BEING THE FOURTH YEAR SINCE THE LAST LEAP-YEAR, AND THE TWEN-
TY-FOURTH OF THE INDEPENDENCE OF THE UNITED STATES OF AMERICA, WHICH
BEGAN JULY 4TH, 1776. CONTAINING ALL THAT IS USUAL IN AN ALMANACK, AND A
VARIETY OF OTHER MATTERS USEFUL AND ENTERTAINING. CALCULATED FOR THE
MERIDIAN OF BOSTON IN AMERICA. LATITUDE 42 DEGREES. 23 MINUTES NORTH.
BUT WILL SERVE FOR ANY OF THE ADJACENT STATES. BY NATHANAEL LOW. [Cut.]
PLANETS. [Seven lines.] ASPECTS [Seven lines.]
*Boston: Printed and sold by John & Thomas Fleet, at the Bible and Heart,
Cornhill. Where may be had their Register & Pocket Almanack, for 1800. [Copy
rights secured.]* [1799.] pp. [24.] 12mo.   AAS. LOC. NYPL. YC.

35747   LOWELL, JOHN   1769–1840
AN ORATION, PRONOUNCED JULY 4, 1799, AT THE REQUEST OF THE INHABITANTS OF
THE TOWN OF BOSTON, IN COMMEMORATION OF THE ANNIVERSARY OF AMERICAN
INDEPENDENCE. BY JOHN LOWELL, JUN. [Fifteen lines of quotations.]
Boston: Printed by Manning & Loring. 1799. pp. (27). 8vo.
AAS. BA. BM. HC. JCB. LOC. MHS. NYHS. NYPL.

35748   LOWNES, Caleb
An Account of the alteration and present state of the penal laws of Pennsylvania. Containing, also, an Account of the gaol and penitentiary house
of Philadelphia — and the interior management thereof. By Caleb
Lownes. Printed by order of the Legislature of Massachusetts.
Printed at Boston, by Young & Minns, State Printers. MDCCXCIX. pp. 36.
8vo.   AAS. BA. BM. JCB. LOC. MHS. NL. NYPL.

35749   LOWTH, Robert   1710–1787
A Short introduction to English grammar. With critical notes. By the
right rev. Robert Lowth, d.d. lord bishop of Oxford. [Five lines of Latin
from] Cicero.
Philadelphia: Printed by R. Aitken, No. 22, Market Street. 1799. *Price
three shillings.* pp. xi, 132. 12mo.   AAS. JCB. NYPL.

35750   LYMAN, Joseph   1749–1828
The Advantages and praises of wisdom. A sermon, delivered at Deerfield,—
Jan. 1, A. D. 1799, at the opening of the Academy in that town; from Prov-
erbs, xii. 8. "A man shall be commended according to his wisdom." By the
rev. Joseph Lyman. a.m. one of the trustees of said Academy.
Printed at Greenfield, by Francis Barker. M,DCC,XCIX. pp. [16.] 8vo.
                            AAS. BA. JCB. NYHS. NYPL. UTS. YC.
Contains. The Address of the Rev. Roger Newton, President, introduc-
ing the preceptor into office.

35751   LYNCHBURG Weekly Gazette. Vol. i. Num. xxxii. Saturday, January 5, [—
Vol. ii. Num. xxxi. Saturday, December 28, 1799.]
[Lynchburg, Va.:] Printed by John Carter & Co. 1799. fol.
Early in this year publication was made by John Carter, alone, and so
continued.

35752   LYON, Patrick
The Narrative of Patrick Lyon, who suffered three months severe imprison-
ment in Philadelphia jail, on merely a vague suspicion of being concerned
in the robbery of the Bank of Pennsylvania, with his remarks thereon.
Philadelphia: Printed by Francis and Robert Bailey. 1799. pp. 76. 8vo. LOC.
Advertised as, "Just published and for sale at Mr. Dobson's Stone House,
Second Street — Mr. Bailey, No. 122 Market Street — Mr. W. Woodward, No. 17, Chesnut Street — and by the Author, at his smith's shop,
in Lombard between Front and Second Streets — Mr. Rawle, near the
George Tavern, Second Street — Mr. Ormrod, Chesnut Street. Booksellers will be supplied by Mr. Bailey. 1799.

35753   McCALLA, Daniel   1748–1800
The Mystery of the Gospel to be published with boldness. A sermon,
preached to the United Independent or, Congregational church of Dor-
chester and Beach-Hill, May 8th, 1799, at the ordination of the revd.
James Adams, to the pastoral charge of said church, by the revd. Daniel
McCalla, a.m. Together with the revd. dr. Keith's Charge delivered on
the same occasion. [Ornament.]
Charleston: Printed by W. P. Harrison, Bay. [1799.] pp. 42. 8vo. NYHS. PU.

35754   McCLURE, David   1748–1820
The New-Year. A sermon, delivered at East-Windsor, first society, on the
first Lord's day, after the commencement of the year 1799. By David
McClure.
Printed at East Windsor by Luther Pratt. 1799. pp. 29. 16mo.   CLA. YC.

35755   M'CULLOCH, John
M'Culloch's Pocket Almanac, for the year 1800. Being a centurial year, not bissextile. And 24-25 of American independence. Vulgar notes and moveable feasts. [Four lines.] In the 6th column of the calendar pages, under the title Moon's age, observe the following signs: [Four lines.]
Philadelphia: Printed and sold by J. M'Culloch, No. 1, North Third Street. [1799.] pp. (32), interleaved. 32mo.   AAS.

35756   M'DONALD, John   –1821
The Danger of America delineated. An address. Delivered at Cooperstown, in the County of Otsego, State of New-York, April 25th, 1799, the fast day recommended by the President of the United States. By J. M'Donald, A.M. Published at the particular request of the hearers.
Cooperstown: Printed by Elihu Phinney, 1799. pp. (28). 8vo.   AAS. NYPL.

35757   —— The Duty of America enforced. An exhortation. Delivered at Cooperstown, on the evening of the national fast, April 25th, 1799. By John M'Donald, A.M. Published at the request of the hearers.
Cooperstown: Printed by Elihu Phinney, 1799. pp. (20). 8vo.   AAS. NYPL.

35758   MACKENZIE, Henry   1745–1831
The Man of the world. In two parts. Virginibus puerisque canto. — Hor. Second American edition.
Philadelphia: Printed for George Gibson, by David Hogan, No. 222, South Third Street. 1799. pp. 260, 7, (1). 12mo.   AAS. NYPL.
Contains, a seven-page list of Subscribers' names.

35759   McMILLAN, ——
Julia, or the adventures of a curate's daughter. By Mr. McMillan. [Ornament.]
Printed at Walpole, Newhampshire, for Thomas and Thomas, by David Carlisle, and sold at their Bookstores. 1799. pp. 84. 12mo.   AAS.

35760   MADISON, James   1751–1836
Caption title: A Letter to a member of Congress [Thomas Evans]; respecting the Alien and Sedition laws. Sir, I have lately been favoured with the perusal of "An Address to the people of Virginia, respecting the alien and sedition laws" which your friends ascribe to you; . . . Columbus, Virginia, June 6th, 1799.
[Richmond: Printed by Meriwether Jones, 1799.] pp. (48). 8vo.   HC. LOC.

For some time the writer has been convinced that the several publications appearing in previous volumes of this work, attributed to Columbus, *pseudonym,* were written by no less a personage than James Madison, afterwards fourth President of the United States. When this question was put, directly, to the late Gaillard Hunt — editor of the Writings of James Madison — he showed some embarrassment, but denied belief; and, in deference to his opinion, such publications have before been entered under the pseudonym. As the weight of expressed opinion, on any subject, is, or should be, proportionate to the known abilities of the person making them, the writer has determined to credit this publication, on one of the most important public questions, at this time, to Mr. Madison; and, inferentially, correct the previous "Columbus" entries.

35761   MADISON, James   1749–1812
An Address, to the members of the Protestant Episcopal Church in Virginia. By Bishop Madison.
Richmond: Printed by T. Nicolson, first house below the Capitol. 1799. pp. 24. 8vo.   HC. LOC.

35762   THE MAID WITH A BOSOM OF SNOW. SUNG WITH GREAT APPLAUSE BY MR. HODGKIN-
SON AT THE PHILHARMONIC SOCIETY. COMPOSED BY J. MAZZINGHI.
> [*New-York:* 1799.] pp. (4). 4to.

35763   MAIR, JOHN
AN INTRODUCTION TO LATIN SYNTAX: OR, AN EXEMPLIFICATION OF THE RULES OF
CONSTRUCTION, AS DELIVERED IN MR. RUDDIMAN'S RUDIMENTS, WITHOUT ANTICI-
PATING POSTERIOR RULES. CONTAINING, I. THE RULES OF SYNTAX, WITH A BRIEF
ILLUSTRATION. II. EXPLANATORY NOTES. III. EXAMPLES, TAKEN FOR THE MOST PART
FROM THE CLASSIC AUTHORS. IV. ENGLISH EXERCISES. TO WHICH IS SUBJOINED,
AN EPITOME OF ANCIENT HISTORY, FROM THE CREATION TO THE BIRTH OF CHRIST.
INTENDED AS A PROPER MEAN TO INITIATE BOYS IN THE USEFUL STUDY OF HISTORY,
WHILE, AT THE SAME TIME, IT SERVES TO IMPROVE THEM IN THE KNOWLEDGE OF
THE LATIN TONGUE. TO WHICH IS ADDED, A PROPER COLLECTION OF HISTORICAL AND
CHRONOLOGICAL QUESTIONS; WITH A COPIOUS INDEX. BY JOHN MAIR, A.M. THE
FIRST AMERICAN EDITION.
> *Philadelphia: Printed for Campbell, Conrad, & Co. by J. Bioren.* 1799. pp.
> x, 299, (1). 12mo.   NYHS.

35764   MALL, THOMAS
A SHORT COLLECTION OF THE HISTORY OF THE MARTYRS, EPITOMIZED. A CLOUD OF
WITNESSES; OR, THE SUFFERER'S MIRROUR. VOL. I.
> *Suffield: Printed by Edward Gray.* 1799. pp. 48. 12mo.

35765   MALLET DU PAN, JACQUES   1749–1800
THE HISTORY OF THE DESTRUCTION OF THE HELVETIC UNION AND LIBERTY. BY J.
MALLET DU PAN. [Five lines from] PREFACE p. 5.
> *Boston: Printed by Manning & Loring, for J. Nancrede, No. 49, Marlbro'-
> Street. March,* 1799. pp. 264, frontispiece. 12mo.   AAS. BA. HC. JCB. MHS. NYPL.
> Contains, a four-page list of Books published by J. Nancrede.

35766   —— — THE HISTORY OF THE DESTRUCTION OF THE HELVETIC UNION AND LIBERTY.
BY J. MALLET DU PAN. [Five lines from] PREFACE, p. 4, 5. SECOND AMERICAN
EDITION.
> *Boston: Printed by Manning & Loring, for J. Nancrede, No. 49, Marlbro'-
> Street. August,* 1799. pp. 240, frontispiece. 12mo.   AAS. JCB. LOC.
> Contains, a six-page list of Books for sale by J. Nancrede.

35767   THE MANUAL OF A FREE MAN, OR REASONABLE EXPOSITION OF THE FUNDAMENTAL
POINTS OF UNIVERSAL POLITICAL RIGHT. (ORIGINALLY PUBLISHED IN HOLLAND BE-
FORE THE FRENCH REVOLUTION.) TRANSLATED FROM THE FRENCH BY A CITIZEN
OF VIRGINIA, WITH NOTES BY THE TRANSLATOR. LIBERTY, IS A SACRED THING, AND
OF DIVINE RIGHT; THEREFORE CONNECTED BY THE CREATOR WITH THE NATURE OF
MAN; SO THAT TO ATTACK IT IS A CRIME, TO CIRCUMVENT IT IS IMPIOUS, TO OVER-
COME IT IS ABOMINABLE. GRAVINA, DE JURE NATURALI —
> *Richmond: Printed by John Dixon.* M.D.CC.XCIX. pp. [108], (1). 12mo.
>   AAS. NYHS.

35768   MAP OF THE STATE OF DELAWARE AND EASTERN SHORE OF MARYLAND, WITH THE
SOUNDINGS OF THE BAY OF DELAWARE.
> *Philadelphia:* [1799.]   LCP.

35769   MARMONTEL, JEAN FRANÇOIS   1723–1799
THE WIDOW OF THE VILLAGE; OR, ADVENTURES OF INNOCENCE. A MORAL TALE, BY
THE CELEBRATED MARMONTEL. TRANSLATED FROM THE ORIGINAL FRENCH, BY MR.
HERON. TO WHICH IS ADDED, THE ERROR OF A GOOD FATHER.
> *New-Haven: Printed by George Bunce.*—1799.—pp. 145. 18mo.   AAS.

35770   MARSHALL, CHARLES
AN INTRODUCTION TO THE KNOWLEDGE AND PRACTICE OF GARDENING, BY CHARLES
MARSHALL, VICAR OF BRIXWORTH, NORTHAMPTONSHIRE. [Three lines from] BA-
CON'S ESSAYS. FIRST AMERICAN, FROM THE SECOND LONDON EDITION. CONSIDER-
ABLY ENLARGED AND IMPROVED. TO WHICH IS ADDED, AN ESSAY ON QUICK-LIME,
AS A CEMENT AND AS A MANURE, BY JAMES ANDERSON, L.L.D. F.R.S. F.A.S. &C.
VOL. I. [— II.]
> *Boston: Printed by Samuel Etheridge, for Joseph Nancrede, No. 49, Marlboro'-*
> *Street.* 1799. 2 vols. pp. x, 276; (2), 134; 115, (4). 12mo.
>   AAS. BA. HC. JCB. LOC. NYPL.

Second title: AN ESSAY ON QUICK-LIME, AS A CEMENT AND AS A MANURE. BY JAMES
ANDERSON, L.L.D. F.R.S. F.A.S. &C. AUTHOR OF "ESSAYS RELATING TO AGRICUL-
TURE AND RURAL AFFAIRS." 3 VOLS. 8VO, AND OF SEVERAL OTHER PERFORMANCES.
HONORARY MEMBER OF THE SOCIETY OF ARTS, AGRICULTURE, &C. AT BATH; OF THE
PHILOSOPHICAL, AND OF THE AGRICULTURAL SOCIETIES IN MANCHESTER; OF THE
SOCIETY FOR PROMOTING NATURAL HISTORY, LONDON; OF THE ACADEMY OF ARTS,
SCIENCES, AND BELLES LETTRES, DIJON: OF THE PHILOSOPHICAL SOCIETY, PHILA-
DELPHIA; OF THE ROYAL ECONOMICAL SOCIETY, BERLIN; AND CORRESPONDENT
MEMBER OF THE ROYAL SOCIETY OF AGRICULTURE, PARIS. [Four lines from]
SWIFT.
> *Boston: Printed by Samuel Etheridge, for Joseph Nancrede, No. 49, Marlboro'-*
> *Street.* 1799. pp. 115.

35771   MARSHALL, WILLIAM   1740–1802
SOME REMARKABLE PARTICULARS IN THE LIFE AND DEATH OF THE REV. THOMAS
BEVERIDGE, LATE MINISTER OF THE GOSPEL TO THE ASSOCIATE CONGREGATION
OF CAMBRIDGE, WASHINGTON COUNTY, STATE OF NEW-YORK. BY WILLIAM MAR-
SHALL, A.M.
> *Philadelphia: Printed by David Hogan.* 1799. pp. (26), (2). 18mo.   BM.

35772   —— A THEOLOGICAL DISSERTATION, ON THE PROPRIETY OF REMOVING FROM THE SEAT
OF THE PESTILENCE; PRESENTED TO THE PERUSAL OF THE SERIOUS INHABITANTS OF
PHILADELPHIA AND NEW-YORK. BY WILLIAM MARSHALL, A.M. MINISTER OF THE
GOSPEL TO THE ASSOCIATE CHURCH IN PHILADELPHIA. [Two lines from] JER.
XXXVIII. 2.
> *Philadelphia: Printed and sold by David Hogan, No. 222, South Third-*
> *Street.* 1799. pp. [22], (2). 8vo.   AAS. LCP. LOC. NYPL.

35773   MARTINET, JOANNES FLORENTIUS   1729–1795
THE CATECHISM OF NATURE; FOR THE USE OF CHILDREN. BY DOCTOR MARTINET,
PROFESSOR OF PHILOSOPHY AT ZUTPHEN. TRANSLATED FROM THE DUTCH. READ
NATURE — NATURE IS A FRIEND TO TRUTH. YOUNG.
> *Philadelphia: Printed by John Bioren, No. 88, Chesnut-Street.* 1799. pp.
> (108). 18mo.   AAS. JCB.

The printed covers give the alphabet and numbers.

35774   MARYLAND. STATE.
BY HIS EXCELLENCY BENJAMIN OGLE, ESQUIRE, GOVERNOR OF MARYLAND. A PROC-
LAMATION. WHEREAS THE LEGISLATURE OF THIS STATE, PENETRATED BY REGRET
FOR THE DEATH OF THE ILLUSTRIOUS PATRIOT GENERAL GEORGE WASHINGTON,
. . . DO HEREBY RECOMMEND AND ADVISE ACCORDINGLY, THAT THE ELEVENTH DAY
OF FEBRUARY NEXT, BE OBSERVED THROUGHOUT THIS STATE, AS A DAY OF MOURN-
ING, HUMILIATION AND PRAYER FOR THE DECEASED. . . . GIVEN IN THE COUNCIL
CHAMBER, AT THE CITY OF ANNAPOLIS, UNDER THE SEAL OF THE STATE OF MARY-
LAND, THIS EIGHTEENTH DAY OF DECEMBER, IN THE YEAR OF OUR LORD ONE
THOUSAND SEVEN HUNDRED AND NINETY-NINE. BENJAMIN OGLE. BY THE GOV-
ERNOR, NINIAN PINKNEY, CLERK TO THE GOVERNOR AND COUNCIL.
> *[Annapolis: Printed by Frederick Green.* 1799.]

MARYLAND. State, continued.
PROCEEDINGS OF THE NEW-HAMPSHIRE LEGISLATURE. . . . STATE OF NEW-
HAMPSHIRE. IN THE HOUSE OF REPRESENTATIVES. DECEMBER 30, 1799. VOTED,
THAT ONE HUNDRED COPIES OF THE FOREGOING, TOGETHER WITH THE FAREWELL
ADDRESS OF GENERAL GEORGE WASHINGTON AT THE TIME HE RESIGNED THE CHAIR
OF GOVERNMENT, BE PRINTED, AND THAT ONE COPY BE GIVEN TO EACH OF THE
STUDENTS OF PHILLIPS' EXETER ACADEMY. SENT UP FOR CONCURRENCE. JOHN
PRENTICE, SPEAKER. IN SENATE, THE SAME DAY READ AND CONCURRED. NATHL.
PARKER, DEP'Y SEC'Y.

    [Portsmouth: Printed by John Melcher. 1799 ?] Broadside. fol.

35775 —— THE LAWS OF MARYLAND, TO WHICH ARE PREFIXED THE ORIGINAL CHARTER,
WITH AN ENGLISH TRANSLATION, THE BILL OF RIGHTS, AND CONSTITUTION OF THE
STATE, AS ORIGINALLY ADOPTED BY THE CONVENTION, WITH THE SEVERAL ALTERA-
TIONS BY ACTS OF ASSEMBLY, THE DECLARATION OF INDEPENDENCE, THE ARTICLES
OF CONFEDERATION, THE CONSTITUTION OF THE GENERAL GOVERNMENT, AND THE
AMENDMENTS MADE THERETO, WITH AN INDEX TO THE LAWS, THE BILL OF RIGHTS,
AND THE CONSTITUTION. IN TWO VOLUMES. REVISED AND COLLECTED, UNDER THE
AUTHORITY OF THE LEGISLATURE, BY WILLIAM KILTY, ATTORNEY AT LAW. VOL-
UME I.

    Annapolis: Printed by Frederick Green, Printer to the State. 1799. pp. (2),
(2), (40), (717), (194). 4to.   AAS. BM. JCB. LOC. NYPL.

35776 —— MARYLAND. BY THE HOUSE OF DELEGATES. JANUARY 1, 1799. WHEREAS IT IS
HIGHLY EXPEDIENT THAT EVERY CONSTITUTIONAL BARRIER SHOULD BE OPPOSED TO
THE INTRODUCTION OF FOREIGN INFLUENCE . . .

    [Annapolis: Printed by Frederick Green. 1799.] Broadside. fol. JCB. RISL.

35777 —— THE MILITIA LAW OF THE STATE OF MARYLAND, COMPLETE; BEING COMPRISED
UNDER THE REGULATIONS MADE RELATIVE THERETO, BY THE DECLARATION OF
RIGHTS — THE CONSTITUTION AND FORM OF GOVERNMENT — THE LAWS PASSED ON
THAT SUBJECT AGREEABLY TO THE ACTS OF CONGRESS — AND THE SUPPLEMENTARY
ACT, PASSED NOVEMBER SESSION, 1798. TO WHICH IS ANNEXED, BARON STUBEN'S
[*sic*] MANUAL EXERCISE. A WELL REGULATED MILITIA IS THE PROPER AND NATURAL
DEFENCE OF A FREE GOVERNMENT. — DECLARATION OF RIGHTS.

    —*Baltimore:*—*Printed for Thomas Herty, by Warner & Hanna.* M.DCC.-
XCIX. pp. (24). 8vo.   LOC.

35778 —— A SUPPLEMENT TO THE MILITIA ACT, PASSED NOVEMBER SESSION, 1798.
    Hagerstown: Printed by Thomas Grieves. 1799.

35779 —— VOTES AND PROCEEDINGS OF THE HOUSE OF DELEGATES OF THE STATE OF MARY-
LAND. NOVEMBER SESSION, 1798. BEING THE FIRST SESSION OF THIS ASSEMBLY.
[— 20 JANUARY, 1799.]

    [Annapolis: Printed by Frederick Green, 1799.] pp. 147. fol.   LOC.

35780 THE MARYLAND GAZETTE. LIV TH YEAR. No. 2712. THURSDAY, JANUARY 3, [—
LV TH YEAR. No. 2763. THURSDAY, DECEMBER 26, 1799.]

    Annapolis: Printed by Frederick and Samuel Green. 1799. fol.

35781 THE MARYLAND HERALD, AND EASTERN SHORE INTELLIGENCER. VOL. IX TH. No.
447. TUESDAY, JANUARY 1, [—VOL. X TH. No. 489. TUESDAY, OCTOBER 29, 1799.]

    Easton: Printed by James Cowan. 1799. fol.   MDHS.

    With the issue for November 5th, the title was changed to *Herald and
Eastern Shore Intelligencer.*

35782 THE MARYLAND HERALD, AND ELIZABETH-TOWN ADVERTISER. VOL. II. No. 97. THURSDAY, JANUARY 3, [— VOL. III. No. 148. THURSDAY, DECEMBER 26, 1799.]
Elizabeth (Hager's) Town: Printed (every Thursday) by Thomas Grieves, near the Court-House. 1799. fol.
MDHS.

35783 MASON, JOHN 1646–1694
SELECT REMAINS OF THE REV. JOHN MASON, M.A. LATE RECTOR OF WATER-STRATFORD, IN THE COUNTY OF BERKS. AUTHOR OF THE SONGS OF PRAISE TO ALMIGHTY GOD. CONTAINING A VARIETY OF DEVOUT AND USEFUL SAYINGS ON DIVERS SUBJECTS, DIGESTED UNDER THEIR PROPER HEADS; RELIGIOUS OBSERVATIONS; SERIOUS ADVICE TO YOUTH; OCCASIONAL REFLECTIONS, &C. AND CHRISTIAN LETTERS. RECOMMENDED BY THE REV. ISAAC WATTS, D.D. WITH A PREFACE, GIVING SOME ACCOUNT OF THE AUTHOR.
Salem: Printed by Joshua Cushing, for B. B. Macanulty. 1799. pp. 189. 8vo.
AAS. EI. JCB. LOC. NYPL.

35784 MASON, THOMAS 1769–1851
A SERMON, DELIVERED AT MIDDLEBURY, VERMONT; ON OCCASION OF THE ANNIVERSARY THANKSGIVING, 1798. BY THOMAS MASON. . . .
Printed at Rutland, Vermont, by John Walker, jun. for the Subscribers. 1799. pp. 18. 8vo.
BM. CHS. LOC. NHHS.

35785 MASON, WILLIAM 1764–1847
A SERMON, DELIVERED AT CASTINE, JANUARY 13TH, 1799. BEING THE SABBATH SUBSEQUENT TO THE INTERMENT OF A YOUNG LADY OF THAT TOWN [Miss Nancy Mann] WHO DIED IN THE 20TH YEAR OF HER AGE. BY WILLIAM MASON, A.M. PASTOR OF THE CHURCH IN CASTINE.
Printed at Castine, (Maine) by David J. Waters. MDCCXCIX. pp. 17. 12mo.
BA. HC. NYHS.

35786 MASSACHUSETTS. STATE.
[Arms.] ACTS AND LAWS, PASSED BY THE GENERAL COURT OF MASSACHUSETTS: AT THE SESSION BEGUN AND HELD AT BOSTON, IN THE COUNTY OF SUFFOLK, ON THURSDAY, THE TENTH DAY OF JANUARY, ANNO DOMINI, 1799. [Colophon:]
Boston: Printed by Young & Minns, State Printers. [1799.] pp. 237–294. fol.
AAS. LOC. NYPL.

35787 —— [Arms.] ACTS AND LAWS, PASSED BY THE GENERAL COURT OF MASSACHUSETTS: AT THE SESSION BEGUN AND HELD AT BOSTON, IN THE COUNTY OF SUFFOLK, ON WEDNESDAY, THE TWENTY-NINTH DAY OF MAY, ANNO DOMINI, 1799. [Colophon:]
Boston: Massachusetts: Printed by Young & Minns, Printers to the honorable General Court. [1799.] pp. 295–339. fol.
AAS. LOC. NYPL.

35788 —— THE BOARD OF HEALTH. COMMONWEALTH OF MASSACHUSETTS. IN THE YEAR 1799. AN ACT TO EMPOWER THE TOWN OF BOSTON TO CHOOSE A BOARD OF HEALTH.
[Boston:] Russell & Cutler, Printers. [1799.] Broadside. fol.

35789 —— [Arms.] COMMONWEALTH OF MASSACHUSETTS. BY HIS EXCELLENCY INCREASE SUMNER, ESQ. GOVERNOR OF THE COMMONWEALTH OF MASSACHUSETTS. A PROCLAMATION, FOR A DAY OF SOLEMN FASTING, HUMILIATION & PRAYER. . . . APPOINT THURSDAY, THE FOURTH OF APRIL NEXT, . . . AND I DO EARNESTLY RECOMMEND THAT ALL SERVILE LABOUR AND RECREATION MAY BE SUSPENDED ON THE SAID DAY. GIVEN AT THE COUNCIL CHAMBER IN BOSTON, THIS TWENTY-EIGHTH DAY OF FEBRUARY, IN THE YEAR OF OUR LORD, ONE THOUSAND SEVEN HUNDRED AND NINETY-NINE, AND IN THE TWENTY-THIRD YEAR OF THE INDEPENDENCE OF THE UNITED STATES OF AMERICA. INCREASE SUMNER. BY HIS EXCELLENCY'S COMMAND, WITH THE ADVICE AND CONSENT OF THE COUNCIL, JOHN AVERY, SECRETARY. GOD SAVE THE COMMONWEALTH OF MASSACHUSETTS! [Colophon:]
[Boston:] Printed by Young and Minns, State Printers. [1799.] Broadside. fol.
AAS. MHS.

MASSACHUSETTS. STATE, continued.

35790 —— [Arms.] COMMONWEALTH OF MASSACHUSETTS. BY HIS HONOR MOSES GILL, ESQ'R. LIEUTENANT-GOVERNOR AND COMMANDER IN CHIEF IN AND OVER THE COMMONWEALTH OF MASSACHUSETTS, A PROCLAMATION FOR A DAY OF PUBLIC THANKSGIVING. . . . THURSDAY, THE TWENTY-EIGHTH DAY OF NOVEMBER NEXT, . . . AND I DO ALSO RECOMMEND TO THE GOOD PEOPLE OF THIS COMMONWEALTH, TO ABSTAIN FROM ALL SERVILE LABOR AND RECREATION UNSUITABLE TO THE RELIGIOUS SOLEMNITIES OF THE SAID DAY. GIVEN AT THE COUNCIL CHAMBER IN BOSTON, THIS SEVENTEENTH DAY OF OCTOBER, IN THE YEAR OF OUR LORD, ONE THOUSAND SEVEN HUNDRED AND NINETY-NINE, AND IN THE TWENTY-FOURTH YEAR OF THE INDEPENDENCE OF THE UNITED STATES OF AMERICA. MOSES GILL. BY HIS HONOR'S COMMAND, WITH THE ADVICE AND CONSENT OF THE COUNCIL. JOHN AVERY, SECRETARY. GOD SAVE THE COMMONWEALTH OF MASSACHUSETTS.

[Boston: Printed by Young and Minns. 1799.] Broadside. fol.   AAS. MHS.

35791 —— GENERAL ORDERS. HEAD-QUARTERS, ROXBURY, MARCH 30, 1799. . . . WILLIAM DONNISON, ADJ. GEN. [Colophon:]

[Boston:] Printed by Young and Minns, Printers to the State. [1799.] Broadside.   EI. MHS.

35792 —— THE COMMITTEE, APPOINTED BY THE LEGISLATURE OF MASSACHUSETTS, TO CONDUCT THE FUNERAL OF HIS (LATE) EXCELLENCY, GOVERNOR SUMNER, REQUEST YOUR ATTENDANCE. . . .

[Boston: Printed by Young and Minns. June 10, 1799.] Broadside.   MHS.

35793 —— ORDER OF PROCESSION FOR THE FUNERAL OF THE LATE GOVERNOR SUMNER. . . .

[Boston: Printed by Young and Minns. 1799.] Broadside.   MHS.

35794 —— THE PERPETUAL LAWS, OF THE COMMONWEALTH OF MASSACHUSETTS, FROM THE ESTABLISHMENT OF ITS CONSTITUTION TO THE SECOND SESSION OF THE GENERAL COURT, IN 1798. IN TWO VOLUMES. VOL. II. CONTAINING THE LAWS FROM MAY, 1788, TO JANUARY, 1799. [BY ISAIAH THOMAS.] [Three lines.]

Printed at Worcester by Isaiah Thomas. 1799. pp. 510. 8vo.   AAS. NL.

The first volume was printed at Worcester, in 1788.

35795 —— REPORT ON THE VIRGINIA RESOLUTIONS, RELATIVE TO THE ALIEN AND SEDITION LAWS, PASSED BY THE CONGRESS OF THE UNITED STATES, MADE BY A COMMITTEE OF THE LEGISLATURE OF MASSACHUSETTS, AS AMENDED BY THE HONORABLE SENATE. [Four columns. Colophon:]

[Boston:] Printed by Young & Minns, Printers to the State. [1799.] Broadside. fol.   AAS.

35796 —— [Arms.] RESOLVES, &C. OF THE GENERAL COURT OF MASSACHUSETTS. PASSED AT THE SESSION BEGUN AND HELD AT BOSTON, ON THURSDAY, THE TENTH DAY OF JANUARY, ANNO DOMINI 1799. [— 1 MARCH, 1799.]

[Boston: Printed by Young and Minns, 1799.] pp. (37)–84. fol.

AAS. LOC. NYPL.

35797 —— —— RESOLVES OF THE GENERAL COURT OF THE COMMONWEALTH OF MASSACHUSETTS. TOGETHER WITH THE LIEUTENANT GOUERNOR'S [*sic*] COMMUNICATIONS, &C. TO THE COURT. BEGUN AND HELD AT BOSTON, IN THE COUNTY OF SUFFOLK, ON WEDNESDAY THE TWENTY-NINTH DAY OF MAY, ANNO DOMINI—M.DCC.XCIX. [— 22 JUNE, 1799.] [Arms.]

Boston: Printed by Young and Minns, Printers to the honorable the General Court. [1799.] pp. 34. fol.   AAS. LOC. NYPL.

35798   MASSACHUSETTS, STATE, continued.
—— TAX FOR THE YEAR 1799. COMMONWEALTH OF [arms] MASSACHUSETTS. PELEG
COFFIN, ESQUIRE, TREASURER AND RECEIVER-GENERAL OF SAID COMMONWEALTH.
TO THE SELECTMEN OR ASSESSORS   GIVEN UNDER MY HAND AND SEAL, AT
BOSTON THE   DAY OF   IN THE YEAR OF OUR LORD, ONE THOUSAND
SEVEN HUNDRED AND NINETY-NINE.

   [Boston: Printed by Young and Minns. 1799.] Broadside. fol.   AAS. LOC.

35799   —— TAX FOR THE YEAR 1799. [Arms.] COMMONWEALTH OF MASSACHUSETTS. IN
THE YEAR OF OUR LORD ONE THOUSAND SEVEN HUNDRED AND NINETY-NINE. AN
ACT TO APPORTION AND ASSESS A TAX OF ONE HUNDRED AND THIRTY-THREE THOU-
SAND, FOUR HUNDRED AND THIRTY-FIVE DOLLARS AND THIRTEEN CENTS, AND PRO-
VIDING FOR THE REIMBURSEMENT OF TWENTY-ONE THOUSAND, FOUR HUNDRED AND
THIRTY-EIGHT DOLLARS PAID OUT OF THE PUBLIC TREASURY, TO THE MEMBERS OF
THE HOUSE OF REPRESENTATIVES FOR THEIR ATTENDANCE THE TWO LAST SESSIONS
OF THE GENERAL COURT.

   [Boston: Printed by Young and Minns. 1799.] pp. 20. fol.   AAS. HSP. LOC.

35800   —— THE STATE OF MASSACHUSETTS FROM THE BEST INFORMATION, 1799.
   New-York: 1799. 9 x 7.

35801   MASSACHUSETTS MISSIONARY SOCIETY.
[Constitution, list of officers and members, and Address] TO ALL, WHO ARE DESIR-
OUS OF THE SPREAD OF THE GOSPEL OF OUR LORD JESUS CHRIST. [Signed, in
behalf of the Society, Nathaniel Emmons, president. Done in Boston, May 28th,
1799. Attest: Samuel Austin, secretary.]
   [Boston: 1799. pp. [8.] 8vo.   AAS. JCB.

35802   MASSACHUSETTS SOCIETY FOR PROMOTING AGRICULTURE.
PAPERS ON AGRICULTURE, CONSISTING OF COMMUNICATIONS MADE TO THE MASSACHU-
SETTS SOCIETY FOR PROMOTING AGRICULTURE, WITH EXTRACTS FROM VARIOUS
PUBLICATIONS; RECOMMENDED TO THE ATTENTION OF FARMERS, BY THE TRUSTEES
OF THE SOCIETY.
   *Boston: Printed by Young and Minns, Printers to the State and to the Agri-
cultural Society.* 1799. pp. 103, plate. 8vo.   AAS. BM. JCB. LOC. NYPL.

35803   MASSACHUSETTS TURNPIKE CORPORATION.
BY LAWS OF THE SIXTH MASSACHUSETTS TURNPIKE CORPORATION, FOR ESTABLISHING
A TURNPIKE ROAD, FROM AMHERST TO SHREWSBURY.
   Worcester: Printed by Mower & Greenleaf. [1799.] pp. (18). (2). 12mo. AAS.

   Contains also, An Act for establishing a corporation by the name of the
   Sixth Massachusetts Turnpike Corporation. And advertisement of its
   shares.

35804   MASSACHUSETTS [arms] MERCURY. NO. 1, OF VOL. XIII. TUESDAY, JANUARY 1,
[— NO. 52 OF VOL. XIV. TUESDAY, DECEMBER 31, 1799.]
   *Boston: Printed by Young and Minns, Printers to the honorable the General
Court.* 1799. fol.   AAS. BA. MHS.

35805   MATILDA, A FAVORITE BALLAD SUNG BY MRS. CHAMBERS IN THE COMEDY OF LOVE'S
FRAILTIES.
   Philadelphia: Printed and sold by G. Willig Market Street No. 185. [1799.]
pp. (2). 4to.   LOC.

35806   MAXCY, JONATHAN   1768–1820
AN ORATION, DELIVERED IN THE FIRST CONGREGATIONAL MEETING-HOUSE, IN PROVI-
DENCE, ON THE FOURTH OF JULY, 1799. BY JONATHAN MAXCY, A. M. PRESIDENT
OF RHODE-ISLAND COLLEGE.
   *Providence: Printed by John Carter, jun. at the new Printing-Office, Market-
Street. 1799. pp. 16. 8vo.*   AAS. BA. BM. CLS. JCB. LOC. MHS. NYPL. RIHS.

35807   MAY, ARTHUR   –1812
AN INAUGURAL DISSERTATION ON SYMPATHY: SUBMITTED TO THE EXAMINATION OF
THE REV. JOHN EWING, S. T. P. PROVOST; THE TRUSTEES & MEDICAL FACULTY, OF THE
UNIVERSITY OF PENNSYLVANIA, ON THE SIXTH DAY OF JUNE, 1799, FOR THE DE-
GREE OF DOCTOR OF MEDICINE. BY ARTHUR MAY, OF PENNSYLVANIA. [One line
of Latin.]
   *Philadelphia: Printed by Way & Groff, No. 48, North Third-Street. 1799.
pp. 30. 8vo.*   AAS. JCB. LOC. NYPL. SGO.

35808   THE MEDICAL REPOSITORY. VOL. II. [NO. I-IV.] [Three lines of Latin from] VIRGIL.
   *New-York: Printed by T. & J. Swords, Printers to the Faculty of Physic of
Columbia College, No. 99 Pearl-Street. 1799. pp. (7), (2), (2), 478, plate by Tis-
dale. 8vo.*   AAS. BA. SGO.

      76th, and 78th New York District Copyright, issued to Samuel Latham
   Mitchell, and Edward Miller, as Proprietors, 4 February, 9 May, 1799.

35809   THE MEDLEY OR NEWBEDFORD MARINE JOURNAL. NO. 11 OF VOLUME VII. WHOLE
NUMBER 323. FRIDAY, JANUARY 4, [— NUMBER 52 ? OF VOLUME VII. WHOLE NUM-
BER 364 ? FRIDAY, OCTOBER 18, 1799.]
   *Newbedford (Massachusetts) Printed and published by John Spooner, at his
office, corner of Water & Prospect Streets. 1799. fol.*   AAS.

      Discontinued at the end of the seventh volume as above.

35810   MELLEN, JOHN, JUNIOR   1752–1828
A DISCOURSE ON NATURAL RELIGION, DELIVERED IN THE CHAPEL OF HARVARD UNI-
VERSITY, IN CAMBRIDGE, SEPTEMBER 4TH, 1799. AT THE LECTURE FOUNDED BY
THE HON. PAUL DUDLEY, ESQ. BY JOHN MELLEN, JUN. PASTOR OF THE EAST CHURCH
IN BARNSTABLE.
   Boston: Printed by Manning & Loring. 1799. pp. [27.] 8vo.
                                    AAS. BA. BM. HC. JCB. LOC. NYPL.

35811   ——— A SERMON PREACHED AT BARNSTABLE, APRIL 28TH, 1799; OCCASIONED BY THE
DEATH OF THE HON. DANIEL DAVIS, ESQ. WHO DEPARTED THIS LIFE ON THE 22D,
IN THE EIGHTY-SIXTH YEAR OF HIS AGE. BY JOHN MELLEN, JUN. PASTOR OF THE
EAST CHURCH IN BARNSTABLE.
   Boston: Printed by Manning & Loring. 1799. pp. [23.] 8vo.
                                              AAS. BA. JCB. LOC.

35812   MERCANTILE [cut] ADVERTISER. OPEN TO ALL PARTIES, BUT INFLUENCED BY NONE.
No. 2012. TUESDAY MORNING, JANUARY 1, [—No. 2317. TUESDAY MORNING, DE-
CEMBER 31, 1799.]
   *Printed and published by John Crookes, for the Proprietor, No. 68 Pine-Street,
New-York. 1799. fol.*   NYHS.

      With the issue for April 22d, it was "Printed and published by James
   Chevalier," who for the past eighteen months had had the direction of
   the paper, at his death August 23d. With the issue for August 27th, it
   was, again, "Printed and published, by John Crookes, for the Proprietor, No. 1, Duane-Street," changed to, No. 68 Pine-Street, in December.

35813   MERCIER, Louis Sébastien   1740–1814
         Memoirs of the year two thousand five hundred. Le tems present est
         gros de l'avenir. Leibnitz. Translated from the French. By William
         Hooper, m.a.

            Richmond: 1799. pp. 360. 12mo.   BM.

35814   MESSER, Asa   1769–1836
         A Discourse, delivered in the chapel of Rhode-Island College, to the senior
         class, on the Sunday preceding their commencement, 1799. By Asa Mes-
         ser, a.m. professor of the learned languages.

            Providence: Printed by John Carter, jun. at the new Printing-Office, Market-
         Street. 1799. pp. 16. 4to.   AAS. JCB. NYPL. RIHS.

35815   —— A Discourse, delivered on thanksgiving-day the 29th of November, 1798,
         at the Congregational meeting-house, in the first precinct in Rehoboth.
         By Asa Messer, a.m. professor of the learned languages in Rhode-Island
         College. Published at the request of the hearers.

            Providence: Printed by John Carter, jun. at the new Printing-Office. Market-
         Street. [1799.] pp. (2), 16. 8vo.   AHTS.

35816   MESSENGER, or MESSINGER, Rosewell   1776–1844
         A Sermon preached at York [Maine] October 21, 1798, by the reverend
         Rosewell Messinger; being the first sermon after his solemn inaugura-
         tion into the Gospel ministry, as colleague pastor with the reverend mr.
         Lyman. Published at the request of the hearers.

            Printed by Samuel Hall, No. 53, Cornhill, Boston. 1799. pp. 23. 8vo.
                                         AAS. BA. BM. JCB. MHS.

35817   A METHOD of raising and training pointers, with instructions and precau-
         tions in selecting them; an account of the several disorders to which they
         are subject, and the proper treatment and medicines in such cases. Trans-
         lated from a celebrated Italian author and found by the experience of
         the translator to be the most effectual.

            Charleston: No. 260, King-Street. 1799.

35818   METHODIST EPISCOPAL CHURCH in America.
         Minutes taken at the several conferences of the Methodist Episcopal
         Church, in America, for the year 1799.

            Philadelphia: Printed by Henry Tuckniss, and sold by Ezekiel Cooper, No.
         47, North Fourth-Street, near Race-Street. MDCCXCIX. *[Price nine cents.]* pp.
         [24.] 12mo.   AAS.

35819   MIDDLESEX COUNTY. Massachusetts. Middlesex Canal.
         Middlesex Canal Navigation. The public are informed that a large boat,
         called Washington, carrying upwards of thirty tons, . . .

            [Boston: 1799.] Broadside.   BPL.

35820   MIDDLESEX Gazette. Vol. xiv. Numb. 685. Friday, January 4, [— Vol. xv.
         Numb. 736. Friday, December 27, 1799.]

            Middletown—(Connecticut)—Printed and published every Friday, by T. Dun-
         ning. 1799. fol.   CHS.

35821 MILLER, SAMUEL 1769–1850
A SERMON, DELIVERED FEBRUARY 5, 1799; RECOMMENDED BY THE CLERGY OF THE
CITY OF NEW-YORK, TO BE OBSERVED AS A DAY OF THANKSGIVING, HUMILIATION,
AND PRAYER, ON ACCOUNT OF THE REMOVAL OF A MALIGNANT AND MORTAL DISEASE,
WHICH HAD PREVAILED IN THE CITY SOME TIME BEFORE. BY SAMUEL MILLER, A. M.
ONE OF THE MINISTERS OF THE UNITED PRESBYTERIAN CHURCHES IN THE CITY OF
NEW-YORK. PUBLISHED BY REQUEST.

New-York: Printed by George Forman. 1799. pp. 36. 8vo.
AAS. BA. CHS. HC. JCB. LOC. NYHS. NYPL. UTS.

35822 THE MINERVA, A LITERARY WEEKLY PAPER.

Richmond: Published by James Lyon. 1799.

Subscriptions were solicited in Norfolk, in July.

35823 THE MIRROR. VOL. VII. No. 323. MONDAY, JANUARY 7, [— VOL. VII. No. 357.
MONDAY, SEPTEMBER 2, 1798.]

Printed and published every Monday morning, by Moses Davis, in Concord,
Newhampshire. 1799. fol. AAS.

In April, "Columbian Independence, twenty-third year. Federal government, eleventh year," was added. The above is the last number
located. On August 27th, Moses Davis established at Hanover, the
Dartmouth Gazette.

35824 —— THE NEWSBOY'S NEW YEAR'S ADDRESS.

[Concord: Printed by Moses Davis. 1799.] Broadside.

35825 THE MIRROR. VOL. II. No. 15. MONDAY, JANUARY 7, [— VOL. II. No. 52 ? TUES-
DAY, SEPTEMBER 7 ? 1799.]

Newburgh, [N. Y.] Published by J. W. Barber. 1799. fol.

In December, Barber entered into partnership with Jacob Schultz, and
established The Orange County Gazette.

35826 THE MIRROR. FIRM, FREE, AND TEMPERATE. VOL. II. No. 17. SATURDAY, JANU-
ARY 5, [— VOL. III ? No. 14 ? SATURDAY, DECEMBER 19, 1799.]

Washington (K.) Printed and published (weekly) by Hunter & Beaumont,
. . . 1799. fol.

On December 19th, the partnership of Hunter & Beaumont was dissolved, and publication of The Mirror ceased.

35827 MIRROR OF THE TIMES, & GENERAL ADVERTISER. [Motto.] VOL. I. No. 1. WEDNES-
DAY, 20TH NOVEMBER, [— No. 12, SATURDAY, 28TH DECEMBER, 1799.]

Wilmington: (Del.) Printed (Wednesdays & Saturdays) by James Wilson,
south side of the upper Market, High-Street. 1799. fol. DHS.

Established by James Wilson, in continuation of The Delaware Gazette,
and continued by him to the issue for the 22 August, 1806, when publication ceased. The motto reads: Here sovereign truth for man's just
rights contends—Alike un-aw'd by foes, un-sway'd by friends.

35828   MISSISSIPPI. TERRITORY.
LAWS OF THE MISSISSIPPI TERRITORY; PUBLISHED AT A SESSION OF THE LEGISLATURE
BEGAN IN THE TOWN OF NATCHEZ, IN THE COUNTY OF ADAMS, AND TERRITORY
AFORESAID, UPON THE 22D DAY OF JANUARY, ANNO DOMINI 1799, AND IN THE 23D
YEAR OF THE INDEPENDANCE [*sic*] OF THE UNITED STATES OF AMERICA: AND
CONTINUED BY ADJOURNMENTS TO THE 25TH DAY OF MAY, IN THE SAME YEAR. BY
AUTHORITY.
> *Natchez: Printed by A. Marschalk, and sold at the Store of messrs. Hunts, &*
> *Co.* 1799. pp. (2), ii, 209. 1 8vo.   NYPL.

35829   MONITEUR DE LA LOUISIANE. No. 116. SAMEDI, 5 JANVIER, [— No. 167. SAMEDI,
28 DÉCEMBRE, 1799.]
> *Nouvelle Orleans:* 1799. 4to.

35830   THE MONITOR. VOL. 15. No. 699. WEDNESDAY, JANUARY 2, [— VOL. 15. No.
750. WEDNESDAY, DECEMBER 25, 1799.]
> *Litchfield, (Connecticut): Printed by Thomas Collier.* 1799. fol.   LOC.

35831   THE MONTHLY MAGAZINE, AND AMERICAN REVIEW, FOR THE YEAR 1799: FROM
APRIL TO DECEMBER INCLUSIVE. [One line of Latin from] VIRGIL. VOL. I. [cut.]
> *New-York: Printed and sold by T. & J. Swords, No. 99 Pearl-Street.* 1800.
> pp. iv, 480. 8vo.   AAS. BA. BM. HC. HSP. LCP. LOC. NYHS. NYPL. NYSL. WHS. YC.

35832   MOODY, or MOODEY, ELEAZAR
THE SCHOOL OF GOOD MANNERS. COMPOSED FOR THE HELP OF PARENTS, IN TEACHING
THEIR CHILDREN HOW TO BEHAVE IN THEIR PLACES, DURING THEIR MINORITY.
> *Dover: Printed by Samuel Bragg, jun.* 1799.

35833   MOORE, GEORGE
GRASVILLE ABBEY: A ROMANCE. IN TWO VOLUMES. VOL. I. [— II.]
> *Salem: Printed by Joshua Cushing, for T. C. Cushing, and B. B. Macanulty.*
> 1799. 2 vols. in one. pp. 170. 16mo.   AAS. EI.

35834   MOORE, JOHN HAMILTON   –1807
THE NEW PRACTICAL NAVIGATOR; BEING AN EPITOME OF NAVIGATION, CONTAINING
THE DIFFERENT METHODS FOR WORKING THE LUNAR OBSERVATIONS, AND ALL THE
REQUISITE TABLES USED WITH THE NAUTICAL ALMANAC, IN DETERMINING THE
LATITUDE AND LONGITUDE AND KEEPING A COMPLETE RECKONING AT SEA. ILLUS-
TRATED BY PROPER RULES AND EXAMPLES. THE WHOLE EXEMPLIFIED IN A JOURNAL
KEPT FROM ENGLAND TO THE ISLAND OF TENERIFFE: ALSO, THE SUBSTANCE OF
INFORMATION EVERY CANDIDATE FOR THE AMERICAN NAVY OUGHT TO BE AC-
QUAINTED WITH, PREVIOUS TO HIS BEING APPOINTED. THIS WITH THE SEA TERMS,
ARE PARTICULARLY RECOMMENDED TO THE ATTENTION OF ALL YOUNG GENTLEMEN
DESIGNED FOR, OR BELONGING TO THE SEA. THE FIRST AMERICAN FROM THE
THIRTEENTH ENGLISH EDITION OF JOHN HAMILTON MOORE, IMPROVED BY THE
INTRODUCTION OF SEVERAL NEW TABLES, AND BY LARGE ADDITIONS TO THE FORMER
TABLES, AND REVISED AND CORRECTED BY A SKILFUL MATHEMATICIAN AND NAVI-
GATOR. ILLUSTRATED WITH COPPER PLATES. TO WHICH ARE ADDED, SOME GENERAL
INSTRUCTIONS AND INFORMATION TO MERCHANTS, MASTERS OF VESSELS, AND OTHERS
CONCERNED IN NAVIGATION, RELATIVE TO THE MERCANTILE AND MARITIME LAWS
AND CUSTOMS.
> *Newburyport: Printed by Edmund M. Blunt.* [1799.] pp. 574, plates and
> diagrams. 8vo.   AAS. BM.

167th Massachusetts District Copyright, issued to Edmund M. Blunt, as
Proprietor, 24 May, 1799.

MOORE, John Hamilton, continued.

35835 —— The Young gentleman and lady's monitor, and English teacher's assist-ant: being a collection of select pieces from our best modern writers: calculated to eradicate vulgar prejudices and rusticity of manners; im-prove the understanding; rectify the will; purify the passions; direct the minds of youth to the pursuit of proper objects; and to facilitate their reading, writing, and speaking the English language, with elegance and propriety. Particularly adapted for the use of our eminent schools and academies, as well as private persons, who have not an opportunity of perusing the works of those celebrated authors, from whence this collection is made. Divided into small portions for the ease of reading in classes. The latest edition. By J. Hamilton Moore. Author of the Practical navigator and Seaman's new daily assistant.

New-York: Printed by John Tiebout, No. 358, Pearl-Street, for R. Macgill, J. Reid, J. Harrisson, E. Duyckinck, C. Davis, Brown and Stansbury, T. B. Jan-sen, S. Stevens, N. Judah, T. Arden, A. Summervill, and Bell and Smith. 1799. pp. vi, 370, (6), 4 plates. 12mo.   AAS.

Second heading: Elements of gesture. [By John Walker.] pp. (335)–370. 4 plates.

35836 MOORE, Thomas, pseudonym.
Gaine's New-York Pocket Almanack, for the year 1800: and 24th of American independence, 'till 4th July. Calculated for this and the neighbouring States. Signs, planets, and aspects. [Twelve lines.] By Thomas Moore, philo.

New-York: Printed by H. Gaine, at the Bible, in Pearl-Street. [1799.] pp. (26), interleaved. 32mo.   AAS. LOC.

35837 MORSE, Jedidiah   1761–1826
An Address, to the students at Phillips Academy, in Andover. Delivered July 9, 1799. Being the day of the anniversary exhibition. By Jedidiah Morse, d.d. Published at the request of the trustees.

Tharlestown [sic]: Printed by Samuel Etheridge. 1799. pp. [16.] 8vo.
AAS. BA. BM. JCB. LOC. MHS. NYHS. NYPL. YC.

35838 —— A Sermon, exhibiting the present dangers, and consequent duties of the citizens of the United States of America. Delivered at Charlestown, April 25, 1799. The day of the national fast. By Jedidiah Morse, d.d. pastor of the church in Charlestown. Published at the request of the hearers.

Charlestown: Printed and sold by Samuel Etheridge. 1799. pp. 50. 8vo.
AAS. BA. BM. CHS. CLA. HC. JCB. LOC. NYHS. NYPL. YC.

Second title: La Sagesse. No. 2660. Tableau des F. F. qui composent la Loge Provinciale Francaise, sous le titre distinctif de la Sagesse: a l'orient de Portsmouth en Virginie, etat de l'Amerique Septentrionale, a l'epoque de la St. Jean, 5798.

Norfolk: Imprime par Willett & O'Conner [sic.] [1798.]

Third title: Wisdom. No. 2660. Table of the brethren who compose the Provincial French Lodge, under the distinctive title of Wisdom: in the east of Portsmouth, in Virginia, State of North America. In the epoch of St. John, 1798.

Norfolk: Printed by Willett & O'Conner [sic.] [1798.] pp. 36–45.

MORSE, JEDIDIAH, continued.

35839 —— — A SERMON, EXHIBITING THE PRESENT DANGERS, AND CONSEQUENT DUTIES OF THE CITIZENS OF THE UNITED STATES OF AMERICA. DELIVERED AT CHARLESTOWN, APRIL 25, 1799. THE DAY OF THE NATIONAL FAST. BY JEDIDIAH MORSE, D.D. PASTOR OF THE CHURCH IN CHARLESTOWN. PUBLISHED AT THE REQUEST OF THE HEARERS. [Ornament.]

Charlestown, Printed: Hartford: Re-printed by Hudson and Goodwin. 1799. pp. 42. 8vo.   CHS. JCB. NYPL. UTS. YC.

Second title: LA SAGESSE. No. 2660. [In cut:] TABLEAU DES F. F. QUI COMPOSENT LA LOGE PROVINCIALE FRANCAISE, SOUS LE TITRE DISTINCTIF DE LA SAGESSE: A L'ORIENT DE PORTSMOUTH, EN VIRGINIE, ETAT DE L'AMERIQUE SEPTENTRIONALE, A L'EPOQUE DE LA ST. JEAN, 5798.

Norfolk: Imprime par Willett & O'Conner [sic]. [1798.] pp. (28)–32.

Third title: WISDOM. No. 2660. TABLE OF THE BRETHREN WHO COMPOSE THE PROVINCIAL FRENCH LODGE, UNDER THE DISTINCTIVE TITLE OF WISDOM: IN THE EAST OF PORTSMOUTH, IN VIRGINIA, STATE OF NORTH AMERICA. IN THE EPOCH OF ST. JOHN, 5798.

Norfolk: Printed by Willett and O'Conner [sic]. 1798. pp. (33)–37.

35840 —— — A SERMON, EXHIBITING THE PRESENT DANGERS, AND CONSEQUENT DUTIES OF THE CITIZENS OF THE UNITED STATES OF AMERICA. DELIVERED AT CHARLESTOWN, APRIL 25, 1799, THE DAY OF THE NATIONAL FAST. BY JEDIDIAH MORSE, D.D. PASTOR OF THE CHURCH IN CHARLESTOWN. PUBLISHED AT THE REQUEST OF THE HEARERS.

New-York: Printed for and sold by Cornelius Davis, No. 94, Water-Street. 1799. pp. (36). 8vo.   AAS. BM. JCB. LOC. MHS. NYHS. NYPL. UTS.

Second title: WISDOM. No. 2660. TABLE OF THE BRETHREN WHO COMPOSE THE PROVINCIAL FRENCH LODGE, UNDER THE DISTINCTIVE TITLE OF WISDOM: IN THE EAST OF PORTSMOUTH, IN VIRGINIA, STATE OF NORTH AMERICA. IN THE EPOCH OF ST. JOHN, 5798.

Norfolk: Printed by Willett and O'Conner [sic.] [1798.]

35841 —— A SERMON, PREACHED AT CHARLESTOWN, NOVEMBER 29, 1798. ON THE ANNIVERSARY THANKSGIVING IN MASSACHUSETTS. WITH AN APPENDIX, DESIGNED TO ILLUSTRATE SOME PARTS OF THE DISCOURSE; EXHIBITING PROOFS OF THE EARLY EXISTENCE, PROGRESS AND DELETERIOUS EFFECTS OF FRENCH INTRIGUE AND INFLUENCE IN THE UNITED STATES. BY JEDEDIAH [sic] MORSE, D.D. PASTOR OF THE CHURCH IN CHARLESTOWN.

Printed at Worcester, Massachusetts, by Daniel Greenleaf, July 10, 1799. pp. 88. 8vo.   AAS. BM. JCB. LOC. NYHS.

35842 —— — A SERMON, PREACHED AT CHARLESTOWN, NOVEMBER 29, 1798, ON THE ANNIVERSARY THANKSGIVING IN MASSACHUSETTS. WITH AN APPENDIX, DESIGNED TO ILLUSTRATE SOME PARTS OF THE DISCOURSE; EXHIBITING PROOFS OF THE EARLY EXISTENCE, PROGRESS, AND DELETERIOUS EFFECTS OF FRENCH INTRIGUE AND INFLUENCE IN THE UNITED STATES. BY JEDIDIAH MORSE, D.D. PASTOR OF THE CHURCH IN CHARLESTOWN. SECOND EDITION.

Boston: Printed by Samuel Hall. 1799. pp. [79.] 8vo.

AAS. BA. BM. CHS. HC. JCB. LOC. NYPL. UTS. YC.

35843 —— — A SERMON, PREACHED AT CHARLESTOWN, NOVEMBER 29, 1798, ON THE ANNIVERSARY THANKSGIVING IN MASSACHUSETTS. WITH AN APPENDIX, DESIGNED TO ILLUSTRATE SOME PARTS OF THE DISCOURSE; EXHIBITING PROOFS OF THE EARLY EXISTENCE, PROGRESS, AND DELETERIOUS EFFECTS OF FRENCH INTRIGUE AND INFLUENCE IN THE UNITED STATES. BY JEDIDIAH MORSE, D.D. PASTOR OF THE CHURCH IN CHARLESTOWN. THIRD EDITION.

Printed by Samuel Hall, No. 53, *Cornhill, Boston.* 1799. pp. 79. 8vo.   NYHS.

35844   MORTON, SARAH WENTWORTH APTHORP   1759–1846
THE VIRTUES OF SOCIETY. A TALE, FOUNDED ON FACT. BY THE AUTHOR OF THE
VIRTUES OF NATURE. [Two lines from] CARTWRIGHT. PUBLISHED ACCORDING TO
ACT OF CONGRESS.

     Boston: Printed by Manning & Loring, for the Author. 1799. pp. [46.]
4to.   AAS. BA. BU. JCB. LOC. NYHS. NYPL.

     In verse. A poem entitled "To Time," pp. 39-46. 170th Massachusetts
District Copyright, issued to Perez Morton, as Proprietor for the benefit
of the Author, 19 July, 1799.

35845   MORTON, THOMAS   1764–1838
SECRETS WORTH KNOWING: A COMEDY, IN FIVE ACTS. AS PERFORMED AT THE THE-
ATRE ROYAL, COVENT GARDEN. BY THOMAS MORTON, ESQ. . . .

     London: Printed: New-York: Re-printed by J. Buel. 1799. pp. 48. 12mo.
           NYPL.

35846   THE MOTHER'S GIFT; OR A PRESENT FOR ALL LITTLE CHILDREN WHO WISH TO BE
GOOD.

     Printed at Worcester, Massachusetts, by Isaiah Thomas, jun. 1799.

35847   MOTHER GOOSE'S MELODY: OR SONNETS FOR THE CRADLE. IN TWO PARTS. PART I.
CONTAINS THE MOST CELEBRATED SONGS AND LULLABIES OF THE GOOD OLD NURSES
CALCULATED TO AMUSE CHILDREN AND TO EXCITE THEM TO SLEEP. PART II. THOSE
OF THAT SWEET SONGSTER AND NURSE OF WIT AND HUMOR, MASTER WILLIAM
SHAKESPEARE. EMBELLISHED WITH CUTS, AND ILLUSTRATED WITH NOTES AND MAX-
IMS HISTORICAL, PHILOSOPHICAL AND CRITICAL. THE THIRD WORCESTER EDITION.

     *Printed at Worcester, Massachusetts, By Isaiah Thomas, jun. Sold wholesale
and retail by him.*—1799. pp. 94, (2), frontispiece. 32mo.   AAS.

     Reprinted in facsimile in Boston, in 1892.

35848   MOUNSEER NONG TONG PAW.

     *Boston: Published at P. A. von Hagen, jun. and Co's, No. 55 Marlboro'
Street.* 1799.

35849   THE MOUNT-PLEASANT COURIER. VOL. I. NO. 1. JUNE 19, [— 1799.]
     Mount-Pleasant, New-York. Published by John Patterson. 1799. fol.

     Established, as a weekly, by John Patterson, from the same Office, and
in continuation of *The Mount-Pleasant Register,* and only known
through a single copy, as above, in private hands.

35850   MULLEN, JOHN
THE BALTIMORE DIRECTORY FOR 1799   A REGISTER OF THE EXECUTIVE, LEG-
ISLATIVE, AND JUDICIAL OFFICERS OF THE UNITED STATES — THE CONSTITUTION
OF THE UNITED STATES — THE OFFICERS OF THE COMMONWEALTH OF MARYLAND,
MAGISTRATES OF THE CITY. WITH AN ACCURATE TABLE OF THE DUTIES ON GOODS,
WARES AND MERCHANDIZE. TOGETHER WITH A GENERAL ABSTRACT FROM THE
REVENUE LAWS, RELATIVE TO THE DUTIES OF MASTERS OF VESSELS — OF THE OWN-
ERS OR CONSIGNEES OF GOODS — OF OFFICERS OF THE CUSTOMS — OF PAYMENT OF
DUTIES, &C. — AND THE FORM OF ENTRY AT THE CUSTOM-HOUSE ON THE IMPORTA-
TION OF GOODS. TO ALL WHICH ARE ADDED, AN ACCOUNT OF THE POST OFFICE
ESTABLISHMENT — THE BANKS — TABLES OF MONIES, &C. — WITH AN ALPHABETICAL
LIST OF THE STREETS, LANES AND ALLEYS. BY JOHN MULLEN.

     *[Baltimore:] Printed for the Editor, by Warner & Hanna, No. 2, North Gay
Street.* 1799. pp. [142.] 12mo.   MdHS.

35851   MURRAY, LINDLEY   1745–1826
THE ENGLISH READER: OR, PIECES IN PROSE AND POETRY, SELECTED FROM THE BEST
WRITERS. DESIGNED TO ASSIST YOUNG PEOPLE TO READ WITH PROPRIETY AND
EFFECT; TO IMPROVE THEIR LANGUAGE AND SENTIMENTS, AND TO INCULCATE SOME
OF THE MOST IMPORTANT PRINCIPLES OF PIETY AND VIRTUE. WITH A FEW PRE-
LIMINARY OBSERVATIONS ON THE PRINCIPLES OF GOOD READING. BY LINDLEY
MURRAY, AUTHOR OF "ENGLISH GRAMMAR ADAPTED TO THE DIFFERENT CLASSES
OF LEARNERS," &C.

     New-York: Printed and sold by Isaac Collins, No. 189. *Pearl-Street.* 1799.
pp. xxxvi, 359. 16mo.   JCB.

35852   —— EXTRACTS FROM THE WRITINGS OF DIVERS EMINENT AUTHORS, OF DIFFERENT
RELIGIOUS DENOMINATIONS; AND AT VARIOUS PERIODS OF TIME, REPRESENTING
THE EVILS AND PERNICIOUS EFFECTS OF STAGE PLAYS, AND OTHER VAIN AMUSE-
MENTS. BY LINDLEY MURRAY, WITH SOME ADDITIONS.

     Philadelphia: Reprinted by Benjamin & Jacob Johnson, No. 147, *High Street.*
1799. pp. 24. 8vo.   AAS. BM. LOC. NYPL.

35853   —— THE POWER OF RELIGION ON THE MIND, IN RETIREMENT, AFFLICTION, AND AT
THE APPROACH OF DEATH: EXEMPLIFIED IN THE TESTIMONIES AND EXPERIENCE OF
PERSONS DISTINGUISHED BY THEIR GREATNESS, LEARNING, OR VIRTUE. [Three lines
from] YOUNG. FROM THE SEVENTH EDITION, CORRECTED AND MUCH ENLARGED.

     New-Bedford: Printed by Abraham Shearman, jun. 1799. pp. viii, 232.
12mo.   AAS. JCB.

     Second title: APPENDIX: CONTAINING AN ACCOUNT OF THE PLAGUE IN LONDON;
AND SOME EXTRACTS FROM THE WRITINGS OF PIOUS AND EMINENT MEN, AGAINST
THE ENTERTAINMENTS OF THE STAGE, AND OTHER VAIN AMUSEMENTS. pp. (2),
(183)–232.

35854   MYSERAS, LAMBRECHT
LAMBRECHT MYSERAS IN MIDDELBURG EMPFINDUNGEN UND ERFAHRUNGEN DER
FROMMEN AUF DEM WEGE NACH DEM HIMMEL EHEMAL AUS DEM HOLLÄNDISCHEN
IN DAS HOCHTEUTSCHE ÜBERSETZET. NUNMEHRO ABER VERBESSERT UND MIT
EINIGEN ANMERKUNGEN VERMEHRET. VIERTE AUFLAGE.

     York: Gedruckt bey Salomon Mäyer. 1799. pp. 395. 12mo.   AAS. HSP. LOC.

TO BE CONTINUED IN THE NEXT VOLUME.

BEERS, ANDREW, *cont.*
Farmer's, 1799   33389
Same, 1800   35167
Same, 1800   35168
Franklin's, 1799   35169
Greenleaf's, 1799   33390
Same, 1800   35170
Same, 1800   35171
Hutchin's, 1800   35172
Stoddard's, 1799   33391
Same, 1800   35173
Webster, 1799   33392
Same, 1800   35174
BEGGARLY boy   35297
BELAIR, ALEXANDRE, P. J. DE
Fortification   35175
BELKNAP, JEREMY, 1744–1798
Account of J. Clarke   34642
American biography, Vol. II 33393
Fast sermon, 1798   33394
BELL, SAMUEL
Masonic oration, 1798   33736
BELL, WILLIAM, 1731–1816
Lord's Supper   35176
BELLAMY, JOSEPH, 1719–1790
Gospel of Christ   33397
Theron, Paulinus, etc.   33396
BELLAMY, THOMAS
Fatal effects of seduction   34307
BELLINGER, JOHN SKOTTOWE
Pneumony   35177
BENEZET, ANTHONY, 1713–1784
Account of Quakers   35178
Same, Baltimore   35518
Considerations on war   35518
BENHAM, ASAHEL
Social harmony   33398
BENJAMIN, ASHER, 1773–1845
Country builder   33399
BENJAMIN, JONATHAN
Harmonia cœlestis   35179
BENNETT, AGNES MARIA, –1808
Beggar girl   33401
BENNETT, JOHN
Letters to young lady   33402
Same, Worcester   33403
BENNEVILLE, GEORGE DE, 1703–93
Lebenslauf   33404
BENTLEY, WILLIAM, 1759–1819
Masonic address, 1798   35180
Masonic charge, 1798   33405
Robison's Proofs   35181
BERESFORD, RICHARD, 1755–1803
Learned languages   35182

BERINGTON, SIMON, 1680–1755
Gaudentio di Lucca   35183
BERKELEY Intelligencer, 1799 35184
BERKSHIRE Gazette, 1798   33406
Same, 1799   35185
BERNE. Œconomical Society
Essays   33407
Same, 1799   35186
BERRIMAN, JACOB M.
Monstrous snake   35187
BETTY Brown, the orange girl 35298
BIBLIA
Holy Bible   33408
Same, Philadelphia   35188
Same, Worcester   33409
Same, Worcester   35189
The Bible. 9th edition   33410
Same   35190
History of the Bible   33411
BIBLIA. O. T. Genesis
Jewish tradition of Moses   35297
BIBLIA. O. T. Psalms
Psalms of David   33412
Carefully suited to worship 35191
Imitated. Boston   35192
Same, Brookfield   35193
Same   35194
Same, Hartford   35195
Same, Northampton   35196
PSALMS in metre   33414
Same, New York   34420
Tate and Brady   35222
BIBLIA. New Testament
Same, New-Haven   33415
Same   35199
Same, Philadelphia   35197
Same   35198
Same, Wilmington   33416
Same, for children   33417
Same   35458
BIBLIA. N. T. Gospels
Four Gospels. Tr. Campbell 35200
Same, in Arawak   35201
BIBLIA. N. T. Matthew
Spiegel für alle menschen   35202
BICKERSTAFF, ISAAC. 1735–1787
Ambrose Gwinett   33418
BICKNELL, ALEXANDER, –1796
Philip Quarll   35203
BIGELOW, TIMOTHY, 1767–1821
Oration, int. S. Dana   33419
BIGLOW, WILLIAM, 1773–1874
Education   35204
New Year's Address   34511

BINGHAM, CALEB, 1757–1817
American preceptor. 5th ed. 33420
Same, 6th edition   35205
Same, 7th edition   35206
Same, Walpole   35207
Astronomical catechism   33421
Columbian orator, 2d ed.   35208
Young lady's accidence,
11th edition   35209
BIRCH, SAMUEL, 1757–1841
Adopted child   33422
Songs in   33423
BIRCH, THOMAS LEDLIE, –1808
Letter from Irish emigrant 33424
Same, Philadelphia   35210
BISHOP, ABRAHAM, 1763–1844
Georgia speculation. Part II. 33425
BLACK GILES, the poacher   35298
BLACKSTONE, Sir WILLIAM
Commentaries. 4 vols.   35211
BLAIR, HUGH, 1718–1800
Rhetoric   33426
BLAIR, SAMUEL, 1741–1818
Fast discourse, 1798   33427
Funeral discourse, J. B. Smith 35212
BLAKE, WILLIAM P.
Catalogue of books   33428
BLATCHFORD, SAMUEL, 1767–1828
Address, 4 July, 1798   33429
Presbyterian ordination   33430
BLAUVELT, ABRAHAM
Almanac, 1799   33431
Same, 1800   35213
Same, Pocket   35214
Same, Sheet   35215
BLOODY Indian battle, 1791 33432
BLUNT, EDMUND MARCH
Navigator   33433
BONNY Wully: ballad   33809
BOOTH, ABRAHAM, 1734–1806
Reign of grace   33434
BORDLEY, JOHN BEALE, 1727–1804
Country habitations   33435
Hemp   35217
Husbandry   35216
BOSTON, Mass.
Notification: Boylston will 35218
Schedule of expenses   35219
To President and Congress 33436
BOSTON. Board of Health
To constituents   35220
BOSTON. Charitable Fire Society
Performances   33437
BOSTON. Marine Insurance Co.
Incorporation   35221
BOSTON. Mutual Fire Insurance Co. Rules   33438

HAMILTON, JOSEPH
Small-pox   33835
Same, New York   35582
HAMPSHIRE COUNTY. Associa-
tion. Sermons   35583
HAMPSHIRE Gazette, 1798   33836
Same, 1799   35584
HAENDEL, GEORG FRIEDRICH
Water music   33837
HANSFORD, THEODOSIUS
Debate on Alien and Sedi-
tion laws   34935
HANWAY, JONAS, 1712–1786
Travels   35585
HAPPY waterman   35297
HARDIE, JAMES, 1758–1826
Fever in New York   35586
HARPER, ROBERT G., 1765–1825
Georgia sales   35587
Same   35588
Letter, to constituent   33838
Observations, 3d edition   33841
Same, 4th edition   33842
Same   33843
Speech, conduct of France   33844
Speech, foreign intercourse   33839
Same   33840
Same   33842
Same   33843
Speech, the navy   35589
HARRIS, THADDEUS M., 1768–1842
Century sermon, 1799   35590
Fast sermon, 1798   33847
Free masonry   33846
Masonic discourse, 1798   33845
Masonic sermon, 1798   35591
Masonic sermon 1798   35592
HARRIS, WALTER, 1761–1843
Fast discourse, 1799   35593
HARRIS, WILLIAM, 1765–1829
Convention sermon, 1799   35594
HARRISON, RALPH, 1748–1810
English grammar   33848
Same   33849
HART, JOSEPH, 1712–1768
Hymns, 15th edition   35595
HART, LEVI, 1738–1808
Funeral discourse, T. Stone   33850
HARTFORD, CONN.
Funeral observance for
Washington   35596
Grammar school   33555
Turnpike road   33560
HARTMANN, HENRICH
Besondere Kunst   33851
Wahre Brantewein-Bren-
nerey   33851

HARVARD UNIVERSITY
Laws   33854
Order of exercises, 1798   33852
Same, 1799   35597
Theses, 1798   33853
Same, 1799   35598
HARVEST home   35297
HARWOOD, JOHN E., 1771–1809
Ellen arise   33855
HASWELL, ANTHONY, 1756–1816
Almanac, 1800   35600
Oration, Bennington, 1799   35599
Lyon's release   35601
HASWELL, LYDIA B., 1759–1799
Family records   35602
HAVEN, SAMUEL, 1727–1806
Dudleian lecture, 1798   33857
Oration, 4 July, 1799   35603
Poetic miscellany   33856
HAVERHILL Federal Gazette,
1798   33858
Same, 1799   35604
HAWEIS, THOMAS, 1734–1820
Word in season   34312
HAWKESWORTH, JOHN, 1725–1773
Almoran and Hamet   33859
HAWKINS, JOSEPH, 1772–
Lottery for his benefit   33861
Voyage to Africa   33860
HAWLES, Sir JOHN, 1645–1716
Englishman's right   33862
HAY, GEORGE, 1765–1830
Liberty of the press   35605
HAYDN, FRANZ JOSEPH, 1732–1809
Rondo   35606
Sonatina   33863
HAYES, JOEL, 1753–1827
Family religion   35583
HAYNES, LEMUEL, 1753–1833
Civil government   33864
HAYWOOD, JOHN, 1762–1826
Reports of cases   35607
HEATH, WILLIAM, 1737–1814
Memoirs   33865
HEAVING the lead   33908
HEIDELBERG Catechism   33412
Same, in German   33866
Same, Albany   35609
Same   35453
HEIRESS of Devon   34525
HELME, ELIZABETH
History of Louisa   33867
Rambles in London   35610
HENING, WILLIAM W., 1768–1828
New Virginia justice   35611
Same   35612

HENRY, MATTHEW, 1662–1714
Communicant's companion   33868
HERALD and Eastern Shore-
Intelligencer, 1799   35613
HERALD of Freedom, 1799   35614
HERALD of Liberty, 1798   33869
Same, 1799   35615
HERALD of United States,
1798   33870
Same, 1799   35616
HERMIT of the forest   33871
HERTY, THOMAS
Digest of Maryland laws   35617
HERVEY, JAMES, 1714–1758
Meditations   33872
HESTER WILMOT   35298
HETH, WILLIAM, 1750–1807
Infallible cure   33873
Same   33874
HEWITT, JAMES
How happy my lot   35618
HILLIARD, JOSEPH, –1843
Duties of pastor and people   33875
HINDMAN, WILLIAM, 1743–1822
French aggression   35619
HINT to Free-masons   35620
HISTORY of American Revo-
lution   33879
HISTORY of boy under hay-
cock   33876
HISTORY of Charles Mortimer   33615
HISTORY of Constantius &
Pulchera   33877
HISTORY of Goody Two Shoes   35621
HISTORY of Kitty Pride   35622
HISTORY of Mr. Fantom   35298
HISTORY of little Ann   33878
HISTORY of Pauline   34525
HISTORY of British Empire   33879
HISTORY of Duchess of C.   33880
HISTORY of plague, 1665   35287
Same   35853
HISTORY of Tommy Careless   33881
Same, Worcester   35623
HISTORY of Tommy Ginger-
bread   33882
HITCHCOCK, ENOS, 1745–1803
Sermon ord. E. Fisk   35624
THE HIVE, 1798   33883
HOBBY, WILLIAM J., –1841
Oration, 4 July, 1798   33884
Oration, 4 July, 1799   35625
HOBSON, JOHN
Liberal education   35626
HOCH-DEUTSCHE Ameri-
canische Calender, 1799   33885
Same, 1800   35627

PITT, C. I.
Poor blind girl   34383
PITTSBURGH Gazette, 1798   34384
PLAIN account of baptism   34385
PLEA for peace   34312
PLEASANT, Mrs., pseud.
Story book   34386
POCKET miscellany   34387
POETIC miscellany   34388
POLITE lady   34389
POLITICAL address   34390
POLITICAL Focus, 1798   34391
POLITICAL Repository, 1798   34392
POMMERUEL, F.R.J.DE, 1745–1823
Buonaparte in Italy   34393
POOR ROBIN, pseud.
Almanack, 1799   34394
POOR WILL, pseud.
Almanack, 1799   34396
Pocket Almanack, 1799   34397
POPE, ALEXANDER, 1688–1744
Essay on man   34398
PORCUPINE's Gazette, 1798   34399
PORTER, ELIPHALET, 1758–1833
Fast discourse, 1798   34401
PORTER, NATHANIEL, 1745–1837
Friendly monitor   34402
PORTLAND, ME. Marine
Society. Laws   34403
PORTLAND Gazette, 1798   34404
Same, 1799   35668
POTE, JEREMY
Narrative   34405
POTOMAK Guardian, 1798   34406
POTTER, ISAIAH, 1746–1817
Sermon, death of two men   34407
POUGHKEEPSIE Journal, 1798   34408
POWNALL, MARY A. W., –1796
Jemmy of the glen   34409
PRESBYTERIAN CHURCH in
U. S. A. Acts, 1798   34410
PRICE, ISAAC
Jersey man's common sense   34411
PRIDEAUX, HUMPHREY, 1648–1724
Life of Mahomet   34412
PRIESTLEY, JOSEPH, 1733–1804
Catechism   34413
PRINCE, JOHN, 1751–1836
Fast discourse, 1798   34414
Same, 2d edition   34415
Same, 3d edition   34416
PRINCE of Brittany   34417
PRIOLEAU, PHILIP GENDRON
Acids, in diseases   34418
PROTESTANT EPISCOPAL CHURCH
in N.J. Proceedings, 1798   34419

PROTESTANT EPISCOPAL CHURCH
in United States.
Book of common prayer   34420
Catechism, Ed. Clarke   33519
PROUD, ROBERT, 1728–1813
History of Pennsylvania.   34421
PROUDFIT, ALEXANDER M.
Sermon, Missionary society   34422
PROVIDENCE, R. I. Congrega-
tional Church. Catechism   34424
PROVIDENCE, R. I. Mechanics
Association. Charter, etc.   34423
PROVIDENCE Gazette, 1798   34425
PUCKLE, JAMES, 1667–1724
Grey-cap for green-head   34426
PUTNAM, AARON, 1734–1813
Being of God   34427
PUTNEY Argus, 1798   34428

QUINCY, JOSIAH,, 1772–1864
Oration, 4 July, 1798   34429
Same, 2d edition   34430
Same, Philadelphia   34431

RAMSAY, ALLAN, 1685–1758
Gentle shepherd   34432
RANLET, HENRY
Almanack, 1799   34433
RANLET's Federal Miscellany,
1798   34434
READING, PA. Theatre.
Play-bill   34435
REDFIELD, LEVI, 1745–
Life   34436
REFORMED DUTCH CHURCH
Catechism   33412
Confession of faith   33412
Government and discipline   33412
Liturgy   33412
Psalms and hymns   33412
RELIGIOUS Monitor, 1798   34437
REMARKABLE duel   33533
REMARKABLE prophecy   34438
REPLY to Address, by great I   34439
REPUBLICAN Journal, 1798   34440
RHEES, MORGAN J., 1760–1804
Altar of peace   34441
Liberty and slavery   34442
RHOADS, ASA
American spelling-book   34443

RHODE ISLAND
Acts, 1797–1798   34444
Assessors of lands   34451
Militia   34448
Proclamation of Laws   34449
Public laws   34453
Rhode-Island Brigade   34455
Tax, $20,000   34450
RHODE ISLAND COLLEGE
Catalogus eorum, 1798   34456
Junior exhibition, 1798   34458
Senior exhibition, 1798   34459
Order of exercises, 1798   34457
Theses, 1798   34460
RHODES, JOHN, 1755–
Adventures   34461
RICHARD, OLD FATHER. pseud.
Almanack, 1799   34462
RICHARDSON, SAMUEL, 1689–1761
Clarissa Harlowe   34463
Same, Philadelphia   34464
Sir Charles Grandison   34465
RICHMOND, EDWARD, 1767–1842
Sermon, ord. L.Wadsworth   34467
RIGHTS of man (Winter), 1798   34468
RIGHTS of man (Moffett),
1798   34469
RILEY, GEORGE
Beauties of creation   34470
RIPLEY, EZRA, 1751–1841
Prayer   34150
Sermon, ord. R. Messinger   34471
RIPLEY, HEZEKIAH, 1743–1831
Sermon, instal. W.R.Ripley   34472
RISING SUN, 1798   34473
THE RISING Sun, 1798   34474
ROBERTS, WILLIAM, 1767–1849
Eugenio and Amelia   34475
ROBERTSON, JOHN
Latitude and departure   35670
ROBERTSON, WILLIAM, 1721–1793
History of America. 2 vols.   34476
ROBISON, JOHN, 1739–1805
Proofs of conspiracy   34477
Same, 4th edition   34478
Extracts from Proofs   35181
ROBSON, JOHN C.
Monarchies in world   34479
ROCHE, REGINA M. D., 1764–1845
Children of the Abbey   34480
Clermont   34481
RODGERS, JOHN, 1727–1811
Charge to missionary   35738
ROGERS, RANSFORD
Morris-Town ghosts   34482
ROLAND DE LA PLATIERE, M. J. P.
Appeal to posterity   34483

BIBLIOGRAPHY.

FRANKLIN, MASS. Parish Library. Benjamin Franklin donation   33673
NEW YORK. Caritat's Circulating Library. Catalogue 35279
PHILADELPHIA. Library Company. 4th Supplement   34357
TRENTON, N. J. Library Company. Regulations   34679
WAREHAM, MASS. Social Library. Catalogue   34955
SALE catalogues: 33428, 33497, 33982, 34165, 35267, 35278, 35279
WRITING: 33703, 34177, 34315, 35578
PRINTING and publishing: 34030, 34110, 34310, 34466, 35316, 35419, 35489, 35646, 35713

BIOGRAPHY.

ANTHONY, SUSANNA. By S. Hopkins   35635
BELKNAP, J. American biography   33393
BENNEVILLE, GEORGE DE. By himself   33404
BEVERIDGE, THOMAS. By W. Marshall   35771
BURROUGHS, STEPHEN. Memoirs   33478
CALVIN, JOHN. Life   35737
COBBETT, WILLIAM. By J. Carey   33493
DECALOGUE, JEAN MARIE. Life   35390
FRANCIS XAVIER, saint. Life 33754
FRANKLIN, BENJAMIN. By himself   33755–33758, 33497, 33498
FRASER, D. Select biography 33760
GODWIN, MARY WOLLSTONECRAFT. By W. Godwin   35556
HASWELL, L. B. Family records   35602
HEATH, WILLIAM. By himself   33865
JONES, MRS. —— Anonymous   35079
JOSEPH. By J. Macgowan   34037
LUTHER, MARTIN. Life   35737
MIDDLETON, E. Evangelical biography   34808

MOHAMMED. By H. Prideaux 34412
MUNSON, LENT. By A. V. Griswold   33827
NAPOLEON BUONAPARTE. By —— Paultier   34551
OSBORN, SARAH. By S. Hopkins   35636
PHILLIPS, CATHERINE P. Memoirs   34371
POTE, JEREMY. Narrative   34405
PUTNAM, ISRAEL. By D. Humphreys   33914
REDFIELD, LEVI. By himself 34436
SCOTT, JOB. Journal   34518
SMITH, VENTURE. By E. Niles 34560
STILES, EZRA. By A. Holmes 33889
TRENCK, F. VON DER. By himself   34678
WASHINGTON, GEORGE. By T. Condie   34365, 35334
WHITEFIELD, GEORGE. By J. Gillies   33799
WOODBRIDGE, ASHBEL. Family records   35739

FUNERAL SERMONS.

ANDROS, MRS. By T. Andros 33305
ARNOLD, WELCOME. By J. Maxcy   34086
BELKNAP, JEREMY. By J. T. Kirkland   33964
BLAKSLEE, LUCY. By A. V. Griswold   33825
BUELL, SAMUEL. By H. Daggett   35372
CHAMBERLAIN, ERASTUS. By I. Potter   34407
CLARKE, JOHN. By P. Thacher 34642
COOPER, SAMUEL. By C. Caldwell   35262
CURRIER, REUBEN. By I. Potter   34407
DANA, SAMUEL. By T. Bigelow   33419
DAVIS, DANIEL. By J. Mellen, jun.   35811
DICKINS, JOHN. By E. Cooper 35353
DIX, SAMUEL. By S. Farrar 33716, 35465
FULLER, JEREMIAH. By. S. Palmer   34304
GILL, REBECCA. By J. Russell 34501
By P. Thacher   34641
GOODHUE, JOSIAH. By W. Wells   34999
HARMON, MARTIN. By D. C. Sanders   34512

HUNTINGTON, BETHIAH. By Z. Ely   35442
MANN, NANCY. By W. Mason 35785
MERRILL, JOHN. By S. Swift 34624
MOOR, WALTER. By D. Avery 35130
PALMER, EDWARD. By W. Wells   35000
PIERCE, MARY. By E. Vining 34933
PRUDDEN, AGNES. By C. Backus   35135
ROWLAND, SARAH. By J. Buckminster   33471
RUSSELL, JAMES. By J. Morse 34144
SILVESTER, DAVID. By T. Whiting   35021
SMITH, JOHN B. By S. Blair 35212
STEVENS, JOHN. By J. Catlin 35288
STONE, TIMOTHY. By L. Hart 33850
STORRS, SARAH. By C. Backus 33354
SUMNER, INCREASE. By A. Holmes   35629
Funeral exercises   35792–93
TAYLOR, PARDON. By W. Wells   35000
THAYER, ATHERTON. By E. Weld   34997
VARNUM, POLLY. By H. Packard   34289
WASHINGTON, GEORGE. Funeral observances   35596, 35774
WATTLES, NATHANIEL. By J. Bacon   33355
WHITE, ELIZABETH. By T. Allen   33386, 35095
WHITE, MARY. By S. Magaw 34042
WOODBRIDGE, JERUSHA. By W. Lockwood   35739

HISTORY.

GOLDSMITH, O. Roman history   33805
JOSEPHUS, F. Works   35675

ALGIERS.

FOSS, J. Captivity   33746–47
UNITED STATES   34808

FRANCE.

BARRUEL, A. DE. Jacobinism 35153
CHARACTERISTICS of French Republic   33507
CLÉRY, J. B. Confinement of Louis XVI   35314

CLASSIFIED SUBJECT INDEX

GEORGIA.

ANDERSON, J. E. Western
   Territory   35111
BISHOP, A. Georgia specu-
   lation   33425
HARPER, R. G. Georgia sales
   on Mississippi   35587–88
NEW ENGLAND MISSISSIPPI
   LAND COMPANY. Articles 34178
   Memorial   34179
UNITED STATES: 34783–84

LOUISIANA.

BANDO de buen Gobierno   34016
ORDRE du Roi   34017
REGULATIONS   35741

TENNESSEE.

PARRINGTON, J. R. Map, and
   description   34310
UNITED STATES: 34886

NORTHWEST TERRITORY.

CONNECTICUT Reserve: 33565,
   34317, 34780, 35345, 35526

SAINT DOMINGO.

MOREAU DE ST. MÉRY, M. L. E.
   Partie Francaise   34137
   Spanish part   34138

GEOGRAPHY AND TRAVELS.

BINGHAM, C. Geographical
   catechism   33421
BLUNT, E. M. Navigator   33433
BRAAM HOUCKGEEST, A. E. VAN
   La Chine   33448
BRUCE, J. Travels in
   Abyssinia   33466
BRYDONE, P. Sicily and
   Malta   33467
CAMPBELL, D. Journey to
   India   33487, 35265
CARLETON, O. Plan of Boston 35005
DAVIES, B. Map of Penn-
   sylvania   35385
DECALVES, A. Travels to
   westward   33615–16, 35391
DWIGHT, N. Geography 33653–54,
   35428
FURLONG, L. American
   coast pilot   33772

GIBSON, J. Atlas minimus   33974
HANWAY, J. Travels through
   Russia   35585
HAWKINS, J. Voyage to
   Africa   33860
HELME, E. Rambles in London 35610
HUNTER, W. Ohio navi-
   gator   33915–16
JOHNSON, E. Northwest
   voyage   33936
LONGWORTH, D. New York
   Directory, 1798   34012
   Same, 1799   35740
MOORE, J. H. New Navigator 35834
MORSE, J. American gazetteer 34143
   Elements of geography   34145
   Geography made easy   34146
MULLEN, J. Baltimore Di-
   rectory   35850
NORMAN, J. American pilot 34239
PAYNE, J. Universal geog-
   raphy   34316
RHODES, J. Adventures   34461
SCOTT, J. Universal gazetteer 34519
STAFFORD, C. W. Philadelphia
   Directory   34593
VOLNEY, C. F. C. B. DE.
   Syria and Egypt   34949
WEED, E. JUN. Geographical
   spelling-book   34987
WEST, J. Boston Directory 35005
WILLIAMS, H. M. Residence
   in France   33797, 35030
WILLIAMS, W. Geography   35032
WILLOCK, J. Voyages   35035
MATHEMATICAL geography: 33795,
   35406, 35670
MAPS: 33448, 33794, 33796, 34137,
   34143, 34145–47, 34316–17,
   34421, 34519, 35005, 35385,
   35768

LANGUAGES.

ARAWAK.

GESCHICHTE von der marterwoche. In Arawak   35201

ENGLISH LANGUAGE.

ALEXANDER, C.
   Grammatical system   35092
   Spelling book   35093
   AMERICAN Primer   33295, 35107
ASH, J. Grammatical insti-
   tutes   33317

BABCOCK, E. Spelling book 33346
BALTIMORE Primmer   33366
BINGHAM, C. American
   preceptor   33420
   Same, 6th edition   35205
   Same, 7th edition   35206
   Same, Walpole   35207
   Young ladies accidence   35209
CAREY, M. Reading book   35271
CHILD'S reading book   35301
COLUMBIAN Primer   35330
COLUMBIAN spelling and
   reading book   33545
DILWORTH, T. New guide   35409
ELY, J. Child's instructor   35441
FENNING, D. Spelling book 35748
GROUT, J. JUN. Child's acci-
   dence   35571
HALE, E. Spelling book   35579
HARRISON, R. English gram-
   mar   33848–49
HEATON, B. Spelling book 35608
KENTUCKY Primer   33956
KENTUCKY Spelling-book   33957
LOWTH, R. English grammar 35749
MOORE, J. H. Monitor   35835
MURRAY, L. English exer-
   cises   34163
   English grammar   34164
   English reader   35851
NEW-ENGLAND Primer 34180–90,
   35107, 35330
O'KELLY, J. Preceptor's
   guide   34270
PERRY, W. Only sure guide 34843
RHOADS, A. Spelling-book   34443
WEBSTER, N. JUN. American
   selection, 13th Conn. ed. 34975
   American spelling-book,
     Thomas' 17th edition   34976
   Same, Thomas' 18th ed.   34977
   Same, Thomas' 19th ed.   34978
   Same, 20th Conn. edition 34979
   Little reader's assistant   34982
   Same, 4th edition   34983
WEED, E. JUN. American
   orthographer   34986
WILSON, S. English grammar 35039
WORCESTER, N. Natural
   teacher   35053

FRENCH LANGUAGE.

WORKS in French: 33363, 33448,
   33579, 33608, 33765, 33780,
   33928, 34017, 34123, 34137,
   34151–52, 35246–47, 35278,
   35838–39, 35533, 35829

GERMAN LANGUAGE.

HOCH-DEUTCHES A B C   33886
WORKS in German: 33299, 33300,
  33311, 33404, 33525, 33625,
  33631, 33701, 33793, 33804,
  33851, 33866, 33885-86,
  33941, 33976, 34010, 34024,
  34098, 34169-76, 34338-40,
  34368-69, 34911, 34916-17,
  34972, 35110, 35201, 35403,
  35449-50, 35453, 35475,
  35544, 35475, 35627, 35709,
  35854

LATIN LANGUAGE.

ADAM, A. Latin grammar   35073
CLARKE, J. Making of Latin 35311
DAVIDSON, J. Latin tongue 33604
MAIR, J. Latin syntax   35763
Ross, J. Latin grammar   34486
RUDDIMAN, T. Latin tongue 34491,
  35763
WORKS in Latin: 33599, 33853,
  34456, 34460, 35098

SPANISH LANGUAGE.

FERNANDEZ, F. Grammar   33731

EDUCATION

GENERAL works: 33601, 33800,
  34558, 34981, 35204, 35434,
  35476, 35626, 35690
CHARLESTOWN, VA. Academy 33509
DARTMOUTH UNIVERSITY
  Catalogue of graduates,   35381
  Catalogus eorum   33599
  Works relating to: 34624
DEERFIELD, MASS. Academy 35750
HARTFORD, CONN. Grammar
  school   33555
HARVARD UNIVERSITY
  Laws   33854
  Order of exercises, 1798 33852
  Same, 1799   35597
  Theses, 1798   33853
  Same, 1799   35598
  Works relating to: 33344, 33857,
    33962, 34629, 35158, 35204,
    35810
LITCHFIELD, CONN. School 34140
NEW JERSEY. COLLEGE OF
  Works relating to   35404

PHILLIPS (ANDOVER) ACAD-
  EMY   35837
PHILLIPS EXETER ACADEMY 35574
RHODE ISLAND COLLEGE
  Catalogus eorum   34456
  Exhibition, junior, 1798 34458
  Exhibition, senior, 1798 34459
  Order of exercises, 1798 34457
  Theses, 1798   34460
  Works relating to: 34085-86,
    34658-59, 34744, 34971,
    35255, 35814
WILLIAMS COLLEGE
  Works relating to: 35137, 35486
YALE COLLEGE
  Catalogue of members, 1797 35058
  Same, 1798   35059
  Scheme of exhibitions, 1796 35060
  Same, 1797   35061
  Same, 1798   35062
  Works relating to 34046-47, 34267

LITERATURE.

DRAMA.

BIRCH, S. Adopted child   33422
BURK, J. D. Female patriot-
  ism   33475
DUNLAP, W. Andre   33652
KOTZEBUE, A. F. F. VON
  Constant lover   35693
  Same, New York   35694
  Count Bergowsky   35695
  Lovers' vows   35696
  Same, New York   35697
  Pizarro   35698
  Same, Charlestown   35699
  Same, New York   35700
  Same, Philadelphia   35701
  Self immolation   35702
  The Stranger   35703
  Same, Salem   35704
  Same, New York   35705
LEWIS, M. G. Castle spectre 34000
  Same, Salem   35730
LITTLE trifler   34005
MARTIN, A. A New scene 34050-51
MORTON, T. Cure for heart-
  ache   34153
  Secrets worth knowing   35845
MUNFORD, R. The Candidates 34158
  The Patriot   34158
MURDOCK, J. The Politicians 34160
OLIVER, P. Adopted son   34271
PINCHARD, Mrs. ──
  Dramatic dialogues   34381

RAMSAY, A. Gentle shepherd 34432
SENSIBILITY   34526
SMITH, E. H. Alcuin   34553
STEARNS, C. Dramatic dia-
  logues   34600

FABLES.

ÆSOPUS. Fables 33273-74, 35085
DODSLEY, R. Fables   33545
FENN, E. F. Fables for
  children   33728
MILNS, W. Fables from Eng-
  lish writers   34112
MOORE, E. Fables for female
  sex   34128

FICTION.

ADVENTURING in the lottery 35297
ADVERTISEMENT for a hus-
  band   35084
ALBERT and Emma   34525
ALCANDER and Rosilla   34307
AMBROSE and Eleanor   35098-99
AMELIA, or faithless Briton 33290,
  33533, 33741
AMELIA, or malevolence de-
  feated   33290, 33741
ARNAUD, F. T. M. DE B. D'
  Fanny   35117
BARZONI, V. Romans in
  Greece   35160
BEGGARLY boy   35297
BELLAMY, T. Fatal effects of
  seduction   34307
BENNETT, A. M. Beggar girl 33401
BERINGTON, S. Gaudentio
  di Lucca   35183
BETTY BROWN, the orange
  girl   35298
BICKERSTAFF, I. Ambrose
  Gwinett   33418
BICKNELL, A. Philip Quarll 35203
BLACK Giles, the poacher   35298
BROWN, C. B. Arthur Mervyn 35243
  Same   34992
  Edgar Huntly   35244
  Ormond   35245
  Same, in French   35246
  Weiland   33461
  Same, in French   35247
BUTLER, J. Fortunes foot-
  ball   33481
CHARLES JONES, the footman 35298
CHARLES MORTIMER   33615
CHARIESSA and Leontine   34417

ELECTION SERMONS—NEW
    HAMPSHIRE.

1798 ROBERT GRAY   33813

ELECTION SERMONS—VERMONT.

1798 DANIEL C. SANDERS   34513
1799 WILLIAM FORSYTH   35491

     CHURCH HISTORY.

ASSOCIATE REFORMED
    CHURCH   33319, 35120
AUSTIN, D. Prophetic leaf   33341

BOWDOINHAM ASSOCIATION   33442,
    35224
CHARLESTON ASSOCIATION   33508,
    35294
CONGREGATIONAL CHURCH   35338–
    35340
DOVER ASSOCIATION   35420
FRIENDS. Society of   33767–68
GILDERSLEEVE, C. Century
    sermon   33798
KETOCKTON ASSOCIATION   35686
METHODIST EPISCOPAL
    CHURCH   34103, 35818
MOSHEIM, J. L. VON. Ec-
    clesiastical history   34154

NEW YORK ASSOCIATION   34223
NEWTON, J. Ecclesiastical
    history   34234
PHILADELPHIA ASSOCIATION   34353
PRESBYTERIAN CHURCH   34410
PROTESTANT EPISCOPAL
    CHURCH   34419, 35594
ROMAN CATHOLIC CHURCH   35580,
    35581
STONINGTON ASSOCIATION   34607
WARREN ASSOCIATION   34956
WARWICK ASSOCIATION   34957
MARTYRS: 35764
MISSIONS: 33552–53, 34312, 34422,
    34441,   34599,   34639–40,
    35362, 35738, 35801

PRINTING INSTITUTED IN
CONNECTICUT, 1709, A. D.

CHELSEA LANDING, 1796.

CHESHIRE, 1782.

DANBURY, 1789.

NATHAN DOUGLAS, Printer, publisher and Bookseller. Douglas and Nichols, near the Court House, 1798–1799.

STILES NICHOLS, Printer. Douglas and Nichols, 1798–1799.

EAST WINDSOR, 1799.

LUTHER PRATT, Printer. 1799.

FAIRFIELD, 1786.

HARTFORD, 1764.

ELISHA BABCOCK, Printer and publisher. 1798–99.

JOHN BABCOCK, Printer and Bookseller. 1798–1799.

I. COOKE, Bookseller. O. D. and I. Cooke, 1798–99.

OLIVER D. COOKE, Bookseller. O. D. and I. Cooke, Booksellers and Stationers, 1798–1799.

HENRY DWIER, Bookseller. Ten rods north of the Court House, 1798.

GEORGE GOODWIN, Printer. Hudson and Goodwin, 1798–1799.

BARZILLAI HUDSON, Printer, publisher and Bookseller. Hudson and Goodwin, at their Bookstore, opposite the North Meeting House, 1798–1799.

LITCHFIELD, 1784.

THOMAS COLLIER, Printer and publisher. 1798–99.

MIDDLETOWN, 1785.

TERTIUS DUNNING, Printer and publisher. 1798–99.

NEW HAVEN, 1754.

ISAAC BEERS, Bookseller. 1798.

GEORGE BUNCE, Printer. 1798–1799.

AMOS DOOLITTLE, Engraver, and Plate Printer. 1798–1799.

SAMUEL GREEN, Printer. T. and S. Green, 1798.

THOMAS GREEN, Printer and publisher. 1. T. and S. Green, opposite the Post Office. 2. Thomæ et Samuelis Green, Universitatis Typographorum, 1798–1799. 3. Thomas Green and Son, near the College, 1799.

THOMAS GREEN, JUNIOR, Printer. Thomas Green and Son, 1799.

—— MORSE, Printer. Read and Morse, 1799.

EDWARD O'BRIEN, Printer and publisher. 1798.

—— READ, Printer. Read and Morse, 1798.

MOSES HAWKINS WOODWARD, Printer and Bookseller. In State Street, 1798.

NEW LONDON, 1709.

SAMUEL GREEN, Printer, publisher and Bookseller. At his Office, adjoining the Bank, 1798–1799.

CHARLES HOLT, Printer and publisher. At his Printing Office, the house occupied by Mr. John Throop, Innholder, a few doors below the old stand, and directly opposite Mr. James Tilley's, 1798–1799.

JAMES SPRINGER, Printer, publisher and Bookseller. Beach Street, dwelling house and store lately occupied by Dr. Pelouze, opposite the Market, 1798–1799.

NEWFIELD, 1795.
(Near Fairfield.)

LAZARUS BEACH, Printer. Bookseller and Stationer. Opposite Mr. Hinman's Inn, 1798–1799.

NORWICH, 1773.

THOMAS HUBBARD, Printer, publisher and Bookseller. (Chelsea Society), 24 rods west of the Meeting House, 1798–1799.

JOHN STERRY, Bookseller. John Sterry and Co. 1798.

JOHN TRUMBULL, Printer, publisher and Bookseller. A few rods west of the Court [Meeting] House, 1798–1799.

STONINGTON PORT, 1798.

SAMUEL TRUMBULL, Printer and publisher. 1798–99.

SUFFIELD, 1797.

REECOME D. ALBRO, Printer. Gray and Albro, 1798.

HAVILA FARNSWORTH, Printer. H. and O. Farnsworth, 1798.

OLIVER FARNSWORTH, Printer. H. and O. Farnsworth, 1798.

EDWARD GRAY, Printer and publisher. 1. Gray and Albro, 1798. 2. Edward Gray, 1799.

WALLINGFORD.

ASAHEL BENHAM, Music publisher. 1798.

WINDHAM, 1791.

JOHN BYRNE, Printer and publisher. In the lower [north] room of the Court House, 1798–1799.

PRINTING INSTITUTED IN
DELAWARE, 1761, A. D.

NEW CASTLE, 1796.

JOHN ADAMS, Printer. Samuel and John Adams, 1798–1799.

SAMUEL ADAMS, State Printer. Samuel and John Adams, nearly opposite the Court House, 1798–1799.

WILMINGTON, 1761.

JOHN ADAMS, Printer. S. and J. Adams, 1798–99.

SAMUEL ADAMS, Printer and publisher. S. and J. Adams, corner of King and High Streets, 1798–1799.

VINCENT BONSAL, Printer and Bookseller. Bonsal and Niles, 1798–1799.

PETER BRYNBERG, Printer, publisher and Bookseller. In Market Street, 1798–1799.

DANIEL COLEMAN, Printer. Vaughan and Coleman, 1799.

HEZEKIAH NILES, Printer. Bonsal and Niles. 1798–1799.

WILLIAM CATHERWOOD SMYTH, Printer and publisher. Two doors below Mr. Brinton's Tavern, High Street, 1798–1799.

JOHN VAUGHAN, Printer and publisher. Vaughan and Coleman, Market Street, 1799.

JAMES WILSON, Printer, publisher, Bookseller and Stationer. 1. At his Bookstore, at the Sign of Shakespeare, No. 5 High Street, opposite the upper Market, 1798–1799. 2. South side of the upper Market, High Street, 1799.

PRINTING INSTITUTED IN
DISTRICT OF COLUMBIA, 1795, A. D.

CITY OF WASHINGTON, 1795.

BENJAMIN MORE, Printer and publisher. At the house next west of the Hotel, 1798.

PRINTING INSTITUTED IN
EAST FLORIDA, 1783, A. D.

ST. AUGUSTINE, 1783.

PRINTING INSTITUTED IN
GEORGIA, 1762, A. D.

AUGUSTA, 1785.

WILLIAM J. BUNCE, Printer. Randolph and Bunce, 1799.

ALEXANDER M'MILLAN, Printer and publisher. Printer to the State, 1798.

GEORGE F. RANDOLPH, Printer. Randolph and Bunce, in Washington Street, 1799.

JOHN ERDMAN SMITH, Printer and publisher. Printer to the State, 1798–1799.

LOUISVILLE, 1798.

AMBROSE DAY, Printer and publisher. Day and Hely, 1799.

JAMES HELY, Printer. Day and Hely, 1799.

ALEXANDER M'MILLAN, Printer to the State. 1798–1799.

ELISHA H. WALDO, Printer for A. M'Millan. 1799.

SAVANNAH, 1762.

NICHOLAS JOHNSTON, Printer and publisher. Nicholas Johnston and Co., Broughton Street, 1798–1799.

GURDON I. SEYMOUR, Printer and publisher. Seymour and Woolhopter, on the Bay, 1798–1799.

PHILIP D. WOOLHOPTER, Printer. Seymour and Woolhopter, 1798–1799.

PRINTING INSTITUTED IN
KENTUCKY, 1787, A. D.

FRANKFORT, 1795.

WILLIAM H. BEAUMONT, Printer. Hunter and Beaumont, 1798–1799.

JAMES M. BRADFORD, Printer and publisher. 1. John Bradford and Son, 1798–1799. 2. James M. Bradford, Main Street, 1799. 3. At the corner of Montgomery and St. Clair Streets, 1799.

JOHN BRADFORD, Printer and publisher. Printer to the Commonwealth. John Bradford and Son, at the Capitol, 1798–1799.

WILLIAM HUNTER, Printer and publisher. Hunter and Beaumont, 1798–1799. Printers to the Commonwealth, 1799.

LEXINGTON, 1787.

JOHN BRADFORD, Printer and publisher. Printer to the Commonwealth. Main Street, 1798–1799.

JAMES H. STEWART, Printer and publisher. 1798.

PARIS, 1797.

DARIUS MOFFET, Printer and publisher. 1798.

WASHINGTON, 1797.

WILLIAM H. BEAUMONT, Printer and publisher. Hunter and Beaumont, 1798–1799.

WILLIAM HUNTER, Printer and publisher. Hunter and Beaumont, 1798–1799.

PRINTING INSTITUTED IN
LOUISIANA, 1794, A. D.

NEW ORLEANS, 1794.

PRINTING INSTITUTED IN
DISTRICT OF MAINE, 1785, A. D.

AUGUSTA, 1797.

PETER EDES, Printer, publisher and Bookseller. Near the Court House, 1798–1799.

CASTINE, 1799.

DAVID J. WATERS, Printer and publisher. 1799.

FALMOUTH, 1785.

FRYEBURG, 1798.

ELIJAH RUSSEL, or RUSSELL, Printer and publisher, 1798–1799.

HALLOWELL, 1794.

PETER EDES, Printer, publisher and Bookseller. Near the Court House, 1799.

HOWARD S. ROBINSON, Printer. 1798.

HARRINGTON, 1797.

PORTLAND, 1786.

JOHN KELSE BAKER, Printer. Baker and George, Fish Street, 1798–1799.

WILLIAM BURDICK, Printer. Rand and Burdick, 1798–1799.

DANIEL GEORGE, Printer. Baker and George, 1798–1799.

ELEZER ALLEY JENKS, Printer and publisher. At his Office in Middlestreet, 1798–1799.

JOHN RAND, Printer and publisher. 1. At his Office in Middle Street, near the head of Fish Street, 1798–1799. 2. Rand and Burdick, 1798–1799.

BENJAMIN TITCOMB, Printer. In Middle Street, 1798–1799.

WISCASSET, 1796.

HENRY HOSKINS, Printer and publisher. 1. Hoskins and Scott, at their Office, corner of Main and Water Streets, 1798. 2. Henry Hoskins, 1799.

—— LAUGHTON, Printer and publisher. Laughton and Rhoades, 1798.

EBENEZER RHOADES, Printer. Laughton and Rhoades, 1798.

JOHN W. SCOTT, Printer. Hoskins and Scott, 1798.

YORK.

DANIEL SEWALL, Almanac maker. At his office, 1798.

PRINTING INSTITUTED IN
MARYLAND, 1726, A. D.

ANNAPOLIS, 1726.

FREDERICK GREEN, Printer and publisher. 1. Printer to the State, 1798–1799. 2. F. and S. Green, 1798–1799.

SAMUEL GREEN, Printer. F. and S. Green, 1798–99.

BALTIMORE, 1765.

VINCENT BONSAL, Bookseller. Bonsal and Niles, No. 173 Market Street, 1799.

MATTHEW BROWN, Printer. Yundt and Brown, 1798–1799.

SAMUEL BUTLER, Bookseller. Thomas, Andrews and Butler, 1798–1799.

ISAAC CARR, Music publisher. No. 6 Gay Street, 1798–1799.

THOMAS E. CLAYLAND, Printer and publisher. Clayland and Dobbin, No. 36 Market Street, opposite the Vendue Store, 1798.

SOLOMON COTTON & Co., Booksellers. 1798.

THOMAS DOBBIN, Printer and publisher. T. E. Clayland and T. Dobbin, 1798–1799.

MICHAEL DUFFEY, Printer. 1798.

H. GREENE, Printer. A. Hanna and H. Greene, 1798.

JOHN HAGERTY, Bookseller. No. 104 Market Street, 1798.

ANDREW HANNA, Printer and publisher. 1. A. Hanna and H. Greene, No. 27 Market Street, next door to the Vendue Store, 1798. 2. Warner and Hanna, 1799.

JOHN [JEAN] HAYES, Printer. No. 8 Baltimore Street, 1798–1799.

GEORGE HILL, Bookseller. 1798.

GEORGE KEATINGE, Printer and Bookseller. In Market Street, No. 149, three doors above Light Lane, 1798–1799.

HENRY S. KEATINGE, Bookseller. 1798–1799.

ALEXANDER MARTIN, Printer and publisher. 1799.

HEZEKIAH NILES, Bookseller. Bonsal and Niles, 1799.

WILLIAM PECHIN, Printer and publisher. No. 15 Baltimore [Market] Street, 1798–1799.

JAMES RICE, Bookseller. J. Rice and Co. [Jacques Rice et Comp.], Market Street, corner of South Street, 1798.

SAMUEL SAUR [or SOWER], Printer, publisher and Bookseller. At his Printing Office, No. 67 Market Street, and his Book Store, in Fayette Street [in der Fayettestrasse], 1798–1799.

BALTIMORE, *continued.*

ISAIAH THOMAS, Bookseller. Thomas, Andrews and Butler, No. 184 Market Street, 1798–1799.

—— WARNER, Printer and Bookseller. 1. Warner and Hanna, Harrison Street, 1799. 2. No. 2 North Gay Street, 1799.

LEONARD YUNDT, Printer and publisher. 1. Yundt and Brown, No. 3 Calvert Street, near the Court House, 1798. 2. No. 12 South Gay Street, 1799.

CHESTERTOWN, 1793.

EASTON, 1790.

JAMES COWAN, Printer and publisher. 1798–1799.

ELIZABETH (HAGER'S) TOWN, 1790.

THOMAS GRIEVES, Printer and publisher. Near the Court House, 1798–1799.

JOHANN GRUBER, Printer and publisher. 1798–99.

FREDERICK TOWN, 1779.

MATTHIAS BARTGIS, Printer and publisher. At his English and German Printing Office, the upper end of Market Street [at the corner of Market and Patrick Streets], 1798–1799.

JOHN D. CAREY, Publisher. At the Office of the Federal Gazette, in Market Street, 1798.

JOHN WINTER, Printer and publisher. At his Office in Patrick Street, near Mr. Samuel Duvall's, 1798–1799.

PRINTING INSTITUTED IN
MASSACHUSETTS, 1639, A. D.

ANDOVER, 1799.

—— AMES, Printer. Ames and Parker, 1799.

—— PARKER, Printer. Ames and Parker, 1799.

ATTLEBOROUGH, 1777.

BOLTON.

ASA HOUGHTON, Almanac maker. 1798–1799.

BOSTON, 1675.

THOMAS ADAMS, Printer and publisher. At his Printing Office, opposite the Court House, in Court Street, 1798–1799.

EBENEZER TURELL ANDREWS, Bookseller. Thomas and Andrews, 1798–1799.

CALEB BINGHAM, Author Bookseller. At his Book Store, No. 44 Cornhill, 1798–1799.

LEMUEL BLAKE, Bookseller. W. P. and L. Blake, 1798–1799.

WILLIAM P. BLAKE, Bookseller. W. P. and L. Blake, at the Boston Bookstore, No. 1 Cornhill, 1798–1799.

DANIEL BOWEN, Printer. At his Press, head of the Mall, under the Columbian Museum Office, 1798–1799.

JOHN BOYLE, Bookseller. No. 18 Marlborough Street, 1798.

JOSEPH BUMSTEAD, Printer and Bookseller. No. 20 Union Street, 1798–1799.

JAMES CUTLER, Printer. 1. At the Printing Office, in Quaker Lane, 1798–1799. 2. Russell and Cutler, 1799.

BENJAMIN EDES, Printer and publisher. In Kilby Street, 1798–1799.

BENJAMIN EDES, JUNIOR, Printer. No. 22, Marlborough Street, 1798.

SAMUEL ETHERIDGE, Printer. At his Printing Office, No. 9 Newbury Street, 1798–1799.

JOHN FLEET, Printer and Bookseller. John and Thomas Fleet, at the Bible and Heart, Cornhill, 1798–1799.

THOMAS FLEET, Printer and Bookseller. Thomas and John Fleet, at the Bible and Heart, in Cornhill, 1798–1799.

JOHN WEST FOLSOM, Printer and Bookseller. At his Book Store and Printing Office, No. 30 Union Street, 1798.

—— GREENLEAF, Bookseller. West and Greenleaf, 1799.

P. A. VON HAGEN, JUNIOR, Music publisher. At the Musical Magazine, No. 62 Newbury Street, 1798.

SAMUEL HALL, Printer and Bookseller. No. 53 Cornhill, 1798–1799.

JOSEPH HAWKINS, Author Bookseller. At the Sign of the Blue Bell, Marlboro' Street, 1798.

SAMUEL HILL, Engraver. 1798–1799.

EBENEZER JOHNSON, Author Bookseller. 1798.

BENJAMIN LARKIN, Bookseller. No. 46 Cornhill, 1798–1799.

EBENEZER LARKIN, JUNIOR, Bookseller and Stationer. No. 47 Cornhill, 1798–1799.

SAMUEL LARKIN, Bookseller. E. and S. Larkin, 1799.

—— LAUGHTON, Printer. Rhoades and Laughton, 1798.

FRANCIS LINDLEY, Printer and Bookseller. Lindley and Moore, No. 19 Marlborough Street, 1798.

JAMES LORING, Printer. Manning and Loring, 1798–1799.

WILLIAM MANNING, Printer and Bookseller. Manning and Loring. 1. In Spring Lane, 1798. 2. No. 2 Cornhill, 1798–1799.

BOSTON, *continued*.

THOMAS MINNS, Printer. Young and Minns, 1798–1799.

JOHN MOORE, Printer. Lindley and Moore, 1798.

PAUL JOSEPH GUERARD DE NANCREDE, Bookseller. No. 49 Marlbro' Street, 1798–1799.

JONATHAN NICHOLS, Bookseller. 1799.

WILLIAM NORMAN, Bookseller and Stationer. At his Bookstore, No. 75 Newbury Street, nearly opposite the Sign of the Lamb, 1798.

SAMUEL S. PARKER, Printer and publisher. At Parker's Printing Office, south side State Street, east corner Kilby Street, 1799.

EBENEZER RHOADES, Printer. 1. Rhoades and Laughton, Court Street, 1798. 2. Ebenezer Rhoades, 1799.

BENJAMIN RUSSELL, Printer and publisher. Printer of the Laws of the Union for the Northern States, south side State Street, next to the Coffee House, 1798–1799.

JOHN RUSSELL, Printer and publisher. 1. At his Office in Quaker Lane, near State [Water] Street, 1798–1799. 2. Russell and Cutler, 1799.

WILLIAM SPOTSWOOD, Bookseller. 1. W. Spotswood and C. P. Wayne, 1798. 2. Spotswood and Etheridge, 1798. 3. No. 22 Marlborough Street, 1798–1799.

ISAIAH THOMAS, Printer, publisher and Bookseller. Isaiah Thomas and Ebenezer T. Andrews, Faust's Statue, No. 45 Newbury Street, 1798–1799.

CALEB P. WAYNE, Printer and publisher. 1. W. Spotswood and C. P. Wayne, 1798. 2. No. 17 Kilby Street, three doors from State Street, 1798.

DAVID WEST, Bookseller. 1. No. 56 Cornhill, 1798–1799. 2. West and Greenleaf, 1799.

JOHN WEST, Bookseller and Stationer. No. 75 Cornhill, 1798–1799.

JAMES WHITE, Bookseller and Stationer. At Franklin's Head, Court Street, 1798–1799.

JAMES WHITE, Printer and Bookseller. Near Charles River Bridge, 1798.

ALEXANDER YOUNG, Printer and publisher. Young and Minns, Printers to the honourable the General Court of the Commonwealth of Massachusetts. Printers to the State, 1798–1799.

BROOKFIELD, 1794.

EBENEZER MERRIAM, Printer. E. Merriam and Co., 1798–1799.

CAMBRIDGE, 1639.

CHARLESTOWN, 1785.

SAMUEL ETHERIDGE, Printer. Next door to the Warren Tavern, 1799.

JOHN LAMSON, Printer. At his Office, near the Bridge, 1798.

CHELMSFORD, 1775.

CONCORD, 1776.

DEDHAM, 1796.

JAMES H. ADAMS, Printer. Mann and Adams, 1798.

HERMAN MANN, Printer and publisher. 1. Mann and Adams, 1798. 2. H. Mann, about 60 rods east of the Court House, 1798–1799.

DEERFIELD.

EPAPHRAS HOYT, Author Bookseller. 1798.

GREENFIELD, 1792.

FRANCIS BARKER, Printer, publisher and Bookseller, 1798–1799.

THOMAS DICKMAN, Printer, publisher and Bookseller. 1798–1799.

—— RIPLEY, Bookseller. Russell and Ripley, 1798.

—— RUSSELL, Bookseller. Russell and Ripley, 1798.

HAVERHILL, 1790.

ANGIER MARCH, Printer and publisher. 1798.

SETH H. MOORE, Printer and publisher. Moore and Stebbins, at their Printing Office, 1798–99.

CHESTER STEBBINS, Printer. Moore and Stebbins, 1798–1799.

LEOMINSTER, 1795.

CHARLES PRENTISS, Printer and publisher. 1. Charles and John Prentiss, south of the Meeting House, 1798–1799. 2. Charles Prentiss, 1799.

JOHN PRENTISS, Printer. 1798–1799.

LONG MEADOW.

NATHANIEL ELY, JUNIOR, Bookseller. 1798.

MEDFORD, 1798.

NATHANIEL COVERLY, JUNIOR, Printer and Bookseller. 1798–1799.

MENDON.

EPHRAIM GOODALE, Bookbinder. 1798.

MIDDLEBOROUGH, 1787.

New Bedford, 1792.

ABRAHAM SHEARMAN, JUNIOR, Printer and publisher. 1798–1799.

JOHN SPOONER, Printer, publisher and Bookseller. 1. Corner of Union and Sixth Streets, 1798–1799. 2. Corner of Water and Prospect Streets, 1799.

Newburyport, 1773.

EDMUND MARCH BLUNT, Printer, publisher and Bookseller. At the Newburyport Book Store, Sign of the Bible, State Street, 1798–1799.

ANGIER MARCH, Printer and publisher. Middle Street, 1798–1799.

JOHN MYCALL, Printer. 1798–1799.

—— PARKER, Printer. Parker and Robinson, 1799.

—— ROBINSON, Printer. Parker and Robinson, 1799.

Northampton, 1786.

SIMEON BUTLER, Bookseller. 1798–1799.

WILLIAM BUTLER, Printer and publisher. 1798–99.

ANDREW WRIGHT, Printer. 1798–1799.

DANIEL WRIGHT AND COMPANY, 1798–1799.

Pittsfield, 1787.

NATHANIEL HOLLY, Printer. Holly and Smith, 1798.

ORSAMUS C. MERRILL, Printer. Merrill and Smith, 1798.

CHESTER SMITH, Printer. 1. Chester Smith and Co., 1798–1799. 2. Merrill and Smith, 1798. 3. Holly and Smith, 1798–1799. 4. Chester Smith, 1799.

Plymouth, 1785.

Princeton.

THOMAS THACHER, Bookseller. 1798.

Rehoboth, 1776.

Salem, 1768.

NATHANIEL COVERLY, Printer and Bookseller. N. and J. Coverly, at their Bookstore, Faust's Statue, Essex Street, 1798–1799.

JOHN COVERLY, Bookseller. N. and J. Coverly, 1798–1799.

JOSHUA CUSHING, Printer. 1799.

THOMAS C. CUSHING, Printer and publisher. Essex Street, between Washington and Market Streets, 1798–1799.

JOHN DABNEY, Bookseller. 1798.

BERNARD B. MACANULTY, Bookseller. 1799.

Springfield, 1782.

TIMOTHY ASHLEY, Printer and publisher. 1799.

EDWARD GRAY, Printer. At the corner of Meeting House Lane, 1798.

FRANCIS STEBBINS, Printer and publisher. 1798–1799.

Sterling.

AARON THOMAS, Bookseller. R. B. and A. Thomas, 1798–1799.

ROBERT BAILEY THOMAS, Almanac maker, Bookseller and Stationer. R. B. and A. Thomas, 1798–1799.

Stockbridge, 1789.

BENJAMIN ROSSETER, Printer and publisher. 1. Rosseter and Willard, 1798. 2. Benjamin Rosseter. 1798.

HERMAN WILLARD, Printer and publisher. 1. Rosseter and Willard, 1798. 2. H. Willard, 1799.

Taunton.

DANIEL BREWER, Bookseller. 1798–1799.

West Springfield, 1795.

RICHARD DAVISON, Printer. 1798.

Worcester, 1775.

DANIEL GREENLEAF, Printer. 1. Mower and Greenleaf, 1799. 2. Daniel Greenleaf, 1799.

GEORGE MERRIAM, Bookseller. 1798–1799.

—— MOWER, Printer. Mower and Greenleaf, 1799.

ALEXANDER THOMAS, Bookseller. Thomas, Son and Thomas, 1798.

ISAIAH THOMAS, Printer, publisher, Bookseller, Stationer, Binder and Paper Manufacturer. Thomas, Son and Thomas, at the Worcester Bookstore, 1798–1799.

ISAIAH THOMAS, JUNIOR, Printer and Bookseller. 1. At his Bookstore, Sign of Johnson's Head, opposite the Gaol, 1798–1799. 2. Isaiah Thomas and Son, at their respective Bookstores, 1798–99.

LEONARD WORCESTER, Printer and publisher. At his Office, near the South Meeting House, 1798–1799.

Wrentham, 1795.

BENJAMIN HEATON, Printer. Nathaniel and Benjamin Heaton, 1798–1799.

NATHANIEL HEATON, JUNIOR, Printer. 1. Nathaniel and Benjamin Heaton, 1798–1799. 2. Nathaniel Heaton, junior, 1799.

PRINTING INSTITUTED IN
MISSISSIPPI, 1799, A. D.

NATCHEZ, 1799.

ANDREW MARSCHALK, Printer. And sold at the Store of Messrs. Hunts, and Co., 1799.

PRINTING INSTITUTED IN
NEW HAMPSHIRE, 1756, A. D.

AMHERST, 1794.

CHARLES CAMBRIDGE, Bookseller. 1799.

SAMUEL PRESTON, Printer and publisher. A few rods west of the Meeting House, 1798–1799.

CONCORD, 1789.

MOSES DAVIS, Printer and publisher. 1798–1799.

GEORGE HOUGH, Printer and publisher, 1798–99.

JOSHUA LEAVITT, Printer. 1799.

CONWAY, 1798.

A. HAYDEN LEONARD, Printer. T. and A. H. Leonard, 1798.

THEODORE LEONARD, Printer and publisher. 1. T. and A. H. Leonard, 1798. 2. Theodore Leonard, 1798.

DOVER, 1790.

JOHN ASPLUND, Travelling Bookseller. 1798.

SAMUEL BRAGG, JUNIOR, Printer and publisher. At his Printing Office, near the Court House, 1798–1799.

EXETER, 1775.

JOHN LAMSON, Printer. 1798–1799.

HENRY RANLET, Printer, publisher and Bookseller. At his Book Store, in Water Street, 1798–1799.

GILMANTON, 1799.

ELIJAH RUSSELL, Printer and publisher. 1799.

HANOVER, 1793.

MOSES DAVIS, Printer and publisher. On the College Plain, 1799.

BENJAMIN TRUE, Printer and publisher. 1. At the northwest corner of College Square, in the Academy, 1798–1799. 2. Leuphanie, Typis Benjamin True, 1798.

B. WOODWARD, Bookseller. Dartmouth College, 1799.

HAVERHILL, 1796.

KEENE, 1787.

ELIJAH COOPER, Printer and publisher. 1798.

JOHN PRENTISS, Printer. 1799.

CORNELIUS STURTEVANT, JUNIOR, Printer, publisher and Bookseller. Cornelius Sturtevant, jun. and Co., 1798.

PORTSMOUTH, 1756.

SAMUEL G. HART, Printer. Treadwell and Hart, 1798–1799.

SAMUEL LARKIN, Bookseller and Stationer. At the Portsmouth Book Store, in Market Street, 1798.

JOHN MELCHER, Printer, publisher and Bookseller. 1. At his Office, corner of Market Street, 1798–1799. 2. Printer to the State, 1798–1799.

CHARLES PEIRCE, Printer, publisher and Bookseller. At the Oracle Press [Columbian Book-Store] No. 5 Daniel Street, 1798–1799.

WILLIAM TREADWELL, Printer and publisher. 1. Treadwell and Hart, at their Printing Office, opposite Mr. Greenleaf's Inn, Congress Street, 1798–1799. 2. William Treadwell, 1799.

WALPOLE, 1793.

DAVID CARLISLE, Printer, publisher and Bookseller. 1. David Carlisle, in the Main Street, 1798–1799. David Carlisle, for Isaiah Thomas [and Thomas and Thomas] 1798–1799.

ALEXANDER THOMAS, Publisher. Thomas and Thomas, 1798–1799.

ISAIAH THOMAS, Publisher. Isaiah Thomas [and Thomas and Thomas.] 1798–1799.

PRINTING INSTITUTED IN
NEW JERSEY, 1755, A. D.

BRIDGETOWN, 1795.

BURLINGTON, 1765.

CHATHAM, 1779.

ELIZABETH TOWN, 1786.

SHEPARD KOLLOCK, Printer, publisher and Bookseller. At his Printing Office and Book Store, 1798–1799.

MONMOUTH, 1795.

MORRIS TOWN, 1797.

ELIJAH COOPER, Printer and publisher. E. Cooper and Co., 1798.

JACOB MANN, Printer and publisher. Nearly opposite the Academy, 1798–1799.

MOUNT HOLLY, 1799.

SAMUEL C. USTICK, Printer. 1799.

MOUNT PLEASANT,
NEAR MIDDLETOWN-POINT, 1794.

NEW BRUNSWICK, 1783.

ABRAHAM BLAUVELT, Printer and publisher. In Albany Street, 1798–1799.

NEWARK, 1776.

DANIEL DODGE, Printer and publisher. A. Pennington and D. Dodge, 1798–1799.

STEPHEN GOULD, Printer. S. Pennington and S. Gould, 1799.

JACOB HALSEY, Printer and publisher. Jacob Halsey and Co., at the Office of the Gazette, 1798.

JABEZ PARKHURST, Printer and publisher. J. Parkhurst and S. Pennington,. 1799.

AARON PENNINGTON, Printer and publisher. Pennington and Dodge, 1798–1799.

SAMUEL PENNINGTON, Printer. Parkhurst and Pennington 1799.

JOHN H. WILLIAMS, Printer and publisher. For the Proprietors, 1798.

JOHN WOODS, Printer and publisher. For the Proprietors. Near the Episcopal Church, 1798.

NEWTON, 1796.

ELIOT HOPKINS, Printer and publisher. 1. Eliot Hopkins and Co., 1798. 2. E. Hopkins and P. Smith, 1798.

P. SMITH, Printer. E. Hopkins and P. Smith, 1798.

PATERSON.

WILLIAM REID, Bookseller. 1799.

PRINCETON, 1790.

SALEM, 1799.

WILLIAM BLACK, Printer. Black and North. 1799.
—— NORTH, Printer. Black and North, 1799.

TRENTON, 1778.

WILLIAM BLACK, Printer. G. Craft and W. Black, 1798.

GERSHOM CRAFT, Printer and publisher. 1. G. Craft and W. Black, at their Office, in Second Street, opposite J. Milnor's Store, 1798. 2. G. Craft, Printer of the Laws of the United States for the District of New Jersey. Printer to the State, at his Office in Main Street, between the Indian Queen and City Hall, 1799.

WOODBRIDGE, 1755.

PRINTING INSTITUTED IN
NEW YORK, 1693, A. D.

ALBANY, 1771.

LORING ANDREWS, Printer and publisher. 1. Loring Andrews and Co. Printers to the State, at the Printing Office in Maiden Lane, 1798. 2. Court Street, a few rods south of the City Hall, 1798–1799. 3. Loring Andrews, 1798–1799.

JOHN BARBER, Printer and publisher. Barber and Southwick, at their Printing Office, Sign of Faust's Statue, lower end of State Street. Or at their Book Store, two doors north of the City Hall, in Court Street, 1798–1799.

JOSEPH FRY, Printer and publisher. 1. Fry and Southwick, corner of Dock Street and Mark Lane. 1798. 2. Joseph Fry, lower end of State Street, 1798.

OBADIAH PENNIMAN, Bookseller. Thomas, Andrews and Penniman, 1798–1799.

HENRY COLLINS SOUTHWICK, Printer. Fry and Southwick, 1798.

SOLOMON SOUTHWICK, Printer. Barber and Southwick, 1798–1799.

THOMAS SPENCER, Bookseller. Spencer and Webb, Market Street, 1798–1799.

ISAIAH THOMAS, Bookseller. Thomas, Andrews and Penniman, at the Albany Book Store, Sign of Franklin's Head, State Street, 1798–1799.

THOMAS SMITH WEBB, Bookseller. Spencer and Webb, 1798–1799.

CHARLES R. WEBSTER, Printer, publisher and Bookseller. Charles R. and George Webster, in the White House, corner of State and Pearl Streets, opposite the City Tavern, 1798–1799.

GEORGE WEBSTER, Printer. Charles R. and George Webster, 1798–1799.

BALLSTON, 1798.

INCREASE CHILD, Printer and publisher. I. and W. Child, at their Printing Office, nearly opposite the Court House, 1798–1799.

WILLIAM CHILD, Printer. I. and W. Child, 1798–1799.

BATH, 1796.

JAMES EDIE, Printer. Kersey and Edie, 1798.

WILLIAM KERSEY, Printer and publisher. Kersey and Edie, 1798.

BROOKLYN, 1799.

THOMAS KIRK, Printer and publisher. 1799.

CANAAN, 1794.

CANAJOHARIE.

J. DWIGHT, Bookseller. 1799.

CANANDAIGUA, 1798.

LUCIUS CARY, Printer and publisher. 1798–1799.

CATSKILL, 1792.

MACKAY CROSWELL, Printer and publisher. 1. T. and M. Croswell, 1798. 2. Mackay Croswell, 1798–1799.

COOPERSTOWN, 1795.

ELIHU PHINNEY, Printer and publisher. At his Printing Office, first door south [east] of the Court House, 1798–1799.

FISHKILL, 1776.

GENEVA, 1796.

GOSHEN, 1789.

JOHN G. HURTIN, Printer and publisher. John G. and William Hurtin, 1798–1799.

WILLIAM HURTIN, Printer. 1798–1799.

HUDSON, 1785.

ASHBEL STODDARD, Printer, publisher and Bookseller. 1798–1799.

JOHNSTOWN, 1795.

JACOB DOCKSTADER, Printer and publisher. 1798.

DAVID HOLDEN, Printer and publisher. Holden and Smith, 1798–1799.

JAMES SMITH, Printer. Holden and Smith, 1798–99.

KINGSTON, 1777.

WILLIAM COPP, Printer and publisher. Copp and Freer, 1798.

SAMUEL FREER, Printer and publisher. 1. Copp and Freer, 1798. 2. Samuel Freer and Son, 1798–1799.

SAMUEL S. FREER, Printer. Samuel Freer and Son, 1798–1799.

LANSINGBURGH, 1787.

JESSE BUEL, Printer. R. Moffitt and Co. 1798.

ROBERT MOFFITT, Printer and publisher. R. Moffitt and Co. 1798.

JOHN SHAW, Bookbinder. 1798.

GARDINER TRACY, Printer and publisher. At the Printing Office, in King's Street, 1798–1799.

CHARLES R. WEBSTER, Publisher. 1798.

MOUNT PLEASANT, 1797.

WILLIAM DURELL, Printer and publisher. 1798.

JOHN PATTERSON, Printer and publisher. 1799.

NEW WINDSOR, 1797.

ABRAHAM LOTT, Printer. Schultz and Lott, 1798.

JACOB SCHULTZ, Printer and publisher. 1. Schultz and Lott, 1798. 2. Jacob Schultz, 1799.

NEW YORK CITY, 1693.

THOMAS ALLEN, Bookseller and Stationer. 1798.

T. S. ARDEN, Bookseller. 1799.

EBENEZER BELDEN, Printer and publisher. E. Belden and Co. No. 40 Pine Street, 1799.

NATHANIEL BELL, Bookseller and Stationer. Bell and Smith, corner of Magazine and Chatham Streets, 1799.

—— BROWN, Bookseller. Brown and Stansbury, 1799.

JOHN BUEL, Printer and Bookseller. No. 74 William Street, 1798–1799.

THOMAS BURLING, JUNIOR, Printer. Tiebout and Burling, 1798.

SAMUEL CAMPBELL, Bookseller and Stationer. No. 124 Pearl Street, 1798–1799.

HOCQUET CARITAT, Bookseller, and Circulating Library. No. 153 Broadway, 1798–1799.

BENJAMIN CARR, Music publisher. At his Musical Repository, No. 131 William Street, 1798.

JAMES CHEVALIER, Printer. Crookes and Chevalier, 1798–1799.

ISAAC COLLINS, Printer and Bookseller. No. 189 Pearl Street, 1798–1799.

JOHN CROOKES, Printer and publisher. 1. For the Proprietor, No. 68 Pine Street, 1798–1799. 2. Crookes and Chevalier, 1798–1799.

CORNELIUS DAVIS, Bookseller and Stationer. No. 94 Water Street, 1798–1799.

MATTHEW L. DAVIS, Printer. 1. P. Freneau and M. L. Davis, 1798. 2. M. L. and W. A. Davis, 1798–1799.

WILLIAM A. DAVIS, Printer. 1. W. A. Davis and Co., 1798. 2. M. L. and W. A. Davis, No. 26 Moore Street, 1798–1799.

DANIEL DUNHAM, Bookseller. 1798.

WILLIAM DURELL, Printer. 1799.

EVERT DUYCKINCK, Bookseller and Stationer. E. Duyckinck and Co., 110 Pearl Street, 1798–99.

JOHN FELLOWS, Bookseller. 1798.

GEORGE FORMAN, Printer. No. 94 Water Street, between Coenties and the Old Slip, 1798–1799.

NEW YORK CITY, *continued.*

PHILIP FRENEAU, Printer and publisher. P. Freneau and M. L. Davis, No. 26 Moore Street, near Whitehall, 1798.

JOHN FURMAN, Printer. No. 102 Pearl Street, third door below the corner of Old Slip, 1799.

HUGH GAINE, Printer, Bookseller and Stationer. 1. At his Book Store and Printing Office, at the Bible, in Pearl Street, 1798–1799. 2. Gaine and Ten Eyck, in Pearl Street, 1798.

JAMES GIBBONS, Teacher of Arithmetic, &c., 1798.

GEORGE GILFERT, Music publisher. G. Gilfert and Co., at their Musical Magazine, Apollo's Head, No. 177 Broadway, 1798–1799.

BENJAMIN GOMEZ, Bookseller and Stationer. No. 97 Maiden Lane, 1798–1799.

ANN GREENLEAF, Printer, publisher and Bookseller. No. 54 Wall Street—six doors from the Tontine Coffee House, 1798–1799.

THOMAS GREENLEAF, Printer, publisher and Bookseller. 1. No. 54 Wall Street — six doors from the Tontine Coffee House, 1798. 2. Printed at Constantinople [Philadelphia, by James Carey] at the Sign of the heads of Traytors Arnorld, Gobbet and Blount, and next door to the Knights of "the Last Ditch," 1798.

JOSEPH HAMILTON, Author Bookseller. 1798–99.

JAMES HARDIE, Author Bookseller. 1799.

JOHN HARRISSON, Printer and Bookseller. At his Book Store and Printing Office, (Yorick's Head) No. 3 Peck Slip, 1798–1799.

JAMES HEWITT, Music publisher. 1. Musical Repository, No. 131 William Street, 1798. 2. No. 23 Maiden Lane, 1799.

GEORGE FOLLET HOPKINS, Printer and publisher. No. 40 Pine Street, Printer of the Laws of the United States for the District of New York, 1798–1799.

ROBERT M. HURTIN, Printer. 1. At the Literary Printing Office, No. 29 Gold Street, 1798. 2. Hurtin and M'Farlane, 1799.

THOMAS B. JANSEN, Bookseller and Stationer. No. 344 Water Street, near the New Slip, 1798–1799.

NAPTHALI JUDAH, Bookseller and Stationer. Sign of Paine's Head, No. 47 Water Street, near Coenties Slip, 1798–1799.

THOMAS KIRK, Printer. No. 112 Chatham Street, next door to the Tea-Water Pump, 1798–1799.

THOMAS LANG, Printer. M'Lean and Lang, 1798.

—— LEE, Bookseller. Lee and Stokes, No. 25 Maiden Lane, 1798–1799.

DAVID LONGWORTH, Directory publisher. No. 66 Nassau Street, 1798–1799.

JOHN LOW, Bookseller. At the Shakespeare Head, No. 322 Water Street, 1798.

MONTEITH M'FARLANE, Printer. Hurtin and M'Farlane, 1799.

ROBERT MACGILL, Bookseller. No. 105 Maiden Lane, 1798–1799.

ARCHIBALD M'LEAN, Printer and publisher. 1. Franklin's Head, No. 116 Pearl Street, 1798. 2. M'Lean and Lang, 1798.

PETER A. MESIER, Bookseller. 1798.

WILLIAM MILNS, Author Bookseller. At the Literary Printing Office, No. 29 Gold Street, 1798.

JOHN MORTON, Printer to the State. 1798–1799.

JACOB S. MOTT, Printer, publisher and Bookseller. No. 7 Vesey Street, 1798.

JAMES ORAM, Printer and publisher. No. 33 Liberty Street, 1798–1799.

JOHN and M. PAFF, Music publishers. 1799.

CLAUDE PARISOT, Printer and publisher. No. 51 Pearl Street, 1798–1799.

JOHN REID, Bookseller and Stationer. No 106 Water Street, 1798–1799.

WILLIAM REID, Bookseller. No. 442 Pearl Street, 1798.

WILLIAM ROBINS, Printer for the Proprietor [John Morton] Printer to the State, at the State Printing Office, No. 71 Pine Street, 1798.

ROBERT SAUNDERS, Printer. No. 25 Maiden Lane, 1798.

CHARLES SMITH, Publisher. No. 51 Maiden Lane, 1798–1799.

CHARLES SNOWDEN, Printer. For the Proprietor [John Morton], No. 71 Pearl Street, 1798–1799.

ALEXANDER SOMERVILLE, Bookseller. 1798–1799.

—— STANSBURY, Bookseller. Brown and Stansbury, 1799.

S. STEVENS, Bookseller. 1799.

—— STOKES, Bookseller. Lee and Stokes, 1798–1799.

JAMES SWORDS, Printer. T. and J. Swords, 1798–1799.

THOMAS SWORDS, Printer, publisher and Bookseller. 1. T. and J. Swords, No. 99 Pearl Street, 1798–1799. 2. Printers to the Faculty of Physic of Columbia College, 1798–1799.

JOHN TIEBOUT, Printer and publisher. At Homer's Head, No. 358 Pearl Street. 1. Tiebout and Burling, 1798. 2. John Tiebout, 1799.

NEW YORK CITY, *continued*.

JOHN C. TOTTEN, Printer. J. C. Totten and Co., No. 66 Nassau Street, 1799.

ARONDT VAN HOOK, Proprietor of the Reading Room. 1798.

GEORGE WAITE, Printer. G. and R. Waite, 1799.

R. WAITE, Printer. G. and R. Waite, 1799.

NOAH WEBSTER, JUNIOR, Editor and publisher. 1. George F. Hopkins and Co., 1798. 2. E. Belden and Co., 1799.

JOHN MASON WILLIAMS, "Anthony Pasquin," publisher. 1799.

ROBERT WILSON, Printer and Bookseller. No. 149 Pearl Street, 1798.

NEWBURGH, 1793.

JOSEPH W. Barber, Printer and publisher. 1798–1799.

DAVID DENNISTON, Printer and publisher. 1798.

PHILIP VAN HORNE, Printer and publisher. 1798.

POUGHKEEPSIE, 1777.

NICHOLAS POWER, Printer and publisher. 1. At the Post Office, 1798. 2. Power and Southwick, near the Court House, 1798.

HENRY COLLINS SOUTHWICK, Printer. Power and Southwick, 1798.

JOHN WOODS, Printer and publisher. 1798–1799.

ROME, 1799.

EBENEZER EATON, Printer and publisher. Eaton and Walker, 1799.

THOMAS WALKER, Printer. Eaton and Walker. 1799.

SAG HARBOR, 1791.

DAVID FROTHINGHAM, Printer and publisher. 1798–1799.

SALEM, 1794.

HENRY DODD, Printer and publisher. In the house formerly occupied by Thomas Barrow, a few rods north of the Court House, 1798–1799.

ST. JOHN HONEYWOOD, Editor. 1798.

SCHENECTADY, 1794.
(On the Banks of the Mohawk.)

CORNELIUS P. WYCKOFF, Printer, publisher and Bookseller. Corner of State and Washington Streets, 1798.

SCIPIO, 1798.

ROGER DELANO, Printer and publisher, 1798–1799.

STILLWATER, 1794.

TROY, 1795.

DAVID BUEL, Bookseller. 1798.

ROBERT MOFFITT, Printer and publisher. 1. R. Moffitt and Co., at their Office, Franklin's Head, 1798. 2. A few doors north of Mr. Peirce's Inn, opposite Messrs. G. and B. Tibbitt's Store, 1799.

LUTHER PRATT, Printer and publisher. Pratt and Co., near the Ferry, 1798.

UPTON, 1794.

UTICA, 1798.

WILLIAM M'LEAN, Printer and publisher. 1798.

WATERFORD, 1797.

WHITESTOWN, 1793.

—— Lewis, Printer. Lewis and Webb, 1798.

WILLIAM M'LEAN, Printer and publisher. Opposite the Meeting House, 1798.

—— WEBB, Printer. Lewis and Webb, 1798.

PRINTING INSTITUTED IN
NORTH CAROLINA, 1751, A. D.

EDENTON, 1788.

HENRY WILLS, Printer and publisher. Joint Printer to the State with A. Hodge, 1798.

JAMES WILLS, Printer and publisher. 1798–1799.

FAYETTEVILLE, 1787.

ABRAHAM HODGE, Printer and publisher. Hodge and Boylan, 1798.

HALIFAX, 1782.

ABRAHAM HODGE, Printer and publisher. 1. Joint Printer to the State with H. Wills, 1798. 2. Printer to the State, 1798–1799.

HILLSBOROUGH, 1788.

NEWBERN, 1751.

JOHN C. OSBORN, Printer, publisher and Bookseller. J. C. Osborn and Co., 1798–1799.

RALEIGH, 1799.

JOSEPH GALES, Printer. 1799.

SALISBURY, 1798.

MICHAEL BROWN, Printer. 1798.

FRANCIS COUPEE, Printer and publisher. 1798.

JOHN. M. SLUMP, Printer. At Michael Brown's English and German Printing Office, 1798.

WILMINGTON, 1764.

ALLMAND HALL, Printer and publisher. Printer to the State, 1798.

PRINTING INSTITUTED IN
OHIO, 1793, A. D.

CINCINNATI, 1793.

JOSEPH CARPENTER, Printer. 1799.

EDMUND FREEMAN, Printer and publisher. 1. S. Freeman and Son, 1798. 2. Edmund Freeman, 1798-1799.

SAMUEL FREEMAN, Printer and publisher. S. Freeman and Son, 1798.

PRINTING INSTITUTED IN
PENNSYLVANIA, 1685, A. D.

BEDMINSTER, 1798.

STEPHEN C. USTICK, Printer. 1798.

BRISTOL, 1799.

AURORA PRESS, for the heirs of B. F. Bache, 1799.

BUSTLETON, 1799.

WILLIAM COBBETT, Printer and publisher. 1799.

CARLISLE, 1785.

GEORGE KLINE, Printer, publisher and Bookseller. 1798-1799.

ARCHIBALD LOUDON, Bookseller. 1798-1799.

JOHN S. M'CLEAN, Printer. Steel and M'Clean, 1798.

JAMES STEEL, Printer and publisher. Steel and M'Clean, at the Sign of the Printing Press in York Street, 1798.

JOHN P. THOMPSON, Printer and publisher. 1799.

CHAMBERSBURG, 1790.

GEORGE KENTON HARPER, Publisher. 1799.

ROBERT HARPER, Printer and publisher. 1798-99.

JAMES MAGEE. Printer. G. K. Harper, 1799.

WILLIAM M'CORKLE, Printer. Snowden and M'Corkle, 1798-1799.

JAMES ROSS, Author Bookseller. 1798.

JOHN M. SNOWDEN, Printer and publisher. Snowden and M'Corkle, in Market Street, near the Bridge, 1798-1799.

EASTON, 1793.

SAMUEL LONGCOPE, Printer and publisher. 1799.

CORNELIUS N. WEYGANDT, Printer. Jacob Weygandt und Sohn, 1798.

JACOB WEYGANDT, Printer and publisher. Jacob Weygandt und Sohn, in der Neuen Buchdruckerey, 1798.

EPHRATA, 1745.

BENJAMIN MAYER, Printer. 1798.

FRIEDENSTHAL BEI BETHLEHEM, 1763.

GERMANTOWN, 1738.

MICHAEL BILLMEYER, Printer, publisher and Bookseller. 1798-1799.

DAVID C. and SEPTIMUS CLAYPOOLE, 1798.

PETER LEIBERT, Printer and Bookseller. 1798.

GREENSBURGH, 1799.

WILLIAM M'CORKLE, Printer. Snowden and M'Corkle, 1799.

JOHN M. SNOWDEN, Printer. Snowden and M'Corkle, 1799.

HANOVER, 1793.

WILLIAM DANIEL LEPPER, Printer. Stellingius and Lepper, 1798.

E. STELLINGIUS, Printer and publisher. Stellingius and Lepper, 1798.

HARRISBURGH, 1789.

JOHN WYETH, Printer and publisher. At his Office in Mulberry Street, 1798-1799.

HUNTINGDON, 1797.

MICHAEL DUFFEY, Printer and publisher. 1798.

JOHN RIVINGTON PARRINGTON, Printer and publisher. 1799.

LANCASTER, 1747.

JOHANN ALBRECHT, Printer, publisher and Bookseller. Johann Albrecht und Comp,, in der Neuen Buchdruckerey, in der Prinz Strasse, das 2te Haus, Nordlich vom Gefangniss, 1798-1799.

ROBERT DICKSON, Printer. W. and R. Dickson. 1798-1799.

WILLIAM DICKSON, Printer and Bookseller. W. and R. Dickson, in Queen Street, north of the Courthouse, 1798-1799.

Lancaster, *continued.*

WILLIAM HAMILTON, Printer, publisher and Bookseller. 1. At the German and English Printing Office, Franklin's Head, King Street, west of the Court House, 1798–1799. 2. William Hamilton and Conrad Wortmann, 1798–1799.

CHRISTIAN JACOB HÜTTER, Printer and publisher. In der Neuen Buchdruckerey, in der Konig'-strasse, die 2te Thüre vom Markt, 1799.

JACOB LAHN, Bookseller. 1798.

CONRAD WORTMANN, Printer. Hamilton and Wortmann, 1798–1799.

Lewiston, 1796.

JOHN DOYLE, Publisher. 1798.

JOSEPH DOYLE, Printer. 1798.

Northern Liberties, 1797.

B. SCHEFFLER, Printer. B. Scheffler and Co., 1798.

Northumberland, 1792.

ANDREW KENNEDY, Printer and publisher. 1799.

A. M'DONALD, Bookseller. 1798.

GEORGE SCHUSLER, Printer and publisher. 1798.

Philadelphia, 1685.

ROBERT AITKEN, Printer and Bookseller. No. 22 Market Street, 1798–1799.

—— ALLAIN, Printer and publisher. 1. Allain, Blocquerst et Wilson, Second Rue Nord, No. 147, 1798. 2. Allain et Brocquerst, 1798.

BENJAMIN FRANKLIN BACHE, Printer, publisher and Bookseller. 1. No. 112 Market Street, between Third and Fourth Streets, 1798–1799. 2. Published for the heirs of Benj. Franklin Bache, at No. 112 Market Street, between Third and Fourth Streets, 1799.

FRANCIS BAILEY, Printer and Bookseller. Francis and Robert Bailey, at Yorick's Head, No. 116 High Street, 1798–1799.

ROBERT BAILEY, Printer. F. and R. Bailey, 1798–1799.

ARCHIBALD BARTRAM, Printer. Budd and Bartram, 1798–1799.

JOHN BIOREN, Printer and Bookseller. 1. No. 75 Dock Street, 1798. 2. No. 83 Chesnut Street, four doors below Third Street, 1799.

—— BLOCQUERST, Printer. 1. Allain, Blocquerst et Wilson, 1798. 2. Allain et Blocquerst, 1798.

SAMUEL F. BRADFORD, Printer and publisher. 1. T. and S. F. Bradford, No. 8 South Front Street, 1798–1799. 2. Samuel F. Bradford, 1798–1799.

THOMAS BRADFORD, Printer, publisher, Bookseller and Stationer. 1. T. and W. Bradford, No. 8 South Front Street, 1798. 2. T. and S. F. Bradford, 1798–1799.

WILLIAM BRADFORD, Bookseller. T. and W. Bradford, 1798.

ALEXANDER BRODIE, Bookseller. 1798.

ANDREW BROWN, Printer and publisher. At Washington's Head, in Chesnut Street—No. 29—between Front and Second Streets, 1798.

ANDREW BROWN, JUNIOR, Printer and publisher. In succession, 1798–1799.

HENRY [STACY] BUDD, Printer. Budd and Bartram, No. 58 North Second Street, 1798–1799.

ROBERT CAMPBELL, Bookseller. Robert Campbell and Co. 1. No. 40 South Second Street, 1798. 2. No. 30 Chesnut Street, 1799.

JAMES CAREY, Printer and publisher. 1. No. 19 Carter's Alley, 1798. 2. Next door to Porcupine's Coat of Arms, a Bull's Eye, a Baboon's Head, and a Lion's Tail, 1798. 3. No. 1 South Second Street, 1798. 4. No. 15 Chesnut Street, 1798–1799. 5. No. 7 South Front Street, 1799.

MATHEW CAREY, Bookseller and Map publisher. No. 118 Market [High] Street, 1798–1799.

BENJAMIN CARR AND Co., Music publisher. At his Musical Repository, No. 132 High [Market] Street, 1798–1799.

CHARLES [CARL] CIST, Printer and Bookseller. 1. No. 104 North Second Street, near Race Street, 1798–1799. 2. Carl Cist, in der Zweyten Strasse, No. 104 nahe am Eck der Rehs Strasse, 1798–99.

DAVID C. CLAYPOOLE, Printer and publisher. 1. David C. and Septimus Claypoole, No. 48 Market Street, 1798. 2. David C. Claypoole, 1799.

SEPTIMUS CLAYPOOLE, Printer. David C. and Septimus Claypoole, 1798.

WILLIAM COBBETT, Printer, publisher and Bookseller. Opposite Christ Church, 1798–1799.

ROBERT COCHRAN, Printer. Patterson and Cochran, 1798.

THOMAS CONDIE, Publisher, Bookseller and Stationer. No. 20 Carter's Alley, 1798–1799.

WILLIAM CONOVER, Printer. 1799.

EPHRAIM CONRAD, Bookseller. 1798–1799.

EZEKIEL COOPER, Methodist publications. No. 47 North Fourth Street, near Race Street, 1799.

JAMES CRUKSHANK, Bookseller. Joseph and James Crukshank, 1798–1799.

JOSEPH CRUKSHANK, Bookseller. 1. No. 87 High Street, 1798. 2. Joseph and James Crukshank, 1798–1799.

PHILADELPHIA, *continued.*

BENJAMIN DAVIES, Bookseller. No. 68 High Street, 1798–1799.

ASBURY DICKINS, Bookseller. No. 41 Market Street, between Front and Second Streets, 1799.

JOHN DICKINS, Methodist publications. No. 50 North Second Street, near Arch Street, 1798.

THOMAS DOBSON, Printer, Bookseller and Stationer. At the Stone House, No. 41 South Second Street, 1798–1799.

GEORGE DOUGLAS, Bookseller and Stationer. No. 2 South Third Street, 1798.

WILLIAM DUANE, Editor and publisher. For the heirs of Benj. Franklin Bache, 1799.

JOHN FENNO, Printer and publisher. Printer to the Senate of the United States, No. 119 Chesnut Street, 1798.

JOHN WARD FENNO, Printer and publisher. No. 119 Chesnut Street, 1799.

SAMUEL FINLAY, Printer and publisher. No. 16 Chesnut Street, 1798.

RICHARD FOLWELL, Printer, No. 33 Carter's Alley, 1798–1799.

T. B. FREEMAN, Publisher. No. 39 South Front Street, opposite the Post Office, 1798.

JOSEPH GALES, Printer and publisher. 1. No. 126 North Second Street, 1798. 2. No. 23 South Third Street, 1798–1799.

GEORGE GIBSON, Bookseller. 1798–1799.

—— GROFF, Printer. Way and Groff, 1798–1799.

DAVID HALL, Printer and publisher. Hall and Sellers, at the New Printing Office, near the Market, No. 51 Market Street, 1798–1799.

DAVID HOGAN, Printer and Bookseller. 1. George Street, a few [third door] doors below South Street, 1798. 2. No. 222 South Third Street, 1798–1799.

DANIEL HUMPHREYS, Printer. No. 48 Spruce Street, 1798–1799.

JAMES HUMPHREYS, Printer, publisher and Bookseller. 1. No. 74 North Third Street, corner of Cherry Alley, 1798. 2. Opposite the Bank of the United States, in South Third Street, 1798–1799.

BENJAMIN JOHNSON, Bookseller. B. and J. Johnson, No. 147 Market [High] Street, 1798–1799.

JACOB JOHNSON, Printer. B. and J. Johnson, 1798–1799.

ROBERT JOHNSON, Bookseller. Robert Johnson and Co., No. 147 High Street, 1798–1799.

W. JONES, Bookseller. No. 30 North Fourth Street, 1798.

HEINRICH KAMMERER, JUNIOR, Printer and publisher. Heinrich and Joseph K. Kammerer, junior, 1798.

JOSEPH K. KAMMERER, UND COMP., Printers and publishers. 1798–1799.

FRANCIS C. KING, Bookseller. No. 42 Market Street, 1798.

JOHN LAMBERT, Author Bookseller. 1798.

SAMUEL LONGCOPE, Bookseller. No. 147 Spruce Street, 1798.

PATRICK LYON, Author Bookseller. At his [Black] smith's Shop, in Lombard, between Front and Second Streets, 1799.

WILLIAM M'CORKLE, Printer. Snowden and M'Corkle, 1798.

JOHN M'CULLOCH, Printer and Bookseller. No. 1 North Third Street, 1798–1799.

H. MAXWELL, Printer. No. 3 Lætitia Court, 1798–1799.

M. L. E. MOREAU DE ST. MERY, Printer and Bookseller. 1. No. 84, corner of Front and Walnut Streets, 1798. 2. Au coin de la Premiere rue Nord & de Callow-Hill, 1798.

JOHN MURDOCK, Author Bookseller, Hair dresser. No. 57 Walnut Street, 1798.

JOHN ORMROD, Printer and Bookseller. No. 41 Chesnut Street, 1798–1799.

JOHN H. OSWALD, Printer. No 179 South Second Street, 1798.

WILLIAM T. PALMER, Printer and publisher. No. 18 North Third Street, 1798.

PIERRE PARENT, Printer and publisher. No. 32 South Fifth Street, 1798.

—— PATTERSON, Printer and Bookseller. Patterson and Cochran, No. 148 South Fourth Street, 1798.

JEREMIAH PAUL, Writing-master. 1798.

ISAAC PEARSON, Bookseller. No. 109 Market Street, 1798–1799.

ZACHARIAH POULSON, JUNIOR, Printer and publisher. 1. No. 106 Chesnut Street, between Third and Fourth Streets, nearly opposite to the Bank of North America, 1798–1799. 2. No. 30 North Fourth Street, near the University, 1798.

HENRY RICE, Bookseller. H. and P. Rice, No. 16 South Second Street, 1798–1799.

PATRICK RICE, Bookseller. H. and P. Rice, 1798–1799.

WILLIAM ROSS, Printer. In Locust Street, near the corner of South Ninth Street, 1798–1799.

WILLIAM ROWSON, Bookseller. Stewart and Rowson, 1798.

PHILADELPHIA, *continued.*

BERNARD SCHEFFLER, Printer and publisher. Scheffler and Co., Northern Liberties, 1798.

HEINRICH [HENRY] SCHWEITZER [SWEITZER], Printer, publisher and Bookseller. 1. No. 85 Race Street, 1798–1799. 2. In der Rees-Strasse, Zwischen der Zweiten und Dritten-Strasse, 1798–1799. 3. An der südwestlichen ecke der Rees-und Vierten-Strasse, 1798.

WILLIAM SELLERS, Printer. Hall and Sellers, 1798–1799.

ABRAHAM SMALL, Printer. J. Thompson and A. Small, 1798.

SAMUEL HARRISON SMITH, Printer and publisher. No. 118 Chesnut Street, 1798.

THOMAS SMITH, Printer. S. H. and T. Smith, 1798.

JOHN M. SNOWDEN, Printer. Snowden and M'Corkle, No. 47 North Fourth Street, 1798.

JAMES STEWART, Bookseller. Stewart and Rowson, No. 9 Cherry Street, 1798.

PETER STEWART, Printer. No. 34 South Second Street, 1798.

JAMES THACKARA, Author Bookseller. No. 72 Spruce Street, 1798.

JOHN THOMPSON, Printer. J. Thompson and A. Small, No. 34 Carter's Alley, 1798.

HENRY TUCKNISS, Printer. No. 25 Church Alley, 1798–1799.

STEPHEN C. USTICK, Printer. No. 97 North Third Street, 1798.

JAMES WATTERS, Publisher. James Watters and Co., Willing's Alley, 1798.

—— WAY, Printer. Way and Groff. 1. No. 27 Arch Street, 1798. 2. No. 48 North Third Street, 1798–1799.

GEORGE WILLIG, Music publisher. At his Musical Magazine, No. 185 Market Street, 1798–1799.

—— WILSON, Printer. Allain, Blocquerst et Wilson, 1798.

WILLIAM WALLIS WOODWARD, Printer. No. 17 Chesnut, near Front Street, 1798–1799.

WILLIAM YOUNG, Printer, Bookseller and Stationer. Whitehall Press, No. 52 South Second Street, 1798–1799.

PITTSBURGH, 1786.

JOHN SCULL, Printer, publisher and Bookseller. At his Printing Office, in Front Street, next door to the corner of Market Street, 1798–1799.

READING, 1789.

GOTTLOB JUNGMANN, Printer and publisher. Jungmann und Comp., in der Deutsche-und Englischen Buchdruckerey, in der Callowhill Strasse, sud von dem Courthaus, 1798.

JACOB SCHNEIDER, Printer and publisher. Schneider und Comp., in der Deutsch-und Englischen Buckruckerey in der Pennstrasse, 1798.

SHIPPENSBURGH, 1797.

SOUTHAMPTON, 1797.

UNION TOWN, 1798.

CHARLES MOWRY, Printer. Stewart and Mowry, 1798–1799.

JACOB STEWART, Printer and publisher. Stewart and Mowry, near the Court House, 1798–1799.

WASHINGTON, 1795.

JOHN COLERICK, Printer and publisher. At Office of the Telegraphe, 1798–1799.

A. CUNNINGHAM, Bookseller. 1798.

JOHN ISRAEL, Printer and publisher. 1798–1799.

WEST CHESTER, 1794.

WILKESBARRE, 1796.

JOSIAH WRIGHT, Printer and publisher. 1798.

THOMAS WRIGHT, Publisher. 1799.

YORK, 1777.

JOHN EDIE, Printer and publisher. 1798–1799.

SALOMON MAYER, Printer and publisher. 1798–99.

PRINTING INSTITUTED IN
RHODE ISLAND, 1727, A. D.

NEWPORT, 1727.

HENRY BARBER, Printer and publisher. Near the State House, 1798–1799.

JACOB RICHARDSON, Bookseller. 1798.

HAVILA FARNSWORTH, Printer and publisher. H. and O. Farnsworth, 1798–1799.

OLIVER FARNSWORTH, Printer and publisher. 1. H. and O. Farnsworth, 1798–1799. 2. Oliver Farnsworth, 1799.

PROVIDENCE, 1762.

JOHN CARTER. Printer, publisher, Bookseller, and Stationer. Carter and Wilkinson, at their Book Store, opposite the Market, 1798.

PROVIDENCE, *continued.*

JOHN CARTER, JUNIOR, Printer. At the New Printing Office, Market Street, west side of the Great Bridge, 1799.

JOSEPH J. TODD, Bookseller, and Circulating Library. At the Bible and Anchor, 1798–1799.

ABEL WHEELER, Printer. 1799.

BENNETT WHEELER, Printer and publisher. At his Office, No. 1 Westminster Street, a few rods westward of the Great Bridge and directly opposite the Turk's Head, 1798–1799.

WILLIAM WILKINSON, Printer. Carter and Wilkinson, 1798.

WARREN, 1792.

NATHANIEL PHILLIPS, Printer and publisher. Printer to the State, at the Post Office, 1798–1799.

PRINTING INSTITUTED IN
SOUTH CAROLINA, 1732, A. D.

CHARLESTON, 1732.

—— BAILEY, Bookseller. Bailey, Waller and Bailey, No. 194 Broad Street, 1798–1799.

GABRIEL M. BONNETHEAU, Printer and publisher. Bonnetheau and Evans, 1798.

THOMAS BARTHOLOMEW BOWEN, Printer and publisher. No. 32 Church Street, near the City Theatre, 1797–1799.

JOHN BURD, Printer. Elliott and Burd, 1798–1799.

THOMAS C. COX, Printer. No. 137 Tradd Street, 1798–1799.

ROBERT ELLIOTT, Printer and publisher. Elliott and Burd, 1798–1799.

S. J. ELLIOTT, Printer. No. 47 Bay, 1798–1799.

JOHN J. EVANS, Printer. Bonnetheau and Evans, 1798.

PETER FRENEAU, Printer and publisher. Freneau and Paine, Printers to the City, and the State, No. 47 Bay, 1798–1799.

WILLIAM PRIMROSE HARRISON, Printer. No. 38 Bay, corner of Elliot Street, 1798–1799.

SETH PAINE, Printer. Freneau and Paine, 1798–99.

EBENEZER S. THOMAS, Bookseller. 1798–1799.

BENJAMIN FRANKLIN TIMOTHY, Printer and publisher. 1798–1799.

—— WALLER, Bookseller. Bailey, Waller and Bailey, 1798–1799.

WILLIAM P. YOUNG, Printer and Bookseller. Franklin's Head No. 43 Broad Street, 1798–1799.

COLUMBIA, 1792.

DANIEL FAUST, Printer and publisher. 1. Young and Faust, 1798. 2. Daniel Faust and Company, 1798–1799.

WILLIAM P. YOUNG, Printer and publisher. Young and Faust, Printers to the State, corner of Richardson and Plain Streets, 1798.

GEORGETOWN, 1791.

JOHN BURD, Printer. Elliott and Burd, 1798–1799.

ROBERT ELLIOTT, Printer and publisher. Elliott and Burd, 1798–1799.

PRINTING INSTITUTED IN
TENNESSEE, 1791, A. D.

KNOXVILLE, 1792.

JOHN RIVINGTON PARRINGTON, Printer. Roulstone and Parrington, 1798.

GEORGE ROULSTONE, Printer and publisher. 1. Printer to the State, 1798–1799. 2. Roulstone and Parrington, 1798. 3. Roulstone and Wilson, 1799.

GEORGE WILSON. Printer and publisher. Roulstone and Wilson, 1799.

NASHVILLE, 1799.

JOHN M'LAUGHLIN, Printer. 1799.

ROGERSVILLE, 1791.

PRINTING INSTITUTED IN
VERMONT, 1778, A. D.

BENNINGTON, 1783.

ANTHONY HASWELL, Printer and publisher. At his Office, a few rods south of the Court House, 1798–1799.

BRATTLEBOROUGH, 1797.

LEVI REDFIELD, Author Bookseller. 1798.

BENJAMIN SMEAD, Printer and publisher. At the Printing Office, in the south lower room in the new building adjoining the City Bridge, 1798–1799.

BURLINGTON, 1796

DRESDEN, 1778.

FAIRHAVEN, 1795.

JAMES LYON, Printer. At Voltaire's Head, 1798.

JUDAH P. SPOONER, Printer and publisher. 1798–1799.

NEWBURY, 1793.

PEACHAM, 1798.

AMOS FARLEY, Printer and publisher. Farley and Goss, 1798–1799.

SAMUEL GOSS, Printer. Farley and Goss, 1798–99.

PUTNEY, 1797.

JUSTIN HINDS, Bookseller. 1798.

CORNELIUS STURTEVANT, JUNIOR, Printer and publisher. 1. Cornelius Sturtevant, jun. and Co. 1798. 2. Cornelius Sturtevant, 1798–1799.

ELIAS STURTEVANT, Printer. Sturtevant and Co., 1798.

ABIJAH WILDER, Printer. Sturtevant and Co., 1798.

RUTLAND, 1792.

JOSIAH FAY, Printer. S. Williams and Co., 1798.

JOHN WALKER, JUNIOR, Printer for S. Williams and Co. 1798–1799.

SAMUEL WILLIAMS, Editor and publisher. S. Williams and Co., a few rods south of the State House, 1798–1799.

VERGENNES, 1798.

SAMUEL CHIPMAN, JUNIOR, Printer and publisher. 1798–1799.

GEORGE WAITE, Printer and publisher. G. and R. Waite, at their Printing Office, adjoining the Court House, 1798.

R. WAITE, Printer. G. and R. Waite, 1798.

WESTMINSTER, 1781.

WINDSOR, 1783.

ALDEN SPOONER, Printer and publisher. On the west side of the Main Street, 1798–1799.

PRINTING INSTITUTED IN

VIRGINIA, 1730, A. D.

ALEXANDRIA, 1782.

HENRY GIRD, JUNIOR, Printer. 1. Price and Gird, 1798. 2. Henry Gird, junior, 1798–1799.

ELLIS PRICE, Printer and publisher. 1. Price and Gird, at the east end of the Market House, 1798. 2. Ellis Price, 1798–1799.

JOHN V. THOMAS, Printer and publisher. Thomas and Westcott, in Royal Street, between the Post Office and the Coffee House, 1798.

MASON LOCKE WEEMS, Travelling Bookseller. 1798.

JAMES D. WESTCOTT, Printer. Thomas and Westcott, 1798.

CHARLOTTESVILLE, 1781.

DUMFRIES, 1791.

FREDERICKSBURG, 1787.

GEORGE CARTER, Printer. Mercer and Carter, 1798–1799.

TIMOTHY GREEN, Printer and publisher. 1798–99.

ROBERT MERCER, Printer and publisher. 1. Mercer and Carter, 1798–1799. 2. Robert Mercer, 1799.

GEORGE TOWN, 1789.

DAVID ENGLISH, Printer. Green, English and Co., 1798–1799.

CHARLES D. GREEN, Printer and publisher. Green, English and Co., 1798–1799.

LEESBURG, 1798.

PATRICK M'INTYRE, Printer and publisher. 1798–1799.

LYNCHBURG, 1793.

JOHN CARTER, Printer and publisher. John Carter and Co., 1798–1799.

JOHN DAVIS, Printer and publisher. John Davis and Co., 1798.

MARTINSBURG, 1790.

JOHN ALBURTIS, Printer, and publisher. 1799.

NATHANIEL WILLIS, Printer, and publisher. At his Printing Office, in Burke Street, near the Court House, 1798.

NORFOLK, 1774.

ROBERT HANNAH, Bookseller. Rainbow and Hannah, 1798.

AUGUSTUS C. JORDAN, Printer and publisher. Opposite the Post Office, 1798–1799.

JAMES O'CONNOR, Printer. Willett and O'Connor, 1798–1799.

THOMAS RAINBOW, Bookseller. Rainbow and Hannah, at the Circulating Library, 1798.

CHARLES WILLETT, Printer and publisher. Willett and O'Connor, near the Market, 1798–1799.

PETERSBURG, 1786.

GEORGE DOUGLAS, Printer and Bookseller. The Blandford Press, Ross and Douglas, at the head of Bollingbrook Street, 1799.

WILLIAM PRENTIS, Printer and publisher. 1798.

—— ROSS, Bookseller. Ross and Douglas, 1799.

RICHMOND, 1780.

AUGUSTINE DAVIS, Printer and publisher. Printer to [for] the [Public] Commonwealth, 1798–1799.

JOHN DIXON, Printer and publisher. 1798. 2. Meriwether Jones and John Dixon, 1798–1799. 3. Printer to the Grand Lodge of Virginia, 1799.

MERIWETHER JONES, Printer and publisher. 1. Meriwether Jones and John Dixon, Printers to the Commonwealth, 1798–1799. 2. Meriwether Jones, 1799.

THOMAS NICOLSON, Printer. First house below the Capitol, 1798–1799.

SAMUEL PLEASANTS, JUNIOR, Printer and publisher. Near [third door below] the Vendue Office of M. Vandewall, 1798–1799.

W. PRICHARD, Bookseller. 1798–1799.

W. A. RIND, Printer. Near the Market, 1799.

SHEPHERD'S TOWN, 1791.

STAUNTON, 1793.

JOHN WISE, Printer and publisher. On the Main Street, three doors above the Rising-Sun Tavern, 1798–1799.

WILLIAMSBURG, 1730.

WINCHESTER, 1787.

RICHARD BOWEN, Printer and publisher. Opposite the Episcopal Church, in Loudoun Street, 1798–1799.

END OF THE TWELFTH VOLUME.